Family Patterns, Gender Relations

Second Edition

Edited by
Bonnie J. Fox

OXFORD
UNIVERSITY PRESS

OXFORD

UNIVERSITY PRESS

70 Wynford Drive, Don Mills, Ontario M3C 1J9
www.oup.com/ca

Oxford University Press is a department of the University of Oxford.
It furthers the University's objective of excellence in research, scholarship,
and education by publishing worldwide in

Oxford New York

Auckland Bangkok Buenos Aires Cape Town Chennai
Dar es Salaam Delhi Hong Kong Istanbul Karachi Kolkata
Kuala Lumpur Madrid Melbourne Mexico City Mumbai Nairobi
São Paulo Shanghai Taipei Tokyo Toronto

Oxford is a trade mark of Oxford University Press
in the UK and in certain other countries

Published in Canada
by Oxford University Press

Copyright © Oxford University Press Canada 2001

Canadian Cataloguing in Publication Data

Main entry under title:
Family patterns, gender relations

2nd ed.
Includes bibliographical references and index.
ISBN 0-19-541587-6

1. Family. 2. Sex role. I. Fox, Bonnie, 1948– .

HQ734.F2417 2001   306.85   C00-932290-6

Cover and text design by: Joan Dempsey

5 6 7 8 - 10 09 08 07 06

This book is printed on permanent (acid-free) paper ∞.
Printed in Canada

For Jesse and John

Contents

Preface

This is the third and most ambitious edition of this Family text. Like the two that preceded it, the focus here is on understanding the patterns and dynamics in the relationships through which people care for children, themselves, and each other daily; that focus includes the ways these relationships are shaped by the larger social context and social structure. The articles here build an understanding of the social relations of sexuality, reproduction, parenting, household work, and income distribution—of family, in short. Because these social relations are typically gender relations, the book is as much about gender as it is about family.

The articles in this collection also present a critical focus on the social organization of things that otherwise seem 'natural'. Accordingly, the first part of the book highlights cross-cultural and historical variations in family patterns. I hope that emphasizing the historical creation of the patterns we live with, and highlighting the relationships that constitute them, will encourage students to see ways current arrangements can be changed. To further that goal, the book ends with two articles that review social policy options for Canadians.

Before we can think about the future, we need to challenge ideas that the nuclear-family patterns typical of the 1950s were somehow ideal. So, the book has two articles that examine the dynamics typical of 1950s-style families. It also contains a chapter that reviews long-term and short-term demographic trends central to family—aimed at providing some perspective on the changes occurring in families today.

What especially distinguishes this edition from the last is an additional focus on family diversity. The different family patterns that are associated with racial and ethnic diversity, and those caused by immigrants' adaptation to North America, are discussed in several selections.

Lesbian families and egalitarian families of varying forms are also examined here.

The vast majority of the articles in this book are Canadian. As in previous editions, however, I used non-Canadian material when I thought it was too good to leave out. There are some new pieces—articles by Meg Luxton, Diana Worts, Tracey Adams, and myself. As well, Sedef Arat-Koc, Riann Mahon, and Guida Man updated and revised earlier articles.

There are many people on whom I relied in the production of this book and its previous editions—and to whom I am grateful. Jack Wayne and Canadian Scholars Press made the first edition possible. The second edition benefited from the input of Doreen Fumia and Sherry Franz when they were undergraduates in my Family course; Sedef Arat-Koc, Penni Stewart, and Lorna Erwin wrote for me despite their busy schedules; Ester Reiter gave insightful criticisms at various points in the production of the book; and Sedef Arat-Koc, Jo-Ann Climenhage, Laura Hollingsworth, Lois Jackson, Mary-Beth Raddon, Pamela Sugiman, and Vappu Tyyska gave invaluable teaching assistance in various courses.

This time I worked in greater isolation because I no longer teach the Sociology of Family course at the University of Toronto. So, the people who wrote (and rewrote) for me are the ones to whom I am most grateful: Thanks go to Meg Luxton, Tracey Adams, Diana Worts, Sedef Arat-Koc, Guida Man, and Riann Mahon. I thank Julie McMullin, Pamela Sugiman, and an anonymous reviewer, as well, for helpful advice. Ellen Gee also deserves thanks, although she had to withdraw her offer to write a demography chapter. And when I decided to write one myself, it was Rod Beaujot's answers to my questions about demographic sources that made my article possible. Thank you, Rod. Dennis Magill also deserves thanks for giving me that extra teaching assistant in order to make it possible to do the book while teaching.

Finally, I thank my family. John's terrific cooking keeps us all going and his computer assistance keeps me sane. And Jesse is just a terrific kid; he 'makes my day' every day.

Acknowledgements

Since the copyright page cannot accommodate all the copyright notices, pages xi–xii constitute an extension of the copyright page.

Sedef Arat-Koc. 'The Politics of Family and Immigration in the Subordination of Domestic Workers in Canada', a revised version of 'In the Privacy of Our Own Home' from *Studies in Political Economy*, 28 (Spring 1989). Reprinted by permission of Studies in Political Economy.

Bettina Bradbury. 'Gender at Work at Home: Family Decisions, the Labour Market, and Girls' Contribution to the Family Economy' from *Canadian Labour History*, Gregory S. Kealey and Greg Patmore, eds. (Sydney: Australian-Canadian Studies, 1990). Reprinted by permission.

Agnes Calliste. 'Black Families in Canada: Exploring the Interconnections of Race, Class and Gender' from *Voices: Essays on Canadian Families*, 1st edition, by M.M. Lynn © 1996. Reprinted with permission of Nelson Thomson Learning, a division of Thomson Learning, Fax 800-730-2215.

Jane Collier, Michelle Z. Rosaldo, Sylvia Yanagisako. 'Is There a Family? New Anthropological Views' from *Rethinking the Family: Some Feminist Questions* edited by Barrie Thorne with Marilyn Yalom. Copyright 1992 by the Institute for Research on Women and Gender, Stanford University. Reprinted with the permission of Northeastern University Press.

Stephanie Coontz. '"Leave It to Beaver" and "Ozzie and Harriet": American Families in the 1950s' from *The Way We Never Were* by Stephanie Coontz. Copyright © 1992 by BasicBooks, A Division of HarperCollins Publishers Inc. Reprinted by permission of Basic Books, a member of Perseus Books, L.L.C.

Nancy Cott. 'Domesticity' from *The Bonds of Womanhood* (New Haven, CT: Yale University Press, 1977). Copyright © 1977. Reprinted by permission of Yale University Press.

Patricia Draper. '!Kung Women: Contrasts in Sexual Egalitarianism in Foraging and Sedentary Contexts' from *Toward an Anthropology of Women*, Rayna Rapp Reiter, ed. (New York: Monthly Review Press, 1975). Copyright © 1975 by Monthly Review Press. Reprinted by permission of Monthly Review Foundation.

Felicity Edholm. 'The Unnatural Family' from *The Changing Experience of Women*, Elizabeth Whitelegg et al, eds. (Oxford: Blackwell Publishers, 1982). Reprinted by permission of Blackwell Publishers.

Bonnie Fox. 'Reproducing Difference: Changes in the Lives of Partners Becoming Parents' from *Feminism and Families*, Meg Luxton, ed. (Halifax: Fernwood Publishing, 1997). Published with the permission of Fernwood Publishing Co. Ltd.

Frank F. Furstenburg and Andrew J. Cherlin. 'Children's Adjustment to Divorce' reprinted by permission of the publisher from *Divided Families: What Happens to Children When Parents Part* by Frank F. Furstenburg (Cambridge, Mass.: Harvard University Press, 1991). Copyright © 1991 by the President and Fellows of Harvard College.

Rosemary Gartner, Myrna Dawson, and Maria Crawford Excerpts from 'Woman Killing: Intimate Femicide in Ontario, 1974–1994' from *Resources for Feminist Research*, 26, 3 & 4 (1998). Reprinted by permission.

Jane Gaskell. 'The Reproduction of Family Life: Perspectives of Male and Female Adolescents' from *British Journal of Sociology of Education*, (4) 1983. Reprinted by permission of Taylor & Francis Ltd, PO Box 25, Abingdon, Oxfordshire, OX14 3UE, UK.

Kathleen Gerson. 'Veering Toward Domesticity' from *Hard Choices: How Women Decide About Work, Career, and Motherhood* by Kathleen Gerson. Copyright © 1985 The Regents of the University of California. Reprinted by permission of University of California Press.

Arlie Hochschild. 'The Third Shift' from *The Time Bind: When Work Becomes Home and Home Becomes Work* by Arlie Russell Hochschild, © 1997 by Arlie Russell Hochschild. Reprinted by permission of Henry Holt and Company, LLC.

Wendy Hollway. 'Heterosexual Sex: Power and Desire for the Other' from *Sex and Love* edited by Sue Cartledge and Joanna Ryan, published in Great Britain by The Women's Press Ltd, 1983, 34 Great Sutton Street, London EC1V 0LQ. Reprinted by permission of the author. Wendy Hollway is Professor in Qualitative Psychology at the School of Psychology, University of Leeds.

Eleanor B. Leacock. 'Women in an Egalitarian Society: The Montagnais-Naskapi' from *Encyclopedia of Mankind* (London: Marshall Cavendish, 1978). Reprinted by permission.

Meg Luxton. 'Wives and Husbands' from *More Than a Labour of Love: Three Generations of Women's Work in the Home* (Toronto: Women's Press, 1980). Reprinted by permission of Women's Press.

Guida Man. 'From Hong Kong to Canada: Immigration and the Changing Family Lives of Middle-Class Women from Hong Kong' from *Voices: Essays on Canadian Families*, 1st edition, by M.M. Lynn © 1996. Reprinted with permission of Nelson Thomson Learning, a division of Thomson Learning, Fax 800-730-2215.

Maxine Margolis. 'Putting Mothers on the Pedestal' from *Mothers and Such: View of American Women and Why They Change* (Berkeley: University of California Press, 1984). Reprinted by permission of the author. Maxine L. Margolis is Professor of Anthropology at the University of Florida.

Fiona Nelson. 'Lesbian Families' from *Lesbian Motherhood: An Exploration of Canadian Lesbian Families* (Toronto: University of Toronto Press, 1996). Copyright © 1996. Reprinted with permission of the publisher.

Shelley A. Phipps. 'Lessons from Europe: Policy Options to Enhance the Economic Security of Canadian Families' from *Family Security in Insecure Times*, National Forum on Family Security (Ottawa: The Forum, 1993). Reprinted by permission of the Canadian Council on Social Development.

Harriet Rosenberg. 'Motherwork, Stress and Depression: The Costs of Privatized Social Reproduction' from *Feminism and Political Economy*, 1st Edition, edited by Heather Jon Maroney and Meg Luxton. © 1987. Reprinted with permission of Nelson Thomson Learning, a division of Thomson Learning, Fax 800-730-2215.

Carol Stack. Pages 32–44 from *All Our Kin: Strategies for Survival in a Black Community* by Carol B. Stack. Copyright © 1974 by Carol B. Stack. Reprinted by permission of HarperCollins Publishers, Inc.

Niara Sudarkasa. 'African American Families and Family Values' from *Exploring the African-American Experience* (Lincoln, PA: Lincoln University Press).

Louise Tilly and Joan Scott. 'The Family Economy in Modern England and France' from Louise Tilly and Joan Scott, *Women, Work and Family*, 1978. Reprinted with permission of the authors.

Mariana Valverde. 'Heterosexuality: Contested Ground' from *Sex, Power and Pleasure* (Toronto: Women's Press, 1985). Reprinted by permission of Women's Press.

Part One   **Putting 'Family' in Perspective**

Chapter 1

Perhaps the most important assumption about 'the family' in popular culture is that the nuclear pattern is somehow 'natural', and therefore universal. The nuclear family seems to follow from the biology of reproduction.

This essay challenges all assumptions of universal family patterns. It examines aspects of family life that seem to us to be nearly inevitable—like the relationship between mother and child—and instead shows tremendous diversity across human societies. Edholm's discussion raises the challenge that we should always question the seemingly unquestionable.

The Unnatural Family

Felicity Edholm

It was, and still is, widely argued that some form of the family, and, in some cases, of the nuclear family, was universal, and was found in all societies. Only recently has this accepted wisdom been challenged and it has still not been dislodged. One major reason for its resilience in anthropology, apart from the crucial political, economic, and ideological significance of the family in the nineteenth- and twentieth-century western world, is that groups very similar to those which we identify as the family do exist in the majority of societies known to anthropologists. Furthermore, anthropologists have tended to assume that an adequate explanatory definition of any given social or cultural trait can be extended to similar traits in other cultures. But as one anthropologist has commented: 'because the family seems to be the predominant unit we must not be bemused into thinking that it is the "natural" or "basic" one' (Fox 1967: 38).

It is usually assumed that the family, a co-residential unit containing parents and their own children, is the natural primary unit within which domestic and sexual relations and socialization will take place; that relationships between members of a family are unique and specific, and are recognizably different from relationships with individuals outside the family; that there is, at least for the early years of life, an inevitably deep and necessary dependence between a mother and her children, and that there is some sense of obligation and interdependence between those who are members of the family, particularly between parents and children; that incest taboos operate within the family unit; and that property, status, and positions pass within the family. It is also usually assumed that there is considerable interdependence, both social and sexual, between men and women and that this is revealed within the family/the household.

The most critical areas of kinship to examine in order to have some understanding of the family are those which offer the greatest challenge to preconceptions and which have significant effect on the construction of kinship relations in so far as they affect the assumptions we have outlined above. Five areas will be explored: conception, incest, parent/child relations and adoption, marriage, households, and residence.

Conception

The question of who our kin, our relations, are is answered in numerous ways, even for the primary parent-child relation. Notions of blood ties, of biological connection, which to us seem relatively unequivocal, are highly variable. Some societies of which we have anthropological record recognize only the role of the father or of the mother in conception and procreation. The other sex is given some significance, but is not seen, for example, as providing blood . . . as having any biological connection. Only one parent is a 'relation', the other parent is not. In the Trobriand Islands, for example, it is believed that intercourse is not the cause of conception, semen is not seen as essential for conception (Malinowski 1922). Conception results from the entry of a spirit child into the womb; the male role is to 'open the passage' to the womb, through intercourse, and it is the repeated intercourse of the same partner which 'moulds' the child. A child's blood comes from its mother's side and from her siblings, her mother and mother's brother, not from the father. A child will not be related by blood to its father, but will look like its father since he has through intercourse created its form. Fathers continue after birth to have a very close and intimate relationship with their children and it is this contact which also is seen as creating the likeness, as moulding the child in his/her father's image.

Other societies recognize the crucial importance of semen in the formation of a child, but believe that it is essential for conception that either the semen of more than one man is involved—or that fertility is only possible given a mixture of different semen, thus a newly married woman in Marind Anim society (in New Guinea) is gang-raped at marriage, and on subsequent ritual occasions (Van Baal 1966). Semen is understood as being necessary for growth throughout childhood and adolescence and elaborate male homosexual activities ensure that adolescent boys are in receipt of semen.

The Lakker of Burma on the other hand consider that the mother is only a container in which the child grows; she has no blood connection with her children, and children of the same mother and different fathers are not considered to be related to each other (Keesing 1976). These cases are extreme but have important implications in that they indicate not only that relations which seem to us to be self-evidently biological, are not universally seen as such. 'Natural', 'biological' relations are not inevitably those which organize human relations at a very fundamental level, since what is understood as 'biological' is socially defined and therefore is expressed in different ways.

Incest

Incest is another area of human relations which is widely discussed in terms of some kind of innate, instinctive abhorrence for sexual relations with 'close kin' and is often attributed to a subconscious realization of the genetic danger of inbreeding. (It is not uniformly accepted that inbreeding is inevitably disadvantageous.)

Incest taboos, defined as prohibitions on sexual relations between individuals socially classified as kin, as relations, are nearly universal. But the prohibition does not inevitably apply to the individuals whom we would identify as primary kin. The most dramatic exceptions to incest are found in certain royal dynasties (Egypt, Hawaii) where inbreeding (brother-sister) was enforced in order to keep the purity of the royal line, as well as in Ptolemaic and Roman Egypt where apparently father-daughter and brother-sister sexual relations were relatively common. In most other known societies, sexual relations between those socially recognized as 'biologically' related are taboo. The Trobrianders, for example, do not consider the children of one father and different mothers to be related and sexual relations between those children are thus entirely legitimate, whereas sexual relations with women who have the same mother, or whose mothers are siblings, is taboo. The Lakker of Burma do not consider that the children of the same mother have any kinship links. 'Incest' does not apply to these non-kin and sexual relations are permitted. In other societies in which, for example, the category of mother or sister is extended to include all males or females of the same generation who are descended through one parent from a common grandfather, or great-grandfather, it is frequently this whole group which is sexually unavailable. It is the social definitions of significant kinship relations that are important in defining incest rather than any concept of natural biological imperatives militating against sexual intercourse within a 'natural family unit'.

Parent/Child Relations: Adoption

It is nearly universally accepted in all anthropological texts on the family, however prepared they are to accept the fact that the nuclear family is not ubiquitous, that the 'mother-child tie is inevitable and given', that the 'irreducible and elementary social grouping is surely the mother and her children'. This is seen as determined by the imperatives of infantile dependence and the need for breast-milk, and is also related to other psychological needs on the part both of the mother and of the child. It is in this context instructive to consider the implications of the widespread practice of adoption. In many societies, children do not live with their 'real' parents, but often stay with their mothers until some time after they have been weaned, when as they say in N. Ghana, they have 'gained sense' (at about six). However, throughout Melanesia and Polynesia, children are adopted just after weaning or, in some instances, well before—a phenomenon which is considered as absolutely acceptable. In some instances, babies are adopted and breast-fed by their adopted mother. Margaret Mead (1935: 193) describes such a situation among the Mundugumor in New Guinea: 'even women who have never borne children are able in a few weeks, by placing the child constantly at the breast and by drinking plenty of coconut milk, to produce enough, or nearly enough, milk to rear the child, which is suckled by other women in the first few weeks after adoption'.

In Tahiti, young women often have one or two children before they are considered, or consider themselves to be, ready for an approved and stable relationship. It is considered perfectly acceptable for the children of this young woman to be given to her parents or other close kin for adoption, while she is freed to continue what is seen as the 'business of adolescence'. The girl can decide what her relationship to the children will be, but there is no sense in which she is forced into 'motherhood' because of having had a baby; 'motherhood' in such a situation can be seen as a status reached by women at a particular stage of development, as involving a psychological and social readiness, not something inevitably attached to the physical bearing of children.

In nearly all the societies in which adoption of this kind is common (and where anthropologists have discussed it at length), it is clear that the adopted child will still maintain contact with its 'natural' parents, and will know what their relationship to each other is. A Tahitian man (himself adopted) was asked about children's relations to their parents: 'if you are not adopted you are grateful to your biological mother, because she gave birth to you. On the other hand, when you are taken in your infancy by somebody it isn't worthwhile to think any more about your mother. The woman who took you in is just the same as your biological mother. Your gratitude is because you were an infant and you were taken' (in Levy 1970: 81). One of the interesting aspects of this definition of the relationship between parents and children is the sense in which it is seen as so critically dependent on gratitude—from child to parent—since it is recognized that adults choose to bring up the child, and do not have a necessary sense of responsibility, or instinctive love for it. The implications of such attitudes for all social relations are clearly considerable.

Again, in most of these societies it is agreed that the adopted child is more the foster father's than the true father's. Margaret Mead (1935), writing on the Manus of New Guinea, described the very considerable personality similarities she saw between fathers and their adopted children. The relationship between fathers and children is extremely close, fathers feed and spend a lot of time with their children. The 'likeness', of which the Trobriand Islanders speak, between father and children, is also, in many other Melanesian and Polynesian societies, seen as due to the close personal contact between them. The father-child relationship is seen as a crucial, and above all, as a social relationship; one which is created by social contact, not one which exists because of a 'blood relationship'. In Tahiti, it is considered an ultimate shame for adopted children to leave the house of their adopted parents since the relationship between those who have lived together and have grown 'familiar' ('matau') with each other (the essential ingredient for all good relations) is seen as inevitably far closer than that between biological 'natural' parents.

It is instructive in this context to consider the United Nations' study on the *Adoption of Children in Western Nations*, in which it is argued that in the West, society attributes 'a sacred character . . . to family bonds' (Levy 1970). The extent to which this attribution is ideological is even more evident once we have understood the extraordinary narrowness of our definitions of familiar 'natural' relations.

Marriage

It has been claimed that some form of marriage is found in all human societies. The definitions of marriage, however, again give some indication of the kind of complexity that is involved in the attempt to provide universals. One famous definition by Goodenough (1970: 12–13) defines marriage in these terms:

> Marriage is a transaction and resulting contract in which a person (male or female, corporate or individual, in person or by proxy) establishes a continuing claim to the right of

sexual access to a woman—this right having priority over rights of sexual access others currently have, or may subsequently acquire, in relation to her (except in a similar transaction) until the contract resulting from the transaction is terminated, and in which the woman involved is eligible to bear children.

Other definitions stress above all the significance of marriage in determining parentage—in allocating children to different groups. The definitions have to be understood in relation to the kinds of social arrangements which are entirely inconsistent with our notions of marriage.

The Nayar of Northern India provide one of the most problematic cases of 'marriage' (Schneider and Gough 1972). The basic social group among the Nayar is the Taravad, a unit composed of men and women descended through the female line from a common ancestress. Thus it is brothers and sisters, mothers and children who cohabit. A child becomes a member of the mother's Taravad, not the father's. A Nayar girl was involved, before she reached puberty, in a formal ritual with a man from an equivalent caste to her own, and then was able to take as many lovers as she wished; the 'husband'—the man who had been involved in the ritual—only had a very minimal ritual attachment to his 'wife', although he too could be one of her lovers. (Not all lovers came from the same caste.) Husbands and fathers, in such a context, are entirely peripheral to the domestic life of their wives and children—and never cohabit.

Among the Nuer of the Nile Basin, one of the most common forms of marriage is what has been called 'ghost' marriage (the anthropologist Evans-Pritchard who worked among the Nuer estimates that nearly 50 per cent of all marriages correspond to this form). Ghost marriage refers to the situation in which a man dies, unmarried, or with no children of his own. If this happens, a close kinsman (related to him through his father's line) will marry a wife 'to his name' and children born of this union will be seen as the dead man's children.

A man who has been involved in marrying this way and bearing children for another man will, when he dies and if he has not contracted a second marriage in his own name—only possible if his wife dies—have to become in his turn a proxy father and a subsequent ghost marriage will be contracted. If a married man dies, his widow then should ideally be married by a brother or close male kin of the dead man and again, children born of this union will be considered to be those of the dead man, not of the living husband.

The Nuer also have another contractual form of 'marriage' in which an old and important, usually barren, woman may marry a younger woman. Nuer marriages are contracted through the 'husband' giving the bride price (cattle) to the wife's group. The children born to this younger woman will then, for particular purposes, such as inheritance, be considered as the children of the old woman, their 'father'. Marriages of this kind indicate the importance among the Nuer both of becoming a parent, or rather a male parent, in order to become an ancestor—for only 'fathers' with offspring are remembered and have status as ancestors—and also of the inheritance of property. Nuer marriages also demonstrate that the marriage indicates a contract between a group of related 'men' who are seen in some sense as equivalents and a woman married to one of them.

These two widely differing examples illustrate one of the other critical elements in the relations defined by marriage: the difference between the 'legally' recognized father or mother and the person who was involved in conception, or birth. In both the cases cited above, the person we would see as the father, he who had impregnated the woman, is not given any social recognition at all, it is the person, not necessarily male, who is given the social position of father who is recognized through the ritual of 'marriage'. The two males are distinguished in the anthropological literature thus: the biological father is the *genitor*, the biological mother the *genetrix*, the 'socially' recognized father the *pater*, the socially recognized

mother the *mater*. In cases of polyandry—where a woman is 'married' to more than one man, as is the case among the Toda, one of the men will perform a ritual which makes him the pater, and the child and subsequent children will belong to this group. In some of the societies (very few) in which polyandry exists, it is a group of brothers who share a wife. In some cases a group of sisters will be 'married' to a group of brothers, and in such situations the children belong to the family group. Individual paternity is thus socially less important than membership of a family unit.

Paternity is of crucial importance in societies in which status, positions, and property are transmitted through the male line. The notion of the group, related through the male line, can in some societies have such force that sexual relations between a woman and any male from the same group as that into which she was born (and such a group can include a considerable number of individuals, all the descendants of a common great-grandfather, for example) are regarded as incestuous. We can see with the example of the Nayar (although the Nayar do constitute an exceptional case) that paternity has far less social significance if all important social attributes are gained through inheritance down the female line. (It is important to recognize that such a system of inheritance does not imply that men are marginalized . . . but that it is brothers rather than husbands who are the significant social males.)

Even in situations in which the attribution of paternity is so important we cannot simply assume that the concepts of legitimacy and illegitimacy are clearcut. In many societies of this kind there are all kinds of arrangements for the allocation of children—which are not wholly dependent on the concepts of the determining factor of parenthood.

Household and Residence

Our conception of what constitutes the family is dependent not only on what we have called kinship ties but equally in terms of residence, domestic units, or households. Given the range of kinship relations that we have briefly explored, it is inevitable that a wide range of different residential patterns exist. Moreover, households will not only be composed of individuals whose relations to each other are based on different criteria, but the size and composition over time of such households will vary, as will their relation to production, to other units, and to social positions.

There are three basic forms of residence as isolated by anthropologists: vivilocal, where a married couple and their children live with the kin of the husband; matrilocal, where the couple live with the kin of the wife; and neolocal, where the couple live independently of either group of kin. This scheme is however further complicated by the fact that in many societies in which descent is traced through the female line (matrilineal societies), the children might initially live with the mother and father with the father's kin, and then later move to live with their mother's kin; in other words, with their mother's brothers, those from whom they will inherit property, status, or position. Often in such societies (such as the Trobriand Islanders) daughters never live with their mother's kin—they stay with their fathers until they marry and then move to their husband's kin. The complication of residence patterns is considerable—one of the factors which these different patterns demonstrate is that households as units of parents and their children are not a necessary or permanent social arrangement. The extent to which individuals are identified with any one household, both as children and as adults, varies considerably. In most matrilineal societies men will circulate and often a man will split his available time and space between kin and conjugal roles. In some societies of this kind, men will live alternately in two places, or will frequently visit two different units, or move at different stages from one to another. In the case of the polyandrous Toda, a woman married to different men

will circulate between their different households (Rivers 1906). Children similarly will shift residence in many societies—in many instances, because of the 'institution' of fostering whereby from the age of about five, children are sent to be brought up by non-parental kin. Claims to have a foster child are formally expressed as the rights held by a man in his sister's children—and by a woman in her brother's daughter—but it is much more extensive than this, and there are many instances of children living with their grandparents (Goody 1969: 192). Households then can often be extremely fluid units, with shifting membership.

In most of the known societies of the world, monogamy is the exception rather than the rule. Some anthropologists claim that over 90 per cent of the world's cultures involve plural polygamous marriages. We have already referred to polyandry, one woman with several husbands, but by far the most common form of polygamy is polygyny—one man with several wives.

In some polygynous societies, almost invariably those in which descent is traced through the male line, households consist of a series of relatively self-contained living quarters, in which a man and his wives, each with her own children, live, one wife in a relatively autonomous domestic unit. In others, domestic arrangements are dominated by a group of brothers, with their wives and their offspring.

The domestic existence of each smaller unit within such a group is determined by the existence of the larger group and is ultimately dependent on the authority of those males who are in control of the unit as a whole.

In such situations it is again difficult to arrive at a useful definition of such a unit if we are concerned to consider households purely as kinship entities. Is such a mother and children unit an entity, or is it a subhousehold within a much larger household?

The Tiv of Nigeria provided an example of this latter form of 'household'. Tiv kinship groups live in compounds, a circular arrangement of huts and granaries, in the centre of which is an open space—'the centre of Tiv family life'. The compound head is the senior, eldest man. He settles disputes, supervises the productive activities of the group and controls magic. His several wives live in separate units in the compound which is also inhabited by his junior children, unmarried daughters, and married sons and their families. In addition, there may be a younger brother and his family, and/or outsiders.

As is argued by the anthropologists involved, while in a sense each wife who has a separate hut and her children constitute a separate domestic unit, the larger compound group—a patrilineal extended family augmented by outsiders—is the central domestic unit of everyday Tiv life and of collective economic enterprise (Bohannon and Bohannon 1968).

It is only when we consider the household in terms of this latter—its productive capacities—that we can make sense of this kind of domestic unit usually found in agricultural communities. Households and domestic units are not only an arrangement of people related to each other through parent-child ties, but in societies such as the Tiv, they form units of production and have to be analyzed and understood as such.

Kinship ties have thus been seen by some anthropologists as constituting the relation of production. The Tiv compound, for example, is essentially a means of reuniting and controlling necessary labour, both productive and reproductive. Clearly households in many societies have to be analyzed as units of production and consumption, and as providers of labour. The form of the household must therefore be analyzed in terms of the economic structure of the society as a whole and cannot simply be seen as a unit containing the 'family', essentially defining sets of affective relations. Precisely because the western ideal of the nuclear family is so ideologically and spatially separated from wage labour, the recog-

nition of the profound economic significance of household formation in other societies has posed considerable problems for anthropologists. It has been even more difficult for western sociologists to re-examine the economic role of the family within their own society in the light of the understanding gained through anthropological analysis.

Polygynous households of the kind described above are common in Africa, south of the Sahara, and however different their form, they are usually crucial productive units. In New Guinea, very different domestic arrangements exist and these cannot be analyzed in terms of the same economic determinants. In Marind Anim and many other New Guinea societies, domestic organization constructs very considerable separation between men and women. Special men's houses provide the focal point for all male life (often including sleeping and eating) and there are often stringent taboos on women having access to such houses and, in general, on contact between males and females.

Conclusion

The family, particularly the nuclear family, can be seen, through comparative analysis, as just one very specific means of organizing the relations between parents and children, males and females. It is not, as has so often been claimed, some kind of 'natural' instinctive and 'sacred' unit. Even the bond between mothers and their own children, which is seen in almost mystic terms as the fundamental biologically determined relationship, can be seen as far less important than we are generally led to believe. Universal definitions of human relations must be constantly questioned and the whole notion of the 'natural' must, in terms of human relations, be challenged, and the 'unnatural'—in these terms the social construction of relationships—must be fully recognized.

References

Bohannon, P., and L. Bohannon. 1968. *Tiv Economy* (Northwestern University Press).

Carroll, V. 1970. *Adoption in Eastern Oceania* (The University of Hawaii Press).

Evans-Pritchard, E.E. 1951. *Kinship and Marriage among the Nuer* (Oxford: Clarendon Press).

Fox, R. 1967. *Kinship and Marriage* (Harmondsworth, UK: Pelican).

Goodenough, W.H. 1970. *Description and Comparison in Cultural Anthropology* (Chicago: Aldine Publishing).

Goody, J.R. 1969. *Comparative Studies in Kinship* (London: Routledge and Kegan Paul).

Keesing, R.M. 1976. *Cultural Anthropology, A Contemporary Perspective* (New York: Holt, Rinehart and Winston).

Levy, R.I. 1970. 'Tahitian Adoption as a Psychological Message' in *Adoption in Eastern Oceania*, ed. V. Carroll (The University of Hawaii Press).

Malinowski, B. 1922. *Argonauts of the Western Society* (London: Routledge and Kegan Paul).

Mead, M. 1935. *Sex and Temperament in Three Primitive Societies* (New York: William Morrow & Co.).

Rivers, W.H.R. 1906. *The Todas* (New York: Macmillan).

Schneider, D., and E.K. Gough. 1972. *Matrilineal Kinship* (Berkeley: University of California Press).

Van Baal, J. 1966. *The Dema: Description and Analysis of Culture (South New Guinea)* (The Hague: Martinius Nijhoff).

Chapter 2

This essay takes up where the last left off—with the insight that family is not determined by biology, and in fact is socially constructed. Specifically, anthropologists Collier, Rosaldo, and Yanagisako argue that family is an idea situated in the development of complex societies with distinct public and private spheres. Their discussion addresses the question why in industrial-capitalist societies family is seen as so important.

The work of Bronislaw Malinowski has most influenced anthropologists' thinking about family. So,

a consideration of his ideas is central in this article. While Malinowski's work may be unfamiliar to sociology students, his ideas have had a strong impact on sociological approaches to the study of family life: Talcott Parsons was his student. And Parsons' functionalist perspective on nuclear families—which held them to be the best arrangement for raising children and for meeting the emotional needs of adults—has had a lasting influence.

Is There a Family? New Anthropological Views

Jane Collier, Michelle Z. Rosaldo, and Sylvia Yanagisako

This essay poses a rhetorical question in order to argue that most of our talk about families is clouded by unexplored notions of what families 'really' are like. It is probably the case, universally, that people expect to have special connections with their genealogically closest relations. But a knowledge of genealogy does not in itself promote understanding of what these special ties are about. The real importance of The Family in contemporary social life and belief has blinded us to its dynamics. Confusing ideal with reality, we fail to appreciate the deep significance of what are, cross-culturally, various ideologies of intimate relationship, and at the same time we fail to reckon with the complex human bonds and experiences all too comfortably sheltered by a faith in the 'natural' source of a 'nurture' we think is found in the home.

This essay is divided into three parts. The first examines what social scientists mean by The Family. It focuses on the work of Bronislaw Malinowski, the anthropologist who first convinced social scientists that The Family was a universal human institution. The second part also has social scientists as its focus, but it examines works

by the nineteenth-century thinkers Malinowski refuted, for if—as we shall argue—Malinowski was wrong in viewing The Family as a universal human institution, it becomes important to explore the work of theorists who did not make Malinowski's mistakes. The final section then draws on the correct insights of nineteenth-century theorists to sketch some implications of viewing The Family, not as a concrete institution designed to fulfil universal human needs, but as an ideological construct associated with the modern state.

Malinowski's Concept of the Family

In 1913 Bronislaw Malinowski published a book called *The Family Among the Australian Aborigines* in which he laid to rest earlier debates about whether all human societies had families. During the nineteenth century, proponents of social evolution argued that primitives were sexually promiscuous and therefore incapable of having families because children would not recognize their fathers (Morgan 1877). Malinowski refuted this notion by showing that Australian aborigines, who were widely believed to practice 'primitive promiscuity', not only had rules regulating who might have intercourse with whom during sexual orgies but also differentiated between legal marriages and casual unions. Malinowksi thus 'proved' that Australian aborigines had marriage, and so proved that aboriginal children had fathers, because each child's mother had but a single recognized husband.

Malinowski's book did not simply add data to one side of an ongoing debate. It ended the debate altogether, for by distinguishing *coitus* from conjugal relationships, Malinowski separated questions of sexual behaviour from questions of the family's universal existence. Evidence of sexual promiscuity was henceforth irrelevant for deciding whether families existed. Moreover, Malinowski argued that the conjugal relationship, and therefore The Family, had to be universal because it fulfilled a universal human need. As he wrote in a posthumously published book:

> The human infant needs parental protection for a much longer period than does the young of even the highest anthropoid apes. Hence, no culture could endure in which the act of reproduction, that is, mating, pregnancy, and childbirth, was not linked up with the fact of legally-founded parenthood, that is, a relationship in which the father and mother have to look after the children for a long period, and, in turn, derive certain benefits from the care and trouble taken (Malinowski 1944: 99).

In proving the existence of families among Australian aborigines, Malinowski described three features of families that he believed flowed from The Family's universal function of nurturing children. First, he argued that families have to have clear boundaries, for if families were to perform the vital function of nurturing young children, insiders had to be distinguishable from outsiders so that everyone could know which adults were responsible for the care of which children.

Malinowski thus argued that families formed bounded social units, and to prove that Australian families formed such units, he demonstrated that aboriginal parents and children recognized one another. Each aboriginal woman had a single husband, even if some husbands occasionally allowed wives to sleep with other men during tribal ceremonies. Malinowski thus proved that each aboriginal child had a recognized mother and father, even if both parties occasionally engaged in sexual relations with outsiders.

Second, Malinowski argued that families had to have a place where family members could be together and where the daily tasks associated with childrearing could be performed. He demonstrated, for example, that aboriginal parents and their immature children shared a single fire—a home and hearth where children were fed and nurtured—even though, among nomadic aborigines, the fire might be kindled in a different location each night.

Finally, Malinowski argued that family members felt affection for one another—that parents who invested long years in caring for children were rewarded by their own and their children's affections for one another. Malinowski felt that long and intimate association among family members fostered close emotional ties, particularly between parents and children, but also between spouses. Aboriginal parents and their children, for example, could be expected to feel the same emotions for one another as did English parents and children, and as proof of this point, Malinowski recounted touching stories of the efforts made by aboriginal parents to recover children lost during conflicts with other aborigines or with white settlers and efforts made by stolen aboriginal children to find their lost parents.

Malinowski's book on Australian aborigines thus gave social scientists a concept of The Family that consisted of a universal function, the nurturance of young children, mapped onto (1) a bounded set of people who recognized one another and who were distinguishable from other like groups; (2) a definite physical space, a hearth and home; and (3) a particular set of emotions, family love. This concept of The Family as an institution for nurturing young children has been enduring, probably because nurturing children is thought to be the primary function of families in modern industrial societies. The flaw in Malinowski's argument is the flaw common to all functionalist arguments: because a social institution is observed to perform a necessary function does not mean either that the function would not be performed if the institution did not exist or that the function is responsible for the existence of the institution.

Later anthropologists have challenged Malinowski's ideas that family always includes fathers, but, ironically, they have kept all the other aspects of his definition. For example, later anthropologists have argued that the basic social unit is not the nuclear family including father but the unit composed of a mother and her children: 'Whether or not a mate becomes attached to the mother on some more or less permanent basis is a variable matter' (Fox 1967: 39). In removing father from the family, however, later anthropologists have nevertheless retained Malinowski's concept of The Family as a functional unit, and so have retained all the features Malinowski took such pains to demonstrate. In the writings of modern anthropologists, the mother-child unit is described as performing the universally necessary function of nurturing young children. A mother and her children form a bounded group, distinguishable from other units of mothers and their children. A mother and her children share a place, a home and hearth. And, finally, a mother and her children share deep emotional bonds based on their prolonged and intimate contact.

Modern anthropologists may have removed father from The Family, but they did not modify the basic social science concept of The Family in which the function of childrearing is mapped onto a bounded set of people who share a place and who 'love' one another. Yet it is exactly this concept of The Family that we, as feminist anthropologists, have found so difficult to apply. Although the biological facts of reproduction, when combined with a sufficiently elastic definition of marriage, make it possible for us, as social scientists, to find both mother-child units and Malinowski's conjugal-pairs-plus-children units in every human society, it is not at all clear that such Families necessarily exhibit the associated features Malinowski 'proved' and modern anthropologists echo.

An outside observer, for example, may be able to delimit family boundaries in any and all societies by identifying the children of one woman and that woman's associated mate, but natives may not be interested in making such distinctions. In other words, natives may not be concerned to distinguish family members from outsiders, as Malinowski imagined natives should be when he argued that units of parents and children have to have clear boundaries in order for child-rearing responsibilities to be assigned efficiently. Many languages, for example, have no word to identify the unit of parents and children that English speakers call a 'family'. Among the Zinacantecos of southern Mexico, the basic social unit is identified as a 'house', which may include from one to twenty people (Vogt 1969). Zinacantecos have no difficulty talking about an individual's parents, children, or spouse; but Zinacantecos do not have a single word that identifies the unit of parents and children in such a way as to cut it off from other like units. In Zinacantecos society, the boundary between 'houses' is linguistically marked, while the boundary between 'family' units is not.

Just as some languages lack words for identifying units of parents and children, so some 'families' lack places. Immature children in every society have to be fed and cared for, but parents and children do not necessarily eat and sleep together as a family in one place. Among the Mundurucu of tropical South America, for example, the men of a village traditionally lived in a men's house together with all the village boys over the age of thirteen; women lived with other women and young children in two or three houses grouped around the men's house (Murphy and Murphy 1974). In Mundurucu society, men and women ate and slept apart. Men ate in the men's house, sharing food the women had cooked and delivered to them; women ate with other women and children in their own houses. Married couples also slept apart, meeting only for sexual intercourse.

Finally, people around the world do not necessarily expect family members to 'love' one another. People may expect husbands, wives, parents, and children to have strong feelings about one another, but they do not necessarily expect prolonged and intimate contact to breed the loving sentiments Malinowski imagined as universally rewarding parents for the care they invested in children. The mother-daughter relationship, for example, is not always pictured as warm and loving. In modern Zambia, girls are not expected to discuss personal problems with, or seek advice from, their mothers. Rather, Zambian girls are expected to seek out some older female relative to serve as confidante (Shuster 1979). Similarly, among the Cheyenne Indians who lived on the American Great Plains during the last century, a mother was expected to have strained relations with her daughters (Hoebel 1978). Mothers are described as continually admonishing their daughters, leading the latter to seek affection from their fathers' sisters.

Of course, anthropologists have recognized that people everywhere do not share our deep faith in the loving, self-sacrificing mother, but in matters of family and motherhood, anthropologists, like all social scientists, have relied more on faith than evidence in constructing theoretical accounts. Because we *believe* mothers to be loving, anthropologists have proposed, for example, that a general explanation of the fact that men marry mother's brothers' daughters more frequently than they marry father's sisters' daughters is that men naturally seek affection (i.e., wives) where they have found affection in the past (i.e., from mothers and their kin) (Homans and Schneider 1955).

LOOKING BACKWARD

The Malinowskian view of The Family as a universal institution—which maps the 'function' of 'nurturance' onto a collectivity of specific persons (presumably 'nuclear' relations) associated with specific spaces ('the home') and specific affective bonds ('love')—corresponds, as we have seen, to that assumed by most contemporary writers on the subject. But a consideration of available ethnographic evidence suggests that the received view is a good deal more problematic than a naïve observer might think. If Families in Malinowski's sense are *not* universal, then we must begin to ask about the biases that, in the past, have led us to misconstrue the ethnographic record. The issues here are too complex for thorough explication in this essay, but if we are to better understand the nature of 'the family' in the present, it seems worthwhile to explore the question, first, of why so many social thinkers continue to believe in Capital-Letter Families as universal institutions, and second, whether anthropological tradition offers any alternatives to a 'necessary and natural' view of what our families are. Only then will we be in a position to suggest 'new anthropological perspectives' on the family today.

Our positive critique begins by moving backward. In the next few pages, we suggest that tentative answers to both questions posed above lie in the nineteenth-century intellectual trends that thinkers like Malinowski were at pains to reject. During the second half of the nineteenth century, a number of social and intellectual developments—among them, the evolutionary researches of Charles Darwin; the rise of 'urban problems' in fast-growing cities; and the accumulation of data on non-Western peoples by missionaries and agents of the colonial states—contributed to what most of us would now recognize as the beginnings of modern social science. Alternately excited and perplexed by changes in a rapidly industrializing world, thinkers as diverse as socialist Frederick Engels (1955) and bourgeois apologist Herbert Spencer (1973)—to say nothing of a host of mythographers, historians of religion, and even feminists—attempted to identify the distinctive problems and potentials of their contemporary society by constructing *evolutionary* accounts of 'how it all began'. At base, a sense of 'progress' gave direction to their thought, whether, like Spencer, they believed 'man' had advanced from the love of violence to a more civilized love of peace or, like Engels, that humanity had moved from primitive promiscuity and incest toward monogamy and 'individual sex love'. Proud of their position in the modern world, some of these writers claimed that rules of force had been transcended by new rules of law (Mill 1869), while others thought that feminine 'mysticism' in the past had been supplanted by a higher male 'morality' (Bachofen 1861).

At the same time, and whatever else they thought of capitalist social life (some of them criticized, but none wholly abhorred it), these writers also shared a sense of moral emptiness and a fear of instability and loss. Experience argued forcefully to them that moral order in their time did not rest on the unshakable hierarchy—from God to King to Father in the home—enjoyed by Europeans in the past (Fee 1974). Thus, whereas Malinowski's functionalism led him to stress the underlying continuities in all human social forms, his nineteenth-century predecessors were concerned to understand the facts and forces that set their experiential world apart. They were interested in comparative and, more narrowly, evolutionary accounts because their lives were torn between celebration and fear of change. For them, the family was important not because it had at all times been the same but because it was all at once the moral precondition for, the triumph of, and the victim of developing capitalist society. Without the family and female spheres, thinkers like Ruskin feared we would fall victim

to a market that destroys real human bonds (Ruskin 1907). Then again, while men like Engels could decry the impact of the market on familial life and love, he joined with more conservative counterparts to insist that our contemporary familial forms benefited from the individualist morality of modern life and reached to moral and romantic heights unknown before.

Given this purpose and the limited data with which they had to work, it is hardly surprising that the vast majority of what these nineteenth-century writers said is easily dismissed today. They argued that in simpler days such things as incest were the norm; they thought that women ruled in 'matriarchal' and peace-loving states or, alternatively, that brute force determined the primitive right and wrong. None of these visions of a more natural, more feminine, more sexy, or more violent primitive world squares with contemporary evidence about what, in technological and organizational terms, might be reckoned relatively 'primitive' or 'simple' social forms. We would suggest, however, that whatever their mistakes, these nineteenth-century thinkers *can* help us rethink the family today, at least in part because we are (unfortunately) their heirs, in the area of prejudice, and partly because their concern to characterize difference and change gave rise to insights much more promising than their functionalist critics may have thought.

To begin, although nineteenth-century evolutionary theorists did not believe The Family to be universal, the roots of modern assumptions can be seen in their belief that women are, and have at all times been, defined by nurturant, connective, and reproductive roles that *do not* change through time. Most nineteenth-century thinkers imaged social development as a process of differentiation from a relatively confused (and thus incestuous) and indiscriminate female-oriented state to one in which men fight, destroy their 'natural' social bonds, and then forge public and political ties to create a human 'order'. For some, it seemed reasonable to assume that women dominated, as matriarchs, in the undifferentiated early state, but even these theorists believed that women everywhere were 'mothers' first, defined by 'nurturant' concerns and thus excluded from the business competition, cooperation, social ordering, and social change propelled and dominated by their male counterparts. And so, while nineteenth-century writers differed in their evaluations of such things as 'women's status', they all believed that female reproductive roles made women different from and complementary to men and guaranteed both the relative passivity of women in human history and the relative continuity of 'feminine' domains and functions in human societies. Social change consisted in the acts of men, who left their mothers behind in shrinking homes. And women's nurturant sphere was recognized as a complementary and necessary corrective to the more competitive pursuits of men, not because these thinkers recognized women as political actors who influence the world, but because they feared the unchecked and morally questionable growth of a male-dominated capitalist market.

For nineteenth-century evolutionists, women were associated, in short, with an unchanging biological role and a romanticized community of the past, while men were imaged as the agents of all social process. And though contemporary thinkers have been ready to dismiss manifold aspects of their now-dated school of thought, on this point we remain, perhaps unwittingly, their heirs. Victorian assumptions about gender and the relationship between competitive male markets and peace-loving female homes were not abandoned in later functionalist schools of thought at least in part because pervasive sexist biases make it easy to forget that women, like men, are important actors in *all* social worlds. Even more, the functionalists, themselves concerned to understand all human social forms in terms of biological 'needs', turned out to strengthen earlier beliefs associating action, change, and interest with the deeds of men because they thought of kinship in terms of biologically given ties, of 'families' as units geared to

reproductive needs, and finally, of women as mere 'reproducers' whose contribution to society was essentially defined by the requirements of their homes.

If most modern social scientists have inherited Victorian biases that tend ultimately to support a view uniting women and The Family to an apparently unchanging set of biologically given needs, we have at the same time failed to reckon with the one small area in which Victorian evolutionists were right. They understood, as we do not today, that families—like religions, economies, governments, or courts of law—are *not* unchanging but the product of various social forms, that the relationships of spouses and parents to their young are apt to be different things in different social orders. More particularly, although nineteenth-century writers had primitive society all wrong, they were correct in insisting that *family* in the modern sense—a unit bounded, biologically as well as legally defined, associated with property, self-sufficiency, with affect and a space 'inside' the home—is something that emerges not in Stone Age caves but in complex state-governed social forms. Tribal peoples may speak readily of lineages, households, and clans, but—as we have seen—they rarely have a word denoting Family as a particular and limited group of kin; they rarely worry about differences between legitimate and illegitimate heirs or find themselves concerned (as we so often are today) that what children and/or parents do reflects on their family's public image and self-esteem. Political influence in tribal groups in fact consists in adding children to one's home and, far from distinguishing Smith from Jones, encouraging one's neighbours to join one's household as if kin. By contrast, modern bounded Families try to keep their neighbours out. Clearly their character, ideology, and functions are not given for all times. Instead, to borrow the Victorian phrase, The Family is a 'moral' unit, a way of organizing and thinking about human relationships in a world in which the domestic is perceived to be in opposition to a politics shaped outside the home, and individuals find themselves dependent on a set of relatively noncontingent ties in order to survive the dictates of an impersonal market and external political order.

In short, what the Victorians recognized and we have tended to forget is, first, that human social life has varied in its 'moral'—we might say its 'cultural' or 'ideological'—forms, and so it takes more than making babies to make Families. And having seen The Family as something more than a response to omnipresent, biologically given needs, they realized too that Families do not everywhere exist; rather, The Family (thought to be universal by most social scientists today) is a moral and ideological unit that appears, not universally, but in particular social orders. The Family as we know it is not a 'natural' group created by the claims of 'blood' but a sphere of human relationships shaped by a state that recognized Families as units that hold property, provide for care and welfare, and attend particularly to the young—a sphere conceptualized as a realm of love and intimacy *in opposition* to the more 'impersonal' norms that dominate modern economies and politics. One can, in nonstate social forms, find groups of genealogically related people who interact daily and share material resources, but the contents of their daily ties, the ways they think about their bonds and their conception of the relationship between immediate 'familial' links and other kinds of sociality, are apt to be different from the ideas and feelings we think rightfully belong to families we know. Stated otherwise, because our notions of The Family are rooted in a contrast between 'public' and 'private' spheres, we will not find that Families like ours exist in a society where public and political life is radically different from our own.

Victorian thinkers rightly understood the link between the bounded modern Family and the modern state, although they thought the two related by a necessary teleology of moral progress. Our point resembles theirs not in the *explanations* we would seek but in our feeling that if we, today,

are interested in change, we must begin to probe and understand change in the families of the past. Here the Victorians, not the functionalists, are our rightful guides because the former recognized that *all* human social ties have 'cultural' or 'moral' shapes, and more specifically, that the particular 'morality' of contemporary familial forms is rooted in a set of processes that link our intimate experiences and bonds to public politics.

Toward a Rethinking

Our perspective on families therefore compels us to listen carefully to what the natives in other societies say about their relationships with genealogically close kin. The same is true of the natives in our own society. Our understanding of families in contemporary American society can be only as rich as our understanding of what The Family represents symbolically to Americans. A complete cultural analysis of The Family as an American ideological construct, of course, is beyond the scope of this essay. But we can indicate some of the directions such an analysis would take and how it would deepen our knowledge of American families.

One of the central notions in the modern American construct of The Family is that of nurturance. When antifeminists attack the Equal Rights Amendment, for example, much of their rhetoric plays on the anticipated loss of nurturant, intimate bonds we associate with The Family. Likewise, when pro-life forces decry abortion, they cast it as the ultimate denial of nurturance. In a sense, these arguments are variations of a functionalist view that weds families to specific functions. The logic of the argument is that because people need nurturance, and people get nurtured in The Family, then people need The Family. Yet if we adopt the perspective that The Family is an ideological unit rather than merely a functional unit, we are encouraged to subject this syllogism to closer scrutiny. We can ask, first, what do people mean by nurturance? Obviously, they mean more than mere nourishment—that is, the provision of food, clothing, and shelter required for biological survival. What is evoked by the word nurturance is a certain kind of relationship: a relationship that entails affection and love, that is based on cooperation as opposed to competition, that is enduring rather than temporary, that is noncontingent rather than contingent upon performance, and that is governed by feeling and morality instead of law and contract.

The reason we have stated these attributes of The Family in terms of oppositions is because in a symbolic system the meanings of concepts are often best illuminated by explicating their opposites. Hence, to understand our American construct of The Family, we first have to map the larger system of constructs of which it is only a part. When we undertake such an analysis of The Family in our society, we discover that what gives shape to much of our conception of The Family is its symbolic opposition to work and business, in other words, to the market relations of capitalism. For it is in the market, where we sell our labour and negotiate contract relations of business, that we associate with competitive, temporary, contingent relations that must be buttressed by law and legal sanctions.

The symbolic opposition between The Family and market relations renders our strong attachment to The Family understandable, but it also discloses the particularity of our construct of The Family. We can hardly be speaking of a universal notion of The Family shared by people everywhere and for all time because people everywhere and for all time have not participated in market relations out of which they have constructed a contrastive notion of the family.

The realization that our idea of The Family is part of a set of symbolic oppositions through which we interpret our experience in a particular society compels us to ask to what extent this set of oppositions reflects real relations between people and to what extent it also shapes them. We do not adhere to a model of culture in which ideol-ogy is isolated from people's experience. On the other hand, neither do we construe the connection between people's constructs and people's experience to be a simple one of epiphenomenal reflection. Rather, we are interested in understanding how people come to summarize their experience in folk constructs that gloss over the diversity, complexity, and contradictions in their relationships. If, for example, we consider the second premise of the aforementioned syllogism—the idea that people get 'nurtured' in families—we can ask how people reconcile this premise with the fact that relationships in families are not always simple or altruistic. We need not resort to the evidence offered by social historians (e.g., Philippe Ariès [1962] and Lawrence Stone [1977]) of the harsh treatment and neglect of children and spouses in the history of the Western family, for we need only read our local newspaper to learn of similar abuses among contemporary families. And we can point to other studies, such as Young and Willmott's *Family and Kinship in East London* (1957), that reveal how people often find more intimacy and emotional support in relationships with individuals and groups outside The Family than they do in their relationships with family members.

The point is not that our ancestors or our contemporaries have been uniformly mean and non-nurturant to family members but that we have all been both nice and mean, both generous and ungenerous, to them. In like manner, our actions toward family members are not always motivated by selfless altruism but are also motivated by instrumental self-interest. What is significant is that, despite the fact that our complex relationships are the result of complex motivations, we ideologize relations with The Family as nurturant while casting relationships outside The Family—particularly in the sphere of work and businesss—as just the opposite.

We must be wary of oversimplifying matters by explaining away those disparities between our notion of the nurturant Family and our real actions toward family members as the predictable failing of imperfect beings. For there is more here than the mere disjunction of the ideal and the real. The American construct of The Family, after all, is complex enough to comprise some key contradictions. The Family is seen as representing not only the antithesis of the market relations of capitalism; it is also sacralized in our minds as the last stronghold against The State, as the symbolic refuge from the intrusions of a public domain that constantly threatens our sense of privacy and self-determination. Consequently, we can hardly be surprised to find that the punishments imposed on people who commit physical violence are lighter when their victims are their own family members (Lundsgaarde 1977). Indeed, the American sense of the privacy of the things that go on inside families is so strong that a smaller percentage of homicides involving family members are prosecuted than those involving strangers (Lundsgaarde 1977). We are faced with the irony that in our society the place where nurturance and noncontingent affection are supposed to be located is simultaneously the place where violence is most tolerated.

There are other dilemmas about The Family that an examination of its ideological nature can help us better understand. For example, the hypothesis that in England and the United States marriages among lower-income ('working-class') groups are characterized by a greater degree of 'conjugal role segregation' than are marriages among middle-income groups has generated considerable confusion. Since Bott observed that working-class couples in her study of London families exhibited more 'segregated' conjugal roles than 'middle-class' couples, who tended toward more 'joint' conjugal roles, researchers have come forth with a range of diverse and confusing findings (Bott 1957). On the one hand, some researchers have found that working-class couples indeed report more segregated conjugal role-relationships—in other words, clearly differentiated male and female tasks, as well as inter-

ests and activities—than do middle-class couples (Gans 1962; Rosser and Harris 1965). Other researchers, however, have raised critical methodological questions about how one goes about defining a joint activity and hence measuring the degree of 'jointness' in a conjugal relationship (Zelditch 1964; Turner 1967; Platt 1969). Platt's findings that couples who reported 'jointness' in one activity were not particularly likely to report 'jointness' in another activity is significant because it demonstrates that 'jointness' is not a general characteristic of a relationship that manifests itself uniformly over a range of domains. Couples carry out some activities and tasks together or do them separately but equally; they also have other activities in which they do not both participate. The measurement of the 'jointness' of conjugal relationships becomes even more problematic when we recognize that what one individual or couple may label a 'joint activity', another individual or couple may consider a 'separate activity'. In Bott's study, for example, some couples felt that all activities carried out by husband and wife in each other's presence were

> similar in kind regardless of whether the activities were complementary (e.g., sexual intercourse, though no one talked about this directly in the home interview), independent (e.g., husband repairing something while the wife read or knitted), or shared (e.g., washing up together, entertaining friends, going to the pictures together). It was not even necessary that husband and wife should actually be together. As long as they were both at home it was felt that their activities partook of some special, shared, family quality (Bott 1957).

In other words, the distinction Bott drew among 'joint', 'differentiated', and 'autonomic' (independent) relationships summarized the way people thought and felt about their activities rather than what they were observed to actually do. Again, it is not simply that there is a disjunction between what people say they do and what they in fact do. The more cogent point is that the meaning people attach to action, whether they view it as coordinated and therefore shared in some other way, is an integral component of that action and cannot be divorced from it in our analysis. When we compare the conjugal relationships of middle-income and low-income people, or any of the family relationships among different class, age, ethnic, and regional sectors of American society, we must recognize that our comparisons rest on differences and similarities in ideological and moral meanings as well as differences and similarities in action.

Finally, the awareness that The Family is not a concrete 'thing' that fulfils concrete 'needs' but an ideological construct with moral implications can lead to a more refined analysis of historical change in the American or Western family than has devolved upon us from our functionalist ancestors. The functionalist view of industrialization, urbanization, and family change depicts The Family as responding to alterations in economic and social conditions in rather mechanistic ways. As production gets removed from the family's domain, there is less need for strict rules and clear authority structures in the family to accomplish productive work. At the same time, individuals who now must work for wages in impersonal settings need a haven where they can obtain emotional support and gratification. Hence, The Family becomes more concerned with 'expressive' functions, and what emerges is the modern 'companionate family'. In short, in the functionalist narrative The Family and its constituent members 'adapt' to fulfil functional requirements created for it by the industrialization of production. Once we begin to view The Family as an ideological unit and pay due respect to it as a moral statement, however, we can begin to unravel the more complex, dialectical process through which family relationships and The Family as a construct were mutually transformed. We can examine, for one, the ways in which people and state institutions acted, rather than merely reacted, to assign certain functions to groupings of kin by making them legally responsible for these functions. We can investigate the manner in which the increasing limitations placed on agents of the community and the state with regard to negotiating the relationships between family members enhanced the independence of The Family. We can begin to understand the consequences of social reforms and wage policies for the age and sex inequalities in families. And we can elucidate the interplay between these social changes and the cultural transformations that assigned new meanings and modified old ones to make The Family what we think it to be today.

Ultimately, this sort of rethinking will lead to a questioning of the somewhat contradictory modern views that families are things we need (the more 'impersonal' the public world, the more we need them) and at the same time that loving families are disappearing. In a variety of ways, individuals today *do* look to families for a 'love' that money cannot buy and find; our contemporary world makes 'love' more fragile than most of us hope and 'nurturance' more self-interested than we believe (Rapp 1978). But what we fail to recognize is that familial nurturance and the social forces that turn our ideal families into mere fleeting dreams are *equally* creations of the world we know *today*. Rather than think of the ideal family as a world we lost (or, like the Victorians, as a world just recently achieved), it is important for us to recognize that while families symbolize deep and salient modern themes, contemporary families are unlikely to fulfil our equally modern nurturant needs.

We probably have no cause to fear (or hope) that The Family will dissolve. What we can begin to ask is what we *want* our families to do. Then, distinguishing our hopes from what we have, we can begin to analyze the social forces that enhance or undermine the realization of the kinds of human bonds we need.

References

Ariès, P. 1962. *Centuries of Childhood*, trans. R. Baldick (New York: Vintage).

Bachofen, J.J. 1861. *Das Mutterrecht* (Stuttgart).

Bott, E. 1957. *Family and Social Network: Roles, Norms, and External Relationships in Ordinary Urban Families* (London: Tavistock).

Engels, F. 1955. *The Origin of the Family, Private Property and the State* in *Karl Marx and Frederick Engels: Selected Works*, v. 2 (Moscow: Foreign Language Publishing House).

Fee, E. 1974. 'The Sexual Politics of Victorian Social Anthropology' in *Clio's Consciousness: Raised*, eds M. Hartman and L. Banner (New York: Harper & Row).

Fox, R. 1967. *Kinship and Marriage* (London: Penguin).

Gans, H.J. 1962. *The Urban Villagers* (New York: Free Press).

Hoebel, E.A. 1978. *The Cheyennes: Indians of the Great Plains* (New York: Holt, Rinehart and Winston).

Homans, G.C., and D.M. Schneider. 1955. *Marriage, Authority, and Final Causes* (Glencoe, IL: Free Press).

Lundsgaarde, H.P. 1977. *Murder in Space City: A Cultural Analysis of Houston Homicide Patterns* (New York: Oxford University Press).

Malinowski, B. 1913. *The Family Among the Australian Aborigines* (London: University of London Press).

———. 1944. *A Scientific Theory of Culture* (Chapel Hill: University of North Carolina Press).

Mill, J.S. 1869. *The Subjection of Women* (London: Longmans, Green, Reader and Dyer).

Morgan, L.H. 1877. *Ancient Society* (New York: Holt).

Murphy, Y., and R. Murphy. 1974. *Women of the Forest* (New York: Columbia University Press).

Platt, J. 1969. 'Some Problems in Measuring the Jointness of Conjugal Role-Relationships', *Sociology* 3: 287–97.

Rapp, R. 1978. 'Family and Class in Contemporary America: Notes Toward an Understanding of Ideology', *Science and Society* 42: 278–300.

Rosser, C., and C. Harris. 1965. *The Family and Social Change* (London: Routledge and Kegan Paul).

Ruskin, J. 1907. 'Of Queen's Gardens' in *Sesame and Lilies* (London: J.M. Dent).

Shuster, I. 1979. *New Women of Lusaka* (Palo Alto, CA: Mayfield).

Spencer, H. 1973. *The Principles of Sociology*, v. 1, *Domestic Institutions* (New York: Appleton).

Stone, L. 1977. *The Family, Sex, and Marriage in England 1500–1800* (London: Weidenfeld and Nicolson).

Turner, C. 1967. 'Conjugal Roles and Social Networks: A Re-examination of an Hypothesis', *Human Relations* 20: 121–30.

Vogt, E.Z. 1969. *Zinacantan: A Mayu Community in the Highlands of Chiapas* (Cambridge, MA: Harvard University Press).

Young, M., and P. Willmott. 1957. *Family and Kinship in East London* (London: Routledge and Kegan Paul).

Zelditch, Jr, M. 1964. 'Family, Marriage and Kinship' in *A Handbook of Modern Sociology*, ed. R.E.L. Faris (Chicago: Rand McNally), 680–707.

Chapter 3

If there is no universal pattern of family, and indeed 'family' makes no sense in societies without a distinction between public and private, how might we conceptualize family as we try to understand cross- cultural variations and historical changes in it? This essay offers a definition of family that informs many of the discussions in the rest of the book.

Conceptualizing Family

Bonnie Fox and Meg Luxton

When people use the term *family*, they usually assume that what they mean by it is clear. Yet, depending on the context, the term has a variety of meanings. An adult man who talks about working to support his family probably means his wife and young children. An adult woman who plans to quit her job to have a family is referring to children. A university student going home to spend the holidays with her family likely means her parents and siblings. Someone who explains that his family was killed in the Holocaust probably means an extended kin group. Still someone else who describes a group of friends as 'my real family' is identifying those who give significant emotional and personal support. At the same time, when a play or film is advertised as 'family entertainment', the implication is that few people will find anything offensive in it. And when politicians claim to support 'family values' they usually mean something quite different from gays and lesbians who claim 'we are family, too'.

These diverse usages show how slippery the term is. In this paper, we review various common-sense, scholarly, and government definitions of *family*, as well as some of the practical implications of these definitions. We then raise some questions of pressing concern and propose a way of approaching the study of family life that may eventually generate answers to the questions.

The Familiar and the Commonsensical

We suggest that the complexities, contradictions, and confusions surrounding the way *family* is used derive from several often poorly understood issues. Perhaps the most important of these issues is that because almost everyone is a member of a family and lives for significant periods of time in a family, they assume that they know very well what *family* means. As well, getting married, having children in the context of marriage, and living as a nuclear family, are such widely accepted patterns in Canadian society they often seem natural. For many people, the pattern of marriage and nuclear families is so taken for granted that it is difficult to question.

Even more problematic, there is often a confusion of common-sense ideas, moral judgments, and actual practices. The fact that the majority of women and men marry and live as couples, for example, reinforces for many people the idea that families should be based on heterosexual monogamous couples. Such beliefs may easily lead to moral assessments that those who do not live in such relationships are inferior, or immoral, or to be pitied. Moreover, it is commonly assumed that other family patterns cause problems, especially for children.

The ease with which people accept marriage and nuclear family forms comes in part from the way ideas about marriage and 'the family' are central to common-sense ideologies. The belief that biology is a 'given', that it determines various social phenomena—such as personality and behaviour, as well as institutions like 'the family'—is strong in this culture. Thus, the biology of reproduction seems to 'naturally' produce the nuclear-family pattern.

Reinforcing that popular assumption, conservative politicians and activist groups calling themselves 'pro-family' have played on people's anxieties and anger about the social changes transforming their lives, and focused those feelings on changing family patterns. 'The family' has been very effectively invoked to symbolize a mythical (and lost) past (Coontz 1992, and this text). And under the guise of 'family values', policies are promoted that could actually undermine people's welfare.

Finally, family relationships are often so emotionally profound and so deeply tied to unconscious feelings that the assumptions of those who grew up in nuclear families are even harder to question. Nevertheless, notions that the nuclear family is a natural unit must be interrogated, if for no other reason than that they have important practical consequences for most of us.

For instance, *family* is a legal term. It involves particular definitions and entails specific legal rights and obligations for certain people. Biological and adoptive parents are required to provide material support and emotional nurturing for their children and are normally entitled to custody of, or access to, those children. Other people who may have deep emotional relations with the children are not recognized in law. Thus, a divorced father's lover who may have lived with the children on a daily basis and cared for them for years has no legal claim to them, while the father's parents do—even though they may have seen the children only once a year as they grew up.

State-regulated institutions such as schools or hospitals use marriage and family relations to determine which people will be informed and consulted about the status of someone in the institution. Thus, critically ill patients may find that family members with whom they have had little contact are admitted to their rooms and entitled to make significant medical decisions whereas friends who have provided daily support and who best know their wishes are excluded. Similarly, even when someone designates an heir in a will, the 'immediate family' has some legal grounds to challenge that will and claim a right to the inheritance. Finally, until 1999 in Ontario a wife of only weeks was entitled to a widow's pension while a same-sex lover of twenty years was not. Only recently are same-sex partners gaining the rights and privileges heterosexual spouses take for granted: In the 1990s, same-sex partners of employees of the federal government and Manitoba became eligible for benefits such as health care and Canada pension (Larson et al. 2000). In 1997, British Columbia became the first jurisdiction in North America to extend the definition of *spouse* to include same-sex partners living together for at least two years (Larson et al. 2000).[1]

In short, how we conceptualize *family* matters. Embodying a set of cultural assumptions, the concept informs legislation, policies, and practices that govern our lives. It also shapes decisions we make as individuals about how to live our lives. It limits or expands our imaginations as we think about the future.

Formal Definitions

Standard definitions of *the family* centre on a number of characteristics to identify a kind of social unit—rather than focus on social relationships involved in specific activities and bearing special emotional significance. The former tendency makes apparent sense to governments, which need to count and classify their populations to assess the need for social services, and even to social scientists when their chief concern is classification. Accordingly, Statistics Canada's definition of a *census family* is: 'A husband and wife [including common-law couples] (with or without children who are unmarried), or a lone parent with one or more children who have never married (regardless of age), living in the same dwelling unit.' This is differentiated from an *economic family*, which is a group of two or more persons who are related to each other by blood, marriage, or adoption, and who live in the same dwelling. In both definitions, if a woman and man live together, they are treated as if married, regardless of their legal status (Statistics Canada 1984 viii–ix and Table 4).

In restricting family to heterosexual partners and people related by blood or marriage, and by insisting on co-residence, this definition excludes some people in relationships involving the dependency and daily caring relationships that are characteristic of families and who consider themselves a family. In fact, it is no doubt because activities and functions are not specified—much less the social relations responsible for them—that biology and legal status are so easily accepted as determinants of family. Lesbian and gay partners living together as married couples; elderly friends sharing financial resources and providing each other necessary daily support; and people in other types of relationships who share material resources, provide daily support services, and have deep emotional connections are all excluded.

As Margrit Eichler (1988) has argued, this definition, when used to establish eligibility for policies supposed to support families, can threaten the welfare of individuals and undermine the economic bases of some families (e.g., the 'married exemption' for income taxes excludes same-sex couples). When used to set policy on access to loved ones, it can separate needy people from those who give them care and support (e.g., visiting rights in hospitals).[2]

It is generally problematic to specify relationships determined by blood, marriage, or residence, and exclude some *social* relationships of

exactly the same nature.[3] Anthropologists (see, e.g., Sahlins 1976; Goody 1976; and Collier et al. 1982, and this text) have shown persuasively that family and kinship are social creations and not products of biology. Even in the simplest human societies, biological ties do not establish the domestic groups that provide mutual support and nurturance of children (Lee 1979). Through human history, the composition and organization of domestic groups have varied tremendously. In other words, the group that lives together, cooperates to produce its subsistence, and cares for children has not always consisted of people tied by blood or marriage. Logically, then, social functions and not biological relations might be the way to identify family.

Different Approaches to Conceptualizing Family

Through the years, dozens—perhaps even hundreds—of definitions of family have been proposed. Indeed, different definitions may be required to serve different purposes: Scholarly definitions may necessarily look different than those used for setting social policy or administering social services (e.g., immigration policy and social work). For the sake of developing a sociological analysis of family and family problems, a definition must accommodate family diversity—both across cultures and within our own culture. Nevertheless, many definitions offered by sociologists suffer from the problem of ethnocentric exclusion of certain types of functioning families. They reflect a familistic ideology most North Americans believe—namely that relations of marriage and blood are the only ones that truly involve (and *can* involve) strong commitment to people's welfare, and especially to the nurturance of children.

Reflecting the influence of Bronislaw Malinowski and his student Talcott Parsons on family sociology, many definitions suffer from the same problems that pervaded structural-functionalist sociology in the 1950s and 1960s. In order to discover regularities and patterns in a complex social world, Parsons and Bales (1955) and fellow structural functionalists abstracted from most detail and constructed highly general models of social reality. For Parsons, the family involved a man and a woman in a basic division of labour; that gendered division of labour was functional (see also Zelditch 1960).

North American experimenters had found in the lab that small groups responsible for performing a task tended to produce and perhaps require both a 'task leader' and an 'emotional leader'. Parsons held families to be a type of small group, with the same properties. For Parsons, the central task families perform is having and raising children—a task functional and necessary to all societies. A short step from this argument was the common assumption, and explicit argument, that since nuclear families were the best units for rearing children, they were universal and essential. Of course, once nuclear families are defined as the best unit for childrearing, their necessity is virtually given. The provocative question whether it *is* best for children to grow up in nuclear families is one this argument sidesteps.

Astounding evidence of Parsons' sexism was his labelling of the work women do—specifically, the provision of childcare, the socialization of children, and the maintenance and management of the household—as 'emotional' and not 'instrumental'. Indeed, in emphasizing the functional nature of the division of household labour by gender, Parsons' work blatantly rationalized the gender inequality characteristic of 1950s North America. Further, by asserting that the family form predominant among white middle-class Americans was functional and natural, Parsons paved the way for those who insisted that other family forms—especially those common in the African-American community (Stack 1974)—were 'deviant' or inadequate.

Parsons' work, influential though it was—and close as it still is to some popular views of family—

was soundly criticized and largely dismissed some time ago by most sociologists (see Morgan 1975). The theme of a functional fit of family to society could not predict the changes that are now so evident in families. More important, his assumption that what was functional (or good) for society was good for the individual could not withstand the feminist critique of the organization of nuclear families. Indeed, sociology had to reconceptualize *family* after feminist theorists made a public issue of the private oppression of full-time housewives (see Friedan 1963; Luxton 1980). Insisting that women's experience of marriage was very different from men's, that private housework was isolating, unrewarding, and connected with economic dependency, and that there was a power differential central to marriage (which too often was expressed through men's violence against their wives), feminist social scientists irrevocably transformed sociology's depiction of family life (Barrett and McIntosh 1982; Thorne and Yalom 1982; Mandell and Duffy 1988; Fox 1997).

Reacting to the inadequacies of old conceptualizations, and surveying the variety of family patterns excluded in these old definitions, some sociologists today conclude that there is no such thing as 'the family'. In other words, people's experiences of family life, and the kinds of families they live in, are infinitely varied. This conclusion, unfortunately, ignores activities in which these different types of families might all be involved; it ignores the common patterns that establish the institutional nature of family.

It is a short step from the conclusion that the family does not exist to the argument that the family is essentially only a symbol system or ideology (Barrett and McIntosh 1982; Gittins 1985). In short, for some writers, the family is a set of ideas; and in this society we are all subject to a hegemonic (or dominant) ideology about families. Specifically, familism, which sees the nuclear family as universal and necessary, constitutes an ideology that characterizes Western capitalist societies (Barrett and McIntosh 1982).

Equating family with familistic discourse is problematic, however. Although it is true that symbol systems make social life meaningful and therefore profoundly shape our lives, it is also the case that there is a material reality to personal life that must be understood. There are social processes and social relations involved in family—which often assume patterned regularity—that cannot be reduced to sets of ideas, however intricately bound up with ideas they are. So what are these social processes and social relations that constitute family?

Towards Definition and Conceptualization

Before the eighteenth century in Europe, there was no term of reference for people related by blood, marriage, or common residence: The term *family* was not used (Flandrin 1979). Even in cultures and historical times when the nuclear unit was present, it was not necessarily distinguished from the larger groupings of which it was a part. Yet, throughout history children have been raised and (many) adults' basic needs for food, shelter, and care have been met—although how these were defined has varied tremendously.

Most basically, it is arguable that this is what we are concerned with when we study family—the maintenance of life on a daily and generational basis. Specifically, the social relationships that people create to care for children and other dependants daily and to ensure that the needs of the adults responsible for these dependents also are met constitute family. Feminist social scientists refer to this work as social reproduction. As Barbara Laslett and Johanna Brenner (1989: 382–3) have stated:

> Among other things, social reproduction includes how food, clothing, and shelter are made available for immediate consumption, the ways in which the care and socialization of children are provided, the care of the infirm and elderly, and the social organiza-

tion of sexuality. Social reproduction can thus be seen to include various kinds of work—mental, manual, and emotional—aimed at providing the historically and socially, as well as biologically, defined care necessary to maintain existing life and to reproduce the next generation.

In every social system there is a relationship between the way people produce their subsistence and wealth—the food, shelter, clothing and other goods, including the tools to produce those goods—and the way the human population is produced. This relationship is never simple or direct. However, the type of work people do to sustain life—whether that involves foraging, pastoralism, agriculture, or industrial capitalist production—creates conditions for certain patterns of childbearing and rearing. In a similar way, certain practices of childbearing and rearing both require and make possible other types of work.

For example, foraging economies tend to produce later ages of childbearing for women, greater birth spacing and thus comparatively fewer numbers of live births per woman than peasant societies (Howell 1979). And because there is little wealth to inherit in foraging societies, there is neither social concern over the legitimacy of children nor control over women's sexuality (Leacock 1981). Instead, all children are welcomed as members of the society; biological parents are known, but the group as a whole tends to accept responsibility for the children (Turnbull 1962; Lee 1979). In such societies, because children are cared for collectively, and also because work is under the control of the worker, women are not required to concentrate on childcare instead of participating in the other work necessary to sustain community life (Lee 1979; Leacock 1981).

In contrast, peasant farmers who individually hold land and must produce their subsistence by working that land, tend to have more children, more closely together. As a result, women become more tied to childrearing and the work they do must be compatible with childcare (Draper 1975; Tilly and Scott 1978; Harris 1981; and this text). In societies where kin groups own great wealth, inheritance becomes a major social concern and certain children are clearly designated as the legitimate heirs of specific individuals. In many agricultural societies where kin membership in the father's lineage both entitles the individual to rights in the land and its produce and legitimates the individual's claim to inheritance rights, child legitimacy is ensured by powerful social controls over women's sexuality (Lerner 1986).

Today, as an evolving legacy of life in a capitalist economy, the number of children per woman is very low. This is understandable given that parents do not have the means to ensure their children's material success (e.g., land they can pass on to sons who will farm it as their parents did). Indeed, they feel they must devote enormous amounts of energy preparing their children emotionally and intellectually so as to maximize their chances of success in systems that are out of their control (i.e., the schools and then the labour market) (Petchesky 1985). Amidst this long-term decline in birthrates, the state in most capitalist societies has assumed a variety of pronatalist policies (e.g., anti-abortion laws) to induce (white) women to have children. Meanwhile, until recently, women have devoted much of their lives to raising their children. Household responsibilities were too great to combine this with waged work, and employers deliberately refused to employ married women (Strong-Boag 1988). Only in recent decades, since there is both need and opportunity for married women to hold jobs, are women trying to combine employment with domestic responsibilities defined as theirs.

Aside from the relationship between the organization of production and reproduction, the nature of wealth and the requirements of production have also been related systematically to the form, composition, and structure of households. Thus, in societies where people had to forage daily to meet subsistence needs, a near-communal organization in which scarce resources were shared and economic decisions collectively made was the wisest survival strategy.

In contrast, in the feudal and early modern periods, as in earlier Roman and Germanic societies—when agricultural and artisanal production constituted the economy—the household was the organizing centre for economic production. Indeed, the word *economy* comes from the Greek word for household. In medieval times, recruitment to the household and household membership were dictated primarily by changing household labour requirements. All workers and servants had the same position in the family as biological children: They were under the authority of the male property owner and household head (Mitterauer and Sieder 1982).

Thus, the subsequent separations of place of residence and site of production for household use, on the one hand, from the site of the production of goods and services for the market, on the other—occurring as capitalism developed—generated a major transformation in households and families. Among other things, the separation destroyed the ease with which parents had previously been able to coordinate childcare and their other work. From the nineteenth century, increasingly, middle-class European households became centres exclusively for raising children and doing domestic labour (Davidoff and Hall 1987).

Today, as in the past, the household, or residential unit, is often the unit of social reproduction. That is, it is a unit of production, reproduction, and consumption, in which people work and pool resources so as to ensure that their own and their dependants' subsistence and emotional needs are met. But this is not always the case. For instance, women commonly have coped with poverty and financial insecurity—and raised their children despite them—by creating support networks of kin and non-kin that extend across households and involve the pooling of all kinds of resources (from money to clothing to time). Decades ago, Carol Stack (1974, and this text) documented such a pattern of coping among poor African Americans, whose men face nearly impossible obstacles in the way of achieving the role of 'breadwinner'. Similar patterns exist in other cultures (Tanner 1974; Rogers 1980) and, in a modified form, in traditional white working-class communities in Western, industrial societies (Young and Willmott 1957; Gans 1962). Carol Stack's (1974: 32) definition of family is worth considering: 'Ultimately I defined "family" as the smallest, organized, durable network of kin and non-kin who interact daily, providing domestic needs of children and assuring their survival.' Because the relationships responsible for social reproduction in our society vary in content, at least by social class, sexual orientation, and race, such a broad definition is useful.

Forces Creating Families

Once family is defined as the relations of social reproduction, the question arises how people are attracted to form such relations. That is, once we understand that biology does not simply produce family, the question of what social mechanisms do create family arises. Bridging the distance between ideas and social relations, Rayna Rapp (1982) has argued that family is the ideological, normative concept that recruits people to household relations of production, reproduction, and consumption. Certainly, family is an idea as well as a set of relationships: The strong belief in this society that only people related by blood or marriage can be truly committed to each other, and that the nuclear family is a natural formation, is a critical force pulling people together to form families. And once together, bound by marriage vows or parenthood, people imbue these relationships with a special significance.

Less obviously, heterosexuality pulls women and men together, while notions of romantic love can induce them to make long-term commitments. Heterosexuality itself is no more biologically determined than is the family (Weeks 1981; Valverde 1985, and this text). Thus, among the social forces creating family are those processes that create heterosexuality as the normative sexual pattern. The profound belief in gender differences and accompanying differential treatment of boys and girls; the subtle and unsubtle repression of 'inappropriate' sexual and gender expression in children and young people, especially boys; and the general eroticization of relationships between girls and boys, women and men, all produce men and women who are likely to be drawn to each other. In turn, the complicated dynamics of romantic love are so compelling that people enter marriage far more easily than seems rational, given the responsibilities it entails.

Aside from these largely ideological forces, that both recruit people into families and themselves constitute family as an idea, there are material forces promoting family formation. A consideration of economic matters makes clear that the organization of the labour market—whereby men typically are paid higher wages than women, and indeed women often are not remunerated sufficiently to support themselves, much less children—is an important force behind the coming together of men and women in marriage (Luxton 1980; Armstrong and Armstrong 1994). Many women are still dependent on finding a man for economic security, as recent data on women and poverty indicate (Gunderson and Muszynski 1990; National Council of Welfare 1999). Moreover, to the extent that boys are still growing up in a world that handicaps their acquisition of the social skills necessary to forge close friendships with men and women who are not sex partners, they continue to be emotionally dependent on finding 'that special woman' (Messner 1990; cf. Walker 1990 and Wellman 1992). In short, because current social organization creates gender differences—whether these be psychological or about material opportunities—it promotes the mutual dependence, and coming together, of women and men.

Additionally, there has been a persistent privatization of the responsibilities attached to social reproduction over time, and this also induces people to form families, based on marriage. That is, without strong community support of women raising children, for example, women are induced to marry. More generally, in many ways the social world is organized around the nuclear-family unit. Fairly devoid of community, this society creates for people the need to form families—and not just for the sake of caring for children.

In connecting children to a particular woman and man, marriage (and thus the state that has constituted marriage as a legal contract) aims to ensure their survival. More generally, though, the ideology of motherhood, which makes women responsible for young children's every need, ensures their survival—and thus this particular ideology is an important social force constructing families (Hays 1996).

In short, families are products of ideologies (especially those of gender difference, normative heterosexuality, romantic love, motherhood, and familism itself), legal practice (especially marriage laws), and economic organization (namely the gender inequality characteristic of the labour market). These forces recruit people to produce children, share their resources, raise their children, and care for each other. Most importantly, they give children a claim on social resources and ensure social reproduction.

Interestingly, those forces that in the past recruited most people to form nuclear families have weakened in recent decades. Heterosexuality is no longer the only socially viable form of sexual expression. The ideologies of romantic love and even motherhood—as women's primary career, often entailing full-time work and relegating all else to the background—now compete against some other ideas, albeit only vaguely developed ones. And the majority of women do not need men economically in the same way they did decades ago.

To return to our objective, though, to conceptualize *family*, we think it most useful to think of family as the relationships that bring people together daily to share resources for the sake of caring for children and each other. Certainly, the care of children is at the heart of what we mean by family. More broadly, we think it most productive to think of family as the relationships that

mobilize resources especially for the sake of generational and daily reproduction—for social reproduction, in short. And while we have emphasized the social forces exerting their influence on people, we must emphasize that people *actively create* their families.[4]

There is still something missing from our definition of family, however. Focusing on the relationships that gather and redistribute resources, and so provide for people's daily sustenance, privileges the material aspect of the relations that constitute families as productive and reproductive units. Yet the emotional connection that so ties people of different generations and households together 'til death do us part'—more so than marriage, it seems—must be central to our conceptualization of family. The power of familism, and kinship ideology in general, in this society attests to the tremendous intensity of the psychic connections among close family. As others have argued, the privatization of family life in this society, and the exclusivity of the mother-child relationship, is no doubt behind this intensity (Mitterauer and Sieder 1982; Coontz 1988).[5]

A Look at Social Reproduction

A peculiarity of the development of industrial capitalism is that (paid) labour that produces subsistence goods and (unpaid) domestic labour came to be physically separated and socially differentiated. In the process, traditional divisions of labour between women and men took on new significance: Women's work was increasingly privatized. It developed a new character as paid work left the home and women themselves were increasingly defined in terms of domestic qualities (Davidoff and Hall 1987; Coontz 1988). In turn, because housework is privatized (i.e., done in a private situation, and defined as 'the family's' responsibility), it was virtually ignored as *work* until feminism revised our thinking. Nevertheless, household work is essential, not only to family members' maintenance but also to the capitalist economy.

Household work involves housework; that is, all the chores necessary to maintain people physically (from meal preparation to clothing care), childcare (from changing diapers to listening to an upset teenager), adult care (from nursing the sick to providing emotional support), and 'making ends meet' (balancing incoming money against the needs of household members). Although it is apparent that this work is necessary to household members' well-being, it is less obvious that it is also central to the operation of the marketplace. In this economy, employers are not responsible for the daily recuperation of their labour force—unlike in feudal economies, where landlords had some obligations to their peasants and master craftsmen housed and fed their apprentices. Thus, the domestic labour that rejuvenates the worker's ability to work not only is important to his or her success in the labour market but also is important to the employer.

Of course, since World War II, in Canada and the United States, when households are unable to make ends meet, the state typically has provided a safety net of minimal assistance, at least for the short term. Yet, unlike in Europe (see Phipps and Mahon, this text), there has been persistent reluctance by the state to assume the responsibilities of social reproduction; consistently, law and policy have enforced families' assumption of those responsibilities (Eichler 1988; Morton 1988). Accordingly, state provision of good quality daycare is unlikely—though perhaps partly because of the specific nature of the work of caring for children (Blumenfeld and Mann 1980). At the same time, in a society where the public sphere seems increasingly inhospitable, and even dangerous, there is some ambivalence on the part of parents about shifting children's daytime care from home to community facilities. Given the alternatives presented by a society increasingly dominated by the marketplace, the comforts of a private haven, nourishing home-cooked meals, etc., remain attractive. All that is entailed by privatized social reproduction seems essential to the quality of life in a society that is essentially anti-social.

Of course, women do the vast majority of the tasks that create the house as a comfortable home and the family as a supportive environment (Luxton 1980, and this text). Indeed, women do the bulk of this work even when they also have full-time employment (Michelson 1983; Hochschild 1989; Morris 1990; Frederick 1995; Luxton, Chapter 21 this text). This gendered division of household responsibility constitutes a serious concern for us all: Those women balancing the demands of family and employment (and they represent the majority of Canadian women) have less sleep, less leisure, and less time for friends than men; and they experience considerable stress trying to coordinate two fundamentally incompatible kinds of jobs (Michelson 1983; Hochschild 1989, 1997).

We must confront the question how much longer women can continue their balancing act, in the context of very little substantial change in the organization of paid work and occupational careers, community services and gender ideology. In turn, this question raises another: Is it possible, in a capitalist society, to de-privatize family life, or at least some of the responsibilities still attached to 'the family'?

Before we can tackle such large questions, we need a firm understanding of both contemporary and historical family patterns. The lessons to be gained from examining history should contribute to an understanding of the social forces shaping family organization today. Unless these are understood, and assessed as structural obstacles to change or forces promoting change, we cannot successfully move on to tackle current problems and explore avenues of change for solving them. Our hope is that with the definition of family that we have proposed (and that emerges from feminist theory) fruitful questions about family will arise, including ones about the nature of current changes in family life and obstacles to a family organization that ensures people's well-being and empowerment. Perhaps we can even begin to find answers to our questions.

Notes

1. At the time of writing, legislation had been introduced by the Canadian federal government which would amend all federal laws to ensure that same-sex partners have the same obligations and rights as heterosexual partners. In response to protest, they also introduced a point of clarification which specified that only heterosexual couples could marry.

2. The emphasis in Eichler's criticism is that family membership, and treatment as a family member, handicaps individuals. Individuals' marital or family status—and not their personal characteristics—establishes their eligibility for state benefits: family relationships may disqualify people for benefits (e.g., a handicapped person loses disability if attached to a spouse with a reasonable income). Eichler's solution is to treat people as individuals, in terms of claims on social resources. We agree, but are concerned about the implicit juxtaposition in her argument between individual and collective/community. The social forces that individualize and isolate us are so strong that advocating another such force is unsettling. The problem, as Eichler points out, is that the state is seeking to shift responsibility for people's welfare onto families, and simultaneously undermining them. Promotion of universal social services, as well as guaranteed individual access to them and to a decent income, would alleviate the problem.

3. The term *blood* continues in both popular and scholarly usage to connote genetic ties.

4. We should remember as well, from the perspective of the larger social order, that families are the chief mechanisms in our society for allocating people to their positions as adults. Although we think of our educational system as the mechanism that assesses people's abilities, streams them in the direction of appropriate adult jobs, and trains them accordingly, family background actually determines much about all of the opportunities children will face. Despite some upward social mobility from one generation to the next, people's class backgrounds have a huge impact on their material situations as adults (Brym with Fox 1989).

5. In turn, we suspect that the emphasis placed upon biology in this society (which generates belief in sociobiological explanations of social phenomena without any evidence, for example) is emblematic of these same emotional bonds among parents and children, and the ideology that expresses them.

References

Armstrong, P., and H. Armstrong. 1994. *The Double Ghetto: Canadian Women and their Segregated Work*, 3rd edn (Toronto: McClelland & Stewart).

Barrett, M., and M. McIntosh. 1982. *The Anti-Social Family* (London: Verso).

Blumenfeld, E., and S. Mann. 1980. 'Domestic Labour and the Reproduction of Labour Power: Towards an Analysis of Women, the Family and Class' in *Hidden in the Household: Women's Domestic Labour Under Capitalism*, ed. B. Fox (Toronto: The Women's Press).

Brym, R., with B. Fox. 1989. *From Culture to Power: The Sociology of English Canada* (Toronto: Oxford University Press).

Collier, J., M. Rosaldo, and S, Yanagisako. 1982. 'Is There a Family? New Anthropological Views' in *Rethinking the Family: Some Feminist Questions*, eds B. Thorne and M. Yalom (New York: Longman).

Coontz, S. 1988. *The Social Origins of Private Life* (London: Verso).

———. 1992. *The Way We Never Were: American Families and the Nostalgia Trap* (New York: Basic Books).

Davidoff, L., and C. Hall. 1987. *Family Fortunes: Men and Women of the English Middle Class 1780–1850* (London: Hutchinson).

Draper, P. 1975. '!Kung Women: Contrasts in Sexual Egalitarianism in the Foraging and Sedentary Contexts' in *Toward an Anthropology of Women*, ed. R. Reiter (New York: Monthly Review Press).

Eichler, M. [1983] 1988. *Families in Canada Today* (Toronto: Gage).

Flandrin, J.-L. 1979. *Families in Former Times: Kinship, Household and Sexuality in Early Modern France*, trans. R. Southern (Cambridge: Cambridge University Press).

Fox, B. 1997. 'Another View of Sociology of the Family in Canada: A Comment on Nett', *Canadian Review of Sociology and Anthropology* 34 (1): 93–9.

Frederick, J. 1995. 'The Struggle to Juggle, Baby Boomers, 25 to 44', Statistics Canada, cat. no. 89-544E (Ottawa: Supply and Services).

Friedan, B. 1963. *The Feminine Mystique* (New York: Dell).

Gans, H. 1962. *The Urban Villagers* (New York: Free Press).

Gittins, D. 1985. *The Family in Question: Changing Households and Familiar Ideologies* (London: Macmillan).

Goody, J. 1976. *Production and Reproduction: A Comparative Study of the Domestic Domain* (Cambridge: Cambridge University Press).

Gunderson, M., and L. Muszynski. 1990. *Women and Labour Market Poverty* (Ottawa: Canadian Advisory Council on the Status of Women).

Harris, O. 1981. 'Households as Natural Units' in *Of Marriage and the Market*, eds K. Young, C. Wolkowitz, and R. McCullough (London: CSE Books).

Hays, S. 1996. *The Cultural Contradictions of Motherhood* (New Haven: Yale University Press).

Hochschild, A. 1989. *The Second Shift: Working Parents and the Revolution at Home* (New York: Avon).

———. 1997. *Time Bind: When Work Becomes Home & Home Becomes Work* (New York: Metropolitan Books).

Howell, N. 1979. *Demography of the Dobe Area !Kung* (New York: Academic Press).

Larson, L., J.W. Goltz, and B.E. Munro. 2000. *Families in Canada: Social Contexts, Continuities and Changes* (Toronto: Prentice-Hall Allyn and Bacon).

Laslett, B., and J. Brenner. 1989. 'Gender and Social Reproduction: Historical Perspectives', *Annual Review of Sociology* 15.

Leacock, E. 1981. *Myths of Male Dominance: Collected Articles on Women Cross-Culturally* (New York: Monthly Review Press).

Lee, R. 1979. *The !Kung San Men, Women, and Work in a Foraging Society* (New York: Cambridge University Press).

Lerner, G. 1986. *The Creation of Patriarchy* (Oxford: Oxford University Press).

Luxton, M. 1980. *More Than a Labour of Love: Three Generations of Women's Work in the Home* (Toronto: The Women's Press).

Mandell, N., and A. Duffy. 1988. *Reconstructing the Canadian Family: Feminist Perspectives* (Toronto: Butterworths).

Messner, M. 1990. 'Boyhood, Organized Sports, and the Construction of Masculinities', *Journal of Contemporary Ethnography* 18 (4): 416–44.

Michelson, W. 1983. *From Sun to Sun* (New Jersey: Rowman & Allanheld).

Mitterauer, M., and R. Sieder. 1982. *The European Family* (Oxford: Basil Blackwell).

Morgan, D. 1975. *The Family and Social Theory* (London: Routledge and Kegan Paul).

Morris, L. 1990. *The Workings of the Household* (London: Polity).

Morton, M. 1988. 'Dividing the Wealth, Sharing the Poverty: The (Re)formation of "Family" in Law in Ontario', *Canadian Review of Sociology and Anthropology* 25 (2).

National Council of Welfare. 1999. *Poverty Profile 1997* (Ottawa: Public Works and Government Services).

Parsons, T., and R.F. Bales. 1955. *Family, Socialization and Interaction Process* (New York: Free Press).

Petchesky, R. 1985. *Abortion and Women's Choice: The State, Sexuality and Reproductive Freedom* (Boston: Northeastern University Press).

Rapp, R. 1982. 'Family and Class in Contemporary America: Notes Toward Understanding of Ideology' in *Rethinking the Family: Some Feminist Questions*, eds B. Thorne and M. Yalmon (New York: Longman).

Rogers, B. 1980. *The Domestication of Women: Discrimination in Developing Societies* (London: Tavistock).

Sahlins, M. 1976. *The Use and Abuse of Biology* (Ann Arbor, MI: University of Michigan Press).

Stack, C. 1974. *All Our Kin: Strategies for Survival in a Black Community* (New York: Harper & Row).

Statistics Canada. 1984. *1981 Census of Canada. Economic Families in Private Households, Income and Selected Characteristics*, cat. no. 93–937 (Ottawa: Supply and Services).

Strong-Boag, V. 1988. *The New Day Recalled: Lives of Girls and Women in English Canada, 1919–1939* (Markham: Penguin).

Tanner, N. 1974. 'Matrifocality in Indonesia and Africa and Among Black Americans' in *Woman, Culture and Society*, eds M.Z. Rosaldo and L. Lamphere (Stanford: Stanford University Press).

Thorne, B., and M. Yalmon, eds. 1982. *Rethinking the Family: Some Feminist Questions* (New York: Longman).

Tilly, L., and J. Scott. 1978. *Women, Work and Family* (New York: Holt, Rinehart and Winston).

Turnbull, C. 1962. *The Forest People* (Garden City, NY: Doubleday).

Valverde, M. 1985. *Sex, Power and Pleasure* (Toronto: Women's Press).

Walker, K. 1990. '"I'm Not Friends the Way She's Friends": Ideological and Behavioral Construction of Masculinity in Men's Friendships', *Masculinities* 2 (2): 38–55.

Weeks, J. 1981. *Sex, Politics, and Society: The Regulation of Sexuality Since 1800* (New York: Longman).

Wellman, B. 1992. 'Men in Networks: Private Communities, Domestic Friendships' in *Men's Friendships*, ed. P. Nardi (Newbury Park, CA: Sage) 74–114.

Young, M., and P. Willmott. 1957. *Family and Kinship in East London* (Baltimore: Penguin).

Zelditch, M. 1960. 'Role Differentiation in the Nuclear Family' in *A Modern Introduction to the Family*, eds N. Bell and E. Vogel (New York: The Free Press).

Part Two | **Examining Family Diversity Across History and Culture**

Section 1   Foraging Societies: Communal Households

To understand family patterns, it is important to get a sense of the dynamic relationship between the way production is organized, on the one hand, and the way the social relations involved in sexuality, reproduction, childrearing, and daily consumption are organized, on the other. Here are two ethnographic accounts of foraging societies by anthropologists especially sensitive to this relationship. Patricia Draper's article discusses a foraging society in Botswana in the late 1960s. The selection from Eleanor Leacock's writings is about an aboriginal society in Canada that survived on hunting. Leacock's research was based on records left by seventeenth-century missionaries, as well as her own fieldwork.

While both writers focus on the nature of gender relations in these societies, because gender relations organize the activities we associate with family, their descriptions provide a sketch of family life in simple societies. Clear in these descriptions are the benefits of non-privatized family patterns—including individual autonomy (even in marriage), collective sharing of childcare responsibilities, the inhibition of violence, and egalitarian gender relations. Each selection traces some of the historical changes that have promoted more privatized living.

Chapter 4

This is Patricia Draper's summary of her impressions of the specific factors and more general social organization that together produced egalitarian gender relations among the !Kung San Bushmen living in the Kalahari Desert in Botswana in the late 1960s. She compares !Kung foragers with !Kung who abandoned a nomadic way of life for settlement, and in so doing offers interesting insights about the connections between privatized family life and unequal relations between women and men.

!Kung Women: Contrasts in Sexual Egalitarianism in Foraging and Sedentary Contexts

Patricia Draper

Most members of the Harvard !Kung Bushman Study Project who have thought about the subject of !Kung women's status agree that !Kung society may be the least sexist of any we have experienced. This impression contradicts some popularly held stereotypes about relations between the sexes in hunting and gathering societies. Because sex is one of the few bases for the differentiation of social and economic roles in societies of this type, it has probably been attributed more weight than it deserves. The men are commonly depicted in rather romantic terms, striving with their brothers to bring home the precious meat while their women humbly provide the dull, tasteless vegetable food in the course of routine, tedious foraging. Contrary evidence is now emerging from several researchers that men and women of band-level societies have many overlapping activities and spheres of influence (Gale 1970). The distinction between male and female roles is substantially less rigid than previously supposed, though there is variation among band-level peoples in the degree of autonomy and influence that women enjoy.

This paper describes relations between the sexes for two groups of !Kung: those living a traditional hunting and gathering life at /Du/da and those who have recently adopted a settled way of life in the !Kangwa Valley and who are now living by agriculture, animal husbandry, and a small amount of gathering.

The point to be developed at some length is that in the hunting and gathering context, women have a great deal of autonomy and influence. Some of the contexts in which this egalitarianism is expressed will be described in detail, and certain features of the foraging life which promote egalitarianism will be isolated. They are: women's subsistence contribution and the control women retain over the food they have gathered; the requisites of foraging in the Kalahari which entail a similar degree of mobility for both sexes; the lack of rigidity in sex-typing of many adult activities, including domestic chores and aspects of child socialization; the cultural sanction against physical expression of aggression; the small group size; and the nature of the settlement pattern.

Features of sedentary life that appear to be related to a decrease in women's autonomy and influence are: increasing rigidity in sex-typing of adult work; more permanent attachment of the individual to a particular place and group of people; dissimilar childhood socialization for boys and girls; decrease in the mobility of women as contrasted with men; changing nature of women's subsistence contribution; richer material inventory with implications for women's work; tendency for men to have greater access to and control over such important resources as domestic animals, knowledge of Bantu language and culture; wage work; male entrance into extra-village policies; settlement pattern; and increasing household privacy.

Background to !Kung Research

The !Kung Bushmen of the Kalahari Desert are one of the better-described primitive cultures, with the literature steadily increasing in the last twenty years. The work of Lorna Marshall, John Marshall, and Elizabeth Marshall Thomas gives a background to !Kung social organization and economy. The publications of the Marshall family concern primarily !Kung living in South-West Africa in the Nyae nyae area.

Since the early 1960s other researchers have entered the field of !Kung studies, in particular members of the Harvard !Kung Bushman Study Project. This team worked in western Botswana with populations of !Kung who overlap with the !Kung of South-West Africa first studied by the Marshall expedition. Members of the Harvard research team have focused on more narrow, specialized topics.

Ethnographic Background to the !Kung: Traditional Population

The !Kung are a hunting and gathering people living today mostly on the western edge of the Kalahari sand system in what is now southern Angola, Botswana, and South-West Africa. The great majority of !Kung-speaking people have abandoned their traditional hunting and gathering way of life and are now living in sedentary and semi-squatter status in or near the villages of Bantu pastoralists and European ranchers. A minority of !Kung, amounting to a few thousand, are still living by traditional hunting and gathering techniques. It is to these bush-living peoples and a few groups of very recently settled !Kung that this paper refers.

The bush-living peoples subsist primarily on wild vegetable foods and game meat. They are semi-nomadic, moving their camps at irregular intervals of from several days to several weeks. The average size of individual groups (also referred to as bands or camps) is about thirty-five people, though the numbers range from seventeen to sixty-five people. Season and the availability of water are the chief factors affecting group size. During the rainy season (October to March), group censuses are lower due to the fact that water and bush foods are widely available in most regions of the !Kung range. Smaller numbers of people in the form of two- and three-family groups spread out over the bush. As the dry season approaches, the small, temporary water pans dry up and the people begin to regroup and fall back on the remaining water sources that continue throughout the dry season. As there are relatively few water sources in the heart of the drought, as many as two or three different camps may be found within one to three miles of the same water hole.

The rules governing the composition of these bands are extremely flexible. It appears there is no such thing as 'band membership'. Close relatives move together over much of the year, though individuals and segments of large kin groups frequently make temporary and amicable separations to go live some miles distant with other relatives and affines.

Material technology is extremely simple. Men hunt with small bows and arrows (tipped with poison) and metal-pointed spears. Women's tools include a simple digging stick, wooden mortar and pestle, and leather kaross which doubles as clothing and carrying bag. Both sexes use leather carrying bags, hafted adzes, and net slings made from handwoven vegetable fibre. Clothing, particularly among the bush people, consists of leather garments; in addition, various cloth garments are worn, especially by the settled !Kung, but also by the peoples of the bush.

Settled Population

As stated before, the great majority of !Kung-speaking peoples are settled around the villages of technologically more advanced peoples and have been there for as many as three generations. Among other !Kung, sedentarization is much more recent. In the case of the Mahopa people, in the !Kung area of Botswana, !Kung commitment to settled life is perhaps fifteen to twenty years old. I observed these people and the people of /Du/da for two years in 1968 and 1969.

About fifty !Kung lived in three separate villages around the permanent water hole at Mahopa. Bantu-speaking pastoralists also lived at Mahopa and watered their herds of cattle, horses, donkeys, and goats at the Mahopa well. These Bantu were chiefly of the Herero tribe and, like the !Kung, lived in about six villages, whose total population consisted of perhaps fifty people. Some !Kung lived in the Herero villages, but my research and remarks here do not refer to them.

The Mahopa people whom I describe lived in villages composed only of !Kung. The decision of the !Kung to avoid close proximity with the Herero is conscious, for relations between the two groups are not entirely amicable—Bantu of the area have a superior attitude and often (according to the !Kung) do not treat !Kung people fairly. Bantu see the !Kung as irresponsible, poor workers who are prone to killing occasional steers from Bantu herds.

The subsistence practices of the recently settled !Kung are mixed. The women continue to gather bush food, but not with the effort or regularity of the women of the traditional groups. Hunting by Mahopa men has virtually ceased. The people keep small herds of goats and plant small gardens of sorghum, squash, melons, and corn. For the most part, the Mahopa !Kung do not own their own cattle (at least, they did not during my fieldwork). Some !Kung women receive milk in payment for regular chores they do for nearby Herero women.

In the first discussion of !Kung women my remarks will pertain to women of the bush-living groups, unless otherwise specified. Description of the women's life in the settled Mahopa villages of the !Kung area will be handled second. The traditional, or bush-living !Kung lived in the /Du/da area, which straddles the border of Botswana and South-West Africa and stretches over a north-south distance of about seventy miles.

Self-esteem Derived from Subsistence Contribution

Women are the primary providers of vegetable food, and they contribute something on the order of 60 to 80 per cent of the daily food intake by weight (Lee 1965). All !Kung agree that meat is the most desirable, most prestigious food, but the hunters cannot always provide it. Without question, women derive self-esteem from the regular daily contribution they make to the family's food.

A common sight in the late afternoon is clusters of children standing on the edge of camp, scanning the bush with shaded eyes to see if the returning women are visible. When the slow-moving file of women is finally discerned in the distance, the children leap and exclaim. As the women draw closer, the children speculate as to which figure is whose mother and what the women are carrying in their karosses.

Often when women return in the evening they bring information as well as bush food. Women are skilled in reading the signs of the bush, and they take careful note of animal tracks, their age, and the direction of movement. On several occasions I have accompanied gathering expeditions in which, when the group was about thirty to forty minutes out of camp, one of the women discovered the fresh tracks of several large antelope. This find caused a stir of excitement in the group. Quickly the women dispatched one of the older children to deliver the report to the men in camp. In general, the men take advantage of women's reconnaissance and query them routinely on the evidence of game movements, the location of water, and the like.

A stereotype of the female foraging role in hunting and gathering societies (in contrast with men's work, which is social in character) is that the work is individualized, repetitive, and boring (Service 1966: 12). Descriptions of the work of gathering leave the reader with the impression that the job is uninteresting and unchallenging— that anyone who can walk and bend over can collect wild bush food. This stereotype is distinctly inappropriate to !Kung female work, and it promotes a condescending attitude toward what women's work is all about. Successful gathering over the years requires the ability to discriminate among hundreds of edible and inedible species of plants at various stages in their life cycle. This ability requires more than mere brute strength. The stereotype further ignores the role women play in gathering information about the 'state of the bush'—presence of temporary water, evidence of recent game movements, etc. On a given day, !Kung hunters consciously avoid working the same area in which women are foraging, knowing that movements of the women may disturb the game, but also knowing that the women can be questioned at the end of the day (Yellen, personal communication).

!Kung women impress one as self-contained people with a high sense of self-esteem. There are exceptions—women who seem forlorn and weary—but for the most part !Kung women are vivacious and self-confident. Small groups of women forage in the Kalahari at distances of eight to ten miles from home with no thought that they need the protection of the men or of the men's weapons should they encounter any of the several large predators that also inhabit the Kalahari (for instance, hyena, wild dog, leopard, lion, and cheetah). It is unusual, but not exceptional, for a lone woman to spend the day gathering. In the times I observed at the /Du/da camps, the solitary foragers were either postmenopausal women or young, unmarried women who were still without

children. Women with children or adolescent, unmarried girls usually gather bush food in the company of two or more other women. The !Kung themselves claim that lovers (as well as married couples) sometimes arrange to meet privately in the bush. !Kung sleeping arrangements may promote these tactics, for at night whole families sleep outdoors together gathered around individual campfires and within a few feet of other families sleeping at their own fires.

Control by Women over Gathered Food

Not only do women contribute equally, if not more than men, to the food supply; they also retain control over the food they have gathered after they return to the village. This is even more true of the vegetable food of women than of the meat brought in by the men. Lorna Marshall and Richard B. Lee have described how the distribution of meat is circumscribed by social rules as well as by the spontaneous demands of fellow camp members. With the exception of small game kills, a hunter has little effective control over the meat he brings into the camp. In contrast, the gatherer determines the distribution of vegetable food, at least when it concerns anyone outside her immediate family. An example may help to illustrate this point. One late afternoon I watched N!uhka return from an unusually long gathering trip. Her kaross was bulging with food, and her face showed fatigue from the weight and from dust, heat, and thirst. She walked stolidly through camp to her own hut. When she reached her hearthside, still stooping with the load, she reached to her shoulder, where the kaross was knotted. Wearily she gave the knot one practised yank. The bush food spilled out of the kaross, clattering and thumping onto the sand behind her. She had not even squatted before releasing the burden. At the sound, several people looked up, but only briefly. No one greeted her or came over to look at the day's collection. N!uhka sat down at her hut, reached inside for an ostrich-egg shell, and slowly drank water from it for several minutes, sitting with her elbows on her knees and staring blankly ahead. Fifteen minutes later her grown daughter and a younger son joined her. The daughter, without talking, blew the coals back to life and started a fire. By then N!uhka had regained her strength, the listlessness had gone, and she picked up a wooden poke and began raking some of the freshly picked =/nd=/dwa bean pods into the hot ashes for roasting. This done, she began gathering up the bush food she had dropped earlier. Most of it she heaped into the rear of her own hut, but she also made two additional small piles. Calling next door to her twelve-year-old grand-nephew, she said, 'Take this to your grandmother' (her brother's wife), and she motioned for him to take one of the heaps of bean pods. Later, when her daughter rose to return to her own fire, N!uhka had her take away the second pile for her own use. It is common for women to make these individual gifts, but it is not mandatory. Food that is brought in by women may also be redistributed during a family meal when other people visit at the fire and are served along with family members.

The fact that !Kung women retain control over their own production is, of course, related to the simplicity of !Kung economy, technology, rules of ownership, and social organization. In more complex societies, there are kin groups, lineages, or other corporate units that control essential resources. Even in the relatively rare cases (matrilineages) where women nominally own the land and household property, it is usually men who control the production and distribution of resources. The gathering work of !Kung women can be done by women alone. They do not need to ask permission to use certain lands; they do not need the assistance of men in order to carry out their work, as in the case of many agricultural societies where men must do the initial heavy work of clearing fields, building fences, and the like, before the less strenuous work of women can begin.

Similar Absenteeism for Men and Women

A similarity in the gathering work of women and the hunting work of men is that both activities take adults out of the camp, sometimes all day for several days each week. The pattern of both sexes being about equally absent from the dwelling place is not typical of most middle-range, agriculturally based tribal societies. In these latter groups one finds an arrangement whereby women, much more than men, stay at home during child tending, domestic chores, food preparation and the like, while the men are occupied with activities that take them outside the household and keep them away for many hours during the day. Frequent (daily) male absence may result in viewing men as a scarce commodity with higher value than women, who are constantly present in the household. If men in this sense are a scarce commodity, their homecoming must have greater significance to those who stay at home, and their influence even in routine domestic affairs may be heightened simply because others are less habituated to their presence. Among the !Kung a case could be argued for the equal, or nearly equal, scarcity value of men and women. Both leave the village regularly, and the return of both is eagerly anticipated—as illustrated earlier in this paper with reference to women.

It seems likely that !Kung men and women have similar knowledge of the larger hunting and gathering territory within which their kin and affines range. Both men and women range out from the camp in the course of their subsistence work, and they are equally affected by group moves in search of bush food, game, and water. More recently, however, /Du/da men have gained larger knowledge of the 'outside' world, for some young men have spent months, and even years, doing wage work at such towns as Ghanzi, Gobabis, and Windhoek. Women are less likely to have had these experiences. Henry Harpending (1972, 1976) has collected demographic data on the !Kung of the !Kangwa and /Du/da areas which shows that the space occupied over a lifetime does not differ for the two sexes. For example, the distribution of distances between birthplaces of mates and birthplaces of parents and offspring are almost identical for the two sexes, both currently and for marriages that took place prior to substantial Bantu contact in these areas.

The absence of warfare or raiding, either among !Kung themselves or between !Kung and neighbouring Bantu, undoubtedly facilitates the freedom of movement of the women. If threat of enemy attack were a recurrent fact of life, many features of !Kung social organization undoubtedly would change, particularly in the area of political leadership, but probably in the area of sex egalitarianism as well. (See Murdock 1949: 205 for a discussion of conditions, including warfare, that increase status discrepancy between the sexes.)

Sexual Division of Labour

When asked, !Kung will state that there is men's work and women's work, and that they conceive of most individual jobs as sex-typed, at least in principle. In practice, adults of both sexes seem surprisingly willing to do the work of the opposite sex. It often appeared to me that men, more than women, were willing to cross lines.

One afternoon while visiting in one of the /Du/da camps, I came across Kxau, a rather sober middle-aged man, industriously at work building his own hut. Building huts is predominantly women's work, and I had never seen such a thing. It happened that Kxau's wife was away visiting at another settlement many miles distant, or she would have made the hut. However, Kxau's daughter, an unmarried girl about seventeen years old, was in camp, and even she did not offer to make the hut or help him once he had started. Kxau proceeded to build the structure methodically and without embarrassment. I deliberately stayed in the vicinity to observe the reaction of other people. No one commented or joked with him about how his women were lazy.

Gathering is women's work, but there are times when men also gather. Some married couples collected mongongo nuts together, but in my observation, the couples most likely to do this were elderly couples and a young couple who had been married for several years but had no children. Water collection is normally considered to be women's work, particularly when the water source is close to camp, perhaps fifteen to twenty minutes' walk. However, when the people are camped several miles from water, men participate regularly in carrying water back to camp. In the months of August, September, and October of 1969, I observed two of the /Du/da camps where water was three miles distant. In this situation men and women both worked at bringing in water. Only on the occasions when several of the men were absent from camp for several nights on hunting trips did their wives collect water daily for the remaining members of the family.

I mentioned earlier that men seemed more willing (or accustomed) than women to do work normally associated with the opposite sex. Gathering and water-collecting are outstanding examples of female tasks that frequently involve men. While there are undoubtedly sound economic and evolutionary reasons for the male monopoly on hunting (Brown 1970), there is one aspect of male hunting tasks that could easily absorb female help but typically does not. I refer here to the job of carrying the meat back to camp from the kill site.

A common pattern among the hunters of /Du/da was for a group of three or four hunters to stay out three or more nights in a row. Frequently by the fourth or fifth day one of their number would appear back in camp with the news that an antelope had been killed and that volunteers were needed to carry in the meat. On such occasions the remainder of the original hunting party stayed with the carcass, cutting the meat into biltong and allowing it to dry and lose much of its weight and volume. Always the helpers recruited were men. Often, but not necessarily, they were young males in late adolescence who had not yet begun serious hunting. I personally never knew of a woman (or women) assisting in such a venture, and never heard of any woman having done it.

The !Kung recognize no taboo against women being present at a kill site. On the contrary, when one or two hunters have killed a large animal some distance from camp, one of the hunters will return to camp and bring back his own and the other hunter's family to camp temporarily by the slain animal. Quite possibly the !Kung could verbalize their feelings about why it would be inappropriate to ask women to carry butchered meat. Unfortunately, while I was in the field it never occurred to me to ask; such blind spots are apparently an unavoidable hazard of fieldwork. Professor Cora Dubois warned me of this problem a few months before I began my work in the Kalahari: 'Beware that the scale of custom will form over your eyes and you will no longer see.'

Childrearing Practices and Sexual Equality

As children grow up there are few experiences which set one sex apart from the other. Living in such small groups, !Kung children have relatively few playmates to choose from.[1] Play groups, when they do form, include children of both sexes and widely differing ages. This habit of playing in heterogeneous play groups probably minimizes any underlying, biologically based sex differences in style—differences which in other societies may be magnified and intensified by the opportunity of playing in same-sex, same-age play groups.

The child nurse is a regular feature of many African agricultural societies. The custom of assigning child-tending responsibility to an older child (usually a girl) in a family is one example of sex-role typing which can begin at an early age. This responsibility shapes and limits the behaviour of girls in ways not true for boys, who are usually passed over for this chore. The training a girl receives as an infant caretaker doubtless has bene-

fits for her eventual role performance and more immediately for the family economy, since she frees the mother from routine childcare and allows her to resume subsistence production. However, the typical nine year old who is saddled with carrying and supervising a toddler cannot range as widely or explore as freely and independently as her brothers. She must stay closer to home, be more careful, more nurturant, more obedient, and more sensitive to the wishes of others. Habits formed in this way have social value, but my point is that such girls receive more training in these behaviours and that they form part of the complex of passivity and nurturance which characterizes adult female behaviour in many cultures.[2]

!Kung do not use child nurses of either sex on a routine basis; this fact follows from the long birth intervals and the pattern of adult subsistence work. The average birth interval is approximately four years (Howell 1976). !Kung mothers can and do give lengthy, intensive care to each child because no new infant arrives to absorb their attention. Such mothers are comparatively unpressured and do not need to delegate the bulk of child-tending responsibility to another caretaker. Naturally, older children interact with younger children and in the process give help, protection, and attention to them. But one or more older children are rarely, if ever, the sole caretakers of younger charges for an appreciable length of time.

The rhythm of adult work also makes the role of child nurse unnecessary. !Kung adults work about three days per week, and they vary their time of being in and out of the camp, with the result that on any given day one-third to one-half of the adults are in camp. They can easily supervise their own children and those whose parents are absent. Older children are helpful in amusing and monitoring younger children, but they do so spontaneously (and erratically), and not because they are indoctrinated with a sense of responsibility for the welfare of a particular child or children.

A reflection of !Kung women's effectiveness in family life is the fact that a mother deals directly with her children when they are in need of correction. A different type of maternal strategy is common in cultures where women's status is clearly subordinate to that of the fathers and husbands. David Landy's study (1959) of rural Puerto Rican socialization techniques, Robert A. and Barbara LeVine's study (1963) of East African Gussi child training practices, and the L. Minturn and John T. Hitchcock study (1963) of childrearing among the Rajputs of Khalapur are particularly good examples of how a mother's ability to control her children is undermined by male superordinance, particularly when accompanied by patrilineal structures and patrilocal residence rules. Such mothers will hold up the father as the ultimate disciplinarian in an attempt to underscore their own power. !Kung do not resort to the threat, 'I'll tell your father . . . !'

Among the !Kung, both parents correct the children, but women tend to do this more often because they are usually physically closer to the children at any given time than the men. When such situations arise, a mother does not seek to intimidate the children with the father's wrath. In this milieu children are not trained to respect and fear male authority. In fact, for reasons which will be elaborated later, authoritarian behaviour is avoided by adults of *both* sexes. The typical strategy used by !Kung parents is to interrupt the misbehaviour, carry the child away, and try to interest him or her in some inoffensive activity.

This way of disciplining children has important consequences in terms of behaviours that carry over into adulthood. Since parents do not use physical punishment, and aggressive postures are avoided by adults and devalued by the society at large, children have relatively little opportunity to observe or imitate overtly aggressive behaviour. This carries over into relations between adult men and women in the society. Among the !Kung there is an extremely low cultural tolerance for aggressive behaviour by anyone, male or female. In societies where aggressiveness and dominance are valued, these behaviours accrue disproportionately to males, and the females are common targets, resulting in a lowering of their status. !Kung women are not caught by this dimension of sex-role complementarity. They customarily maintain a mild manner, but so do their men.

Relations of Men with Children

A further example of the equality between the sexes and the amount of overlap in their activities is the relationship between men and their children. In cultures where men have markedly superordinant status, women and children are expected to show deference to the male head of the family by staying away from him, observing routine formalities. !Kung fathers, in contrast, are intimately involved with their children and have a great deal of social interaction with them. The relation between fathers and young children is relaxed and without stylized respect or deference from the children. In fact, the lack of tact with which some children treated their parents was at first quite shocking to me.

As an example, I can relate an incident in which Kxau was trying to get his youngest son, Kashe, to bring him something from the other side of camp. Kxau was sitting at one edge of the village clearing with another man older than himself. Kxau repeatedly shouted to his son to bring him his tobacco from inside the family hut. The boy ignored his father's shouts, though !Kung camps are small, and the boy clearly could hear his father. Finally Kxau bellowed out his command, glaring across at his son and the other youngsters sitting there. Kashe looked up briefly and yelled back, 'Do it yourself, old man.' A few minutes later Kxau did do it himself, and Kashe received no reprimand.

Most fathers appear ill at ease when they hold very young infants, although by the time a child is nine or ten months old it is common to see the father playing with the child and holding it close to his face, blowing on its neck, and laughing. In the late afternoon and evening in a !Kung camp one often sees a father walking among the huts with a two- or three-year-old boy perched on his shoulder. The father ambles along, accepting an offer of a smoke at one hut, then moving on to squat elsewhere while watching a kinsman scraping a hide or mending a tool. At such times the father is mindful of the boy at his shoulder but pays him no special attention, aside from now and then steadying the child's balance.

There are certain aspects of childcare that men unanimously eschew. Most prefer not to remove mucus from the runny nose of a child. Most adults of both sexes have a rather high tolerance for this sight, but occasionally a man will see his child with an especially unwholesome-looking smear on his upper lip, and will call out to his wife, 'Ugh! Get rid of that snot.' Men are also loath to clean up feces left by children. Usually the mother or an older child will scoop up the offending mess with a handful of leaves. If however, a child's defecation has gone unnoticed by all except the father, he will call out to his wife to remove it.

Effect of Group Size and Settlement Pattern on Relations Between the Sexes

!Kung camps are typically quite small; the average camp size at /Du/da was thirty-four with a range of seventeen to sixty-five. The small group size is related to the low order of specialization of sex roles. Given the rather small numbers of able-bodied adults who manage group life and subsistence in these camps, the lack of opposition (or specialization) of the sexes is highly practical. Especially in the rainy seasons when local group size falls to about fifteen people, it is useful and necessary for adults to be relatively interchangeable in function.

Observing the way people group themselves during leisure hours in a !Kung camp gives one a feeling for the tone of informal heterosexual interaction. Men and women (children, too) sit together in small clusters—talking, joking, cracking and eating nuts, passing around tobacco. Individuals pass among these groups without causing a rift in the ambiance, without attracting attention. In general, the sexes mix freely and unselfconsciously without the diffidence one might expect to see if they thought they were in some way intruding.

If there were a prominent opposition between the sexes, one would expect some expression of this in the organization and use of space within the !Kung camps. However, there are no rules and definitions that limit a person's access to various parts of the village space on the basis of sex. The overall small size of the settled area almost removes this type of symbolism from the realm of possibility.

To an outsider, particularly a Westerner, the small size of !Kung camps and the intimate, close living characteristic of them can seem stifling.[3] Essentially, thirty to forty people share what amounts to (by our standards) a large room. The individual grass scherms, one to each married couple, ring an elliptical village space. The huts are often placed only a few feet apart and look a mere forty to fifty feet across the cleared, central space into the hearth and doorway of the hut on the opposite side of the circle. Daily life goes on in this small, open space. Everything is visible with a glance; in many camps conversations can be carried on in normal tones of voice by people sitting at opposite ends of the village. In this setting it is easy to see why the sexes rub elbows without embarrassment. In other societies, where sex roles and the prerogatives which attach to them are more exclusively defined, one generally finds architectural features used to help people manage their interaction and/or avoidance: walls, fences, separate sleeping and/or eating arrangements, designated spaces allocated to only one sex, etc.

In summary, many of the basic organizing features of this hunting and gathering group contribute to a relaxed and egalitarian relationship between men and women. The female subsis-

tence role is essential to group survival and satisfying to the women. The foregoing remarks have
illustrated a framework within which egalitarian
relations are a natural or logical outcome. There
are other issues bearing on the question of women's
influence and control which are not answered
here. Decision-making is one such issue.
Leadership and authority are difficult problems to
research in band-level societies generally, and in
this one in particular. Still, the question of whether
women or men more often influence group or family decisions is an empirical one, albeit one on
which I have no data. Other areas that bear on the
topic of women's influence and power are marital
relations, access to extramarital relations, the influence of young women in determining the selection
of their first husbands, changes in women's influence over their life cycles, etc.[4] So far as I know,
these issues have yet to be researched in a systematic way among the !Kung.

The Sedentary !Kung of Mahopa

As stated earlier, my fieldwork was conducted in
two areas of northwestern Botswana: the /Du/da
area and the !Kangwa area. The second area was
the locus of research similar to that conducted on
the social life of the bush-living !Kung at /Du/da.
Within the !Kangwa area (about seventy miles
from the /Du/da water hole) I worked at Mahopa,
one of several permanent water sources in the
!Kangwa Valley. Around Mahopa are various settlements, of which three were the focus of my
study. The three settlements were composed
almost exclusively of !Kung. (Of about fifty persons living there, only one was !Kung—a middle-
aged Tswana man married to a !Kung woman.)

The Mahopa 'well' forms a small pan, or pool
of standing water, in the rainy season; but in the
dry season it shrinks to a muddy, clay-ringed ditch.
This ditch is dug out periodically during the dry
season to ensure seepage of an adequate amount of
water to supply the approximately one hundred
human residents of the Mahopa area and the vari-

ous domestic animals owned by !Kung and non-
!Kung alike. Mahopa is like other settlements of the
!Kangwa area such as !Goshi, !Ubi, !Kangwa, and
!Xabi in these respects: it has the only permanent
water source in its immediate environs, and it hosts
a mixed population of !Kung and Bantu-speaking
pastoralists of the Tswana and Herero tribes. At all
of these water holes a variety of villages are found,
some having non-!Kung only, some having !Kung
only, some having a mixture of both.

During my fieldwork at Mahopa I deliberately avoided those villages in which both !Kung
and Bantu lived. I was concerned with observing
the effects of sedentism on a pattern of life which
I had observed in the bush. I was not directly
interested in the nature of !Kung-Bantu interaction. It goes without saying that in some respects
(especially goat herding and crop planting) the
local pastoralists were a model for the subsistence
practices of the sedentary !Kung.

The additional question—whether or not
Bantu sex-role ideals influence the changes in
!Kung sex roles, especially in the direction away
from egalitarianism—will not be answered in this
discussion. Adequate handling of this topic
would require greater knowledge of (particularly)
Herero social organization and the dynamics of
!Kung-Bantu acculturation than I possess. It
remains, however, an important research question, both for the full description of !Kung sedentarization and for understanding general factors
that accompany or produce shifts in status relations between the sexes. I will confine myself here
to dealing with the sedentary !Kung and some of
the changes in the relations between the sexes
which appear to follow from the shift from
nomadism to sedentism.

The Effect of Sedentism
on Sex Egalitarianism

Stated most simply, my strong impression is that
the sexual egalitarianism of the bush setting is
being undermined in the sedentary !Kung vil-

lages. One obvious manifestation of status inequality is that at Mahopa sex roles are more rigidly defined, and at the same time women's work is seen as 'unworthy' of men. In the bush setting, although adult roles are sex-typed to some extent—particularly with respect to the exclusive male hunting, and the fact that gathering is primarily done by women—men do not lose face when they do work typically done by women, such as gathering. But in the sedentary villages of Mahopa there is definitely a feeling that it is unmanly for a man to do the jobs that should be done by women. The following example is offered as an illustration of this and of how the community brings social pressure on women (not, in this case, men) to conform.

At the largest of the three Mahopa villages lived a wife, !Uku, about sixteen years of age, and her husband /Gau, about thirty. Like many first marriages of !Kung women, this union was not happy and had not been for some time. The primary source of discontent was the wife's refusal to do the normal domestic chores expected of her. Her husband ranted publicly, claiming that she refused to collect water for their household. !Uku in those days was looking sullen; she avoided her husband and refused to sleep with him. This kind of marital standoff was not unusual among any of the !Kung I knew. !Kung brides are notorious for being labile, uncooperative, and petulant. Young husbands, though usually five to ten years older than their wives, can also be fractious and emotionally ill-equipped to make a first marriage last. !Kung have an expression which invariably crops up when one or both partners to a young marriage sabotage domestic life. They say 'Debi !oa kxwia // wa,' which translates literally: 'Children spoil marriage.'

The atypical feature of the Mahopa couple's difficulty was that the husband made a continuing issue of it. He berated his wife's behaviour loudly in public and enlisted her relatives to 'shame' her into good behaviour, etc. Though I never observed a precisely parallel episode in the bush, my prediction is that such a husband would have grumbled quietly, shrugged his shoulders, and either collected the water himself or tried to drink the water of friends and relatives. He also might have waited until his wife complained that he never provided her with meat and then reminded her that he could not spend all day hunting and still have to supply his own water.

By the time I was living at Mahopa and knew of this marital problem, it appeared to me that the elders of the village were working harder at trying to keep the couple together than would be usual in the bush. In the bush concerned relatives will work to keep a young couple together up to a certain point, but if the individuals themselves feel mismatched, there are few, if any, arguments that will persuade them to stay together. When (as often happens) the young couple divorces, no one loses a great deal—no property of any economic weight has changed hands, etc. If both the ex-spouses (together with some of their respective kin) go their separate ways, their departure causes no special disruption in the context of routinely shifting residence patterns.

At Mahopa there were larger political factors at work in the village that may have accounted for the pressure on the couple to get along. Both spouses were related in different ways to the most influential couple of the largest of the three villages. The wife, !Uku, was indirectly related as 'niece' to the man who was spoken of as the 'owner' of the village. !Uku's husband, /Gau, was the actual brother of the village 'owner's' wife. This older, influential couple needed to attract stable, permanent residents to their village. They were extremely 'progressive' in comparison with other !Kung of the !Kangwa area. Both had had many years of experience living in various Bantu cattle camps but were now striving to maintain a separate community of sedentary !Kung who could live by agriculture and animal husbandry. Their village needed personnel; /Gau and !Uku were, in theory, ideal recruits to the village on account of their age and kin connections.

What is important for us here is that certain influential persons had vested interests in the success of the marriage, and that the bulk of social criticism was directed at the wife, not the husband. In this sedentary situation various persons stood to lose a good deal in the event of a divorce. From the point of view of the village 'owner' and his wife, a divorce might result in both young people leaving the village. This would be undesirable for reasons already stated. From the point of view of !Uku's parents, who also lived in this village, if their daughter divorced the brother of the 'landlady', then their own welcome in the village might become jeopardized.

Although social pressure was being brought to bear on !Uku, it appeared that these pressures were not having the desired effect. !Uku's mother told me privately that she was disgusted with her daughter, that she had tried to get her to change her ways, but that !Uku was obdurate and had even used insulting language to her. !Uku at this time seemed to go out of her way to irritate her husband, had seriously offended her mother, and appeared quite regressive in her behaviour. For example, although she was sixteen years old, she spent hours each day playing dolls with three other girls, ten, nine, and seven years of age. From the bush-living groups I was well acquainted with five adolescent females (both married and unmarried, and approximately the age of !Uku), but I never observed any of them playing so continuously and with such absorption with children five or six years younger.

In the sedentary situation individuals have a different kind of commitment to the place and the persons with whom they are living. People have invested time and energy in building substantial housing, collecting a few goats, clearing and planting fields, and processing and storing the harvested food. It is not easy for an individual to leave these resources behind merely because he or she is at odds with someone else in the village. The couple just described were aware of what they had to lose; the head couple needed neighbours and village mates, not only for the purposes of economic cooperation but because they wanted the human company that would come of a stable settlement around them.

The unhappy marriage remained with no solution or even the hint of one during the time I observed it. Neither party to the marriage appeared ready to leave, so their plight festered and spread into the lives of other people in the village. It was not clear to me why the greatest criticism was levelled at the wife. At sixteen, she was at least fifteen years younger than her husband (a greater age difference than usual for !Kung couples), and as a juvenile she may have been an easier target than her mature husband. /Gau was known for his hot temper and general unpredictability. The concerned parties may have felt uneasy about urging him to a compromise. Such a marriage in the bush setting would have had a different history. !Uku would have left her husband long before, in all likelihood to spend another year or two in casual flirtations before marrying again.

Childhood Practices and the Greater Separation of Adult Sex Roles

Previously I have stated that in the bush children of both sexes lead very similar lives. Girls and boys do equally little work within the village. For similar reasons both girls and boys are not encouraged to routinely accompany adults of the same sex on their respective food-getting rounds. Children sometimes accompany the women on gathering trips (particularly in the rainy season when the women do not have to carry drinking water for them), but up to about twelve years of age the children make little or no contribution to the collected food which their mothers carry home. Children do, however, pick their own food and eat it during the trek.

In the settled life children continue to have a great deal of leisure, but there is a shift in the adult attitude toward a child as a potential or real worker.[5] Boys, for example, are expected to help with the animal tending.[6] They do not herd the animals during the day, but at sundown they are expected to scout the outskirts of the village and to hasten the returning animals into their pens. In each of the three Mahopa villages there was one boy who was primarily responsible for herding chores. In the largest village there were other boys also available, and these youths were frequently asked to help with the herding. Girls were not expected to help in the animal tending, and they in fact made no regular contribution.

An important feature of the herding work of the boys was that it regularly took them out of the village, away from adults and out on their own. There was no comparable experience for girls. They tended to stay in or near the village, unless they were accompanying older women to the water hole to collect water. On such occasions they quickly walked the mile or more to the well, where they filled their buckets and then returned more or less promptly to the village. In contrast, the boys drove their animals to the water and then, their work done, they lingered at the water hole. Herero men also came to the well, driving animals to water. Herero and Tswana women frequently came to the well to wash clothing. !Kung boys hung around the fringes of this scene, listening and observing. Experiences like these are no doubt related to the superior knowledge of Bantu languages which !Kung men exhibit in comparison to !Kung women. Such experiences must foster for boys a better and earlier knowledge of the greater !Kangwa area and a more confident spirit when moving within it—or outside of it, for that matter.

Women and girls appear to inhabit more restricted space—that space being largely their own village or neighbouring villages. The Mahopa women gather wild plant foods, but they do this infrequently and forage in an area much closer to the village and for shorter intervals as compared with the bush women.

Overall, the Mahopa women seem homebound, their hands are busier, and their time is taken up with domestic chores.[7] A number of factors enter into this change. Under settled conditions food preparation is more complicated, although the actual diet is probably less varied in comparison with that of the foragers. Grains and squash must be brought in from the fields and set up on racks to dry. Sorghum and corn are pounded into meal; squash and melons are peeled and then boiled before eating. Women do the greatest part of the cooking, and they also do most of the drying and storing.

The material inventory of the settled villagers is richer than that of the bush-living !Kung. People have more possessions and better facilities, and all of these things require more time and energy for maintenance. Housing, for example, is more substantial than in the bush. Round, mud-walled houses with thatched roofs are replacing the traditional grass scherms at Mahopa. More durable structures are a response to at least two changes. Once committed to settled life, it makes sense to build better and more permanent shelters. Also, the presence of domestic animals in and near the villages means that grass houses are either protected by barricades or they are literally eaten up. Most people believe it is easier to build the mud-dung earth houses and to close them with inedible doors, rather than being continually on the lookout against stock. These structures provide better shelter, but they also require more upkeep. The women periodically resurface the interior walls and lay new floors. The men do some domestic maintenance work, but it is more likely to be fencing, roof-thatching, and other nonroutine work. It appears that the Mahopa men are becoming peripheral to their households in ways that are completely uncharacteristic of the easy integration of bush-living men into their own households. More will be said about this later.

At Mahopa the work of adult women is becoming more specialized, time-consuming, and homebound, and these women are quite willing to integrate their daughters into this work. Girls have no regular chores to compare with the herding work of some of the boys, but their mothers give them frequent small tasks such as pounding grain, carrying away a troublesome toddler, fetching earth from termite hills to be used in making mud, etc. The little girls are usually on the premises and easy targets for their mothers' commands; little boys seem to be either gone from the village (on errands already described) or else visible but distant enough from the women so that their help cannot be enlisted conveniently.

Earlier in this paper I suggested that bush-living men and women are about equally absent from their respective households, due to the similarities in the location and frequency of their work. This is less true at Mahopa. Women are in the village a great deal. The greatest part of their work takes place there, and foraging occupies only a small part of their weekly work. Mahopa men are increasingly absent from the households as their women become more consistently present. There are tasks and activities for men in the village which have already been described, though they are not routine. What work the men do often takes them away from the village. They water animals, and when the goats are giving birth to kids the men who own pregnant goats check on the grazing herd during the day to make sure the newborn are not lost or rejected by the mothers. During planting season the men clear the fields and erect brush fences around the gardens to keep out the animals. Some men leave home for several days at a time to do wage work for Bantu employers living at other settlements in the !Kangwa Valley.

It is difficult to specify precisely what effect this increasing male absenteeism had on family life or relations between the sexes. The activities of the sedentary men are different not only in form but in content from those of the women. They leave home more frequently, travel more widely, and have more frequent interaction with members of other (dominant) cultural groups. In their own villages the men carry an aura of authority and sophistication that sets them apart from the women and children. For example, occasionally some incident, such as a legal case pending before the Tswana headman at !Xabi, would attract attention in the !Kangwa area. In the afternoons I often saw a group of men composed of several !Kung and one or two Hereros sitting in a shady area of one of the !Kung villages. The men would be discussing the case, carrying on the talks in a Bantu language. Women never joined these groups, and even children seemed to give these sessions a wide berth.

What these episodes conveyed to me is that at Mahopa political affairs are the concern of men, not women. Why or how women have been 'eased out' (at least in comparison with the influence they had in the bush) is not clear. The /Du/da people, so long as they remained in the bush, had only rare and fleeting contacts with members of different cultural groups. If one postulates that men are the natural political agents in intergroup contacts, then the /Du/da milieu would not elicit that potential of the male role. At Mahopa three cultural groups mixed. !Kung men, as already described, were more sophisticated than the women, and on those occasions when !Kung became involved in extragroup events, the !Kung men came prominently to the fore.

Organization of Space and Privacy in the Bush Setting

To recapitulate, in the bush, village space is small, circular, open, and highly intimate. Everyone in the camp can see (and often hear) everyone else virtually all of the time, since there are no private places to which people can retire. Even at nightfall people remain in the visually open space, sleeping singly or with other family members around the fires located outside the family huts (Draper 1973). Elsewhere (Draper 1976), I have suggested that !Kung egalitarianism and commitment to sharing are more than coincidentally associated. The intensity of social pressure, in combination with the absence of privacy, makes hoarding virtually impossible, at least for individuals who wish to remain within the group. I am suggesting that the nature of village space in the bush acts as a 'lock' on other aspects of culture that are congruent but capable of sliding apart. While it is true that !Kung values oppose physical fighting and anger, ranking of individuals in terms of status, material wealth, and competition, the context in which social action occurs is such that the earliest and subtlest moves in these directions can be perceived immediately by the group. Various forms of negative reinforcement can be employed by anyone and everyone, and the effect is to discourage anti-social behaviour, whatever form it may take.

Obviously a continuous socialization process is not unique to the !Kung. All of us experience our fellows shaping our behaviour throughout our lives. What I would like to stress about the !Kung is that in this small, face-to-face society it is much more difficult to compartmentalize one's motives, feeling states, and (most of all) actions. In ways not true of our life, !Kung remain in continuous communication, though they may not be directly conscious of the exchanges of information that are occurring.

This potential for continuous socialization exists among the !Kung; if it works in the ways I have suggested, it need have no single effect on sexual egalitarianism among hunter-gatherers. There is, for example, abundant literature on other band-level peoples (notably Australian aborigines), where similar technology, economy, and settlement patterns produce at least formally similar settings for social action without attendant equality in male and female statuses (Hart and Pilling 1960; Hamilton 1970; Hiatt 1970; Peterson 1970; White 1970). In the !Kung case, a number of factors appear to be working directly and indirectly to insure high autonomy of females and immunity of females to subordination by males. Several of these factors have been isolated in the foregoing discussion in an attempt to 'explain' sexual egalitarianism from *inside* the system—to show how sexual egalitarianism is a logical outcome given the realities of the !Kung life.

Looked at from the point of view of factors *outside* the normative system, another argument can be made for why an egalitarian, mutual interdependence prevails among these people. The nature and distribution of the resources used by the hunting and gathering !Kung probably have indirect consequences for potential competition between and within !Kung groups. Both vegetable and animal foods are thinly and unevenly distributed over the bush. This is particularly true of the large antelope, which move erratically and seldom in the large herds that are more typical in East Africa and Arctic North America. Under conditions as these, hunting success for a particular individual depends as much on luck as it does on skill. Among the !Kung, even the best hunters readily admit that there are times when game is unavailable or when conditions do not permit the stalk-and-close approach to game required by bow-and-arrow hunting. As a result, any individual man cannot count on success, and in this context sharing of meat is an essential form of social insurance—a way of distributing food to the have-nots against the time when their fortunes change. Not surprisingly, the rules about sharing meat constitute one of the most important values in !Kung culture. My guess is that in such a system where males are continually levelled and divested of their ownership of the single most valued item (meat), the potential for male competition is largely removed. The strict sharing ethic, together with the values against interpersonal aggression described earlier, are checks on male agonistic behaviour that leave the field open for female autonomy and influence.[8]

Organization of Space and Privacy in the Settled Villages

In the settled villages the organization of space and the notion of privacy have undergone some interesting changes. Instead of the circular, closed settlement pattern of the bush, the settled villages typically are arranged in an open crescent; individual households have moved farther apart; and household privacy is substantially increased, particularly for those people who have acquired more material wealth. With individual houses farther apart, the pattern of social usage of the village space is different. The average distance between interactive clusters of people also increases. In the settled village different activities are more typically separated in space, as contrasted with the bush setting where it is typical to find people carrying on a conversation and/or activity while sitting back-to-back with other people who are engaged in a wholly different enterprise.

At the time I was living at Mahopa a few families already lived in permanent mud-walled houses and some other families were in the process of building Bantu-style rondavels to replace their smaller grass scherms. Occupants of the completed rondavels build log fences around their houses; slender logs or poles are placed upright in the ground, reaching to a height of five to six feet, and spaced one to two inches apart. These fences encircle individual households and create an inner courtyard. Obviously, privacy is increased substantially by the changed house type, settlement pattern, and fencing.

When I asked settled villagers why people erected the fences, the typical response was that it is a means of keeping domestic animals away from people's living quarters. Goats, in particular, can be a nuisance. They steal food, knock over pots, even come into houses in search of food. Their fresh dung attracts flies which are also bothersome. If domestic animals entail a new style of building, the solid, roomy houses, fences, and more linear placement of separate households also change the quality of social interaction in the villages. There are internal boundaries within the village space, which people recognize and manipulate in ways completely foreign to the bush setting. In the bush people can see each other and determine, on a variety of grounds,[9]

whether it is appropriate or timely to initiate social interaction. In the Mahopa villages one heard such exchanges as 'So-and-so, are you at home?' and 'Shall I enter [your space]?'

There are differences in material wealth among the people of the settled villages that would not be tolerated in the bush. These differences are manifest in terms of household size and elaborateness of construction, unequal ownership of domestic animals, clothing, jewellery, and food reserves. The differences are not large in an absolute sense, but in comparison with the similar material wealth of individuals in the bush, the differences are impressive. Some !Kung live simply, still using grass scherms and owning few possessions; others are better off, though the men in particular seem to avoid some kinds of ostentation. For example, the two men who were the most influential males in their villages often dressed very simply and did not have the outward appearance of 'big men'.[10] Yet, if invited into their houses, one would see a remarkable collection of *things*: clothing, dishes, blankets, bottles, trunks with locks, etc. As a guest in such a house one could sit on the floor, lean back against the cool, sound-deadening wall, and enjoy being *alone* with one's host while he or she made tea and murmured small talk.

Ranking of individuals in terms of prestige and differential wealth has begun in the settled villages. Men, more than women, are defined as the managers or owners of this property. One would hear, for example, such expressions as 'Kxau's [a man's name] house' or 'Kxau's village'. Children are most often identified as being the child of the father rather than the child of the mother. Goats are also referred to as belonging to one or another adult male, though in fact a given man's herd generally includes several animals which in fact belong to his wife or other female relatives. These expressions can be heard in the bush setting, for individual ownership exists among the foragers as well, but the 'owners' referred to are as likely to be women as men. At Mahopa this linguistic custom is being replaced by one in which the adult male stands as the symbol of his domestic group. It is a linguistic shorthand, but I believe it signifies changes in the relative importance attached to each sex.

Earlier I referred to the increasing peripheralization of males in the settled villages and the opposite centripetal moving of women to the local domestic sphere. As households and possessions become private, I believe women are becoming private as well. (Perhaps this is one reason the women can afford to be ostentatious of their wealth.) In contrast bush men and women are equally 'public', mobile, and visible. I believe this exposure of women is a form of protection in the bush setting. For instance, residence choices of bush-living couples are such that over time the couples live about equally (often simultaneously) with the kin of both husband and wife (Lee 1974). (At present there is not even an ideal of patrilocal residence, so far as my own interviews could establish.) This means that the wife typically has several of her own close kin nearby. These people are already on the premises and can support her interests should they conflict with the interests of her husband or his close kin. When husbands and wives argue, people are at hand to intervene if either spouse loses self-control. Wife-beating in these settings is extremely difficult to effect.

Once, during my work in Mahopa, I had a conversation with two middle-aged women who lived in the largest of the settled villages where I was camped. I often asked !Kung adults about the Herero, what they thought of them, how they perceived the differences between the groups, mainly because for reasons already stated I seldom visited the Herero settlements and knew little from direct observation about the pattern of life there. In one such conversation I asked Kxarun!a, a woman of about fifty, 'Who do you think has the better life—a !Kung woman or a Herero woman?' She answered in a serious, thoughtful way, 'The !Kung women are better off. Among the Herero if a man is angry with his wife he can put her in their house, bolt the door and beat her. No one can get in to separate them. They only hear her screams. When we !Kung fight, other people get in between.' The other woman sitting with us agreed earnestly.

It would be unwise to attach too much significance to this remark. People are always accusing the people 'over there' of various dread offences ranging from wife-beating to much worse practices. Still, the remark chilled me and I remember deliberately not looking at the Bantu-style rondavels which were going up in the middle of the village where we sat.

In this paper I have pointed out differences in sexual egalitarianism in the hunting and gathering groups versus the settled groups of !Kung. I have discussed factors in the bush setting which favour high autonomy for females and freedom from subordination by males. Once the !Kung shift their subsistence to animal husbandry and crop planting, a number of changes occur in the area of sex roles. A major aspect of this change is the decrease in women's autonomy and influence relative to that of the men.

Notes

Fieldwork for this project was supported by National Institute of Mental Health Grant No. MH-136111 to Irven DeVore and Richard B. Lee. This paper has benefited from my discussions with many people. Dr Nancy Howell (University of Toronto, Scarborough College) and I have discussed these issues for several years, beginning with our common experience in the Kalahari. Drs Carol Smith and Henry Harpending (University of New Mexico), with whom I taught the undergraduate course, 'Bio-Cultural Bases of Sex Roles', have done much to further my thinking in the area of human sex roles.

1. The average size of camps in the /Du/da area was thirty-four persons of whom an average of twelve were children ranging from newborn to fourteen years of age.

2. See Barry, Bacon, and Child (1957) and Whiting and Whiting (1973) for further discussion of cross-cultural regularity and variability in sex differences in nurturance training.

3. For further discussion of living density of !Kung camps, see Draper (1973).

4. Some of these issues are discussed by Shostak (1976).

5. The Barry, Child, and Bacon (1957) cross-cultural study reported this as a general attribute of societies with a high degree of accumulation of surplus.

6. See Whiting and Whiting (1973) for a discussion of factors that affect the development of responsibility in boys.

7. Unfortunately, during the period of study I collected systematic information on adult work effort only at /Du/da and not at any of the settled !Kung villages.

8. Lee (1969) provides a fascinating description of how an anthropologist's pride in making a gift of meat to a !Kung village was deflated by the !Kung expertise in putting down boastfulness.

9. My impression while working in the field was that a student of proxemics would find a wealth of material in the area of nonverbal communication among the foraging groups of !Kung.

10. Yet the middle-aged wives of these men often wore jewellery and clothing beyond the means of other women living in the settled villages.

References

Barry, H.H., M.K. Bacon, and I.L. Child. 1957. 'A Cross-Cultural Survey of Some Sex Differences in Socialization', *Journal of Abnormal and Social Psychology* 55: 327–82.

Brown, J.K. 1970. 'A Note on the Division of Labor by Sex', *American Anthropologist* 72: 1073–8.

Draper, P. 1973. 'Crowding Among Hunter-Gatherers: The !Kung', *Science* 182: 301–3.

———. 1976. 'Social and Economic Constraints on Child Life Among the !Kung' in *Kalahari Hunter-Gatherers*, eds R.B. Lee and I. DeVore (Cambridge, MA: Harvard University Press).

Gale, F., ed. 1970. *Woman's Role in Aboriginal Society*. Australian Aboriginal Studies No. 36. Canberra: Australian National Institute of Aboriginal Studies.

Hamilton, A. 1970. 'The Role of Women in Aboriginal Marriage Arrangements' in *Woman's Role in Aboriginal Society*. Australian Aboriginal Studies No. 36. Canberra: Australian Institute of Aboriginal Studies.

Harpending, H. 1972. '!Kung Hunter-Gatherer Population Structure'. Ph.D. diss., Harvard University.

———. 1976. 'Genetic and Demographic Variation in !Kung Populations' in *Kalahari Hunter-Gatherers*, eds R.B. Lee and I. DeVore (Cambridge, MA: Harvard University Press).

Hart, C.W.M., and A.R. Pilling. 1960. *The Tiwi of North Australia* (New York: Holt, Rinehart and Winston).

Hiatt, B. 1970. 'Woman the Gatherer' in *Woman's Role in Aboriginal Society*. Australian Aboriginal Studies No. 36. Canberra: Australian Institute of Aboriginal Studies.

Howell, N. 1976. 'The Population of the Dobe Area !Kung' in *Kalahari Hunter-Gatherers*, eds R.B. Lee and I. DeVore (Cambridge, MA: Harvard University Press).

Landy, D. 1959. *Tropical Childhood* (Chapel Hill: University of North Carolina Press).

Lee, R.B. 1965. 'Subsistence Ecology of !Kung Bushmen'. Ph.D. diss., University of California, Berkeley.

———. 1969. 'Eating Christmas in the Kalahari', *Natural History* 78.

————. 1974. 'Male-Female Residence Arrangements and Political Power in Human Hunter-Gatherers', paper presented at the workshop in 'Male-Female Behavior Patterns in Primate Societies' at the IV International Congress of Primatology.

LeVine, R.A., and B. LeVine. 1963. 'Nyansongo: A Gusii Community' in *Six Cultures*, ed. B. Whiting (New York: John Wiley).

Minturn, L., and J.T. Hitchcock. 1963. 'The Rajputs of Khalapur, India' in *Six Cultures*, ed. B. Whiting (New York: John Wiley).

Murdock, G. 1949. *Social Structure* (New York: Macmillan).

Peterson, N. 1970. 'The Importance of Women in Determining the Composition of Residential Groups in Aboriginal Australia' in *Woman's Role in Aboriginal Society*. Australian Aboriginal Studies No. 36. Canberra: Australian Institute of Aboriginal Studies.

Service, E.R. 1966. *The Hunters* (Englewood Cliffs, NJ: Prentice-Hall).

Shostak, M. 1976. 'A Shun/twa Woman's Memories of Childhood' in *Kalahari Hunter-Gatherers*, eds R.B. Lee and I. DeVore (Cambridge, MA: Harvard University Press).

White, I.M. 1970. 'Aboriginal Woman's Status: A Paradox Resolved' in *Woman's Role in Aboriginal Society*. Australian Aboriginal Studies No. 36. Canberra: Australian Institute of Aboriginal Studies.

Whiting, J.W.M., and B.B. Whiting. 1973. 'Altruistic and Egoistic Behavior in Six Cultures' in *Cultural Illness and Health*, eds L. Nader and T.W. Maretzki (Washington: American Anthropological Association).

Chapter 5

These selections from the writings of the late anthropologist Eleanor B. Leacock provide rich descriptions of gender and family relations among the Montagnais-Naskapi, an aboriginal people (the former now known as the Innu) in Labrador. Leacock provides an especially close look at the organization of economic activities underlying the egalitarian gender relations typical of foraging societies. As well, Leacock discusses relationships among (a) how these people satisfy their subsistence needs, (b) the organization of families (around the nuclear unit or a larger unit), and (c) the nature of relations between women and men.

Women in an Egalitarian Society: The Montagnais-Naskapi of Canada

Eleanor Leacock

In the past, the Montagnais-Naskapi of the eastern Labrador Peninsula lived by hunting moose, caribou, beaver, bear, hare, porcupine, and other small game; by fishing, and by catching water fowl. The Indians hunted with bows and arrows, spears, and a variety of traps. Meat that was not eaten was smoke-dried for storage. In the summer they gathered nuts, berries, and roots.

The Montagnais-Naskapi lived in tents constructed of twenty to thirty poles, converging at the top and covered with large rolls of birch bark and animal hides. A tent might be shared by about eighteen people. They wore breechcloths, leggings and moccasins, and robes with detachable sleeves, made from leather by the women. In the winter, travel was by foot on snowshoes and long narrow sledges, which were dragged along forest trails by a cord strung across the chest. Canoes made of birch bark were used in the summer.

Until very recently, the Montagnais-Naskapi still lived for the most part in tents, wore moccasins, and often the women retained their traditional hairstyle with the hair wound on two little wooden knobs over the ears. They manufactured their own canoes, snowshoes, fish spears, sleds, and toboggans, using the 'crooked knife'—a sharpened steel file, curved upwards at the end and hafted in a piece of wood. They seldom settled in one place for more than a few weeks; entire families moved hundreds of miles or more in the course of a year.

The Indians spoke their own language, told their own stories, and taught their children to read and write in the phonetic script they developed long ago when European books and letters gave them the idea. Thus, many anthropologists considered the Indians' use of some modern technology, and their adoption of some Western social and religious practices, to be the sum total of the changes that have taken place in their lifestyle.

However, a close study of the observations made centuries ago by traders and missionaries shows what profound changes have taken place in the way the Montagnais-Naskapi live. Le Jeune, a Jesuit missionary, lived with a Montagnais band in the winter of 1633–4, and his accounts give a picture of their life in the days when they depended on hunting, not only for food, but for everything from clothes to snowshoe-webbing. Three or four families, usually related, lived together in a single large tent; men, women, and children travelled together, each working and contributing to the group to the extent he or she was able.

Le Jeune relates that three tent groups joined forces and decided to winter together on the south shore of the St Lawrence River some miles below Quebec. Leaving their canoes at the coast, they went inland and travelled about, shifting their camp twenty-three times in the period from November 12 to April 22. The winter was a hard one, since the lack of snow made it impossible to trace moose successfully. One of the three tent groups left the other two, so that they might spread out over a wider area.

Eventually a heavy snowfall alleviated the situation, and large game was killed in sufficient numbers so that some of the meat could be dried and stored. In the spring, the tent group Le Jeune was with split up temporarily, some members keeping to the highlands to hunt moose, the others following the stream beds where beaver were to be found. Gradually the entire party collected again at the coast where the canoes had been cached.

Within the group, the social ethic called for generosity, cooperation, and patience, and Le Jeune commented on the good humour, the lack of jealousy, and the willingness to help that characterized daily life. Those who did not contribute their share were not respected, and it was a real insult to call a person stingy.

The Montagnais had no leaders; the 'chiefs' Le Jeune referred to were apparently men of influence and rhetorical ability. Everyone was impressed with the skill of the speaker who put forth the Montagnais view of French-Indian relations when he greeted Champlain in 1632. Such men were spokesmen, who acted as intermediaries with the French or with other Indian groups, but they held no formal power, a situation the Jesuits tried to change by introducing formal elections.

*   *   *

Important matters were resolved through considered discussion. Le Jeune was impressed by the patience with which people listened as others spoke, rather than all talking at once. At that time leadership in specific situations fell to the individual who was most knowledgeable. For instance, during Le Jeune's stay when food was scarce and the Indians had to move in search of it, he wrote: 'When our people saw that there was no longer any game within three or four leagues of us, a Savage, who was best acquainted with the way to the place where we were going, cried out in a loud voice, one fine day outside the cabin, "Listen men, I am going to mark the way for breaking camp tomorrow at daybreak".'

The principle of autonomy extended to relations between men and women. Though some observers saw women as drudges, Le Jeune saw women as holding 'great power' and having, 'in nearly every instance . . . the choice of plans, of undertakings, of journeys, of winterings'. Indeed, independence of women was considered a problem to the Jesuits, who lectured the men about 'allowing' their wives sexual and other freedom and sought to introduce European principles of obedience.

Compare this lifestyle with that of an Indian man living to the northeast of Quebec a few decades ago, who depended upon the produce of his trap line for most of his livelihood. He worked within a definite territory which was probably passed down to him by his father, father-in-law, or another older relative. During the trapping season he left his family at a permanent camp, or perhaps even at the fur trading post, and he travelled back and forth along his line of some 300 to 400 steel traps, preferably in the company of a partner or grown son, but at times alone. Only in the summer did he join his fellow band members at the trading post, and only in this season would all the trappers live together with their families for a reasonably long period of time.

The change in this Indian's life had come about because he was no longer primarily a hunter. He was first and foremost a trapper, dependent upon the goods his furs procured for him at the local trading post. True, his ancestors always hunted and traded furs. Avenues of exchange and communication in aboriginal America had apparently been kept open from time immemorial. However, this trade was primarily for luxury items and for social purposes. It was not of great economic importance; the economy of the Indians was still based almost entirely on hunting for immediate use.

Then Europe, breaking the bonds of the small self-contained feudal communities of the Middle Ages, slowly began to develop into a commercial and urban civilization. Explorers covered the earth; trade with American Indians, and the fur trade in particular, was of no small importance. Even before the end of the sixteenth century, British and French companies were competing among themselves for a monopoly of the St Lawrence trade.

To the Indians, the trade opened up a source of new and more effective tools and weapons, of cloth which did not have to be tanned and worked, and of foods which could be more readily transported and stored. However, it demanded an unending flow of furs, and trapping fur-bearing animals began to displace the hunting of large game in the Indian economy. Within a few generations the Indians near the earliest trade centres around Quebec had become dependent upon trade goods as the mainstay of their existence. When the fur-bearing animals in their immediate area became scarce, they became the middlemen between the Europeans and the Indians who lived further to the north and west.

On the face of it, there seems little reason why it should make much difference when men turned to trapping rather than hunting as a major pursuit. But through the fur trade it came to supersede and replace all other basic economic activities. And tending a trap line was a more individual type of activity than hunting. When men became trappers, the sexual definition of functions and spheres of interest became sharper, for the wife and children began to be set apart as the family who were provided for, as compared to the men who were the providers. At the same time, there was a breaking up of the 'family bands' (the two or three tent groups that usually stayed together) into smaller units approaching the 'nuclear' family.

A connected change that took place in Montagnais-Naskapi life was an increasingly clear-cut differentiation between the spheres of men's work and women's work. In the past, both sexes were almost continuously engaged in satisfying the immediate needs of the extended family group. There was a rough and ready division of labour, based on expediency, with the men doing most of the large game hunting, and the women preparing the food, making the clothes and tents, and tending the small children. When necessary, the women helped with the hunting, and if a woman was busy elsewhere, a man would readily look after the children. The Mistassini Diaries, written a century ago by Hudson's Bay Company members, mention Indian women in western Labrador who were the heads of families and even handled their own traps.

The lack of a marked division of labour prevailed until recently in the camp of the Northwest River Indians. A man and his wife would come together from the woods, each carrying a log. A father and daughter might saw wood together. A man might hold a fussing child, while the mother calmly did something else, feeling no compulsion to take over. A whole family would go off in a canoe to pull in the fish nets. Two young women would pick up some guns and go off to hunt rabbits. It is only when one comes to the technical processes that one noticed a division of skills that seems to be rigid: the men were the wood workers, making the canoes and snowshoes, and the women handled the skins, scraping, tanning, working, and sewing them.

Another change that can be observed among the Montagnais-Naskapi is a shift towards smaller family units. Only on rare occasions did two or three Indian families of eastern Labrador still share a tent. One result of the breaking up of large 'extended' families into smaller units based on a married couple and their children, was that the circle of people upon whom the children depend began to shrink. Le Jeune reveals the feelings of a seventeenth-century Indian father, who chided the French, saying, 'Thou hast no sense. You French people love only your own children; but we love all the children of our tribe.' In 1950, however, there was a growing emphasis among the Indians on having one's 'own' son who will help one on the trap line.

On the other hand, it must be said that the general loving attitude toward all children still prevailed. Time and again one noticed an adult's casual and spontaneous concern for the needs of whatever child happened to be around. Nor could one pick out an orphan or 'adopted' child by the way he or she was treated. Such children were in no way set apart from the life of the group, but were gratefully taken in and cherished by another family.

These are only a few of the developments that have been taking place in Montagnais-Naskapi life. Any number of others could be studied—changing forms of property and attitudes towards possessions, courtship practices, recreation and amusement, methods of childrearing, and so on. However, the same fundamental point would be made by examination of any important area of living: that the Montagnais-Naskapi Indians are not a people who simply accepted some European traits and rejected others, but a people who actively adjusted their whole way of life to meet the demands of a new occupational calling.

By 1950, most Montagnais-Naskapi had moved into relatively large centres of permanent settlement. Three important towns were Schefferville, near a large interior iron mine; Seven Islands, a railhead on the St Lawrence River; and Happy Valley, near the Goose Bay Air Base on the eastern coast. While most Indians who lived in these towns were wages labourers at the enterprises near their homes, work was often seasonal, and some still derived a major part of

their income from winter trapping. Many young Indians were moving to cities for work and schooling and some were joining local and national Indian groups that concern themselves with the problems and futures of native Canadians. As part of this future many young Indians found that they wanted to retain some of the Indian tradition of a close group life, in tune with the waters and forests, the animals and bird life, the natural surroundings of their ancestors.

*   *   *

Montagnais-Naskapi Economy and Decision-making

The Montagnais-Naskapi lived by hunting and trapping wild game—caribou, moose, beaver, bear, hare, porcupine, and water fowl, by fishing, and by gathering wild berries and other vegetable foods. Like foraging peoples everywhere, they followed a regular pattern of seasonal movement according to the provenience of the foods on which they depended. The Montagnais with whom Le Jeune worked summered on the shores of the St Lawrence River, where groups of several hundred people gathered to fish, socialize, and make and repair canoes, snowshoes, and other equipment. In the fall, groups of some thirty-five to seventy-five people separated out to ascend one or another of the rivers that emptied into the St Lawrence. During the winter hunting season, these bands might split up into smaller groups in order to spread out over a wide area in search of game. However, they kept in touch with each other so that if some were short of food, they could turn to others for help.

The smallest working unit was the group that lived together in a large cone-shaped lodge— some ten to twenty people, or, in Western terms, several nuclear families. In early times, as later, residential choices were probably flexible, and people moved about in accord both with personal likes and dislikes and with the need for keeping a reasonable balance in the working group between women and men and young and old. Upon marriage, however, a man ideally moved into his wife's lodge (Thwaites 1906: 31, 169). Accordingly, mentions of a Montagnais man's family might include the man's wife's sister, or a son-in-law, or a father-in-law (6: 125; 9: 33; 14: 143–5). Yet three brothers and their wives shared the lodge in which Le Jeune lived. Le Jeune is silent about the relationships among the wives who, judging from hunting-group compositions in recent times, could easily have been sisters or parallel cousins.[1] In any case, Le Jeune's diary shows that the arrangement was not permanent.

Ethnographic evidence as well as the *Jesuit Relations* indicates that decisions about movements were made by the adult members of whatever group was involved. There is no question about women's importance in making such decisions. In fact, one recorder stated that 'the choice of plans, of undertakings, of journeys, of winterings, lies in nearly every instance in the hands of the housewife' (68: 93). Individuals might be chosen as spokespersons to mediate with the French, but such 'chiefs' held no formal authority within the group. Le Jeune noted that 'the Savages cannot endure in the least those who seem desirous of assuming superiority over the others; they place all virtue in a certain gentleness or apathy' (16: 165).

> They imagine that they ought by right of birth, to enjoy the liberty of wild ass colts, rendering no homage to anyone whomsoever, except when they like. They have reproached me a hundred times because we fear our Captains, while they laugh at and make sport of theirs. All the authority of their chief is in his tongue's end; for he is powerful insofar as he is eloquent; and, even if he kills himself talking and haranguing, he will not be obeyed unless he pleases the Savages (6: 243).

Le Jeune was honest enough to state what he saw as the positive side of Montagnais egalitarianism:

As they have neither political organization, nor office, nor dignities, nor any authority, for they only obey their Chief through good will toward him, therefore they never kill each other to acquire these honors. Also, as they are contented with mere living, not one of them gives himself to the Devil to acquire wealth (6: 231).

In his final judgement, however, Le Jeune remained bound by his culture and his missionizing commitment: 'I would not dare assert that I have seen one act of real moral virtue in a Savage. They have nothing but their own pleasure and satisfaction in view' (6: 239–41).

The Jesuit Program for Changing Montagnais Marriage

As indicated above, Le Jeune's original assumption—that he could win the Montagnais to Christianity through converting the men—changed when he learned how far Montagnais family structure was from that of the French. He realized that he would have to give special attention to women as well as men if he was to eliminate the Montagnais' unquestioned acceptance of divorce at the desire of either partner, of polygyny, and of sexual freedom after marriage.

'The young people do not think that they can persevere in the state of matrimony with a bad wife or a bad husband', Le Jeune wrote. 'They wish to be free and to be able to divorce the consort if they do not love each other' (16: 41). And several years later, 'The inconstancy of marriages and the facility with which they divorce each other, are a great obstacle to the Faith of Jesus Christ. We do not dare baptise the young people because experience teaches us that the custom of abandoning a disagreeable wife or husband has a strong hold on them' (22: 229).

Polygamy was another right that women as well as men took for granted: 'Since I have been preaching among them that a man should not have more than one wife, I have not been well received by the women; for, since they are more numerous than the men, if a man can only marry one of them, the others will have to suffer. Therefore, this doctrine is not according to their liking' (12: 165). And as for the full acceptance of sexual freedom for both women and men, no citation can be more telling of the gulf between French and Montagnais society than Le Jeune's rendition of a Montagnais rebuff.

> I told him that it was not honorable for a woman to love any one else except her husband, and that this evil being among them, he himself was not sure that his son, who was there present, was his son. He replied, 'Thou hast no sense. You French people love only your own children; but we all love all the children of our tribe.' I began to laugh, seeing that he philosophized in horse and mule fashion (6: 255).

*   *   *

Converts to Christianity wrestled with the dilemmas posed by the French faith. A recently married young man wished to be faithful to his wife, but felt himself 'inclined toward infidelity'. Deeply disturbed by his criminal wish, he entreated to be imprisoned or publicly flogged. When his request was refused, 'He slips into a room near the Chapel and, with a rope that he finds, he beats himself so hard all over the body that the noise reaches the ears of the Father, who runs in and forbids so severe a penance' (22: 67).

*   *   *

Women and children alike suffered punishment at the hands of the converts. 'A young Christian, getting into a passion, beat his wife, who had insolently provoked him,' Le Jeune wrote. The man then repented of his sin and went to the chapel to pray to God for mercy. Le Jeune had the couple brought to him. 'They were properly reprimanded,' he reported, 'especially the

woman, who was more guilty than the husband' (18: 155). As for the children,

> they are all in an incredible state of satisfaction at having embraced the Faith. 'We punish the disobedient,' said they. A young girl who would not go to the nets, where her father sent her, was two days without food as a punishment for her disobedience. Two boys, who came late to prayers in the morning were punished by having a handful of hot cinders thrown upon their heads with threats of greater chastisement in case the offenses were repeated (18: 171).

Several Christians even had a drunken, young, pagan relative thrown into prison—in Le Jeune's view, 'an act fit to astonish all those who know the customs of the Savages, who cannot endure that any one should touch their kinsmen; but God has more power than nature' (20: 153).

In 1640, eight years after Le Jeune's arrival in New France and the setting up of a Jesuit mission, the governor called together a group of influential Montagnais men, and 'having recommended to the Christians constance in their marriages—he gave them to understand that it would be well if they should elect some chiefs to govern them' (18: 99). Accordingly, the Montagnais sought advice from the Jesuits, who supervised the election of three captains. The men then 'resolved to call together the women, to urge them to be instructed and to receive holy Baptism'. The women were used to holding councils of their own to deal with matters of concern to them and reported surprise at being lectured to by the men.

> Yesterday the men summoned us to council, but the first time that women have ever entered one; but they treated us so rudely that we were greatly astonished. 'It is you women,' they said to us, 'who keep the Demons among us; you do not urge to be baptized . . . when you pass before the cross you never salute it,

you wish to be independent. Now know that you will obey your husbands and you young people know that you will obey your parents, and our captains and if any fail to do so, we will give them nothing to eat (18: 107).

Women's responses ranged from zealous compliance to rebelliousness. An incident illustrating compliance with a husband's wishes, and suggesting the internalization of guilt, occurred when a Christian woman joined some 'games or public recreation' of which her husband did not approve.

> Having returned, her husband said to her, 'If I were not Christian, I would tell you that, if you did not care for me you should seek another husband to whom you would render more obedience; but having promised God not to leave you until death, I cannot speak to you thus, although you have offended me.' This poor woman asked his forgiveness, without delay, and on the following morning came to see the Father who had baptized her, and said to him, 'My Father, I have offended God, I have not obeyed my husband; my heart is sad; I greatly desire to make my confession of this' (18: 35).

Other women continued to have lovers, to solicit married men to take a second wife, and to defy or leave their husbands. One convert complained, 'My wife is always angry; I fear that the Demons she keeps in my cabin are perverting the good that I received in holy Baptism.'

*   *   *

Another particularly revealing incident offers an important comment on Montagnais ethics, and indicates the growing distance between the missionized Montagnais, with their acceptance of corporal punishment, and the unconverted. A Jesuit called some 'chief men' together and, after commending them on putting a stop to 'the dis-

orderly conduct that occasionally occurred among them', expressed astonishment at their permitting a young baptized woman to live apart from her husband. The captain responsible for her replied that 'he had tried all sorts of means to make her return to her duty and that his trouble had been in vain; that he would, nevertheless, make another effort.' The Jesuit father counseled him to consult his people and decide upon what was to be done for such disobedience. 'They all decided upon harsh measures. "Good advice," they said, "has not brought her to her sense; a prison will do so." Two Captains were ordered to take her to Kebec and . . . have her put in a dungeon.' The woman fled, but they caught her and tried to take her by canoe to Quebec. At this

> some Pagan young men, observing this violence, of which the Savages have a horror, and which is more remote from their customs than heaven is from Earth, made use of threats, declaring that they would kill any one who laid a hand on the woman. But the Captain and his people, who were Christians, boldly replied that there was nothing that they would not do or endure, in order to secure obedience to god. Such resolution silenced the infidels.

To avoid being imprisoned, the woman 'humbly begged to be taken back to Saint Joseph, promising thence forward she would be more obedient'. Le Jeune stated,

> Such acts of justice cause no surprise in France, because it is usual there to proceed in that manner. But, among these peoples . . . where everyone considers himself from birth, as free as the wild animals that roam in their great forest . . . it is a marvel, or rather a miracle, to see a peremptory command obeyed, or any act of severity or justice performed.

*   *   *

Long-Range Impact
of the Jesuit Program

*   *   *

Perhaps no incident in the *Relations* more poignantly reveals the cultural distance to be spanned by Montagnais converts than that in which a French drummer boy hit a Montagnais with his drumstick, drawing blood. The Montagnais onlookers took offense, saying, 'Behold, one of thy people has wounded one of ours, thou knowest our custom well; give us presents for this wound.' The French interpreter countered, 'Thou knowest our custom; when any of our number does wrong, we punish him. This child has wounded one of your people; he shall be whipped at once in [their] presence.' When the Montagnais saw the French were in earnest about whipping the boy, they began to pray for his pardon, alleging he was only a child, that he had no mind, that he did not know what he was doing; but as our people were nevertheless going to punish him, one of the Savages stripped himself entirely, threw his blanket over the child and cried out to him who was going to do the whipping; 'Strike me if thou wilt, but thou shalt not strike him.' And thus the little one escaped (5: 219).

This incident took place in 1633. How was it possible that scarcely ten years later, adults could be beating, withholding food from, and even, if the report is accurate, doing such things as throwing hot ashes on children and youths? Above, I have referred to the punitiveness toward the self and others that accompanied the often tormented attempt on the part of converts to reject a familiar set of values and replace it with another. This psychological response is familiar. To say this, however, merely presses the next questions: Why did some Montagnais feel so strongly impelled to make this attempt? The answer is that the Jesuits and their teachings arrived in New France a full century after the economic basis for unquestioned cooperation, reciprocity, and respect for individual autonomy began to be undercut by the trading of furs for European goods. On the basis of new economic ties, some Montagnais-Naskapi were interested in attaching themselves to the mission station and the new European settlement, thereby availing themselves of the resources these offered. By the same token, some were prepared to accept the beliefs and ritual practices of the newcomers, and to adopt—or attempt to adopt— new standards of conduct.

Elsewhere, I have documented the process whereby the stockpiling of furs for future return, to be acquired when the trading ships arrived, contradicted the principles of total sharing based on subsistence hunting, fishing, and gathering (Leacock 1954). The process has subsequently been well described for the Canadian sub-Arctic generally, and it has been pointed out that parallel processes are involved when a horticultural people become involved in exchange relations with a market economy (Murphy and Steward 1955).

At the same time that the fur-trade was undercutting the foundation for Montagnais-Naskapi values and interpersonal ethics, the terrible scourge of epidemic disease, the escalation (or introduction) of warfare, and the delusion of relief from anxiety offered by alcohol were also undermining Montagnais-Naskapi self-assurance. Alfred Goldsworthy Bailey (1969) has described the effects of these developments in a review of the conflict between European and eastern Algonkian cultures during the sixteenth and seventeenth centuries. Fear of disease, particularly smallpox which raged in the decade after the priests' arrival, was only equaled by fear of the Iroquois. The prolonged and intricate torture of Iroquois prisoners, into which women entered with even more zeal than men, was a grim expression of profound fearfulness and anger. Alcohol, which temporarily elated the spirits, led to fights around the European settlement; in 1664 there is a reference to a case of rape committed under its influence (48: 227).

This is not to say, however, that Montagnais-Naskapi society as a whole was thoroughly disrupted. The violence that occurred around the European settlement contrasts not only with the friendliness, gaiety, and lack of quarreling that Le Jeune described during the winter he spent in the interior in 1633–4, but also with the general cooperativeness and good will—albeit laced with raucous banter and teasing—that characterized Montagnais-Naskapi life in later centuries in the rest of the Labrador Peninsula. Quebec was, after all, a gateway to the North American interior, and fur-trading posts and mission stations pushed ever westward. The non-racist policy of building a French colony in part with resocialized Indians was abandoned and replaced by a hardening color line. In time, all Montagnais-Naskapi became Catholic, but without the closer supervision of the Jesuits, they retained established religious practices and added Catholic sacraments and prayer. During the summer of 1951, the 'shaking-tent rite', in which a religious practitioner converses with the gods, both gaining useful information and entertaining the audience in the process, was still being practiced in eastern Labrador.

The pace of change in most of the Labrador Peninsula was slow, as Indians living far from centres of early settlement and trade gradually became drawn into a fur-trapping economy. In the summer of 1950, I was able to document the final stages of transition in southeastern Labrador, at a time when the next major change was about to transform life for French and English fishermen and fur-trappers as well as Montagnais-Naskapi hunter-trappers; a railroad was being built into a huge iron mine deep in the north-central part of the peninsula. When I was there, conditions in the north woods were still such that the traditional Montagnais-Naskapi ethic of cooperativeness, tolerance, and non-punitiveness remained strong.

What about the relations between women and men? As in the seventeenth-century accounts, one can still find contrasting judgments. Burghesse (1944) has written that

labour is fairly equitably divided between the sexes under the economic system of the Montagnais. Each sex has its own particular duties but, within certain limits, the divisions between the types of work performed are not rigid. A man would not consider it beneath his dignity to assist his wife in what are ordinarily considered duties peculiar to the woman. Also, women are often enough to be seen performing tasks which are usually done by men. On being questioned in regard to this aspect of their economics, the Montagnais invariably reply that, since marriage is an union of co-equal partners for mutual benefit, it is the duty of the husband to assist his wife in the performance of her labors. Similarly, it is the duty of the wife to aid the husband. . . .

The Montagnais woman is far from being a drudge. Instead she is a respected member of the tribe whose worth is well appreciated and whose advice and counsel is listened to and, more often than not, accepted and acted upon by her husband (4–7).

*   *   *

Women retained control over the products of their labour. These were not alienated, and women's production of clothing, shelter, and canoe covering gave them concomitant practical power and influence, despite formal statements of male dominance that might be elicited by outsiders. In northern Labrador in the late nineteenth century, dependence on trading furs for food, clothing, and equipment was only beginning. Band cohesion was still strong, based on the sharing of meat, fish, and other necessities and on the reciprocal exchange of goods and services between women and men.

By the middle of this century, the economic balance had tipped in favour of the ultimate dependence upon the fur-trade (and, in many cases, wage labour) throughout the entire Labrador Peninsula. The Montagnais-Naskapi lived in nuclear family units largely supported by the husband and father's wages or take from the trap line. Nonetheless, the resources of the land were still directly used, were still available to anyone, were acquired cooperatively insofar as it was most practical, and were shared. Furthermore, partly through their own desire and partly in accord with the racist structure of Western society, the Montagnais-Naskapi main-tained their status as a semi-autonomous people and were not separated into an elite minority versus a majority of marginal workers. Thus, a strong respect for individual autonomy and an extreme sensitivity to the feelings of others when decisions were to be made went with a continuing emphasis on generosity and cooperativeness, which applied to relations between as well as within the sexes.

Note

1. Parallel cousins are the children of two sisters or two brothers (and their spouses). Children of a brother and a sister (and their spouses) are called 'cross-cousins'. As is common in many kin-based societies, the Montagnais-Naskapi terms for parallel cousins were the same as for siblings, while the terms for cross-cousins, who were desirable marriage partners, connoted something like 'sweetheart' (Strong 1929).

References

Bailey, A.G. 1969. *The Conflict of European and Eastern Algonkian Cultures, 1504–1700* (Toronto: University of Toronto Press).

Burghesse, J.A. 1944. 'The Woman and the Child Among the Lac-St-Jean Montagnais', *Primitive Man* 17.

Leacock, E. 1954. 'The Montagnais "Hunting Territory" and the Fur Trade', *American Anthropologist* 78.

Lips, J. 1947. 'Naskapi Law', *Transactions of the American Philosophical Society* 37.

Murphy, R.F., and J.H. Steward. 1995. 'Tappers and Trappers: Parallel Processes in Acculturation', *Economic Development and Cultural Change* 4.

Speck, F.G. 1931. 'Montagnais-Naskapi Bands and Early Eskimo Distributions in the Labrador Peninsula', *American Anthropologist* 33.

———. 1942. 'Montagnais-Naskapi Bands and Family Hunting Districts of the Central and Southern Labrador Peninsula', *American Philosophical Society* 85.

Strong, W.D. 1929. 'Cross-Cousin Marriage and the Culture of the Northeastern Algonkians', *American Anthropologist* 31.

Thwaites, R.G., ed. 1906. *The Jesuit Relations and Allied Documents*. 71 vols (Cleveland: Burrows Brothers).

Tyrrell, J.B., ed. 1931. *Documents Relating to the Early History of Hudson Bay* (Toronto: Champlain Society).

| Section 2 | **Preindustrial Europe and North America: The Household Economy** |

*Y*ears ago, researchers laid to rest the myth that preindustrial families were typically extended (i.e., consisting of three generations living together under one roof). Yet the dynamics of preindustrial households, which have been described by social historians studying peasant and artisan households from medieval times through the eighteenth century, cast a new perspective on the matter. Although the nuclear family arrangement may have been dominant at any point in time across much of Europe, its existence was premised on cross-generational ties (through which land—the prerequisite of marriage—was passed). So, while mortality limited the chances that children would live with their grandparents, extended kin ties were fundamental to family existence. Moreover, nuclear families' continued existence was often predicated on the willingness or need of other households to take in their children at various points in their childhood and youth, as well as on the labour of people who lived in the household but were not related by blood or marriage (e.g., farm workers, servants, etc.). In short, there was nothing self-contained or privatized about nuclear families in preindustrial Europe. They bore little resemblance to nuclear families today—in their composition, degree of stability, the care of children and the emotional tenor of households.

Chapter 6

Between images of warm, extended families and argu-ments about parents neglecting their children, there is a range of confusing ideas about preindustrial European *families. After a careful reading of major social histori-ans, Tracey Adams presents a useful summary of the evidence on family life in medieval England.*

Women, Men, and the Family in Medieval England

Tracey L. Adams

Question 2.

In medieval England, the family or household was the basic social unit. Virtually all members of soci-ety spent most of their lives living and working with a family—even if that family was not their own. The family was a unit of production, as well as a unit of consumption. While in medieval times the family was likely the centre of life and love for those within it, it was primarily an economic unit in which individuals worked together to gain a livelihood. For the majority of English peas-antry—the main focus of this examination—gain-ing a livelihood was a struggle that required the constant and diverse labour of all family members. Within the family, there was a marked division of labour, with husbands and wives, and boy and girl children, expected to perform different tasks and fulfill different roles within the family. The contri-bution of all members of the family toward gain-ing subsistence was essential and valued; however, the status of each member of the family was not equal. The husband was the representative of the family and legal authority figure while his wife and children were viewed as his dependants.

This chapter examines medieval English fam-ilies as units of production and consumption, and it looks within these units to consider the nature of the relations between husbands and wives, and between parents and children. It considers both the internal dynamics of families and how fami-lies were integrated into the broader community. Before delving into a discussion of medieval fam-ilies, however, it is necessary to describe the con-text in which medieval families lived and worked. Family strategies to gain a livelihood, and even family structure itself, were responses to the exi-gencies of life and production in medieval village communities.

Production and the Village Community

In the fourteenth and fifteenth centuries, England was an overwhelmingly agrarian economy. While there were many towns inhabited by tradesmen, merchants, and people practising a range of occu-pations, most of the population were peasants engaged in agricultural production. Farms were located in communities or villages—collective settlements of peasant households that were usu-ally bound to a manor (Postan 1972: 123). Although in the west of England many farms were consolidated tracts of land that were usually hedged or fenced, the dominant pattern of farm-ing throughout much of England was the open-field system (Ault 1972; Bennett 1987). Under the open-field system, peasants did not have con-solidated holdings; they held strips of land located in many different fields. These strips were not fenced, but lay open, with one family's land adjacent to another's. Under the open-field sys-tem, agricultural production was organized and regulated by the members of the community. What was planted, and when and where it was planted, were matters decided by the community as a whole, not by individuals.

This emphasis on community interaction and regulation influenced the family, and ensured that families were not isolated from each other. Many families relied on the help and assistance of their neighbours. For instance, not all peasants in a community would own oxen and plows. Those without plows and/or oxen could borrow from those who had them and, in turn, exchange their own equipment or labour. Neighbours further relied on one another for other kinds of exchanges of favours and goods. The community interaction and regulation that characterized production also affected family relations. Conflicts between families were regulated by the community. Activities within the family could be regulated in a similar way. Neighbours would intervene and voice their disapproval if they believed a husband was being cruel to his wife or was not providing for her properly, or if a husband or wife was committing adultery (especially if the extramarital affair affected the husband's provision for his wife or his treatment of her) (Hanawalt 1986a: 208–9; Bennett 1987). Behaviour that was socially unacceptable was seen as detrimental to the community and, thus, the community at large felt the responsibility to intervene to bring the behaviour of the offending party back in line with social expectations. This kind of community regulation and interaction was concomitant with a lack of family privacy. Community members were aware of what was going on within and between other families. Privacy was not something particularly valued or pursued by medieval families.[1]

As noted, peasant farming communities were generally linked with a manor. The social relations of production during much of this period were 'feudal'. Most of the peasants in the village were *villeins* or tenants (serfs) of the lord of the manor. The relationship between a lord and his tenants was somewhat complex in England at this time. The peasants were technically 'unfree'. The land they farmed was held by the lord of the

manor, who rented the land to his tenants. The lord also expected his tenants to pay him regular fines or taxes, as well as 'rent' which, through much of the period, was due in the form of labour—working on land that remained in the lord's possession. Complicating the picture of a village community, there were also tenants who were *freeholders*. Freeholders were peasants who held land in the community, but who did not owe service to the lord of the manor. However, they did pay money rents to the lord, and were still subject to some fines and payments.

Although the peasants in a village community did not technically 'own' the land they farmed, they 'held' it. The land was theirs to farm, and they could pass it on to their heirs. On the death of a landholder, the lord would take possession of the deceased's best beast, and would issue a new lease to the heirs, or confirm that the heirs now possessed the land. The lord also required various payments from his tenants, and imposed fines upon them for certain behaviours and misdemeanours. For instance, peasant maidens were expected to pay a fee upon marriage, and could be fined for having sex before marriage or for bearing illegitimate children. These fines, however, were somewhat variously imposed. Only when a peasant was wealthy enough to pay was the marriage tax required (Hanawalt 1986a; Gies and Gies 1987; Bennett 1987). Fines for premarital sex or illegitimate children were more likely to be exacted when the lord was short of money and had to raise some quick funds. For instance, in Wakefield, the lord of the manor sought to finance his divorce by rounding up most of the young women in the village in January of 1316 and fining them for fornication outside of marriage and bearing illegitimate children (Gies and Gies 1987: 170; Hanawalt 1993: 195).

Overall, the relationship between lord and tenant involved a complex system of mutual obligations, in which the lord of the manor held a great deal of power that was in actuality variously exercised. His power was not absolute, however, as his actions were constrained by manorial custom and tenant compliance which waned towards the end of the medieval period. Although the peasants technically did not 'own' their land, the land they farmed was theirs for all intents and purposes. There was a very active land market in medieval times, and tenants bought and sold land according to their means and their ability to farm it.

Within the village community, there were substantial inequalities amongst the peasantry. Historians record three identifiable groupings. At the top of peasant society were those peasants who possessed a fair amount of land (a *virgate*), that provided enough food to not only support their families, but also enough to trade in the market. These families also tended to hold positions of influence within the village and its regulatory bodies. Next were a group of 'middling' peasants who possessed enough land to feed themselves; in a good year, they *may* have had some left over to sell on the market. These families had less influence, but they were often active in village society and the manorial courts. Towards the bottom of peasant society were those *cottars* who did not possess enough land to feed themselves, and who had to rely on bye-industries and wage work to get by. For families in this latter group, existence was a struggle. Although these inequalities were fairly persistent as a pattern, a family's position within this hierarchy was not necessarily stable from one generation to the next. High mortality rates, inheritance patterns, and vagaries of fortune or misfortune, ensured that there was a fair amount of both upward and downward mobility within the village community. These inequalities within the community are significant as the nature of family life, marriage, and childhood, as well as family strategies for survival, varied across social groups.

Family life, social inequality, and the lord-tenant relationship changed significantly during the period under investigation. In 1348–9, the Black Plague hit England, after devastating much of Europe. It is estimated that the Plague wiped out between one-third to one-half of the entire population (Postan 1972). The Plague ultimately led to an end of feudalism, as lords, now in need of tenants, found that they could not afford to alienate them through extensive labour rents and fines. Peasants became 'free' of many feudal fines and labour requirements. Moreover, the Plague altered families' strategies for gaining subsistence and survival. For instance, one way for people to gain land before the Plague was to marry a widow. This strategy became much less appealing after the Plague when land and wage labour were more in abundance. The Plague also affected inequalities in the village, to some extent making it easier for poorer peasants to get land, but also making it easier for wealthy peasants to expand and increase their holdings.

It was within this context of lord-peasant relations, inequalities, community regulation of production and social life, and high mortality rates, that medieval peasants formed families, reproduced, and lived their lives. It is to these families, we will now turn our attention.

Family or Household?

In medieval times, the household was the main unit of production and consumption. The extent to which this household was synonymous with the family has been a matter of debate among historians. What historians agree on is that the core of the medieval household and family was a married couple. Married couples almost always had their own homes, which were relatively easy to construct and not very expensive (Hanawalt 1986a; Bennett 1987). They did not live with extended family members, either parents or brothers and sisters, except under unusual circumstances. The couple's children also lived in the household. What historians disagree about is how often others, outside this nuclear-family unit, were present within the household. It is likely that when children were young, families found it useful to employ servants to help them with household production (Bennett 1987). These servants were often older children, employed for an extensive period of time, who lived with the families that employed them and were basically treated as members of the family.

The extent to which servants were employed in homes, however, is uncertain. As Hanawalt (1986a) argues, by the fifteenth and sixteenth centuries, it was common for families to send children out to service or apprenticeship between the ages of 7 and 14. This was often done when a family had more mouths than it could feed; yet spending time in service or an apprenticeship was also seen as part of growing up in this later era. In the thirteenth and fourteenth centuries, hiring servants and sending children out to be servants was also quite common in towns (Hanawalt 1993). However, it does not seem to be quite as common among medieval peasants. When peasants needed help and could afford it, they hired someone to help them. This help was not necessarily long term; it could be temporary and/or seasonal. There was a large labour supply in the overpopulated countryside before the Plague. Families also relied on their neighbours for mutual help and assistance. Thus, families had other strategies they could pursue if they could not afford a year-round servant and felt that they needed some assistance with production.

According to Hanawalt (1986a), households typically contained nuclear families. Although employing a servant was perhaps not so rare as to be described as atypical, it was also probably not the standard case either. It is important to note, however, that while historians emphasize the importance of nuclear families as the main unit within village society, medieval people had no word for *family*. They themselves would have placed more emphasis on household. In speech, they specified the relationship of household members to the household head—not membership in a family. Thus, people were described as 'Margery wife of Robert' or 'John son of Robert'.[2]

In medieval records, servants were rarely distinguished from other household dependants (especially children), except for the purposes of inheritance. There was no sentimentalized notion of a 'family' in the medieval era, which drew sharp boundaries between family members and those outside. For medieval peasants, the household was the important social unit, and this household consisted of a nuclear family and any servants they may have had in their employ.

Medieval Marriages

In medieval times, the vast majority of peasants would have spent some time in a marriage relationship. There were few options for peasant men and women beyond marriage. Life and production within village communities centred around a married couple. It was very difficult for a man to farm alone, without a wife, as it was difficult for a woman to farm and gain subsistence without a husband. A peasant marriage was 'a classic partnership in which each person contributes a specialized skill that complements the other' (Hanawalt 1986b: 17). Each partner needed the other, and each made essential contributions to family survival.

That marriage in medieval times was regarded as a partnership is evident in the way marriages were negotiated. Marriage was a contractual agreement that not only joined husband and wife together, but also joined their land and goods. Women had to bring a dowry into marriage. The size of the dowry was generally negotiated between the families of the potential bride and groom. The dowry might consist of land, but more commonly involved money and a number of goods and household items such as linens, cooking pots, spoons, and so on. The size of the dowry was of some importance. Women with larger dowries would be more attractive in the marriage market. A large dowry would also help a woman attract a man with property and good prospects. Virtually all women—whether rich or poor—

needed a dowry. As a women could not marry without one, poor women often engaged in wage work as adolescents and young women to earn a dowry so that they could marry when older.

The husband brought land into the marriage. The marriage contract involved the negotiation of *dower*. Before a marriage occurred, it was necessary for the husband to stipulate what *dower land* a potential wife would receive, upon his all-too-likely early death. Dower lands were generally half of the husband's land holdings, but could be as little as a third or as much as the entire holding.[3] This land was to be held by the widow, so that she would have some means of support during her widowhood, until her death, at which time the land would revert back to the couples' heir. The size of dower lands was important in the negotiation of a marriage contract; women from wealthier families with good dowries would seek out the most favourable dower arrangements. Negotiations surrounding the marriage contract were most often performed by the parents of the couple involved.

The importance of property to medieval marriages ensured that economic factors were the predominant consideration when negotiating a marriage. Particularly in marriages between people with property, such as members of the aristocracy, the gentry, and even wealthy peasants, economic considerations loomed large (Power 1975; Acheson 1992). However, historians suggest that love was also sometimes a factor in medieval marriages, especially among the peasantry (Acheson 1992; Hanawalt 1986a, 1993). Although information is scarce, it appears that many husbands and wives loved each other. The love found in these marriages was not a romantic love, but a sense of attachment that developed from living together and working together.[4] It was not common for a couple to marry for love, but if they did, they could not ignore economic considerations. In the words of one medieval historian, only the poor and 'the foolish could marry for love or sexual attraction alone' (Hanawalt

1993: 208). But for those with property, as for those with little, personal attraction might *influence* a decision to marry, especially for men (Gies and Gies 1987; Acheson 1992). While people would seek marriage partners with the appropriate dowry, dower, and means, they could choose the most appealing person from among a number of potential partners. It seems likely that men had more latitude in making this kind of choice than did women, who were often married off by their parents to the person who gave the best offer (Power 1975; Gies and Gies 1987).[5]

Given that economic considerations were so important in negotiating marriages, age at marriage was not typically young. There were, of course, many instances of propertied, and often orphaned, women married at very young ages. Heiresses were in such demand that they were often betrothed while still children. However, for a marriage to be considered legal and binding, the church required that boys were at least fourteen and girls at least twelve years old when they consented to marry (Gies and Gies 1987). A marriage could be dissolved if the parties involved so wished when they reached this age (Gies and Gies 1987). Nonetheless, in medieval times, early marriage was the exception, not the rule. Before marriage, a man had to acquire some property, while a woman had to acquire property, household goods, or money. In pre-Plague England, where land was scarce and wages low, the average age at marriage was relatively late. Couples generally did not marry until they were in their twenties, and often not until they were older. After the Plague, the greater abundance of land and high wages encouraged earlier marriages, but even at this time, it is believed that men and women waited until they were in their twenties.[6]

On marriage, both a man and a woman experienced a change of status. Before marriage, both were 'semi-independent'. Although they were generally still dependants of their fathers, they were independent enough to own land, to attend manorial courts as landholders, and to hold jobs and acquire some goods of their own (Bennett 1987). After marriage, men became fully independent. They were now entitled to hold offices in village courts and administration, and they became more fully citizens of the community. They were landholders and household heads with all the duties and responsibilities that accompanied those statuses. Women had a very different experience on marriage: they left their semi-independent status behind, and became dependants of their husbands (Bennett 1987). Any property, goods or income that a woman brought into a marriage, or even acquired during a marriage, were administered by her husband. A married woman could not buy or sell land, or enter contractual agreements, without her husband. She had virtually no participation in the political life of the village community. Ultimately, a married woman was not seen as an individual, but as a dependant of her husband, and he had a great deal of authority over her (Bennett 1987).

This authority was extensive. In a medieval marriage, the husband controlled his wife's financial assets and her public behaviour. He could freely enforce his will through physical violence since wife beating was considered to be a normal part of marriage (Bennett 1987: 103). The village community upheld husband's rights over their wives and it too helped to ensure that wives remained dependent and obedient to their husbands. Gender relations within medieval families and medieval communities more generally were patriarchal in nature, and men had extensive authority over their wives and other dependants.

Juxtaposed against this substantial political and social inequality between husband and wife was the economic partnership involved in gaining subsistence to maintain the family. Men and women within the family were mutually dependent on one another for survival and subsistence (Hanawalt 1986a). There was a sexual division of labour within the family: men typically concentrated their labour in the fields, while women's work was centred in and around the home and

garden. This division of labour was not rigid, and it varied somewhat with the seasons. During harvest-time, and other times during the main farming season, women would work in the fields alongside men, while during the winter months men spent more of their time closer to the house with women (Hanawalt 1986a).

Within this division of labour, the work of men was generally concentrated on one (or perhaps two) primary tasks: men were busy with the work of agricultural production. Some men combined agricultural labour with a trade practised part-time. Common trades included carpentry, blacksmithing, weaving, and tailoring. Women's tasks were a great deal more varied than were men's. Women maintained the home and tended the animals (who frequently shared the home with them), tended a large garden, looked after children, cooked, foraged and gathered fuel, did laundry and dairying chores, went to market, and sometimes participated in brewing and spinning (Hanawalt 1986a; Bennett 1987).[7] As noted, women also worked in the fields with their husbands, and/or helped with the latter's trade work when needed. Although there is little concrete evidence of how husbands and wives regarded this division of labour, wills from the era as well as literature suggest that each felt the other made a valued contribution (Hanawalt 1986a). Moreover, it seems that husbands regarded their wives as true economic partners, as most men who left wills preferred to have their wives rather than children, extended kin, or close friends handle their estates.

Whereas husbands were the political representatives of their families as well as family authority figures, it appears that both husband and wife worked together for family prosperity and to maintain subsistence. As Bennett (1987: 103) argues, although they were 'theoretically powerful, husbands probably often shared domestic decisions with their wives'. It should be noted that the division of labour between men and women in the family varied between prosperous and less prosperous families. More prosperous peasants were more likely to hire others to help in the fields, and thus would have relied less on women's labour in this context, while poorer families with fewer resources or help would have relied more heavily on the labour of women in agricultural pursuits and likely in bye-industries as well (Middleton 1979; Bennett 1987). Whatever the family's means, however, the labour of women was indispensable to family survival and well-being (as was men's).

The ability of a family to obtain subsistence could be jeopardized by the death of one of the spouses. In this era of high mortality rates, widowhood was a very common occurrence—so common that provisions for widows after their husband's death were negotiated prior to marriage, as we have seen. Men rarely remained widowers for long. They typically remarried quickly after the death of a wife, especially if they had young children. They needed a wife's labour. The length of time women remained widows varied across this period. As we saw, land was so scarce before the Plague that a young or middle-aged widow with property was likely to be in demand in the marriage market; after the Plague, widows were less attractive marriage partners and thus more likely to remain widows for an extended period of time.

As widows, women had political and economic rights they did not possess when married. They had control over their lands and could participate in manorial courts as landholders. They were able to carry on a business, buy and sell land, and control their own profits—just as their husbands used to do, and just as they might have done as single women. However, widows' economic well-being was often precarious. Their prosperity depended on having someone to farm their land, and a widow without grown sons would have to hire someone to do farm work for her. This expense would strain the finances of many, unless they were moderately wealthy. During widowhood, women's political and economic freedoms were balanced against this economic fragility. Life and production in a village centred around a husband and wife team; it was difficult for men and women to maintain production with one partner missing.

Children

Children also had an important role in the family economy. For most families, attaining subsistence required the work of every member of the household. Thus, from a very young age, children did chores for their family and helped out when they could. From the age of four, children might be expected to help fetch water, gather berries or fuel for the household, as well as watch over younger siblings. Children's contributions to the household expanded as they got older. Children became most useful to their parents during the ages eight through twelve when they became more independent from their parents, and were given many independent chores to do (Hanawalt 1986a). At this age, children started to be trained for the work they would do as adults. Thus, older girls did chores similar to those of their mothers, while boys more often helped their fathers with their work in the fields. Families needed the labour of their children to help feed them. When they had more mouths than they could feed, they sent their children off to live with other families as servants. This latter strategy could be of some advantage to poor children, as such service work might enable them to earn money that they could use when older for a dowry, or perhaps for the purchase of some land.

Although children were expected to contribute to the household, there was also plenty of time for play. While some historians have claimed that children were treated like little adults, the bulk of the historical evidence suggests that this was not the case (Hanawalt 1986a, 1993). Young children had very few chores and were expected to spend much of their time playing either by themselves or with other children. Even by adolescence, medieval peasants did not spend the majority of their time working, but actually spent a great deal of time in play and other leisure pursuits. It was only on entering adulthood that they appear to have worked in the same manner as their parents. Children who were sent out to service or an apprenticeship probably worked more than other children. However, during this era, the age at which children were sent out was raised. It became more common to keep children at home, engaged in play (and for some education), until they were at least fourteen (Hanawalt 1993).

Looking after children was the responsibility of the mother. The exigencies of peasant production, however, ensured that it was not her only responsibility, nor generally was it her primary responsibility. The importance of medieval women's work to family well-being often meant that they could not watch their children as closely as they would have liked (Hanawalt 1986a; Gies and Gies 1987: 298). This fact, combined with the fact that the home and its environs were quite hazardous, sometimes led to tragedy. Although mothers usually sought a babysitter for their children when they were busy, they were generally forced to use people whose labour was not required elsewhere, such as young children or elderly people, who were not always the most competent caretakers (Hanawalt 1986a). Ultimately, it was a mother's responsibility to care for children, raise them, and keep them safe.

Despite people's efforts, mortality was high during medieval times. Not only were there many deaths from accidents, but also from illness and disease. Children were particularly affected by the Great Plague. Inadequate nutrition, especially among the poor, made children more vulnerable to illness and disease. Thus, life for children was precarious in medieval times.

With high mortality, and relatively low fertility as a result of inadequate nutrition among the poor, many families would not have a large number of children living to adulthood. Estimates of household and family size during the period suggest an average of just below five (Postan 1972). This estimate would suggest that medieval families

had, on average, three children (living at a time). Of course, these estimates are approximate, and obscure variation among households. Wealthier households are believed to have had many more children, and regardless, would have had a higher household size because they were more likely to employ servants. Poorer households were generally smaller (Hanawalt 1986a; Bennett 1987).

Given their contributions to the family economy and the high mortality rates, children were likely regarded as very precious. However, in the past, historians have disagreed over how highly children were valued, and how parents felt about their children. Aries (1962) has argued that children were not particularly valued in medieval society, except insofar as they contributed to the family economy, and that men and women in this society did not have a sentimentalized view of childhood. More recently, historians examining the relations between parents and their children have come to different conclusions. Even though medieval men and women did not sentimentalize childhood to the extent that we do today, they certainly exhibited concern and care for their children. Hanawalt's (1993) study of medieval childhood illustrates that parents went to a great deal of trouble to get their children established in the world. They sought land for their children and/or worked to establish them in good apprenticeship or service contracts. When their children were living with other families under such contracts, parents were careful to monitor their progress, and quick to intervene on behalf of their children if they felt that the contract was not being honoured and/or their children were not being treated properly. Both parents and community authorities kept watch in an effort to ensure that children were being treated properly, especially when separated from their parents.

Hanawalt (1986a) argues that parents' concern for their children is evident in the actions they took to protect them. In her analysis of medieval accidental death reports, she found stories of mothers rushing into burning buildings to try to rescue their children, only to perish in the fire, as well as stories of parents anxiously searching for lost children who had wandered off, only to find them dead. Although there is no way of accurately assessing how much medieval people loved their children, there is ample evidence that medieval people had great concern for children, and that they actively tried to protect them and promote them in the world.[8] Hanawalt (1986a: 186–7) also finds in medieval stories some evidence that children were sentimentalized, although to a much lesser extent than is common today. Children clearly had a value in medieval society, and this value was not entirely reducible to their contribution to the family economy.

One way, perhaps the last way, parents tried to provide for their children was through inheritance. The typical inheritance pattern in medieval England was primogeniture: the eldest son inherited his family's land (although in some villages, the youngest son inherited it). Thus, families endeavoured to establish their other children, if they could, before they died. They would purchase land for their other sons and possibly their daughters as well. They would also try to provide their children with education, an apprenticeship, or—if they could not afford these—a service contract whereby their children could earn their own money toward their future. Daughters would have to be provided with a dowry, and parents were often active in trying to secure the most favourable marriage match for their daughters. In their wills, fathers also provided for their children. In addition to granting the family holding to the eldest son, they left their remaining children other parcels of land, household goods, or money, as they were able.

Inheritance patterns affected children's future well-being and their future social ties. The eldest son had a good chance of keeping the social standing and prosperity his parents had earned, and possibly more, through their efforts or his own. Later children were less secure in their status, however. While some parents were wealthy enough to provide for all of their children, even they could not ensure that their younger children would attain the same social standing as their eldest children. When grown, brothers and sisters seem to have interacted more with others in their village who had a similar or slightly higher status than their own. Collateral ties between siblings were not that strong, it appears, and contact between siblings with very different social statuses may not have been common (Bennett 1987). In fact, data from medieval times suggests that adult siblings did not interact frequently with each other or their more extended kin.[9] Interactions seem to have been strongest within the nuclear family and household, and between these households and those of nearby neighbours within the village community.

Discussion

For medieval families, as for other precapitalist agrarian families, the nature of production and consumption shaped not only family structure, but also family relations. Families had to produce enough to cover their consumption needs. For most families in these economies, the labour of all household members was required to meet consumption. In this context, the labour of each family member was highly valued.

Families engaged in many strategies to ensure household subsistence, and ideally, prosperity. Balancing labour and consumption was one important strategy. Families could expand their household size by hiring a servant if they required more labour and could afford to feed another; however, if they had enough workers and too many mouths to feed, they could send a child to live with another family as a servant. Moreover, families relied on neighbours for assistance and support in production.

Families also endeavoured to ensure that children were established and secure as adults so that they could form families of their own. Good marriages could help determine the fortunes of both sons and daughters. The precariousness of survival in these societies ensured that families placed importance upon the marriage relationship as an economic partnership. As we have seen, although substantial gender inequality existed within the family and in medieval society more generally, marriage relations were flexible enough to enable wives to engage in a variety of work roles to care for their families, and even to take over for their husbands when the latter were unavailable due to illness, death, or other absence.[10] This flexibility enabled a family to pursue many strategies in order to gain subsistence, and at times, to prosper.

It is this flexibility, and the wide range of strategies open to medieval families, that seem to distinguish them most from families in later centuries. With the rise of capitalism, beginning in the sixteenth century, there was a gradual decline in flexibility; a more rigid sexual division of labour gradually took hold. Family subsistence strategies also changed dramatically as landholding began to polarize. The ability of many peasants to support themselves on the land was diminished. From the sixteenth century on, they increasingly were forced to leave the land and look for wage work in the towns and cities.

Notes

1. Indeed, entire families and their servants often slept in the same room, and sometimes in the same bed or pallet. Privacy was not necessarily a priority for family members, nor would it have been easily attained given the simple nature of medieval dwellings, and the closeness of many medieval houses.

2. While last names were becoming increasingly common during the period, they were somewhat variously applied, and might differ even from one generation to the next. Moreover, they were generally used in conjunction with reference to the household head, as in 'Margery wife of Robert Baker'.

3. Customary law (the law of the manor and village community) granted a wife half of her husband's lands upon his death, but common law (the law of the country) guaranteed a wife only one-third. In their wills, husbands could specify any amount of land over these limits, and sometimes granted their wives use of the entire holding.

4. Notions of romantic love did arise during this period among the aristocracy. 'Courtly love' was a romantic love celebrated in literature and songs during the thirteenth century. Courtly love involved an attachment between a knight and a married woman who was not his wife. To prove his love, the knight would perform noble deeds and worship his lady according to a complicated set of formalities and codes. Courtly love was a platonic love, and it could not occur between husband and wife (Power 1975).

5. For a marriage to be considered valid and binding by the church, both husband and wife had to give their free consent. Studies suggest, however, that this consent, particularly for women, could be forced or given under extreme family pressure (Gies and Gies 1987; Acheson 1992).

6. In towns, where apprenticeships were more common than in the countryside, men had to wait until their apprenticeship was completed before they could marry. This ensured that few married before their early twenties and, by the end of the period, before their late twenties. Women in apprenticeships or in service generally had no such restrictions on their marriage.

7. The presence of markets in medieval England meant that families did not have to produce everything they consumed; they could concentrate on the production of some food or goods, and purchase other food or goods on the market. Some agricultural societies, such as preindustrial Ontario, were not as market-oriented, and thus, the family likely produced a higher proportion of what they consumed. The labour of family members, particularly of wives and daughters, was extremely important in these latter agrarian societies (Cohen 1988).

8. Medieval parents were also quite concerned about disciplining their children. At the time, discipline entailed a liberal use of physical punishment. They believed in the maxim 'spare the rod, spoil the child'.

9. Extended kin, including godparents, were generally not a large part of the everyday lives of medieval family members. Rather, they seem to have functioned as a resource that could be drawn on for assistance, for verification of identity or age for inheritance purposes, or as a contact that might help locate service jobs or apprentice positions (Hanawalt 1986a, 1993).

10. Within the gentry and aristocracy, a wife sometimes took over her husband's business and monitored her husband's affairs while he was away on business or off fighting in a war. On widowhood, women often took over for their husbands in trade, farming, or business (Power 1975; Gies and Gies 1987).

References

Acheson, E. 1992. *A Gentry Community: Leicestershire in the Fifteenth Century, c. 1422–c.1485* (Cambridge: Cambridge University Press).

Ariès, P. 1962. *Centuries of Childhood: A Social History of the Family*, trans. R. Baldick (London: Vintage Books).

Ault, W.D. 1972. *Open-Field Farming in Medieval England: A Study of Village By-Laws* (London: Allen and Unwin).

Bennett, J.M. 1987. *Women in the Medieval English Countryside: Gender and Household in Brigstock Before the Plague* (London: Oxford University Press).

Cohen, M.G. 1988. *Women's Work, Markets, and Economic Development in Nineteenth-Century Ontario* (Toronto: University of Toronto Press).

Gies, F., and J. Gies. 1987. *Marriage and the Family in the Middle Ages* (Harper & Row).

Hanawalt, B.A. 1986a. *The Ties that Bound: Peasant Families in Medieval England* (London: Oxford University Press).

———, ed. 1986b. *Women and Work in Preindustrial Europe* (Bloomington: Indiana University Press).

———. 1993. *Growing Up in Medieval London: The Experience of Childhood in History* (London: Oxford University Press).

Middleton, C. 1979. 'The Sexual Division of Labour in Feudal England', *New Left Review*: 113–14, 147–68.

Postan, M.M. 1972. *The Medieval Economy and Society: An Economic History of Britain in the Middle Ages* (Penguin).

Power, E. 1975. *Medieval Women*, ed. M.M. Postan (Cambridge: Cambridge University Press).

Chapter 7

What follows is part of Louise Tilly and Joan Scott's book Women, Work and Family, *which examines women's work in England and France between 1700 and 1950. The selection is long, because of its fine description of the dynamics of preindustrial households, which were both units of the production of subsistence and units of consumption, and thus in continual need to balance labour supply against consumption require-* *ments (by altering household composition). That much of the nature of family life, and even the quality of personal relationships, was dictated by economic considerations and pressures is evident in this selection. As well, Tilly and Scott's focus on the position of women gives us a pretty clear picture of the division of labour by gender, and the differential power of men and women, which constitute the roots of gender relations today.*

The Family Economy in Modern England and France

Louise A. Tilly and Joan W. Scott

Economy and Demography

In the cities and the countryside of eighteenth-century England and France economic life was organized on a small scale. The visual image one gets from reports of the period is of small farms dotting the countryside and of small shops lining the crowded narrow streets of cities. . . . The centre of life for rural people, whatever the size of their holding, was a farm. The centre of the farm was the household in which they lived and around which work was organized.

For those engaged in rural and urban manufacturing the household was both a shop and a home. . . . In the craftshop and on the land most productive activity was based in a household, and those labouring often included family members. This form of organization is often referred to as the household or domestic mode of production. It had important consequences for family organization. The labour needs of the household defined the work roles of men, women, and children. Their work, in turn, fed the family. The interdependence of work and residence, of household labour needs, subsistence requirements, and family relationships constituted the 'family economy'.

The specific form of the family economy differed for craftsmen and peasants. And in the city and the country there were important differences between the prosperous and the poor, between those families with property and those who were propertyless. Nonetheless, in all cases production and family life were inseparably intertwined. And the household was the centre around which resources, labour, and consumption were balanced.

RURAL ECONOMIES

Most people lived in rural areas and worked in agriculture during the eighteenth century. Estimates based on scattered local studies show that in 1750 agriculture employed about 65 per cent of all English people and about 75 per cent of the French population (Cipolla 1976: 74). The forms of agricultural organization differed in France and England.

In France, the most typical rural household in the eighteenth century was the peasant household. In the course of the century the pressures of increased population and of high rents and taxes drove many families off the land or left them severely impoverished. . . . Some families barely subsisted on their land, others not only produced for themselves but marketed a crop of grapes, grains, olives, and the like. Some families manufactured cloth or clothing to supplement their earnings. Others hired themselves out as part-time labourers as well as tilled their own soil. Whatever the expedients they adopted to make ends meet, these rural people remained peasants, and the family's life ultimately was organized around the property, no matter how small the holding (Baehrel 1961; Goubert 1965b: 148; Hufton 1974, 1975).

The composition of the peasant household could vary considerably over the years. At any time those living and working together constituted a 'family' whether or not they were related by blood. 'The peasant concept of the family includes a number of people constantly eating at one table or having eaten from one spot . . . peasants in France included in the concept of the family the groups of persons locked up for the night behind one lock' (Thorner, Kerblay, and Smith 1966; Flandrin 1976: 103).

Although the terms *family* and *household* were often used interchangeably, and although servants took their meals with family members, the number of non-kin in the household of a propertied peasant depended on the composition of his own family. The propertied peasant had to balance labour and consumption. His resource—land— was fixed. The amount of work to be done and thus the number of labourers needed changed in the course of the family's life cycle. A young couple could adequately provide for its own needs, with the assistance perhaps of some day labourers at planting and harvest times. As children were born, they also had to be fed, and the availability of the mother to work away from the hearth decreased. The consumption needs of the family exceeded its labour power, and so at this point outside labour was recruited. Young men and women were added to the household as servants. They usually worked in exchange for room and board, rarely for cash wages. They were available for work because their own families either could not support them or did not need their labour.

(One study suggested that 30 per cent of all rural workers in England at the end of the seventeenth century were servants, and that 60 per cent of all those fifteen to twenty-four years old in rural England were servants.) As the peasant's own children grew up, the need for outside help diminished. When several children lived in the household, there might be more labour available than the size of the landholding warranted. At this point, farmers might rent or buy additional land. More typically, in the land-poor regions of Western Europe, children would leave home to seek employment. They usually worked in other households as servants (Macfarlane 1970: 209; Berkner 1972; Kussmaul-Cooper 1975b).

In England some people still supported themselves on small farms during the eighteenth century, but they were a decreasing group. The growth of agricultural capitalism, particularly in the form of sheep-herding to produce wool for sale, led to the enclosure of large areas of land and the gradual, and violently resisted, dispossession of small farmers. Despite their protests and resistance, English farmers lost the struggle to retain their land and their right to farm it (see Thompson 1975 and Hay et al. 1975 for details). By 1750 land ownership was concentrated 'in the hands of a limited class of very large landlords, at the expense both of the lesser gentry and the peasants . . .' (Hobsbawm 1968: 15).

The dispossessed became agricultural labourers working for wages on the large farms, or they turned to cottage industry. Those involved in cottage industry worked at home on account for a merchant entrepreneur. In England the typical form of cottage or domestic industry was wool and, later, cotton weaving. In both England and France, merchants brought raw materials to rural cottages and then picked up the woven cloth which they had finished in towns or large villages. By having cloth woven in the countryside, the merchants managed to escape the control of the guilds, organizations of urban craftsmen, which closely supervised production in the cities. Although cottage weavers, like agricultural labourers, worked for wages, they worked in their own households, controlling the pace and organization of production. The family was the unit of production and of consumption, the household was the locus of work and residence. The family economy thus existed in the cottages of domestic weavers (and hosiers and nail or chain-metal workers) as it did in the households of propertied peasants.

Agricultural labourers, on the other hand, left home to earn wages elsewhere. 'Thus an amazing number of people have been reduced from a comfortable state of partial independence to the precarious condition of hireling' (Davies 1965: 41). Family members often worked together. And the aim of everyone's work was to secure enough to support the family, both by bringing home some cash and by labouring in exchange for food. Among these families family membership meant shared consumption, but not shared production. In this case the family economy became a 'family wage economy'. The unit's need for wages, rather than for labourers, defined the work of family members.

WORK IN URBAN SOCIETY

Cities in both England and France had similar economic and occupational structures in the early modern period. They were essentially centres of consumer production and of commerce. The dominant form of activity differed from city to city. Yet city life differed markedly from life in the country. Gathered within city walls was a diverse population linked by an exchange of goods, services, and cash.

The varieties of urban life can be illustrated by examining several cities. For the early modern period, we will describe York, England, and Amiens, France. Both these cities were typically 'preindustrial' in economy and social structure. York was a Cathedral town, engaged in commerce, while the principal business of Amiens was small-scale, largely artisanal textile manufacture. . . .

The specific jobs available to men and women differed according to the economic struc-

ture of each city. In York most manufacture involved luxury products: bell casting, glass painting, and pewter and clock making were among those listed. The cocoa, chocolate, and confectionery business which was to dominate the late-nineteenth-century economy of York had its origins in small eighteenth-century family businesses. In addition, there were jobs connected with the river trade from York to the seaport of Hull. Butter, grain, coal, salt, and wool were regularly shipped through York. And, although the fortunes of the city (once the 'second capital' of English society) seemed to be declining by the end of the eighteenth century, it remained a centre of handicrafts and trade. . . .

In the provincial capital of Amiens most people were engaged in the woollen trades. Various tax lists enable us to determine the occupations of others in the city, although these lists give out a partial description, since only the wealthier people in the city were taxed. Most artisans and shopkeepers on the lists were in textiles, food, and the building trades. A list from 1722 indicates a number of servants, too (Deyon 1967: 546).

Despite differences in specific trades in each city, the forms of organization were similar. Economic units were small, often overlapping with households. The scale of production was also small, for the quality and quantity of activity in commerce and manufacture were controlled by guild or other forms of regulation and by the availability of only limited amounts of capital. Life was more specialized in urban than in rural society. Food and clothing production, for example, was carried on in separate settings from the households of most urban residents. Rather than make most of what it needed, the urban family bought what it needed in the market or in shops. Shoemakers, for example, made shoes for sale, but they purchased their other clothing and food. Because of this division of labour, urban families were involved in many more consumer activities than their rural counterparts, and cash was regularly used as a means of exchange.

Manufacture and trade, however, were geared primarily to the demand of the local population. Hence the production of food and clothing and the construction of housing were the largest urban manufacturing sectors. Together they employed, according to one estimate, from 55 to 65 per cent of a city's working population (Cipolla 1976: 75).

In Amiens, as in York, guilds regulated the training and activities of skilled craftsmen. The number of workers in a trade was limited and, except in a few cases such as millinery and shawl making, the masters and apprentices were male. Craftsmen often worked at home or in small shops assisted by family members, apprentices and journeymen, and servants. Indeed, the dynamic of the self-employed artisan's household was much like that of the peasant's, for labour supply and consumption needs had to be balanced. An artisan had to produce and sell enough goods so that he could feed his family. Competition from others in the trade was controlled by guilds, which limited the numbers of those who became masters. Yet labour demands were variable within a trade; some work was seasonal, there were periods of great activity, other periods of slump. An artisan's family members often served as extra hands, as unpaid assistants in time of high demand. In addition, if family members alone could not furnish the necessary labour, an artisan hired assistants, who lived in the household as long as their labour was needed. On the other hand, if he could not use the labour of his family members at his trade, a craftsman often sent them off to find work elsewhere. His children joined another household as apprentices or domestic servants.

Although craftsmen produced most goods in workshops in their homes and used their families as labour units, the economy of the city provided many opportunities for work away from home. Men and women earned wages as servants or as street merchants, or as assistants to artisans or construction workers. The wage workers included journeymen who had no chance to advance to mastership, masters who had lost their small capital in bad times and now worked for others, daughters and sons of craftsmen whose shops could not absorb their labour, migrants to the city, unskilled workers, and widows with no capital but with a family to support.

Servants formed a substantial portion of urban populations in the seventeenth and eighteenth centuries. Their precise numbers are often difficult to determine since they were not always listed separately in tax and demographic records. Nonetheless, from those records which clearly identified servants, it has been estimated that perhaps 16 per cent of those between the ages of fifteen and sixty-five in European cities in this period were servants. Hufton suggests that in eighteenth-century French cities, servants could represent as much as 13 per cent of the working population. In Aix in 1695, some 27 per cent of the working population were servants. The term *servant* designated a broad category of employment (Hufton 1974: 4). Any household dependent, whether performing domestic or manufacturing tasks, was a servant. There were servants in the households of the rich and in the households of craftsmen and petty artisans. They were young men or women who joined a family economy as an additional member. Indeed the language used to describe servants denoted their dependent and age status. 'Servant' was synonymous with 'lad' or 'maid'—a young, unmarried, and therefore dependent person.

Wage labourers, on the other hand, lived in households of their own, bound together, like the families of agricultural labourers, by the need to earn money which would pay for their subsistence. Their presence in cities is attested to by the rolls of charitable organizations, which gave them bread when they could not earn enough, and by the complaints of guilds against their activity. Petty artisans, unskilled and casual labourers, carters, and street hawkers were commonly listed. In Paris in 1767, when an Order in Council enjoined the registration of non-guild members selling food, clothing, or lodging to the public, the list included 'retailers and repairers of old clothes and hats, of rags and of old ironware, buckles and hardware . . . sellers of medicines for eyes, corns, and assorted afflictions. . . .' The inventory of lawsuits against non-guild members in York in 1775 included many of these same trades (Allison and Tillot 1961: 216; Kaplow 1972: 45). In the families of wage labourers, all members old enough to seek employment did so.

The work of each person brought little remuneration; the combined earnings of family members were often barely enough for the support of the group. In these families, individuals sold their labour power in order to support the family unit; they were 'in fact if not in principle . . . proletarian[s]' (Landes 1969: 44). Theirs was a 'family wage economy'.

PRODUCTION AND CONSUMPTION

In both England and France, in city and country, people worked in small settings, which often overlapped with households. Productivity was low, the differentiation of tasks was limited. And many workers were needed. The demand for labour extended to women as well as men, to everyone but the youngest children and the infirm. Jobs were differentiated by age and by sex, as well as by training and skill. But among the popular classes, some kind of work was expected of all able-bodied family members. The work of individuals was defined by their family positions. An observer of twentieth-century French peasants described their household economy in terms which also portray peasant and artisan families in the seventeenth and eighteenth centuries: 'The family and the enterprise coincide: the head of the family is at the same time the head of the enterprise. Indeed, he is the one because he is the other . . . he lives his professional and his family life as an indivisible entity. The members of his family are also his fellow workers' (Mendras 1970: 76). But whether or not they actually

worked together, family members worked in the economic interest of the family. In peasant and artisan households, and in proletarian families, the household allocated the labour of family members. In all cases, decisions were made in the interest of the group, not the individual. This is reflected in wills and marriage contracts which spelled out the obligation of siblings or elderly parents who were housed and fed on the family property, now owned by the oldest son. They must work 'to the best of their ability' for 'the prosperity of the family' and 'for the interest of the designated heir' (Bernard 1975: 30). Among property-owning families the land or the shop defined the tasks of family members and whether or not their labour was needed. People who controlled their means of production adjusted household composition to production needs. For the propertyless, the need for wages—the subsistence of the family itself—sent men, women, and children out to work. These people adjusted household composition to consumption needs. The bonds holding the proletarian family together, bonds of expediency and necessity, were often less permanent than the property interest (or the inheritable skill) which united peasants and craftsmen. The composition of propertied and propertyless households also differed. Nevertheless, the line between the propertied and the propertyless was blurred on the question of commitment to work in the family interest.

One of the goals of work was to provide for the needs of family members. Both property-owning and proletarian households were consumption units, though all rural households were far more self-sufficient than urban households. Rural families usually produced their own food, clothing, and tools, while urban families bought them at the market. These differences affect the work roles of family members. Women in urban families, for example, spent more time marketing and less time in home manufacture. And there were fewer domestic chores for children to assist with in the city. In the urban family, work was oriented more to the production of specific goods for sale, or it involved the sale of one's labour. For the peasant family, there were a multiplicity of tasks involved in working the land and running the household. The manner of satisfying consumption needs thus varied and so affected the kinds of work family members did.

When the number of household members exceeded the resources available to feed them, and when those resources could not be obtained, the family often adjusted its size. Non-kin left to work elsewhere when children were old enough to work. Then children migrated. Inheritance systems led non-heirs to move away in search of jobs, limited positions as artisans forced children out of the family craftshop, while the need for wages led the children of the propertyless many miles from home. People migrated from farm to farm, farm to village, village to town, and country to city in this period. Although much migration was local and rural in this period, some migrants moved to cities, and most of these tended to be young and single when they migrated. Indeed, in this period cities grew primarily by migration; for urban death rates were high and deaths often outnumbered births, a result largely of the crowded and unsanitary conditions that prevailed. Migrants came to the city from nearby regions. Deyon examined parish registers, apprenticeship contracts, and civil enfranchisement registers from Amiens and found that most migrants came from Picardy, the province of which Amiens was the capital. Village compatriots tended to live near one another. Young men and boys often migrated to be apprenticed to a craftsman who himself came from their village. Young women and girls followed their brothers to Amiens and became domestic servants (Deyon 1967: 7–10).

Migration increased in times of economic crisis, when food was scarce and when, even with everyone working, families could not feed all their members. The precariousness of life in rural and urban areas in the seventeenth and eighteenth centuries has been documented dramati-

cally in studies such as those by Pierre Goubert and Olwen Hufton. These studies have shown that large numbers of ordinary people barely survived on the fruits of their labour. At the end of a lifetime of work, an artisan or peasant might have nothing more than a few tools or the small piece of land with which he began. Simply feeding one's family in these circumstances was a constant preoccupation. An increase in the price of bread, the basic staple in the diet of the popular classes, could easily make a family's earnings inadequate for its survival. Thus Goubert charts the fortunes of the Cocu family in terms of the price of bread:

> The family earned 108 sols a week, but they ate 70 pounds of bread among them. With bread at one half sol a pound their livelihood was secure. With bread at 1 sol a pound, it began to get difficult. With bread at 2 sols, then at 3.2, 3.3 and 3.4—as it was in 1649, 1652, 1662, 1694, 1710—it was misery (Goubert 1965b: 344; see also Hufton 1974).

Even if the price of bread remained stable, other factors might unbalance a family's budget. Agricultural or trade depressions could severely strain a family's resources. At these times there were bread riots as people collectively sought food for their families. If matters did not improve, individual families might send children off to seek their fortunes away from home, as servants, apprentices, or vagrants. Sometimes the father of the family left home in search of work. He thereby relieved the household of the need to feed him, since he could contribute nothing to its support. He also left the family to an uncertain, but probably poverty-stricken, future.

If the adult members of the family could continue working, then young children were sent away to restore the balance between consumption and work. When families were desperate, parents might expose or abandon a last-born child. Older children, still too young to work productively, were sent off also, to whatever their fate might hold. Fictional characters such as Hansel and Gretel and Hop-O'-My-Thumb, children deliberately lost by parents who could not feed them, had real counterparts. Deyon's study of seventeenth-century Amiens indicates that during food shortages in 1693–4 and 1709–10 the number of abandoned children rose. These were not only infants, but children as old as seven (Deyon 1967: 357). Another recent study of the records of charity in eighteenth-century Aix-en-Provence reveals that children were regularly enrolled at an orphanage because their families could not feed them. Only a third of these were actually orphans. Once a child entered the orphanage, he or she was likely to be joined by a sibling. In other cases, a child would return home and be replaced in the orphanage by a sibling. Families used the orphanage as a temporary measure, enrolling a child and then withdrawing him or her as economic circumstances allowed. Hence one girl entered the Aix orphanage in 1746, 'rejoined her family briefly in 1747, then returned . . . later left again, and . . . reentered . . . in 1755' (Fairchilds 1976: 10).

The location and organization of work differed among the households of rural and urban people and among the propertied and the propertyless. So did the levels of consumption vary and the manners of satisfying family needs. Yet in all cases the family was both a labour unit and a consumption unit, adjusting its size and assigning work to its members to meet its needs in both spheres.

DEMOGRAPHY: MARRIAGE

The demographic patterns of early modern England and France reflected the need to balance people and resources. Death frequently influenced these patterns. Perhaps the most sensitive indicator of the relationship between resources and population was the age at which couples married. The precise age at marriage varied from city to country and from region to region depending on inheritance laws and on specific conditions. Yet among the popular classes the crucial differences were between the propertied and the propertyless.

Marriage was, among other things, an economic arrangement, the establishment of a family economy. It required that couples have some means of supporting themselves and, eventually, their children. For peasant children this meant the availability of land; for artisans, the mastery of a skill and the acquisition of tools and perhaps a workshop. Wives must have a dowry or a means of contributing to the household. Among families with property these resources most often were passed on from generation to generation.

In England, inheritance by the oldest son prevailed. In France this custom of primogeniture was not universal. In some areas of France, particularly in the west, an heir and his wife lived with his parents, in a stem family arrangement. In northern France, on the other hand, a young man had to postpone marriage until a house was vacant. This meant until the death of one or both parents. Land was passed to one child—usually, though not necessarily, the oldest son. He paid his siblings a cash settlement which represented their share of the family land. A brother could use his money to buy some land of his own or to set himself up in a trade. A sister used her money as a dowry. Often the heir had to mortgage the property to pay off his sisters and brothers. Sometimes, too, the money was not available. Then the heir's siblings might remain on the family farm as unmarried labourers in their brother's household, working in exchange for room and board. 'A peasant reckons this way; my farm can feed no more than one, at most two, sons; the others may have to remain unmarried or seek their fortune elsewhere' (Braun 1966: 46; see also Flandrin 1976: 180–1).

Among artisans, trade regulations prevented early marriage. Apprentices and journeymen were not allowed to marry until they had completed their training. In some cases, the duration of apprenticeship was as much a function of the artisans' desire to control workers' access to their trade as it was of the difficulty of the skills taught. Apprentices' and journeymen's associations reinforced the control by expelling from their ranks anyone who married. A young man was ready to marry only when he had an established niche in the system of production.

The need for a dowry meant that young women, too, often had to wait for the death of their parents to receive a settlement. In the weaving centre of Manchester, for example, in the period 1654–7, more than half of the girls marrying for the first time had recently lost their fathers. Other girls, those who worked to accumulate savings for a dowry, had to spend many years gathering a small sum (Armengaud 1975: 145).

The result of these requirements was a relatively late age at marriage in both England and France; women were generally twenty-four or twenty-five years old, men twenty-seven. The late age at marriage of women meant that couples had fewer children than they would have had if the woman had been nineteen or twenty at marriage. If she married at twenty-five, the woman was actively engaged in childbearing for only a portion of her fertile years. (There was little sexual intercourse outside of marriage, and very low rates of illegitimacy. During the eighteenth century in France, the illegitimacy rate increased from 1.2 to 2.7 per cent of all births.) Thus relatively late marriage functioned as a kind of birth control, in the sense that it limited the size of the completed family (Goubert 1965a; Henry 1965).

Among the propertyless, there were no resources to inherit. When a young man and woman were able to earn wages, they could marry. Not only must an individual be able to work, however, but work which paid wages must be available. (Servants, for example, could not marry since a requirement of their jobs was that they live in the household they served, that they remain unmarried, and that they receive much of their payment in room and board, not cash.) One study has shown that in Shepshed, England, during the seventeenth century, the coming of domestic industry provided jobs and cash wages and led to a lowered age of marriage (Levine

1976; see also Braun 1966). In other areas, the growth of commercial agriculture, and the consequent demand for agricultural labourers, may have had the same effect.

Among the poorest, marriage sometimes did not take place at all. The absence of property and the lack of any expectation that it would be acquired, made legalization of sexual relationships unnecessary. From the seventeenth century comes this comment on the urban poor: 'They almost never know the sanctity of marriage and live together in shameful fashion' (Fairchilds 1976: 33). These people, however, were exceptions. In general, those without property did marry. They married younger than their peasant and artisan counterparts, and as a result, their wives bore more children over the course of the marriage. But most expected to be able to live on the fruits of their labour. A couple marrying in Amiens in 1780 acknowledged their poverty, but wrote a contract anyway, agreeing that if they did manage to make some money, the future bride would have 'by preciput 150 livres of the estate and the survivor would have the bed and bedclothes, . . . his or her clothes, arms, rings, and jewels' (Deyon 1967: 254).

Some people never married, of course. In general, permanent celibacy was more common in cities than in the country. There were examples of unmarried brothers or sisters remaining sometimes on farms with a married sibling. More commonly, however, these individuals migrated to a city in search of work. The occupational structure of particular cities often determined the marital fate of many of its migrants. In Lyons, for example, the women who came to work in the silk industry greatly outnumbered the men. As a result, during the eighteenth century, some 40 per cent of adult women were still single at age fifty in that city. (In towns where men outnumbered women, more women were married.) In Amiens, with its mixed occupational structure, 20 per cent of the women over forty in one wealthy parish were single at death. The rate was 13 per cent in two poorer parishes. Domestic servants in the wealthy parish account for the difference. Cities housed most people whose occupations by definition precluded marriage—members of religious orders, soldiers, servants, and prostitutes were typically urban residents (Deyon 1967: 42; Armengaud 1975: 30; see also Knodel and Maynes 1976).

BIRTH AND FERTILITY

Once a couple married, at whatever age, they began to have children. About half of all first babies were born less than a year after their parents' marriage. Studies of French villages indicated that subsequent children were then born about twenty-five to thirty months apart. This interval was apparently the result of two factors, postpartum abstinence from intercourse, and nursing, which postpones the onset of ovulation. Among working-class families in cities, birth intervals were shorter because mothers sent their children to wet nurses rather than nursing them themselves and because infant mortality was high. In both cases, women became fertile sooner than they would have if they had nursed an infant. In Amiens, for example, in a parish of small shopkeepers, artisans, and workers, children were born about two years apart. In Lyons, where work in the silk industry demanded a great deal of a mother's time and where children were regularly sent to wet nurses, birth intervals were even shorter: births occurred there at the rate of one per year (Wrigley 1969: 124; Armengaud 1975: 52; Flandrin 1976: 197).

There is some evidence to indicate that couples sometimes practised deliberate birth control. One study, of the English village of Colyton in Devon in the seventeenth century, seems to show that couples were deliberately limiting the size of their families. Its author, E.A. Wrigley, suggests that a longer than usual interval between the next-to-last and the last birth is an indicator of attempted fertility control. This first attempt of couples to avoid conception failed, of course, but

the longer birth interval is evidence of their effort. Such control as there was was probably achieved by means of *coitus interruptus*, or withdrawal, the most widely known and widely practised technique (Wrigley 1966: 123). Most other studies, however, using the same kinds of data and the same method of family reconstitution, do not point to deliberate family limitation before the late eighteenth century. Yet complete families were not large: four or five children at most, more often only two or three who lived to adulthood. Why?

First, standards of nutrition and health were very low. Analyses of the diet of the popular classes in this period show consistent evidence of malnutrition, a factor which inhibited conception and which promoted miscarriage. Poor nutrition of a mother increased the likelihood that her infant would be stillborn or weak. And it affected the supply of milk she had to nurse it. In addition, poor nutrition made many women infertile before forty or forty-five—the usual age of menopause (Meuvret 1965; Le Roy Ladurie 1969).

Second, mortality rates were very high. If infants did not die at birth because of unsanitary or crude childbirth procedures, they died within the first year of life. Young children, too, died in large numbers. Finally, many marriages were shortened by the death of one of the spouses. Childbirth resulted in a high incidence of maternal death. In one fishing village in France, one-third of all marriages were broken by death within fifteen years. Men's opportunities for remarriage were usually greater than those of women. As a result, women did not engage in intercourse during all of their fertile years and hence did not bear children. Given the odds that death would strike a young child or a spouse, there was little need to employ birth control (Armengaud 1975: 53). Death was the natural regulator of family size in early modern England and France.

DEATH AND MORTALITY

Premature death was a frequent experience of family life in this period. Death rates nearly matched birth rates, producing a very slow growth of population. The crude birth rate was about 35 per thousand; the death rate 30 per thousand. Moreover, until around 1730, there were years with dramatically high death rates, reaching 150, 300, and even 500 per thousand in some localities. These deaths were the result of widespread crop failures and consequent starvation, or of epidemics of diseases like the plague. The last plague epidemic struck in southern France in 1720–2 (Cipolla 1964: 77; Clarkson 1971: 28–9), but new diseases caused killing epidemics well into the twentieth century. Demographers usually place the end of extreme and widespread mortality due to disease and starvation in the early eighteenth century.

Yet even in relatively stable times, death rates were very high by modern standards—a rate of 30 per thousand is more than triple the present-day rate in Western Europe. Studies of French villages show that about one-quarter of all infants born alive died during their first year of life, another quarter died before they reached the age of twenty. Urban death rates were even higher. In Amiens, for example, during the seventeenth century, 60 to 70 per cent of all burials were of persons under twenty-five. Although rates varied from parish to parish and among villages, the overall situation was similar in England and France. Goubert aptly summarized the mortality experience of preindustrial families: 'It took two births to produce one adult' (Goubert 1965a: 468).

The life expectancy at birth for people in this period was thirty years. Of course, that figure included infant and child mortality. If a person lived to age twenty-five, the likelihood was much greater than at birth that she or he would live to fifty or sixty. Yet, although systematic evidence is hard to accumulate, it is clear that adult mortality was also quite high. The figures on orphans and widows are revealing in this connection. Laslett's analysis of the English village of Clayworth found that during the period 1676–88, '32 per cent of all resident children [under 14] had lost one or

both of their parents'. A study of all children in households in nineteen English communities from 1599 to 1811 indicates that some 20 per cent were orphans. For France, Jean Fourastié has drawn a hypothetical portrait of family life, for a man at the end of the seventeenth century. In that situation marriage would be broken by the death of a spouse after an average of twenty years. The average ages of a child orphaned in this way would be fourteen years (Fourastié 1959: 427; Laslett 1974; Armengaud 1975: 74–7).

Many children were left orphans when their mothers died in childbirth. Ignorance of the need for sanitary conditions, the crude attempts of midwives to force a baby from the womb, and the general poor health of pregnant women made for high rates of maternal mortality. Age-specific mortality tables drawn for small seventeenth- and eighteenth-century villages show women dying in larger numbers than men between ages twenty-four and forty—the childbearing years. In Amiens, in the parish of Saint-Rémy in 1674–6, fifty-three women and forty men aged fifteen to forty-five died. In another parish in 1665–8, deaths were recorded for ninety-one women and only fifty-two men in that age range (Deyon 1967: 39).

The death of a parent left not only orphans, but widows or widowers. The existence of these people is attested to by notices of second marriage, particularly of men, and by charity rolls and tax lists, on which widows' names predominated. Fourastié's calculations show that 1,000 men married at age twenty-seven and surviving to age fifty, nearly half would have lost their wives. Many of these men would have remarried and would have also lost a second wife. (The calculations for women would be similar except that fewer widows remarried.) Overall, in eighteenth-century France 'at least 30 per cent of all marriages were second weddings for one of the partners'. Most parishes had many widows in them. In Châteaudun, at least half of the seamstresses and spinners listed on tax rolls in 1696 were widows. In eighteenth-century Bayeux, over 46 per cent of all textile workers in the linen and woollen trades were widows (Fourastié 1959: 425; see also Couturier 1969: 64; Lebrun 1971: 190; Hufton 1974: 116; Baulant 1976: 105). The poor widow, struggling to support her children, was a familiar figure in the towns and villages of the period.

Early modern populations could do little medically to control mortality. Nutrition was poor, little was known about hygiene, and medical science had not developed. In 1778, a French demographer noted that 'it is still a problem whether medicine kills or saves more men' (Armengaud 1975: 70; see also Dupaquier 1976). The result was that every person who survived to adulthood experienced the loss of close relatives: a father, mother, sisters, and brothers. Few children knew their grandparents, few grandparents lived to see the birth of a first grandchild. Orphanhood, widowhood, and the loss of children were common experiences. In calculations about family size, about fertility and household labour supply, the expectation of death played an important part.

These, then, were the economic and demographic characteristics of England and France during the seventeenth and eighteenth centuries. Agriculture was more important than manufacturing, and most people lived in rural areas. In France, small-scale property holding and artisanal manufacture were typical. In England, by 1750, there had been consolidation of agricultural holdings and a consequent increase in the size of farms, on the one hand, and in the proportion of people without property, on the other hand. Work in both countries was relatively undifferentiated and productivity was low. On the demographic side, fertility and mortality were both high, so population growth was very slow. A relatively high age of marriage and a degree of non-marriage served to reduce fertility. From the perspective of the household, most aspects of life were affected by the need to maintain scarce resources and consumers in a delicate balance. Family life and economic organization were inseparably entwined.

Premature death was a familiar experience in each household. Within this context were shaped the position and activities of women.

Single Women in the Family Economy

Most single women belonged to households, either as daughters or servants. Most were young, but whatever their age, single women were regarded as dependants of the household in which they lived and worked. Under the domestic mode of production most work was organized around a household, the basic unit of which was a married couple. Girls either worked at home or for another family. If they were to escape this state of dependency, they had to marry, for single adult women were effectively children. The language of the day equated a girl with a maid, a maid with a servant. Age, marital status, and occupation were inseparably intertwined.

Single women were often effectively servants for their families, if not in the households of strangers. Those employed in other areas, textiles for example, usually lived with a family or with other women like themselves. Even in religious orders, single women joined a family of celibate sisters. Prostitutes usually lived in groups. Economically it was extremely difficult to be single and independent. In the best of jobs female wages were low, one-third to one-half of what men's were (Hauser 1927; Hufton 1975). The only way for a woman to achieve a measure of economic security, as well as adult status, was to marry. If she did not marry, her position was anomalous. If she became a nun, of course, she gained protection and recognition, although her role and autonomy were limited. An unmarried woman outside a convent was vulnerable to material hardship and sexual exploitation.

Although aggregate figures are not available for this period, local studies indicate that in rural areas marriage took place at a relatively late age and nearly all women did marry. In urban areas, rates of celibacy among women could be higher because of differences in sex ratios and as a result of the concentration of specialized occupations for single women (Hollingsworth 1969: 160–8). Most of these occupations, like domestic service or religious orders, involved a familylike dependency.

SINGLE WOMEN'S WORK

All women began their working lives as daughters, serving the family economy of which they were a part. The specific jobs they did were a consequence of their family's place in the productive process, of the nature of the enterprise in which it was engaged.

A daughter began assisting at home as soon as she was able to work. Indeed, at an early age, her role was no different from that of male children, and many accounts make no distinction when describing children's work. Girls and boys were given small tasks to do as early as four or five years of age. In rural areas they cared for farm animals and helped at harvesting and gleaning. In cottages where families engaged in rural industry, young children washed and sorted wool or learned to spin. . . . As they grew older, girls usually assisted their mothers, boys their fathers. In agricultural areas, daughters helped with dairying, cared for poultry, prepared food, and made cloth and clothing. During planting and harvesting they joined family members and hired hands in the fields. . . .

When their mothers took on industrial work, daughters assisted them. In the villages around the silk-weaving centre of Lyons in France, mothers and daughters cultivated silkworms and mulberry leaves. When industry kept the father from farm work, mothers and daughters took care of the farm. Female family members were farmers along the coasts of France, for example, because males were fishermen who were at sea for long periods of time (Garden 1970; Armengaud 1975: 36).

In cities also, daughters worked for their families. The craftsman's household was also his workshop and his family members were among his assistants, whether he wove silk or wool, sewed shoes or coats, made knives, or baked

bread. . . . If the father worked elsewhere, daughters assisted their mothers as market women, laundresses, or seamstresses. When she worked at home a daughter served a kind of apprenticeship to her mother, learning the domestic, agricultural, or technical skills she would need as an adult.

Not all girls remained working at home until marriage, however. The labour needs of her family defined the type of work a daughter might do at home, but also whether or not she would remain there. Family labour was differentiated by age and sex. So, if a family had no need for a daughter's labour, she would be sent to a job somewhere else. Peasants with two or three working children and more than one daughter would send younger daughters away to earn their keep. Weavers, who needed several spinners to supply thread for their looms, jealously guarded their daughters at home, while bakers or shoemakers whose sons, male apprentices, and wives were an ample labour force, regularly sent their daughters away. Families thus adjusted their labour supply by sending off daughters not suited for certain work and taking on male apprentices in their stead.

The ability of a family to feed its children was another influence on where a daughter worked. For subsistence farmers with small holdings, the cost of maintaining a daughter might be greater than the value of her labour. It would be cheaper to hire and feed a few local labourers during the harvest season than to provide for one's own child all year long. Moreover, in time of economic crises, the numbers of 'surplus children', those who could not be supported, would grow, and daughters and sons would be sent off to seek jobs as servants or apprentices.

Death was yet another factor which sent daughters to work away from home. The death of a parent often left the widow or widower less means to support the children. In the French town of Châteaudun during the sixteenth to eighteenth centuries, for example, daughters of winegrowers remained at home until marriage. They participated in all aspects of domestic and household work and were given ample dowries when they married. The death of a father, however, immediately changed the pattern. At that point, the mother took up a trade and sold the family holding or passed it to one of her sons. Daughters who were too young to marry or 'who could not marry immediately became chamber maids in town or farm servants in the country'. The luckiest of these found places at the homes of other winegrowers (Couturier 1969: 181).

The remarriage of a widowed parent could also result in the dislocation of the children of the first marriage, either because the step-parent resented feeding and caring for children who were not his or her own or because conflicts and jealousies became unbearable. Folk tales such as Cinderella and Snow White capture an aspect of these relationships. . . .

Even if both parents were alive, however, the economic resources of the family might be insufficient for the establishment of more than one child with the means to live independently as a married adult. Daughters needed a dowry, and families customarily provided them with it. In rural areas, depending on laws of inheritance, a girl was given either a sum of money or movable property, usually household and farm furnishings. Again depending on local practices, she might receive a full settlement at her marriage or be promised a payment after the death of her parents. In cities, craftsmen gave their daughters household furnishings, cash, skills, or tools. In country and city, the size of the family contribution to a dowry or settlement was very small among the lower classes. Often, the family's contribution had to be supplemented. An artisan's daughter had an advantage over her rural counterpart in this situation, for the skills she had were highly valued. Unlike the heavy manual labour of a farm, trade skills guaranteed a lifetime of relatively high wage-earning possibilities or of assistance to one's husband at his trade. These were acceptable as substitutes for the dowry required of rural girls. But, in either case, if a

dowry was needed for a woman's contribution to a marriage and the family (or some other source) could not provide it, a girl had to earn it herself (Clark [1919] 1968: 194; Hufton 1975: 9).

When for one or a combination of reasons daughters left home to work, they usually entered another household. In the country, domestic service was the typical occupation of a young girl. Of course, in areas of rural textile manufacture, particularly in England, in the early eighteenth century, spinners were in great demand. It took the work of four spinners to supply thread enough for one weaver. One Englishman complained about 'Maid-Servants who choose rather to spin, while they can gain 9s/week by their Labour than go to service at 12d a week to the Farmer's Houses as before' (Clark [1919] 1968: 115–16). Spinsters lived either at home or in the weaver's household. But even in areas where spinning and lacemaking jobs were available, girls sometimes went into service at age twelve or thirteen, after having done textile work as a child. Cities offered other opportunities and urban-born girls took advantage of them. Such girls might be apprenticed to a crafts- or tradeswoman. Others might work for wages in a local enterprise, usually related to textile or garment manufacture. In Caen, France, the lace industry employed girls between ages five and fifteen. They were first apprenticed for two months and their parents paid both for their training and for a place at the workbench. When the lessons were completed, the girls began to earn a daily wage. But in cities, as in the country, the main occupation for young girls was domestic service. In Ealing in 1599, for example, almost 'three quarters of the female children [between ages fifteen and nineteen] seem to have been living away from their parents', most often as servants (Macfarlane 1970: 209; Perrot 1975: 425).

In a period when most productive activity was organized within or around a household, service was the major occupation for young single women. Service involved a variety of chores, not only the ones the twentieth century associates with domestic work. A servant was a household dependant who worked in return for board and wages. The low cost of her labour, the availability of young, single women to work, the need in producing households for an extra hand, made the employment of a servant a fairly common practice. Service was the customary means by which households exchanged labour supply and balanced their own labour and consumption needs.

In upper-class families a girl 'in service' was a maid of one kind or another, a laundress, charwoman, serving maid, or nursemaid. In household productive units she was an extra hand, available to do whatever work was required. She might be a dairymaid or harvester on a farm; in textile towns she was 'a resident industrial employee'. In Lyons, for example, a *servante* did domestic chores and helped prepare the silk to be woven. As with a daughter, the nature of the family enterprise defined her work, except that a servant girl usually did the dirtiest and most onerous of the chores that needed to be done (Le Roy Ladurie 1969: 477; Hufton 1975: 3). In return for her work she was fed, housed, and clothed and paid a wage at the end of her term, which usually lasted a year. This meant that a servant had little or no money to spend on herself during the year and was entirely dependent on her employers. The year term also meant frequent moves for a girl from one household to another. Moves might be even more frequent for some girls. Employers might fire them at any point, refusing to pay anything for their services. The failure of a small business inevitably sent the servant girl packing, with no payment of her wages, no matter how long she had worked.

When daughters left home to work they did not always sever family ties. Their parents often helped them find jobs, and provided homes for them between terms of service. One study suggests that female farm servants in England returned to their families far more frequently than did males (Kussmaul-Cooper 1975a: 6). Moreover, kin networks were a common means used by those seeking jobs. In the country, peasants and agricultural labourers sought work for their daughters at neighbouring farms or in a nearby village or large town. On market days and at fairs, local women learned from other women of available positions for their daughters. In some areas, there were more formalized ways of securing jobs as servants. Young girls would come on their own to annual hiring fairs in search of employment. Sometimes, if a brother or father journeyed to another area, as Savoyard men did to Lyons or as men from Rouergue did to the Herault vineyards, a sister or daughter might accompany him. In some areas of eighteenth-century France, Hufton suggests, male family members seem to have set the patterns of female migrations (Hufton 1975: 5). In cities, artisans or their wives used trade, neighbourhood, and kin connections to secure apprenticeships for their daughters. Unskilled labourers introduced their children to whatever jobs they did in the urban labour market.

A girl's ability to maintain contact with their family depended on how far she had journeyed from home. Some girls did travel alone from their country villages to large textile centres or regional and state capitals, becoming permanent urban residents. Rural-born girls migrated cityward, while urban girls tended to remain closest to home, working and marrying in the city of their birth. In general, however, the continuing demand for cheap female labour in towns and on farms made it possible for most girls to remain within a short distance of home, sustained by occasional visits, by parcels of food, and by the expectation of returning there to marry.

The death of a girl's parents, of course, modified this pattern. Orphans were on their own, lacking family connections to help them find work or to sponsor their migrations. Without resources, with no one to turn to for help, orphans had to settle for whatever work they could find, throwing themselves on the mercy of an employer, a charitable organization, or the state. They were more vulnerable, more open to exploitation, more likely to end up in trouble as criminals, prostitutes, and mothers of illegitimate children. A sixteenth-century English magistrate described the 'dells' of his day as delinquent girls on the road 'through the death of their parents and nobody to look after them. . .' (Pinchbeck and Hewitt 1969: 99). In a society where family membership was important for economic and social survival (as well as for social identity), the lack of a family had only negative effects.

The work of a young single woman was circumscribed by a limited range of occupational opportunities. The type and location of her work was defined by her family's needs. A daughter worked, as everyone did in lower-class families in this period, to help support the unit of which she was a part. In addition, her work prepared her for marriage, by giving her training and skills and sometimes also by enabling her to accumulate the capital she needed for a dowry.

COURTSHIP AND MARRIAGE

A girl was ready for marriage when she had accumulated some capital or received it from her family, when she was ready to help establish a productive unit, a household. The amount was not necessarily very large. In France, some cash, a bed, sheets, and some pots were frequently all a girl brought to her new household. . . . Often a girl's small earnings supplemented the family contribution.

Unless she migrated far away, or unless she was an orphan, a girl's marriage usually involved her family in a variety of ways. First, her family's economic situation limited her choice of a husband to someone of roughly comparable means. The size of the dowry the family promised or provided was a reflection of its property holdings or trade prosperity. An artisan's craft position was itself an important consideration, for access to a tightly controlled craft might be gained for a son-in-law. Among property-owning peasants, parents often vetoed suitors whose family holdings did not measure up to their own. Marriage was a chance to extend or renew family capital. Less

directly parental and community expectations imbued children with the idea that they would repeat their parents' experience. They usually did not expect to rise in the world, only to remain at their parents' level. Hence they sought partners among their social and economic peers.

Second, the parental community of residence and work was most often the one within which a girl found a husband. In rural areas, young women met young men in the village, at local social gatherings, or in the household of an employer. In France, the *veillée* offered young people a means of meeting one another, under the watchful eye of parents and neighbours and in activities which were usually segregated by sex. The *veillée* was the rural custom of gathering in the largest, warmest barn on cold winter evenings. The animals and the groups of people created warmth, and the company an occasion for socializing. 'People sat on benches, chatting, laughing, complaining about taxes and tax collectors, gossiping about young men and women . . .' (Flandrin 1976: 106).

In the city, a girl might marry an apprentice or journeyman in her father's shop, or the son of another craftsman. Networks of labour and trade were important sources of marriage partners. In Amiens, such 'corporative endogamy' was the rule. Young men in the same trades married one another's sisters with great frequency; apprentices married their master's daughters or widows (Deyon 1967: 340). But apprentices or journeymen might also choose a servant girl in the household. The small capital she had saved from her service brought to the couple the possibility of buying a loom and setting up a shop of their own (Hufton 1975: 7–9). Since social, occupational, and family life were so closely intertwined, one's associate at work often became a marriage partner.

Among the propertyless, of course, marriage crossed occupational lines, but geographic endogamy was the norm. Artisans and peasants as well as the unskilled and propertyless tended to marry others from the same parish or a neighbouring one. One study of early-eighteenth-century Bayeux found that 63 per cent of all women married in Bayeux came from there, or from one of fourteen neighbouring parishes (Couturier 1969: 132, 137; El Kordi 1970: 125; Gouesse 1972: 1145; Armengaud 1975: 36). A community might also extend beyond the parish. Trade routes and paths of migration for labourers extend the boundaries of the effective social community. Local market systems probably were the largest social unit within which marriage partners were chosen.

Social and geographic endogamy had important implications for marriage and for premarital sexual behaviour. It meant that family and communal ties, as well as the relationship between the two individuals, bound a couple together and governed their behaviour. In many areas, engaged couples began sleeping or living together before marriage. Local custom varied, of course. In areas of France and England, studies have documented the practice. In addition, the fact that rates of prenuptial conception tended to be higher in cities than in rural areas suggests that such cohabitation was more common in cities. Premarital sexual activity was tolerated because marriage was expected to and usually did take place. Hence, although some brides were pregnant at the altar, bastards were relatively few. Using marriage and birth registers from seventy-seven parishes in rural England, from 1540 to 1835, P.E.H. Hair found that between one-third and one-sixth of all brides were pregnant at their weddings (Hair 1966; Hollingsworth 1969: 194). Indeed, pregnancy often seems to have precipitated a couple's marriage. In small village communities, or among groups of urban craftsmen, families could put a great deal of pressure on a young man who had begun to regret his choice of a mate and was hesitating about marriage. Such social pressure tended to ensure that marriage usually followed engagement, especially if pregnancy intervened.

The women who bore illegitimate children were often those with no ties to their families of origin. Several English studies have indicated that most illegitimate births came from the poorest and most vulnerable women in the community. One study suggests the existence of a subgroup of 'bastard bearers' (Laslett and Oosterveen 1973: 284). These were people whose sexual behaviour was not that different from their more prosperous counterparts. The difference was that 'the relatively more secure position [of the better-off] meant that their behaviour was more certain of ultimate legitimation' (Levine and Wrightson 1980). In other words, prosperous parents were in a better position to enforce the promise of marriage which had compromised their daughters. On the other hand, girls with no parents or those who were a long distance from home were most vulnerable. Servant girls in cities were often open to exploitation by their employers or by young men they met. Indeed, rates of illegitimacy and of child-abandonment were highest among domestic servants. These women could not appeal to parental, religious, or community authority to help them make a seducer keep his promise.

Young women were protected not only by their parents but by community institutions as well. In many rural areas, the rituals of courtship and marriage involved vigilant groups of young people who regulated the morals and sexual activity of the village. Adolescent boys particularly policed the behaviour of courting couples, sometimes even influencing a man's choice of a mate. A wide discrepancy in the ages of the couple, for example, or promiscuity or adultery, could attract the ridicule of local youths. They would engage in elaborate rituals, following the couple, mocking them, singing profane songs under the woman's window. A bad-smelling bush planted before a girl's door indicated her low moral standing. A group of young men might fight or fine strangers courting local girls (Davis 1971; Gillis 1974: 20). Unwed mothers as well as married men who seduced single girls would be 'charivaried' or, in England, hear the sound of 'rough music' at their door. . . . In the village community these proceedings had the effect of legal sanctions. The charivari set and enforced standards of acceptable sexual conduct. Natalie Davis has pointed out that they also regulate the activities of the youths themselves, preventing too-early marriage and premarital promiscuity.

Organizations of craftsmen, too, watched over the activities of journeymen and apprentices. The rules of journeymen's organizations included the requirement that members not marry until they had completed their training and were in a position to help support a family. Guilds also had rules which prohibited young men from seducing girls and which enforced their regulations with fines and expulsion (Cadet 1870: citing S. Daubie, 118). Of course, those outside the guild structure were not subject to such rules. In general, the movement of people into, out of, and within cities made the regulation of sexual and social behaviour more difficult, especially among the unskilled. Hence rates of illegitimacy were higher in cities, and concubinage was a more common practice.

A woman's courtship and her marriage involved her family in a number of important ways. A young man usually asked a young woman's family for her hand. Then the families of the engaged couple assembled to draw up a contract which specified the economic terms of the marriage. The wedding was celebrated by family and community members. In the country, whole villages turned out to eat, drink, and dance in celebration of the consecration of a union; in cities all the craftsmen of a particular trade (many of whom were also related) attended the festivities. Among the propertyless and the unskilled the wedding might be less elaborate, but dancing was free and people could clap and sing if there was no money to hire music. These rituals and festivities marked the couple's entry into adulthood, the creation of a new family, the beginning of an independent existence. Among property holders marriage might ally two families and joint property holdings. In the lower ranks of society marriage was simply the establishment of a new family economy, the

unit of reproduction and of work without which 'one cannot live' (Armengaud 1975: 144; Stone 1975: 48–9).

The characteristics of marriage among the popular classes clearly were different from those in the upper classes. Among wealthy families there was strict parental control over marriage. Parents sought to preserve their status and wealth by allying their children with a limited group of similarly wealthy families. Children's marriages extended networks of power and influence. The lineage must be protected, the patrimony enlarged and transmitted from one generation to the next. In these cases property was the basis for status and political power, hence family control over children's marriages was vital for the preservation of the élite position of aristocrats or local notables. There was, for example, a close association between the transmission of wealth and political power in Vraiville, a French village studied by Martine Segalen. There all the mayors for ten generations were descendants of, or married to, one of the thirteen most eminent families (Segalen 1972: 104). The families carefully chose spouses for their children from among a very small group of large property holders.

Among the popular classes parental consent and family contracts did not mean the same thing. Within the social and economic limits already described, individual choice of a spouse was permitted. Parental consent functioned as a verification of the couple's resources. Parents wanted to be sure a child would find his or her new family situation roughly equal to that of the family or origin. Moreover, the contract involved not the acquisition of resources for the patrimony, but the surrendering of resources by families to the new family. Families, rather than the individuals to be married, drew up the contracts because they were the units of social identification and of membership for all individuals. The children were leaving one family to establish another and they were transferring their resources, their means of support, from one household to another. Relatively few persons, men or women, went through an intermediate stage of independence—economic or social—as they passed from their family of origin to their family of procreation. Individuality in the modern sense was socially and legally limited.

The age of marriage was constrained by the fact that family and social resources were limited. Like their husbands, wives were expected to bring a contribution to the marriage, in the form of capital, household furnishings, or marketable skills. Marriage itself signified the beginning of a new enterprise, of an economic partnership of husband and wife. It was 'the founding of a family' (Armengaud 1975: 144). And it was the emergence of this new family, the re-creation of a social and economic unit, the beginning of a new enterprise that families and communities celebrated at a wedding.

During the time she was single a young woman usually worked in a household. Family labour and consumption needs determined whether or not she worked at home. But wherever she worked, she was dependent on the household in which she lived. Her work was both a means of contributing to her family's economy and a means of supporting herself. It also prepared her for marriage by helping accumulate the resources she would need to establish a family of her own.

Married Women in the Family Economy

The married couple was the 'simple community of work, the elementary unit', in the preindustrial household (Gouesse 1972: 1146–7). The contribution of each spouse was vital for the creation and survival of the family. From its outset, marriage was an economic partnership. Each partner brought to the union either material resources, or the ability to help support each other. Peasant sons brought land, craftsmen brought their tools and skill. Daughters brought a dowry and sometimes a marketable skill as well. The dowry of a peasant or artisan daughter was usually a contribution to the establishment of the couple's house-

hold. These might include 'a bit of cash, furniture, linen, tools. Sometimes a loom, one or two skeins of wool, several pounds of wool and silk, a boat, a thousand eels for a fish merchant, sometimes a house or part of a house in the city, a meadow and some plots of land in the country' (Deyon 1967: 341).

Among the propertyless there was only the promise of work and wages. In Amiens in 1687, François Pariès, a mason, and Marie Hugues declared in their contract that they had no material possessions and that 'they are mutually satisfied with their well-being and with one another' (Deyon 1967: 254). The point was that the wife as well as the husband made an economic contribution (or a promise of one) which helped set up the new household. In addition, however, it represented a commitment to help support the new family. The resources brought to the marriage were only a beginning. The continuing labour of each partner was required to maintain the couple and, later, its children. In the course of a lifetime, the work of husband and wife was the major source of the family's support. Families were productive and reproductive units, centres of economic activity and creators of new life. Married women contributed to all aspects of family life and thus fulfilled several roles within their households. They engaged in production for exchange and production for household consumption, both of which contributed to the family's economic well-being. And they performed the reproductive role of bearing and raising children.

Married Women's Work

A married woman's work depended on the family's economic position, on whether it was involved in agriculture or manufacturing, whether it owned property or was propertyless. But whether labour or cash were needed, married women were expected to contribute it. The fact that a woman bore children influenced the kind of work she did, but it did not confine her to a single set of tasks, nor exclude her from participation in productive activity. The organization of production in this period demanded that women be contributing members of the family economy. It also permitted women to control the time and pace of their work, and to integrate their various domestic activities.

Within the preindustrial household, whether on the farm or in the craftshop, among property holders and wage earners, there was a division of labour by age and by sex. The levels of skill expected of children advanced with age, with young children performing the simplest and crudest chores. Certain kinds of heavy work were reserved for men, but women also did many heavy tasks which today are considered too arduous for females. Hauling and carrying were often women's tasks. Rural and urban wives sometimes had occupations of their own, or they shared their husbands' occupations performing specified tasks within the productive process. Indeed, the jobs women did reflected the fact that they performed several functions for the family. The normative family division of labour tended to give men jobs away from the household or jobs which required long and uninterrupted commitments of time or extensive travel, while women's work was performed more often at home and permitted flexible time arrangements.

Rural Women

On farms, men worked in the fields, while women ran the household, made the family's clothes, raised and cared for cows, pigs, and poultry, tended a garden, and marketed surplus milk, vegetables, chickens, and eggs. A French peasant saying went: 'No wife, no cow, hence no milk, no cheese, neither hens, nor chicks, nor eggs . . .' (Armengaud 1975: 75). The sale of these items often brought in the only cash a family received. Women's participation in local markets reflected their several family roles. They earned money as an out-growth of activities concerned with family subsistence; and they might use the money to purchase food and supplies for their families. Their domestic and market activities overlapped,

and both served important economic functions for the family. Moderately prosperous farm families owed their success to a variety of resources, not the least of which was the wife's activity.

*   *   *

Wives of propertyless labourers also contributed to the family economy. They themselves became hired hands, 'working in the fields and doing all kinds of hard jobs'. Others became domestic textile workers. Still others alternated these activities. When Vauban, justifying his fiscal recommendations under Louis XIV, described the family of an agricultural labourer, he emphasized the importance of the wife's ability to earn money: 'by the work of her distaff, by sewing, knitting some stockings, or by a bit of lace-making, according to the region' (Morineau 1972: 236; see also Flandrin 1976: 113). Without this and her cultivation of a garden and some animals, 'it would be difficult to subsist'. Home work most commonly involved spinning or sewing. Lacemaking, straw plaiting, glovemaking, knitting, and needlework were the major areas of domestic manufacture. Pinchbeck estimates that lacemaking alone employed as many as 100,000 women and children in seventeenth-century England. About a million women and children worked in the clothing trades as a whole in England in that period (Pinchbeck [1930] 1969: 203; Clark [1919] 1968: 97). And in France, as rural industry took hold in some areas, the numbers of women employed in spinning rose. Women earned low wages spinning, perhaps five sous a day in Picardy at the end of the seventeenth century (Guilbert 1966: 30–1). Male weavers earned double that amount. Yet the individual wage a married woman could earn was less important than was her contribution to a joint effort. Spinning and weaving together were the complementary bases of the family economy.

When no home work was available, a wife marketed her household activities, shopping for others at the market, hawking some wares: extra pieces of linen she had woven or lengths of thread she had spun and not used. Rural women also became wet nurses, nursing and raising the children of middle-class women and of urban artisans who could afford to pay them. In the countryside around Paris and around the silk-weaving centre of Lyons, for example, wet nursing was a common way for a rural woman to earn some additional money while caring for her own child. In areas around big cities in France particularly, this might be an organized enterprise. In Paris, for example, men or women (called *meneurs* or *messagères*) located rural nurses, recruited urban babies, then transported the infants in carts to the country, where they often remained until they were three or four years old, if they survived infancy. One late-eighteenth-century estimate places at about 10,000 the number of Parisian infants sent out to nurse. Maurice Garden suggests that close to a third of all babies born in Lyons (some 2,000 of 5,000 to 6,000) were carted off to the countryside. Until the late eighteenth century these included the children of the upper classes as well as of artisan and shopkeeping families (Garden 1970: 324). Most often, however, the more prosperous families hired wet nurses who lived in the household. The wet-nurse 'business' was most developed, it appears, in large preindustrial urban centres where married women played an active role in artisan and commercial enterprise. There was little supervision of the nurses in this period. The job could be fairly lucrative and demand was high, so some women 'nursed' babies long after their own children had grown and their milk dried up.

Married women, then, would often alternate different kinds of work, putting together a series of jobs in order to increase their earnings or to earn enough to help their families survive. Indeed the absence of employment for the wives of wage earners was often given as the reason for a family's destitution.

Although women tended to work at or near home, they did not do so exclusively. On farms,

the rhythm of the seasons with their periods of intensive labour brought women into the fields to sow and harvest, as well as to glean. . . . In areas where small property holders worked as agricultural labourers or as tradesmen, women tended the family plot and men worked away from home 'except for about a week in hay harvest, and for a few days at other times, when the gathering of manure or some work which the women cannot perform' required the men's assistance (Pinchbeck [1930] 1969: 20). In the vineyards of the Marne 'the wife [was] really the working partner of her husband: she share[d] all of his burdens', cultivating the grapes (Flandrin 1976: 113).

On the other hand, there was household work which included the entire family. In villages in France, for example, the kneading and preparation of bread (which was baked in a communal oven) 'mobilized the energies of everyone in the house every other week in the summer and once a month in winter' (Bernard 1975: 30). And the winter slaughter of a pig took all family members and sometimes some additional help. When the farm or the household needed labour, it incorporated all hands, regardless of sex, in periods of intense activity. At other times, though work roles were different, they were complementary. The family economy depended upon the labour of both husband and wife.

Urban Women

Wives of skilled craftsmen who worked at home usually assisted their husbands, sharing the same room, if not the same bench or table. The wife sometimes prepared or finished materials on which the husband worked. Thus wives spun for their weaver husbands, polished metal for cutlers, sewed buttonholes for tailors, and waxed shoes for shoemakers. Sometimes a wife's work was identical to her husband's. . . . If the wife was not her husband's constant companion at the loom, however, or if spinning was her customary job, she still must be able to take his place when he had other tasks, when he was ill, or when he died. . . . The fact that all family members worked together and benefited jointly from the enterprise meant that some jobs were learned by both sexes and could be interchangeable. It meant, too, . . . that the family's joint economic activity was the first priority for everyone.

If the products made at home were sold there, then a craftsman's wife was usually also a shop-keeper. She handled transactions, kept accounts, and helped supervise the workers in the shop. Many of these women hired servants to free them from 'the routine of domestic drudgery'. When work pressed, as it did in the Lyonnais silk trade (where the typical female occupation was silk spinning or assistance with weaving), mothers sent their infants off to nurses rather than break the rhythm of work in the shop (Clark [1919] 1968: 156; see also Hufton 1975: 12).

Yet, if a wife was her husband's indispensable partner in many a trade, and even if her skill equalled his, she remained his assistant while he lived. Married women were granted full membership in certain guilds only after their husbands had died and then so long as they did not remarry. Occupational designations in all but the food and clothing trades usually were male. Women were referred to as the wives of the craftsmen, even when they were widows and practising in the trade on their own. Hence, Mrs Baskerville, a widow of a printer and letter founder, 'begs leave to inform the Public, . . . that she continues the business of letter founding, in all its parts, with the same care and accuracy that was formerly observed by Mr Baskerville' (Pinchbeck [1930] 1969: 284–5). The practice reflected a family division of labour which undoubtedly took into account a woman's domestic tasks: her other activities might claim her time while the husband could be a full-time craftsman. In addition, in the most skilled trades, an investment in long years of training might be unwise for a woman in the light of the lost time, the illnesses, and the higher mortality of women usually associated with childbirth (Deyon 1967: 39). The exclusion of women also

represented a means of controlling the size of a craft. Only when labour was scarce were women permitted to practise certain trades. The press of numbers, however, led to their exclusion from goldsmithing, for example, in England by 1700. (Women were employed, however, as unskilled assistants—often called servants—in large shops. But these were usually young, single women.) By and large, in the home-based skilled trades, married women were part of the family labour force.

Some women did have crafts or trades of their own in the cities of England and France in 1700. Most of these were associated with the production and distribution of food and clothing. The all-female *corporations* in seventeenth-century France include seamstresses, dressmakers, combers of hemp and flax, embroiderers, and hosiers. In addition, there were fan and wig makers, milliners, and cloak makers (Guilbert 1966: 21–2). Lists from English cities are similar.

In many of these trades women regularly took on apprentices. In millinery, for example, an apprenticeship lasted from five to seven years and required a substantial fee. The women ran their enterprises independently of their husbands, whose work often took them away from home. . . .

Women were represented, too, in the retail trades, assisting their husbands and running their own businesses as well. In England, brewing once was a female monopoly. It was so no longer by the eighteenth century, but women still practised the trade. Women were also bakers, grocers, innkeepers, and butchers. At least one woman butcher in eighteenth-century London 'lived by killing beasts in which . . . she was very expert' (Pinchbeck [1930] 1969: 295).

By far the most numerous group of married women working independently were the wives of unskilled labourers and journeymen. They were women in precarious economic situations, since their husbands never earned enough money to cover the household needs. These women had no skills, nor did they have capital for goods or a shop. No family productive enterprise claimed their time. So they became petty traders, and itinerant peddlers selling such things as bits of cloth or 'perishable articles of food from door to door' accompanied by their children (Clark [1919] 1968: 150, 290; Hufton 1974). The street was their shop; their homes were their workplaces; and their work required no investment in tools or equipment. On the list of non-guild members in Paris cited on page 62 there were 1,263 women and only 486 men. The women were lodging-house keepers and retailers or 'repairers of old clothes and hats, of rags and old ironware, buckles and hardware' (Kaplow 1972: 45). When they did not sell items they had scavenged or repaired, they sold their labour, carting goods, water, or sewage, doing laundry, and performing a host of other unskilled services which were always in demand in the city and usually outside the control of the guilds. Their work was an aspect of 'the economy of makeshift' which characterized their entire lives. As such, the time spent earning wages was sporadic and discontinuous. . . .

The time required of women differed greatly in different situations. During harvesting and planting, wives worked day and night in the fields. Wives of urban butchers and bakers spent many hours in the family shop. Lyons' silk spinners paid others to nurse their babies. Women doing casual labour had to spend long hours earning a few pence or sous. Yet the work of most married women permitted a certain flexibility, some control over the time and pace of work. Some studies estimated that in the course of a year, a woman probably spent fewer days at cash-earning activities than did her husband. While a man worked about 250 days a year, a woman worked about 125 to 180 days. The studies, based on contemporaries' analyses of family budgets of French weavers in 1700 and agricultural labourers in 1750, assumed that a married woman worked less 'because of the supplementary demands of her sex: housekeeping, childbirth, etc' (Morineau 1972: 210, 221). In the

fields, women could stop work to nurse a baby or feed a young child. In craft and retail shops, they could allocate some time for domestic responsibilities. In addition, they could include young children in certain aspects of their work, teaching them to wind thread or clean wool. Those who walked the street, selling their wares, were invariably accompanied by their children. Yet rather than 'working less', as contemporaries described it, it seems more accurate to say that demands on women's time were more complex. In this period, the type of work women did meant that even if home and workplace were not the same, a woman could balance her productive and domestic activities.

WIDOWS

We have described so far a 'normal' situation, in which both husband and wife were alive. Yet mortality statistics indicate that quite frequently death changed this picture. The death of a husband disrupted the family division of labour and left the wife solely responsible for maintaining the family. Sometimes, of course, there were children to assist her, to run the farm, or earn some wages. But often they were too young or too inexperienced to contribute much.

In the best of circumstances, a widow gained the right to practise her husband's craft. She became legal representative of the family, and her mastery and autonomy were publicly recognized. . . .

Widowhood, however, was usually a difficult situation. Deprived of a husband's assistance, many women could not continue a family enterprise and instead sought new kinds of work. In the French town of Châteaudun, for example, wives of vineyard owners, who had managed the household side of the family enterprise while their husbands lived, took in sewing and spinning when they died. The wife could not do the heavy work of harvesting the grapes herself. And she could rarely afford to pay hired help. The few opportunities for her to earn money—usually as

a seamstress—were poorly paid and were insufficient to keep up the activities of the vineyard
(Baulant 1976: 106). In cities, women who did
the most onerous jobs were often widows whose
need led them to take any work they could find.
Many of these women were unable to support
themselves despite their work, for wages were so
low. The jobs available to these women—as
seamstresses, or unskilled workers—were noto-
riously poorly paid. Hence it was impossible for
women and their families to live on earnings
alone. So they often sent their children off to
charitable institutions, or to fend for themselves.
Widows and orphans made up the bulk of names
on charity lists in the seventeenth and eighteenth
centuries. . . .

Remarriage was clearly the happiest solution
for a widow, since an economic partnership was
the best means of survival. Widows and widowers did remarry if they could. One study of the
Parisian region found that in the sixteenth, seventeenth, and eighteenth centuries men remarried
within a few months or even weeks of their wives'
deaths (Baulant 1976: 104). Among the lower
classes, the rates of remarriage were much higher
than among the upper classes, who were protected from penury by the money or property
specifically designated for widowhood in marriage contracts. Prosperous widows were sometimes prevented from remarrying by children
who did not want their inheritance threatened. If
she could find a husband, a second marriage for
a widow of the popular classes meant a restora-
tion of the household division of labour. If she
had a craftshop or some land, a widow might
attract a younger man eager to become a master
craftsman or a farmer. (As the husband of a master's widow a man was legally entitled to take over
the mastership.) But if she had no claim to property or if she had to relinquish those claims
because of the difficulty of maintaining the enterprise alone, she would marry a man whose economic situation was considerably worse than her
first husband's. In these instances, farm wives, for

example, would become agricultural field labourers or, perhaps, spinners (Couturier 1969: 139).

In most cases, however, widows failed to find
new spouses and they had to manage on their
own. Widowers more often chose younger, single
women as their second wives. A widow's
advanced age or the fact that she had children
lessened her chances of finding a husband.
(Sometimes the price of remarriage was the abandonment of her children, since a prospective husband might be unwilling or unable to contribute
to their support. But even this alternative might
be preferable to the precarious existence of a
widow on her own who might have to abandon
her children anyway.) The charity rolls and hospital records of the seventeenth and eighteenth
centuries starkly illustrate the plight of a widow
with young children or of an elderly widow, desperately struggling and usually failing to earn her
own bread. 'Small wonder,' comments Hufton
(1974: 117), 'the widow and her brood were
common beggars. What other resource had they?'

Although there were fewer of them (they
either remarried or simply abandoned their children), widowers too were on the charity lists. Like
the widows, these men had great difficulty supporting themselves and their dependent children.
Such men and women were eloquent testimony to
the fact that the line between survival and starvation, between poverty and destitution, was an
extremely thin one. They clearly demonstrate as
well that two partners were vital to family survival.
The family division of labour reflected an economy based on the contributions of husband and
wife. The loss of one partner usually meant the
destruction of the family economy. Although the
jobs they performed may have differed, the work
of husband and wife were equally necessary to the
household. It was this partnership of labour that
struck one observer in eighteenth-century France:

> In the lowest ranks [of society], in the coun-
> try and in the cities, men and women
> together cultivate the earth, raise animals,

manufacture cloth and clothing. Together they use their strength and their talents to nourish and serve children, old people, the infirm, the lazy and the weak. . . . No distinction is made between them about who is the boss; both are. . . (Hufton 1974: 38).

It is not entirely clear that a partnership of labour meant there existed a 'rough equality' between husband and wife in all areas of family life (this is the position of Power 1975: 34). It is clear, however, that the survival of the family depended on the work of both partners. . . . Tasks performed were complementary. The differentiation of work roles was based in part on the fact that women also had to bear children and manage the household, activities which were necessary, too, to the family economy. The family economy reproduced itself as the basic economic unit of production. Children were important as well for the sustenance of aged and dependent parents.

MARRIED WOMEN'S DOMESTIC ACTIVITY

The wife's major domestic responsibility was the provision of food for the family. The work of all family members contributed directly or indirectly to subsistence, but wives had a particular responsibility for procuring and preparing food. In the peasant family, 'the duties of the mother of the family were overwhelming; they were summed up in one work: food' (Le Roy Ladurie 1969: 481). In the unskilled labourer's home, too, the wife raised chickens, a cow, a pig, or a goat. Her garden supplemented the miserable wages she earned sewing and those her husband made in the fields. Urban wives frequented markets, where they haggled and bargained over the prices of food and other goods. Some also kept small gardens and few animals at home. Whether she grew food or purchased it—whether, in other words, she was a producer or consumer—the wife's role in providing food served her family. A wife's ability to garden and tend animals, or to bargain and to judge the quality of items for sale,

could mean the difference between eating decently and not eating at all. In more desperate circumstances, women earned the family's food by begging for it or by organizing their children to appeal for charity. They supervised the 'economy of makeshift', improvising ways of earning money or finding food, and going without food in order to feed their children. One curé in Tours compared such women to 'the pious pelican of the *Adoro Te*, who gave her blood to feed her young'. Hufton's careful study of the poor in eighteenth-century France has led her to conclude that 'the importance of the mother within the family economy was immense; her death or incapacity could cause a family to cross the narrow but extremely meaningful barrier between poverty and destitution' (Hufton 1971: 92).

Food was the most important item in the budgets of most families. Few families had any surplus funds to save or to spend on anything other than basic necessities. A French artisan's family, for example, whose members earned 43 sols a day, spent in 1701 approximately 36 sols on food: bread, herring, cheese, and cider. Poorer families ate less varied fare. Rural and urban wage earners in eighteenth-century France could spend more than half of their income on bread alone (Lefebvre 1962: 218; Morineau 1972: 210; Hufton 1974: 46–8).

The fact that she managed the provision of food gave the wife a certain power within the family. She decided how to spend money, how to allocate most of the family's few resources. She was the acknowledged manager of much of the monetary exchange of the family and her authority in this sphere was unquestioned. Legally, women were subordinate to their husbands. And some were clearly subject to physical mistreatment as well. Recent studies of criminality, violence, and divorce among the lower classes during the seventeenth and eighteenth centuries indicate that wife beating occurred and that women were at a disadvantage in seeking redress in court.

The law tolerated male adultery and punished it in females; and it also tolerated violence by men against their wives (Abbiateci et al. 1971; Castan 1974; Phillips 1976). The studies, of course, focus on examples of family breakdown and disharmony which reached the criminal courts. They do not, therefore, adequately describe the day-to-day dealings of husband and wife, nor do they detail *distribution* of power within the household. Yet it is precisely the distribution that is important. Men had the physical and legal power, but women managed the poor family's financial resources. Within the households of the popular classes there seem to have been not just one, but several sources of power. Men did not monopolize all of them. Wives' power in the household stemmed from the fact that they managed household expenditures for food. Among families which spent most of their money on food this meant that the wife decided how to spend most of the family's money.

WOMEN IN POPULAR POLITICS

The wife's role in providing food could lead to her involvement in public, political actions. Household concerns and economic issues overlapped in this period; the family was a public as well as a private institution. The politics of the disenfranchised popular classes was a politics of protest. Groups of people gathered to complain about what they considered unjust prices or taxes. And, lacking any other means of influencing the élites who governed them, they often took matters into their own hands, refusing to pay high prices or taxes, and burning tolls and fiscal records. Women and men engaged in these disturbances, the most typical of which was the bread or grain riot.

The bread riot was usually a protest against the adulteration of flour by millers, the hoarding of wheat and bread, or what the crowd considered unjust prices. These demonstrations were often led by women, and women formed a large proportion of their participants. George Rudé and E.P. Thompson have analyzed bread-and-grain riots at length. They have shown that the demonstrations were a means used by the popular classes to protest the introduction of *laissez-faire* capitalist practices. When local authorities reduced their customary attempts to control the price of grain and bread, as was done in England and France in the eighteenth and early nineteenth centuries, prices soared, especially in time of shortage. People rioted in the name of traditional justice, demanding that prices once again be fixed so that the poor, too, might eat. The rioters were not the abject poor but representatives of the industrious classes, peasants and artisans, tradesmen and their wives. Women frequently began the protests as they waited outside a bakery to buy their families' bread or as they arrived at the market and learned that the price of grain had increased, or that no grain was available. Crowds of women and their children, joined by men, then descended on the miller or the baker, seizing his supplies and selling them at a 'just price', punishing him by damaging machinery or simply distributing available flour or bread. . . .

Natalie Davis has argued that in the sixteenth century women's preponderant role in these and other disturbances reflected popular views which saw women as inclined to passion and disorder. They were also legally exempt from punishment, hence not responsible to the authorities for their behaviour. She suggests, too, that women, particularly if they were mothers, were understood to have a moral right to speak the truth and denounce injustice (Davis 1975). In addition, of course, the bread riots flowed from the concrete and collective experiences of women as they carried out their family role of consumer and food provider. These women were responsible for marketing, and they best knew the consequences for their families of higher prices, of products of inferior quality and of deprivation. . . .

CHILDBIRTH AND NURTURE

The role of food provider was an important aspect of a married woman's productive economic activity and it was also tied to her reproductive role. For it was she who bore and nurtured children, she who clothed and cared for them. Children were the inevitable consequence of marriage; childbearing was an exclusively female activity. Married women expected to spend much of their married lives pregnant or caring for young children. High infant mortality rates and ensuing high fertility meant that at least two-thirds of a wife's married years involved reproductive activity. For women the risks and pain of childbirth, the need to spend some time nursing an infant, the supervision and feeding of children were all part of the definition of marriage.

The activities surrounding childbirth were almost exclusively performed by females. Midwives sometimes assisted at the birth of a child. These were usually local women who had 'inherited' the few skills they had from their own mothers or from another woman in the community. But a midwife's services cost money and often women simply helped another, with no previous training or experience. The lack of knowledge contributed to maternal and infant disability and death. . . .

The presence of another woman was helpful to a mother for a practical and legal reason. . . . If the baby died, she could serve as a witness that it had not been deliberately murdered by its mother. In the seventeenth century, in both England and France, male doctors began to take an interest in childbirth. They developed new methods of assistance and regulated the practice of midwifery. Books of instruction were prepared, and investigations of local practices were made. In France, regulation of midwives was partly a consequence of a drive by church officials to increase the custom of baptism. One clergy man, Mgr Rochefoucauld, visited every parish in the diocese of Bourges early in the eighteenth century. He found many women helping one another in childbirth and urged all women to get together and elect one or two 'official' midwives, who would be trained and certified by the state and church. In the villages and towns he visited, some women apparently followed his instruction. But the reforms did not change the practice in most regions.[1] Well into the nineteenth

century babies were delivered by untrained women. As Hufton (1974: 14) has put it, 'The actual birth of the child was surrounded by a "complicity" of females.' Childbirth created a bond among women. They not only shared the experience, but also assisted and nursed one another as best they could.

Yet after the birth of a baby, in the list of household priorities the care of children ranked quite low. Work and the provision of food for the family had first claim on a married woman's time. In the craftshop or on the farm, skilled or unskilled, most labour was time-intensive. Men and women spent the day at work, and what little leisure they had was often work-related. Hence in the rural *veillée* people would gather in barns on winter evenings to keep warm, to talk, but also to repair farm tools, to sew, to sort and clean fruit and vegetables. In cities when women were not formally employed or when their paid work was through, they put in long hours spinning, buying and preparing food, or doing laundry. Household tasks were tedious and no labour-saving technology lightened the chores of a working woman. She simply did not have time to spare to devote specifically to children. The demands of the family enterprise or the need to earn wages for the unskilled could not be postponed or put aside to care for children, who, in their earliest years, represented only a drain on family resources. Busy mothers in French cities sent their babies out to be nursed by wet nurses if they could afford it. Silk spinners in Lyons, as well as the wives of butchers and bakers, entrusted newborn infants to strangers rather than interrupt their work to care for them, even when this increased the likelihood that the infant would die (Garden 1970: 324; Hufton 1974: 318; Sussman 1975). Indeed, death rates among children put out to nurse were almost twice as high as among infants nursed by their own mothers. Even infants who remained at home, however, did not receive a great deal of care. The need for special attention for young children simply was not recognized. As Pinchbeck and Hewitt (1969:

8) have put it, 'Infancy was but a biologically necessary prelude to the sociologically all important business of the adult world.'

Philippe Ariès' pathbreaking book on family life demonstrated that ideas about children and the experience of childhood have had an important history. Before about the eighteenth century, children were not central to family life. They were dressed as miniature adults almost as soon as they could walk, and they were included in all aspects of adult activity, work as well as games. While childhood was understood as a stage of dependency, there nonetheless was no special treatment prescribed for children, no notion that their physical and emotional needs might differ from those of adults. New ideas about childhood began to spread among the upper classes by the latter half of the seventeenth century, but Ariès indicates that these did not reach the popular classes until late in the nineteenth century. So in seventeenth- and eighteenth-century working-class and peasant families, children from infancy to about ages seven were dependent beings, but their presence in no way altered family priorities. Children were incorporated into ongoing activities, and had only a minimal claim on material resources and parental time.

The position of children in a family was the result of several factors: high infant and child mortality rates and a relative scarcity of both time and material resources. The likelihood was great that a child would die before it reached maturity. Parents' treatment of their children clearly took these odds into account. They often gave successive children the same name, anticipating the fact that only one would survive. Since the life of any child was so fragile, there was no reason to try to limit or prevent pregnancy. Moreover, as two historians have put it:

> The high rates of mortality prevailing amongst children inevitably militated against the individual child being the focus and principal object of parental interest and affec-

tion. . . . The precariousness of child life also detracted from the importance of childhood as an age-status. In a society where few lived to grow old, age was of less significance than survival (Pinchbeck and Hewitt 1969: 7).

The needs of family economy and not children's individual needs or the needs of 'childhood' determined whether or not children remained at home from infancy onward. If they were not put out to a wet nurse, children might be sent into service or apprenticeship at age seven or eight. They were expected to work hard and were sometimes subjected to harsh treatment by their masters and mistresses. (Court records are full of accounts of young servants and apprentices fleeing from cruel employers.) On the other hand, if the family needed their labour, children worked at home.

Children were a family resource only if their labour could be used. In propertied families, of course, one child was also important as an heir. As soon as they were able, young children began to assist their parents in the work of the household. In time of scarcity, those not working might be abandoned or sent away, for they were of limited usefulness to the household as it attempted to balance labour and food.

As family labourers, children were accorded no special treatment. They simply worked as members of the family 'team'. Their interest and their needs were not differentiated from the family interest. The mother's services to the family were therefore services to them as well. Although she spent time as a childbearer, a mother allocated little time to activities specifically connected with childrearing. Children were fed and trained to work in the course of the performance of her other responsibilities. Married women allocated their time among the three major activities. The organization of production in this period permitted them to integrate their activity, to merge wage work, production for household consumption, and reproduction.

Production was most often located in the household, and individuals for the most part controlled the time and pacing of their work. Production for the market was often an outgrowth of production for household consumption. Although household chores were time-consuming, they did not demand a broad range of skill or expertise. Childbirth interrupted a woman's routine and claimed some of her time, but after a few days, a woman was usually back to work, taking time out only to nurse the infant. Views of children and standards of childcare were such that children were either sent away at a young age or were incorporated into adult routines and adult work. Hence it was possible for a married woman to earn wages or to produce for the market, to manage her household, and to bear children. Each activity influenced the others, but no single activity defined her place nor claimed all of her time. In the course of her lifetime, indeed in the course of a year or a day, a married woman balanced several types of activity and performed them all. She was the cornerstone of the family economy.

Note

1. Archives Departementales, Cher, Cote 1, MI 23. This reference was given to us by Nancy Fish of UCLA. We are grateful for her help.

References

Abbiateci, A. et al. 1971. *Crimes et criminalité en France, XVIIe–XVIIIe siècles* (Paris: Colin).

Allison, K.J., and P.M. Tillot. 1961. 'York in the Eighteenth Century' in *A History of Yorkshire*, ed. P.M. Tillot (London: The Institute of Historical Research).

Armengaud, A. 1975. *La famille et l'enfant en France et en Angleterre du XVIe au XVIIIe siècles: Aspects démographiques* (Paris: Société d'édition d'enseignement supérieur).

Baehrel, R. 1961. *Une Croissance: La Basse Provence rurale (fin du XVIe siècle–1789)* (Paris: SEVPEN), 109–20.

Baulant, M. 1976. 'The Scattered Family: Another Aspect of Seventeenth-Century Demography' in *Family and Society*, eds R. Forster and O. Ranum (Baltimore: Johns Hopkins).

Berkner, L. 1972. 'The Stem Family and the Development Cycle of the Peasant Household: An Eighteenth Century Austrian Example', *American Historical Review* 77 (April): 398–418.

Bernard, R.-J. 1975. 'Peasant Diet in Eighteenth-Century Gevaudan' in *Diet from Pre-Industrial to Modern Times*, eds Forster and Forster (New York: Harper & Row).

Braun, R. 1966. 'The Impact of Cottage Industry on an Agricultural Population' in *The Rise of Capitalism*, ed. D. Landes (New York: Macmillan).

Cadet, E. 1870. *Le Mariage en France* (Paris: Guillamin).

Castan, N. 1971. 'La Criminalité familiale dans le ressort du Parlement de Toulouse, 1690–1730', in *Crimes et criminalité en France, XVIIe-XVIIIe siècles*, ed. A. Abbiateci et al. (Paris: Colin).

Castan, Y. 1974. *Honnêteté et relations sociales en Languedoc (1715–1780)* (Paris: Plon).

Cipolla, C. 1964. *The Economic History of World Population*, rev. edn (Baltimore: Penguin).

———. 1976. *Before the Industrial Revolution: European Society in the Eighteenth Century* (New York: Norton).

Clark, A. [1919] 1968. *The Working Life of Women in the Seventeenth Century* (London: G. Routledge & Sons; reissued by Frank Cass).

Clarkson, L.A. 1971. *The Pre-Industrial Economy of England, 1500–1750* (London: Batsford).

Couturier, M. 1969. *Recherches sur les structures sociales de Châteaudun, 1525–1789* (Paris: SEVPEN).

Davies, D. 1965. 'The Case of Labourers in Husbandry, 1795' in *Society and Politics in England, 1780–1960,* ed. J.F.C. Harrison (New York: Harper & Row).

Davis, N. 1971. 'The Reasons of Misrule: Youth Groups and Charivaris in Sixteenth-Century France', *Past and Present* 50: 42–75.

———. 1975. 'Women on Top' in *Culture and Society in Early Modern Europe,* ed. N.Z. Davis (Stanford: Stanford University Press).

Deyon, P. 1967. *Amiens, Capitale provinciale: Etude sur la société urbaine au 17e siècle* (Paris, The Hague: Mouton).

Dupaquier, J. 1976. 'Les Caractères originaux de l'histoire démographique française au XVIIIe siècle', *Revue d'histoire moderne et contemporaine* 23 (April–June).

El Kordi, M. 1970. *Bayeux au XVIIe et XVIIIe siècles* (Paris, The Hague: Mouton).

Fairchilds, C. 1976. *Poverty and Charity in Aix-en-Province, 1650–1789* (Baltimore: Johns Hopkins University Press).

Flandrin, J.-L. 1976. *Familles: Parenté, maison, sexualité dans l'ancienne société* (Paris: Hachette).

Fourastié, J. 1959. 'De la vie traditionnelle à la vie "tertiaire"', *Population* 14.

Garden, M. 1970. *Lyon et les lyonnais au XVIIIe siècle* (Paris: Les Belle-Lettres).

Gillis, J.R. 1974. *Youth and History* (New York: Academic Press).

Goubert, P. 1965a. 'Recent Theories and Research on French Population between 1500 and 1700' in *Population in History: Essays in Historical Demography,* eds D.V. Glass and D.E.C. Eversley (Chicago: Aldine).

———. 1965b. 'The French Peasantry of the Seventeenth Century: A Regional Example' in *Crisis in Europe, 1540–1660: Essays from Past and Present,* ed. T. Aston (London: Routledge and Kegan Paul) and *Beauvais et le Beauvaisis.*

Gouesse, J.-M. 1972. 'Parenté, famille et mariage en Normandie aux XVIIe et XVIIIe siècles', *Annales: Economies, Sociétés, Civilisations* 27.

Guilbert, M. 1966. *Les Fonctions des femmes dans l'industrie* (Paris, The Hague: Mouton).

Hair, P.E.H. 1966. 'Bridal Pregnancy in Rural England in Earlier Centuries', *Population Studies* 20 (Nov.): 233–43.

Hajnal, J. 1965. 'European Marriage Patterns in Perspective' in *Population in History: Essays in Historical Demography,* eds D.V. Glass and D.E.C. Eversley (Chicago: Aldine).

Hauser, H. 1927. *Ouvriers du temps passé* (Paris: Alcan).

Hay, D. et al. 1975. *Albion's Fatal Tree* (New York: Pantheon).

Henry, L. 1965. 'The Population of France in the Eighteenth Century' in *Population in History: Essays in Historical Demography,* eds D.V. Glass and D.E.C. Eversley (Chicago: Aldine).

Hobsbawm, E.J. 1968. *Industry and Empire: An Economic History of Britain since 1750* (London: Weidenfeld and Nicolson).

Hollingsworth, T.H. 1969. *Historical Demography* (London: The Sources of History Limited in Association with Hodder and Stoughton Ltd.).

Hufton, O. 1971. 'Women in Revolution, 1789–1796', *Past and Present* 53.

———. 1974. 'Women and Marriage in Pre-Revolutionary France', unpublished paper.

———. 1974. *The Poor of Eighteenth Century France, 1750–1789* (Oxford: Clarendon Press).

———. 1975. 'Women and the Family Economy in Eighteenth Century France', *French Historical Studies* 9 (Spring): 1–22.

Kaplow, J. 1972. *The Names of Kings: The Parisian Laboring Poor in the Eighteenth Century* (New York: Basic Books).

Knodel, J., and M.J. Maynes. 1976. 'Urban and Rural Marriage Patterns in Imperial Germany', *Journal of Family History* 1 (Winter).

Kussmaul-Cooper, A. 1975a. 'The Mobility of English Farm Servants in the Seventeenth and Eighteenth Centuries', unpublished paper, University of Toronto (cited with permission).

———. 1975b. 'Servants and Laborers in English Agriculture', unpublished paper, University of Toronto (cited with permission).

Landes, D. 1969. *The Unbound Prometheus* (Cambridge: Cambridge University Press).

Laslett, P. 1974. 'Parental Deprivation in the Past: A Note on the History of Orphans in England', *Local Population Studies* 13 (Autumn): 11–18.

———, and K. Oosterveen. 1973. 'Long-term Trends in Bastardy in England: A Study of the Illegitimacy Figures in the Parish Registers and in the Reports of the Registrar General, 1461–1960', *Population Studies* 27.

Le Roy Ladurie, E. 1969. 'L'Amenorrhée de famine (XVIIIe-XXe siècles)', *Annals: ESC* 24e Année (Nov.–Dec.): 1589–601.

Lebrun, F. 1971. *Les Hommes et la mort en Anjou aux 17e et 18e siècles* (Paris, The Hague: Mouton).

Lefebvre, G. 1962. *Etudes Orléannaises*, v. 1 (Paris: CNRS).

Levine, D. 1976. 'The Demographic Implications of Rural Industrialization: A Family Reconstitution Study of Shepshed, Leicestershire, 1600–1851', *Social History* (May): 177–96.

———, and K. Wrightson. 1980. 'The Social Context of Illegitimacy in Early Modern England' in *Bastardy and Its Comparative History*, ed. P. Laslett (Cambridge: Cambridge University Press).

Macfarlane, A. 1970. *The Family Life of Ralph Josselin* (Cambridge: Cambridge University Press).

Mendras, H. 1970. *The Vanishing Peasant: Innovation and Change in French Agriculture*, trans. J. Lerner (Cambridge, MA: MIT Press).

Meuvret, J. 1965. 'Demographic Crisis in France from the Sixteenth to the Eighteenth Century' in *Population in History: Essays in Historical Demography*, eds D.V. Glass and D.E.C. Eversley (Chicago: Aldine).

Morineau, M. 1972. 'Budgets populaires en France au XVIIIe siècle', *Revue d'histoire économique et sociale* 50.

Perrot, J.-C. 1975. *Genèse d'une ville moderne: Caen au XVIIIe siècle* (Paris, The Hague: Mouton).

Phillips, R. 1976. 'Women and Family Breakdown in Eighteenth Century France: Rouen 1780–1800', *Social History* 2 (May): 197–218.

Pinchbeck, I. [1930] 1969. *Women Workers and the Industrial Revolution, 1750–1850* (London: G. Routledge; reissued by Kelley).

———, and Hewitt, M. 1969. *Children in English Society*, v. 1 (London: Routledge and Kegan Paul).

Power, E. 1975. *Medieval Women* (Cambridge: Cambridge University Press).

Segalen, M. 1972. *Nuptialité et alliance: Le Choix du conjoint dans une commune de l'Eure* (Paris: G.P. Maisonneuve Larose).

Stone, L. 1975. 'The Rise of the Nuclear Family in Early Modern England' in *The Family in History*, ed. C. Rosenberg (Philadelphia: University of Pennsylvania Press).

Sussman, G. 1975. 'The Wet-Nursing Business in Nineteenth Century France', *French Historical Studies* 9 (Fall): 304–23.

Thompson, E.P. 1975. *Whigs and Hunters* (London: Allen Lane).

Thorner, D., B. Kerblay, and R.E.F. Smith, eds. 1966. *A.V. Chayanov on the Theory of Peasant Economy* (Homewood, IL: Richard D. Irwin).

Wrigley, E.A. 1966. 'Family Limitation in Pre-Industrial England', *Economic History Review*, 2nd series, 19 (April): 89–109.

———. 1969. *Population and History* (London: Cambridge University Press).

Chapter 8

Working-class youth were expected to contribute to household subsistence in the nineteenth century. Historians have documented a pattern of gender differences in the way their earnings were treated—girls typically turning over nearly all of their wages to parents, boys typically paying room and board. Less explored is the issue of gender differences in the allocation of sons' and daughters' labour. Bettina Bradbury explores this issue in her examination of families in two working-class areas in Montreal in the late nineteenth century.

Of course, reliance on the earnings of teens and young adults signifies the impoverished existence of many working-class people in early industrial capitalism. During the first half of the nineteenth century, the solution they began to fight for involved men earning a 'family wage'—one high enough to support themselves as well as a wife and children. Although such an ideal was not approximated for most working-class men until much later, it involved notions of gender— women (and children) defined as dependants and men defined as breadwinners—that had a lasting legacy.

Gender at Work at Home: Family Decisions, the Labour Market, and Girls' Contributions to the Family Economy

Bettina Bradbury

'Gender at work' can be read in two ways. In the first, work is a noun, and the central question is 'How do definitions of skill, of appropriate work for men and women, get negotiated within the workplace by men and women, workers and capital?' Recent discussions of the sexual division of labour in diverse industries, of 'gender at work', the social construction of skill and of the role of unions in perpetuating women's unequal position in the workforce have made major contributions to our understanding of the complexities of the relationships between gender and class, between patriarchy and capitalism. Historical research in this field is rich and fascinating, and is reshaping both women's history and working-class history in Canada as elsewhere.[1]

'Gender at work' can also be read, if my grammar is correct, as a verb. Here the question posed would be 'How does gender work as a process in society which means that men and women end up with different work and life experiences?' To answer this question involves consid-

eration of factors other than those found in the workplace. In this paper I would like to argue that while workplace-centred approaches go a long way toward explaining sex segregation within specific trades, they ignore different levels of decision-making and other institutions that have already gendered the workforce before it arrives at the factory gate.[2] Equally, while approaches stressing the strength of patriarchal ideology or the importance of domestic labour help explain why married women remain out of the workplace they fail to grasp the complex interactions between patriarchy and capitalism. Furthermore they are more difficult to apply when dealing with the work of daughters rather than their mothers.

Within families decisions were made about who should stay home to look after children and do housework and who should earn wages which had wide-reaching impact on the composition of the workforce. Such decisions were never made in an ideological or economic vacuum, they represented a complex and often unconscious balance between basic need, existing ideology and practise regarding gender roles, the structure of the economy, and the particular economic conjuncture. Schools taught specific skills and implanted tenacious ideas about future roles. At its broadest level this paper represents a simple plea to those looking at divisions of labour in the workplace to also consider the work done by historians of the family and education. In Canada such work offers some clues about this broader process, although little research systematically examines the question.[3] To the extent that historians interested in how gender is worked out within the workplace and in the unions ignore what happens prior to men and women's arrival at work, their explanations will fail to consider the wider and deeper sexual division of labour, which not only relegated women to jobs defined as less skilled in workplaces shared with men and to feminine ghettos, but also determined that large numbers would simply not enter the workforce or would do so only sporadically.

More specifically the paper focuses on one aspect of the question, namely how family decisions in interaction with the nature of local labour markets influenced sons' and in particular daughters' contribution to the family economy.[4] The paper concentrates on the micro-level, examining what I have been able to deduce about family decision-making processes regarding which family members should seek wage labour in two Montreal working-class wards between the 1860s and 1890s. A brief description of the major sectors employing males in Montreal is followed by an assessment of the importance of additional wage earners to working-class families. The respective work of sons and daughters within the family economy is evaluated.

The sexual division of labour within the family, and the need for additional domestic workers as well as extra wage labourers, I argue, meant that the context, timing, and contours of boys' and girls' participation in wage labour were dif-

ferent. By looking at the role of girls in the family economy and not just in the labour market,[5] we can better see how the major changes accompanying the emergence of industrial capitalism in Montreal did not modify the dominant sexual division of labour.

Montreal Families and Wage Labour, 1860–90

The years 1860 to 1890 were characterised by the growing dominance of industrial capital in the economic structure of Montreal, the increasing dependence on wage labour of a major proportion of its population. Canada's first and largest industrial city, 'the workshop' of Canada, had a wide and complex array of industries. Most important were those relating to rail and water transportation, shoemaking, clothing, and food and beverages. The metallurgy sector, dominated by production for the railroads, provided jobs for skilled immigrants from Great Britain, and some French Canadians with a long tradition of working in metal. In shoemaking and dressmaking, as in numerous other smaller trades, artisanal production was rapidly, if unevenly, giving way to production in large factories. Minute divisions of labour accompanied the utilisation of new types of machinery throughout the period, drawing immigrants and French Canadians new to the city into the myriad of largely unskilled jobs that were being created. Broadly speaking, the male workforce was divided into four groups. Best paid and most secure were the relatively skilled workers involved in the new trades that emerged with the industrial revolution—the engineers, machinists, moulders and others who worked in the foundries and new factories. More subject to seasonal and conjectural unemployment were skilled workers in the construction trades. A third group comprised those workers in trades undergoing rapid deskilling and re-organisation, most important amongst these were the shoemakers. General unskilled labourers made up the other major subgroup within the working class. About twenty-five cents a day separated the average wage of each of these groups, setting the stage for potential differences in their standard of living, and their family economy.[6] Women and girls worked largely in separate sectors of the economy, particularly as domestic servants, dressmakers, and in specific kinds of factory work. In virtually every sector, their wages were half those of males or less.[7]

The Importance of Additional Earners in the Family Wage Economy

These disparities of approximately twenty-five cents a day had the potential to separate the working class into identifiable fractions, each capable of achieving a different standard of living in good times, each vulnerable in diverse ways to the impact of winter, cyclical depressions and job restructuring. Throughout most of the period the most skilled had more flexibility in their budget and a greater chance of affording to eat and live at a level that may also have helped to ward off the diseases that spread only too quickly through the poorly constructed sewers and houses of the city. This greater margin of manoeuvre which higher daily wages, greater job security, and the possession of skills that were scarce and usually in demand gave to the skilled, was not constant. It was particularly likely to be eroded in times of economic depression or of rapid transformations in the organisation of work.

While some skilled workers organised successfully during this period, the major element of flexibility in the family income, for skilled and unskilled alike, lay not so much in the gains that organisations could offer, but in the ability to call on additional family members to earn wages, to gain or save money in other ways, or to limit the necessity of spending cash. Decisions about who additional family workers would be were therefore crucial in determining the contours of the family economy and of the labour force. An examination of the importance of secondary wage

earners, and of who they were in terms of their age and sex allows a better grasp of the interaction between family labour deployment decisions, the 'gendering' of the workforce and the structure of the economy. This section therefore assesses the importance of additional wage earners in families headed by men in different types of occupations.[8] The following section then attempts to determine who such workers were.

The average number of workers reported by the families of the two working-class areas studied here, Ste Anne and St Jacques wards, fluctuated over the family life cycle. Amongst young couples who had not yet borne children, the wife would occasionally report an occupation, sometimes another relative lived with the couple, contributing to the number of workers in the household, so that until 1881 families averaged just over one worker at this first stage of a couple's married life. Most families then passed through a long period of relative deprivation as children were born, grew, and required more food, clothing and larger living premises. Between the time when the first baby was born and some children reached twelve or thirteen, the families of Ste Anne and St Jacques continued to have only slightly more than one worker. Then children's contribution began to make up for the difficult years. In 1861, families where half the children were still under fifteen averaged 1.34 workers; once half were fifteen or more they averaged 1.97. In subsequent decades the expansion of wage labour made children's contribution even more important. Whereas in 1861 the average family with children over the age of eleven had only .48 of them at work, in 1881 it had 1.16. By 1871 the average family with offspring aged fifteen or more had nearly as many children living at home and working as there had been total number of workers a decade earlier. From .85 children at work, the number reported increased to 1.85. The total number of family workers increased from an average of under two at this stage in 1861 to nearly three a decade later. Children's wages became more and more important as children came to constitute a wage-earning family's major source of security.

The prosperity that this number of workers could have secured was temporary. It depended largely on the ability of parents to keep their wage-earning children in the household. As older sons or daughters began to leave home to work or marry, the average dropped down again. If both members of a couple survived they would find themselves struggling again in their old age on a single wage, or no wage at all. For aged working-class widows and widowers, the situation was particularly bleak if there were no children able to help.[9]

Over these years the patterns of the working-class and non-working-class families diverged. In 1861 the non-working class, particularly in St Jacques, included a high proportion of artisans and shopkeepers, men whose family economy required not the wages, but the work of wives and children. As a result, the average number of workers and of children at work in their families was higher than in all other groups except the unskilled. Over the next two decades, artisans became less and less common. Family labour was increasingly limited to enterprises like small corner groceries. Professionals and some white collar workers became more important among the non-working-class populations. After 1871, the reporting of jobs by children was least likely amongst this group.

It was within the working-class family economy that the most dramatic changes occurred over this period, although there were significant and changing differences between the skilled, the unskilled, and those in the injured trades. The inadequacy of the $1.00 a day or less that a labourer could earn remained a constant throughout this period. As a result, unskilled families consistently relied on additional workers when they were able to. In 1861 they averaged 1.45 workers, compared to 1.27 among the skilled. Over the next two decades the growing number of jobs available allowed them to increase the average number of family workers to 1.62 then 1.66. Amongst those with working-age offspring, the average number at work increased by 123 per cent from .60 in 1861 to 1.34 two decades later.

For these unskilled workers the period before children were old enough to work was the most difficult. It is worth examining how some such families managed at the critical stage of the family life cycle and after as children matured. Olive Godaire, wife of labourer Pierre, worked, probably at home as a dressmaker in 1861, to help support their three children aged two to eight. Ten years later, it was her eighteen-year-old daughter who was taking in sewing, while a ten-year-old boy was apprenticed to be a tinsmith.[10] In the case of labourer John Harrington's family, the period when the father was the only earner within the nuclear family lasted for at least eighteen years. When John and Sarah's children were under ten, they took in boarders and had John's fifty-year-old father, also a labourer, living in the household. Whatever money these extra family and household members contributed would have helped compensate for John's low wages or irregular work and they continued to take in boarders over the next ten years. Their oldest son Timothy was still going to school in 1871 and the family was cramped in a rear dwelling where rent was minimal. Somewhere between 1871 and 1881, the boys joined their father in seeking general labouring jobs. For the first time the family lived alone, without additional household members, and with three wage earners, even three labourers, must have enjoyed a standard of living that was relatively high compared to the previous year.

The degradation of work conditions and lower wages that typified trades like shoemaking appear to have been counteracted by sending growing numbers of family members to seek steady work. In 1861 such families had only 1.08 workers—fewer than any other group. By 1881 they averaged 1.62 workers. Most dramatic was the increased importance of the contribution of children resident at home. The average number of children reporting a job amongst those families with children of working age nearly tripled over the two decades, from .55 to 1.51. At that date a few families like that of Angeline and Alexis Larivière had four workers. Their two daughters, twenty-two-year-old Josephine and sixteen-year-old Marie-Louise worked as general labourers. The twenty-year-old son Charles was a stone-cutter.[11]

The relative superiority of the wages of skilled workers seems clear in 1861 when they appear to have been able to manage with fewer workers than other groups—averaging only 1.27. A decade later, with 1.5 workers, they still needed fewer than the rest of the working class. The depression that hit in 1874, however, appears to have eroded much of the superiority of the skilled workers. In 1881 after seven years of major depression, which was only just lifting and which must have left many a family heavily indebted, the pattern of family labour deployment was similar to that of the unskilled and those in the injured trades.

This convergence of experiences within the working class over this period is not surprising, given the impact of the depression, combined with the degeneration of work conditions in some skilled trades. In the metal-working trades, for example, trade was said to be dead in the winter of 1878. Half the local unionised workers were said to be 'working at any kind of labouring work.' Two years earlier, a moulder drew attention to the desperate condition of Montreal mechanics, 'working on a canal at 60 cents per day, men who have served years in securing a trade, the wages they receive being only a mockery of their misery.'[12]

Families clearly attempted to shape their own economies by adjusting the numbers of wage earners to fit their expenses when they were able to do so. Additional wage earners were not only needed, but were used by all fractions of the working class, with differences stemming from the economic conjuncture, the nature of the labour market, their own life cycle and earning power. In so

doing, they influenced the city's labour pool and enhanced their own survival. The increasing availability of wage labour in the factories, workshops, and construction sites of Montreal meant that even in times of depression more and more sons and daughters could and did find work. The reliance of employers in certain sectors on women and youths resident at home depressed male wages generally, while offering families the opportunity to counter a father's low earnings.

Economic transformation thus interacted dialectically with family needs, reshaping the labour market, the family economy, and the life course of children. This interaction is clearest in the case of workers in those sectors undergoing most dramatic transformation. The continued reorganisation of production in trades like shoe-making was reflected not only in the greater increase in the number of their children seeking waged work over the period, but also in the tendency to delay marriage and reduce family size. In the labour market in general, children living at home became a much more significant proportion of workers.[13] In the sewing trades, for example, one quarter of the workers had been co-resident children in 1861; by 1881, 55 per cent were.

Age, Gender, and Additional Family Earners

To try to grasp the decision-making processes behind these patterns of change in the average numbers of family members reporting work over this period, it is necessary to determine who the family workers were in terms of age and gender, and to examine the families from which they came.

Older sons still living at home were the most usual second earners in a family. The number of really young children or married women reporting a job was insignificant beside the importance of children in their late teens or twenties, despite the attention focused on such young workers by contemporaries.[14] Once sons in particular reached fifteen or sixteen, they were expected to work. 'In our culture,' reported Alice Lacasse, the daughter of a French-Canadian immigrant to New Hampshire, 'the oldest children always went to work.'[15] Wage labour for boys over fifteen became the norm in this period, as more and more were drawn into the labour force. Growing numbers of girls did report a job, but the proportion of boys at work remained consistently higher than that for girls in all age groups. And, the pattern of involvement over a girl's life course continued to be completely different from a boy's.

By the age of fifteen or sixteen, 30 per cent of the boys who lived at home in these two wards were reporting a job in 1861. Others no doubt sought casual labour on the streets, working from time to time, at other times roaming together in the gangs of youths that dismayed middle-class contemporaries, and filled up the local police courts. In 1871, when times were good, and industrial capitalism more entrenched, nearly 46 per cent of boys this age could find a job, while in the depression of the 1870s and early 1880s, the percentage dropped back to 37 per cent. After the age of sixteen, and increasingly over the period, boys' involvement with wage labour or other work would grow steadily as they aged. At ages seventeen to eighteen, 50 per cent reported a job in 1861, nearly 68 per cent two decades later. By age twenty-one nearly 90 per cent of boys listed a job at the end of the period.

Among the girls of Ste Anne and St Jacques wards, the work found and the pattern of job reporting over their lives was very different from that of the boys. Once boys passed their early teens they found work in a wide variety of jobs in all sectors and workplaces of Montreal. Girls, in contrast, remained concentrated within specific jobs and sectors. For girls as for boys, the chances of finding work clearly expanded with the growth of Montreal industry. At ages 15 to 16, for instance, only 13 per cent reported a job in 1861 compared to 30 per cent in 1881. At the peak age at which girls reported working, nineteen to twenty, 25 per cent worked in 1861, nearly 38

per cent did so in 1871, then 35 per cent in 1881. Even then, however, the visible participation rate of girls was only half that of boys.[16] After age twenty, the experiences of boys and girls diverged quickly and dramatically, as most, but never all women, withdrew from the formal labour market while most men found themselves obliged to seek work for the rest of their lives.

For those girls who did earn wages, then, paid labour was apparently undertaken for a brief period of their lives prior to marriage. At any one time, most girls aged fifteen or more who remained at home with their parents in these wards reported no job at all. Joan Scott and Louise Tilly have suggested that within the 'industrial mode of production' 'single women are best able to work, since they have few other claims on their time.'[17] The discrepancy in the formal wage labour participation rates for boys and girls in these two Montreal wards suggests to me that single women did, in fact, have other claims on their time. In particular, the heavy and time-consuming nature of nineteenth-century housework, the prevalence of disease, the wide age spread amongst children in most families, and the myriad of other largely invisible pursuits and strategies necessary to survival for the working-class family, meant that many of these girls were needed by their mothers to help with work at home. Their role in the division of labour within the family is highlighted on one census return where members' roles were explicitly described. Louis Coutur, a carter who was fifty in 1861, reported that his twenty-one-year-old son was a shoemaker, his wife's job was 'housework'.[18] It seems fair to assume, making allowance for the under-enumeration of steady labour and casual work among daughters, that most of the girls who listed no job or school attendance, worked periodically, if not continually, at domestic labour as mother's helpers in and around the home. It is thus in the light of family decisions about the allocation of labour power at home, as well as in the structure of jobs available in the marketplace, that the patterns of children's wage labour as well as of their schooling must be interpreted.

At home, girls served an apprenticeship in the reproduction of labour power—in babysitting, cleaning, mending, sewing, cooking, and shopping, and by the end of the century in nursing and hygiene.[19] Religious leaders were explicit about the need for mothers to educate their daughters in their future roles. 'Apply yourselves especially to the task of training your daughters in the functions they will have to perform for a husband and family, without neglecting your other children,' wrote Père Mailloux in a manual for Christian parents that was republished several times between the middle and the end of the nineteenth century.[20] When girls attended school, the subjects learned were not very different. Education for females, except in a few expensive academies, out of reach of the working class, taught only the most basic and general of subjects and housekeeping-type skills. Whereas boys' schools offered book-keeping and geography, girls' schools offered music, needlework, and sewing.[21] Curriculums aimed to prepare girls for their future role as housekeeper, wife, and mother.[22] The minister of education was explicit. He feared that too many young women were being educated above their station in life, and suggested that bookkeeping and domestic economy constituted the best basis of female education.[23] In separate schools, with curriculum that moulded life roles based on gender distinctions, girls were not going to reshape their futures dramatically by slightly increasing the average number of years that they spent at school and in the workplace over this period.

Girls, then, did become secondary wage earners within the working-class family economy, were increasingly likely to do so over this period, but remained less likely to report a job than were boys. The importance of their contribution to domestic labour, the lower wages they could make in the formal labour market, or an ideological repulsion to girls' labour either within the working class or amongst capitalists, constitute partial explanations for their lower rate of participation. In the absence of interviews or written memoirs, it is important to examine the work patterns of specific families more closely to see what reasons can be deduced from the evidence.[24]

Even among the families apparently in greatest need, sons seem to have been sent out to work in preference to daughters. If any families needed to draw on as many workers as possible, it should have been those headed by the labourers or shoemakers of these wards. In such families, food costs alone for a family with several growing children rapidly outstripped a man's incoming wages. Yet even these families appear to have avoided sending girls out to work, if possible. Among labourer's families in Ste Anne in 1881, for example, 66 per cent of those who had boys over ten reported having a son at work, while only 28 per cent of those with girls the same age did so. If older brothers were working, girls generally did not. Girls of age twenty or more would stay at home while a teenage son worked. Their respective roles seem clearly defined. Twenty-six-year-old Ellen Mullin, for example, reported no occupation. Two brothers, aged nineteen and twenty-three worked as carters. Ellen's role was to help her mother with the domestic labour for the three wage earners and her fourteen-year-old younger brother.[25]

In Ste Anne, even families without sons, or without young sons only, seem to have been either unwilling to send girls to work or unable to find work that was seen as suitable in the neighbourhood. Forty-two-year-old Octave Ethier must surely have had trouble supporting his four daughters aged one to seventeen and his wife on his labourer's wages. Yet neither seventeen-year-old Philomène, nor fifteen-year-old Emma reported having a job.[26]

The girls in labourers' families who did report an occupation fell into two categories. Half were the oldest child, either with no brothers or only brothers who were much younger than they were. Nineteen-year-old Sarah Anne Labor, for instance, was the oldest in a family of six children. The closest brother was only seven. She worked as a soap maker. Her wages, and the fact that the family shared the household with several other families, must have helped make ends meet.[27]

The second group of girl workers in Ste Anne and St Jacques came from labourers' families that sent almost all their children to work regardless of gender. Catherine Harrigan, for instance, was fourteen. She worked as a servant. Her two brothers aged fifteen and twenty were labourers like their father. In the family of St Jacques labourer Damase Racette, four girls aged seventeen to twenty-five were all dressmakers, as was his wife, Rachel. A twenty-seven-year-old son, was a cigar maker.[28] This latter group of families appears the most desperate, perhaps because of recurrent illness, or the habitual drunkenness of a parent. When Commissioners Lukas and Blackeby were examining the work of children in Canadian mills and factories in 1882, they reported finding too many cases in the cities and factory districts where parents with 'idle habits' lived 'on the earnings of the children, this being confirmed' in their eyes by one instance where three children were at work, having a father as above described.[29] Yet, such a family could simply have been taking advantage of the fact of having more children of working age to make up for years of deprivation on the inadequate wages most family heads could make. Two years later, reports made to the Ontario Bureau of Industries stressed the inadequate wages of family heads as the major cause of children working, while mentioning that dissipation of the husband or father was less often a cause.[30] When a father was chronically ill, or a habitual drunkard, the wages of several children would indeed have been necessary to support a family. The use of daughters and of children aged ten to twelve to earn wages in this minority of labourers' families contrasts with the absence of such workers in other labourers' families, highlighting the relative infrequency of a daughter's work, even among those in greatest need.

Was it in part working-class ideology that kept girls at home if at all possible, seeing the workplace as unfit for them, or was it rather a pragmatic response to the fact that boys' wages rapidly outstripped those of girls? Pragmatism, made necessary by the exigencies of daily existence, must certainly have played an important part. It made good sense to have boys earn wages rather than girls, for while young children of each sex might earn a similar wage, once they reached fifteen or sixteen, girls' wages were generally half those of a young man. On the other hand, when there was work available that girls could do, more were likely to report a job. Thus the labourers of St Jacques were more likely to have daughters at work than those of Ste Anne. An equal percentage of those with children eleven or over had girls at work as had boys. The fact that nearly 80 per cent of these girls worked in some branch of the sewing industry shows how advantage was taken of the availability of this kind of work in the neighbourhood.

Family labour deployment decisions, then, were forged in the context of their own needs, invariably arising partly from the size, age, and gender configurations of the family, as well as from the kind of work the family head could find. They were realised in relationship with the structure of the local labour market, of job possibilities, and of local wage rates for men and women, boys and girls. And they were influenced by perceptions, ideologies, and gut reactions about what was appropriate for sons and daughters. Thus, it was not just the fact that sewing was available in St Jacques ward that made this such a popular choice for daughters living in that ward, for putting out could theoretically operate anywhere in the city or the surrounding countryside. It was, I suspect, the very fact that it could be done at home that was crucial. For, while domestic service no doubt took some young women from families in these wards away from their own families and into the homes of others, sewing usually kept daughters working at home.[31]

Home-work offered parents, and mothers in particular, several advantages. Firstly, they could oversee their daughters' work and behaviour, avoiding the individualism that working in a factory might encourage, and skirting the dangers and moral pitfalls that at least some contemporaries associated with factory work for young, unmarried women.[32] More importantly, girls sewing at home, like their mothers, could combine stitching and housework, could take care of younger children, run odd errands, or carry water as needed, because they were right there and were always paid by the piece.

The clustering of two to five family members, all seamstresses, commonly found in the census returns for St Jacques ward suggests very strongly that here was a centre of the home-work that was crucial to Montreal's sewing and shoemaking industries during this period. It was not uncommon to find three to four sisters, ranging in age from eleven to twenty-eight all working, presumably together, as sewing girls. In the Mosian family of St Jacques ward, for instance, four daughters worked as seamstresses in 1871. The father was a labourer, and although the wife reported no occupation, she probably also did some sewing at home at times.[33] In 1881, the family of Marie and Michel Guigère had reached a relatively secure stage in their family life cycle. With nine children at home aged two to twenty-three, this joiner's family reported seven workers. Four of the girls, aged thirteen to twenty-three, were seamstresses, one son worked as a labourer, and the thirteen-year-old son was an apprentice. The girls could combine sewing with helping their mother keep house for other workers, caring for the younger children, shopping, cooking, cleaning, and also looking after her husband's seventy-year-old father who lived with them. Marie too probably helped sporadically with sewing.[34]

Some parents with the liberty to choose must have been reluctant to expose their daughters to the long hours, continual supervision, exhausting work, and brutal forms of discipline that existed in some of Montreal's workshops and factories. Work at home could counteract such factors of 'repulsion'[35] in some of the sectors employing girls. Cigar-making factories provided jobs for girls and boys in Ste Anne and St Jacques alike. While some manufacturers appear to have been decent men, neither fining nor beating their employees, others, in an apparently desperate attempt to control their youthful workforce, resorted to physical violence, heavy fines, even locking up children as they strove to mould this young generation of workers to industrial work. Children, like adults, in these factories worked from six or seven in the morning until six at night, and sometimes later.[36] Unlike adult males, they were subject to a vast array of disciplinary measures aimed at making them more productive and more responsible as workers. One child reported:

> If a child did anything, that is, if he looked on one side or other, or spoke, he would say: I'm going to make you pay 10 cents fine, and if the same were repeated three or four times, he would seize a stick or a plank, and beat him with it.[37]

Mr Fortier's cigar-making factory was described as a 'theatre of lewdness'. There was said to be 'no such infamous factory as M Fortier's . . . nowhere else as bad in Montreal.' There, one cigar maker described apprentices as being 'treated more or less as slaves'.[38] It was the evidence of the treatment of one eighteen-year-old girl that really shocked both the public and the commissioners examining the relations between labour and capital in 1888. Georgina Loiselle described how Mr Fortier beat her with a mould cover because she would not make the 100 cigars as he demanded.

> I was sitting, and he took hold of me by the arm, and tried to throw me on the ground. He did throw me on the ground and beat me with the mould cover.

Q. Did he beat you when you were down?

A. Yes, I tried to rise and he kept me down on the floor.[39]

The case of Mr Fortier's cigar factory was not typical. It created a sensation when the evidence was heard. At least some of the mothers of girls working there got together, perhaps encouraged by Mr Fortier, to give evidence to counteract the impact of such bad publicity. 'I am the mother of a family and if I had seen anything improper I would not have stayed there,' explained a Mrs Levoise. 'I have my girl working there.'[40]

While conditions in other Montreal factories were not as extreme, there was sufficient evidence of beatings, other draconian forms of discipline and heavy fines to explain why many girls and their parents may have wished to avoid factory labour. In cotton factories there was some evidence of boys and girls being beaten. Furthermore, fines in at least one Montreal cotton factory could reduce pay packages by between $1.00 and $12.00 in two weeks. Work there began at 6:25 a.m. and finished at 6:15 p.m. When extra work was required, employees had to stay until 9 p.m., often without time off for supper.[41] There were some perks to work in the textile industry. Nineteen-year-old Adèle Lavoie explained that the girls were accustomed to 'take cotton to make our aprons'. Apparently this was usually allowed, but on at least one occasion she was accused by the foreman of having taken forty to fifty yards. When a search of her house produced no results, she reported that the foreman returned to the factory to insult and harass her sister. When she did not produce the cotton, 'he stooped at this time and raising the skirt of my sister's dress, he said she had it under her skirt.'[42]

Airless, hot, dusty factories, such sexual abuse by foremen, work conditions, and the long hours, were all factors that may have discouraged parents from sending girls into factory work. More significant were the wages they earned. For children under fourteen or so, wages varied little by sex. After that, male and female differentials hardened. Girl apprentices in dressmaking, mantlemaking, and millinery sometimes earned nothing for several years until they learned the trade; then they received around $4.00 a week only. 'Girls' in shoe manufactories received $3.00 to $4.00 compared to the $7.00 or $8.00 earned by men. A girl bookbinder made between $1.50 and $6.00 weekly, compared to an average of $11.00 for male journeymen. Even on piece-work, girls and women generally received less than men. In general, wage rates for women were approximately half those of men.[43]

Duties at home and low wages, whether they worked in or outside the home, meant that whereas over this period more and more working-class boys would have reached manhood accustomed to wage labour, their sisters were much more likely to move backwards and forwards between paid work and housework in response to the family's economic needs, and their position in the household. Once boys, and particularly those who had been fortunate enough to acquire a skill in demand in the marketplace, reached their late teens, their earning power might rival that of their father. Wage labour offered such children potential freedom from their family in a way that had not been possible in family economies based on shared work and the inheritance of property. Such freedom was seldom possible for girls, unless they were willing to complement wage labour with prostitution.

Age, Gender, and Changing Patterns of Residence, Schooling, and Domestic Labour

Yet, boys in general do not appear to have taken dramatic advantage of such potential freedom. Nor did girls.[44] In 1861, living with others was still an important stage in the lives of some young people of both sexes. Amongst the seventeen-year-old girls residing in Ste Anne and St Jacques, 35 per cent were boarding with other families, living with relatives or working and living in as a servant. Twenty years later, only 12 per cent of girls that age were not living with their parents, and half of these were already married. Amongst boys aged eighteen 34 per cent were not living with their parents in 1861 compared to only 17 per cent two decades later. Living longer at home with their parents was a fundamental change in the life cycle of boys and girls alike during this period of industrial expansion.[45]

Behind the percentages of children living with their parents or elsewhere lies a complex history of tension between family needs and individual desires, of children balancing off the advantages of the services offered at home against the relative independence that living with strangers, or even relatives might offer.[46] For all families who had passed through at least fifteen years of budget stretching, house sharing, and debt building while their children were young, the relative prosperity that several workers could offer was to be jealously guarded. It was precisely 'because young adults could find jobs' that it 'was in the interest of parents to keep their children at home as long as possible'.[47] The patterns of residence of children suggest that, whatever conflicts there were overall, in these two wards of Montreal between 1861 and 1881 it was increasingly the parents who were the winners.

The motives behind individual decisions, the weight of traditions of family work, are difficult to grasp in the absence of written records. The factors constraining or encouraging one choice or another are clearer. Most children would have left home once they had a job only if their wages were adequate to pay for lodgings and they felt no commitment to contributing to the family income.[48] Clearly more older boys earned enough to pay for room and board than did girls. Thus, in 1871, when work was readily available, 29 per cent of the twenty-three-year-old males living in these wards were boarding or with relatives; 39 per cent were living with their parents and 32 per cent had married. Amongst girls the same age, the low

wages they could make severely limited their options. Only 15 per cent were boarding; 41 per cent were still with their parents, and 44 per cent were already married. The contraction of work and lower wages that accompanied the Great Depression, which hit in 1874, limited the possibility of leaving home to lodge with others or to marry. In 1881, the percentage of twenty-three-year-old boys married had dropped to 25 per cent; only 10 per cent were boarding or living with relatives. Sixty-five per cent remained at home with their parents, presumably pooling resources to survive the difficult times. The depression appears to have hastened the decline of this stage of semi-autonomy. What occurred in subsequent years remains to be determined.

The different roles of boys and girls in the family economy are confirmed in the different patterns of school attendance by age and sex. In general, school and work appear to have been complementary rather than in competition. Some children began school at four years old. By age seven approximately 60 per cent of boys and girls were receiving some education. In 1881 this percentage rose to a peak of 78 per cent for eight- and nine-year-old boys, and of around 80 per cent for girls aged nine to twelve, then fell off rapidly once both sexes reached thirteen. The proportion of children receiving some schooling increased, but not dramatically, between 1861 and 1881. Age, gender, and the economic conjuncture created variations within this overall trend. Most important was the more erratic pattern in the attendance of boys that hints at relationships between age, gender, schooling, and wage labour that require further investigation. Overall the percentage of ten- to fourteen-year-old girls at school increased slowly but steadily from 57 per cent in 1861 to 68 per cent in 1881.[49] The increase was greater in St Jacques than Ste Anne, but the pattern was similar. Amongst boys in each ward, in contrast, the proportion at school was lower in 1871 than any other year, and the proportion of ten- to nineteen-year-olds at work increased. In Ste Anne, in particular, the factories, workshops, and general labouring jobs attracted growing numbers of these youths. The percentage of fifteen- to nineteen-year-old boys reporting working in that ward increased from thirty-eight in 1861 to sixty-four a decade later. While a certain number of families appear to have taken advantage of boom periods to draw their sons, in particular, out of school, the majority of families appear to have got the best of both worlds. Most working-class boys went to school for varying lengths of time before they reached thirteen or so, and then sought wage labour.

These figures confirm the greater importance of a son's wage contribution to the family economy. Girls' role is clear in the high proportion that continued to report neither a job, nor school attendance. Transformations of the economy and the passage of time were slow to modify this gender difference in the relationship between girls' and boys' schooling, and their roles in the family economy. A study conducted in Quebec in 1942, just before schooling was finally made compulsory in that province, found that among children quitting school before the age of sixteen, 61 per cent of girls gave as their reason, 'Maman avait besoin de moi,' while 50 per cent of boys stated, 'Ma famille avait besoin d'argent.' Only 10 per cent of girls gave that reason.[50] The centrality of girls' domestic labour in a different Canadian city, Toronto, is corroborated by evidence showing that potential foster parents in that city at the turn of the century were four times more likely to seek girls than boys, specifically for their usefulness as domestics and nursemaids.[51]

Conclusion

Gender was clearly at work in both senses of the word in nineteenth-century Montreal. On the one hand, the labour market was characterised by a sexual division of labour which, despite the rapid and dramatic changes occurring in the period, limited the numbers of jobs where capitalists considered employing women. This was not immutable, as the cases where 'girls' were used as strikebreakers made clear. Montreal's labour market included major sectors, particularly sewing and shoemaking, that employed large numbers of girls and women. Yet, the figures of labour-force participation rates for the two wards studied here suggest strongly that girls and women seldom entered the workforce in proportions equivalent to their brothers or boys the same age, and that over their life courses their participation was totally different.

The reasons why lie at least partially within the workings of the family wage economy. Working-class families in Montreal clearly both needed and used additional family workers to counteract low wages, and to improve their standard of living. The number of extra workers varied with the skill of the family head, and the worth of that skill in the labour market. Thus, while in good times, skilled workers managed with fewer family workers than the unskilled or those in injured trades, economic depression eroded such superiority. Yet in whatever complex and probably tension-loaded decisions were made about who would seek what kind of work, boys were much more likely to be the auxiliary wage earners than girls.

To explain why brings us, in a sense, to the heart of the debate about the relative importance of patriarchy and capitalism in explaining women's oppression.[52] That the domestic labour of wives has been crucial both to family survival and to women's inequality has long been recognised both empirically and theoretically. But where do daughters fit in? Fathers, one could argue, by keeping girls at home along with their mothers to serve their daily need for replenishment, ensured that the work of all women was viewed as intermittent and secondary to that of the major wage earners.[53] Alternatively, the accent can be put on the nature of specific industries, or more generally on the capitalism labour market, which, by setting women's wage rates at half those of men, made it logical to send boys to work rather than girls.[54] Unequal access to work on the same terms as men thus not only perpetuated women's position in the home, but tragically disadvantaged those single women and widows who alone, or supporting children or elderly parents, had to live on such wages.

Clearly a dialectic is at work here. Neither empirically, nor theoretically, can the workings of patriarchy, or of capitalism, be neatly separated from each other.[55] The nature of the interaction between the two and the weight of one over the other will vary historically and geographically. Among Montreal families, decisions were made in part in relation to existing jobs and wage rates, and such decisions perpetuated, reified the idea that women's work was temporary, performed before marriage or in moments of family crisis.[56] Admitting the dialectic adds complexity to the explanation but remains, I suspect, insufficient. It does so because the emphasis remains on the formal, wage-earning labour market. Domestic labour in the nineteenth century was fundamental to family survival, to the transformation of wages into a reasonable standard of living, and to the reproduction of the working class. Historians have recognised the importance of this job for the working-class wife and mother; the role of daughters has been examined less explicitly.[57] Yet, for nineteenth-century mothers whose children were widely spaced in age, in whose homes technology had made virtually no inroads to lighten their labour, the help of daughters was invaluable. Housewives had no control over the amount of wages the husband earned, and little over how much was turned over to them. Housework was labour intensive and time consuming. One of the only ways in which wives could control the content and intensity of their work was to get children to help. Wherever possible, once girls reached an age where they could be of use to the mother, they were used to babysit, to run errands, to clean, sew, and cook. If this could be combined with wage-earning activities as in the case of home-work in the sewing industry, then such girls did work more formally. If there were no brothers of an age to earn, daughters might work in factories, offices, shops or as domestics. But the need of mothers for at least one helper at home would mean that the rate of formal labour-force participation for girls would generally be lower than that for boys.[58] Patriarchal ideas within the working class, elements of male pride and self-interest, economic pragmatism and the daily needs of mothers and housewives thus interacted, creating a situation in which most girls served an apprenticeship in domestic labour prior to, or in conjunction with, entering the workforce.[59] In cities and towns where the labour market was completely different, where whole families or women were explicitly sought by employers, this division of labour, indeed, the very institutions of marriage and the family could be modified. The question of how to ensure that the necessary domestic labour was performed, however, would remain fundamental.[60] The working out of roles by gender at home would continue to influence the configurations of gender at work.

Notes

1. Heidi Hartmann, 'Capitalism, Patriarchy, and Job Segregation by Sex', *Signs* 1 (Spring 1976): 137–69; Judy Lown, 'Not So Much a Factory, More a Form of Patriarchy: Gender and Class During Industrialisation' in E. Garmarnikow et al., *Gender, Class, and Work* (London, 1983); Sonya O. Rose, 'Gender at Work: Sex, Class, and Industrial Capitalism', *History Workshop Journal* 21 (Spring 1986): 113–31; Nancy Grey Osterud, 'Gender Divisions and the Organization of Work in the Leicester Hosiery Industry' in Angela V. John, *Unequal Opportunities, Women's Employment in England 1800–1918* (Oxford: Basil Blackwell, 1986), 45–70; Sylvia Walby, *Patriarchy at Work:*

Patriarchal and Capitalist Relations in Employment (Minneapolis: University of Minnesota Press, 1986); Ruth Milkman, *Gender at Work: The Dynamics of Job Segregation by Sex during World War II* (Urbana: University of Illinois Press, 1987). For Canadian articles touching the question see: Gail Cuthbert Brandt, 'The Transformation of Women's Work in the Quebec Cotton Industry, 1920–1950' in Bryan D. Palmer, ed., *The Character of Class Struggle: Essays in Canadian Working Class History, 1840–1985* (Toronto: McClelland & Stewart, 1986); Mercedes Steedman, 'Skill and Gender in the Canadian Clothing Industry, 1890–1940' in Craig Heron and Robert Storey, eds, *On the Job: Confronting the Labour Process in Canada* (Montreal and Kingston: McGill-Queen's University Press, 1986), 152–76; Marta Danylewycz and Alison Prentice, 'The Evolution of the Sexual Division of Labour in Teaching: A Nineteenth-Century Ontario and Quebec Case Study', *Histoire sociale/Social History* 6 (1983): 81–109; Marta Danylewycz and Alison Prentice, 'Teachers, Gender and Bureaucratising School Systems in Nineteenth-Century Montreal and Toronto', *History of Education Quarterly* 24 (1984): 75–100; Jacques Ferland, 'Syndicalisme parcellaire et syndicalisme collectif: Une interpretation socio-technique des conflits ouvriers dans deux industries québecoises, 1880–1914', *Labour/ Le Travail* 19 (Spring 1987): 49–88.

2. This argument is obviously not mine alone. It is fundamental to much of the discussion of the workings of patriarchy and to the domestic labour debate, where too often it remains at an abstract theoretical level or based on cursory historical data. It is worth making here because much theoretical work places too much emphasis on either capitalist relations or reproduction and patriarchy, simplifying the complexity of relations between the two, while historical literature on the workplace or the family tend to treat the relation between the two simplistically.

3. Joy Parr's recent articles offer the first major sustained analysis in which decisions and conditions in the home and in the workplace and the relationship between the two are constantly and systematically examined. See especially 'Rethinking Work and Kinship in a Canadian Hosiery Town, 1910–1950',

Feminist Studies 13, 1 (Spring 1987): 137–62; and also 'The Skilled Emigrant and Her Kin: Gender, Culture, and Labour Recruitment', *Canadian Historical Review* 68, 4 (Dec. 1987): 520–57, reprinted in Veronica Strong-Boag and Anita Clair Fellman, eds, *Rethinking Canada: The Promise of Women's History*, 2nd edn (Toronto: Copp Clark Pitman, 1991), 33–55. Gail Cuthbert-Brandt does so in a different sense in 'Weaving It Together: Life Cycle and the Industrial Experience of Female Cotton Workers in Quebec, 1910–1950', *Labour/Le Travailleur* 7 (Spring 1981). Mark Rosenfeld's recent article '"It Was a Hard Life": Class and Gender in the Work and Family Rhythms of a Railway Town, 1920–1950', *Historical Papers* (1988), and reprinted in the volume, carefully unravels how the rhythms of work in the running trades structured the family economy and gender roles in Barrie, Ontario, a railway town.

4. No Canadian works directly confront this question either in the econometric sense in which Claudia Goldin poses it in 'Family Strategies and the Family Economy in the Late Nineteenth Century: The Role of Secondary Workers', in Theodore Hershberg, *Philadelphia, Work, Space, Family and Group Experience in the Nineteenth Century* (New York: Oxford University Press, 1981), 277–310, or in the more feminist and qualitative way that Lynn Jamieson poses it in 'Limited Resources and Limiting Conventions: Working-Class Mothers and Daughters in Urban Scotland c. 1890–1925' in Jane Lewis, ed., *Labour and Love: Women's Experience of Home and Family, 1850–1940* (Oxford: Basil Blackwell, 1986), 49–69.

5. Marjorie Cohen makes a similar argument without elaborating on its implications for daughters in stating that 'the supply of female labour was limited by the labour requirements of the home'. *Women's Work, Markets, and Economic Development in Nineteenth-Century Ontario* (Toronto: University of Toronto Press, 1988), 139. Her insistence on the importance of domestic production and women's work in the home for rural and urban families alike and for an understanding of the wider economy represents an important contribution to economic history as well as to the history of women and the family in Canada.

6. On the average, in the early 1880s, for example, a labourer earned around $1.00 a day, a shoemaker $1.25, a carpenter $1.50, and various more highly skilled workers anything from $1.75 (blacksmith) up. See Bettina Bradbury, 'The Working-Class Family Economy, Montreal, 1861–1881' (Ph.D. diss., Concordia University, 1984), 18; *Canada, Parliament, Sessional Papers, 1882, Paper No. 4, Appendix 3, Annual Report of the Immigration Agent*, 110–11, lists wages in a variety of trades.

7. In this, Montreal and Canada were little different from other cities and counties, nor has much of the discrepancy been eliminated today.

8. The figures used in this paper are derived from research done for my Ph.D. thesis, currently under revision for publication. A 10 per cent random sample was taken of households enumerated by the census takers in Ste Anne and St Jacques in 1861, 1871, and 1881. This resulted in a total sample of 10,967 people over the three decades. They resided in 1851 households and 2,278 families as defined by the census takers.

9. For a brief and preliminary examination of how widows of all ages survived, see my 'Surviving as a Widow in Nineteenth-Century Montreal', *Urban History Review* 17, 3 (1989): 148–60, reprinted in Strong-Boag and Fellman, eds, *Rethinking Canada*, 2nd edn.

10. These life histories were recreated by tracing families between the censuses of 1861, 1871, and 1881.

11. Mss. Census, St Jacques, 1881, 17, p. 110.

12. *Iron Moulders Journal*, Jan. and June, 1878, Report of Local 21; *Iron Moulders Journal*, Jan. 1876, Report of Local 21 and open letter from Local 21 to the editor, cited in Peter Bischoff, 'La formation des traditions de solidarité ouvrière chez les mouleurs Montréalais: la longue marche vers le syndicalisme, 1859–1881,' *Labour/Le Travail* 21 (Spring 1988), 22. Bischoff suggests, sensibly, that amongst moulders the homogenising experience of these years of depression left them more open to the idea of including less skilled workers in their union in the 1880s. The widespread appeal of the Knights of Labour could be seen in the same light.

13. In 1861, for example, only 16 per cent of those reporting jobs in these two wards were children residing at home; twenty years later nearly one-third of all reported workers were offspring living with their parents. Peter Bischoff found a similar trend amongst moulders. The percentage of moulders for the entire city of Montreal that were sons living with their parents rose from 25 per cent in 1861 to nearly 40 per cent in 1881. Peter Bischoff, 'Les ouvriers mouleurs à Montréal, 1859–1881' (MA thesis, Université de Québec à Montréal, 1986), 108.

14. There is no doubt that the wage labour both of young children and married women was under-enumerated. However, as no labour laws existed in Quebec until 1885, and education was not compulsory until 1943, it is unlikely that fear of repercussions would have inhibited parents from responding as it might have elsewhere. It seems fair to assume that the under-reporting of children's jobs, and probably married women's, would have been no greater in Montreal than in other cities of Canada, England, or America, and possibly less.

15. Tamara K. Hareven and Randolph Langenbach, *Amoskeag: Life and Work in an American Factory City* (New York: Pantheon Books, 1978), 262.

16. Caution has to be exercised when using reported jobs for women and children. There is a tendency now in some of the literature on the subject to suggest that gender differentials in workforce participation are largely a result of women's work not being adequately enumerated. While I am sure that some under-enumeration of women's work occurred in Montreal, as elsewhere, I don't think that under enumeration can explain away the differential. Nor is the phenomenon easy to measure. More important, I think, was the nature of women's work, which because of its lack of regularity, its more informal nature, was less likely to be reported. On the problem of under-reporting see, in particular, Sally Alexander, 'Women's Work in Nineteenth-Century London: A Study of the Years 1820–1850', in Juliett Mitchell and Ann Oakley, eds, *The Rights and Wrongs of Women* (London: Penguin Books, 1976), 63–6; Karen Oppenheim Mason, Maris Vinovskis, and Tamara K. Hareven, 'Women's Work and the Life Course in Essex County, Massachussetts, 1880', in

Tamara K. Hareven, *Transitions: The Family and the Life Course in Historical Perspective* (New York: Academic Press, 1979), 191; Margo A. Conk, 'Accuracy, Efficiency and Bias: The Interpretation of Women's Work in the U.S. Census of Occupations, 1890–1940', *Historical Methods* 14, 2 (Spring 1981): 65–72; Edward Higgs, 'Women, Occupations, and Work in the Nineteenth-Century Censuses', *History Workshop* 23 (Spring 1987).

17. Joan Scott and Louise Tilly, *Women, Work, and Family* (New York: Holt, Rinehart and Winston, 1979), 231.

18. Mss. Census, 1861, St Jacques, 11, p. 7750.

19. By the end of the century the need for this kind of education of daughters was being explicitly preached by Montreal doctors and by church representatives, and was formalised in Quebec with the creation of écoles menagères after the 1880s. Carole Dion, 'La femme et la santé de la famille au Québec, 1890–1940' (MA thesis, Université de Montréal, 1984).

20. A. (Père) Mailloux, *Le manuel des parents Chrétiens* (Quebec, 1851, 1910), cited in Carole Dion, 'La femme et la santé de la famille', 60–5.

21. L.A. Huguet-Latour, *L'Annuaire de Ville Marie: Origine, utilité, et progrès des institutions catholiques de Montréal* (Montreal, 1877), 165–70.

22. Marie-Paule Malouin, 'Les rapports entre l'école privée et l'école publique: L'Academie Marie-Rose au 19e siècle', in Nadia Fahmy-Eid and Micheline Dumont, eds, *Maîtresses de maison, maîtresses d'école* (Montreal: Boreal Express, 1983), 90.

23. Québec, *Documents de la Session*, 1874, 'Rapport du Ministre de l'instruction publique', vii.

24. In Lynn Jamieson's study of working-class mothers and daughters in Scotland, which is based on interviews, she makes it clear that mothers made different demands upon boys and girls in terms of the contributions they should make to the family economy. Mothers 'pre-occupied with their housekeeping responsibilities' were much more likely to keep girls home from school to help with housework than to encourage boys to go out and earn. If a father died, for example, daughters or sons might enter full-time paid employment, but if a mother died 'only daughters left school early to become full-time housekeepers,' 'Working Class Mothers and Daughters in Scotland', in *Labour and Love*, 54, 65.

25. Mss. Census, Ste Anne, 1881, 5, p. 1.

26. Ibid.

27. Ibid., 9, 208.

28. Ibid., 17, 340.

29. 'Report of the Commissioners Appointed to Enquire into the Working of the Mills and Factories of the Dominion and the Labour Employed therein', Canada, Parliament, *Sessional Papers*, 1882, Paper No. 42, 2.

30. Annual Report of the Ontario Bureau of Industries, 1884, cited in Cohen, *Women's Work*, 128.

31. The fact that domestic service was Montreal's leading employment for girls, and that it usually involved living in, complicates this analysis of the work of children. Girls could work away from home as a domestic and contribute their pay to their parents; they would not, however, figure among the average number of workers found in census families, nor would their experience be captured in the proportion of girls having a job. On the other hand, neither is that of any boys who left to find work in construction shanties, lumbering camps, railroad work, etc. The figures given in the text are always the percentages of those living in the ward, and with their parents who reported a job. Those who lived and worked elsewhere are thus always removed from both the numerator and the denominator.

32. On the commissioners' concerns about this see Susan Mann Trofimenkoff, 'One Hundred and One Muffled Voices', in Susan Mann Trofimenkoff and Alison Prentice, *The Neglected Majority: Essays in Canadian Women's History* (Toronto: McClelland & Stewart, 1977). How the working class viewed these morality issues requires examination.

33. Mss. Census, St Jacques, 1871, 6, p. 137.

34. Mss. Census, St Jacques, 1881, 12, p. 101.

35. Sydney Pollard, *The Genesis of Modern Management: A Study of the Industrial Revolution* (London: Edward Arnold, 1965), 162.

36. *Quebec Evidence*, evidence of Wm. C. McDonald, tobacco manufacturer, 529.

37. RCRLC, *Quebec Evidence*, anonymous evidence, 42.

38. Ibid., 44–7.

39. Ibid., 91.

40. Ibid., evidence of Mrs Levoise.

41. Ibid., evidence of a machinist, Hudon factory, Hochelaga, 273–4.

42. Ibid., evidence of Adèle Lavoie, 280–2.

43. Ibid., evidence of Patrick Ryan, cigar maker, 37; machinist Hudon Mills, 271; Samuel Carsley, dry goods merchant, 15; Oliver Benoit, boot and shoe-maker, 365; Henry Morton, printer, 297; F. Stanley, foreman at the Star, 331.

44. Here I am referring to the percentage of children at home as opposed to boarding, living with relatives, or living in someone else's house as a servant. The samples taken in each census do not allow me to follow children over time and identify those who actually left home.

45. The same process occurred in Hamilton, and in other cities that have been studied. See Michael Katz, *The People of Hamilton*, 257, 261; Mary P. Ryan, *The Cradle of the Middle Class: The Family in Oneida County, New York, 1790–1865* (New York: Cambridge University Press, 1981), 168–9; Richard Wall, 'The Age at Leaving Home', *Journal of Family History* 8 (Fall 1983): 238.

46. For a careful analysis of the relationship between women's wages, costs of board, and decisions about where to live see Gary Cross and Peter Shergold, 'The Family Economy and the Market: Wages and Residence of Pennsylvania Women in the 1890s', *Journal of Family History* 11, 3 (1986): 245–66.

47. Paul Spagnoli, 'Industrialization, Proletarianization, and Marriage', *Journal of Family History* 8 (Fall 1983): 238.

48. Michael Anderson's careful analysis of which children left home shows that boys in Preston, Lancashire, were more likely to do so than girls. He believes children made 'a conscious calculation of the advantages and disadvantages, in terms of the standard of living which they could enjoy', based on the wages they could make, their father's wage, and the amount they were required to hand over to their parents. *Family Structure* 67: 127–9.

49. A similar, but greater, increase in girls' school attendance is described for Hamilton by Michael B. Katz and Ian E. Davey in 'Youth and Early Industrialization' in John Demos and Sarane Spence Boocock, eds, *Turning Points: Historical and Sociological Essays on the Family*.

50. 'Le problème des jeunes qui ne frèquent plus l'école', *École Social Populaire* 351 (April 1941): 26, cited by Dominique Jean, 'Les familles québécois et trois politiques sociales touchant les enfants, de 1940 à 1960: Obligation scolaire, allocations familiales et loi controlant le travail juvenile' (Ph.D. diss., Université de Montréal, 1988).

51. 'First Report of Work Under the Children's Protection Act', 26; 'Third Report of Work Under the Children's Protection Act', 10, cited in John Bullen, 'J.J. Kelso and the "New" Child-Savers: The Genesis of the Children's Aid Movement in Ontario', paper presented to the CHA Annual Meeting, Windsor, Ont., June 1988, 35–8.

52. The usefulness of taking a category of women other than wives and mothers to test the soundness of contemporary feminist theory on this question is clear in the article of Danielle Juteau and Nicole Frenette who start with an examination of the role of Nuns in late nineteenth- and early twentieth-century Quebec, and use their insights to critique much contemporary feminist theory. 'L'évolution des formes de l'appropriation des femmes: des religieuses aux "meres porteuses"', *Canadian Review of Sociology and Anthropology* 25, 2 (1988).

53. One of the great advantages of the domestic labour debate was its recognition of the importance of housework and reproduction of labour power to capitalism. Less clear in much of the writing was the failure of most writers to acknowledge the interest of men in the perpetuation of domestic labour. For an elaboration of this critique see Walby, *Patriarchy at Work*, 18–19.

54. Ruth Milkman criticizes labour-segmentation theory, early Marxist-feminist writing, as well as

Hartmann's description of patriarchy for paying insufficient attention to the effect of industrial structure on the sexual division of labour and struggles over 'women's place' in the labour market. Looking much more concretely than theorists have done at specific industries, she argues that 'an industry's pattern of employment by sex reflects the economic, political, and social constraints that are operative when that industry's labour market initially forms'. *Gender at Work*, 7.

55. Herein lies the problem of the 'dual systems' approach of Hartmann and others. Heidi Hartmann, 'Capitalism, Patriarchy and Job Segregation by Sex', *Signs* (1977); Varda Burstyn, 'Masculine Dominance and the State' in Varda Burstyn and Dorothy Smith, *Women, Class, Family, and the State* (Toronto: Garamond Press, 1985). Sylvia Walby succeeds better than others in drawing out the links between the two, but insists on their relative autonomy in *Patriarchy at Work*.

56. Canadian historians, whether in women's history or working-class history are only just beginning to unravel this complex, dialectical relationship between the structure of the economy and the needs of the family, in interaction with both capital and labour's definitions of gender roles. It is an unravelling that must continue if we are to understand how gender was at work and continues to work outside the workplace as well as within it.

57. Some of the problems faced by feminist theoreticians grappling with the relationship between women's oppression by males within marriage, their subordination in the labour market, and the wider forces of patriarchy, stem from the assumption that only wives perform domestic labour. This seems to me a profoundly historical view, and one that downplays the importance of the family as a place of socialization and training.

58. Here would be an example of mothers making choices that made their lives easier, but which in the long run perpetuated, even exaggerated, men's more privileged position in the marketplace. On this see Gerder Lerner, *The Creation of Patriarchy* (Oxford: Oxford University Press, 1986), cited in Bonnie Fox, 'Conceptualizing Patriarchy', *Canadian Review of Sociology and Anthropology* 25, 2 (1988): 165.

59. Psychological, Freudian theories about gender identity seem less important here than the practical day-to-day experience in the home and the role model of the mother. Nancy Chodorow, *The Reproduction of Mothering* (Berkeley: University of California Press, 1978).

60. For a superb description of the complex ways in which women in Paris, Ontario—a knitting town where job opportunities for women were much greater than for men—dealt with domestic labour, see Joy Parr, 'Rethinking Work and Kinship in a Canadian Hosiery Town, 1910–1950', *Feminist Studies* 13, 1 (Spring 1987): 137–62.

Chapter 9

Nancy Cott highlights the political function nine-teenth-century domestic ideology served. She also draws out the implications of the 'cult of domesticity' for gender. The only issue she does not explore here is that of the source of these ideas. The evidence is that middle-class women themselves were forging an identity amidst the erosion of the household economy, and using this domestic ideology to claim status for themselves and increase their own power in the household.

Domesticity

Nancy F. Cott

In 1833, when Esther Grout returned to Hawley, Massachusetts, from her travels in search of employment, and wrote in her diary 'Home is sweet'—'there is no place like home'—those phrases were freshly minted clichés (Grout 1833). A host of New Englanders were using the printed word to confirm and advance her sentiments. Essays, sermons, novels, poems, and manuals offering advice and philosophy on family life, childrearing and women's role began to flood the literary market in the 1820s and 1830s, with a tide that has not yet ceased. These early works fall into five categories. There were those primarily on the mother's (less frequently, the father's) responsibilities, such as the Reverend John S.C. Abbott's *The Mother at Home*, Lydia Maria Child's *The Mother's Book*, William Alcott's *The Young Mother*, and Theodore Dwight's *The Father's Book*. A closely related group, including Herman Humphrey's *Domestic Education*, Louisa Hoare's *Hints for the Improvement of Early Education*—a fictional version—Catherine Sedgwick's *Home*, offered principles for childrearing. Others such as Sally Kirby Fales's *Familiar Letters on Subjects Interesting to the Minds and Hearts of Females* and Lydia H. Sigourney's *Letters to Young Ladies* assess women's social role in a general way. A fourth sort more specifically considered the appropriate education for women: Abigail Mott's *Observations on the Importance of Female Education* and Almira Phelps's *The Female Student*, for instance, did so. A slightly different number, with titles such as *The Young Lady's Home* or *The Young Lady's Friend*, followed the etiquette tradition, prescribing manners for women and men.[1] At the same time, magazines addressing an audience of 'ladies' multiplied rapidly, carrying essays, stories, and advice of a similar domestic slant. Despite some minor differences and contradictions among the views expressed in this rash of words, altogether they revealed a single canon—of domesticity.

The central convention of domesticity was the contrast between the home and the world. Home was an 'oasis in the desert', a 'sanctuary' where 'sympathy, honor, virtue are assembled', where 'disinterested love is ready to sacrifice everything at the altar of affection'. In his 1827 address on female education a New Hampshire pastor proclaimed that 'It is at home, where man . . . seeks a refuge from the vexations and embarrassments of business, an enchanting repose of affection: where some of his finest sympathies, tastes, and moral and religious feelings are formed and nourished;—where is the treasury of pure disinterested love, such as is seldom found in the busy walks of a selfish and calculating world.' The ways of the world, in contrast, subjected the individual to 'a desolation of feeling', in the words of the *Ladies'*

Magazine; there 'we behold every principle of justice and honor, and even the dictates of common honesty disregarded, and the delicacy of our moral sense is wounded; we see the general good, sacrificed to the advancement of personal interest, and we turn from such scenes, with a painful sensation . . .' (Burroughs 1827: 18–19; *Ladies' Magazine* May 1830).

The contradistinction of home to world had roots in religious motives and rhetoric. Christians for centuries had depreciated 'the world' of earthly delights and material possessions in comparison to Heaven, the eternal blessings of true faith. In the 1780s and 1790s British Evangelicals doubled the pejorative connotation of 'the world', by preferring bourgeois respectability above the 'gay world' of aristocratic fashion. Living in an era of eroding public orthodoxy, they considered family transmission of piety more essential than ever to the maintenance of religion; consequently they conflated the contrasts of Heaven versus 'the world' and bourgeois virtue versus the 'gay world' with the contrast between the domestic fireside and the world outside.[2] In that tradition, when Esther Grout wrote in her diary, 'oh how sweet is retirement. The pleasantest & I think some of the most profitable moments of my life have been spent in retirement', she was referring to her withdrawal from the world in solitary religious devotion and *also* to her repose *at home* (Grout 1830).

The rhetorical origins of the contrast between home and world demand less interpretation than the canon of domesticity built upon it. That contrast infused the new literature because, in simplest terms, it seemed to explain and justify material change in individuals' lives. Between the Revolution and the 1830s New England's population became more dense and more mobile, its political system more representative and demanding of citizens, its social structure more differentiated and its economic structure more complex than in earlier years when the business of 'the world' had mostly taken place in households. Economic growth and rationalization and the entry of the market mechanism into virtually all relations of production fostered specialized and standardized work and a commercial ethic. Because of regional division of production and marketing, agriculture production itself became more specialized and more speculative. The farmer's success was not in his own hands when he produced for distant markets. In handicrafts the functional differentiation of wholesale merchant, retail merchant, contractor or 'boss', and pieceworker replaced the unified eighteenth-century pattern in which an artisan made and sold his wares from his residence. Masters (now employers) and their journeymen or apprentices no longer assumed a patriarchal relationship; wages and prices defined their relationship to one another and to the merchants above them. Trends such as the decline of traditional determinants of deference, the assertion of an individualist ethos, increasing extremes of wealth and poverty, and replacement of unitary association networks by pluralistic ones, indicated deep change in social relations (Common 1909; Montgomery 1968; Fischer 1974). Differentiation and specialization characterized this transformation of society. These were portrayed and symbolized most powerfully in the separation of production and exchange from the domestic arena—the division between 'world' and 'home'.

The canon of domesticity encouraged people to assimilate such change by linking it to a specific set of sex-roles. In the canon of domesticity, the home contrasted to the restless and competitive world because its 'presiding spirit' was woman, who was 'removed from the arena of pecuniary excitement and ambitious competition'. Woman inhabited the 'shady green lanes of domestic life', where she found 'pure enjoyment and hallowed sympathies' in her 'peaceful offices'. If man was the 'fiercest warrior, or the most unrelenting votary of stern ambition', 'toil-worn' by 'troubled scenes of life', woman would 'scatter roses among the thorns of his appointed track'. In the 'chaste, disinterested circle of the fireside' only—that is, in the hearts and minds of sisters, wives, and mothers—could men find 'recipro-cated humanity . . . unmixed with hate or the cunning of deceit' (*Ladies' Magazine* 1830b; Cary 1830: 4.7; *The Discussion* 1837: 225–6; *Ladies Companion* 1840). The spirit of business and public life thus appeared to diverge from that of the home chiefly because the two spheres were the separate domains of the two sexes.

In accentuating the split between 'work' and 'home' and proposing the latter as a place of salvation, the canon of domesticity tacitly acknowledged the capacity of modern work to desecrate the human spirit. Authors of domestic literature, especially the female authors, denigrated business and politics as arenas of selfishness, exertion, embarrassment, and degradation of soul. These rhetoricians suggested what Marx's analysis of alienated labour in the 1840s would assert, that 'the worker . . . feels at ease only outside work, and during work he is outside himself. He is at home when he is not working and when he is working he is not at home' (Marx [1844] 1967: 292–3). The canon of domesticity embodied a protest against that advance of exploitation and pecuniary values. Nancy Sproat, a pious wife and mother who published her own family lectures in 1819, warned that 'the air of the world is poisonous. You must carry an antidote with you, or the infection will prove fatal.' (A latter-day Calvinist, she clearly gave 'the world' dual meaning, opposing it to both 'home' and 'Heaven'. Her antidote, likewise, was a compound, of domestic affection and religious faith.) No writer more consistently emphasized the anti-pecuniary bias of the domestic rhetoric than Sarah Josepha Hale, influential editor of the Boston *Ladies' Magazine* from 1828 to 1836 and subsequently of *Godey's Lady's Book* in Philadelphia. 'Our men are sufficiently money-making,' Hale said. 'Let us keep our women and children from the contagion as long as possible. To do good and to communicate, should be the motto of Christians and republicans.' She wished 'to remind the dwellers in this "bank-note world" that there are objects more elevated, more worthy

of pursuit than wealth.' 'Time is money' was a maxim she rejected, and she urged mothers to teach their children the relative merits of money and of good works.[3]

Yet the canon of domesticity did not directly challenge the modern organization of work and pursuit of wealth. Rather, it accommodated and promised to temper them. The values of domesticity undercut opposition to exploitative pecuniary standards in the work world, by upholding a 'separate sphere' of comfort and compensation, instilling a morality that would encourage self-control, and fostering the idea that preservation of home and family sentiment was an ultimate goal. Family affection, especially maternal affection, was portrayed as the 'spirit indefatigable, delighting in its task', which could pervade the 'regenerate' society. Furthermore, women, through their reign in the home, were to sustain the 'essential elements of moral government' to allow men to negotiate safely amid the cunning, treachery, and competition of the marketplace.[4] If a man had to enter the heartless and debasing world, his wife at home supplied motive and reward for him, to defuse his resentment:

O! what a hallowed place home is when lit by the smile of such a being; and enviably happy the man who is the lord of such paradise. . . . When he struggles on in the path of duty, the thought that it is for *her* in part he toils will sweeten his labours. . . . Should he meet dark clouds and storms abroad, yet sunshine and peace await him at home; and when his proud heart would resent the language of petty tyrants, 'dressed in a little brief authority', from whom he receives the scanty remuneration for his daily labors, the thought that she perhaps may suffer thereby, will calm the tumult of his passions, and bid him struggle on, and find his reward in her sweet tones, and soothing kindness, and that the bliss of home is thereby made more apparent ('Essay on Marriage' 1834).

The literature of domesticity thus enlisted women in their domestic roles to absorb, palliate, and even to redeem the strain of social and economic transformation. In the home, women symbolized and were expected to sustain traditional values and practices of work and family organization. The very shrillness of the *cri de coeur* against modern work relations, in the canon of domesticity meant that women's role in the home would be inflexibly defined.

Recoiling from the spirit of self-interest and self-aggrandizement they saw in the marketplace, rhetoricians of domesticity looked to the home for a sanctuary of 'disinterested' love; because women at home presumably escaped exposure to competitive economic practices, they became representatives of 'disinterestedness'. (In fact, women at home who engaged in 'given-out' industry as increasing numbers did, brought the economic world into the home.) More profoundly and authentically, married women represented 'disinterestedness' because they were economically dependent. Because their property and earnings by law belonged to their husbands, married women could not operate as economic individuals.[5] Wives lacked the means and motive for self-seeking. The laws of marriage made the social model for striving for wealth irrelevant to them. Beyond equating wives' economic dependence with disinterestedness, the canon of domesticity went a further step and prescribed women's appropriate attitude to be selflessness. The conventional cliché 'that women were to live for others' was substantially correct, wrote the author of *Woman's Mission*, for only by giving up all self-interest did women achieve the purity of motive that enabled them to establish moral reference points in the home (*Woman's Mission* 1840: 48–52). Thus women's self-renunciation was called upon to remedy men's self-alienation.

Furthermore, the canon of domesticity required women to sustain the milieu of task-oriented work that had characterized earlier family organization. This requirement made service to others and the diffusion of happiness in the family women's tasks. Women's household service alone remained from the tradition of reciprocal service by family members. Since it highlighted that aspect of women's role, the canon of domesticity in its early formulation directed them not to idleness or superficial gentility but to a special sort of usefulness. Sarah Hale maintained, for instance, that women's principles of unselfishness and magnanimity should be manifest in their acts of service. A female author of *Letters on Female Character* similarly preferred to view woman as 'a rational being, whose intelligent and active exertions are to afford a perennial source of comfort to mankind', rather than as a romantic goddess to be worshipped (*Ladies' Magazine* 1830b: 445; Cary 1830: 174).

Assuming that women would be happy insofar as they served others and made them happy, these writers reinforced women's orientation toward interpersonal goals in the emotional realm rather than self-reliant accomplishment.[6] 'In every thing I must consult the interest, the happiness and the welfare of *My Husband*,' Eunice Wait of Hallowell, Maine, wrote on the day she married a Universalist evangelist, '. . . may it be my constant study to make him contented and happy, and then will my own happiness be sure' (Cobb 1822). In a similar vein Mary Orne Tucker congratulated herself, after four years of marriage, on her husband's happiness at home: 'His *happy home* I say, and I say it too with *pride*, and *pleasure*; it is no small compliment to my own abilities, to my own powers to please, my temper is somewhat wayward, but I hope it has not been discovered in scenes of domestic life, to shine as a good wife, is an object of my highest ambition, there are many humble duties to fulfill and to fulfill them with honor and chearfulness [*sic*] is a consideration which ought not to be beneath the notice of every reflecting woman.'[7]

The amorphousness of such requirements as 'to please' or 'to serve' did not make women's role any less demanding. Ironically, the rhetoric that intended to distinguish 'home' and 'woman' from 'the world' and 'man' tended to make the two spheres analogous and comparable. It was the paradox of domesticity to make women's work-roles imitate men's; despite the intent to stress how they differed, domestic occupations began to mean for women what worldly occupations meant for men. A businessman in a *Godey's Lady's Book* story admonished his young wife, who had repeatedly neglected to have his midday meal ready on time:

> Your error lies in a false idea which you have entertained, that your happiness was to come somewhere from out[side] of your domestic duties, instead of in the performance of them—that they were not part of a wife's obligations, but something that she could put aside if she were able to hire enough servants. I cannot, thus, delegate my business duties to any one; without my governing mind and constant attention, every thing would soon be in disorder, and an utter failure, instead of prosperity, be the result of my efforts. By my carefulness and constant devotion to business, I am enabled to provide you with every comfort; surely, then, you should be willing also to give careful attention to your department, that I may feel home to be a pleasant place (Arthur [1841] 1972: 169).

Business provided one analogy, politics another. 'I think it is my humble desire to be as a wise Legislator to my little province,' wrote Susan Huntington, a minister's wife who knew the domestic canon by heart before publications rehearsed it, 'to enact as few statutes as possible, & those easy and judicious—to see that all things are done at the proper time, & in the proper way, so far as is practicable, that our family may be a quiet, well organized, regular family' (Huntington 1819).

Defining it as her province, the canon of domesticity made woman's household occupation her vocation. The very attempt to immobilize woman's role in the home transformed her household duties into a discrete, specialized, and objective work-role. Domesticity as a vocation meant, furthermore, that woman's work-role imitated man's while lacking his means of escape. If man could recover from his work 'at home', woman's work was 'at home'. She provided for his relief. Since her sex-role contained her work-role, for her there was no escape. 'A law of her being' appointed her vocation, according to the canon. 'To render *home* happy, is woman's peculiar province; home is *her world*.' She was 'neither greater nor less than man, but different, as her natural vocation is different, and . . . each is superior to each other in their respective departments of thought and action.' Even if woman's vocation was 'natural', however, it required preparation and instruction. Not only the numerous books of advice to the wife and mother but also new institutions to educate girls for those roles, heralded the rationalization of women's domestic occupations into a 'profession'.[8]

Notes

1. All of the titles mentioned were published in New England (primarily Boston) between 1830 and 1840, except Hoare's, published in London in 1819, republished in New York, 1820, and then in Salem in 1829; Mott's, published in New York in 1825; and Sedgwick's 1835 novel—though a New Englander she published with Harper & Bros. in New York.

2. For examples of Evangelical writings see T. Gisborne, *An Enquiry into the Duties of the Female Sex* (London, reprinted Philadelphia, 1798), and H. More, *Stricture on the Modern System of Female Education*, vol. 1, 9th edn (London, 1801); see also M.G. Jones, *Hannah More* (Cambridge, 1952); Gordon Rattray Taylor, *The Angel-Makers: A Study in the Psychological Origins of Historical Change*

1750–1850 (London: Heinemann, 1958) esp. 12–36; Christopher Hill, 'Clarissa Harlowe and her Times', *Essays in Criticism* 5 (1955): 320; Keith Thomas, 'The Double Standard', *Journal of the History of Ideas* 20 (1959): 204–5; and I. Watt, 'The New Woman, Samuel Richardson's Pamela', R.L. Coser, ed., *The Family: Its Structure and Functions* (New York: St Martin's, 1964): 286–8.

3. Mrs N. Sproat, *Family Lectures* (Boston, 1819); *Ladies' Magazine* 3 (Jan. 1830): 42–3; (July 1830): 325; 3 (Feb. 1830): 49–55. Hale maintained that women's empire in the home was 'purer, more excelled and spiritual than the worldly scope of regulating by laws the intercourse of business', *Ladies Magazine* 5 (Feb. 1832); 87. Cf. Catharine Beecher's declaration in *Suggestions Respecting Improvements in Education* (Hartford, CT, 1829): 53: 'The dominion of woman [in contrast to man's] may be based on influence that the heart is proud to acknowledge.'

4. *Woman's Mission* (New York, 1840): 20–1; *The Discussion*: 225. Cf. Mary Ryan's conclusion in 'American Society and the Cult of Domesticity, 1830–1860' (Ph.D. diss., University of California, Santa Barbara, 1971), esp. 70–1, that the literature of domesticity of the 1840s included a complete theory of the psychologically specialized and socially integrative functions of the family in industrial society. Ryan observes that women in the home instilled in their husbands and children national values and an ethic of social control; 'by sustaining their husbands through the discomforts of modern work situations, and gentry restraining them from antisocial behavior, American women facilitated the smooth operation of the industrial system.' The nineteenth-century definition of 'social integration' was 'the moral power of woman' (70, 337).

5. Nor did wives, on the whole, fail to understand their dependence 'First when I received the $5 bill I kissed it,' a Cambridge woman wrote to her absent husband in thanks, 'because it seemed to me proof that my dear Husband did not lose me from his mind as soon

as from his sight: then, I thought I would use it very prudently.' Elizabeth Graeter, Cambridge, MA, to Francis Graeter, 14 Aug. 1836, Hooker Collection.

6. In children's books in the 1840s, there is a discernible contrast between the achievement motivation encouraged in boys and the affiliation motivation encouraged in girls. J.S.C. Abbott's *The School Boy*, for instance, stressed that the boy must aim for correctness and truth, even at the expense of popularity. Girls' books by Lydia Maria Child and Lydia Sigourney also advocated purity and correct principle, but stressed that girls should attain these by loving others, treating them nicely, following the Golden Rule, etc. In his *Rollo* series, Jacob Abbott portrayed Rollo (nine years old) as an independent little man who followed the truth and wished to succeed, but made Rollo's sister Jane passive, cautious, nervous, and dependent on her brother. Bernard Wishy discussed these books in *The Child and the Republic* (Philadelphia, 1968): 57–8.

7. She continued, 'I am every day amply repaid for all my endeavors to please, every look from my master is certificate of my success, and the plaudit of my own conscience affords sweet peace.' Diary of Mary Orne Tucker, 1 May 1802.

8. Quotations from *Ladies' Magazine* 3 (May 1830): 218; Caleb Cushing, 'The Social Condition of Woman', from the *North American Review*, April 1836, reprinted in *Essays from the North American Review*, ed. Allen Thorndike Rice (New York, 1879): 67. Catharine Beecher popularized the idea that wife-and-motherhood was woman's 'profession' in her mid-nineteenth century, but that usage began, I believe, with Hannah More's *Strictures on the Modern System of Female Education*, originally published in 1799 and widely read by women in the United States for decades after. More wrote, 'The profession of ladies, to which the bent of their instruction should be turned, is that of daughters, wives, mothers, and mistresses of families' (v. 1, 9th edn [London, 1801]: 112).

References

Arthur, T.S. [1841] 1972. 'Sweethearts and Wives', *Godey's Lady's Book* 23 (Dec.) reprinted in *Root of Bitterness: Documents of the Social History of American Women*, ed. N.F. Cott (New York: Dutton, 1972).

Burroughs, C. 1827. *An Address on Female Education, Delivered in Portsmouth, N.H., Oct. 26, 1827* (Portsmouth).

Cary, V. 1830. *Letters of Female Character,* 2nd edn (Philadelphia).

Cobb, E.H.W. 1822. Diary, v. 1 (10 Sept.), 29, BPL.

Common, J.R. 1909. 'American Shoemakers, 1648–1895', *Quarterly Journal of Economics* 24: 39–84.

The Discussion of the Character, Education, Prerogatives, and Moral Influence on Women. 1837. (Boston).

'Essay on Marriage'. 1834. *Universalist and Ladies' Repository* 2 (Apr. 19): 371.

Fischer, D.H. 1974. 'America: A Social History,' v. 1, 'The Main Lines of the Subject 1650–1975', unpublished MS, esp. ch. 4, 42–3; ch. 12, 20–2.

Grout, E. 1830. Diary (13 Sept.), Pocumtuck Valley Memorial Association Library Collections, HD.

————. 1833. Diary (4 Aug.), Pocumtuck Valley Memorial Association Library Collections, HD.

Huntington, S.M. 1819. Diary (14 June), SML.

Ladies' Companion. 1840. 'Influence of Woman—Past and Present', 13 (Sept.).

Ladies' Magazine. 1830a. 'Home' by L.E., 3 (May): 217–18.

————. 1830b. Quotations from 'Woman', probably by S.J. Hale, 3 (Oct.): 441, 444.

Marx, K. 1844. 'Alienated Labor', in *Writing of the Young Men on Philosophy and Society*, eds and trans L.D. Easton and K.H. Guddat (Garden City, NY: Anchor Books, 1967).

Montgomery, D. 1968. 'The Working Classes of the Pre-Industrial American City', *Labor History* 9: 3–22.

Women's Mission. 1840. (New York).

Chapter 10

The feature of family life on which it is perhaps most difficult to get perspective is the mother-child relationship. Intensive mothering seems to us the only way to raise children. This selection traces the historical development of the ideas that define motherhood as we know it. Maxine Margolis situates the rise of new ideas about childhood and motherhood in the changes occurring in family life, and also links these ideas to the developing needs of an industrial-capitalist society. The broad changes she describes occurring in the United States were happening in Canada as well.

Certainly, the erosion of the household economy, which not only provided women with a critical produc-tive role but also allowed both parents to train their children (and others) for adulthood, established the context for new definitions of women's role and parenting. What is not clear in this piece, though, is who produced this ideology; in fact, Margolis emphasizes the imposition of these ideas on women. In contrast, social historian Mary Ryan, in Cradle of the Middle Class, has shown that middle-class women themselves had a hand in fashioning these ideas—in reaction to the loss of their economic role and in anticipation of the problem of preparing their children for a quickly changing economy (in which parents were losing the possibility of passing on either land or skills to the next generation).

Putting Mothers on the Pedestal

Maxine Margolis

> Motherhood as we know it today is a surpris-ingly new institution. In most of human his-tory and in most parts of the world even today, adult, able-bodied women had been, and still are, too valuable in the productive capacity to be spared for the exclusive care of children.
>
> Jessie Bernard,
> *The Future of Motherhood*, 1974

Debates about the conflict between motherhood and work have lessened in intensity over the last decade as millions of middle-class wives and mothers have taken jobs and as employment for these women has become the norm rather than the exception. But these developments have not met with unanimous approval. Just think of the demand by groups like the Moral Majority for a return to 'traditional family values', code words for the presence of a full-time housewife-mother in the home. Nevertheless, biting denunciations of working mothers—so common during much of

this century—are much less frequent today. Most women are pleased to be living in an era in which they are free to take a job or even pursue a career and in which their economic contribution to their families is recognized. They probably feel less uneasy about working because it is no longer an article of faith that their employment is harmful to their children. But what is often overlooked is that this is not the first time in American history when work and motherhood were thought compatible and when women's productive activities were seen as essential to their families' well-being.

Ideas about the 'correct' maternal role have often changed over the last 250 years in the United States. Not until the nineteenth century, for example, did a child's development and well-being come to be viewed as the major, if not the sole responsibility of his or her mother, who was then urged to devote herself full-time to her parental duties. In contrast, during the eighteenth century childrearing was neither a discrete nor an exclusively female task. There was little emphasis on motherhood *per se* and both parents were simply advised to 'raise up' their children together.

These and other changes in ideas about motherhood are not isolated cultural artifacts resulting from random ideological fashions. I will argue that these value changes were and are moulded by changes in the nature of the family and the American economy. I intend to review the process whereby motherhood as a full-time career for middle-class women first arose as women's role in the domestic economy diminished, 'work' was removed from the household, the family became more isolated from the larger community, the need for education and skilled children increased, and the birthrate declined. As a result of these developments, with minor variations, the exclusivity of the mother-child dyad and the incessant duties of motherhood emerged beginning in the 1830s as givens in American child-rearing manuals and other prescriptive writings aimed at the middle class.

One of the principal factors that have influenced the middle-class mother's role and the ideology surrounding it is the decline of domestic production. During the colonial period when women were responsible for the manufacture and use of a wide variety of household products essential to daily living, women could not devote themselves full-time to motherhood. But in the early nineteenth century, as manufacturing left the home for the factory, middle-class women found themselves 'freed up' to spend more time on childcare. And before long they were told that such full-time care was essential.

The daily presence or absence of men in the home also shaped the American definition of motherhood. During colonial times when men, women, and children all worked together in or near the household, there were no firm distinctions in parental responsibilities. It was the duty of both parents to rear their children, and fathers were thought to be especially important to a proper religious education. But when a man's work began to take him away from the home for most of the day—an arrangement that began with the onset of industrialization nearly 200 years ago—childrearing responsibilities fell heavily on the mother. And, once again, middle-class mothers were told that this was in the nature of things.

Household size and its contacts with the outside world have also influenced the mother role. Prior to the nineteenth century, when most households were larger than the nuclear family, when they consisted of more people than just a married couple and their children, the presence of other adults who could take a hand in childcare diluted maternal responsibility. Because the household was the site of both life and work, because there was a constant coming and going of people, the mother-child tie was but one of many relationships. As the country industrialized in the nineteenth century, however, the home and the place of work became separate. Women then remained as the only adults in the household and the mother-child relationship was thrown into sharp relief. Mothers took on all the burdens of childcare, and their performance of these tasks became a major concern. Why? Because the middle-class mother was advised that she and she alone had the weighty mission of transforming her children into the model citizens of the day.

Fertility rates also influence the mother role, but not always in the way one might expect. It seems logical that the more children a woman has, the more she will be defined by her maternal role, for the care and feeding of a large brood demand so much time. But this was not always the case. The emphasis on motherhood in the nineteenth century *increased* as fertility among the middle class *decreased*. One explanation of this anomaly lies in what has been called the 'procreative imperative' (Bernard 1974: 7; Harris 1981: 84). This refers to the promotion of cheap population growth by powerful elements in society which benefit from the rearing of 'high quality' children. As industrialization continued, the need for skilled labour correspondingly increased. Thus, the reification of maternity during the nineteenth century reflects a dual attempt to stem the falling birthrate in the middle class and increase the quality of children through long-term mother care. The emphasis on maternity was also a way of solving what became known as 'the woman question'. Once a woman's productive skills were no longer needed, what was to occupy her time? The answer was summarized in a single word: *motherhood*.

This preoccupation with motherhood and the corollary assumption that an exclusive mother-child relationship is both natural and inevitable is by no means universal. Ethnographic evidence clearly points out the variability of childcare arrangements and the ideologies that justify them. One study of 186 societies from around the world, for example, found that in less than half—46 per cent—mothers were the primary or exclusive caretakers of infants. In another 40 per cent of the societies in the sample primary care of infants was the responsibility of others, usually siblings. An even more striking finding is that in less than 20 per cent of the societies are mothers the primary or exclusive caretakers *after* infancy. The authors of this study conclude: 'According to our ratings, in the majority of these societies mothers are not the principal caretakers or companions of young children' (Weisner and Gallimore 1977: 170; for information on cross-cultural differences in childrearing values see Lamber, Hamers, and Frasure-Smith 1979).

How are we to explain this conclusion which contradicts the deeply held modern American belief in the central role of the mother in childcare? A number of factors are involved in the explanation, but one clue is that the living arrangement we take so much for granted—the married woman's residence in a nuclear family household made up exclusively of parents and children—is extremely rare cross-culturally. Such households are found in only 6.1 per cent of the societies listed in the massive Human Relations Area Files, the largest systematic compilation of cross-cultural data in the world (Weisner and Gallimore 1977: 173). So in the majority of societies other kin present in the household relieve the mother of some of the burden of childcare.

Another factor that influences the degree of maternal responsibility is the nature and location of women's productive activities. In societies with economies based on hunting and gathering or agriculture, young children typically are taken care of by an older sibling or by their mother or other female relative while these women are gathering or gardening. But in industrial societies where the workplace and the household are separate, production and childcare are incompatible. It is in these same societies—ones in which women's activities typically are limited to the domestic sphere—that we find the duties of parenting weighing most heavily on the mother (Brown 1970: 1073–8; Klevana 1980).

A study of mothers in six cultures points up the relative rarity of western industrial childcare patterns. In the American community represented in the study 92 per cent of the mothers said that they usually or always took care of their babies and children by themselves. The other five societies displayed considerably less maternal responsibility for childcare. In the words of the authors: 'The mothers of the US sample have a significantly heavier burden (or joy) of baby care than the mothers in any other society.' They explain: 'Living in nuclear families isolated from their relatives and with all their older children in school most of the day the [American] mother spends more time in charge of both babies and older children than any other group' (Minturn and Lambert 1964: 95–7, 100–1, 112–13).[1]

These studies suggest that the preoccupation of American experts with the mother-child relationship almost certainly is a result of social and economic developments in the United States and Western industrialized societies in general, societies that are characterized more than most others by exclusive mother-childcare arrangements. What we have come to think of as inevitable and biologically necessary is in great measure a consequence of our society's particular social and economic system. We are certainly not unique in believing that our brand of mother-child relationship is natural and normal. People in every culture firmly believe that *their* childrearing practices stem from nature itself (Berger and Luckmann 1966: 135).[2]

*   *   *

Raise Up Your Children Together: The Colonial Period to 1785

A distinct maternal role would have been incompatible with the realities of life during colonial times. The mother-child relationship was enmeshed in the myriad daily tasks women performed for their families' survival. They kept house, tended gardens, raised poultry and cattle, churned milk into butter and cream, butchered livestock, tanned skins, pickled and preserved food, made candles, buttons, soap, beer, and cider, gathered and processed medicinal herbs, and spun and wove wool and cotton for family clothes. The wives of farmers, merchants, and artisans were kept busy with these duties and the wives of merchants and artisans often helped in their husbands' businesses as well. Childrearing therefore largely centred on teaching children the skills needed to keep the domestic economy going. Childrearing was not a *separate* task; it was something that simply took place within the daily round of activities. It is little wonder that in 1790 a New England mother could write that her two children 'had grown out of the way' and are 'very little troble [sic]' when the younger of the two was still nursing (quoted in Cott 1977: 58; quoted in Bloch 1978b: 242).

The agrarian economy of the seventeenth and eighteenth centuries presented no clear-cut separation between the home and the world of work; the boundary between the preindustrial family and society was permeable. Male and female spheres were contiguous and often overlapped, and the demands of the domestic economy

ensured that neither sex was excluded from productive labour. Fathers, moreover, took an active role in childrearing because they worked near the household. Craftsmen and tradesmen usually had their shops at home and farmers spent the long winter months there. The prescriptive literature of the day rarely or imprecisely distinguished between 'female' or domestic themes and the 'masculine' world of work. The few colonial domestic guides addressed both men and women under the assumption that they worked together in the household (Sklar [1841] 1977; Ariès 1965).

Scholars now agree that the colonial family was not an extended one as was once thought; the best estimates are that at least 80 per cent were nuclear (but not nuclear in the same way as the small isolated nuclear family of the industrial era). The colonial family was nuclear in the formal sense in that parents and children were at its core, but mothers and fathers usually were not the only adults living in the household. Some families took in maiden aunts, or perhaps an aged parent, others had apprentices or journeymen, while domestic servants were common in the households of the prosperous. Moreover, because the typical colonial couple had six to eight offspring, children ranging from infancy to adolescence were commonly found in the same household. Finally, the practice of 'putting out' children and taking others in ensured that at least some children were not brought up exclusively by their parents. What is central to the discussion here is that during the colonial period children's relationships were not nearly as mother-centred as they later came to be in the smaller industrial variant of the nuclear family. Given the composition of the colonial American household, children must have received support from and been disciplined by a number of adults—their parents, apprentices or servants, older siblings, and perhaps other relatives as well (Demos 1970; Greven Jr 1973b; Bloch 1978b; Degler 1980: 5).

Children themselves were hardly recognized as a separate human category in the American colonies of the seventeenth and eighteenth centuries. 'There was little sense that children might somehow be a special group with their own needs and interests and capacities,' writes one historian. Virtually all of the childrearing advice of the day emphasized that children were 'meer Loans from God, which He may call for when He pleases'. Parents were told to bring up their children as good Christians and discipline was emphasized, but no mention was made of developing the child's personality, intelligence, or individuality. Quite to the contrary, most sermons dwelt on the importance of breaking the child's 'will' (Wadsworth [1712] 1972; Mather [1741] 1978; Demos 1970: 57–8).

Some children were 'put out' to work as early as six or seven years of age, and those who remained with their parents were expected to help with household chores. Girls as young as six could spin flax and boys helped in farming tasks or fetched wood. Childhood was at best a span of years lasting considerably less than a decade. Even had a family wanted a prolonged, leisurely childhood for its offspring, this was a luxury few could afford (Calhoun [1917] 1960; Demos 1970: 141).

Since infant mortality rates were high, parents expected to lose some of their children. Infant mortality in the seventeenth century, for example, ranged from 10 to 30 per cent in different parts of the colonies; this high rate was acknowledged in the sermons of the day. . . .

Although not a great deal is known about seventeenth- and eighteenth-century advice on childrearing and parental roles—the few manuals of the period were of English origin—we can glean some indication of parental duties in the American colonies from the sermons of the day. In a 1712 sermon entitled 'The Well Ordered Family or, Relative Duties', Benjamin Wadsworth, pastor of the Church of Christ in Boston, distinguished mothers' responsibilities from fathers' when he urged the former to 'suckle their children'. But then he went on to say: 'Having given these hints about Mothers, I may say of Parents (Comprehending both Father and Mother) they should provide for the outward supply and comfort of their Children. They should nourish and bring them up.' In the lengthy discussion of religious instruction and the teaching of good manners and discipline that followed, all of Wadsworth's injunctions were addressed to 'Parents'. . . .

Colonial clergymen were generally consistent in their sermons treating parental roles. Fathers were to supervise the secular and religious education of their children, teaching them to fear and respect God, but mothers also were advised of their responsibilities in this training. Both parents were admonished to set good examples for their children, and both were held responsible for their children's general well-being. Except for the greater authority bestowed on the father as head of the family, the prescribed roles for parents made no important distinctions on the basis of sex. Similarly, even in funeral sermons for women, there was little mention of motherhood as opposed to the more generalized concept of parenthood. In the few sermons specifically addressed to mothers, the duties laid out were the same as those addressed to both parents, and 'none of these were distinctly maternal obligations' (Frost 1973; Masson 1976; Bloch 1978a: 106; Ulrich 1979).[3]

To be sure, women were thought to have special ties to their children during infancy, and infants were described as 'hers' by both men and women. The realities of reproduction were certainly recognized, and here we find special advice to mothers. A number of clergy inveighed against the practice of wet nursing, which in fact was quite rare in the American colonies. In describing the duties of a righteous woman Cotton Mather admonished: 'Her care for the Bodies of her Children shows itself in the nursing of them herself. . . . She is not a Dame that shall scorn to nourish in the world, the Children whom she has already nourished in her Womb.' Wet nursing was condemned because it was thought contrary to God's will and dangerous to the physical health of the child, not because it was believed to interfere with the development of a bond between mother and child. Some ministers actually warned women against 'excessive fondness' for their children (Mather [1741] 1978: 105; Bloch 1978a: 105; Norton 1980: 90, 94).

Once children reached the age of one or two, when their survival was more certain, all directives regarding childrearing were addressed to *both* parents. Fathers were expected to take a larger role once children reached an educable age. This was particularly true among the Puritans, who believed that the 'masculine' qualities of religious understanding and self-discipline were essential in childrearing. One of the few distinctions made in the sermons of the day was in vocational training; this was the responsibility of the parent of the same sex as the child, although sometimes responsibility was removed from the family entirely. Children, particularly boys, often were sent out at age nine or ten to apprentice in other households while children from other families were taken in to serve as apprentices (Ryan 1975: 60; Bloch 1978a: 107; Bloch 1978b: 242; Kessler-Harris 1981: 29).

A cult of motherhood did not exist because it would have been incongruous in this setting. Women were far too busy to devote long hours to purely maternal duties, and fathers, older siblings, and other adults were also on hand to see to children's needs and discipline. Moreover, because of high mortality rates, a woman was not likely to become obsessive about her children, some of whom would not survive to adulthood. It is not surprising that, as one scholar had remarked of the colonial period, '. . . motherhood was singularly unidealized, usually disregarded as a subject, and even at times actually denigrated.' Although women bore and cared for very young children, this role received less emphasis in the prescriptive literature than nearly any other aspect of women's lives. Motherhood, when it was discussed at all, was merged with the parental, domestic, and religious obligations of both sexes (Bloch 1978a: 101, 103–4).

The Transition: 1785–1820

The cult of motherhood is usually associated with the middle and late nineteenth century, but we can see its roots in the prescriptive literature of the very late eighteenth century and the first decades of the nineteenth century. During these years the earliest hints of a special and distinct maternal role began appearing in sermons, domestic guides, medical volumes, and childrearing manuals; for the first time writers began stressing the critical importance of maternal care in early childhood.

It is significant that these years also witnessed the beginnings of the industrial revolution. Markets slowly expanded, agriculture efficiency increased, transportation costs decreased—all developments that led to greater specialization in the economic division of labour. What is centrally important to my argument is that home industry, which typified the colonial period, began to wane. Gradually home manufacture for family use was replaced by standardized factory production for the wider market. The first industry that moved from the home to the factory was textile manufacture, one of women's traditional household tasks. As early as 1807 there were a dozen large textile mills in New England, and by 1810 farm families could buy cloth in village shops and from itinerant peddlers (Smith 1796: 58; Brownlee 1974: 77; Ryan 1975: 91; Cott 1977: 24).

The replacement of homespun by manufactured goods was nonetheless a gradual process. In 1810 Secretary of Treasury Albert Gallatin estimated that 'about two-thirds of the clothing, including . . . house and table linen used by the inhabitants of the United States, who do not reside in cities, is the product of family manufactures.' In terms of monetary value this was about ten times the amount produced outside the home. Class membership and place of residence were primary factors in the reduction of home manufacture; more prosperous families, urban dwellers, and those living in the older settled areas of the East led the way in the substitution of store-bought goods for homemade ones (quoted in Degler 1980: 361).

While women's role in the domestic economy gradually diminished, important changes also were taking place in the family. By the late eighteenth century the domestic sphere had begun to contract; there were fewer servants than there had been earlier, the practice of taking in apprentices and journeymen had all but ceased, and with the expansion of economic opportunities fathers were spending less time at home. The physical separation of the home and the place of work already was under way for artisans, merchants, and professionals. But while fewer adults remained in the household, children were now living in it until they reached adolescence. With the demise of the 'putting out' system, middle-class children were no longer apprenticed to other families and by 1820 they generally lived at home until about the age of fifteen. The nuclear family itself became smaller as the birthrate declined, particularly in the more densely populated eastern regions of the country. A study of Gloucester, Massachusetts, found that women who married before 1740 had an average of 6.7 children while those who married after that date averaged 4.6 children. Similarly, by the late eighteenth century in Andover, Massachusetts, women typically had five or six children when their grandmothers had averaged seven or eight (Greven 1970; Bloch 1978a: 114; Bloch 1978b: 251; Degler 1980).

Not only was the middle-class household smaller in size but with the onset of industrialization it was no longer a wholly self-contained unit whose members were bound by common tasks. For the first time the place, scope, and pace of men's and women's work began to differ sharply. As a distinct division of labour gradually arose between the home and the world of work, the household's contacts with the outside decreased. By the first decades of the nineteenth century the term *home* had come to be synonymous with *place of retirement or retreat* (Cott 1977).

Ideologies about the nature of children also began to change. By 1800 the Calvinist belief in infant damnation had begun to give way to the Lockean doctrine of the *tabula rasa*, which stressed the lack of innate evil (or good), and the importance of experience in moulding the child. In 1976 one physician wrote, '. . . that any children are born with vicious inclinations, I would not willingly believe.' Children, at least middle-class children, began to be seen as individuals. They were no longer viewed as 'miniature adults' whose natural inclinations toward evil had to be broken: childhood was becoming a distinct period in the life cycle. The dictum that children were to be treated as individuals with special needs and potentials requiring special nurturing placed a new and heavy responsibility on parents; failure in childrearing could no longer 'be blamed on native corruption', explains one historian (Smith 1796: 108; Frost 1973: 87; Slater 1977).

These altered views of children coincided with the decline of the birthrate in the late eighteenth and early nineteenth centuries. The decline in New England, for example, was greatest between 1810 and 1830, and, according to one scholar, during these years 'the new sensibility towards children first became highly visible' (Slater 1977: 73). But the lower birthrate, implying fewer children per family and perhaps more attention paid to each child, only partially explains the fundamental change in thinking about children. Both the gradual redefinition of women's role and the redefinition of childhood were linked to larger societal changes affecting middle-class life.

The prescriptive literature on childcare in these years was in many ways transitional between the stark dicta of the colonial clergy and the effusive writings of the later nineteenth-century advice givers. Prior to about 1830 such literature did not enjoy mass circulation but appeared in periodical articles, printed sermons, and occasional treatises. All of it came under the rubric 'domestic education' and was written by ministers, physicians, and parents for a white middle-

and upper-middle-class audience. Most pertinent here was the transitional image of the role of middle-class mother. Motherhood in fact was being revamped. Duties that had once belonged to both mothers and fathers or to fathers alone were now becoming the near exclusive province of mothers. One historian of the period notes that 'now fathers began to recede into the background in writings about the domestic education of children.' Treatises on the treatment of childhood diseases, diet, hygiene, and exercise for young children now addressed mothers alone. Some of the medical texts also offered advice on the psychological management of young children, stressing for the first time the importance of the mother's influence during the impressionable years (Slater 1977; Bloch 1978a: 112–13).

Arguments against wet nursing also took on a new cast. Whereas earlier commentators condemned the practice for its ill effects on a child's health, writers now added that wet nursing tainted the child's character. One of the earliest references to a special relationship between mother and child appears in this context. A 1798 tract printed in England (but read in America) urged women to nurse their children so as to avoid 'the destruction, or at least the diminution of the sympathy between mother and child'. Nursing was no longer simply a woman's religious duty but the key to her future happiness as well. 'Those children who are neglected by their mothers during their infant yeas,' wrote Dr Hugh Smith in 1796, 'forget all duty and affection towards them, when such mothers are in the decline of life.' The same author exalted in the joys of breast feeding: 'Tell me you who know the rapturous delight, how complete is the bliss of enfolding in your longing arms the dear, dear fruits of all your pains!' . . . (Smith 1796: 54, 57; quoted in Frost 1973: 72).

*   *   *

Another early guide is Dr William Buchan's *Advice to Mothers*, published in Boston in 1809. The growing importance of the maternal role is obvious here. 'The more I reflect on the situation of a mother, the more I am struck by the extent of her powers,' wrote Dr Buchan. Clearly not all mothers are equal: 'By a mother I do not mean the woman who merely brings a child into the world, but her who faithfully discharges the duties of a parent—whose chief concern is the well-being of her infant.' But mothers walked a narrow line between neglect and overindulgence. 'The obvious paths of nature are alike forsaken by the woman who gives up the care of her infant to a hireling . . . who neglects her duties as a mother; and by her who carries these duties to excess; who makes an idol of her child' (Buchan [1809] 1972: 3, 77). This is the first mention of a theme that was to be heard over and over again in the prescriptive writings of the nineteenth and much of the twentieth centuries. Mothers must be ever on guard to do their job properly—always lurking in the background of the advice books were the pitiful figures of mothers who had failed, mothers who had not taken their duties seriously, or mothers who had performed them with excessive zeal. . . .

Emphasis on the mother role was not limited to advice manuals. Between 1800 and 1820 a new theme appeared in many New England sermons: mothers are more important than fathers in shaping 'the tastes, sentiments, and habits of children'. One New Hampshire minister proclaimed in 1806: 'Weighty beyond expression is the charge devolved to the female parent. It is not within the province of human wisdom to calculate all the happy consequences resulting from the persevering assiduity of mothers.' While sermons of the day did not deny all paternal responsibility, they made clear that raising children was a specialized domestic activity that was largely the province of mothers. As one scholar of the period notes, this 'emphasis departed from (and undermined) the patriarchal family ideal in which the mother, while entrusted with the physical care of her children, let their religious, moral, and intellectual guidance to her husband' (quoted in Cott 1977: 86; quoted in Bloch 1978a: 112).

Although little is known about the actual childrearing practices in the early nineteenth century, it is clear that the aim of the advice manuals and the sermons dealing with the topic was to increase the amount of time and attention mothers devoted to infants and small children. For the first time in American history the care of young children was viewed as a full-time task, as a distinct profession requiring special knowledge. What had once been done according to tradition now demanded proper study. Even arguments favouring women's education now came to be couched in terms of the woman's role as mother; women were to be educated because the formation of the future citizens of the republic lay in their hands (Sicherman 1975: 496). It is ironic, indeed, but by no means coincidental, that as their sphere narrowed and became more isolated, middle-class women were told that their sphere's importance to the future of the new nation was boundless.

Historian Ruth H. Bloch notes that economic factors exercised a 'push-pull' effect on childrearing responsibilities. As the domestic production of middle-class mothers began to wane and their domestic work lost its commercial value, fathers began to spend more and more time working outside the home, as did other adults who had once resided in the household (Bloch 1978b: 250). Women, left alone at home with their children, who were now living there until adolescence, began to assume almost complete responsibility for childcare. The prescriptive literature, with its newly expanded definition of motherhood, was thus a response to these structural changes in society. In essence, as the female role in domestic production declined, the middle-class woman was told to focus on reproduction.

Motherhood, A Fearful Responsibility: 1820–70

The concept of the mother role which prevailed from the late eighteenth century to about 1820 was, in the words of one historian, 'a rare and subdued hint of the extravagant celebration of motherhood to come' (Abbott 1833: 162; Calhoun [1918] 1960: 52; Ryan 1975: 126). Beginning in the 1820s and gaining momentum in the 1830s and 1840s, a flood of manuals and periodical articles gave advice on the maternal role, exulted in the joys of motherhood, and told women that good mothering was not only the key to their own and their children's happiness but crucial to the nation's destiny as well.

This period between 1820 and 1860 was one of rapid industrialization; industrial production in fact doubled every decade. . . . The most salient change occurring during these years was the eventual demise of the self-sufficient household. The growth of industry, technological advances, improvements in transportation, and the increasing specialization of agriculture made more goods available, and the household became more and more reliant on the market to meet its needs. In simple terms the period between 1820 and 1860 witnessed the substitution of store-bought goods for home-manufactured goods, and this development had a profound impact on women's work. Even as early as the 1820s women's domestic production had diminished in scope and variety to the extent that they were left with only a residue of their former household duties. In New England by 1830 home spinning and weaving were largely replaced by manufactured textiles, and by mid-century women's productive skills had become even more superfluous; butter, candles, soap, medicine, buttons, and cloth were widely available in stores. By 1860 women's contribution to household production continued to a significant extent only in remote frontier regions. The noted feminist and abolitionist Sarah Grimké remarked on the decline of home manufacture in 1838: 'When all manufactures were domestic, then the domestic function might well consume all the time of a very able-bodied woman. But nowadays . . . when so much of woman's work is done by the butcher and the baker, by the tailor and the cook, and the gas maker . . . you see how much of woman's time is left for other functions' (Cott 1977; Ehrenreich and English 1978; quoted in Degler 1980).

The removal of production from the home to the factory led to the breakdown of the once close relationship between the household and the business of society. For the first time 'life', that is, the home, was divided from 'work'. Not only had the two spheres become separate, they were now seen as incompatible; the home was a retreat from the competitive world of commerce and industry, a place of warmth and respite where moral values prevailed. The business of the world no longer took place at home.

These economic and social developments were of course not unique to the United States. A similar series of events occurred in England in the seventeenth century. There, in the words of one scholar of the period, 'the old familial economic partnership of husband and wife was being undermined. The wife was being driven from her productive role. The concept of the husband supporting his family was replacing mutuality in earning power . . . [the wife's] place might still be in the home, but her husband was no longer an integral part of it' (Thompson 1974: 75).

The American household continued to shrink throughout the nineteenth century. By 1850 the ancillary household members had moved out—an unmarried sister might be teaching school in town and greater numbers of domestic servants were leaving the middle-class household to take factory jobs. . . . Part of this decrease, however, resulted from a falling birthrate.

Ideas about the nature of children continued to evolve. The neutral *tabula rasa* of the first decades of the nineteenth century was supplanted by the idea of the 'sweet angels of the Romantic era'. After 1830 children were routinely depicted as beings of great purity and innocence. They were naturally close to God and their virtuous proclivities had only to be gently moulded to ensure eternal salvation. Closely allied with this idealized image of the young was the conviction

that *mothers and mothers alone* had the power to transform malleable infants into moral, productive adults. For this reason many warned against the dangers of hiring nurses, for even the best nurse was never an adequate substitute for the mother herself. Only a mother's care and influence, not that of fathers, older siblings, relatives, or servants, could fulfil the special physical and spiritual needs of the growing child. Motherhood had not only become a careerlike responsibility but the responsibility had grown longer and longer in duration. By the mid-nineteenth century middle-class children remained at home until well into adolescence, and throughout the century there was a tendency to prolong dependence. Children left home at a later and later age (Slater 1977; Wishy 1968: 40; Degler 1980: 69).

Some scholars claim that the nineteenth century's concern with the child as an individual and with proper childrearing methods was the result of a decline in infant mortality. Parents, they argue, became more certain that their children would grow to adulthood and so were willing to invest more time and energy in them. Historian Carl Degler faults this thesis, citing data that suggests that infant mortality did not decline. In fact, infant mortality might even have been higher than the official statistics indicate with the likelihood of a high mortality rate among unreported births. One could argue on this basis that at least part of the growing concern for the child was because infant mortality rates did remain so high. Catherine Beecher and other manual writers contended that proper childcare would help to prevent the deaths of infants and young children (Beecher [1841] 1977; Degler 1980: 72–3).

Population growth from reproduction did in fact decline steadily as the birthrate fell throughout the nineteenth century. By 1850 the average white woman was bearing only half as many children as her grandmother had. Even more striking is the 50 per cent decline in the completed fertility rate for the century as a whole; it fell from 7.04 children per white woman in 1800 to 3.56 in

1900. The question, of course, is why did women bear fewer children? In the words of anthropologist Marvin Harris, in an industrializing, urbanizing society children 'tend to cost more and to be economically less valuable to their parents than children on farms' (Degler 1980: 181; Kessler-Harris 1981: 34; Harris 1981: 81).

Children in agrarian societies cost relatively little to raise and they help out by doing a variety of tasks even when they are young. But in cities the expense of rearing children increases as does their period of dependency; most or all of the items a child needs must be purchased, and schooling is required before the child can become economically independent. In essence, urban children contribute less and cost more. Therefore, as the nineteenth century progressed, the shift in the costs and benefits of having children particularly affected the middle class, whose children required longer and longer periods of socialization before they could make it on their own outside the home. The rearing of 'quality' children, children who enjoyed a long period of dependency while they were schooled to take their 'rightful' position in society, was an ever more costly process. Is it any wonder then that the average middle-class family had fewer and fewer children as the century progressed?

The immense outpouring of advice manuals and other prescriptive writings after 1830 cannot be adequately explained by continued high levels of infant mortality or even by the fact that women were having fewer children and simply had the time to make a greater investment in each one. Another factor in the advice-giving boom was the nation's slowly growing need for children who would be reared to become professionals or to take the business and management positions being created by the industrializing process. What better and cheaper way to accomplish this than by urging middle-class women to devote many years and large quantities of their (unpaid) time and energy to nurturing the future captains of business and industry?

Another key to understanding the paeans to motherhood is the falling fertility rate of the middle class. But the relationship is by no means a simple one. It seems logical that if women had been taking these paeans seriously they would have had more rather than fewer children, and it is of course naïve to assume that fertility decisions are made on the basis of advice books. I believe the line between the two is as follows: as fertility declined among the white middle class, there was growing alarm in certain quarters. Where were the future leaders in business and industry to come from? Who was going to manage the nation's burgeoning industries? At a time when the fertility of the nonwhite and the foreign-born was higher than that of native-born whites, the country's élite feared that the 'backbone' of the nation was being diluted by 'lesser types'. The glorification of maternity which was directed at potential mothers of the 'backbone', was an attempt, albeit an unsuccessful one, to encourage their reproductive activity.[4]

Scholars are not certain just how people in the nineteenth century controlled their fertility, but there is evidence that American women began practising abortion more frequently after 1840. One historian estimates one abortion for every twenty-five or thirty live births during the first decades of the century, a proportion that rose to about one in every five or six live births during the 1850s and 1860s. Most contemporary physicians agreed that the primary motive for abortion was control of family size, and they cited as evidence the fact that by far the largest group practising abortion was married women. It is significant that prior to the nineteenth century there were no laws prohibiting abortion during the first few months of pregnancy. The procedure was not illegal until 'quickening', that is, until the first movements of the fetus are felt at about four months. The first laws banning abortion were passed between 1821 and 1841; during those two decades ten states and one territory specifically outlawed its practice. By the time of the Civil War nearly every state had laws prohibiting abortion at all stages of fetal development (Gordon 1977: 52, 57n; Mohr 1978: 50, 20).

I do not think that mere coincidence accounts for concern about the falling birthrate, laws banning abortion, and the publication of numerous childcare manuals and articles lauding the maternal role, all appearing at roughly the same time. The outpourings of the advice givers reflected the wider anxiety about middle-class women's declining fertility and sought to counteract it by dwelling on the joys of motherhood for their white, middle-class audience.

The contraction of women's productive activities in the now smaller and more isolated nuclear household provided the necessary setting for this expanding emphasis on the mother role. There was now a sizeable, literate audience of home-bound women who could be advised of the importance of motherhood and given suggestions of time-consuming methods for its proper discharge. In short, as the domestic sphere contracted and middle-class women found their lives increasingly centred around their husbands and children, they were advised of the gravity of their redefined role. What higher calling was there than shaping the future leaders of the nation?

Maternal Ideals

A number of recurrent themes in nineteenth-century childrearing manuals and periodical articles were only weakly developed or were entirely absent from the prescriptive writings of an earlier era. Foremost among these are that childcare is the exclusive province of women, that motherhood is their *primary* function, and that mothers, and mothers alone, are responsible for their children's character development and future success or failure. By the 1830s motherhood had been transformed into a mission so that 'the entire burden of the child's well-being in this life and the next' was in its mother's hands (*The Ladies' Museum* 1825; Sunley 1963: 152). These themes, moreover, were

not limited to childrearing manuals. Popular novels, poems, and biographies of famous men all stressed the important role of the mother in shaping her child's fate. Middle-class women were told that they had it in their power to produce joy or misery, depending on how they performed their parental duties. These sentiments were echoed in a burgeoning literature on 'female character' which claimed that women were innately nurturant, domestic, and selfless, all qualities that made them 'naturals' at childrearing.

One of the most striking features of the childrearing advice of the mid-nineteenth century is the disappearance of references to fathers. While some earlier tracts were addressed exclusively to mothers, most were written for 'parents', and there was even an occasional 'advice to fathers' manual. This shift from *parental* to *maternal* responsibility is evident in Philip Greven's collection of sermons, treatises, and other sources of advice on childrearing dating from 1628 to 1861 (Greven Jr 1973a). The first eight excerpts, originally published between 1629 and 1814, are all addressed to 'parents'. It is not until John Abbott's 1833 essay 'On the Mother's Role in Education' that the maternal role is highlighted and mothers are given the primary responsibility for childcare.

Mothers were offered abundant advice on the feeding, dressing, washing, and general management of infants and young children. They were told how to deal with teething, toilet training, masturbation, and childhood diseases. But the mother's physical care of her children was a minor task compared to her job of socializing them. Women were advised that their every thought and gesture, no matter how seemingly inconsequential, carried a message to the child. Women were to be ever on their guard lest they impede their offspring's moral development.

Many writers stressed the sentimental benefits of an activity that received no material rewards. 'How entire and perfect is the dominion over the unformed character of your infant. Write what you will, upon the printless tablet, with your wand of love,' wrote Mrs Sigourney in *Letters to Mothers* (1838).

Women's education is justified, some advice givers claimed, because of women's influence on the next generation. *Maternal* education, however, was what they really sought. In an 1845 tome, for example, Edward Mansfield cited three reasons for educating women: '. . . that they should as *mothers*, be the fit teachers of infant men. That they should be the fit teachers of American men. That they should be the fit teachers of Christian men' (Mansfield 1845: 105, emphasis in original).

Motherhood, as depicted in the prescriptive writings of the mid-nineteenth century, was a full-time occupation demanding time-consuming unpaid labour. 'It truly requires all the affection of even a fond mother to administer dutifully to the numerous wants of a young child,' wrote William Dewees. Mrs Sigourney agreed. She saw a mother as 'a sentinel who should never sleep at her post', recommending that women get household help to perform manual tasks so that the mother 'may be able to become the constant directress of her children'. There is no question that mothering was work; infants should be fed on demand, and toilet training and 'moral education' should begin at a few months of age. Cleanliness was stressed and clothes were to be washed often and changed as soon as they got dirty. Furthermore, the good mother would keep careful records of her children's behaviour and development. The Reverend Abbott told mothers to 'study their duty', while Mrs Sigourney urged women to 'study night and day the science that promotes the welfare of our infant' (Abbot 1833: 169; Sigourney 1838: 28, 82, 87; Dewees 1847: 64–5).

Mothers, according to the advice givers, were perfectly suited to care for their children; no one else could do the job as well or, one might add, as cheaply. As far as the mother's duties permitted, she was to 'take the entire care of her own child', advised the popular domestic writer, Lydia Maria Child. During the first 'sacred' year, concurred

Mrs Sigourney, 'trust not your treasure too much to the charge of hirelings. Have it under your superintendence night and day. The duty of your office admits of no substitute.' But what of other family members? Are they of no help? Yes: '. . . brothers and sisters, the father, all perform their part, but the mother does the most,' opined the author of a *Parents Magazine* article, who went on to issue a stern warning. Children whose mothers did not 'take the entire care of them' faced real danger; a mother 'cannot be long relieved without hazard or exchanged without loss' (Child [1831] 1972: 4; Sigourney 1838: 16, 32, 87; *Parents Magazine* 1841: 156).

A corollary of the focus on mothers was the disappearance of fathers from the childrearing manuals of the nineteenth century. Advice books assumed that children spent most of their time with their mothers, not their fathers, even though by law and custom final authority was patriarchal. Paternal responsibilities were rarely spelled out. For example, in answering the question 'Is there nothing for fathers to do?' Reverend Abbott responded that there are many paternal duties 'which will require time and care'. But the only duties he actually stipulated for fathers were 'to lead their families to God' and to teach their children to 'honor' their mother. Although some advice givers saw fathers as the primary disciplinarians in the family, others urged mothers to punish their children's misbehaviour before fathers returned home in the evening. Even daily prayers, once led by the father as head of the household, had now become the province of the mother (Abbott 1833: 155–6).

The occasional references to fathers in the prescriptive writings of the day either remarked on their sovereignty in the home or noted their real responsibilities outside of it. A father's duties, advised the *Ladies' Companion*, are 'the acquisitions of wealth, the advancement of his children in worldly honor—these are his self-imposed tasks'.

*   *   *

By the mid-nineteenth century a gooey senti-mentality had come to distinguish motherhood from fatherhood. A sample from a 'ladies' maga-zine' of the day reveals the tone: 'Is there a feeling that activates the human heart so powerful as that of maternal affection? Who but women can feel the tender sensation so strong? The father, indeed, may press his lovely infant to his manly heart, but does it thrill with those feelings which irresistibly overcome the mother?' (*Ladies' Literary Cabinet* 1822: 5).

These patterns of ideological change are also apparent in an analysis of sixteenth- to nine-teenth-century childrearing responsibilities in England. English manuals of the sixteenth and seventeenth centuries told parents to 'co-rear' their children: eighteenth-century manuals depicted mothers as the primary childrearers but expressed some anxiety about this; by the nine-teenth century mothers were the primary rearers 'without anxiety' (Stewart, Winter, and Jones 1975: 701).

In America by mid-century good mothering was not only essential to the well-being and future of the child but the lack of such exclusive care was considered a threat to the very moral fibre of the nation. 'The destiny of a nation is shaped by its character,' Reverend Beckwith proclaimed, 'and that character . . . will ever be found to be molded chiefly by maternal hands.' 'When our land is filled with pious and patriotic mothers, then will it be filled with virtuous and patriotic men,' agreed Reverend Abbott. But it is clear that women's contribution to the young republic was to be indirect. In the words of Daniel Webster: 'It is by promulgation of sound morals in the community, and more especially by the training and instruction of the young that woman performs her part toward the preservation of a free government.' . . . (Abbott 1833: 153; Beckwith 1850: 4; quoted in Kuhn 1947: 34).[5] As part of the effort to convince middle-class women of their crucial role in the nation's destiny—a role wholly dependent on the diligent performance of their maternal duties—moral educators frequently cited the mothers of famous men.

*   *   *

Many advice writers dwelt long and graph-ically on the general evils that sprang from poor mothering. An 1841 issue of *Parents Magazine* contained a case study of a convict, whose life of crime was analysed in the following terms: 'His mother, although hopefully pious, never prayed with him in private. . . . There was no maternal association in the place of their resi-dence.' Then a warning was issued: 'Reader, are you a parent?. . . *Train up a child in the way he should go.*' Even such cataclysms as the French Revolution, with its 'atheism, licentiousness, and intemperance', could be avoided by 'seizing upon the infant mind and training it up under moral and religious influence', suggested another author in the same magazine. Mrs Elizabeth Hall, writing in *The Mother's Assistant*, made the point succinctly; 'Perhaps there is no proposition that is so hackneyed, and at the same time so little understood, as that women are the prime cause of all the good and evil in human actions. . . . Yes, mothers, in a certain sense the destiny of a redeemed world is put into your hands' (Hall 1849: 25; quoted in Kuhn 1947: 67, emphasis in original). Mothers were given a strong message. They were the potential source of *both* evil and good in the world, so that they had best be mindful of the proper per-formance of their maternal duties.

Many authors pointed out that while women should not go out into the world, the mother role, because of its far-reaching influence, still gave women a lofty position in society. 'Though she may not teach from the portico nor thunder from the forum . . . she may form and send forth the sages that shall govern and renovate the world,' wrote Catherine Beecher, the popular domestic educator. 'The patriotism of women,' Mrs Sigourney agreed, 'is not to thunder in sen-ates'—it is to be expressed in the 'office of mater-nal teacher'. A writer in *Ladies' Magazine* noted that a mother's influence is 'unseen, unfelt', but through it 'she is forming the future patriot, statesman, or enemy of his country; more than this she is sowing the seeds of virtue or vice which will fit him for Heaven or for eternal misery' (Beecher 1829: 54; Sigourney 1838: 13, 16; *Ladies' Magazine* 1840: 246).

The rewards of motherhood were extravagantly described by the advice givers. To wit: 'My friends,' wrote Mrs Sigourney, 'if in becoming a mother, you have reached the climax of your happiness, you have also taken a higher place on the scale of being.' Since children have the power to change their mothers for the better and bring them joy, no matter how difficult the tasks of motherhood, a mother 'would willingly have endured a thousand fold for such a payment'. Children also could provide their mothers with eternal salvation. 'Does not the little cherub in his way guide you to heaven, marking the pathway by the flowers he scatters as he goes?' queried Mrs Child. There was no doubt that children were the keys to feminine fulfilment. The love of children, proclaimed an editorial in *Godey's Lady's Book*, 'is as necessary to a woman's perfect development, as the sunshine and the rain are to the health and beauty of the flowers'. Not only was a woman's entire happiness dependent on her civilizing task, her very identity was derived from it. 'A woman is nobody. A wife is everything . . . and a mother is, next to God, all powerful,' trumpeted a writer in a Philadelphia newspaper at mid-century (quoted in Calhoun [1918] 1960: 84–5; Child [1831] 1972: 9; Sigourney 1838: 2, 24; *Godey's Lady's Book* 1860: 272).

This preoccupation with motherhood is baffling unless firmly set within its larger social and economic context. The demise of the self-contained household economy, the isolation of a much reduced living unit, the segregation of the home from the work place, and the resultant segregation of daily life into male and female spheres were all elements in the stage setting in which this ideology emerged. These factors, rather than any strong domestic propensity in women, explain the overweening emphasis on the mother role. On this point I take issue with the historian Carl Degler, who writes that since only women bore and could feed children in the early years, it is not surprising that 'the ideology of domesticity stressed that women's destiny was motherhood'. But hadn't women always borne and nursed children? Why does this ideology appear in full strength only after 1820? In the words of another historian, Mary Ryan, why for the first time was 'childhood socializaton, and not merely the physical care of infants . . . subsumed under the category of motherhood?' Why, asks another student of the subject, if there had always been mothers, had motherhood just been invented? The answer lies in the structural changes occurring in nineteenth-century society, changes that led to the increased seclusion of women and children in the home, the decreasing burden of household manufacture, the need for 'high quality' children, and the growing concern with the declining birthrate of the white middle class. These changes more than adequately explain why motherhood, as never before, 'stood out as a discrete task' (Ryan 1975: 84; Cott 1977: 84; Degler 1980; Dally 1982: 17).

Notes

1. This study does not measure the actual amount of time mothers spent with their infants, only whether mothers had primary or exclusive care of them.

2. This is what has been called 'the most important confidence trick that society plays on the individual—to make appear as necessary what is in fact a bundle of contingencies'.

3. I am indebted to Bloch's two articles for the sources contained in this and the next section of the chapter. They are the most thorough research on the prescriptive literature of the colonial period and early nineteenth century that I have found.

4. Although the fear of 'race suicide' is usually associated with the very late nineteenth and early

twentieth centuries and with the figure of Theodore Roosevelt, there were in fact references to it prior to the Civil War. See L. Gordon, *Woman's Body, Woman's Right* (New York, 1977), ch. 7, and A.W. Calhoun, *A Social History of the American Family: Since the Civil War* (New York, [1919] 1960), ch. 11.

5. Somewhat later the British sociologist Herbert Spencer, who was widely read in the United States, propounded a similar idea when he wrote that 'Children . . . had to be long nurtured by female parents' for 'social progress' to take place (quoted in L. Duffin, 'Prisoners of Progress: Women and Evolution' in *The Nineteenth Century Woman*, eds S. Delmot and L. Duffin [New York, 1978], 78).

References

Abbott, Rev. J.S.C. 1833. *The Mother at Home* (New York: American Tract Society).

Ariès, P. 1965. *Centuries of Childhood* (New York: Vintage).

Beckwith, G.C. 1850. 'The Fate of Nations Dependent on Mothers', *The Mother's Assistant* 15: 4.

Beecher, C. 1829. *Suggestions Respecting Improvements in Education* (New York: Hartford, Packard, and Butler).

———. [1841] 1977. *A Treatise on Domestic Economy* (New York: Schocken).

Berger, P.L., and T. Luckmann. 1966. *The Social Construction of Reality* (New York: Doubleday).

Bernard, J. 1974. *The Future of Motherhood* (New York: Penguin).

Bloch, R.H. 1978a. 'American Feminine Ideals in Transition: The Rise of the Moral Mother, 1785–1815', *Feminist Studies* 4: 106.

———. 1978b. 'Untangling the Roots of Modern Sex Roles: A Survey of Four Centuries of Change', *Signs* 4: 242.

Brown, J.K. 1970. 'A Note on the Division of Labor by Sex', *American Anthropologist* 72: 1073–8.

Brownlee, W.E. 1974. *Dynamics of Ascent: A History of the American Economy* (New York: Alfred A. Knopf).

Buchan, W. [1809] 1972. *Advice to Mothers* reprinted in *The American Physician and Child Rearing: Two Guides 1809–1894* (New York: Arno Press).

Calhoun, A.W. [1917] 1960. *A Social History of the American Family: The Colonial Period* (New York: Barnes and Noble).

———. [1918] 1960. *A Social History of the American Family: From Independence through the Civil War* (New York: Barnes and Noble).

Child, L.M. [1831] 1972. *The Mother's Book* (New York: Arno Press).

Cott, N.F. 1977. *The Bonds of Womanhood: 'Woman's Sphere' in New England, 1780–1835* (New Haven: Yale University Press).

Dally, A. 1982. *Inventing Motherhood* (London: Burnett Books Ltd).

Degler, C.N. 1980. *At Odds: Women and the Family in American from the Revolution to the Present* (New York: Oxford University Press).

Demos, J. 1970. *A Little Commonwealth: Family Life in Plymouth Colony* (New York: Oxford University Press).

Dewees, W. 1847. *A Treatise on the Physical and Medical Treatment of Children*, 10th edn (Philadelphia: Blanchard and Lea).

Ehrenreich, B., and D. English. 1978. *For Her Own Good: 150 Years of the Experts' Advice to Women* (New York: Anchor).

Frost, J.W. 1973. *The Quaker Family in Colonial America: A Portrait of the Society of Friends* (New York: St Martin's Press).

Gordon, L. 1977. *Woman's Body, Woman's Right* (New York: Penguin).

Greven, Jr, P.J. 1970. *Four Generations: Population, Land, and Family in Colonial Andover, Massachusetts* (Ithaca, NY: Cornell University Press).

———. 1973a. *Child Rearing Concepts, 1628–1861* (Itasca, IL: Peacock).

———. 1973b. 'Family Structure in Seventeenth Century Andover, Massachusetts' in *The American Family in Socio-Historical Perspective*, ed. M. Gordon (New York).

Hall, E.S. 1849. 'A Mother's Influence', *The Mother's Assistant* 1: 25.

Harris, M. 1981. *American Now: The Anthropology of a Changing Culture* (New York: Simon and Schuster).

Kessler-Harris, A. 1981. *Women Have Always Worked* (Westbury, NY: The Feminist Press).

Klevana, W.M. 1980. 'Does Labor Time Increase with Industrialization? A Survey of Time Allocation Studies', *Current Anthropology* 21: 279–98.

Kuhn, A.L. 1947. *The Mother's Role in Childhood Education: New England Concepts 1830–1860* (New Haven: Yale University Press).

Ladies' Literary Cabinet. Jan. 1822. 5: 5.

Ladies' Magazine. 1840. 'Influence of Women—Past and Present', 13: 246.

The Ladies' Museum. 1825. 'Maternity' 1 (Sept.): 31.

Lamber, W.E., J.F. Hamers, and N. Frasure-Smith. 1979. *Child Rearing Values: A Cross-national Study* (New York).

Mansfield, E. 1845. *The Legal Rights, Liabilities, and Duties of Women* (Salem, MA: John P. Jewett).

Masson, M.W. 1976. 'The Typology of the Female as a Model for the Regenerate: Puritan Teaching, 1690–1730', *Signs* 2: 304–15.

Mather, C. [1741] 1978. *Ornaments of the Daughters of Zion*, 3rd edn (Delmar, NY: Scholars Facsimiles and Reprints).

Minturn, L. and W.W. Lambert. 1964. *Mothers of Six Cultures* (New York: John Wiley).

Mohr, J.C. 1978. *Abortion in America: The Origins and Evolution of National Policy 1800–1900* (New York: Oxford University Press).

Norton, M.B. 1980. *Liberty's Daughters: The Revolutionary Experience of American Women* (Boston: Houghton Mifflin).

Parents Magazine. March 1841.'The Responsibility of Mothers', 1: 156.

Ryan, M.P. 1975. *Womanhood in America: From Colonial Times to the Present* (New York: New Viewpoints).

Sicherman, B. 1975. 'American History', *Signs* 1: 461–85.

Sigourney. 1838. *Letters to Mothers* (Hartford: Hudson and Skinner).

Sklar, K.K. [1841] 1977. 'Introduction' in C.E. Beecher, *A Treatise on Domestic Economy* (New York: Schocken).

Slater, P.G. 1977. *Children in the New England Mind* (Hamden, CN: Archon).

Smith, H. 1796. *Letters to Married Women on Nursing and the Management of Children*, 2nd edn (Philadelphia: Mathew Carey).

Stewart, A.J., D.G. Winter, and A.D. Jones. 1975. 'Coding Categories for the Study of Child Rearing from Historical Sources', *Journal of Interdisciplinary History* 5: 701.

Sunley, R. 1963. 'Early Nineteenth Century American Literature on Child Rearing' in *Childhood in Contemporary Cultures*, eds M. Mead and M. Wolfenstein (Chicago: University of Chicago Press).

Thompson, R. 1974. *Women in Stuart England and America* (Boston: Routledge and Kegan Paul).

Ulrich, L.T. 1979. 'Virtuous Women Found: New England Ministerial Literature, 1668-1735' in *A Heritage of Her Own*, eds N.F. Cott and E.H. Pleck (New York: Touchstone).

Wadsworth, B. [1712] 1972. 'The Well-ordered Family, or, Relative Duties', in *The Colonial American Family: Collected Essays* (New York: Arno).

Weisner, T., and R. Gallimore. 1977. 'My Brother's Keeper: Child and Sibling Caretaking', *Current Anthropology* 18.

Wishy, B. 1968. *The Child and the Republic: The Dawn of Modern American Child Nurture* (Philadelphia: University of Philadelphia Press).

Part Three   **Twentieth-Century Developments**

Chapter 11

Gender and family ideals that developed in the nine-teenth century became reality for many North Americans in the twentieth century. Looking back on the twentieth century, the dominant image of family life is of the nuclear family in which the man is bread-winner and the woman is a full-time homemaker. The pattern was common at times during the century—in the 1920s and the two or three decades that followed World War II, at least. Idealization of this family pat-tern is often entangled in nostalgia for the 1950s.

Part Three includes two articles that consider the object of this popular idealization. One examines the interpersonal relations typical of breadwinner-homemaker families and the other examines what life was really like in the 1950s in the United States. Part Three begins with an overview of demographic trends shaping family life.

This essay reviews major changes in the per-sonal and family lives of Canadians in the twentieth century. In a climate where images of a family 'crisis' are not uncommon, it is important to have a sense of what has gone before—if only to understand what is truly new and unusual, and what is not. As well, understanding what is causing family changes is essential to creating the kinds of social policies and programs that will support families.

As Times Change: A Review of Trends in Personal and Family Life

Bonnie Fox

That Canadian families are changing, and have been for some time, is undisputed.[1] Declining rates of marriage, low birthrates, high rates of divorce, and an increasing incidence of lone-par-ent families (and inactive fathers) signify changes in an important institution, and in relations between women and men. Advocates of a return to 'family values' see cause for alarm in these changes. Assuming the imminent demise of the nuclear family, they propose that society itself is threatened. For example, American sociologist David Popenoe (1993: 539) has argued that 'today's family decline . . . [is] both unique and alarming' because it is about decline of the 'nuclear unit [which is] the fundamental and most basic unit of the family'.

Popenoe's reasoning resonates very strongly with popular wisdom. Repeating the argument that Talcott Parsons developed in the early post-World War II period, Popenoe states that the nuclear family performs two critical functions—good quality childrearing and the satisfaction of adults' needs for affection. He argues further that 'there is strong reason to *believe*, in fact, that the [nuclear] family is by far the best institution to carry out these functions' (Popenoe 1993: 539, emphasis added). Like Parsons before him, Popenoe's concern is that these functions must be fulfilled for the sake of social order. Although this concern squares with those of many politicians and heads of corporations, for most of us there is another abiding worry—about the needs of the women, men, and especially children who are not in stable and loving families.

Taking issue with the notion of a crisis in 'the family', American social-historian Stephanie Coontz (1997: 2) reviewed the history of family life in the United States to show that 'there never was [in the United States] a golden age in family life, a time when all families were capable of meeting the needs of their members and protecting them from poverty, violence or sexual exploitation'. Instead, her book, *The Way We Never Were*, shows:

> the tremendous variety of family types that have worked—or not worked—in American history. When families succeeded, it was often for reasons quite different than stereotypes about the past suggest—because they were flexible in their living arrangements, for example, or could call on people and institutions beyond the family for assistance or support (1997: 2).

While Popenoe blames individuals, and their increasing selfishness, for 'rejecting the family', Coontz argues that the problems people are experiencing in these times of change stem from the absence of public supports to changing families. This is the conclusion of Canadian sociologist John Conway as well. Conway believes (like Popenoe) that there is a 'crisis' in 'the family' in Canada, but argues that 'the obvious conclusion is to support the new emerging family forms at both personal and policy levels' (1993: 39).

In order to assess the merits of the different arguments in the debate about family change, one has to understand something of the nature and extent of the changes that are occurring in people's personal and family lives, as well as the implications of these changes. The aim of this chapter is to review the key changes in family patterns. We will see that there is significant change occurring recently. In the last few decades, some long-term trends have been reversed. What will also be apparent, though, is that the long-run trends were not smooth. There were changes, and even reversals, before the recent changes that are causing such concern. Moreover, patterns that seem unusual today are not necessarily new.

In this chapter, I describe long-term and recent changes in personal and family patterns. I first discuss the trends that preceded recent changes, and then review recent changes—offer-

ing explanations along the way, and some discussion of the implications of the changes. Finally, I discuss the variety of family patterns today.

Long-term Trends

There are many ways to measure changes in family life. We will ask first what are the ages when women and men typically experience the key life events that are related to family—like marriage and parenthood. Second, we will ask how likely it is that women and men actually experience such life-changing events as marriage, parenthood, and divorce.

We begin our review of long-term trends by examining the typical life course for successive birth cohorts[2] since the mid-nineteenth century. Table 1 shows estimates of the median ages[3] for each major life event, for ten-year birth cohorts, starting with people born between 1831 and 1840, and ending with people born between 1961 and 1970. For each birth cohort, the table presents our best-guess picture of the ages at which important events in women's and men's life cycles typically occurred—first marriage, first and last birth (and thus the period in women's lives taken up with pregnancy and the care of infants), the start of the 'empty nest' (when the last child is twenty years old and presumably leaves home) and (for women) widowhood. This kind of estimate of the typical family life cycle of different birth cohorts seems a satisfying kind of summary, but resulting figures should be taken as only crude indicators of trends and changes. Other demographic analyses have shown that, at least as far back as the 1911–20 birth cohorts, the lives of the majority of people have not followed what is assumed to be the 'typical' sequence for adults (leaving home, then getting married, then having children, raising children and seeing them leave home, etc.) (Ravanera and Rajulton 1996: 145). There is considerable diversity in the paths constituting different people's family life cycles, and this variety has increased especially in recent decades.

Table 1: Median Ages at Family Life-Course Events

	Approximate Birth Cohorts:												
	1831–40	1841–50	1851–60	1861–70	1881–90	1891–1900	1901–10	1911–20	1921–30	1931–40	1941–50	1951–60	1961–70
Females													
Median Age at:													
First Marriage	25.1	26.0	24.9	24.3	25.1	23.4	23.3	23.0	22.0	21.1	21.3	22.5	25.0
First Birth	27.1	28.0	26.9	26.3	27.1	25.4	25.0	25.4	23.5	22.9	23.3	24.5	26.0
Last Birth	41.0	40.0	38.2	36.2	36.2	33.9	29.1	28.8	29.5	29.1	26.7	26.3	27.8
Empty Nest*	61.0	60.1	58.2	56.2	56.2	53.9	49.1	48.8	49.5	49.1	46.7	46.3	47.8
Widowhood	58.2	59.5	58.9	58.3	60.1	59.4	61.3	63.0	67.0	67.2	68.8	69.9	70.0
Males													
Median Age at:													
First Marriage	27.9	29.1	29.2	28.0	28.5	28.4	27.0	26.3	24.3	24.0	23.5	24.6	27.0
First Birth	29.9	31.1	31.2	30.0	30.5	30.4	28.7	28.7	25.8	25.8	25.5	26.6	28.0
Last Birth	43.8	43.1	42.5	39.9	39.6	38.9	32.8	32.1	31.8	32.0	28.9	28.4	29.8
Empty Nest*	63.8	63.1	62.5	59.9	59.6	58.9	52.9	52.1	51.8	52.0	48.9	48.4	49.8

* Age at which last child is 20 years old.

Sources: Gee 1987: 278. For 1961–70 birth cohort: 1991 Census of Canada, cat. no. 84–212, table 1; 1991 Census of Canada, cat. no. 84–210, table 11 and table 15; and DBS, Vital Statistics, cat. no. 84–802. (See Gee 1987: Appendix, for methods used to derive estimates.)

Nevertheless, the figures in Table 1 show some interesting trends and changes. The largest change over time is a product of the decline in birthrates. While women born before the mid-nineteenth century likely spent between twelve and fourteen years pregnant and bearing their five or six children (Gee 1987: 275), the period spent mothering young children shrank over the course of the twentieth century as the birthrate declined. It increased slightly for the women who had their children during the post–World War II 'baby boom': women born in the 1920s and 1930s (and having children in the 1940s and 1950s) spent about six years in the childbearing stage of life. Nevertheless, women born between 1901 and 1910 (and having children in the 1920s and 1930s) spent only four years pregnant and having their babies; and, when the decline in the birthrate continued after the baby boom, women born in the 1950s and 1960s (and having children in the 1970s and 1980s) spent only about two years in this stage of life, usually having one or two children.

The age when women and men typically first married also declined over time, until the 1970s. Together with the decline in birthrates, earlier marriage meant that women were younger when they finished childbearing. It is worth noting as well that the period following World War II, affecting 1921–30 and 1931–40 female birth cohorts, brought a larger decline in age at first marriage than usually occurred from decade to decade. For men born in the 1920s through the 1940s, first marriage also came significantly earlier than for the male cohorts preceding them. In fact, the notable drop in age of marriage in the post-World War II period through 1960—occurring in the 1950s, essentially—is just one indicator of a period significantly different from that preceding it (as we will see).

Before asking why these changes occurred, we should note one other interesting long-term trend, which is clear in Table 1. The 'empty nest' period—the time couples have together after their youngest child has moved out of the home—developed in the twentieth century. With extensions in life expectancy, and declining numbers of children, this stage in life expanded over the course of the century (until, perhaps, recently).

Why have women had fewer and fewer children? The long-term decline in the birthrate reflects changes over time in women's position and in the economic situation of families. Starting in the mid-nineteenth century, women had fewer children despite considerable odds. Until well into the twentieth century, women apparently knew almost nothing about the physiology of reproduction and, until the 1930s at least, doctors were typically unwilling to help patients anxious to reduce the number of pregnancies (McLaren and McLaren 1986). There was reason for doctors' reluctance. Abortion, which was fairly commonly used—and became a principal means by which birthrates were lowered—was illegal (from the moment of conception) after 1837 (McLaren and McLaren 1986: 39).[4] Even the dissemination of information about contraception—as well as its use—was illegal after 1892 (McLaren and McLaren 1986).[5]

Nevertheless, by the nineteenth century many women had developed a conviction that the dangers attached to childbirth were unacceptable (Wertz and Wertz 1979; Leavitt 1986).[6] Moreover, men's interest in limiting family size also apparently grew, whether out of concern about their wives' health and well-being or about the burden of the responsibility for children. Women might resort to abortion without their husbands' help, or even knowledge, but *coitus interruptus*, or withdrawal—which was apparently the chief means of contraception well into the twentieth century—required the man's co-operation (McLaren and McLaren 1986). So the decline over time in the birthrate represents both women's and men's desires for fewer children.

Central to people's desire to have fewer children was, no doubt, the changing economic situation of couples. Through the nineteenth century, a 'household economy' in which husbands and wives had the resources they needed (land or trade skills) to support themselves and their children—and in which women contributed to subsistence—eroded.[7] This kind of economy was, of course, replaced by a capitalist economy in which people had to find waged work (or sell their products or services in the marketplace) in order to survive. At least in the United States, middle-class men began to identify themselves as 'breadwinners' by the middle of the nineteenth century (Kimmel 1996). As men's work moved outside the household, wives became economically more marginal, even though middle-class women continued to contribute to their families' subsistence—gardening and keeping cows or pigs even in cities, until the latter practices were outlawed toward the end of the century (Bradbury 1984).

The erosion of an economy located in households was important. Not only had women done essential productive work when married couples had access to the necessary means of production, but also fathers had provided for their children's future, passing on land or ensuring an apprenticeship in a skilled trade. The longstanding tradition of apprenticeship—whereby youth lived in the household of a man and a woman who trained them in a trade—eroded in the first half of the nineteenth century in urban Canada, according to historian Michael Katz (1975). Until an institutional framework in which to 'contain young adolescents' developed, there was thus a 'crisis of youth' (Katz 1975: 307).

Social historian Mary Ryan (1981) describes a similar problem in upstate New York in the early decades of the nineteenth century, largely because of the fact that numbers of young men were moving from rural areas into towns, and beyond their parents' control, to find work.[8] According to Ryan, middle-class women in these towns addressed the 'youth problem' by assuming the role of socializers or educators, and specifically by setting up activities that would help instill in the young men important civic values—

in addition to housing them. They advocated the 'Protestant Ethic', with its emphasis on hard work and thrift, for example. Within decades, these same women realized that the values they were promoting were critical to their own sons' survival and success in a quickly changing economy. Accordingly, they began keeping their sons (and daughters) home through their teens, to provide for their formal and informal education. Katz (1975) found that in Hamilton between 1851 and 1871 the length of time boys (and girls, to a lesser extent) remained in their parents' homes, and the amount of education they received, increased. (See also Bradbury, Chapter 8, this text.) So, parental responsibilities—which shifted from fathers to mothers—became more labour intensive, requiring long years of attention by mothers. Having a child became a heavier responsibility than earlier. And having fewer children meant that women could devote 'less of their lives to infant care, freeing them to attend to growing children' (Vinovskis and Frank 1997: 55). And over the course of the century, middle-class womanhood was increasingly equated with motherhood (Margolis, Chapter 10 this text).

Thus the 'separate spheres' ideology that developed in the middle class (Cott, Chapter 9 this text; Welter 1966) was not simply imposed on women: middle-class women themselves (as Ryan argues) had a hand in creating an ideology that equated womanhood with motherhood. Because childhood was becoming sentimentalized in this class, and women's moral strength was seen as an uplifting influence on the future generation, the new ideals of womanhood served to increase women's status in the home and their control over both children and their households (Laslett and Brenner 1989). In the long run, of course, domestic ideology was central to women's subordination.

In the 1800s, middle-class women also embraced an image of physical frailty (Wood 1974). This identity seems ironic until its utility as a way of excusing sexual inactivity, and thus a means of reducing numbers of pregnancies, is recognized (Laslett and Brenner 1989). By the end of the nineteenth century, many middle-class women were arguing for 'voluntary motherhood', and thus women's right to refuse to submit to men's sexual demands (Gordon 1974). So, as the weight of childrearing shifted to women's shoulders, and the responsibility it entailed increased, women took action to ensure the successful fulfillment of a role that increasingly defined their lives—namely, motherhood. One way they did that was by having fewer children.

The economics of working-class households suggest that there must have been incentive for them to reduce the number of children through the nineteenth century, and in fact until the 1950s. Except for skilled workers, working-class men were very unlikely to be earning a 'family wage' until as late as the 1950s or 1960s (Fox 1980; Bradbury 1993). Not only did men earn too little to support their families through the nineteenth century, but working-class women were also less able than their middle-class sisters to contribute to family subsistence by extending their domestic work (gardening, keeping animals, taking in boarders). They typically could supplement their husbands' earnings only by doing waged work (Bradbury, Chapter 8 this text; Bullen 1992). Children earned money also and, in fact, were the more important secondary earners until well into the twentieth century. Too much can be made of children's economic value, however. The added cost of each new mouth to feed must have been as salient to parents as whatever added wages a child would eventually bring home. That many working-class families maintained a precarious balance between destitution and subsistence indicates how significant another dependant could be to a family (Bradbury 1982).

Of course, more than economic considerations influence the number of children couples have. Power dynamics in marriage and men's attitudes toward women also matter. The common interest that middle-class husbands and wives

had, in limiting family size in the interest of achieving middle-class respectability, was unlikely for a working-class population without much prospect of improving their lot. In fact, working-class status eroded men's authority in the household, and seems to have fuelled misogynist attitudes and struggles by men to re-assert control over their households (Stansell 1982; Gordon 1988). Negotiations around sexuality were shaped by a feeling of entitlement that no doubt characterized many working-class men's attitudes toward their wives (Stansell 1982). Nevertheless, there is evidence that working-class women were battling with their husbands around definitions of gender, domestic roles and responsibilities, and decent treatment in marriage (Gordon 1988; Laslett and Brenner 1989). Thus, while an economic incentive was at work in reducing the size of working-class families, so were motives that were more exclusively women's.[9]

In the twentieth century, there were non-economic reasons for married couples to want smaller families, which compounded the economic ones already at work. In the early decades of the century, newly won legal rights and improved educational and employment opportunities (especially for single women) raised new possibilities of personal autonomy for middle-class women at least (Strong-Boag 1988). But after marriage, the demands of homemaking and childcare precluded a combination of paid and unpaid work for middle-class women, and made dependence on the male breadwinner inevitable. Joanna Brenner and Barbara Laslett (1991) have argued that this discrepancy between the possibilities that middle-class women faced before marriage and their constraints as mothers and wives is one of the reasons why the emergent consumer culture appealed to these women—with its message that heterosexual romance and marriage were the routes to personal happiness (Rapp and Ross 1986; Brenner and Laslett 1991).

To the extent that women did embrace the ideal of the companionate marriage which became very popular in the early decades of the twentieth century, they had to negotiate a contradiction—between romance and sexual excitement, on the one hand, and motherhood and devotion to children, on the other. Women who took the roles of wife and mother seriously needed to have manageable numbers of children. McLaren and McLaren (1986) found evidence that Canadian women desperate for help with contraception in the early decades of the century were typically married women with several children, who wanted ongoing companionship in their marriage. Of course, in reducing the number of children they raised, women encountered another contradiction, since their role in life was defined (culturally and often personally) in terms of having and raising children. As a result, in the economically prosperous and highly domestic years of the 1950s and early 1960s, the trend of declining birthrates was reversed, and a 'baby boom' occurred.

The 1950s was, in fact, an unusual period: not only did birthrates rise and a major drop in age at marriage occur, but also divorce rates were unusually low among couples who married in that period (Coontz 1992; May 1988).[10] Two factors seem responsible for the changes that marked this period. First, it was the birth cohorts of the 1920s and 1930s who entered adulthood, and thus set the patterns that characterized the postwar period. Having grown up during times of economic depression and war, they apparently were driven by desires for material security and social/emotional tranquility (May 1988).[11] Second, the period was one of economic growth. Steady rises in real earnings meant that most families had at least an expectation of continuing improvement in their economic position, even if sizeable numbers still were not prosperous (Coontz 1992). So, the combination of a birth cohort with an unusual background and an unusual postwar period—of economic growth—together meant that some of the long-term demographic trends were suspended for a time.

Another Long-term Trend

Another set of changes in women's life cycle did not reverse itself in the 1950s—the steep increase in women's, and especially married women's, involvement in the labour force. While only 11.2 per cent of married women were in the paid labour force in 1951, by 1971 37 per cent were; and in 1991 61.4 per cent of married women were in the labour force (Statistics Canada 1953, 1974, 1994). Indeed, in 1991, 64 per cent of married women with children under six years of age, and even 61 per cent of those whose children were under three years of age, were in the paid labour force (Statistics Canada 1994). Meanwhile, more employed women were doing part-time work in the 1970s, 1980s, and 1990s than in the 1950s and 1960s. The proportion of women working part time rose steadily from about 11 per cent in 1953 to 24.9 per cent in 1970, and since then has been between 24 and 25 per cent (Leacy 1983; Statistics Canada 1998).

By 1971, in fact, an interesting change had occurred in women's involvement in the labour force. See Figure 1, which shows the labour force participation rates of 'synthetic cohorts' of women—groups of women who came of age to enter the labour force at the same time.[12] For the first time, in 1971 the labour-force participation rate of women twenty-five to thirty-four—that is, women in their prime childbearing years—was not lower than it had been ten years earlier, when the women were fifteen to twenty-four years old. That is, beginning with the cohort of women who reached adulthood (ages fifteen to twenty-four) in 1961, the earlier life-cycle pattern of reduced labour-force involvement during the child-bearing years (ages twenty-five to thirty-four) ended. For this cohort of women, and those who came after them, labour-force involvement actually *increased* during the period in which women were also having their children. No doubt, this different pattern of labour-force involvement over women's life course attests to

**Figure 1: Women's Age-specific Labour Force
Participation Rates for Synthetic Cohorts**

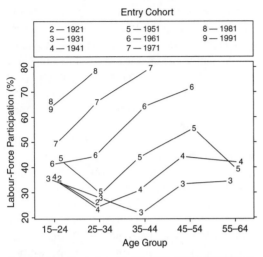

Sources: Leacy, Urquhart, and Buckley 1983. *Historical Statistics of
Canada* (series D107–123); 1971 Census, cat. no. 94–702, table 2;
1981 Census, cat. no. 92–915, table 1; 1991 Census, cat. no.
93–324, table 1.

changed economic circumstances faced by
Canadian couples. While motherhood used to
entail withdrawal from the labour force, women
now attempt to accommodate its demands by an
increase in part-time work (Duffy, Mandell, and
Pupo 1989: 81), and delaying marriage and childbearing (as we will see).

Behind the rise in women's labour-force
involvement were changes in the nature of the
occupational structure and families. In the
labour market, there was increasing demand for
clerical workers for much of the twentieth century, and there was also a shift away from manufacturing jobs and toward service jobs after
World War II. Accordingly, marriage bars and
other barriers to women's involvement in wage
work broke down, especially in the post-World
War II period. From the vantage point of families, about half of Canadian households have
been in need of a second income through the
twentieth century (Fox 1980). Until after World
War II, teenagers, especially boys, were the pre-

ferred second earners, but as school requirements rose women became the main second
earners in families.[13] Also prompting the movement of homemakers into waged work was a
postwar economy in which it increasingly made
more economic sense for women to earn money
than to produce subsistence goods (like clothing)
at home; in fact, it became less possible to substitute home production for the purchase of necessary goods when commodities such as cars
became essential.

Since the 1980s, systematic restructuring of
the economy has meant a decline in real hourly
wages for men under thirty-five years of age, and
a drop in the purchasing power of all men's earnings (Armstrong and Armstrong 1994; Yalnizyan
1998: 19, 25). Consequently, many Canadian
families have maintained their standard of living
through the 1980s and 1990s only because of
women's employment. The restructuring that is
ongoing means a drastic and progressive drop in
the numbers of men earning a family wage, and
thus able to support a family (Bakker 1996). Two
incomes will therefore remain a necessity for most
Canadian households.

To the extent that restructuring has meant
not only lower individual earnings but also
unemployment and the threat of job loss especially for men, it directly undermines marriage
and nuclear families. Research on families in the
1930s Depression, and on male-female relations
in poor African-American communities, indicates
that the damage to men's identity when they fail
at breadwinning directly undermines stable male-
female relationships (Elder 1974; Stack 1974;
Sullivan 1998). Moreover, to the extent that
women are no longer fully dependent on men for
access to a decent standard of living, they have
been able to leave unhappy marriages and choose
not to marry in the first place. Higher rates of
divorce, a decline in marriage, and even a rise in
common-law relationships, make sense given the
changes occurring in the economy—and that is
indeed what has occurred.

Recent Changes

Turning to recent changes in personal life, Table 1 gives some indication of the dramatic change that has occurred recently with respect to marriage. The 1961–70 female and male birth cohorts—marrying mostly in the 1980s and 1990s—typically married about two-and-a-half years later than they did in the 1970s. This is a large change in a statistic that has been quite stable over the centuries in Western culture. Likewise, the cohort of women born between 1961 and 1970 became

parents about a year and a half later than women born between 1951 and 1960. These figures indicate significant change in people's life cycle. In fact, as we will see, they are the products of a postponement of marriage and rise in the popularity of common-law relationships, but also an overall decline in the formation of any kind of heterosexual union.[14]

Table 2 gives an indication of these changes. Here we see age-specific percentages of people who are currently married, people in unions (both marriages and common-law relationships),

Table 2: Per cent of Women and Men Presently Married, in a Union (Married or Cohabiting), Separated or Never Married—1981 and 1991

	1981				1991			
	Married	Total in Union	Separated	Never Married	Married	Total in Union	Separated	Never Married
Women								
15–19	3.6	6.5	0.1	93.4	1.3	4.2	0.1	95.7
20–24	36.5	45.9	2.1	52.0	19.4	33.6	1.2	65.2
25–29	65.9	73.0	3.8	23.2	50.9	65.1	2.7	32.2
30–34	75.5	80.2	9.4	10.5	64.7	75.1	8.6	16.3
35–39	78.1	81.7	11.0	7.3	69.5	77.5	11.7	10.7
40–44	79.2	82.0	11.9	6.1	71.5	77.8	14.3	7.9
45–49	78.8	80.9	13.3	5.8	72.3	77.5	16.2	6.4
50–54	76.4	78.1	15.8	6.0	73.1	76.8	17.5	5.6
Men								
15–19	0.7	1.4	0.1	98.5	0.5	1.1	0.1	98.8
20–24	19.8	26.9	0.9	72.2	8.7	17.8	0.4	81.8
25–29	55.6	63.7	2.6	33.7	37.6	51.5	1.5	47.0
30–34	73.1	79.1	6.0	15.0	58.9	70.2	5.6	24.2
35–39	79.1	83.8	6.8	9.3	68.4	77.3	7.8	14.8
40–44	81.2	84.8	7.4	7.8	73.4	80.8	9.3	9.8
45–49	81.8	84.6	7.9	7.5	75.9	82.4	10.0	7.6
50–54	81.6	83.7	8.4	7.8	78.2	83.3	10.0	6.7

Source: Beaujot, R., E. Gee, F. Rajulton, and Z. Ravanera, 1995: 10, 41.

people who are separated (and for those over thirty, separated, divorced or widowed), and people never married, for 1981 and 1991. What we see first is that the percentage of people who have never married increased between 1981 and 1991, for all age groups except those fifty to fifty-four years of age. Declines in marriage have, in fact, occurred for women since 1961 and for men since 1971 (Beaujot et al. 1995).

Looking at a couple of key age groups highlights the change. Of women in their late twenties (twenty-five to twenty-nine years of age), the decline in the percentage currently married was from 82 per cent in 1971 (not shown in Table 2) to 65.9 per cent in 1981 to 50.9 per cent in 1991. Even after inclusion of the portion of this age group living in common-law relationships, there is still a decline in the percentage living in intimate heterosexual relationships—from 73 per cent in 1981 to 65.1 per cent in 1991. Over a third of women twenty-five to twenty-nine years of age were not in heterosexual unions in 1991, and nearly a third had never married. For men twenty-five to twenty-nine years of age, there was a decline in the percentage currently married from 74 per cent in 1971 to 55.6 per cent in 1981 to 37.6 per cent in 1991—from the vast majority being married to a minority in that state. Indeed, while 63.7 per cent were in an intimate heterosexual union in 1981, only a slim majority, 51.5 per cent, were in 1991.

The decline is evident even for men and women in their late thirties (thirty-five to thirty-nine years of age). The percentage of women that age who were currently married declined from 89 per cent in 1971 to 78.1 per cent in 1981 and 69.5 per cent in 1991. The percentage of women that age in some kind of intimate heterosexual union decreased from 81.7 per cent in 1981 to 77.5 per cent in 1991. For men thirty-five to thirty-nine years of age, the decline in percentage married was from 88 per cent in 1971 to 79.1 per cent in 1981 and 68.4 per cent in 1991. The percentage of men in an intimate heterosexual union fell from 83.8

per cent in 1981 to 77.3 per cent in 1991. Of all people thirty to fifty-four years of age in 1991, 23.1 per cent of women and 22 per cent of men were not in a union—either because they never married or because they were separated, divorced, or widowed (Beaujot et al. 1995: 65). Thus, while being married was the most common state for people in their middle years in 1991, it was not at all the case that nearly everyone was married.

So, there has been not only a postponement of marriage but also a decline in the percentage of people marrying. And the increase in common-law unions has been insufficient to compensate for the fall in marriages. Of course, these statistics vary across provinces, such that common-law unions are significantly more typical, and marriage less typical, in Quebec than elsewhere (Nault and Belanger 1996).

Common-law unions have become popular generally, however: in 1991, of men and women twenty to twenty-four years of age, 51 per cent of men and 42 per cent of women who were in a union were cohabiting, which is about double the proportions in 1981 (Beaujot et al. 1995: 12). Among those twenty-five to twenty-nine years of age, about a quarter of women and men in unions were cohabiting, which is twice the 1981 figure (Beaujot et al. 1995: 12).

These unions are significant for more than their numbers. On the one hand, they are part of the pattern of later marriage since many cohabitors eventually marry each other: according to the 1990 General Social Survey, 37 per cent of married people aged eighteen to twenty-nine had previously cohabited. The estimate from that study is that about 40 per cent of common-law relationships end in marriage within five years (Beaujot et al. 1995: 12). On the other hand, common-law relationships are considerably less stable than marriages. One estimate is that about a third of them end within five years, which is more than double the rate of marriage breakdown (Beaujot et al. 1995: 12). Another estimate is that the average length of time spent in these types of unions was

2.5 years in 1981 and 4.4 years in 1991 (though longer in Quebec) (Nault and Belanger 1996: 20). It is obvious that common-law relationships delay marriage, but it is also true that these kinds of union reduce both people's desire to marry and their likelihood of marrying (Wu 1999). In 1991, it was estimated that as many as 25 per cent of Canadian women and 30 per cent of Canadian men would never marry, if current patterns continued (Nault and Belanger 1996).[15]

That women are now less likely to marry means higher rates of childlessness. Remaining childless indicates perhaps the most dramatically different life course for women. And there has been a rise in the extent of childlessness recently. As Table 3 indicates, rates of childlessness were high for women born in the nineteenth century, and indeed before 1922. The rate was especially high, rising to over 15 per cent, for those women born between 1907 and 1911, who were of childbearing age between 1927 and 1946[16]—in other words, during the 1930s Depression and World War II. For women born after 1922, who entered the childbearing years (mostly) during the postwar period, childlessness declined; and for those who came of age during the 1950s and 1960s (and born between 1932 and 1941), rates of childlessness were very low. The rate of childlessness started to climb again for women born after 1941. These women were less subject to the 'feminine mystique' of the 1950s and faced more options—especially in the form of jobs—than did women entering adulthood in the 1950s.[17] Additionally, many of them came of age largely (given longer time in school and later age of childbearing) in the 1970s, when the economy was tightening up in terms of job creation and wage levels.

That more women are now remaining single has an impact on childbearing, even though sizeable numbers of never-married women are now having children. Considering all women, those who have and have not been married, the rates of childlessness in 1991 were fairly high, and prob-

ably rising. In 1991, over 16 per cent of all women forty to forty-four years of age had never had children, 14 per cent of all women forty-five to forty-nine years of age were childless, and over 12 per cent of all women fifty to fifty-four years of age were childless (Statistics Canada 1993). Aside from never having children, women are also postponing motherhood. In 1961, nearly 90 per cent of women twenty-five to twenty-nine years of age had children; in 1971, 80 per cent of them did; in 1981, slightly more than 70 per cent did; and in 1991, only slightly more than 60 per cent did (Beaujot et al. 1995: 17). These increases in rates of childlessness and the trend toward a postponement of motherhood attest to both changes in women's lives and increased differences among women.

Postponing marriage and motherhood is clearly related to women's increasing education

Table 3: Per cent of Ever-Married Women Who Are Childless

Census Year	Age	Birth Cohort	% Childless
1941	55–64	1877–86	13.2
1941	45–54	1877–96	12.3
1961	50–54	1907–11	15.3
1961	45–49	1912–16	13.1
1971	50–54	1917–21	11.8
1971	45–49	1922–26	9.6
1971	40–44	1927–31	8.2
1981	50–54	1927–31	8.4
1981	45–49	1932–36	7.2
1981	40–44	1937–41	7.3
1991	50–54	1937–41	8.0
1991	45–49	1942–46	9.4
1991	40–44	1947–51	10.7

Sources: Gee 1987: 273; 1971 Census of Canada, cat. no. 92–718, table 24; 1981 Census of Canada, cat. no. 92–906, table 7; 1991 Census of Canada, cat. no. 93–321, table 2.

and need to establish themselves in a labour market where jobs are still incompatible with family responsibilities. What are the sources of the lower rates of marriage, the rise in common-law relationships, and higher rates of childlessness? The continuing reality that women pay a price in the labour market for marriage and motherhood, and continue to shoulder more responsibility for housework and childcare at home than men, indicates pretty clearly why women are postponing and even avoiding marriage and long-term commitments to men. As many writers have pointed out, the place women now have in the labour force has allowed them choice about whether or not to marry; it has eroded a structural imperative that women marry in order to have the possibility of a decent standard of living.[18] Moreover, the erosion of men's ability to support their families highlights the injustice of relationships in which men claim privileges that women do not have—especially taking on less responsibility in the home and thus forcing women to work longer hours every week (Hochschild 1989; Frederick 1995). This privilege, which appeared to be deserved when men earned a 'family wage' (Luxton 1980, and Chapter 12 this text) no longer seems so when two people together support their family. That women are likely to be choosing inequality when they choose to marry is significant.

At the same time, the absence of change in many men, coupled with the failure of state policies and programs to support working mothers (e.g., with good, affordable daycare), and most employers' failure to accommodate family responsibilities (e.g., with shorter work weeks, flexible schedules, good part-time jobs), explain why many women increasingly have felt that they must choose between family and career. Of course, the thorough questioning of conventional gender roles and nuclear-family life that flourished in the 1960s, and especially the Women's Liberation Movement which revived and recreated feminist visions, changed popular culture in a way that enabled people to make different choices than their parents. Thus, the rise of common-law relationships provided a middle ground between marriage and the single state—an intimate heterosexual relationship where sexual activity does not entail having children, and intimacy does not mean 'forever'. And the fact that sizeable numbers of women are now able to have careers means that a fulfilling adult life is possible without children for more women than in older generations. In short, the exchange between men and women that represented the foundation of family for many decades—his financial support for her domestic and sexual services—was undermined by women's increasing labour-force involvement.[19]

There are obvious implications of the trends in marriage, cohabitation, and childbearing, especially having to do with gender. Parenthood typically entails a significantly more gendered division of labour and responsibility between men and women (Fox, Chapter 19 this text). Marriage has a similar, though smaller, effect. American research comparing marriage with common-law relationships indicates a significantly more conventional division of labour among married couples (Blumenstein and Schwartz 1983; South and Spitze 1994).

For women, marriage and motherhood have likely economic costs as well. Beaujot and colleagues (1995: 2) quantify the economic costs: the employment income of single women is 94 per cent of men's, and while 72 per cent of single women are in part-time work so are 66 per cent of single men; in contrast, for women thirty to thirty-four who are married and have children, employment income is 49 per cent of men's, and only 35 per cent of them (as opposed to 81 per cent of men) work full-time. That women are postponing marriage, entering it not only when they are older but also more educated and likely employed than earlier generations, that they are likely to live in common-law relationships first and even instead of marriage, and that they are spending only a small fraction of adulthood in the early years of motherhood, should promote greater gender equality in heterosexual relationships. Moreover, the very fact that there are paths for women that do not involve a lasting relationship with a man—and that some women take these paths—must have an indirect effect on what goes on between men and women in marriage and common-law relationships.

Divorce

Related to these changes is another life-defining trend of significance—that involving divorce. Divorce has apparently been on the rise over the course of the twentieth century. There was a major increase in the rate of divorce in the late 1960s, however, with federal legislation which made divorce easier.[20] While the rise in divorce continued to the late 1980s, divorce rates have fluctuated through the 1990s. Perhaps most interesting is the story told in Figure 2. The two charts show the rates of divorce for every year following marriage, for cohorts of men and women born between 1911 and 1960. Clearly, each birth cohort has been significantly more likely than the one before it to divorce. For example, after ten years of marriage, fewer than 2 per cent of women born between 1911 and 1920 were divorced but nearly 20 per cent of women born between 1951 and 1960 were. The increase is similar for men, except that about 17 per cent of men born between 1951 and 1960 were divorced after ten years of marriage. While slightly over 3 per cent of men and women born between 1911 and 1920 were divorced after twenty years of marriage, almost 35 per cent of women and about 30 per cent of men born between 1951 and 1960 were divorced after two decades of marriage.

It is estimated that if current patterns continue into the future, 31 per cent of marriages contracted in 1991 will end in divorce (Nault and Belanger 1996: 17). Although many people remarry, it is also the case that the propensity to remarry following divorce decreased between the

1980s and the 1990s (and even more so than the decline in the propensity to marry for the first time) (Nault and Belanger 1996: 7).[21]

It is common to attribute the increasing instability of marriage to people's selfishness. Mostly, this means women's 'selfishness', since it is they who typically do more of the emotional work in heterosexual relationships, as well as the housework and child care (Hochschild 1989). That

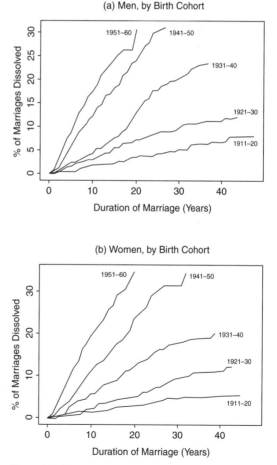

Figure 2: Cumulative Percentages Separated or Divorced by Sex and Birth Cohort, 1911 to 1960

(a) Men, by Birth Cohort

(b) Women, by Birth Cohort

Source: Beaujot et al. 1995. Figure 4.5, p. 133. Data provided by Z. Ravanera.

there are two experiences of any marriage—'his' and 'her' experiences[22]—is overlooked in this glib explanation, which assumes that people should remain in relationships that are problematic.

Of course, many women stay in marriages where they do more of the work, and make compromises they judge to be unfair (Hochschild 1989). At least one (American) study of divorced women, however, found that most of their marriages had ended precisely because of the negative gender dynamics in them (Kurz 1995).[23] Demie Kurz (1995: 45) found, in her representative sample of divorced American women, that almost one-fifth of them (especially the middle-class women) had divorced for reasons involving conventional male behaviour—the man's failure to share housework, childcare, and even emotional work, and/or his need to be in control.[24] Another one-fifth of the women in the study (especially working-class and poor women) ended their marriage because of their partner's violence. Altogether, the majority of reasons for divorce in this study had to do with men's problematic behaviour, since another 19 per cent of the women referred to an 'other woman' as the reason for the breakup, and 17 per cent cited drug/alcohol abuse by the man, and his absence from home, as the key reasons for the divorce (Kurz 1995: 45). Kurz's study suggests that marriages that end in divorce were not providing what we all expect of marriage—love and support. Given the possibility of choice, it is not surprising that women would opt to leave such relationships. Of course, there are many causes of the rise in divorce; some women leave for reasons other than these, and men also take the initiative. Supporting all the individual decisions is a changed cultural climate which makes divorce easier.

For the adults and children who experience it, the emotional and social consequences of divorce are varied. Moreover, it is not at all easy to separate the effects of divorce from the effects of the conflict that caused the divorce (Furstenberg and Cherlin, Chapter 31 this text).

What is clearly a major problem affecting most women who experience divorce, however, is the drop in income that typically occurs. Using longitudinal data tracing the impact of divorce on a representative sample of Canadians, between 1982 and 1986, Ross Finnie (1993: 228) found that as a result of divorce women 'experience a steep decline in economic well-being while men enjoy moderate increases'. Using income-to-needs ratios (which adjust for family size) to measure well-being, Finnie (1993: 225) found the ratio of women's well-being to men's well-being to be about .59 a year after divorce. It improved only slowly over the subsequent years. He also found that over a third of women who were not poor before their divorce became poor in the year following it (compared with about 10 per cent of men) (Finnie 1993: 219).

The aftermath of divorce, for women and children, makes clear the contradictions in the current environment of family life. The old exchange between men and women—involving his financial support for her domestic and sexual services—which was the foundation of nuclear families has broken down, and yet social arrangements predicated on that old pattern remain. So, for example, women's position in the labour force has not changed dramatically: many women still do not earn enough to support themselves and their children. At the same time, provincial family laws governing divorce assume that society has changed in such a way that individuals are now self-sustaining. Since the late 1970s, most provinces stipulate a division of 'family property' into two equal parts, so that the separating man and woman can go on with their lives without continuing dependency on each other. A man's ongoing support of a former wife who stayed home full-time is to be short-term only, and women with any source of income are not expected to need ongoing support. So, women face a dramatic drop in income, and children—who typically live with their mothers—experience a similar drop in their standard of living.

They may also lose their home (in the split of the family assets), which means a loss of friends, a move to a new school and neighbourhood, etc. It is the absence of societal changes—in employment and government policy—that would support women-headed families that has produced much of the current level of child poverty.

For many children, divorce also means the loss of their father, since fathers often lose contact with children not living with them (Conway 1993). Reseach suggests that the reasons have to do with the centrality of family to fatherhood and even manhood. Thus, fathering is difficult in a situation that is removed from normal daily family life and the presence (and facilitation) of the mother (e.g., restricted to eight-hour visits every Sunday). As well, though, men who withdraw from contact with their children may do so as a result of an ongoing battle with their ex-wives—a battle often about 'manhood'. For some men, divorce means loss of the control and authority that was central to their marriage; the need to reaffirm their sense of manhood may mean battling over 'rights' (seen as due them by payment of child support) rather than investing energy in sustaining relationships with the children; or their last vestige of manliness may depend upon maintaining control of their emotions, which means avoiding the stress of visitation (Arendell 1992).

Whatever the reasons why many fathers find it hard to maintain close relations with their children after divorce, many even fail to follow through on their financial obligations to them. Somehow, not living with their children means, for many men, no longer being responsible for them (Eichler 1997). In the 1980s, a majority of men defaulted on court-ordered child-support payments (which were already set at levels below half the cost of raising children); there is no reason to believe that matters have improved significantly since then (Conway 1993: 122). The economic consequences for children are dire: in 1997, the poverty rate for children in lone-parent families headed by women was 60.4 per cent,

which was tremendously higher than the rate of 12.7 per cent for children in two-parent families (National Council of Welfare 1999: 90). Given the difficulty of combining childcare and employment, in the absence of state commitment to affordable childcare facilities, and given the low levels of earnings attached to many of the jobs women are in, it is still the case that women attempting to raise children outside a live-in relationship with a man often have a very hard time. Thus, in one important sense at least—the financial support of children—this society still assumes the nuclear family.

A Diversity of Family Types

Increases in divorce, childbearing outside marriage, the rise in common-law relationships, etc., signify a diversity of family patterns. Yet it is hard to summarize the diversity of family arrangements in Canada today. Some types of families are never surveyed in censuses (e.g., gay and lesbian families). Others would be hard to enumerate (e.g., those extending across different households). Additionally, any summary that offers a 'snapshot' of the population at one point in time ignores the fact that any point in time captures people at different life-cycle stages. So, at best, we can get only some indication of the diversity of living and caring arrangements.

Table 4 presents a summary of the major types of families in Canada, as of 1996. In that year, 86 per cent of families (as defined by Statistics Canada) involved a heterosexual couple living together, and 81 per cent of children were living in families headed by a man and a woman. Of course, a sizeable percentage of these children will experience life in a lone-parent household at some point in their childhood or teens. Moreover, a sizeable number of these families are 'blended', or reconstituted in the wake of divorce. Blended families feature more complicated daily negotiations, with more sets of relationships, than other two-parent families. The role of stepmother is an especially difficult one, while relations beyond the nuclear unit are usually difficult, especially those with former partners (Ahrons and Rodgers 1997). Of necessity, these families have fluid boundaries, so considering them to be nuclear is somewhat problematic.

Table 4: Type of Family of Adults and Never-Married Children, by Adults' Employment Status —1996 Census Data

Family Structure and Adults' Employment Status	Families		Never-Married Sons and Daughters at Home	
	%	Number	%	Number
Married Couples	74	5,779,720	73	6,869,700
With Children	45	3,535,635		
Both Adults Employed	27	2,118,920		
Husband Sole Breadwinner	11	826,380		
Wife Sole Breadwinner	3	201,430		
Without Children	29	2,244,090		
Both Adults Employed	9	744,200		
Husband Sole Breadwinner	4	319,350		
Wife Sole Breadwinner	2	153,895		
Common-Law Couples	12	920,635	8	735,565
With Children	5	434,955		
Both Adults Employed	3	238,975		
Husband Sole Breadwinner	1	101,365		
Wife Sole Breadwinner	0	33,520		
Without Children	6	485,690		
Both Adults Employed	4	319,570		
Husband Sole Breadwinner	1	59,900		
Wife Sole Breadwinner	1	45,120		
Lone-Parent Families	14	1,137,505	19	1,764,485
Male Parent	2	192,275		
Employed	2	125,040		
Female Parent	12	945,230		
Employed	6	480,555		
Total	100	7,837,865	100	9,369,750
	99			

Sources: Statistics Canada, 1999. http://www.statcan.ca/english/census96/june9/f3can.htm and http://www.statcan.ca/english/census96/oct14/fam1.htm

In terms of life on a day-to-day basis, perhaps most significant about two-parent families today, however, is that in a majority of them both adults are employed—60 per cent of married couples with children and 55 per cent of common-law couples with children, in 1996. The women in these families are caught in a web of contradictions, because of the absence of change in society and in men. In dual-earner families, women are pulled in two directions, by two incompatible sets of responsibilities—those of their paid work and those at home (Luxton, Chapter 21 this text). The terms of employment still usually assume a person unencumbered by family responsibilities, while children still need endless amounts of attention. Moreover, although the definition of what children need for healthy development has inflated over the decades, the responsibility for their well-being remains squarely on the shoulders of parents, especially mothers (Hays 1996).

While some commercial services for parents seem to have increased over the years (e.g., psychotherapy) along with greater sensitivity to issues of childhood development, community supports for basic care remain meager (e.g., good, affordable daycare).[25] Indeed, the outrage that such stingy public support warrants has been inhibited by the endurance of old beliefs about mothers' natural abilities and babies and toddlers being better off at home full-time. Of course, there is no evidence to support such beliefs (Eyer 1992). In fact, the evidence is that good-quality daycare is better for toddlers than being home full time with their mothers (Clarke-Stewart 1982). But only a minority of the population can afford to place their children in a daycare facility, and good daycare is getting harder for Canadian parents to find (Picard 2000). So, considering children alone, the 'cost' of employment that women bear remains high.

Meanwhile, men are still not assuming work or responsibility in the home equal to what women do (Luxton, Chapter 21 this text). This inequality is a product of the many factors constituting gender in this society. Gender ideology and the divide between home and 'work' have (since the nineteenth century) gendered the work that goes on in the home. The definition of manhood, based on an opposition to all that is feminine, and featuring notions of achievement, dominance and control, provides an obvious obstacle to sharing (Hochschild 1989). Women's typically lower bargaining power—because of their generally worse position in the labour market and the 'marriage market' (and the higher cost of divorce for women)—affects how much women push men to share, and thus how much they do share (Luxton 1983). And, in the end, the privilege of being cared for is one that many men find hard to surrender.

Stress is clearly an outcome of the 'juggling act' that many women must do daily (see Hochschild, Chapter 22 this text). It is also the case, however, that women's mental and physical health benefits from combining employment and family (see Coontz 1997, Chapter 3, for a literature review). And, in the end, children do not seem to suffer from having mothers in the labour force either (Coontz 1997). What seems to be affected the most when both adults are in the labour force is marriage: when men fail to share the load, tensions in the relationship are common, and divorce more likely (Hochschild 1989; Kurz 1995).

That parenting in dual-earner families is difficult underlines the problems faced by lone-parent families. In 1996, 14.5 per cent of families were lone-parent families, and 19 per cent of dependent children lived in them (see Table 4). The fact that a similar proportion of Canadian families consisted of lone parents in the early decades of the twentieth century does not reduce their significance today.[26] And what appears most significant about them is that most are headed by women, and thus many must struggle with poverty.

As we have already noted, lone-parent families face the difficulty of living in a society organized around nuclear families. When one adult is responsible for both childcare and financial support, poverty is likely: in 1997, 57.1 per cent of lone-parent mothers were living below the poverty line (compared with 11.9 per cent of couples with children) (National Council of Welfare 1999: 36).[27] With very few supportive social policies and programs, the material support of extended kin (e.g., grandparents of the children) is likely the main way many of these families survive. Probably a sizeable portion of them live in extended-family households.[28]

Lone parenthood is just one condition that may move young adults back to live in their parents' home (Boyd and Pryor 1989). While the percentage of young unmarried adults living at home declined in the 1970s, it rose considerably in the 1980s, and also (though less) in the 1990s (Mitchell 1998: 22). Young adults are both leaving their parents' home later than in previous decades (though about the same time as they did in the early part of the twentieth century) and returning home in greater numbers. This state of semidependence is prompted, no doubt, by the rising costs of postsecondary education and the difficulty young people have finding a good job, as well as rising rates of divorce and motherhood outside marriage. What the return of young adults to their parents' home means is that the stresses of a society that is unsupportive of families not only weigh on parents while they are raising their children but also that the pressure is extending over a longer stretch of the life course. Families of origin have become 'a type of social safety net for young adults in times of need' (Mitchell 1998: 41). In turn, this type of privatized social safety net may serve to reproduce inequalities of wealth: how well young adults do is even more dependent on the financial resources of their parents now than it was before.

Much of the diversity in family patterns fails to appear in summary tables such as the one here. Even the simple comparison of two-parent and lone-parent families shows a relationship between family pattern and income inequality, however. Research has shown that different material circumstances induce people to develop different kinds of family arrangements. The fact that economic restructuring is producing a variety of non-

normal types of jobs, and that more people are self-employed, should allow for an increasing diversity of family arrangements. At the same time, the economic instability of many jobs and types of employment today means that people increasingly need the kind of pooling, sharing, and collective support that families can often involve—which means that families (however configured) are not likely to die out.

Additionally, there is ethnic and racial diversity in Canadian families that has yet to be fully explored (but see Calliste, Chapter 26 this text). Immigration also requires big adjustments of families (see Man, Chapter 27 this text). Sizeable numbers of Canadians live in gay and lesbian families, which are increasingly being studied, but which still rest on unions that are not even recognized as marriages (Nelson, Chapter 28 this text). This review has just scratched the surface of an ever changing terrain.

Conclusion

These are times of change in family life. Family patterns frequently change, however. Whenever the material (or economic) foundations of families shift, the adjustments that people have to make are reflected in changing family patterns.

This brief overview highlights key changes in family patterns. The long-term decline in birthrates that has had profound effects on family relations—certainly heightening the emotional intensity of parent-child relations—began with a reconfiguration of families in the nineteenth century. Then, as household economies were undermined, raising children became a more privatized and demanding responsibility. Women assumed the responsibilities of parenting and homemaking while men became primarily breadwinners, and this gendered division of labour between spouses provided the organizational scaffolding of families for decades afterwards. Recently, as women have come to share the responsibilities of financial support, that scaffolding has been shaken. An argument can be made that it is because all else has not significantly changed—except women's move into the labour force—that high rates of separation, divorce, and avoidance of marriage have resulted. In short, mothers who are also in the labour force have not been supported—by necessary changes in social policy (especially state provision of good, affordable daycare facilities), employment practices (especially shorter work weeks, allowances for flexible schedules, and part-time jobs with solid benefits), and men's behaviour (that is, the sharing of household responsibilities). And as the cost of family has risen for women, they have pushed changes in family patterns.

Women's labour-market earnings allow them more choice about how they will live. Thus, the formation of heterosexual unions has declined, rates of divorce have increased, and childlessness has increased; at minimum, marriage and child-bearing are postponed. Nevertheless, while women are both choosing and/or compelled to live in a diversity of family types these days, we still live in a society organized around nuclear families. With very meager support of family in general, those families that deviate from the nuclear pattern often are especially likely to suffer materially. Thus, family patterns are entangled in the social inequality that characterizes this society.

Notes

1. I thank Rod Beaujot for generous help with the literature, and John Fox for turning my pencil drawings into very clear computer-generated figures.

2. Birth cohorts are groups of people who were born in the same year (or decade, in this case).

3. The median age is the age that divides the population evenly—into half below and half above.

4. Abortion was de-criminalized in Canada only in 1988.

5. It remained technically illegal here until 1969, in fact.

6. This conviction would, toward the end of the nineteenth century, lead them to seek medical doctors to attend childbirth, instead of female midwives who were seen as less well trained (Leavitt 1986).

7. Social historian Michael Katz (1975: 293) found that by the mid-nineteenth century women were working alongside their husbands in fewer than half of all households in Hamilton. This gives us some indication of the decline in the household economy in urban Canada.

8. That the same kind of migration was happening in at least Hamilton in mid-nineteenth century is clear from the high numbers of young boarders that Katz (1975) found in evidence.

9. McLaren and McLaren (1986) uncovered evidence of sheer desperation for information about contraception on the part of some working-class women in the early decades of the twentieth century.

10. This paragraph is based on American research. There has not been a Canadian study of the 1950s comparable to those done in the United States, so I assume here that there were strong similarities between the two countries in that era.

11. There is even evidence that children of the Great Depression reacted to the upheaval in family life and gender roles that followed men's unemployment, and especially women's assumption of the role of financial provider (which was a common pattern), by aiming to create families characterized by conventional gender roles (Coontz 1992).

12. These 'synthetic' (or constructed) cohorts, represented by the different lines in the figure, were constructed by taking the age-specific labour-force participation rates for each ascending age category from one census to the next—for example, the rate for fifteen to twenty-four year olds in the 1921 Census, the rate for twenty-five to thirty-four year olds from the 1931 Census, etc. Essentially, we have a picture of participation in the labour force over the life course for people coming of age at different times.

13. In 1931, while only about 3 per cent of married women worked for wages, over 54 per cent of teens fifteen years and older, living in families with both husband and wife present, earned money during the year (Dominion Bureau of Statistics 1933).

14. Of course, what none of the official statistics tell us is the incidence of same-sex unions. So, we may be wrong if we conclude that people are less likely to form unions altogether.

15. These average figures were, however, pulled up by the very high estimates for Quebec: it was estimated that 44 per cent of women and 50 per cent of men in Quebec would never marry. The estimate for Ontario was 18 per cent of women and 22 per cent of men (Nault and Belanger 1996).

16. This assumes that women have children between twenty and thirty-five years of age.

17. This is Betty Friedan's (1965) term. Her best-selling book, *The Feminine Mystique,* argued that women in the 1950s had a 'problem that has no name', because they were subject to a heavy message that personal fulfillment could be found in full-time motherhood and homemaking.

18. While the majority of women in the labour force do not earn as much as men, in about 25 per cent of marriages women earn more than their male partners.

19. This may be a crude way of capturing the exchange between men and women in conventional nuclear families, but Canadian family law understood that to be the exchange—and even defined marriage in those terms (Kronby 1981).

20. In 1968, the first federal legislation on divorce was passed, in the Divorce Act which specified eight grounds for divorce involving fault, and seven ways of establishing marital breakdown (e.g., three years of separation). Apparently the adversarial process the legislation established was cumbersome and time-consuming, however (Richardson 1996). Then, the 1985 Divorce Act made divorce considerably easier: instead of establishing fault, parties simply have to give evidence of marriage breakdown—separation for one year, adultery, or mental and physical cruelty (Richardson 1996: 227).

21. As with the pattern for common-law unions, divorce is considerably higher in Quebec than in the other provinces, and the likelihood of remarrying is lower (Nault and Belanger 1996).

22. The idea of 'his' and 'her' marriage is Jessie Bernard's (1972).

23. Not many researchers have systematically examined why couples divorce. The bulk of research effort has gone to examine the effects of divorce.

24. In the majority of cases, women are the ones who file for divorce; so studying women makes sense.

25. Hospitals' early-release policies following birth are one among many cutbacks in social services which increase the burden of women in families. Early release means not only that babies are at greater physical risk but also that mothers fail to get the instruction, help, and support with basic infant care which is so critical in those first few days of motherhood.

26. While the death of a partner was responsible for a majority of single-mother families early in the century, today separation, divorce, and births outside marriage are responsible for the bulk of these families (Hudson and Galaway 1993).

27. This figure contrasts with Sweden, where, because of solid state support, only 5 per cent of lone mothers are poor (Baker 1995).

28. In the United States in 1991, children living with one parent were four times more likely to live in an extended family than children living with two parents (30 per cent vs. 7 per cent) (Taylor 1997: 79).

References

Ahrons, C., and R. Rodgers. 1997. 'The Remarriage Transition' in *Family in Transition*, 9th edn, eds A.S. Skolnick and J.H. Skolnick (New York: Longman), 185–97.

Arendell, T. 1992. 'After Divorce: Investigations into Father Absence', *Gender & Society* 6 (4): 562–87.

Armstrong, P., and H. Armstrong. 1994. *The Double Ghetto: Canadian Women & Their Segregated Work*, 3rd edn (Toronto: McClelland & Stewart).

Baker, M. 1995. *Canadian Family Policies* (Toronto: University of Toronto Press).

Bakker, I., ed. 1996. *Rethinking Restructuring: Gender and Change in Canada* (Toronto: University of Toronto Press).

Beaujot, R., E.M. Gee, F. Rajulton, and Z.R. Ravanera. 1995. *Family Over the Life Course: Current Demographic Analysis*, cat. no. 91–543E (Ottawa: Industry).

Bernard, J. 1972. *The Future of Marriage* (New Haven: Yale University Press).

Blumenstein, P., and P. Schwartz. 1983. *American Couples* (New York: The Free Press).

Boyd, M., and E.T. Pryor. 1989. 'The Cluttered Nest: The Living Arrangements of Young Canadian Adults. *The Canadian Journal of Sociology* 14 (4): 461–79.

Bradbury, B. 1982. 'The Fragmented Family: Family Strategies in the Face of Death, Illness, and Poverty, Montreal, 1860–1885' in *Childhood and Family in Canadian History*, ed. J. Parr (Toronto: McClelland & Stewart), 93–109.

———. 1984. 'Pigs, Cows and Boarders: Non-Wage Forms of Survival among Montreal Families, 1861–91', *Labour/Le Travail* 14: 9–46.

———. 1993. *Working Families: Age, Gender, and Daily Survival in Industrializing Montreal* (Toronto: McClelland & Stewart).

Brenner, J., and B. Laslett. 1991. 'Gender, Social Reproduction, and Women's Self Organization: Considering the U.S. Welfare State', *Gender & Society* 5 (3): 311–33.

Bullen, J. 1992. 'Hidden Workers: Child Labour and the Family Economy in Late Nineteenth-Century Urban Ontario' in *Canadian Family History*, ed. B. Bradbury (Toronto: Copp Clark), 199–220.

Clarke-Stewart, A. 1982. *Daycare* (Cambridge, MA: Harvard University Press).

Conway, J. [1990] 1993. *The Canadian Family in Crisis* (Toronto: James Lorimer).

Coontz, S. 1992. *The Way We Never Were: American Families and the Nostalgia Trap* (New York: Basic Books).

———. 1997. *The Way We Really Are: Coming to Terms with America's Changing Families* (New York: Basic Books).

Dominion Bureau of Statistics. 1933. 1931 Census. v. 5: 686–7.

Duffy, A., N. Mandell, and N. Pupo. 1989. *Few Choices: Women, Work and Family* (Toronto: Garamond Press).

Eichler, M. 1997. *Family Shifts: Families, Policies and Gender Equality* (Toronto: Oxford University Press).

Elder, G.H., Jr. 1974. *Children of the Great Depression: Social Change in Life Experience* (Chicago: University of Chicago Press).

Eyer, D. 1992. *Mother Infant Bonding: A Scientific Fiction* (New Haven: Yale University Press).

Finnie, R. 1993. 'Women, Men, and the Economic Consequences of Divorce: Evidence from Canadian Longitudinal Data', *Canadian Review of Sociology and Anthropology* 30 (2): 205–43.

Fox, B. 1980. 'Women's Domestic Labour and Their Involvement in Wage Work: Twentieth-Century Changes in the Reproduction of Daily Life'. Ph.D. diss., University of Alberta.

Frederick, J. 1995. 'As Time Goes By . . . Time Use of Canadians', cat. no. 89–544 (Ottawa: Industry).

Friedan, B. 1965. *The Feminine Mystique* (New York: Dell).

Gee, E. 1987. 'Historical Changes in the Family Life Course of Canadian Men and Women' in *Aging in*

Canada: Social Perspectives, ed. V. Marshall (Markham: Fitzhenry and Whiteside), 265–87.

Gordon, L. 1974. Woman's Body, Woman's Right: A Social History of Birth Control in America (New York: Penguin).

———. 1988. Heroes of Their Own Lives: The Politics and History of Family Violence (New York: Viking).

Graham, H. 1987. 'Being Poor: Perceptions and Coping Strategies of Lone Mothers' in Give and Take in Families, eds J. Brannen and G. Wilson (London: Allen & Unwin), 32–56.

Hays, S. 1996. The Cultural Contradictions of Motherhood (New Haven: Yale University Press).

Hochschild, A. 1989. The Second Shift: Working Parents and the Revolution of Home (New York: Viking).

Hudson, J., and B. Galaway, eds. 1993. Single Parent Families (Toronto: Thomson Educational Publishing).

Katz, M.B. 1975. The People of Hamilton, Canada West: Family and Class in a Mid-Nineteenth-Century City (Cambridge, MA: Harvard University Press).

Kimmel, M. 1996. Manhood in America: A Cultural History (New York: The Free Press).

Kronby, M.C. 1981. Canadian Family Law (Don Mills, ON: General).

Kurz, D. 1995. For Richer, For Poorer: Mothers Confront Divorce (New York: Routledge).

Laslett, B., and J. Brenner. 1989. 'Gender and Social Reproduction: Historical Perspectives', Annual Review of Sociology 15: 381–404.

Leacy, F.H., ed. 1983. 2nd edn of Urquhart, M.C., and K.A.H. Buckley, eds, Historical Statistics of Canada (Ottawa: Supply and Services).

Leavitt, J.W. 1986. Brought to Bed: Childbearing in America, 1750 to 1950 (New York: Oxford University Press).

Luxton, M. 1980. More Than a Labour of Love: Three Generations of Women's Work in the Home (Toronto: Women's Press).

———. 1983. 'Two Hands for the Clock: Changing Patterns in the Gendered Division of Labour in the Home', Studies in Political Economy 12: 27–44.

May, E.T. 1988. Homeward Bound: American Families in the Cold War Era (New York: Basic Books).

McLaren, A., and A.T. McLaren. 1986. The Bedroom and the State: The Changing Practices and Politics of Contraception and Abortion in Canada, 1880–1980 (Toronto: McClelland & Stewart).

Mitchell, B. 1998. 'Too Close for Comfort? Parental Assessments of "Boomerang Lid" Living Arrangements', The Canadian Journal of Sociology 23 (1): 21–46.

National Council of Welfare. 1999. Poverty Profile 1997 (Ottawa: Public Works and Government Services).

Nault, F., and A. Belanger. 1996. 'The Decline in Marriage in Canada, 1981 to 1991', cat. no. 84–536 (Ottawa: Statistics Canada, Health Statistics Division).

Picard, A. 2000. 'Good Child Care Harder to Find: Study', The Globe & Mail (25 Jan.).

Popenoe, D. 1993. 'American Family Decline, 1960–1990: A Review and Appraisal', Journal of Marriage and the Family 55: 527–55.

Rapp, R., and E. Ross. 1986. 'The 1920s: Feminism, Consumerism, and Political Backlash in the United States' in Women in Culture and Politics: A Century of Change, eds J. Friedlander, B.W. Cook, A. Kessler-Harris, and C. Smith-Rosenberg (Bloomington: Indiana University Press).

Ravanera, Z., and F. Rajulton. 1996. 'Stability and Crisis in the Family Life Course—Findings from the 1990 General Social Survey', Canadian Studies in Population, 23 (2): 165–84.

Richardson, C.J. 1996. 'Divorce and Remarriage' in Families: Changing Trends in Canada, 3rd edn, ed. M. Baker (Toronto: McGraw-Hill Ryerson), 315–49.

Ryan, M. 1981. Cradle of the Middle Class: The Family in Oneida County, New York, 1790–1865 (Cambridge: Cambridge University Press).

South, S., and G. Spitze. 1994. 'Housework in Marital and Nonmarital Households', American Sociological Review 59 (3): 327–47.

Stack, C. 1974. All Our Kin: Strategies for Survival in a Black Community (New York: Harper & Row).

Stansell, C. 1982. City of Women: Sex and Class in New York, 1789–1860 (Urbana: University of Illinois Press).

Statistics Canada. 1953. 1951 Census, v. 4, table 11, cat. no. 98–1951.

———. 1974. 1971 Census, v. 3, part 7, table 6, cat. no. 94–776.

———. 1993. 1991 Census, v. 1, table 2, cat. no. 93–321.

———. 1994. *Women in the Labour Force*, table 6.3, cat. no. 75–507E.

———. 1998. *Historical Labour Force Statistics*, cat. no. 71–201XBP, p. 18.

Strong-Boag, V. 1988. *The New Day Recalled: Lives of Girls and Women in English Canada, 1919–1939* (Markham: Penguin).

Sullivan, M. 1998. 'Absent Fathers in the Inner City' in *Public and Private Families*, ed. A. Cherlin (Boston: McGraw-Hill), 100–8.

Taylor, R. 1997. 'Who's Parenting? Trends and Patterns' in *Contemporary Parenting: Challenges and Issues,* ed. T. Arendell (Thousand Oaks, CA: Sage), 68–92.

Vinovskis, M., and S.M. Frank. 1997. 'Parenting in American Society: A Historical Overview of the Colonial Period Through the 19th Century' in *Contemporary Parenting: Challenges and Issues,* ed. T. Arendell (Thousand Oaks, CA: Sage), 45–67.

Welter, B. 1966. 'The Cult of True Womanhood: 1820–1860', *American Quarterly* 18 (2): part 1, 151–74.

Wertz, R., and D.C. Wertz. 1979. *Lying In: A History of Childbirth in America* (New York: Schocken Books).

Wood, A.D. 1974. '"The Fashionable Diseases": Women's Complaints and Their Treatment in Nineteenth-Century America' in *Clio's Consciousness Raised*, eds M. Hartman and L.W. Banner (New York: Harper & Row), 1–22.

Wu, Z. 1999. 'Premarital Cohabitation and the Time of First Marriage', *Canadian Review of Sociology and Anthropology* 36 (1): 109–28.

Yalnizyan, A. 1998. *The Growing Gap: A Report on Growing Inequality between the Rich and Poor in Canada* (Centre for Social Justice).

Chapter 12

In 1976–7, Meg Luxton carried out a study of full-time homemakers in working-class families in Flin Flon, Manitoba. She chose Flin Flon because the oldest generation of women in town had raised their families in the most primitive of housing conditions—without running water, electricity, or household appliances. Interviewing three generations of Flin Flon women meant that Luxton was able to learn about how their household work changed as their households modernized. *More Than a Labour of Love, the book that Luxton wrote as a result of this research, is very revealing about the nature of personal relations, and especially gender relations, typical of nuclear families in which women are full-time homemakers and men are breadwinners. What follows is the chapter on wives and husbands.*

Wives and Husbands

Meg Luxton

> *I [woman] take thee [man]*
> *To my wedded husband*
> *To have and to hold*
> *From this day forward*
> *For better for worse*
> *For richer for poorer*
> *In sickness and in health*
> *To love, cherish and to obey*
> *Till death do us part*
> Solemnization of Matrimony

In her marriage vows, a woman promises 'to love, cherish and to obey' her husband. While couples appear to marry on the basis of free choice and love, their dependence on the wage imposes structural imperatives which undermine their freedom and love. The daily requirements of household survival mean that both adults must subject themselves and each other to dictates which, for the most part, are beyond their control and which are not particularly in their interests.

Consequently, marriage is indeed 'for better for worse'. While some aspects of marriage are good and women often mention the pleasure and happiness they derive from their marriages, the underlying imperatives create all sorts of tensions which diminish the marital relationship, binding people to each other not by choice based on love but by dependency and a lack of alternatives.[1]

Wage Labour and Domestic Labour

For many working-class women, supporting themselves independently by wage labour is not an inevitable or even a realistic alternative. The sex segregation of the labour market restricts women to the lowest paid, least secure and most monotonous jobs. Women's wages are so low that it is virtually impossible, especially if they have children, for women to survive.[2] Often in periods of high unemployment or in small towns like Flin Flon, there are simply not enough jobs available for those women who want to work. For these women marriage becomes a primary option—it appears to be the only viable life strategy available to them.

In this way there is a basic economic compulsion to marriage and women's low wages help to keep the nuclear family together. Though women marry on the basis of free choice, they have very few real alternatives because of how those alternatives are structured. By associating themselves with men who are earning relatively higher wages, women probably have a higher standard of living than they might have if they depended on their own wage labour.

This economic dependency permeates and threatens female/male relationships. For family households to survive, the husband must sell his labour power in exchange for wages to an employer on an ongoing, regular basis. Once the men enter the bosses' employ, they are no longer free but come under the direct control of their employer.

The employer's primary objective is to extract from his employees as much of their ability to work as possible, to maximize the product of their labour by the end of the shift. Once workers are employees, they become part of capitalist production and how they work depends on how the capitalist organizes production—his control over his labour force, his capacity to co-ordinate and rationalize the various operations of his enterprise—in other words, his capacity to harness labour in the production process and to utilize his workers' labour power to the hilt.

Marx described this type of labour, showing vividly its implications for the (male) worker's state of being:

> Labour is external to the worker—that is, it is not part of his nature—and the worker does not affirm himself in his work but denies himself, feels miserable and unhappy, develops no free physical and mental energy but mortifies his flesh and ruins his mind. The worker therefore feels at ease only outside work, and during work he is outside himself. . . . The external nature of work for the worker appears in the fact that it is not his own but another person's, that in work he does not belong to himself but to someone else (Easton and Guddat 1967: 292).

From the perspective of the worker, the labour process is not for the satisfaction of needs. Rather it demands the denial of needs. Time spent at work is segregated from 'real life'; it is time spent

for, controlled by, and at the service of another. The man returning after a day of work comes home tired. His capacity to labour has been consumed, so he is spent and depleted. He considers his time off work to be his own, to do with as he pleases. He demands the right to spend his time away from wage work in voluntary activities.

But the experiences of wage work are not so easily shaken. His experiences at work usually leave him tired, frustrated, and irritable. The worker bears the social residue of this alienating labour process and of the oppressive social relations of capitalist production. He needs to find ways of releasing those feelings of tension, of assuaging the dissatisfaction. He wants his leisure time to be free of conflict and to be refreshing, restful, and personally satisfying. He needs the opportunity and the means to re-energize—to reproduce his labour power—before he goes back to work the next day.

A miner who had worked for the Company for forty-one years explained how he experienced this process:

> I work hard, see. And it's not great work. And when I gets home I'm tired and fed up and I want to just rest till I feel better. I come home feeling sort of worn down and I need to loosen up and feel human again. At work there is always someone standing over me telling me I have to do this or that. Well, I don't want any more of that at home. I want to do what I want for a change. I want a chance to live when I'm off work.
>
> (Generation II, b. 1920)[3]

Despite the social relations of production, or perhaps because of them, a man is usually proud of his skill, strength, and intelligence in performing his job. This pride focuses on the wages he receives; a good wage is an expression of his ability as a worker.

For the man the importance of the wage is represented by his home, for it is his wage that buys the house he lives in and provides for his needs and those of his wife and children. A male worker measures his worth by his ability to provide for his family. He is proud to be able to support a wife who can devote all her time and energy to maintaining their household. His self-esteem is derived from his ability to provide and maintain his side of the sexual division of labour. This helps motivate him to continue working. And for his labour he expects that the home will be his castle. For the man there is a distinct separation between his workplace and his home, between work time and leisure time. He usually assumes that his wage labour fulfills his obligations within the division of labour of the family household. When a man comes home he is finished work:

> He is at home when he is not working and when he is working he is not at home. His work, therefore, is not voluntary, but coerced, forced labour. It is not the satisfaction of a need but only a means to satisfy other needs. Its alien character is obvious from the fact that as soon as no physical or other pressure exists, labour is avoided like the plague (Easton and Guddat 1967: 292).

No such separation exists for the woman. Her workplace is her home, and for her, work time and leisure time are indistinguishable. She discharges her obligations within the division of labour by doing all those things that are necessary to ensure that the adult members of the household are available for work every day—able and relatively willing to work. In this way she ensures, as far as possible, the regular continuance of the wage on which she depends in order to meet her own physical and social needs. Because the labour power of her husband is exchanged for a wage, while hers is not, the needs of the husband and the requirements of his wage labour always take precedence over other household considerations. Part of the woman's work includes caring for her husband, creating a well-ordered and restorative home for him to come back to. In the process her work becomes less visible and its importance is less acknowledged. The wife is subordinated to the husband.

The sexual division of labour, although inherently hierarchical, makes the participants mutually dependent. While the dependency of women is greater economically and socially, men are dependent on their wives not only for the physical aspect of domestic labour but also for important psycho-emotional support. Within the household division of labour, it falls to the woman to provide for the immediate needs of the wage worker. All aspects of women's work, from its schedules and rhythms to the most subtle personal interactions, are touched and coloured by the type of wage work the men are doing, by the particular ways in which their labour power is consumed by capital.

If the man is engaged in shift work, the household then operates around two, or sometimes three, often contradictory schedules. It is the woman's task to service each routine and to prevent each of them from coming into conflict. This process is well illustrated by one housewife's day. The woman gets up at 7:00 a.m., feeds the baby, then gets the three older children up, fed, and off to school by 8:45 a.m. Meanwhile, her husband who is on the graveyard shift (midnight to 8:00 a.m.) comes in from work and wants a meal, so once the children are fed she prepares his dinner. Then he goes to bed and sleeps until about 6:00 p.m. During the day she must care for the toddler, do her housework, feed and visit with the older children who come home for lunch from noon to 1:30 p.m. and return again at 4:00 p.m. All of this occurs while 'daddy is sleeping' and the noise level must be controlled to prevent him from being disturbed. At 5:00 p.m. she makes supper for the children and at 6:00 p.m. she makes breakfast for him. By 8:30 p.m., when the children are in bed, he is rested and ready to socialize while she is tired and ready to sleep. Another woman in a similar position described it this way:

It totally disrupts my life, his shift work. I have to keep the kids quiet—I'm forever telling them to shut up—and I can't do my work, because the noise wakes him. It makes my life very difficult.

(Generation II, b. 1941)

The impact of shift work on family life is subtle and difficult to pin down. Workers on weekly rotating shifts cannot sleep properly and their eating patterns are disrupted. The result is general irritability, headaches, constipation, and a host of other physical ailments. The social and psychic effects are more elusive.[4] Flin Flon women generally maintained that the graveyard shift was the hardest for them. Some of them did not like being alone with small children at night. Others said they never had time with their husbands, who went to bed as the women were getting up:

Those changing shifts are awful. It's a constant reminder that his work comes first, over any other needs his family might have. We can never get ourselves organized into any regular pattern because our lives are always being turned upside down.

(Generation III, b. 1947)

The requirements of the husband's wage work affect the women's work in a variety of other ways. Women usually have to pack a lunch for their husbands. They may have to wash and repair work clothes. Most significantly, they have to organize their time around their husband's time. All of the women interviewed said that they got up before their husbands in the morning because it was their responsibility to wake them and get their breakfast ready in time for them to leave for work.

A song from a play about mining towns illustrates how women have to organize their time around the Company's schedules:

'Who says we don't work to the whistle?
With us it just don't show.

We got to have dinner on the table before that whistle blow (Winnipeg Women's Liberation 1978).'

Or, as a Flin Flon housewife described it:

Lots of people say what a housewife does isn't work. Well, it is work, and it's just like men's work only it isn't paid and it isn't supervised. But I have things I have to do at certain times. The main difference is, my work is regulated by his work. And whatever I have to do is somehow always overshadowed by the requirements of his work.

(Generation II, b. 1934)

Beyond doing these immediate tasks, the housewife must enter in to a far more complex and profound relationship with her husband, for she must also ensure his general psycho-emotional well-being.

The types of demands placed on domestic labour in trying to meet the husband's needs are partly a function of the specific way in which the husband's labour power has been consumed by capital. For example, levels of mental or physical fatigue vary according to the job as do the types of stress, kinds of injuries, size of appetite, and so on. What restoring his ability to work actually involves depends to a large extent on the personality and personal preferences of the individuals in the marriage. These various constraints and possibilities account for some of the differences between households.

In many cases the men develop their own ways of dealing with their work-related tensions. Their wives simply have to recognize their patterns and allow them to do what they want. Some men want to be left alone for a while when they get home. Others insist on going to the pub for a few drinks before coming home. Three of the women interviewed said their husbands insisted that supper be on the table when they walked in the door. These men refused to talk to anyone until they had eaten.[5] In some households the wife and children had to be home waiting for him when he arrived home from work:

> Bill likes to play with the kids when he comes in, so I always make sure we're home and the kids are washed and changed.
>
> (Generation III, b. 1955)

In others the children had to be neither seen nor heard when their fathers first returned from work:

> When Mike comes in he likes a quiet time with a beer and no kids, so I have to make sure the kids keep quiet and don't bug him in any way.
>
> (Generation III, b. 1950)

Men who do heavy physical labour such as shovelling muck (broken rock) or very noisy work, such as drilling, may need a quiet time alone to relax when they first get off work. Those working under the direct supervision of a boss may choose to release the tensions generated by drinking, playing with their children, or yelling at their families. Some men like to spend their free time at home watching television. Others like to go visiting or have friends over. Some prefer to go off with their male friends to the bush for hunting or fishing or to the pub for drinking. Others like to be very active in voluntary organizations, municipal politics, union politics, or other activities that take them out of the home and away from their families. Whatever their choice, the women's task is to facilitate.

This is a subtle process. Though the tendency for women is to do things 'his way' women are not powerless within marriage. They do have a certain amount of leeway and considerable influence, and they regularly exercise discretion about how much they let their husbands' needs structure their lives. When the man is not present, the housewife can do things 'her way'. She can sometimes expand and alter his tastes.

Depending on the quality of their relationship, she can even get him to do things her way.

If the relationship is poor, the wife may do all she can to make her husband's life miserable by regularly asserting her own will in deliberate opposition to his. When there is no conflict between them, she may do things his way because she loves him and wants to make him happy. Finally, many women will say that they do things their husband's way because they believe that is the way a household should function. In fact, the events they describe suggest that what is often designated 'his way' is often really 'their way'.

On some level all of the woman's work takes into account her husband's preferences. This was reflected repeatedly in the decisions Flin Flon women made about what to buy, what to cook, what to wear. When asked why they prepared the foods they did, most women replied that they made what their husbands' liked. Often women mentioned that they liked certain foods or were interested in trying a different type of cooking but they refrained because their husbands' tastes had priority. They also bought clothes with their husbands' tastes in mind. A friend and I were shopping for shoes. She tried on a pair that she liked very much. After much indecision she rejected them because 'Henry just wouldn't like them.' In another instance a woman spent several hours preparing her dress and getting ready for a formal party. When her husband came in he took one look at her and commented that he had never liked that dress. She immediately went to change her clothes.

An older woman recalled moving into a new house from a two-room cabin in 1940. The new house was completely modern, and they had enough money to furnish it as they liked:

> We settled in slowly. We did one room at a time. We would sit down and discuss the room and what we wanted to do with it. We would talk it out together, then I would go and buy the things we needed and set it up.

I always did it the way he wanted. After all, it was his money what bought it and he should have his house as he likes.

(Generation II, b. 1915)

This woman described a co-operative process of decision making and then, without mentioning any conflict or deferral, she said it was his way. How much this suggests that her preferences are guided by him and how much it reflects her notion of how things should be is impossible to determine.

Love and Affection

All of these types of interactions have an impact on the social relations of marriage. One of the striking features of marital relations in Flin Flon over the last three generations is that, as soon as limitations imposed by their working conditions were modified, Flin Flon residents altered their marital arrangements. Love, affection, and caring have changed considerably over the last fifty years. Largely because of their respective work patterns, women and men in the early period had little time to spend socializing together. Sometimes men had to work away from home for months at a time. Even when they lived at home, they often worked for twelve and fourteen hours each day six days a week. The woman's housework required long, uninterrupted days.

Older women described their expectations of marriage as 'making a family'. For them the sexual division of labour was explicitly embodied in their interpersonal relations as well. A couple co-operated to form a household and to have children. They recognized very distinct women's and men's spheres in their leisure activities. As working time decreased for both women and men, the quality of their relationships changed. The shortened work week and the improvements in housework meant that men could be at home more often and that women had more opportunities to take a few hours 'off'.[6]

Younger women described their marriages as 'partnerships'. While they adhered to the traditional division of labour based on work, they seemed to share more activities with their husbands and they expected to be 'friends' with them. Over the last fifty years wives and husbands have increasingly spent more time together. Couples seem to expect more demonstrated affection, intimacy, friendship from each other. A young woman described how her marriage differed from her mother's:

They didn't seem to expect much of each other. They lived together and I know they cared, but they each went their own ways. I don't think that's right. I want to have more closeness with my husband. I think husbands and wives should be each other's best friends.

(Generation III, b. 1952)

Comparing observations of an older woman recalling her past and a young woman describing her present confirms this changed perspective:

When we was married [1926] and moved here we knew we each had our own harness to pull. Jake worked for the railway and later for the Company and he worked long hours for most of the week. I recollect he worked twelve to fourteen hours each day Monday to Saturday and on Sunday he slept or went out for a drink with his mates. He brought home the wages; that were his job. Me, I looked after the house and took care of the kids and made sure his clothes were clean and his meals were on the table. That were my job.

(Generation I, b. 1895)

Jim's my best friend in the world. I don't like to do anything unless he can too. Well he works for the Company, eh, and I take care of the house and the kids but all the time he's home we do things together.

(Generation III, b. 1949)

Besides changing work patterns other social forces, such as the increasing isolation of the family, have affected marital relationships. In the early period in Flin Flon social life involved regular collective activities. Large groups of people held dances, floating card games, berry-picking outings, and socials organized by groups of individuals who came together for a specific event. Women were central to organizing these get-togethers.

Over the years there has been a shift from community-based entertainment to smaller family events. The number of communal activities has decreased and are organized either by businesses or formal organizations. Women are still active, but the scope of their decision making and authority has been reduced. Where women once organized for both the community and their families, they now organize primarily for their families.

This shift has reduced women's social horizons and increased their orientation toward the family. An older woman described her experience:

> When we first came here the town was small and there weren't no Trout Festival Association or Rotary or whatnot to organize things. So we did it. Oh I remember lovely times, big dances and lots of fun. The men were all working odd hours so we women would do it and everybody would go. . . . Now it seems everything is done for us. There's this or that event, all organized in advance for you, and families go to them or not. It's not the same somehow.
>
> (Generation I, b. 1901)

As she suggests, this change is partly as a result of the municipal infrastructure. However, other factors have also contributed to the changing social patterns.

Before people in Flin Flon owned cars, groups of people sometimes got rides in horse-drawn wagons into the bush to collect berries or to go hunting, picnicking, or exploring:

> Before we had the car we often used to go in groups for a wagon ride somewhere. Now we just all go off separately in our own cars.
>
> (Generation II, b. 1923)

Another source of major social change was the development of television:

> Before the TV come we used to have a regular, floating card game with the people on the street. We'd go from house to house playing cards and having a whale of a time.
>
> (Generation I, b. 1898)

> Used to be, we'd go visiting. Folks would go out for a walk and drop in and chat, have a beer. Nowadays we just all stay home and watch telly.
>
> (Generation II, b. 1931)

The result of these changes is that families have become more dependent on their own leisure activities. When female and male spheres were quite separate, women were less concerned with entertaining their husbands and more involved with the community at large. Their increased isolation within the family, coupled with the modern expectation of friendship and companionship, has meant that wives and husbands are more dependent on each other and therefore more vulnerable to personal whim:

> I don't like to go out visiting without Mike. It just doesn't seem right. We like to do things together. But he hasn't been feeling like going out since he started working the night shift, so I haven't been going out either. I miss it.
>
> (Generation III, b. 1951)

Sexuality

> I don't know what sex is all about. Sometimes I wish you could just do it because it feels good. But of course you can't. You're not sup-

posed to do it till you're married. You might get pregnant. He wants it and you don't. There's all these different things happening all at once. And you don't know what's right or wrong or why it's all happening. Oh sex! Who would have thought anything so simple could be so complex?

(Generation III, b. 1950)

The 'long arm of the job' stretches from the workplace into the bedroom and exerts its grip on the most intimate part of marriage. Sexuality is so complex that it operates on many levels and has different meanings in different situations. In some ways it is an expression of human need, of pleasure, and of the social togetherness of lovers. In other ways it is an oppressive and repressive relationship which grinds the tenderness and love out of people, leaving behind the frustration, bitterness, and violence. From the perspective of domestic labour, there is an aspect of sexuality that is work. On one level marriage can be understood as an exchange between wife and husband—her domestic work, including sexual access, for his economic support.[7]

This underlying exchange becomes apparent in the prelude to marriage, the period in which women are recruited for domestic labour. The process of dating—of selecting a mate for marriage—is, of course, not experienced as an exchange by the people participating in it. The economic necessity for women and the sexual motivation for men are hidden under massive layers of ideology, propaganda, and confusion. People date and marry for many reasons, often because 'that is the way things work'. They are usually so caught up in the process that they do not have time to reflect on it. Although very few Flin Flon women and men had analyzed the forces that underpin their lives, they did experience the power of those forces. In dating practices, for example, women generally dated men their own age or older. Men rarely dated older women. While a couple may have agreed to share

the costs on a date, men were generally expected to pay. Most significantly, women were not supposed to initiate a relationship. They had to wait until a suitable man approached them.

This means that the balance of forces in any female/male relationship is likely to be unequal. Men tend to have the advantage of being older, having economic power and social authority. Women rarely have access to as much money and they cannot act forthrightly. They are forced to manipulate and insinuate—to set things up so that men will ask them out and, ultimately, ask them to marry.

This inequality permeates sexual activities. Whatever their real feelings (and often they do not know what their real feelings are), both women and men get involved in the process of serious dating where women trade sexual 'favours' for a 'good time' and economic rewards. On some level the participants are aware of this underlying exchange.

The women know that if they hold out too long, they risk losing the man to someone who is less resistant. Three young women were evaluating their relationships with their current steady boyfriends. All three men were working. One woman, age sixteen, had been out with her seventeen-year-old boyfriend six times. She commented:

Tomorrow will be our seventh date. Last time he really wanted me to neck with him but I wouldn't. I only let him kiss me goodnight when he took me home. I don't think I can get away with that again this date. I'm going to have to let him go further or he'll never take me out again.

Her boyfriend had been working for the Company for two years. He owned a car and had sizeable savings. He had also stated publicly that when he married, as a wedding present he would give his wife the downpayment for the house of her choice. Because of his resources he was considered a 'good catch'.

Her fifteen-year-old friend replied:

Yeh, John [age sixteen] and me were necking last weekend and we got real close. He wants to go all the way but I said no way. Not till I get married. But he laughed and said I'd be an old maid if I never made out till then. I'm afraid that if I give in, I'll get pregnant, but if I don't, then I'll lose him.

The third woman, sixteen years old, agreed:

Yeh! Boys always expect you to go all the way. And if you won't, then they go find someone else who will. Andy [her eighteen-year-old boyfriend of six months] said that it wasn't worth his while taking me out all the time, spending his money on me, if I didn't come across.

The men had a similar understanding. One seventeen-year-old man returned from a date in a foul mood. He complained bitterly that he had had a 'lousy time' because:

Jesus, I took her out for supper and we went to a show, and when I took her home she would do nothing but peck my face and say, 'Thank you for the nice time'. I spent all that money on her, and was real nice to her too and that's all the thanks I get.

Men try to cajole and coerce women 'to go all the way'. Women resist, give in a bit, resist some more. Everyone knows the risks involved and when a woman finally 'gives in' and 'allows' the man to go all the way, two related but opposed social expectations come into play. The first is the assumption that pregnancy is the woman's responsibility. If she does not take precautions to prevent conception, she must face the consequences alone. The second is that men do have responsibilities. If a couple have sexual relations and the woman gets pregnant, then they will probably marry.

Once a woman is pregnant, the man is not bound by the same constraints in the situation. Unlike the woman, he can decide or choose whether or not to accept some of the responsibility for her pregnancy. If he does not accept it, then she has been 'knocked up' and as a single woman she is subject to material and social hardships. If the man does accept some responsibility, they get married. For the woman this is clearly the preferred choice. It indicates to her as well as to others that he thinks enough of her to want to marry. It makes her a 'good woman'. However, her dependency on him establishes yet another tension in their relationship.

Many Flin Flon women expressed feelings of gratitude because their husbands had married them. Some spoke of feeling indebted to men who offered to marry them:

Bob is my honey. When I told him I was pregnant he didn't give me no hassle. He just said right off, 'Why then we'll get us married and I'll be a daddy.' He was so good to me.
(Generation III, b. 1955)

I owe him so much. You know, I got that way and I wasn't going to tell him, only my sister said she would if I didn't. At first he was mad. But he agreed we'd get married.
(Generation III, b. 1956)

Many women expressed anxiety that their husbands had married them only because they were pregnant. These women talked about how they and their children were burdens that the man had 'nobly' taken on. One woman, married for over thirty years and the mother of five children, described her fears:

I think maybe he hates me deep down. We had to get married and then I had four more after that one. So he didn't want to marry me. I don't think he ever loved me. But he stuck with us. It was a sort of noble gesture on his part back then. I don't think he knew what it would mean.

(Generation II, b. 1924)

After the first child is born couples are confronted with a series of problems and decisions that focus on sex, children, and domestic work. Here, more than anywhere else perhaps, the different interests of women and men are illuminated. For men the issue seems relatively straightforward. They have an acknowledged and socially recognized desire for sexual intercourse. They tend to assume both that birth control is the responsibility of the woman and that having children is part of marriage. They also generally favour having several children.

For women the question is far more complex. While a few women have come to terms with their sexuality and have apparently satisfying and active sex lives, most young women find sexuality problematic. They say that they rarely enjoy sex except as an indication that their husbands still love them. They are ignorant about their own sexual needs and are terrified of getting pregnant. A standard complaint raised by women of all ages was that their husbands wanted sex 'too often':

He's forever wanting it. Never a weekend goes by but he isn't after me to sleep with him. I don't understand why men want it so often.

(Generation II, b. 1929)

This discrepancy between the experiences of women and men is reflected in interactions between friends or cohorts of the same sex. Men at work joke about making it or 'scoring' with their wives on a regular basis. Older men comment regularly on younger men's work patterns by assuring them that the reputed laziness of the younger men occurs because they have such active sex lives. Older men caution younger men to wait until they have been married for ten years; then they will not have sex so often and will be able to get a good day's work done.

Women regularly console each other for having 'over-sexed' husbands who constantly make demands on them. Older women reassure younger women that after they have been married for ten years or so their husbands will not want sex so much. It will then happen only a couple of times a year and the younger women will not have to worry any more. A young woman who had been married for three years commented:

My husband wants sex too much. I think he is oversexed. If he had his way, we'd make out every day!

(Generation III, b. 1950)

Her older neighbour reassured her:

My man used to be that way too, but he got over it. Just wait a few more years and yours will slow down too. It's hard on you now, but it gets better.

(Generation II, b. 1925)

While the primary reason women give for avoiding sex is the fear of pregnancy, the contradictions they experience are compounded by the fact that their work is continuous and tiring. When a man gets home from work he expects to relax. For a woman home is work and she can rarely relax. Relaxing and concentrating on sex may be almost impossible for the woman if she is listening for the children, or has just finished cleaning up and is trying to organize herself for the next day:

Then he wants to make out, but I just can't. My head is racing, thinking of all the stuff to be done tomorrow morning, and I'm tired and just want to collapse asleep. And part of me is always listening for the baby.

(Generation III, b. 1954)

In general, their tension about pregnancy and the nature of their work combine to make women reluctant sexually. Just as patterns of love, affection, and caring have changed over the last fifty years, so too have patterns of sexuality. In her analysis of 'the marriage bed', Lillian Rubin (1976: 44) found that in the last fifty years American sexual practices have changed tremendously. 'The revolution in American sexual behavior is profound.' She also found that while working-class couples were having sex more frequently and with greater variation, it was at the man's initiative. The women felt great ambivalence and insecurity about sex.

In Flin Flon it also appears that women of the third generation experienced greater confusion, bewilderment, and pressure about sexuality than their mothers and grandmothers did before them. One explanation is that as sexuality is increasingly identified with leisure activities, popularity, and personal expression, it acquires increased significance for both women and men. Another explanation emerges from an analysis developed by Michael Schneider (1975) regarding the dynamic between wage work and male sexuality. Schneider notes the oppressive characteristics of wage work, where the work processes and the machines take over the worker. The body of the worker moves in response to predetermined patterns. His mind has to obey the logic of work processes determined by someone else. Fundamentally, he is denied his humanity.

One area that capitalism does not directly control at work is his sexuality. Because this is one area left to the man, it becomes an important one for him to develop and express. Schneider also notes that as labour has been steadily degraded by capitalism, sex has become increasingly important as a focus of survival for the individual. In sex male workers have increasingly sought solace and release and an assertion of power, which means there is now more sexual pressure on women.

Older Flin Flon women described sex as a duty a woman is obliged to provide for her man. Because they believed that male sexual needs are direct and urgent, they said it was the responsibility of women to meet them. They rarely referred to any sexual drive on the part of women:

> A woman doesn't need that like a man. Men need it regular or they go a bit nutty. So women have to give it to them. You just leave it up to them; just let them do what they want.
> (Generation I, b. 1894)

These women received no direct sexual education. Instead they received extremely contradictory messages. Sex was 'not nice' and something to be avoided. Sex was a duty that a woman performed willingly and passively for her husband. They learned to repress and deny their sexual feelings while submitting to men. Older Flin Flon women said that their usual sexual experience was limited to the missionary position, which maximizes the passivity of women. Younger women described a considerably wider range of sexual activities. The sexual revolution of the 1960s expanded knowledge about sexual physiology and sexual practices. As various studies have shown, more people are practising more variations in their sexual behaviour now than in the 1940s.[8]

Rubin found that men were interested in changing their sexual behaviour and pushed women to experiment. She also found that women viewed men's attitudes, including their concern for female orgasm and gratification, as a mixed blessing. She concluded:

> As long as women's sexuality is subjected to capricious demands and treated as if regulated by an 'on-off' switch, expected to surge forth vigorously at the flick of the 'on' switch or to subside at the flick of the 'off', most women will continue to seek the safest path and remain quietly some place between 'on' and 'off' (Rubin 1976: 92).

'Quietly somewhere between on and off' is an apt description of the way most younger Flin Flon women talked about their sexuality:

Sometimes I get real excited and I really want it but what we do doesn't really do it to me so then I feel frustrated and irritable. So it's better if I never get turned on.

(Generation III, b. 1952)

I usually don't get turned on very much but sometimes he's just so nice and he loves me so much that I feel sort of like it.

(Generation III, b. 1951)

Mostly I don't think about sex, but if I get too turned off then it's awful when he wants it, so I can't shut myself off completely.

(Generation III, b. 1954)

The passive lover is a natural extension of the 'good girl'. Women who for years learned to deny their sexual needs cannot suddenly reverse those years and 'turn on'. But for younger men sexuality is an important part of the way they have learned to express their feelings. As one man explained:

I love her and I want her to know how deeply I feel and I can't understand why she won't let me show her [by having sex].

(Generation III, b. 1945)

His bewilderment was genuine; so was his affection. Rubin (1976: 47) describes the uncertainty that women and men experience when they confront each other's sexual expectations:

The cry for understanding from both men and women is real. Each wishes to make the other understand, yet, given the widely different socialization practices around male and female sexuality, the wish is fantasy. As a result, he asks; she gives. And neither is satisfied.

For women the recent sexual patterns that men have introduced are bound up in contradictions. Men want women to be more active, to participate more energetically in sex, to initiate it

more often. They want greater variety, particularly oral sex. They also want to feel that women are enjoying sex. But women and men have not generally learned how to share mutual pleasure. Instead men tend to exert even more pressure on women and then appropriate women's pleasure for themselves.

So women become more active, take the initiative, and either have orgasms or fake them, still mostly to satisfy the men:

He keeps telling me he wishes I'd start things off sometimes. But when I do he's always busy or too tired or I'm interrupting him. I think he wants me to start things when he wants them to start.

(Generation III, b. 1945)

For some women, sex is still a duty, but a duty that now includes being active:

He wants me to be real turned on and excited. He sort of likes it when I pant and moan and wiggle around.

(Generation III, b. 1941)

Some women do what their husbands want out of resignation or fear:

I don't care any more. I just let him do what he wants, and if he wants me to do something I do it. So what?

(Generation III, b. 1946)

When he wants it he has to get it or he gets mad and beats me up, so I always do as he wants.

(Generation III, b. 1957)

Just as women are afraid when dating that if they hold back they may lose the men, some wives are afraid that if they do not participate in sex, they will lose their husbands to other women, to the pub, or to male friends:

I do whatever he wants. Otherwise I figure he'll run off with other women—ladies of the night types.

(Generation III, b. 1945)

I try to act real interested and sexy just as he's leaving for work so he'll be interested and come straight home after work.

(Generation II, b. 1935)

I always seduce him just before we go to a party. That way I figure he won't be interested in other women. He'll be too pooped.

(Generation III, b. 1946)

For some women sexual co-operation is a way of inducing or rewarding good behaviour. Some even recognize the sexual-economic exchange that underlies marriage:

If I want something, I just get all sexy and loving, and after I tell him what I want.

(Generation III, b. 1956)

If he does something really nice, like help me with the dishes or take me out somewhere to something special, then I always try to make love to him so he'll know I liked what he did.

(Generation II, b. 1933)

When I want something for the house, like a new washing machine or something, then I just make love like crazy for a while and then stop. Then I tell him what I want and say that if he wants more loving he has to buy it.

(Generation III, b. 1949)

For many other women, however, sex is a way of expressing their feelings of affection and caring. For them 'making love' is literally that. Sex both expresses and reinforces the love they feel for their husbands:

I love that guy. So I try to show him.

(Generation III, b. 1947)

He's a sweetie. I love him so I make love with him lots.

(Generation III, b. 1948)

He's a wonderful man. I love him. It's the best way I can let him know.

(Generation III, b. 1953)

Love and affection can hold women back sexually. Some women decide that there is no percentage in 'turning on'. To turn on is to assert one's own needs. Sex traditionally revolves around the man's advances, his schedules, his rhythms, his climax—*his* needs. For a woman to be turned on seems to contest this one-sidedness. Women often subordinate their needs and wants to ensure family harmony. Sublimating their sexuality to their husbands' may be an expression of this pattern, an attempt on the part of the wife to express her love for her husband.

Sometimes I'd like to say stop when he is pounding away at me. Then I'd tell him to slow down, to touch me the way I dream about. And I imagine us making love beautifully. And I like it and I love him. But if I did, I know he'd feel hurt. It's important to him that he thinks I like the way he makes love. If I started suggesting things he'd feel bad. So I don't.

(Generation III, b. 1948)

The sublimation of sexuality, in the interests of marital harmony may be one reason sexual activity apparently decreases as the marriage ages. Sixty of the women interviewed reported that as their marriages progressed, their level of sexual activity decreased. It may be that, faced with their inability to resolve all the contradictions that surround sexuality, many couples give up. They minimize their sexual activities rather than continue to confront the tensions:

When we were first married, sex was really difficult. I never liked it and he knew that and it made him feel bad. Gradually it just didn't seem worth it to go on. So we don't do it much any more.

(Generation II, b. 1931)

Family Violence Is a Hateful Thing

Men and women come to marriage from very different positions and their experiences of work and marriage create different understandings. At best these contrary positions are barriers which must be struggled against. For most couples they become sources of tension and all too frequently the tension leads to hostility and conflict.

At work men are powerless, so in their leisure time they want to have a feeling that they control their own lives. Because they are responsible for the household's subsistence, men often feel that they have the right to control the arrangements of the household and the people who live there. As the wage *earner*, the man is the wage *owner*. He is the property owner in the family; his power is rooted in real property relations. This property prerogative is the basis of the unequal relations of the family. Structured into household relations therefore is a 'petty tyranny' which allows the man to dominate his wife and children. Such male domination derives partly from the fact that domestic labour is predicated on wage labour and therefore caters to the needs of the wage worker. It is reinforced partly by societal norms of male dominance and superiority. Male chauvinism easily flourishes in such a setting. Some men exercise their 'petty tyranny' by demanding that their wives be at home when they get off work. The reason men give for making this demand is partly a reflection of their desire to assert their authority:

She's my wife and she should be there when I get off.

(Generation II, b. 1919)

You [to wife] be home when I get off. That's where you belong.

(Generation III, b. 1946)

Knowing that they can demand that their wives be at home waiting for them is a mechanism for releasing some of the feelings of powerlessness the wage work engenders:

It makes me feel good to know she is at home waiting for me, like there's a place where I'm a man. I think about that when I'm at work.

(Generation III, b. 1953)

One result of the economic relationship between women and their husbands is to bind the men to their jobs. While divorce from the means of production structurally compels men to do wage work, once a man has a dependent wife and children he incurs responsibilities and debts, which means that he cannot afford to stop working. While a single man can choose to quit a particular job when it becomes too unpleasant, a married man cannot. Objectively the woman becomes a force in keeping the man tied to his job. From her position of economic dependency, a wife adds more pressure to the structural compulsion to work.

Historically the Company has hired married men precisely because they create a more stable workforce. Sometimes women themselves recognize this aspect of their relationship:

I know he hates his job. It's a terrible job. But he can't quit 'cause of me and the kids. We need his wages.

(Generation III, b. 1953)

Subjectively women act as pressure to keep their husbands not only at work but working regularly and responsibly. Many men deal with their dislike of work by quitting periodically, or less drastically, by going late, taking time off, or slacking on the job. Such behaviour is directly threatening to the household standard of living as it affects the amount of money the men bring home. It is in the women's interests to try to prevent the men from taking time off. When a man considers doing so, his wife may point out that they are in debt and need his money.

Thus some men see their wives as constantly nagging, forcing them to work when they hate it. This induces tensions between the needs of women as domestic workers and the response of the men to wage work, tensions which are often expressed as hostilities between the sexes. A woman whose husband regularly skipped shifts expressed her sense of frustration and anger at men:

> Men. They're just no good. They are lazy and irresponsible and selfish. Look at Jim, he just skipped another shift and how are we going to make do?
>
> (Generation II, b. 1929)

On the other hand, the responsibility of being breadwinners generates in men all sorts of pressure and fear, which in turn are often projected onto women (Guettel 1974: 14). This hostility is reinforced by women's work as tension managers for their husbands.

When men express their work-related tensions, anxieties, and hostilities at work, it is economically threatening to the employer. When their protest is collectively expressed, for example in a general strike, the results are politically threatening to the capitalist state. Therefore, both employers and the state employ sophisticated means to minimize this potential. The threat of firing is the most significant means of repressing outbursts in the workplace. Labour legislation, especially laws against wildcat strikes, and the armed force of the police protect the interests of the state.

On the other hand, family violence is not directed against either employers or the state. While in recent years, primarily because of pressures from the women's liberation movement, family violence has gradually come to be considered socially deviant, it is still not recognized as a major social problem. Very little is done by either employers or the state to prevent family violence.

If no mechanisms are available by which workers can channel their work-related tensions in to forms of struggle at the workplace, they carry those tensions and angers home with them. Part of reproducing the worker's labour power must therefore include ways of displacing those work-related fears and hostilities:

> When he comes home from work, I really think it's up to me to help him relax and feel good. If he's grumpy and tired, I cheer him up.
>
> (Generation II, b. 1926)

This part of women's work in reproducing labour power is the most hidden and profound. It is also of vital importance for her work and her life. While part of this tension management is done for the sake of the man, another part is for herself and the children. Women do not want to live with fights and the threat of violence everyday. They defuse tension, refrain from a certain argument, or protect their husbands from things that will upset them in order to maintain peace:

> I remember how I always used to try and meet him at the door with a cup of tea. He liked his tea. If I made him feel better after work, then our home was a happy one.
>
> (Generation I, b. 1900)

In some instances, women are the recipients of overt anger and rage. Some examples will illustrate what this means in practice. A thirty-two-year-old man had worked for the Company for sixteen years. His current supervisor did not like him and they had regular clashes at work. He came home almost every night tense and irritable. His wife described what happened at night:

> We go to sleep and then sometimes in the middle of the night I wake up because he is groaning and punching me and crying out angry stuff at his boss. Sometimes he punches me real hard and once he broke my nose. Course he didn't mean to and it wasn't me he was mad at. It was his boss, but still. So I get out of bed and go make tea and wake

him up and talk to him, then he settles down and we go back to sleep. It happens maybe two or three times a week.

(Generation III, b. 1949)

The wife received the brunt of the rage and violence that her husband bottled up and repressed at work. She considered it her duty to get up and make him tea and comfort him, even though she had an infant to feed at 6:00 a.m. She was constantly tired and sometimes dozed off in the middle of a conversation. She apologized for doing so by explaining:

See Joe has a hard time at work so I have to get up with him in the night, so I don't get too much sleep these days.

In another case, a twenty-eight-year-old man had worked for the Company for twelve years. He too had a supervisor with whom he fought regularly. His solution to his work-related tensions was to get drunk or stoned on marijuana every night after work. His wife was concerned for his health and worried that he drank or smoked 'all that hard-earned cash'. When he was 'ripped' he tended to think that she was the hated boss and he lashed out at her:

Once he came at me with the kitchen knife saying I was [the boss] and he wasn't going to take no more shit from me. Another time he took a swipe at me and broke my glasses. Usually though he just yells at me that I can take my fucking job and shove it or something like that. I just keep out of reach till he calms down.

(Generation III, b. 1951)

Growing out of the various power struggles that occur between men and their work and between wives and husbands is sex-based hostility where male contempt for women is expressed through physical violence.

Wife beating is one of the hidden crimes in this society. In recent years the women's liberation movement has pointed out how widespread it is. The few studies that have been done show unequivocally that wife beating is a phenomenon that occurs with equal frequency among families of all classes (Eekelaar and Katz 1975; Borland 1976; D'Oyley 1978; Martin 1978; Renvoize 1978; MacLeod 1980). It is part of the larger problem of generalized violence against women and must be understood in that context. For working-class families, it is compounded by the pressures and dependency generated by the proletarian condition:

My husband beats me, usually on payday. He gets mad and hates me. His violence is a really hateful thing.

(Generation II, b. 1935)

Why do women put up with such treatment? They do so partly because there are no resources to give them the support necessary to deal with the abuse. Flin Flon has no hostels for women; the police will not interfere in what they term 'domestic squabbles'; and economically the women have no resources to leave. Equally important is the fact that most women feel it is their responsibility to 'stick it out' because marriage is 'till death do us part' and tension managing is part of their work. Of the hundred women interviewed, only three were divorced. Most women, when male violence erupts, 'just keep out of reach' until it subsides.

One woman who was beaten regularly by her husband was recovering after a particularly bad attack in which her arm was broken. What she said explains in part why so many women accept the abuse they receive from their husbands:

He puts up with shit every day at work and he only works because he has me and the kids to support. Weren't for us he'd be off trapping on his own, with no boss breathing down his neck. He hates his job. He's got all that mad locked up inside with nowhere for it to go. So sometimes he takes it out on me and the kids. Well I sort of don't blame him I guess.

(Generation II, b. 1935)

Thus a terrible but logical and extreme extension of their roles as tension managers is for women, as the victims, to blame themselves and to feel guilty for having induced male hostility and aggression.

Meeting Women's Needs

Domestic violence is the most extreme form of women's oppression within the family. However, in a myriad of other less obvious ways the subordinate character of domestic labour denies women their full humanity.

Domestic labour is responsible for reproducing the labour power of all the adults of the household. In other words, the woman is responsible for reproducing not only her husband's capacity to work each day but her own as well. In some ways, domestic labour is similar to wage work. It is frequently physically and mentally exhausting and monotonous. While it is not alienated in the sense that wage labour is alienated, it is the epitome of self-sacrificing labour. Because it is unpaid, women can justify it as reasonable and honourable work only by considering it a 'labour of love'. This definition reinforces its self-sacrificing quality and encourages women themselves to underplay the extent to which it is much more than a labour of love. In daily life this means that women's needs are not always met.

When household resources are scarce, it is the women who cut back their consumption first. There is a working-class tradition of women eating less than their husbands and children, denying themselves sustenance they badly need so that other household members can have more.[9]

In many Flin Flon households, on the day before payday there was very little food in the house. A number of women regularly did not eat that day because there was only enough for one or two people.

> He's got to eat or he can't do his work and the baby needs food to grow, but it won't hurt me to skip a meal for once.
>
> (Generation III, b. 1958)

Women's sleeping time is also vulnerable to demands from other household members. In some households where men worked the night shift, their wives got up at 3:00 a.m. either to greet them coming off shift or to send them off to work. When those women had school-aged children, they also had to get up at 7:30 a.m. so their sleep was disrupted and inadequate. When other household members were sick or frightened or simply unable to sleep at night, the women got up with them to comfort, feed, and care for them. A number of women talked about how tired they felt all the time. They attributed this 'housewife's fatigue' to regularly interrupted sleep.

Even when women were ill, they had to carry on with their work. Those women who were actively engaged in domestic labour reported that their husbands were sick enough to stay in bed an average of four days each year. Their husbands went to bed when they got sick, and the women took care of them in addition to doing their regular work. The women themselves were sick enough to warrant staying in bed an average of eight days each year. However, they unanimously agreed that, no matter how sick they were, they could not take time off to go to bed. They continued with their regular work despite their illness. In every case, women took time off work only when they were hospitalized—for a major illness or having a baby. Women said they enjoyed their stays in hospital when their babies were born. They relished the rest and being catered to.

The twenty-two women who were retired said that a similar pattern continued even when the couple was older and nearing retirement. In older people, illness was compounded by the fact that many of the men had work-related injuries or illnesses, which meant they required constant nursing. Even though the women were also often ill or crippled by age-related diseases, such as arthritis and rheumatism, they still continued to nurse the men. A number of women said that dealing with an ill spouse finally forced them to retire:

> I kept on managing my house for twenty years after my husband retired. He had bad lungs [from working underground] and at last he took to bed and needed regular nursing. Well I kept at it for about a year, but I wasn't strong enough so I finally had to give it up.
>
> (Generation I, b. 1888)

Reproducing labour power also involved ensuring that workers have a chance to recuperate, relax, and engage in leisure activities that are not related to their regular work. For domestic workers, especially with young children, meeting this need is almost impossible. There is no time when the woman is totally free from work-related responsibilities. Even when she is relaxing, she is on call. Women recognize that their situation differs from their husbands':

> I guess I have to take care of all of them and then I have to take care of myself too.
>
> (Generation III, b. 1955)

> How come there's no one to take care of me?
>
> (Generation II, b. 1934)

> When they are tired, or can't find something or they want something, I do it for them. When I want something I get it for myself.
>
> (Generation III, b. 1945)

When women described their activities during a typical day, they frequently mentioned periods when they took time 'off' to visit with friends, watch TV, or just sit down for a cup of tea and a cigarette. However, even during these breaks, those with young children must be alert to their activities. And all too often, women described their breaks as time not only to relax but also to 'do a bit of mending or sewing'.

The responsibility of constantly caring for the needs of others means that it is often difficult for women to determine what their own needs are:

> When I wake up early I like to lie in bed and have a think about my life. It's the only time I have to myself and what I need, you know, to get me through my day. Like I know what he needs—his lunch box and a hot supper— and what they need—clean clothes and their lunch. And they all need love I guess. But what do I need?
>
> (Generation II, b. 1936)

Sometimes the work women do becomes so merged with their identity that they have trouble distinguishing them. They confuse their own needs with those of their families. This confusion is reflected in the way women sometimes describe family needs. A woman buying a jacket for her six-year-old child remarked: 'I need this jacket. It's getting cold these days.'

The lack of clarity that women have about their own needs as domestic workers begins with marriage when most couples set up households and the women establish the social relations of their work based on inexperience and lack of knowledge. The first few years of household formation are critical, for it is during this period that patterns of work, personal interactions, and the particular expression of the division of labour within the household are established. Once established they are extremely difficult to change.

A woman with three children under ten years of age observed that when her first baby was born she was so interested and excited by the new baby that she wanted to take care of it herself. She never asked her husband to help out with childcare. When the second and third children were born, the novelty had worn off, her energy was dissipated, and she wanted him to become involved:

> But he just wouldn't. He said he'd never changed a nappy and he wasn't about to start. In fact, he used to point out regularly that I had insisted on doing it alone with the first one and why had I suddenly changed my tune now?
>
> (Generation III, b. 1948)

Because of their initial experience and lack of knowledge, women frequently flounder around for several years trying to understand what is happening to them and trying to get some control over the situation.

At the same time, they are caught up in the demands of young children, keeping a house and relating to their husbands. Many of them end up in the same situation as the Red Queen in Lewis Carroll's *Through the Looking Glass*, having to run as fast as they can simply to stay in one place.[10] An older woman recalled her feelings of bewilderment and confusion during this early period of her marriage:

> I never quite got on top of things. I kept thinking that if I could just get a week of peace I could think things through and then I'd be okay. But everything was always rushing here and there and I didn't ever catch up. Now I sort of have a routine and a pattern of work. But I never chose it. It just happened by default.
>
> (Generation I, b. 1907)

Most women are not deliberate martyrs; they make a concerted effort to ensure that their own needs for relaxation and support are met at some level. They develop strategies, such as organizing their workplace and the social relations of their work in the most convenient and convivial ways possible. This means that women are interested in adopting any new developments in household technology, in the organization of their work or in new products and materials.

Another strategy involves organizing their work so that they can assert themselves as they choose when their husbands are not around. Most women organize this part of their time around their own interests:

> When he's not here I do things how I want. I scrub my floors or do my wash or go visit or play with the kids—whatever I want to do and how I want to do it. When he gets off, I have to make sure I'm on time for work, I have to be home waiting for him and I do what he wants while he's there. That way he feels good, we have a good time together and I get my own time too.
>
> (Generation III, b. 1947)

As a third strategy women establish and maintain networks of co-workers, friends, and neighbours to provide a milieu in which they can pool their knowledge about their work and share information, goods, and services. All of the women interviewed described these networks as vitally important to them. On an average women spent three to four hours each day visiting, either in person or on the phone, with friends and neighbours. During these visits women combine a number of activities. They enjoy each other's company while exchanging information about their work and their lives. Simultaneously they care for their children and continue doing some aspect of their housework, such as ironing or cooking:

> I try to visit with my friends as often as possible. It helps me get through my day. We sit and chat about this and that. We watch the kids. I help do the laundry or whatever.
>
> (Generation III, b. 1949)

They also rely a great deal on assistance and support from female relatives. Of the twenty women interviewed who had mothers living in Flin Flon, nineteen said that they saw their mothers at least twice a week. Of the eighty-eight active domestic workers interviewed, seventy-two said they relied on a close female relative, mother, mother-in-law, daughter, or sister to help out in crisis situations. Women in sixty-three households said they visited with a close female relative at least once each week and that those women provided assistance, information, and affection:

> My sister and my husband's mother are just always there when I need them. If I want to pop out to the store, one of them will mind the baby. If I'm feeling low, I go for a visit.
> (Generation III, b. 1951)

Through their women friends and relatives, housewives can improve the social relations of their work and meet some of their own needs for work-related tension managing. Even women who considered their husbands to be their best friends asserted that women friends were special and important:

> Well, my husband, he's my husband and I love him, and he knows me better than anyone and he's my best friend. But Sarah is something else. I see her everyday and we chat and when I'm down she cheers me up and when I'm in a muddle she sorts me out and when things aren't good with my husband, she hugs me.
> (Generation III, b. 1948)

Frequently, several women got together to do some part of their work collectively. Two or three women went shopping in one car, and as they shopped they pooled ideas about good deals and menu suggestions. They looked out for each other's children and borrowed money from each other. On occasion, several women assembled in one house to spend the day cooking. They usually did this when the food such as pierogies, cabbage rolls, or preserves required lots of chopping or a long cooking time and constant watching. The women prepared a large quantity of food to be shared among all of them. I participated in two collective cooking activities. One day three of us worked from 9:00 a.m. to 5:30 p.m and made 435 pierogies. On another day, four of us worked from 10:30 a.m. to 4:30 p.m. and made 193 cabbage rolls. Working together turned an onerous job into an interesting social occasion.

Most of the women interviewed said that periodically when their children were young they arranged with another woman to exchange child-care services. Two women with children of similar ages took turns looking after each other's children for a number of hours each week. This gave each of the mothers some time 'off' to spend as they wished.

Because individual women work most of the time in the isolation of their own home, these relations with other women combine both the need for co-workers with whom to share information and advice and the need for friends with common interests. It is these relationships that provide much of the tension managing that domestic workers need. Women pointed out that their husbands rarely did domestic work and consistently undervalued both its difficulty and its worth. Other women, who from their own experience understood the requirements and rigours of the work, were more helpful in providing support, reassurance, and comfort for work-related problems:

> Sometimes I feel so tired and out of sorts with my family. I can't really talk to David about it. He tries but he really doesn't understand, and anyway sometimes he's part of the problem, if you know what I mean. My mother or my sister or my neighbour next door, I just go and have a good cry with them and then I feel better.
> (Generation III, b. 1942)

Women's efforts to improve the conditions of their work, and their families' lives, and all the contradictions inherent in that, have an impact beyond their immediate household and friendship networks.

The tension between women's short- and long-term interests as domestic labourers and as members of their class was illustrated during the period of contract negotiations between the union and the Company in 1976. A number of women noted that the negotiations directly affected them and their ability to do their work. One woman pointed out the contradictions between the immediate objective conditions of her work, the long-term interests of that work, and her subjective understanding of her class interests. Her immediate interests were the regularity of the wage, ensuring that money kept coming into the household purse. Her long-term interests as a domestic labourer were concerned with the magnitude of the wage and its increase. As a member of her class she had to grapple with the short-term/long-term trade-offs that are always part of class struggle:

> I don't want a strike because I can't live on strike pay. I just can't feed my kids on strike pay. But I think we should strike because that company makes so much money off those men and it thinks it can get away with murder. We need to stand up to the Company and show them that they can't go on trashing us workers any more.
>
> (Generation II, b. 1926)

There is a long tradition of miners' wives acting militantly in support of the miners in class-struggle situations.[11] In both strikes in Flin Flon, in 1934 and 1971, the wives of strikers played an important role in the union struggles. They organized strike support committees, went on the picket lines and regularly indicated both their support for the men and their own interests in winning the strike.

A woman who was active in the 1971 strike described her experiences and noted the connections between her work in the home and her husband's wage work:

> The men were on strike and their families were hurting. A bunch of us women were talking. Some of them wanted to end the strike—they were scared and just wanted life to be normal again. But others understood better that it was our strike too. We needed more money and better conditions for our men, [and this] meant better conditions at home. Miserable angry workers make rotten husbands. . . . So we went on the picket line and did what we could.
>
> (Generation II, b. 1929)

By seizing the initiative, women begin to gain some control over their working conditions and their lives. This gives them strength to struggle against the inequalities of their marriages. It undermines their subordination and helps to make better, rather than worse, the position of wife in industrial capitalist society.

Notes

1. The most important lack of alternatives is the fact that heterosexual monogamous marriage is generally considered to be the only normal life choice for everyone. People who choose to be single, to have children alone, to have no children, to live with several people, lesbians, homosexuals and bisexuals, even couples who live together without marrying—all are subjected to some degree of social sanction and disapproval. As long as this is so people cannot 'choose' freely to marry.

2. The situation of women wage earners with respect to the sex-segregated job market and the unequal pay differentials between women and men was well

documented in 1970 by the *Report of the Royal Commission on the Status of Women in Canada* (Ottawa: Information Canada, 1970). More up-to-date figures from the Department of Labour, Women's Bureau, are summarized by Pat Armstrong and Hugh Armstrong in *The Double Ghetto* (Toronto: McClelland & Stewart, 1978). These more recent figures confirm that the pay differential between women and men is, if anything, increasing.

3. Luxton interviewed sixty women who had set up their households between the 1920s and 1970s: five did so in the 1920s, fifteen in the 1930s, and ten from each of the later decades. (She interviewed other women as well, but this was her initial sample.) She divided these sixty women into three 'generations' (which she signified with I, II, and III). The first generation established their households in the most primitive of conditions, and the last had houses that were equipped with modern services and technology. Whenever she quotes them, Luxton indicates the birth date (b) of each woman.

4. For a study of the impact of shift work on the social relations of the family, see P.E. Mott, *Shift Work: The Social, Psychological and Physical Consequences* (Ann Arbor: University of Michigan Press, 1965), 18.

5. This is a typical pattern for working-class families. Denis et al. cite the example of the man who threw his supper into the fire even though he admitted that it was particularly good food. His wife had gone out and arranged for another woman to prepare his meals for him. They quoted him when he explained that he threw out the dinner because it was his wife's job to prepare his meal and she could not allocate her work to someone else. N. Denis, F. Henriques, and C. Slaughter, *Coal Is Our Life: An Analysis of a Yorkshire Mining Community* (London: Tavistock Publications, 1969), 182.

6. Michael Young and Peter Willmott in *The Symmetrical Family: A Study of Work and Leisure in the London Region* (London: Routledge and Kegan Paul, 1973) suggest that the shorter work week for wage workers and the improved situation for domestic workers created by household technology have resulted in a new type of family relations where the sexual division of labour is breaking down. They note that men have begun to spend a bit more time around the house helping out with domestic work and that women are increasingly taking on wage work. They hypothesize from these observations that a basic equality is evolving within the family. They are able to make such a statement only because they have never stopped to investigate what actually does constitute domestic labour. While it is true that men are helping out more around the house, they are still 'helping out'. The internal household labour is still the primary responsibility of women.

7. While marriage laws vary, one universal feature is the recognition that legal marriage must be 'consummated'; that is, sexual intercourse must take place. If it does not, the marriage may be annulled, which essentially means that the marriage never occurred.

8. For a summary of the major studies on North American sexuality since Kinsey see Ruth Brecker and E. Brecker, *An Analysis of Human Sexual Response* (New York: Signet, 1966): M. Hunt, *Sexual Behavior in the 1970s* (Chicago: Playboy Press, 1974); Shere Hite, *The Hite Report* (New York: Dell Books, 1976).

9. For a good discussion on how and why women subordinate their needs to those of their husbands, see Laura Oren, 'The Welfare of Women in Labouring Families: England 1860–1950', in M. Hartman and L.W. Banner, eds, *Clio's Consciousness Raised: New Perspectives on the History of Women* (New York: Harper and Row, 1974); M.L. McDougall, 'Working Class Women During the Industrial Revolution, 1780–1860', (Houghton-Mifflin, 1977); Jane Humphries, 'The Working Class Family, Women's Liberation, and Class Struggle: The Case of Nineteenth Century British History', *The Review of Radical Political Economics: Women, Class and the Family* 9, 3 (Fall 1977).

10. In Lewis Carroll's *Through the Looking Glass* (London: Penguin Books, 1971), Alice meets the Red Queen and they begin to run just as fast as they can because they want to stay in the same place. Alice suggests that this is unusual but the Queen assures her: 'Now here you see, it takes all the running you can do to keep in the same place.

If you want to get somewhere else, you must run at least twice as fast as that.' A number of women who had read this story saw a similar pattern in their own lives.

11. For information on the role of women in miners' strikes in North America, see M.E. Parton, ed., *The Autobiography of Mother Jones* (Chicago: Charles H. Kerr, 1974); and Kathy Kahn, *Hillbilly Women* (New York: Avon Books, 1973). The important part that women play in primary resource strike situations was graphically portrayed by Barbara Kopple in her film *Harlan County, USA* (1975). For a sketchy outline of the role of women in the Flin Flon strikes, see Valerie Hedman, Loretta Yauck, and Joyce Henderson, *Flin Flon* (Flin Flon, MB: Flin Flon Historical Society, 1974). *The Wives Tale/L'histoire des femmes*, is a film about the 1978 strike against Inco in Sudbury, Ontario.

References

Borland, M., ed. 1976. *Violence in the Family* (Manchester: Manchester University Press).

D'Oyley, V., ed. 1978. *Domestic Violence* (Toronto: Ontario Institute for Studies in Education).

Denis, N., F. Henriques, and C. Slaughter. 1969. *Coal Is Our Life: An Analysis of a Yorkshire Mining Community* (London: Tavistock Publications).

Easton, L.D., and K.H. Guddat, eds and trans. 1967. *Writings of the Young Marx on Philosophy and Society* (New York: Doubleday).

Eekelaar, J.M., and S.N. Katz. 1975. *Family Violence* (Toronto: Butterworth).

Guettel, C. 1974. *Marxism and Feminism* (Toronto: The Women's Press).

MacLeod, L. 1980. *Wife Battering in Canada: The Vicious Circle* (Ottawa: Canadian Advisory Council on the Status of Women).

Martin, J.P., ed. 1978. *Violence and the Family* (New York: John Wiley).

Renvoize, J., ed. 1978. *Wed of Violence* (London: Routledge and Kegan Paul).

Rubin, L. 1976. 'The Marriage Bed', *Psychology Today* (Aug.): 44.

Schneider, M. 1975. *Neurosis and Civilization* (New York: The Seabury Press).

Winnipeg Women's Liberation. 1978. *Newsletter* (Feb.).

Chapter 13

Writers who argue that 'the family' is in decline invariably use the 1950s as the point of comparison with today. When those same writers argue for a return to 'family values', they represent the 1950s as the last decade of traditional—and therefore ideal— family life. In fact, 1950s family patterns were among the key reasons why the Women's Liberation Movement emerged in the 1960s: many baby-boom women were seeking to develop new ideals of gender and family precisely because of the problems they had witnessed or experienced in their parents' homes. American historian Stephanie Coontz wrote The Way We Never Were *to respond to the range of past popular myths about families that infuse Canadian as well as American culture. What follows is a chapter from that book which discusses the 1950s in the United States.*

'Leave It to Beaver' and 'Ozzie and Harriet': American Families in the 1950s

Stephanie Coontz

Our most powerful visions of traditional families derive from images that are still delivered to our homes in countless reruns of 1950s television sitcoms. When liberals and conservatives debate family policy, for example, the issue is often framed in terms of how many 'Ozzie and Harriet' families are left in America. Liberals compute the percentage of total households that contain a breadwinner father, a full-time homemaker mother, and dependent children, proclaiming that fewer than 10 per cent of American families meet the 'Ozzie and Harriet' or 'Leave It to Beaver' model. Conservatives counter that more than half of all mothers with preschool children either are not employed or are employed only part-time. They cite polls showing that most working mothers would like to spend more time with their children and periodically announce that the Nelsons are 'making a comeback' in popular opinion if not in real numbers (*Boston Globe* 11 Apr. 1989; *Washington Post* 11 June 1989; *Fortune* 25 Mar. 1991; *Washington Post National Weekly Edition* 25 Nov.–1 Dec. 1991).

Since everyone admits that nontraditional families are now a majority, why this obsessive concern to establish a higher or a lower figure? Liberals seem to think that unless they can prove the 'Leave It to Beaver' family is on an irreversible slide toward extinction, they cannot justify introducing new family definitions and social policies. Conservatives believe that if they can demonstrate the traditional family is alive and well, although endangered by policies that reward two-earner families and single parents, they can pass measures to revive the seeming placidity and prosperity of the 1950s, associated in many people's minds with the relative stability of marriage, gender roles, and family life in that decade. If the 1950s family existed today, both sides seem to assume, we would not have the contemporary social dilemmas that cause such a debate.

At first glance, the figures seem to justify this assumption. The 1950s was a profamily period if ever there was one. Rates of divorce and illegitimacy were half what they are today; marriage was almost universally praised; the family was everywhere hailed as the most basic institution in society; and a massive baby boom, among all classes and ethnic groups, made America a 'child-centred' society. Births rose from a low of 18.4 per 1,000 women during the Depression to a high of 25.3 per 1,000 in 1957. 'The birthrate for third children doubled between 1940 and 1960, and that for fourth children tripled' (Chafe 1974: 217).

In retrospect, the 1950s also seem a time of innocence and consensus: gang warfare among youths did not lead to drive-by shootings; the crack epidemic had not yet hit; discipline problems in the schools were minor; no 'secular humanist' movement opposed the 1954 addition of the words *under God* to the Pledge of Allegiance; and 90 per cent of all school levies were approved by voters. Introduction of the polio vaccine in 1954 was the most dramatic of many medical advances that improved the quality of life for children.

The profamily features of this decade were bolstered by impressive economic improvements for vast numbers of Americans. Between 1945 and 1960, the gross national product grew by almost 250 per cent and per capita income by 35 per cent. Housing starts exploded after the war, peaking at 1.65 million in 1955 and remaining above 1.5 million a year for the rest of the decade; the increase in single-family homeownership between 1946 and 1956 outstripped the increase during the entire preceding century and a half. By 1960, 62 per cent of American families owned their own homes, in contrast to 43 per cent in 1940. Eighty-five per cent of the new homes were built in the suburbs, where the nuclear family found new possibilities for privacy and togetherness. While middle-class Americans were the prime beneficiaries of the building boom, substantial numbers of white working-class Americans moved out of the cities into affordable developments, such as Levittown (Mayer 1978; Mason 1982).

Many working-class families also moved into the middle class. The number of salaried workers increased by 61 per cent between 1947 and 1957. By the mid-1950s, nearly 60 per cent of the population had what was labeled a middle-class income level (between $3,000 and $10,000 in constant dollars), compared to only 31 per cent in the 'prosperous twenties', before the Great Depression. By 1960, thirty-one million of the nation's forty-four million families owned their own home, 87 per cent had a television, and 75 per cent possessed a car. The number of people with discretionary income doubled during the 1950s (Chafe 1986: 111–18; May 1988: 165; Mintz and Kellogg 1988: 182–3).

For most Americans, the most salient symbol and immediate beneficiary of their newfound prosperity was the nuclear family. The biggest boom in consumer spending, for example, was in household goods. Food spending rose by only 33 per cent in the five years following the Second World War, and clothing expenditures rose by 20 per cent, but purchases of household furnishings and appliances climbed 240 per cent. 'Nearly the entire increase in the gross national product in the mid-1950s was due to increased spending on consumer durables and residential construction', most of it oriented toward the nuclear family (May 1988: 167; May 1989: 188).

Putting their mouths where their money was, Americans consistently told pollsters that home and family were the wellsprings of their happiness and self-esteem. Cultural historian David Marc argues that prewar fantasies of sophisticated urban 'elegance', epitomized by the high-rise penthouse apartment, gave way in the 1950s to a more modest vision of utopia: a single-family house and a car. The emotional dimensions of utopia, however, were unbounded. When respondents to a 1955 marriage study 'were asked what they thought they had sacrificed by marrying and raising a family, an overwhelming majority of them replied, "Nothing".' Less than 10 per cent of Americans believed that an unmarried person could be happy. As one popular advice book intoned, 'The family is the center of your living. If it isn't, you've gone far astray' (Marc 1989: 50; May 1988: 28; Mintz and Kellogg 1988: 180).

The Novelty of the 1950s Family

In fact, the 'traditional' family of the 1950s was a qualitatively new phenomenon. At the end of the 1940s, all the trends characterizing the rest of the twentieth century suddenly reversed themselves: for the first time in more than one hundred years, the age for marriage and motherhood fell, fertility increased, divorce rates declined, and women's degree of educational parity with men dropped sharply. In a period of less than ten years, the proportion of never-married persons declined by as much as it had during the entire previous half century (Brogue 1959; McLaughlin et al. 1988: 7).

At the time, most people understood the 1950s family to be a new invention. The Great Depression and the Second World War had reinforced extended family ties, but in ways that were experienced by most people as stultifying and oppressive. As one child of the Depression later put it, 'The Waltons' television series of the 1970s did not show what family life in the 1930s was really like: 'It wasn't a big family sitting around a table radio and everybody saying goodnight while Bing Crosby crooned "Pennies from Heaven".' On top of Depression-era family tensions had come the painful family separations and housing shortages of the war years: by 1947, six million American families were sharing housing, and postwar family counselors warned of a widespread marital crisis caused by conflicts between the generations. A 1948 *March of Time* film, 'Marriage and Divorce', declared: 'No home is big enough to house two families, particularly two of different generations, with opposite theories on child training' ('Marriage and Divorce' 1948; Milkman 1976: 84; Ware 1982).

During the 1950s, films and television plays, such as 'Marty', showed people working through conflicts between marital loyalties and older kin, peer group, or community ties; regretfully but decisively, these conflicts were almost invariably 'resolved in favor of the heterosexual couple rather than the claims of extended kinship networks, . . . homosociability and friendship.' Talcott Parsons and other sociologists argued that modern industrial society required the family to jettison traditional productive functions and wider kin ties in order to specialize in emotional nurturance, childrearing, and production of a modern personality. Social workers 'endorsed nuclear family separateness and looked suspiciously on active extended-family networks' (Parsons and Bales 1955; Gordon 1988: 161; Smith 1990).

Popular commentators urged young families to adopt a 'modern' stance and strike out on their own, and, with the return of prosperity, most did. By the early 1950s, newlyweds not only were establishing single-family homes at an earlier age and a more rapid rate than ever before but also were increasingly moving to the suburbs, away from the close scrutiny of the elder generation.

For the first time in American history, moreover, such average trends did not disguise sharp variations by class, race, and ethnic group. People married at a younger age, bore their children earlier and closer together, completed their families by the time they were in their late twenties, and experienced a longer period living together as a couple after their children left home. The traditional range of acceptable family behaviours—even the range in the acceptable number and timing of children—narrowed substantially (Jones 1980: 34; Ryan 1983: 271–2; Van Horn 1988; May 1988: 237).

The values of the 1950s families were also new. The emphasis on producing a whole world of satisfaction, amusement, and inventiveness within the nuclear family had no precedents. Historian Elaine Tyler May (1988: 11) comments: 'the legendary family of the 1950s . . . was not, as common wisdom tells us, the last gasp of "traditional" family life with deep roots in the past. Rather, it was the first wholehearted effort to create a home that would fulfill virtually all its members' personal needs through an energized and expressive personal life.'

Beneath a superficial revival of Victorian domesticity and gender distinctions, a novel rearrangement of family ideals and male-female relations was accomplished. For women, this involved a reduction in the moral aspect of domesticity and an expansion of its orientation toward personal service. Nineteenth-century middle-class women had cheerfully left housework to servants, yet 1950s women of all classes created makework in their homes and felt guilty when they did not do everything for themselves. The amount of time women spent doing housework actually *increased* during the 1950s, despite the advent of convenience foods and new, labour-saving appliances; childcare absorbed more than twice as much time as it had in the 1920s. By the mid-1950s, advertisers' surveys reported on a growing tendency among women to find 'housework a medium of expression for . . . [their] femininity and individuality' (Friedan 1963: 204; Mathews 1987).

For the first time, men as well as women were encouraged to root their identity and self-image in familial and parental roles. The novelty of these family and gender values can be seen in the dramatic postwar transformation of movie themes. Historian Peter Biskind (1983: 252, 255) writes that almost every major male star who had played tough loners in the 1930s and 1940s 'took the roles with which he was synonymous and transformed them, in the fifties, into neurotics or psychotics'. In these films, 'men belonged at home, not on the streets or out on the prairie . . . not alone or hanging out with other men'. The women who got men to settle down had to promise enough sex to compete with 'bad' women, but ultimately they provided it only in the marital bedroom and only in return for some help fixing up the house.

Public images of Hollywood stars were consciously reworked to show their commitment to marriage and stability. After 1947, for example, the Actors' Guild organized 'a series of unprece-

dented speeches . . . to be given to civic groups around the country, emphasizing that the stars now embodied the rejuvenated family life unfolding in the suburbs'. Ronald Reagan's defense of actors' family values was especially 'stirring', noted one reporter, but female stars, unlike Reagan and other male stars, were obliged to *live* the new values as well as propagandize them. Joan Crawford, for example, one of the brash, tough, independent leading ladies of the prewar era, was now pictured as a devoted mother whose sex appeal and glamour did not prevent her from doing her own housework. She posed for pictures mopping floors and gave interviews about her childrearing philosophy (May 1988: 64, 140–2; May 1989: 146).

The 'good life' in the 1950s, historian Clifford Clark points out, made the family 'the focus of fun and recreation'. The ranch house, architectural embodiment of this new ideal, discarded the older privacy of the kitchen, den, and sewing room (representative of separate spheres for men and women) but introduced new privacy and luxury into the master bedroom. There was an unprecedented 'glorification of self-indulgence' in family life. Formality was discarded in favour of 'livability', 'comfort', and 'convenience'. A contradiction in terms in earlier periods, 'the sexually charged, child-centered family took its place at the center of the postwar American dream' (Clark 1986: 209, 216; 1989: 171, 182; May 1988: 162).

On television, David Marc comments, all the 'normal' families moved to the suburbs during the 1950s. Popular culture turned such suburban families into capitalism's answer to the Communist threat. In his famous 'kitchen debate' with Nikita Khrushchev in 1959, Richard Nixon asserted that the superiority of capitalism over communism was embodied not in ideology or military might but in the comforts of the suburban home, 'designed to make things easier for our women' (May 1988: 18; Marc 1989: 50).

Acceptance of domesticity was the mark of middle-class status and upward mobility. In sitcom families, a middle-class man's work was totally irrelevant to his identity; by the same token, the problems of working-class families did not lie in their economic situation but in their failure to create harmonious gender roles. Working-class and ethnic men on television had one defining characteristic: they were unable to control their wives. The families of middle-class men, by contrast, were generally well behaved (Glennon and Bustch 1982; May 1988: 146; Taylor 1989).

Not only was the 1950s family a new invention; it was also a historical fluke, based on a unique and temporary conjuncture of economic, social, and political factors. During the war, Americans had saved at a rate more than three times higher than that in the decades before or since. Their buying power was further enhanced by America's extraordinary competitive advantage at the end of the war, when every other industrial power was devastated by the experience. This privileged economic position sustained both a tremendous expansion of middle-class management and organized labour. During the 1950s, real wages increased by more than they had in the entire previous half century (Potter 1959; Bowles, Gordon, and Weisskopf 1983: 66–7; Chafe 1986: 111–18; Henretta et al. 1987: 852).

The impact of such prosperity on family formation and stability was magnified by the role of government, which could afford to be generous with education benefits, housing loans, highway and sewer construction, and job training. All this allowed most middle-class Americans, and a large number of working-class ones, to adopt family values and strategies that assumed the availability of cheap energy, low-interest home loans, expanding educational and occupational opportunities, and steady employment. These expectations encouraged early marriage, early childbearing, expansion of consumer debt, and residential patterns that required long commutes to work— all patterns that would become highly problematic by the 1970s.

A Complex Reality: 1950s Poverty, Diversity, and Social Change

Even aside from the exceptional and ephemeral nature of the conditions that supported them, 1950s family strategies and values offer no solution to the discontents that underlie contemporary romanticization of the 'good old days'. The reality of these families was far more painful and complex than the situation-comedy reruns or the expurgated memories of the nostalgic would suggest. Contrary to popular opinion, 'Leave It to Beaver' was not a documentary.

In the first place, not all American families shared in the consumer expansion that provided Hotpoint appliances for June Cleaver's kitchen and a vacuum cleaner for Donna Stone. A full 25 per cent of Americans, forty to fifty million people, were poor in the mid-1950s, and in the absence of food stamps and housing programs, this poverty was searing. Even at the end of the 1950s, a third of American children were poor. Sixty per cent of Americans over sixty-five had incomes below $1,000 in 1958, considerably below the $3,000 to $10,000 level considered to represent middle-class status. A majority of elders also lacked medical insurance. Only half the population had savings in 1959; one-quarter of the population had no liquid assets at all. Even when we consider only native-born, white families, one-third could not get by on the income of the household head (Harrington 1962; *Social Security Bulletin* July 1963: 3–13; Miller and Nowak 1977: 122; Chafe 1986: 143; Patterson 1986: 13; Stern 1991: 538).

In the second place, real life was not so white as it was on television. Television, comments historian Ella Taylor, increasingly ignored cultural diversity, adopting 'the motto "least objectionable programming," which gave rise to those least objectionable families, the Cleavers, the Nelsons, and the Andersons'. Such families were so completely white and Anglo-Saxon that even the Hispanic gardener in 'Father Knows

Best' went by the name of Frank Smith. But contrary to the all-white lineup on the television networks and the streets of suburbia, the 1950s saw a major transformation in the ethnic composition of America. More Mexican immigrants entered the United States in the two decades after the Second World War than in the entire previous one hundred years. Prior to the war, most blacks and Mexican-Americans lived in rural areas, and three-fourths of blacks lived in the South. By 1960, a majority of blacks and Mexican-Americans lived in cities. Postwar Puerto Rican immigration was so massive that by 1960 more Puerto Ricans lived in New York than in San Juan (Barnouw 1975; Griswold del Castillo 1984: 113–14; Henretta et al. 1987: 845; Taylor 1989: 40; *Washington Post* 25 June 1989).

These minorities were almost entirely excluded from the gains and privileges accorded white middle-class families. The June Cleaver or Donna Stone homemaker role was not available to the more than 40 per cent of black women with small children who worked outside the home. Twenty-five per cent of these women headed their own households, but even minorities who conformed to the dominant family form faced conditions quite unlike those portrayed on television. The poverty rate of two-parent black families was more than 50 per cent, approximately the same as that of one-parent black ones. Migrant workers suffered 'near medieval' deprivations, while termination and relocation policies were employed against Native Americans to get them to give up treaty rights (Collier 1954; Murrow 1960; Harrington 1962; Riley 1987).

African Americans in the South faced systematic, legally sanctioned segregation and pervasive brutality, and those in the North were excluded by restrictive covenants and redlining from many benefits of the economic expansion that their labour helped sustain. Whites resisted, with harassment and violence, the attempts of blacks to participate in the American family dream. When Harvey Clark tried to move into Cicero, Illinois, in 1951, a mob of 4,000 whites spent four days tearing his apartment apart while police stood by and joked with them. In 1953, the first black family moved into Chicago's Trumball Park public housing project; neighbours 'hurled stones and tomatoes' and trashed stores that sold groceries to the new residents. In Detroit, *Life* magazine reported in 1957, '10,000 Negroes work at the Ford plant in nearby Dearborn, [but] not one Negro can live in Dearborn itself' (*Life* 9 Nov. 1953; *Life* 11 Mar. 1957; Danielson 1976; Miller and Nowak 1977: 199–201; Shapiro 1988).

More Complexities: Repression, Anxiety, Unhappiness, and Conflict

The happy, homogeneous families that we 'remember' from the 1950s were thus partly a result of the media's denial of diversity. But even among sectors of the population where the 'least objectionable' families did prevail, their values and behaviours were not entirely a spontaneous, joyful reaction to prosperity. If suburban ranch houses and family barbecues were the carrots offered to white middle-class families that adopted the new norms, there was also a stick.

Women's retreat to housewifery, for example, was in many cases not freely chosen. During the war, thousands of women had entered new jobs, gained new skills, joined unions, and fought against job discrimination. Although 95 per cent of the new women employees had expected when they were first hired to quit work at the end of the war, by 1945 almost an equally overwhelming majority did not want to give up their independence, responsibility, and income, and expressed the desire to continue working (Trey 1972; Chafe 1974: 178–9).

After the war, however, writes one recent student of postwar reconstruction, 'management went to extraordinary lengths to purge women workers from the auto plants', as well as from other high-paying and nontraditional jobs. As it turned out, in most cases women were not permanently expelled from the labour force but were merely downgraded to lower-paid, 'female' jobs. Even at the end of the purge, there were more women working than before the war, and by 1952 there were two million more wives at work than at the peak of wartime production. The jobs available to these women, however, lacked the pay and the challenges that had made wartime work so satisfying, encouraging women to define themselves in terms of home and family even when they were working (Tobias and Anderson 1973; Milkman 1987; McLaughlin et al. 1988: 24).

Vehement attacks were launched against women who did not accept such self-definitions. In the 1947 bestseller, *The Modern Woman: The Lost Sex*, Marynia Farnham and Ferdinand Lundberg described feminism as a 'deep illness', called the notion of an independent woman a 'contradiction in terms', and accused women who sought educational or employment equality of engaging in symbolic 'castration' of men. As sociologist David Riesman noted, a woman's failure to bear children went from being 'a social disadvantage and sometimes a personal tragedy' in the nineteenth century to being a 'quasi-perversion' in the 1950s. The conflicting messages aimed at women seemed almost calculated to demoralize: at the same time as they labeled women 'unnatural' if they did not seek fulfillment in motherhood, psychologists and popular writers insisted that most modern social ills could be traced to domineering mothers who invested too much energy and emotion in their children. Women were told that 'no other experience in life . . . will provide the same sense of fulfillment, of happiness, of complete pervading contentment' as motherhood. But soon after delivery they were asked, 'Which are you first of all, Wife or Mother?' and warned against the tendency to be 'too much mother, too little wife' (Farnham and Lundberg 1947: 24; Hartmann 1982: 173; 179–80; May 1988: 96–7).

Women who could not walk the fine line between nurturing motherhood and castrating 'momism', or who had trouble adjusting to 'creative homemaking', were labeled neurotic, perverted, or schizophrenic. A recent study of hospitalized 'schizophrenic' women in the San Francisco Bay Area during the 1950s concludes that institutionalization and sometimes electric shock treatments were used to force women to accept their domestic roles and their husbands' dictates. Shock treatments also were recommended for women who sought abortion, on the assumption that failure to want a baby signified dangerous emotional disturbance (Hartmann 1982: 174; Warren 1987).

All women, even seemingly docile ones, were deeply mistrusted. They were frequently denied the right to serve on juries, convey property, make contracts, take out credit cards in their own name, or establish residence. A 1954 article in *Esquire* called working wives a 'menace', a *Life* author termed married women's employment a 'disease'. Women were excluded from several professions, and some states even gave husbands total control over family finances (Miller and Nowak 1977: 164–5). There were not many permissible alternatives to baking brownies, experimenting with new canned soups, and getting rid of stains around the collar.

Men were also pressured into acceptable family roles, since lack of a suitable wife could mean the loss of a job or promotion for a middle-class man. Bachelors were categorized as 'immature', 'infantile', 'narcissistic', 'deviant', or even 'pathological'. Family advice expert Paul Landis argued: 'Except for the sick, the badly crippled, the deformed, the emotionally warped and the mentally defective, almost everyone has an opportunity [and, by clear implication, a duty] to marry' (Miller and Nowak 1977: 154; Ehrenreich 1983: 14–28; Mintz and Kellogg 1988: 181).

Families in the 1950s were products of even more direct repression. Cold war anxieties merged with concerns about the expanded sexuality of family life and the commercial world to create what one authority calls the domestic version of George F. Kennan's containment policy toward the Soviet Union: a 'normal' family and vigilant mother became the 'front line' of defence against treason; anticommunists linked deviant family or sexual behaviour to sedition. The FBI and other government agencies instituted unprecedented state intrusion into private life under the guise of investigating subversives. Gay baiting was almost as widespread and every bit as vicious as red baiting (Caute 1978; Boyer 1985; Schrecker 1986; Henretta et al. 1987; May 1988; Morris 1990).

The Civil Service Commission fired 2,611 persons as 'security risks' and reported that 4,315 others resigned under the pressure of investigations that asked leading questions of their neighbours and inquired into the books they read or the music to which they listened. In this atmosphere, movie producer Joel Schumacher recalls, 'No one told the truth. . . . People pretended they weren't unfaithful. They pretended that they weren't homosexual. They pretended that they weren't horrible' (Eisler 1986: 341).

Even for people not directly coerced into conformity by racial, political, or personal repression, the turn toward families was in many cases more a defensive move than a purely affirmative act. Some men and women entered loveless marriages in order to forestall attacks about real or suspected homosexuality or lesbianism. Growing numbers of people saw the family, in the words of one husband, as the one 'group that in spite of many disagreements internally always will face its external enemies together'. Conservative families warned children to beware of communists who might masquerade as friendly neighbours; liberal children learned to confine their opinions to the family for fear that their father's job or reputation might be threatened (May 1988: 91).

Americans were far more ambivalent about the 1950s than later retrospectives, such as 'Happy Days', suggest. Plays by Tennessee Williams, Eugene O'Neill, and Arthur Miller explored the underside of family life. Movies such as *Rebel Without a Cause* (1955) expressed fears

about youths whose parents had failed them. There was an almost obsessive concern with the idea that the mass media had broken down parental control, thus provoking an outburst of 'delinquency and youthful viciousness'. In 1954, psychiatrist Fredric Wertham's *Seduction of the Innocents* warned: 'The atmosphere of crime comic books is unparalleled in the history of children's literature of any time or any nation.' In 1955, Congress discussed nearly 200 bills relating to delinquency. If some of these anxieties seem almost charmingly naïve to our more hardened age, they were no less real for all that (Gilbert 1986: 3, 8, 66; May 1988: 91).

Many families, of course, managed to hold such fears at bay—and it must be admitted that the suburbs and small towns of America were exceptionally good places for doing so. Shielded from the multiplying problems and growing diversity of the rest of society, residents of these areas could afford to be neighbourly. Church attendance and membership in voluntary associations tended to be higher in the suburbs than in the cities, although contact with extended kin was less frequent. Children played in the neighbourhoods and cul-de-sacs with only cursory warnings about strangers (for a defence of the suburbs see Donaldson 1969; see also Seeley, Sim, and Loosely 1956; Whyte 1956).[1]

In her autobiographical account of a 1950s adolescence, Susan Allen Toth remembers growing up 'gradually' and 'quietly' in a small town of the period: 'We were not seared by fierce poverty, racial tensions, drug abuse, street crimes.' Perhaps this innocence was 'constricting', she admitted, but it also gave a child 'shelter and space to grow'. For Toth, insulation from external problems meant that growing up was a process of being 'cossetted, gently warmed, transmuted by slow degrees' (Toth 1978: 3, 4).

For many other children, however, growing up in 1950s families was not so much a matter of being protected from the harsh realities of the outside world as preventing the outside world from learning the harsh realities of family life. Few would have guessed that radiant Marilyn Van Derbur, crowned Miss America in 1958, had been sexually violated by her wealthy, respectable father from the time she was five until she was eighteen, when she moved away to college (Van Derbur Atler 1991). While not all family secrets were quite so shocking, author Benita Eisler recalls a common middle-class experience:

> As college classmates became close friends, I heard sagas of life at home that were Gothic horror stories. Behind the hedges and driveways of upper-middle-class suburbia were tragedies of madness, suicide, and—most prevalent of all—chronic and severe alcoholism . . .
>
> The real revelation for me was the role played by children in . . . keeping up appearances. Many of my new friends had been pressed into service early as happy smiling fronts, emissaries of family normalcy, cheerful proof that 'nothing was really wrong' at the Joneses (Eisler 1986; Hall 1990).

Beneath the polished facades of many 'ideal' families, suburban as well as urban, was violence, terror, or simply grinding misery that only occasionally came to light. Although Colorado researchers found 302 battered-child cases, including 33 deaths, in their state during one year alone, the major journal of American family sociology did not carry a single article on family violence between 1939 and 1969. Wife battering was not even considered a 'real' crime by most people. Psychiatrists in the 1950s, following Helene Deutsch, 'regarded the battered woman as a masochist who provoked her husband into beating her' (Kempe et al. 1962: 181; Pleck 1987: 169, 182; Mintz and Kellogg 1988: 194).

Historian Elizabeth Pleck (1987) described how one Family Service Association translated this psychological approach into patient counselling during the 1950s. Mrs K came to the Association because her husband was an alcoholic who repeatedly abused her, both physically and sexually. The agency felt, however, that it was simplistic to blame the couple's problems on his drinking. When counselors learned that Mrs K refused her husband's demands for sex after he came home from the night shift, they decided that they had found a deeper difficulty: Mrs K needed therapy to 'bring out some of her anxiety about sex activities'.

We will probably never know how prevalent incest and sexual abuse were in the 1950s, but we do know that when girls or women reported incidents of such abuse to therapists, they were frequently told that they were 'fantasizing' their unconscious oedipal desires. Although incest cases were common throughout the records of case-workers from 1880–1960, according to historian Linda Gordon's study of these documents, the problem was increasingly redefined as one of female 'sex delinquency'. By 1960, despite overwhelming evidence to the contrary, experts described incest as a 'one-in-a-million occurrence'. Not until the 1970s, heartened by a supportive women's movement, were many women able to speak out about the sexual abuse they had suffered in silent agony during the 1950s; others, such as Marilyn Van Derbur, are only now coming forward (Pleck 1987: 156–7; Gordon 1988: 206–22).

Less dramatic but more widespread was the existence of significant marital unhappiness. Between one-quarter and one-third of the marriages contracted in the 1950s eventually ended in divorce; during that decade two million legally married people lived apart from each other. Many more couples simply toughed it out. Sociologist Mirra Komarovsky (1962: 331) concluded that of the working-class couples she interviewed in the 1950s, 'slightly less than one-third [were] happily or very happily married'.

National polls found that 20 per cent of all couples considered their marriages unhappy, and another 20 per cent reported only 'medium happiness'. In the middle-class sample studied by Elaine Tyler May, two-thirds of the husbands and wives rated their marriages 'decidedly happier than average', but an outside observer might well have scaled this back to a percentage much like Komarovsky's, for even the happiest couples reported many dissatisfactions and communication problems. 'The idea of a "working marriage" was one that often included constant day-to-day misery for one or both partners' (May 1988: 202; Mintz and Kellogg 1988: 194).

A successful 1950s family, moreover, was often achieved at enormous cost to the wife, who was expected to subordinate her own needs and aspirations to those of both her husband and her children. In consequence, no sooner was the ideal of the postwar family accepted than observers began to comment perplexedly on how discontented women seemed in the very roles they supposedly desired most. In 1949, *Life* magazine reported that 'suddenly and for no plain reason' American women were 'seized with an eerie restlessness'. Under a 'mask of placidity' and an outwardly feminine appearance, one physician wrote in 1953, there was often 'an inwardly tense and emotionally unstable individual seething with hidden aggressiveness and resentment' (Miller and Nowak 1977: 174; Mintz and Kellogg 1988: 195).[2]

Some women took this resentment out on their families. Surely some of the bizarre behaviours that Joan Crawford exhibited toward her children, according to her daughter's bitter remembrance, *Mommie Dearest*, flowed from the frustration of being forced into a domestic role about which she was intensely ambivalent. Other women tried to dull the pain with alcohol or drugs. Tranquilizers were developed in the 1950s in response to a need that physicians explicitly saw as female: virtually nonexistent in 1955, tranquilizer consumption reached 462,000 pounds in 1958 and soared to 1.15 million pounds merely a year later. Commentators noted a sharp increase in women's drinking during the decade, even

though many middle-class housewives kept their liquor stash hidden and thought no one knew that they needed a couple of drinks to face an evening of family 'togetherness' (Lisansky 1958: 315; Crawford 1978: esp. 51–6, 82–8; Chafe 1986: 126).

But not even 'the four *b*'s', as the mother of a colleague of mine used to label her life in the 1950s—'booze, bowling, bridge, and boredom'—could entirely conceal the discontents. In 1956, the *Ladies' Home Journal* devoted an issue to 'The Plight of the Young Mother'. When *McCall's* ran an article entitled 'The Mother Who Ran Away' in the same year, the magazine set a new record for readership. A former editor commented: 'We suddenly realized that all those women at home with their three and a half children were miserably unhappy.' By 1960, almost every major news journal was using the word *trapped* to describe the feelings of the American housewife. When *Redbook's* editors asked readers to provide them with examples of 'Why Young Mothers Feel Trapped', they received 24,000 replies (Friedan 1963: 44, 59; Eisler 1986: 209–10).

Although Betty Friedan's bestseller *The Feminine Mystique* did not appear until 1963, it was a product of the 1950s, originating in the discontented responses Friedan received in 1957 when she surveyed fellow college classmates from the class of 1942. The heartfelt identification of other 1950s women with 'the problem that has no name' is preserved in the letters Friedan received after her book was published, letters now at the Schlesinger Library at Radcliffe (Mathews 1987).

Men tended to be more satisfied with marriage than were women, especially over time, but they, too, had their discontents. Even the most successful strivers after the American dream sometimes muttered about 'mindless conformity'. The titles of books such as *The Organization Man*, by William Whyte (1956), and *The Lonely Crowd*, by David Riesman (1958), summarized a widespread critique of 1950s culture. Male resentments against women were expressed in the only partly humorous diatribes of *Playboy* magazine (founded in 1953) against 'money-hungry' gold diggers or lazy 'parasites' trying to trap men into commitment (Ehrenreich 1983).

Contradictions of the 1950s Family Boom

Happy memories of 1950s family life are not all illusion, of course—there were good times for many families. But even the most positive aspects had another side. One reason that the 1950s family model was so fleeting was that it contained the seeds of its own destruction. It was during the 1950s, not the 1960s, that the youth market was first produced, then institutionalized into the youth culture. It was through such innocuous shows as 'Howdy Doody' and 'The Disney Hour' that advertisers first discovered the riches to be gained by bypassing parents and appealing directly to youth. It was also during this period that advertising and consumerism became saturated with sex (Friedan 1963: 44, 59; Jones 1980).

In the 1950s, family life was financed by economic practices that were to have unanticipated consequences in the 1970s. Wives and mothers first started to work in great numbers during the 1950s in order to supplement their families' purchasing power; expansion of household comforts came 'at the cost of an astronomical increase of indebtedness'. The labour-management accord of the 1950s helped erode the union movement's ability to oppose the takebacks and runaway shops that destroyed the 'family wage system' during the 1970s and 1980s (Chafe 1986: 144).

Family and gender strategies also contained some time bombs. Women who 'played dumb' to catch a man, as 40 per cent of Barnard College women admitted to doing, sometimes despised their husbands for not living up to the fiction of male superiority they had worked so hard to promote. Commitment to improving the quality of family life by manipulating the timing and spacing of childbearing led to the social acceptability of family planning and the spread of birth-control techniques. Concentration of childbearing in early marriage meant that growing numbers of women had years to spare for paid work after the bulk of their childcare duties were finished. Finally, 1950s families fostered intense feelings and values that produced young people with a sharp eye for hypocrisy; many of the so-called rebels of the 1960s were simply acting on values that they had internalized in the bosom of their families (Chafe 1974: 218; Ryan 1983: 277; Demartini 1985; Chafe 1986: 125; Eisler 1986: 369; May 1988: 149–52).

Teen Pregnancy and the 1950s Family

Whatever its other unexpected features, the 1950s family does appear, at least when compared to families in the last two decades, to be a bastion of 'traditional' sexual morality. Many modern observers, accordingly, look back to the sexual values of this decade as a possible solution to what they see as the peculiarly modern 'epidemic' of teen pregnancy. On closer examination, however, the issue of teen pregnancy is a classic example of both the novelty and the contradictions of the 1950s family.

Those who advocate that today's youth should be taught abstinence or deferred gratification rather than sex education will find no 1950s model for such restraint. 'Heavy petting' became a norm of dating in this period, while the proportion of white brides who were pregnant at marriage more than doubled. Teen birth rates soared, reaching highs that have not been equaled since. In 1957, 97 out of every 1,000 girls aged fifteen to nineteen gave birth, compared to only 52 out of every 1,000 in 1983. A surprising number of these births were illegitimate, although 1950s census codes made it impossible to identify an unmarried mother if she lived at home with her parents. The incidence of illegitimacy was also disguised by the new emphasis on 'rehabilitating' the white mother (though not the black) by putting her baby up for adoption and encouraging her to 'start over'; there was an 80 per cent increase in the number of out-of-wedlock babies placed for adoption between 1944 and 1955 (May 1986: 117, 121, 127; Rothman 1984; Vinovskis 1988: 25; Solinger 1992).

The main reason that teenage sexual behaviour did not result in many more illegitimate births during this period was that the age of marriage dropped sharply. Young people were not taught how to 'say no'—they were simply handed wedding rings. In fact, the growing willingness of parents to subsidize young married couples and the new prevalence of government educational stipends and home ownership loans for veterans undermined the former assumption that a man should be able to support a family before embarking on marriage. Among the middle class, it became common for young wives to work while their husbands finished school. Prior to the 1950s, as David Riesman wrote of his Depression-era classmates, it would not 'have occurred to us to have our wives support us through graduate school' (Rothman 1984; Eisler 1986: 199).

Contemporary teenage motherhood in some ways represents a *continuation* of 1950s values in a new economic situation that makes early marriage less viable. Of course modern teen pregnancy also reflects the rejection of some of those earlier values. The values that have broken down, however, have little to do with sexual restraint. What we now think of as 1950s sexual morality depended not so much on stricter sexual control as on intensification of the sexual double standard. Elaine Tyler May argues that sexual 'repression' gave way to sexual 'containment'. The new practice of going steady 'widened the boundaries of permissible sexual activity', creating a 'sexual brinkmanship' in which women bore the burden of 'drawing the line', but that line was constantly changing. Popular opinion admitted, as the *Ladies' Home Journal* put it in 1956, that 'sex suggestiveness' was here to stay, but insisted that it

was up to women to 'put the brakes on' (May 1986: 101–2; Sanders 1990: 11–12).

This double standard led to a Byzantine code of sexual conduct: 'petting' was sanctioned so long as one didn't go 'too far' (though this was an elastic and ambiguous prohibition); a woman could be touched on various parts of her body (how low depended on how serious the relationship was) but 'nice girls' refused to fondle the comparable male parts in return; mutual stimulation to orgasm was compatible with maintaining a 'good' reputation so long as penetration did not occur.

The success of sexual containment depended on sexual inequality. Men no longer bore the responsibility of 'saving themselves for marriage'; this was now exclusively a woman's job. In sharp contrast to the nineteenth century, when 'oversexed' or demanding men were considered to have serious problems, it was now considered 'normal' or 'natural' for men to be sexually aggressive. The 'average man', advice writers for women commented indulgently, 'will go as far as you let him go'. When women succeeded in 'holding out' (a phrase charged with moral ambiguity), they sometimes experienced problems 'letting go', even after marriage; when they failed, they were often reproached later by their husbands for having 'given in'. The contradictions of this double standard could not long withstand the period's pressures for companionate romance: by 1959, a more liberal single standard had already gained ground among older teenagers across America (Bailey 1989: 90; Rothman 1984).

The Problem of Women in Traditional Families

People who romanticize the 1950s, or any model of the traditional family, are usually put in an uncomfortable position when they attempt to gain popular support. The legitimacy of women's rights is so widely accepted today that only a tiny minority of Americans seriously propose that women should go back to being full-time housewives or should be denied educational and job opportunities because of their family responsibilities. Yet when commentators lament the collapse of traditional family commitments and values, they almost invariably mean the uniquely female duties associated with the doctrine of separate spheres for men and women.

Karl Zinsmeister of the American Enterprise Institute, for example, bemoans the fact that 'workaholism and family dereliction have become equal-opportunity diseases, striking mothers as much as fathers.' David Blankenhorn of the Institute for American Values expresses sympathy for the needs of working women but warns that 'employed women do not a family make. The goals of women (and of men, too) in the workplace are primarily individualistic: social recognition, wages, opportunities for advancement, and self-fulfillment. But the family is about collective goals . . . building life's most important bonds of affection, nurturance, mutual support, and long-term commitment' (Blankenhorn 1990: 10–12; *Washington Post National Weekly Edition* 14–20 Jan. 1991).

In both statements, a seemingly gender-neutral indictment of family irresponsibility ends up being directed most forcefully against women. For Blankenhorn, it is not surprising that *men's* goals should be individualistic; this is a parenthetical aside. For Zinsmeister, the problem with the disease of family dereliction is that it has spread to women. So long as it was confined to men, evidently, there was no urgency about finding a cure.

The crisis of commitment in America is usually seen as a problem associated with women's changing roles because women's family functions have historically mediated the worst effects of competition and individualism in the larger society. Most people who talk about balancing private advancement and individual rights with 'nurturance, mutual support, and long-term commitment' do not envision any serious rethinking of the individualistic, antisocial tendencies in our society, nor any ways of broadening our sources of nurturance and mutual assistance. Instead, they seek ways—sometimes through repression, sometimes through reform—of rebuilding a family in which women can continue to compensate for, rather than challenge, the individualism in our larger economy and polity.

Notes

1. Though Whyte criticized the lack of individualism in the suburbs he described, his description of boring group life might sound rather comforting to many alienated modern Americans.

2. The physician reported that most of these women had fulfilled their wifely and motherly roles for years, in seemingly irreproachable ways, but were nevertheless unfulfilled. Unable to accept the logic of his own evidence, the doctor concluded that their problems were a result of their 'intense strivings for masculinity'.

References

Bailey, B. 1989. *From Front Porch to Back Seat: Courtship in Twentieth-Century America* (Baltimore: Johns Hopkins University Press).

Barnouw, E. 1975. *Tube of Plenty: The Evolution of American Television* (New York: Oxford University Press).

Biskind, P. 1983. *Seeing Is Believing: How Hollywood Taught Us to Stop Worrying and Love the Fifties* (New York: Pantheon).

Blankenhorn, D. 1990. 'American Family Dilemmas', in *Rebuilding the Nest: A New Commitment to the American Family*, eds D. Blankenhorn et al. (Milwaukee: Family Service America).

Bowles, S., D. Gordon, and T. Weisskopf. 1983. *Beyond the Wasteland: A Democratic Alternative to Economic Decline* (Garden City, NY: Doubleday).

Boyer, P. 1985. *By the Bomb's Early Light: American Thought and Culture at the Dawn of the Atomic Age* (New York: Pantheon).

Brogue, D. 1959. *The Population of the United States* (Glencoe, IL: Free Press).

Caute, D. 1978. *The Great Fear: The Anti-Communist Purge Under Truman and Eisenhower* (New York: Simon and Schuster).

Chafe, W. 1974. *The American Woman: Her Changing Social, Economic, and Political Roles, 1920–1970* (New York: Oxford University Press).

———. 1986. *The Unfinished Journey: America Since World War II* (New York: Oxford University Press).

Clark, C. 1986. *The American Family Home, 1800–1960* (Chapel Hill: University of North Carolina Press).

Clark, Jr, C. 1989. 'Ranch-House Suburbia: Ideals and Realities', in *Recasting America: Culture and Politics in the Age of Cold War*, ed. Lary May (Chicago: University of Chicago Press).

Collier, J. 1954. 'Indian Takeaway', *Nation*, 2 Oct. 1954.

Crawford, C. 1978. *Mommie Dearest* (New York: William Morrow).

Danielson, M. 1976. *The Politics of Exclusion* (New York: Columbia University Press).

Demartini, J. 1985. 'Change Agents and Generational Relationships: A Reevaluation of Mannheim's Problem of Generations', *Social Forces* 64.

Donaldson, S. 1969. *The Suburban Myth* (New York: Columbia University Press).

Ehrenreich, B. 1983. *The Hearts of Men: American Dreams and the Flight from Commitment* (Garden City, NY: Anchor Press).

Eisler, B. 1986. *Private Lives: Men and Women of the Fifties* (New York: Franklin Watts).

Farnham, M., and F. Lundberg. 1947. *Modern Woman: The Lost Sex* (New York: Harper and Brothers).

Friedan, B. 1963. *The Feminine Mystique* (New York: Dell).

Gilbert, J.B. 1986. *A Cycle of Outrage: America's Reaction to the Juvenile Delinquent in the 1950s* (New York: Oxford University Press).

Glennon, L., and R. Bustch. 1982. 'The Family as Portrayed on Television, 1949–1978', in *Television and Behavior: Ten Years of Scientific Progress and Implications for the Eighties*, eds David Pearle et al. (Washington: US Department of Health and Human Services).

Gordon, L. 1988. *Heroes of Their Own Lives: The Politics and History of Family Violence, 1880–1960* (New York: Viking).

Griswold del Castillo, R. 1984. *La Familia: Chicano Families in the Urban Southwest, 1848 to the Present* (Notre Dame: University of Notre Dame Press).

Hall, N. 1990. *A True Story of a Drunken Mother* (Boston: South End Press).

Harrington, M. 1962. *The Other America: Poverty in the United States* (New York: Macmillan).

Hartmann, S. 1982. *The Home Front and Beyond: American Women in the 1940s* (Boston: Twayne).

Henretta, J.A. et al. 1987. *America's History*, v. 2 (Chicago: Dorsey Press).

Jones, L. 1980. *Great Expectations: America and the Baby Boom Generation* (New York: Ballantine).

Kempe, C.H. et al. 1962. 'The Battered Child Syndrome', *Journal of the American Medical Association*: 181.

Komarovsky, M. 1962. *Blue-Collar Marriage* (New Haven: Vintage).

Life, 9 Nov. 1953, 151.

Lisansky, E. 1958. 'The Woman Alcoholic', *Annals of the American Academy of Political and Social Sciences*: 315.

Marc, D. 1989. *Comic Visions: Television Comedy and American Culture* (Boston: Unwin Hyman).

'Marriage and Divorce'. 1948. A *March of Time* film, 14, 7.

Mason, J. 1982. *History of Housing in the U.S.: 1930–1980* (New York: Gulf).

Mathews, G. 1987. *'Just a Housewife': The Rise and Fall of Domesticity in America* (New York: Oxford University Press).

May, E.T. 1988. *Homeward Bound: American Families in the Cold War Era* (New York: Basic Books).

May, L. 1989. 'Movie Star Politics', in *Recasting America: Culture and Politics in the Age of the Cold War*, ed. Lary May (Chicago: University of Chicago Press).

Mayer, M. 1978. *The Builders* (New York: Gulf).

McLaughlin, S.D. et al. 1988. *The Changing Lives of American Women* (Chapel Hill: University of North Carolina Press).

Milkman, R. 1976. 'Women's Work and Economic Crisis: Some Lessons from the Great Depression', *Review of Radical Political Economics* 8: 84.

————. 1987. *Gender at Work: The Dynamics of Job Segregation by Sex During World War II* (Urbana, IL: University of Illinois Press).

Miller, D., and M. Nowak. 1977. *The Fifties: The Way We Really Were* (Garden City, NY: Doubleday).

Mintz, S., and S. Kellogg. 1988. *Domestic Revolutions: A Social History of American Family Life* (New York: Free Press).

Morris, R. 1990. *Richard Milhous Nixon: The Rise of an American Politician* (New York: Holt).

Murrow, E.R. 1960. 'Harvest of Shame', CBS Reports, 25 Nov. 1960.

'The Negro and the North', *Life*, 11 Mar. 1957, 163.

Parsons, T., and R. Bales. 1955. *Family, Socialization, and Interaction Process* (Glencoe, IL: Free Press).

Patterson, J. 1986. *America Struggles Against Poverty, 1900–1985* (Cambridge: Harvard University Press).

Pleck, E. 1987. *Domestic Tyranny: The Making of Social Policy Against Family Violence from Colonial Times to the Present* (New York: Oxford University Press).

Potter, D. 1959. *People of Plenty* (Chicago: University of Chicago Press).

Riley, G. 1987. *Inventing the American Woman* (Arlington Heights, VA: Harlan Davidson).

Rothman, E. 1984. *Hands and Hearts: A History of Courtship in America* (New York: Basic Books).

Ryan, M. 1983. *Womanhood in America from Colonial Times to the Present* (New York: Franklin Watts).

Sanders, A. 1990. 'Sex, Politics, and Good Taste in Nabokov's *Lolita* and Ike's America', paper delivered at 'Ike's America, A Conference on the Eisenhower Presidency and American Life in the 1950s', University of Kansas, Lawrence, 4–6 Oct.

Schrecker, E. 1986. *No Ivory Tower: McCarthyism and the Universities* (New York: Oxford University Press).

Seeley, J., R.A. Sim, and E.W. Loosely. 1956. *Crestwood Heights: A Study of Culture in Suburban Life* (New York: Basic Books).

Shapiro, H. 1988. *White Violence and Black Response: From Reconstitution to Montgomery* (Amherst: University of Massachusetts Press).

Smith, J.E. 1990. 'The Marrying Kind: Working Class Courtship and Marriage in Postwar Popular Culture', paper presented at American Studies Association Conference, New Orleans, Oct.: 3.

Social Security Bulletin, July 1963, 3–13.

Solinger, R. 1992. *Wake Up Little Susie: Single Pregnancy and Race in the Pre-Roe v. Wade Era* (New York: Routledge).

Stern, M. 1991. 'Poverty and the Life-Cycle: 1940–1960', *Journal of Social History* 24: 538.

Taylor, E. 1989. *Prime-Time Families: Television Culture in Postwar America* (Berkeley: University of California Press).

Tobias S., and L. Anderson. 1973. 'What Really Happened to Rosie the Riveter', *MSS Modular Publications* 9.

Toth, S.A. 1978. *Blooming: A Small-Town Girlhood* (Boston: Little, Brown).

Trey, J.E. 1972. 'Women in the World War II Economy', *Review of Radical Political Economics*, July.

Van Derbur Atler, M. 1991. 'The Darkest Secret', *People*, 6 July.

Van Horn, S.H. 1988. *Women, Work, and Fertility, 1900–1986* (New York: New York University Press).

Vinovskis, M. 1988. *An 'Epidemic' of Adolescent Pregnancy?: Some Historical and Policy Considerations* (New York: Oxford University Press) .

Ware, S. 1982. *Holding Their Own: American Women in the 1930s* (Boston: Twayne).

Warren, C. 1987. *Madwives: Schizophrenic Women in the 1950s* (New Brunswick: Rutgers University Press).

Whyte, W.H. 1956. *The Organization Man* (New York: Simon and Schuster).

Part Four   **Exploring the Many Facets of Personal Life and Family**

Section 1 | The Social Construction of Gender: Processes Creating Mothers, Wives, and Breadwinners

The gendered division of labour, and gender roles, are basic organizational features of families today. We begin our exploration of family life today with a consideration of how gender differences are created. There is no evidence that biology determines people's behaviour or the roles they assume as adults. For decades, sociologists have turned to the idea of socialization (or learning) to explain why women and men typically end up with somewhat different priorities as adults—women prioritizing family-care responsibilities and men prioritizing the financial support of loved ones (at least in terms of how they typically spend their time). Problems with these explanations have been apparent for some time, however. On the one hand, children still grow up in a culture that is thoroughly saturated with the idea of gender difference, and there is evidence that boys and girls are still subject to different treatment, expectations, and experiences. On the other hand, however, it is not at all clear—according to the evidence— that men and women are different in ways that would account for the different work they do, and responsibilities they bear, as adults. We have to find answers to questions about gender differences in roles and social position somewhere other than in the notion of individual personality characteristics created by childhood socialization. The research described in the next two chapters turns our attention away from individuals, and their socialization, to social organization.

Chapter 14

Researchers still find gender differences in teenagers' expectations about adulthood. Young women expect to prioritize family responsibilities at a certain point in their lives, while young men do not. Moreover, young women realize that this priority will be incompatible

with full-time employment. Although it is tempting to turn to 'socialization' to explain girls' continuing expectations about domestic responsibilities, Jane Gaskell's study, done in the late 1970s, suggests a different explanation.

The Reproduction of Family Life:
Perspectives of Male and Female Adolescents

Jane Gaskell

The literature on the transition from school to work emphasizes the experience of males rather than females, as does a good deal of work in the sociology of education (Acker 1981). . . . This neglect of women's experiences has meant not only that findings on males are misleadingly generalized to 'youth', but also that the analysis remains incomplete, failing to make visible assumptions based on the experience of males; these assumptions become visible only when the experience of females is addressed. One important assumption is the role of domestic labour. When the focus shifts to young women, it is clear that family issues must be addressed alongside issues of paid employment in order to understand the ways young people approach working life. But it is not just the young women who make assumptions about how their family lives will affect their work outside the home. The choices all young people make are embedded in assumptions about family life. For the males, however, family issues have appeared neither important nor problematic. It is assumed that they will get older, marry, and 'settle down' to an uninterrupted work life, provided that a job is available.

When researchers have turned their attention to women's place in the labour force, one of the first variables that is added to the analysis is family plans (Sokoloff 1980). A husband's 'support'

and the necessity of interrupting their work lives for childbearing and rearing differentiate the labour-force behaviour of some women from others (Almquist and Angrist 1975; Bielby 1978).

This leads in the same direction as the argument, made theoretically by Barrett (1980), Kuhn (1978), and others, that the continuing location of women in the family is central to understanding women's subordination in both capitalist and socialist societies. Women continue to be primarily responsible for domestic labour, even as their participation in the labour force increases (Meissner 1975, 1981; Vanek 1974, 1980). Employers and state agencies assume women are primarily located in the family (Coser and Rokoff 1971; Wolpe 1974; Thurow 1975) and by basing policy on this assumption, serve to ensure its continuation. But it is not just women who are located in families. Fully theorizing the organization of families and the role they play in locating people is critical to an adequate notion of how paid work is treated by everyone, not simply to understanding the oppression of women.

This paper will take data gathered in a study of seventeen- and eighteen-year-olds who are just leaving school and entering work and will focus on the way they construct their family lives in relation to their work. It will try to fill in a gap in the literature on the transition to adulthood by addressing the reproduction of family life alongside the reproduction of wage labour. What I will try to explore is how these young people come to expect and plan family lives of their own where the woman will take primary responsibility for domestic work and where the man will 'help out'. Of course, expectations and decision at this age are not binding. Young people's anticipation and planning for domestic life will not take into account all the contingencies they will face or accurately predict their own responses. However, the way they anticipate the future affects what the future will bring them. It is only a first step in determining how the allocation of domestic duties occurs, but it is an important step in reproducing families in which domestic work depends largely on women. . . .

[S]ocialization theories have attempted to explain the continuation of family forms where women take responsibility for childcare and housekeeping, through the internalization of the dominant ideology by young men and women. Educational research on gender has emphasized the way the dominant ideology of women's domesticity is transmitted to the young in parents' and teachers' attitudes, and in school practices and textbooks. This research has exposed an important set of sexist practices that had been hidden. But as Anyon (1981) has pointed out, the assumption is that this socialization is, unfortunately, successful and that little girls emerge content to re-create traditional forms of behaviour. But recent research has begun to take seriously the resistance of young people and the ways the dominant ideology is mediated through a prism of class- and gender-specific life conditions and experiences and only selectively incorporated. The result is a blend of oppositional tendencies and acquiescence, self-interest and acceptance of domination (Hall and Jefferson 1977; McRobbie 1978). This approach allows a more dialectic approach to ideology and structure and makes change possible, open to human agency.

In this paper, I will point to the ways in which structures of capitalism and patriarchy, and dominant ideologies of gender, impinge on the experience of working-class youth, and on the ways they think about organizing domestic work in their own lives. I will present the youth not just as passive recipients of cultural and economic imperatives, but as creative, active participants in making 'sense' and making choices for themselves. They do choose, or at least plan for, patterns of domestic labour that continue women's subordination in the family and in the workplace. But neither the women nor the men are powerless in this process—they resist some aspects of it, they see through some of the inequity, and they find advantages for themselves in traditional patterns. Looking at how they decide to organize domestic labour and why, exposes the structural and ideological factors that become critical in reproducing old patterns, and the factors that might change and lead to different kinds of decisions, with different consequences for themselves and others. It exposes the struggle, the weighing of forces, and the problems confronting them, rather than granting total power to the system.

Methodology

Eighty-three students were interviewed for this study from three schools in different working-class neighbourhoods of Vancouver, British Columbia. They all graduated from Grade 12 in 1977 and planned to go directly into the labour market. Thirty-six of the students were male; 47 were female. The students volunteered to participate in the study during a spare period in school hours and as a result cannot be said to be 'representative' of all the students in the school who were planning to go to work. But the schools were not randomly picked to be representative of Vancouver schools; they also volunteered to participate. And Vancouver is not representative of British Columbia or Canada. The study should then be seen as an exploration of the ways in which a specific group of young people approaches growing up and the ways ideology and structure affect this process. How much the findings can be generalized can be determined only through other similar work.

The first interview took place in May of the students' final high-school year. The interview covered educational plans, job plans, course selection, and attitudes toward the division of labour between men and women in the home, at school, and at work. A second interview took place between February and April, 1978, when eighty of the original students were recontacted. They were asked about their work, about the transition from school to work, and about the ways they were organizing and planning to organize their domestic lives.

The process of coding and using the interview comments was complex. The interviews were transcribed and read over several times. They were then analyzed by recording comments in categories such as division of labour in the home, bringing up children, the importance of work for women, etc. Profiles of individual students were also developed in order to understand the interrelationships among attitudes. The original transcripts were often reread in the process of developing interpretations of the interviews, to check for accuracy and relevant additional information.

Two interviews cannot provide the same depth of information as participant observation over a longer period of time. However, interview comments do reveal ways of thinking that cannot be measured by more standardized procedures. The young people describe the way the world works, what they like about it, and what they do not. They can be pushed to explain what they take for granted and to consider why alternative plans are not feasible. Their explanations and common sense do become clear.

The Girls

All of these girls plan to work outside the home. However, they feel that their right to work outside the home needs to be justified, rather than taken for granted. It is striking how many of them say women 'should be able' to work 'too'; 'It's okay for women to earn money. She [sic] is helping out'; 'I think if she wants to work, she can.'

This is because they all assume they will have primary responsibility for domestic work—for childcare and for housekeeping. They assume that paid work outside the home will be possible only when domestic duties have been taken care of. If they want to make space for other activities, they feel they are responsible for making alternative domestic arrangements—by working harder themselves, by 'bullying' their husbands, finding someone else to care for the children, or buying other necessary services.

This belief that work outside the home will be secondary to work inside the home is critical to understanding how these girls plan their lives and 'voluntarily' choose paths that will tend to reproduce secondary status at work and, paradoxically, in the home. It limits their aspirations, or at least reconciles them to less attractive jobs (Gaskell 1977). As the girls in this study put it:

> If I had a job that was really important, I probably wouldn't be able to raise my own children the way I want to.

> I considered engineering pretty seriously [but] . . . if I'm going to get married that's the most important thing I'm looking forward to.

It also means that whatever job a woman aspires to is treated as less important to her husband's, allowing him to devote time and family resources to performing his job well, while she takes them from hers. Her lack of resources, especially monetary, limits her power in the home, even though she devotes her energy there.

These girls, then, are not part of a new generation of 'liberated' women who reject old roles explicitly. (Some young women today undoubtedly do, and the processes involved in this need to be understood.) In their assumption of domestic responsibilities, these girls fit the abstract models of 'reproducing patriarchal structures' and being 'successfully' socialized. However, the girls arrive at what they expect to do not through a straight-forward response to structural imperatives or through a complete internalization of a domestic ideology. To understand the processes involved, it is necessary to explore both ideological and structural factors, showing how individual beliefs and choices are dialectically related to social forces that are beyond their choice or control.

The Domestic Ideology and the Role of Experience

The dominant ideology tells these girls that putting family responsibilities first is the preferred pattern for women. Domestic work will be as satisfying, fulfilling, and challenging as putting a career first. It reflects a woman's special interests and abilities, making her different from, but not unequal to, a man. The ideology obscures power differences and uses gender, rather than choice or achievement, as the criterion for determining who does what.

To the extent that these girls have been successfully socialized into femininity, they should accept this pattern, prefer to do the domestic work, and see themselves as more suited to it than any man. About a quarter of the girls did this, turning domestic work into a romantic idyll ('Her main job is doing things that you know, he likes. And making the house their own. Making it a nice and comfortable place to come home to. Supporting him and his problems, sort of thing.') They regarded housework as a good alternative to the stresses of a paid job ('I'd rather be at home. I don't want to work the rest of my life. I'd rather do the housework'); a rewarding way to spend time ('The advantage of being a girl is that you have kids and bring up a family'); or just the way it is ('I feel that the woman's place is in the home, and I feel that she should work at making their marriage work'). For these girls, their experiences

have reinforced the notion that they belong in the home. They have become interested in domestic work, they value it, and they like it. As a result, they prefer traditional patterns and use the domestic ideology to defend their choice.

Although we can see them as 'well socialized', this is an active process for them. They find advantages in traditional patterns. They discount experiences that might bring their beliefs into question. A job is nice, they admit, but only for a while. Housework can be a chore, but a tidy house is satisfying.

The other three-quarters of the girls do not describe their experience as so nicely congruent with the domestic ideology. For them, making sense of their everyday experience produces beliefs that run counter to the stereotype of the happy housewife, beliefs that they feel impelled to take seriously.

They have seen that paid work provides status, money, and independence. They are enthusiastic about moving into jobs after high school, despite the low wages and the low-level and boring jobs most had. They find that work provides a period of relative independence in their lives, when parental control is eased, and the school *in loco parentis* disappears. They are treated as responsible adults and paid a wage, signalling that they are competent to perform a task that is of real value to someone else. Furthermore, work provides more free time and the money to enjoy it (Gaskell and Lazerson 1981).

These positive feelings about paid work are projected into the future, and buttressed by their observations of their mothers' lives. Sixty per cent of their mothers work, but the daughters of both working and non-working mothers share the view that life at home is isolating, boring, and cuts you off from the 'real world'.

> You get bored staying at home. Women should get into things more. My mum is at home. She doesn't know what is going on in the world.

I think women should be able to work. My mum did. She didn't do it because we were starving or anything. She did it because she was really bored. She needed to come out of her shell.

Rubin (1976: 169) finds the same attitudes among married working-class women. Despite the fact that they are often forced to work by financial pressures, 'most find the world of work a satisfying place—at least when compared to the world of the housewife'. Work provides independence, and more ability to control one's own life, even when the jobs appear routine, low paying, and dead end. The socialization into femininity that these girls have received has not been enough to convince them that paid work does not matter for a woman and that they should define their achievement simply in terms of a domestic role.

Most of the girls are well acquainted with housework. Eighty-five per cent of them were regularly expected to do household chores and half of them took a major responsibility for housework for the whole family. In their descriptions of how housework gets done in the family, it is clear that mothers take primary responsibility, whether they are working outside the home or not. Female children are the primary helpers and males rarely do much.

> When I was younger my parents were working and me and my sister were young but we swept the floor and vacuumed and washed the dishes and then when Mom came home she'd do the heavy stuff, like washing clothes, and that.

> I don't have to do chores around the house. Like I help my mum with the dishes. Sometimes I'll wash and dry for a week if I feel like it. Sometimes I won't even touch them. But usually, I must admit, I either wash or dry for her, you know. . . . On Saturdays and Sundays, like, I clean the basement, mop

it up and that. Saturday my mom does the upstairs. But I like to cook too, like a lot of times I'll come home and cook dinner.

Even girls who by their own assessment 'didn't do much' were able to list household tasks that they performed fairly regularly. Females' responsibility for this work is so deeply ingrained that it is barely noticed.

Housework is seen as unglamorous and boring work, by and large, not something that provides great rewards. At their most positive, the girls might say, 'Housework is tolerable. I will do it if it has to be done.' This view of housework feeds the desire for work outside the home, which is less boring, more socially rewarding, and more challenging.

Childcare is the most critical and demanding part of domestic work and, although these girls were committed to having families, they were very ambivalent about the joys of mothering. They have experiences in babysitting and they have watched their own mothers. Some of the strongest expressions of the negative impression this left were:

> I don't ever want to have kids. I can't stand being around little kids. They drive me totally out of my mind.

> I think 95 per cent of mothers don't want their kids. You always have to do things you don't want to do. You don't have any respect for yourself. The kids are dirty and crabby and you get treated like dirt by your husband.

In milder language, many described women at home with small children as 'depressed and hypochondriac', 'tired out', and 'really bored'. This ambivalence about motherhood—I want children, but staying home for long periods with children is a nuisance—is also described by Prendergast and Prent (1980). Using a somewhat different methodology, they also discovered some of the accounts most teenage girls give of motherhood are dominated by fears of isolation, boredom, and depression rather than the stereotypical joy in children.

Three-quarters of the girls, then, valued paid work over domestic work. In this, they reflect and find support from the dominant achievement values of the society, if not from feminine values. But they overwhelmingly agree that they would be the ones who would take primary responsibility for domestic work. How did they agree to this, agree to collude in their own subordination, to take on the less desirable tasks, if their socialization had not succeeded in making it a preferred choice for most of them?

Ideology and Structure: The Dialectic of Reproduction

Even though these girls did not accept the whole ideology of domesticity, elements of this ideology continued to exert considerable influence on how they interpreted what they saw around them, and what they took for granted. These elements existed alongside an understanding of the way existing social structures prevented change. The particular mixture of critical awareness, social analysis, and dominant ideology that they produce illustrates both the active part the girls themselves play in reproduction and the role of ideological hegemony and social structure.

MASCULINITY

For many, the barriers to change lie in the nature of men. Men, these girls said over and over again, cannot or will not share domestic work. They are not like that. So if you want a tidy house and you want to live in relative harmony with men, you have to do it yourself.

> Sharing the housework would be wonderful. But it is not going to happen. He'd [her boyfriend] never help with the floors or with the dishes. I know him too well. I don't

expect him to do it because I know he wouldn't.

> I just couldn't picture my husband doing it—cleaning, making beds, making supper. I guess it's picturing my brother and dad.

> Men don't know the first thing about a laundry machine.

Similarly, men are seen as incapable of, or at least not very competent at, bringing up children.

> I can't give a distinct reason why a mother [rather than a father] should bring up her children, but I think it should be the wife that brings them up. It's because the kids really relate better to mothers.

> The woman has more affection for a baby when it is small. Men aren't used to it, and don't want to do it.

> Men are rough, their tone of voice. Babies like softness.

> I don't think men are very good at raising children. From what I have seen of fathers, I don't think they could hack it. I guess that is just the way they were brought up when they were young. Women have a better knack for it than men do.

In all these ways, men are seen as incapable and/or unwilling to be full-time fathers. Their masculinity is threatened by involvement with small children. As one girl put it, 'I always look at them as fags. I really do. I can't help it.'

This view of men, masculinity, and the limits of acceptable or 'natural' male behaviour has been noted before (Oakley 1974: 153–60; Gaskell 1977; Tolson 1977). These beliefs show few signs of change, despite the women's movement and more media attention to the issue. The girls express an enormous amount of incredulity when presented with the notion that men might be domestic.

Their construction of masculinity is rooted in an ideology that suggests that what men are like is what men must be like. Biological explanations of the differences between men and women and the domestic ideology's construction of the special nature of men and women shape their perceptions. A culture based on gender differences makes it easy to incorporate this element into the way they construct their lives.

Their views are also validated by their experience of patriarchal family structures. They have not seen men in domestic roles. Their fathers, brothers, and boyfriends do housework only as a special favour for a woman. The knowledge that some men do housework—that it is not inherent in the nature of man not to do housework—seems hard to come by, but can be powerful when it does. One of the two girls who said they would fight for equal sharing of the housework said:

> He [her boyfriend] is neat and I'm not. The regular way is the way it's mostly done. You don't see people going against it. Why not? I want to be equal. Men and women should share the housework. I know guys who vacuum and sew and do the laundry.

When they were presented with the possibility of having a man stay at home while the woman worked, the girls also alluded to the role their experience played: 'It could be okay, I guess. It's strange because I'm not used to it. I still feel that a child needs his mother.' This view of men is important in shaping the dilemma the girls confront. It limits the way they see their options, to having no children and a messy house, or making the adjustments themselves. Men remain outside the whole process of negotiation.

THE LABOUR MARKET

A further constraint that these girls saw impinging directly on their ability to plan their future

was a realistic assessment of the probable earnings of themselves and the men they would live with. Men earn more money than women. Women can expect, on the average, to earn about 60 per cent of what men earn in Canada. These girls were in and were expecting to continue in jobs that were firmly located within the female part of a sexually segregated labour market. Fifty-four per cent were in clerical jobs, 18 per cent were in sales jobs, and 16 per cent were working as waitresses (Gaskell 1981).

With occupational prospects like these, the girls realized that if they worked and their husbands stayed home to look after the children, the family would not be well off financially. Assuming a parent must stay at home with young children, it makes more financial sense for the woman to be the one who gives up her job, if only for a while. This economic reason for the belief that it should be women who stay home was often used by girls who wanted to keep working: 'It would be quite all right for him to stay home if the wife went to work. As long as she made enough money to support them.'

Girls with more traditional views were also able to point to economic constraints to bolster their views.

> One parent should be able to stay home until the kids are old enough for school. The most practical approach is that the one with the most money would work. But really I'd probably stay home anyway. I'd have more patience.

Financial pressure also has the effect of pushing women into the labour market. These girls are aware of how tenuous the financial position of single-income households has become.

> I think that now most women are going to have to work. In our age it is impossible to buy a house or anything, and I think we are going to have to work and support him and work equally.

I think if only one works, they don't have hardly any money. They don't eat good.

This push, however, is adding the responsibility of earning money on the women's existing domestic duties, not making the responsibility for domestic labour equal. Women will not earn an equal share of the family income and Lein et al. (1977) have pointed out that this tends to make women feel they have to work even harder around the house to 'make up for' their lack of earning power.

The fact that women can expect to earn lower wages than men becomes a critical structural element in reproducing a traditional division of labour in the home. It becomes a financially rational decision. Involved in this decision is the incorporation of an element of dominant ideology, the view that how much you earn determines the importance of your work. Financial criteria become the primary mode of valuing work. Work that brings in a lot of money deserves more respect than work that does not. This, in turn, serves to devalue domestic labour even further, as well as devaluing the work women do outside the home. Again, ideology, along with the structural reality of a sexually segregated labour market, become the elements that combine to lead to 'reproduction'.

CHILDCARE

Finally, the availability of acceptable childcare outside the family limits these girls' notions of how they will handle domestic labour and a paid job. This constraint need not differentially affect men and women. If domestic responsibilities were shared, the problems of finding substitute childcare would be also. But because, as we have seen above, the girls assume responsibility, childcare constrains their job planning and not the boys'.

Their view that childcare is a 'drag' and that paid work is rewarding coexists with the belief that young children need to be cared for by their mothers, if they are to grow up healthy, happy, and well adjusted. This belief is widespread. Public polls

reveal that Canadians overwhelmingly endorse equal opportunities for women, but just as strongly believe that 'when children are young a mother's place is in the home' (Gibbins, Ponting, and Symons 1978; see also Yankelovitch 1974). It is this conflict that the girls must come to terms with.

Women shouldn't work with small children. It's hard on the kids.

One thing I learned in Child Care and feel strongly about, if a woman is working she doesn't get to know the kids. Mothers shouldn't stick the kids with a babysitter until Grade One.

One thing I'm really against is leaving kids when they are really small. Kids come first. Wait till they're a few years into school.

This ideology exerts a powerful influence on these young women. It may be learned in a childcare course, as one of the girls above indicated, or picked up from family, friends, TV, newspapers, magazines, and childcare manuals. The view that one must stay at home with young children is also fed by the inadequacy of any perceived alternatives to childcare by full-time mothers until the school takes over at the age of five or six. Although school is an approved alternative to mother, other publicly available alternatives, such as babysitting and daycare at an earlier age, are seen as 'dumping grounds', lacking in 'love', and alienating parents from children (see also Lein et al. 1977).

You'll be a better mother if you were with the kids, and not throw them out with the babysitter . . . because they learn bad habits.

I don't believe in leaving little kids at home with the babysitter and their mother not knowing them very well. I'd wait to go back to work until they were in about Grade One or Two.

There's a daycare across the street and I feel those children won't grow up as part of those parents. Daycare workers have more influence. If both parents want to work, they should realize they can't give a child what he deserves. They shouldn't have children.

These views reflect the real fact that the availability, quality, and funding of daycare is less than desirable because of the very low priority given to it within the social-service area and the very low salaries that are paid to anybody embarking on a career in daycare. Decent childcare is hard to find, but then, one would argue, so is a decent first grade classroom. The notion that the age of five or six is the desirable age to have children in 'school' is clearly a reflection of the way childcare has been publicly organized— at five the state pays and the state provides subsidies only to parents with low incomes, making daycare a suspect institution, appropriate only for 'inadequate' parents. In this area the ideology of mothering, instead of being contradicted by experience, is supported by it. The organization of society—the structure—produces the experience that validates the ideology and produces constraints that any parent must contend with in order to change traditional patterns of behaviour. Ideology and structure come together to reproduce mother-centred patterns of childrearing for another generation.

The Potential for Change

Although incorporation of elements of the dominant ideology, the constraints of childcare and the labour market, and their experience of men combined to produce in all of these girls the view that domestic work is primarily their responsibility, there are differences in the ways they plan to deal with the domestic responsibilities they assume. Some are more likely to challenge the usual behaviour patterns than others.

A couple of girls, seeing the dilemmas, concluded that marriage and a family were not for them. The only way to stay independent was not to get married, not to have children. Although only two contemplated this as a long-term solution, many commented that they would put off marriage and certainly having children, for a while (at least until age twenty-five, which seemed like a long time to them) to enjoy their independence while it was possible.

It was the potential availability of acceptable alternatives for childcare that was critical in setting apart that quarter of the girls who planned to return to work while their children were preschoolers.

I would work if my mum would take care of the kids.

I guess I'd have to stay at home for a while, at least until they're one and a half or two years old. Unless my husband worked graveyard.

I'd go back to work when they were old enough for daycare—one and a half or two.

The most acceptable alternative forms of childcare are family arrangements, with the husband or with the grandmother. But if daycare is seen as acceptable, it makes it possible to return to work when the child is eighteen months or perhaps three years, instead of when she is five.

There were also a few girls who, while accepting that they 'should' stay home for the sake of the children, were prepared to put their own needs above their responsibilities.

It would be better to stay at home, but personally, I don't think I could.

I hate staying at home. I'd really be going crazy without a job. But with children, part-time is best.

Similarly, a couple of girls were committed enough to sharing housework to be willing to do battle over it.

You should share everything when you're married. Even now my boyfriend does the dishes. He complains and bitches sometimes. Sometimes I do it. He is trying hard to change his habits. It creates tension between us.

This girl's expressed willingness to create tension and take on her boyfriend distinguishes her from the great majority of other girls who, if they do it, do it more quietly, less on principle.

The girls anticipate that experience in the labour market will also make a difference to how much paid work they do, and perhaps to the division of domestic work.

If I really love my job, and the boss needs me, maybe . . .

It should be the husband [who works], unless he's unemployed and I could get outside work.

This suggests that change can occur when a girl takes her own needs seriously and when the social structure provides her with alternatives. Structural factors—the availability of childcare, male unemployment, women getting higher pay—may produce shifts in who does what, if not immediately in whose responsibility it is seen to be. The girls are certainly not so committed to traditional patterns that new opportunity structures would make no difference. These changes in behaviour would then become part of their, and other girls', experience and provide potential challenges to received ideology. Understanding this dialectical relation between ideology and structure allows us to see how reproduction occurs systematically, but it is not a necessary and inevitable outcome of the situation in which these girls find themselves.

The Boys

The boys also make decisions about how they plan to manage domestic work. Although paid work is their primary focus in planning the future, they also want to get married and have children, just as the girls do. They, however, do not plan to take a lot of responsibility for these tasks, which allows them to treat paid work as their main focus of concern.

It is perhaps easier to understand the boys' decision—who wouldn't want to have the more powerful and independent position and to let someone else take responsibility for getting the domestic work done? Who wouldn't like a 'wife'? Because the dominant ideology supports their immediate self-interest, reconstituting this ideology to make it congruent with their experience and desires is not as pressing for them. In this section, I will outline the boys' notion of the division of labour in the home and examine how accurate the girls constructions of the boys' views are.

The Ideology of Domesticity and Self-Interest

Most of the boys accept the traditional view of the division of labour in the home. They are significantly more conservative than the girls, significantly more likely to swallow the 'domestic ideology' whole.

I wouldn't let her work if I could support the family.

If I work and get a lot of money, I wouldn't want her to work. She could look after the kitchen or something. There's a lot to do.

I'm traditional. Women's Lib can never make a husband pregnant. Mother's place is at home until the kids can take care of themselves.

They accept some variations—the woman can 'help' the man by getting a paid job and the man can 'help' the woman around the house. But a differentiation of roles is assumed.

A wife helps out. It's not as important [for her to work] as long as you can get along on his wages. It's not right if she has a kid.

When the kids get to be about sixteen and they're in school all day and she's got five hours to kill she should go out and get a job not far from home so she can get home and make supper.

And a reversal of roles is outrageous.

I'd never let her do that. It's just a person's morals. It's how you're brought up. . . . The man is supposed to go and collect the bread and the woman stays home. . . .

No, if you have a lot of kids, she's got to stay home all the time and he brings in the money. It's the husband's duty to keep the household going. I don't know why. That's the way it's always been.

It became apparent in the interviews that they had not spent a lot of time worrying about it—it's 'just the way it is', they said. Their own households ran along these lines, and they took these patterns for granted.

The males and females don't share the work in our house. The females got nothing else to do. When mother was working, she did all the housework too, but that's because my sister wouldn't do it.

I sleep and eat. Sometimes wash the dishes. Pick up the mail and paper if I step on it. I don't really care if the housework is done. Mother does it. She works part-time.

And they were quite aware of their own self-interest. They did not like domestic work. They did not want to change what was obviously an advantageous status quo. Although they said the same

things as girls—housework is a drag and child-care drives me nuts—they were much more willing to take their own self-interest seriously than the girls were.

I can't picture myself staying at home and looking after the kids for five years, while she works. I'd just feel sheer lazy.

For one thing, I don't like kids and house-work, kids and housework. . . . I wouldn't want to do it all the time.

When they were prodded, they recognized that their assumptions were not quite fair—that they 'should' share. This was clearest in the area of housework.

I don't do a hell of a lot. I'm too lazy . . . I'm bagged after work. I want the weekends for myself. Biking, skiing, my girlfriend. I should help more—there should be two of me—one to stay around. My mum and sister do the work.

If I marry, I should share, but I wouldn't want to.

If I marry my girlfriend, I'd help her out. I don't like doing it. If someone doesn't ask me, I won't do it.

In the area of childcare, it was not so much fairness as a desire to retain their primacy in family affairs that motivated them to take part in domestic work. They set out how important their role in childcare was, retaining their father's prerogatives and his ultimate authority, while leaving women to do the primary caregiving.

There's a difference between raising kids and looking after them. The woman might spend more time with the kids, but the father has the authority.

From age one to seven you are mom's boy; and then from seven to fourteen, you are daddy's boy. The kids need the female, but they need the male image too. They act differently to males and females. They can get away with more with the female, like with their mothers. But the father comes home and he's ready to hit the kid over the head.

In the interview, then, the boys overwhelmingly presented very conservative views. When asked, what came most easily to mind was what their parents did, what the dominant ideology told them, a justification for their own present behaviour. This makes the girls' description of men fairly accurate. They are, as the girls described, unused to and unwilling to do much about domestic duties. They incorporate the dominant ideology gladly, actively to serve their own interests.

Equality and Structural Barriers

The boys were not universally as reactionary as the above views suggest. Some boys did take seriously the notion of women's equal rights, especially to a job.

Sure I think [career women] are a really good idea. But I think it's going to be a long time before women are really into top positions . . . because so many men still feel that women should be at home and doing the routine jobs.

Women should be able to work outside the home. We shouldn't expect them to get married, have babies, and stay home. They do have their own freedom, their own life. They can enjoy it.

The general values of achievement and fairness present a challenge to the traditional views of these boys. They admire women with more independence; they feel everyone should be treated equally. Achieving these goals, however, will involve some concessions by men in the area of domestic labour. Are they willing to follow through? To a certain extent, although it often becomes 'helping' rather than sharing equally. On housework:

Yeh, they [men] should do that, you know; they should just say 'Oh I worked eight hours and I'm tired and I'm gonna go to sleep or something.' They both occupy the same house, and . . . we have to look [after] our own things, and if we can't split the duties. . . .

They should share. It's something that has to be done. I help my fiancée with her housework. She has a two-year-old son.

On childcare:

I think it's sort of an equal responsibility, too. If a man's home, why not be involved? He sort of groans changing those diapers. I'd probably end up doing it. Changing the kid at 2 o'clock in the morning . . . yuk. It's important, like . . . they have to do it.

The way it is in most families is what I *don't* want. I want to have some part in what the kids are doing. I want to be at home; I still want to have something that I would do as a career. . . . But I really think that it should be equally done.

As with the girls, structural barriers become more important in their thinking. For the boys, these come down on the side of not taking equal responsibility at home, which is what they prefer anyway. The labour market makes it more reasonable for women to stay home because they earn less.

I wouldn't mind doing childcare if she had a large income; I would stay at home. But I would prefer to be working and have my wife at home.

Staying at home is a little weird; the guys have to be a little strange, or, unless the guy's a cripple and can't help it. . . . If she'd earn more money than him it would probably work out that she'd go to work and he'd stay home.

And the person who stays home should do the housework; so they can assume women will do it for them.

I figure if I'm gone all day and my wife is home she can clean up.

Whoever has the job shouldn't have to do the housework. It could be either person. But, I'd have the job.

I think the person who spends the most time at home should do the majority of the work.

A woman might handle childcare in some other way besides staying home, but daycare is unacceptable and alternative childcare is hard to come by.

If there was somebody to take care of the kids I wouldn't mind if she worked or when she is very well trained for or involved in her work.

She could have a small part-time job if she wants to. But not with the kids in daycare.

So it becomes 'reasonable' to assume the woman will stay home, even for those more liberal boys who do not assume it is their prerogative to tell their wives what to do, and who do not find the notion of equality absurd before it is even addressed by factors in the real world. The application of universal principles—whoever earns most money, whoever is at home—becomes the reason for women to do the work.

For the more liberal boys, resolving the issue of domestic labour becomes a struggle to integrate principles of fairness and achievement with

relegating women to the home. For the more conservative boys, this is a less difficult issue because they incorporate an ideology of domesticity for women more completely, and they are less concerned about putting their self-interest above fairness. For neither group of boys does their concrete experience play a large role in refracting and forcing them to reinterpret the ideologies they hear. It is a much more abstract issue. It does not have the immediate meaning it has for the girls.

Conclusions

. . . Despite the initial similarity in their enthusiasm for leaving school and finding work, males and females make different long-term assumptions about what a paid job will mean, because of its relation to domestic labour.

In exploring the reasons for this, I have stressed the incorporation of elements of the dominant ideology and their interaction with social institutions, notably the labour market and the provision of childcare, and with their immediate experiences of family and friends. Income differences between men and women, the inadequate provision of public childcare facilities, and the predominance of families with a traditional division of labour are all part of the world these young people know, and they interpret it through incorporation of selected elements of the dominant ideology. Their experience then takes on meanings that lead to an expectation that traditional patterns will be continued. Whether these expectations will come to pass cannot be determined here, but I have suggested that changes in opportunities—a good job for a woman, an excellent childcare facility, a liberal husband—could make a difference. The trouble is that these changes are unlikely to occur on a wide scale.

Both the young men and the young women in this study expect that the young women will add work outside the home to their domestic work. Paid labour for women gets incorporated into the old directives that women be primarily mothers and housekeepers, helpmates to their husbands rather than equal partners in the labour force or the home. It means that while these young women are pleased by their transition from school to work and find their jobs important and rewarding, they still assume they will give them up in a few years, and, for the most part, will not allow the demands of their paid work to interfere with their family life.

There is perhaps nothing surprising about this. Much of the literature tells us that, although paid labour can increase women's power in the household, it does not equalize their power. Women's jobs provide them with less income than men's and are seen as less important. Even working women continue to do most of the domestic labour, both reflecting and producing their 'secondary' status as workers.

These interviews give some insight into the way this pattern begins in the expectations of young people about to embark on adult life and into the factors that begin to produce change in their expectations. A few girls accept happily, indeed glorify, the traditional role of women. They want to be primarily lovers of their husbands, mothers to their children. These see advantages in the traditional pattern; they appropriate the traditional ideology. They recognize often that their attitudes reflect the way they have been brought up, the way they have learned to deal with the world, the skills and abilities that they have developed over time. But they accept these prescriptions.

But most girls do not embrace these traditional tasks so cheerfully. The majority do not particularly like housework, and they see being at home with children as confining. Work brings them independence, responsibility, and money, all of which they are enjoying. Marriage and children bring a return to dependence on a male wage, personalized control and authority in the family, and little time that is not available to the demands of others. However, incorporating domestic duties into their lives seems necessary, given the way they

see the men around them behaving, the state of childcare, and the incomes they can expect. Elements of the domestic ideology still shape the way they see acceptable options. The social organization of childcare, the nature of men, and the fact of segregated labour markets make change unlikely. They therefore determine to cope with their lack of alternatives with good grace, not asking the impossible, not complaining about the inevitable. Facing up, as they feel, realistically, to the constraints of their lives, they accept them and constrain themselves accordingly. Some feel they will be more able to work out individual solutions through struggling with the men in their lives or finding a neighbour to babysit, than others.

In the young people in this study, we can see both the passivity that reproduces traditional roles and the beginning of discontent that provides the possibility of change. There are many youth, most notably a large number of the girls, who would challenge the idea that the traditional division of labour by sex is equally fulfilling for males and females, and that it is the only proper way to organize families and work. But it is clear that this discontent is not enough to bring about equality for men and women. The waning of the domestic ideology among the girls is not enough to stop them planning their lives around it. Life choices come not merely from some abstract principles of the way the world works, what opportunities are open, what paths are possible. In this construction of how the world works, ideological elements incorporated from outside are critical. Young people with more liberal attitudes thought little change seemed realistically possible. Instead of expressing much anger about this or trying to combat it, which might begin a process of change, they resign themselves to it and resolve to get on with life as it presents itself. . . .

Any attempt to give young people a sense of their own agency in the world, to show them that the world is constructed through a series of political and personal actions that might be changed, involves not just talking to them but also showing them that conditions can indeed be altered. In other words, it involves not just ideological work but also political movements for institutional change that demonstrate the possibility of change. This might occur in many ways—for example, in a movement for satisfactory childcare that demonstrates its potential value, or in a struggle for equal pay that shows women's jobs are valuable and can be rewarded. The limits of reform will be set not just by how well an alternative account of the world can be conveyed but also by how much the lived world of such young people can actually be demonstrated to be changeable.

References

Acker, S. 1981. 'No Woman's Land: British Sociology of Education 1960–1979', *Sociological Review* 29 (1): 77–104.

Almquist, E.M., and S.S. Angrist. 1975. *Careers and Contingencies* (Port Washington, NY: Dunnellen).

Anyon, J. 1981. 'Accommodation, Resistance and Female Gender', paper presented at the International Sociology of Education Conference, Birmingham, England.

Barrett, M. 1980. *Women's Oppression Today: Problems in Marxist Feminist Analysis* (London: Verso).

Bielby, D. 1978. 'Career Sex: Atypicality and Career Involvement of College Education Women', *Sociology of Education* 51 (1): 7–28.

Coser, R.L., and G. Rokoff. 1971. 'Women in the Occupational World: Social Disruption and Conflict', *Social Problems* 18 (4): 535–54.

Gaskell, J. 1977. 'Sex Role Ideology and the Aspirations of High School Girls', *Interchange* 8 (3): 43–53.

———. 1981. 'Sex Inequalities in Education for Work: The Case of Business Education', *Canadian Journal of Education* 6 (2): 54–72.

——— and Lazerson. 1981. 'Between School and Work: Perspectives of Working-Class Youth', *Interchange* 11 (3): 80–96.

Gibbins, R., J.R. Ponting, and G. Symons. 1978. 'Attitudes and Ideology: Correlates of Liberal Attitudes Towards the Role of Women', *Journal of Comparative Family Studies* 9 (1): 19–40.

Hall, S., and T. Jefferson. 1977. *Resistance Through Rituals: Youth Subcultures in Post-War Britain* (London: Hutchinson).

Kuhn, A. 1978. 'Structures of Patriarchy and Capital in the Family' in *Feminism and Materialism*, eds A. Kuhn and A.M. Wolpe (Boston: Routledge).

Lein, L. et al. 1977. *Working Family Project Final Report: Work and Family Life* (Wellesley: Wellesley College Research Center for Research on Women).

McRobbie, A. 1978. 'Working Class Girls and the Culture of Femininity', Women's Study Group, Centre for Contemporary Cultural Studies. *Women Take Issue* (Birmingham: Center for Contemporary Cultural Studies, University of Birmingham, Women's Studies Group).

Meissner, M. 1975. 'No Exit for Wives: Sexual Division of Labour and the Cumulation of Household Demands', *Canadian Review of Sociology and Anthropology* 12: 424–39.

———. 1981. 'The Domestic Economy: Now You See It, Now You Don't', paper prepared for SSHRC conference on Women in the Labour Force, Vancouver.

Oakley, A. 1974. *The Sociology of Housework* (New York: Pantheon).

Osterman, P. 1980. *Getting Started: The Youth Labor Market* (Cambridge, MA: MIT Press).

Prendergast, S., and A. Prent. 1980. 'What Will I Do? Teenage Girls and the Construction of Motherhood', *Sociological Review* 28 (3): 517–32.

Rubin, L. 1976. *Worlds of Pain: Life in the Working Class Family* (New York: Basic Books).

Sokoloff, N. 1980. *Between Money and Love* (New York: Praeger).

Thurow, L. 1975. *Generating Inequality* (New York: Basic Books).

Tolson, A. 1977. *The Limits of Masculinity* (London: Tavistock).

Vanek, J. 1974. 'Time Spent in Housework', *Scientific American* 231: 116–20.

————. 1980. 'Household Work, Wage Work and Sexual Equality' in *Women and Household Labour*, ed. S.F. Berk (Newbury Park, CA: Sage).

Willis, P. 1977. *Learning to Labour* (Farnborough: Saxon).

————. 1981. 'Cultural Production Is Different from Cultural Reproduction Is Different from Social Reproduction Is Different from Reproduction', *Interchange* 12 (2–3): 48–67.

Wolpe, A.M. 1974. 'The Official Ideology of Education for Girls', in *Educability, Schools and Ideology*, eds J. Ahier and M. Flude (London: Croom Helm).

Yankelovitch, D. 1974. *The New Morality: A Profile of American Youth in the 1970s* (New York: McGraw-Hill).

Chapter 15

This chapter, from Kathleen Gerson's book Hard Choices *reports on her study of American women who became adults in the 1970s. Gerson was interested in the life choices this cohort made, and interviewed them in the 1980s, when they were in their thirties. Her focus was on the relationship between these women's current priorities—whether family or paid employment/career—and the priorities they held when they were in their early twenties. She found that no matter which priority they held in* early adulthood, the majority of them switched priorities between then and their thirties. Women who abandoned a focus on domesticity, for a focus on their employment or careers, did so for a variety of reasons—dissatisfaction with full-time domesticity, an unstable marriage or relationship with a man, a tight household budget, or good employment opportunities. The women who switched their focus from employment to family are described below, in a chapter from* Hard Choices.

Hard Choices: Veering Toward Domesticity

Kathleen Gerson

The lives of the women analyzed in the first part of this chapter underwent significant change in adulthood. These women traded their earlier work ambitions and aversions to domesticity for motherhood and domestic orientations. They began adulthood with high aspirations and a strong ambivalence toward domestic pursuits, but adult events and experiences intervened to challenge their assumptions and redirect their lives. In contrast to their nontraditional counterparts, these women were exposed to forces in the home and on the job that loosened their psychological and actual ties to work and replaced them with children and domestic aspirations.

The backgrounds of this group's members were not substantially different from those of the other respondents. Indeed, taking socialization factors and starting points alone into account, these women were, if anything, more predisposed to seek out a nondomestic life pattern. Over 60 per cent of those whose early life orientations were nondomestic veered in a domestic direction.

This chapter explains why this group veered toward domesticity and what distinguishes it from those who did not.

Declining Work Aspirations and the Home as a Haven

Like nontraditional women, women who veered toward domesticity experienced events that pushed them off their expected tracks. This group, however, was propelled down a different road. Unlike nontraditional women, they were subjected to the traditional package of incentives and constraints that have historically made domesticity attractive and other options difficult and costly for women to choose. Members of this group were more likely than those who veered toward nontraditional pursuits to become committed to traditional marriages that undermined efforts at career building, insulated them from economic squeezes, and allowed them to implement domestic choices. They were also more likely to encounter blocked work opportunities, which enhanced the pull of motherhood and domesticity. They were thus drawn toward domestic commitments despite the structural changes leading other women to eschew such choices. In this sense, their lives underscore the continuing forces of traditional arrangements, which have persisted even as new alternatives have gained growing numbers of adherents.

THE PRECEDENCE OF PERSONAL RELATIONSHIPS

For those who veered toward domesticity, stable marriages and committed relationships with men provided the conditions that made the bearing and rearing of children possible. Committed heterosexual partnerships also promoted the development of the desire to do so.

Most in this group struck a traditional bargain with male partners. Through a negotiated process, they exchanged allegiance to their partner's career for emotional and financial support. This bargain exacted a sometimes subtle, sometimes obvious cost at the workplace because the male partner's job took precedence over the respondent's own. Long-term commitment to a heterosexual relationship thus gradually undermined these women's work commitments and directed them toward mothering and domesticity.

Developing Commitment to Marriage over Work

Women who traded work accomplishments for a committed relationship confronted an intractable conflict between their public and private commitments. Either directly or circuitously, these women had to *choose between* a valued relationship and the promise of satisfying work. When a relationship was an accomplished fact and a career a risky possibility, the option of family was more compelling than the option of work. This married woman in her late twenties thus relinquished a promising job in a male-dominated occupation in order to preserve a relationship she valued more:

Q: If you were so happy being a customs inspector, why didn't you stay with it?

A: The customs thing was interesting, exciting to me, but at that point I got married and *that* became very important to me. So it was to keep that relationship. It was more desirable to live with Don than to be a customs inspector.

For women faced with a conflict between commitment to work and commitment to an intimate partner, a number of factors promoted the choice of love over work. First, these traditional partnerships were based, at least in part, on a mutual, if often unspoken, assumption that the male partner's work mattered more. Because women in this situation generally perceived that they benefited from their partners' success, they became enlisted in the process of male career building. When conflicts arose between two careers, as they often did, it was the woman who sacrificed job opportunities.

For example, career building often required geographic mobility. When the male partner's career took precedence, women in these relationships were forced to go along with their partners' work demands at the expense of their own. (Papanek 1973 and Kanter 1977a, 1977b discuss how middle-class male careers have historically required the efforts of two persons—a man at the office and a woman at home.) This need to follow where the male career led made it difficult to establish a solid base at the workplace or to take advantage of advancement opportunities when they arose. This homemaker and mother of two declined a promotion so that she could follow her spouse during the early years of their marriage:

A: I did take a job with the telephone company and left when I had my first child and was offered a management position. I know a lot of people at the phone company now, women who are making exorbitant salaries, and then I think, 'Gee, that would have been me if I had stuck with it.' [But] we were doing a lot of moving. . . . I couldn't really make a commitment to anyone, because Jeff was in a training program, and every time he got a promotion, we moved. I go with my husband wherever he goes; that was always a very clear thing.

The threat of losing a valued relationship also posed a powerful obstacle to female career development. When success could be purchased only at the expense of a relationship, women in traditional relationships chose to forgo longstanding dreams as well as real opportunities. This respondent chose to avoid competing with her spouse, for she feared a win at work would entail a greater loss at home:

Q: Why didn't you pursue your interest in retail merchandising?
A: I explored the field when we were first married, but it was a strange situation. We laugh about it now. My husband was at ———. I had an interview with ———, and I thought, 'Well, gee, what if I get to be a buyer and he doesn't? That could really blow a relationship.' So I guess you would say I deferred a little.

Some women translated the fear of losing a relationship into a fear that they lacked the ability to handle a more demanding position. It is difficult to distinguish between fear of success and fear of failure in these instances. Despite this twenty-eight-year-old, childless secretary's elaborate efforts to convince herself that she really did not want a promotion, she acknowledged that her partner wanted it less than she did. She thus perceived that a career could be purchased only at the expense of love, security, and motherhood. Faced with such potentially high costs, she

declined to take advantage of advancement opportunities that arose:

A: I had a couple of opportunities to get into sales, and I passed them up. I don't know if that was wise, but anyway. . .
Q: Why did you pass them up?
A: I know the business and everything, but now I'm living with Bill. He's not a businessman; he's a country boy, and he likes me to spend my time with him. I think my main reason for turning it down was I was scared of it, too, you know. Bill expressed his opinion, although he would never say to me, 'Don't do it.' But I think deep down inside the idea scared me.
Q: Why did the idea scare you?
A: Bill wanted me to be a secretary. And I thought, why should I take on more responsibility and travel and entertain and get involved? So I just decided no. But I think deep down inside it just sounds like such a big challenge for me, and I think I'm scared about it. . . . I'm getting older, the family image. I really want to become a mother someday, and that's really on my mind, I think. And I guess I keep thinking, if I get into sales, that's going to get further and further away [from having a family]. . . . I'm really kind of split right down the middle, because you could eventually make a lot of money being in sales, and I like that part of it. But, like I say, my personal life means so much more to me. I'm really happy with Bill, and that means more to me than my job.

Although it may appear that these women behaved according to Matina Horner's 'motive to avoid success' syndrome (1972), their actions did not result from a psychological handicap peculiar to the female sex. Their choices were rooted in structural circumstances that forced them to choose between love and work and threatened to exact a great price if they chose work over love. In short, these women *did* have something to lose by succeeding. To the extent that they perceived their options correctly, they made sensible choices in an effort to preserve personal happiness. They did not respond in peculiarly 'feminine' and irrational ways.

We must look, therefore, to the decision-making context as a whole to understand when fear of success is experienced and why such fear is acted on rather than overcome or ignored. A psychological process may set up a tension, but it does not predetermine how an actor will resolve it, especially when she experiences a variety of conflicting emotions. Fear is only one of a number of potentially motivating emotions, and not necessarily the most influential on behaviour. We may fear the very goals we are motivated to seek, but fear will not in itself prevent us from seeking them.

Actual choices, as distinct from fears or hopes, thus depend on social circumstances and on how the social context sets up a balance of gains and losses. Because women face different sets of costs and benefits, they vary in the extent to which success at work threatens other valued life pursuits. They also vary in the degree to which they 'fear' success rather than embrace it unambivalently and in the degree to which such fear actually impedes their work mobility. For women in traditional partnerships, who were faced with a choice between love and work, the high cost of work success was simply not deemed worth the price.[1]

If subtler inducements failed to dampen their enthusiasm for work commitment, women sometimes faced more overt opposition from traditional husbands. In these instances, a male partner intervened directly to thwart a woman's work plans so that he might preserve some valued aspect of his life. Patriarchal authority prevailed when this mother of two sought to enter police work:

Q: What happened to your plans to become a policewoman?

A: I got married, and my husband said no. He didn't feel that was a position for his wife and the mother of his kids to be in. It's not an eight-to-five job, and sometimes it's an eighteen-hour job; so he didn't go for that.

Q: Were your plans for becoming a police-woman serious at that time?

A: They were at the point when I realized I had to make a choice, and they became less. I didn't particularly *like* it, but I didn't have much choice.

Men also intervened less directly to dampen women's chances for success at work. In some instances, simply caring for a man led to the loss of workplace opportunities. This homemaker's first husband required as much attention as a child, eventually reducing her career aspirations to the hope of mere economic survival:

A: [In my] early twenties I was very work-oriented. I did get married when I was twenty, a previous marriage, and that sort of sidetracked it. Where before I think I'd been more career-oriented, marrying left it as 'work' rather than career.

Q: What happened?

A: It wasn't a decision. It happened that the man I married was more of a babysitting job; so to maintain the marriage was as much as I could handle. Work became just something I had to do to feed us without really having the energy to put myself into it, to consider it a career. In fact, at the time, I worked at a bank, and they had an opening. But because my personal life was so fouled up, it sort of shot down my possibilities of getting that, which was a bad move on my part.

Thus, through a variety of mechanisms, commitment to a traditional relationship directly and indirectly undermines a woman's work ties. Although the proportion of marriages (or heterosexual partnerships) that operate according to these traditional rules is on the decline, arrangements that grant precedence to the male's career and penalize a woman for having one persist and continue to provide powerful incentives for women's domestic orientations. When a husband has strong incentives to see his wife succeed at work—as in the case of the economically squeezed family—the advantages he gains through her success may offset the marginal power he loses at home. Supportive spouses are not unknown in many modern marriages, and a supportive partner fuels nontraditional aspirations just as surely as a nonsupportive one undermines them. Recent studies show, however, that although husbands support a certain measure of success on the part of their wives, they tend to get uncomfortable when that success, especially as measured by income, equals or surpasses their own. (See, for example, Blumstein and Schwartz 1983; Huber and Spitze 1980.) Patriarchal marriage patterns persist, however, not simply because men continue to benefit from them. Many women, too, continue to uphold patriarchal marriage because they have interests of their own to protect. Income inequality between the sexes, for example, reinforces a traditional sexual division of labour and supports the priority of the male career on practical grounds.[2]

The financial and emotional benefits of traditional partnerships led respondents with declining work aspirations to overlook or minimize the price they were paying. Indeed, this gradual decrease in work commitment was not typically experienced as a cost. Rather, respondents in traditional marriages felt fortunate to retain a domestic foothold in the face of so much change around them. They did not experience 'patriarchy' as domination, but rather greeted it as their good fortune in securing spouses willing to care for them and support their preferences for domesticity. This ex-secretary regarded her dependence on her husband's paycheque not as domination, but as liberation:

A: There's this mystique about the charismatic man, who's not a decent and dependable sort of man. They're movie types. . . . [My husband] goes to work and comes home at five, and [people] say, 'Isn't that boring?' And I say, 'No, not at all,' because it gives me time to [do what I want]. I'm not always struggling down at the bottom of the ladder. Once you get that and taste it, you never want to let that go.

A part-time nurse felt privileged to have an option her husband did not share:

A: [My husband] thinks I'm getting my cake and eating it, too. I get to stay home and am enjoying it. And he has an ulcer.

Commitment to a traditional relationship thus tended to exact gradual, often imperceptible costs at the workplace. Whether or not these costs were perceived as costs, women in this situation faced a choice between a satisfying personal life and satisfying work. This set of options made their choices not a matter of whether they lost, but rather what they chose to lose. For those with declining work aspirations, forgone work opportunities were easier to bear than the loss of emotional ties and a secure family life.

Consequences of Marital Commitment

However it was evaluated, the sequence of events that led these women to choose commitment to a man over commitment to work had two interdependent consequences. First, pressures to maintain a valued relationship diminished the chances of securing satisfying work and ultimately made domesticity more attractive. This mother of two chose homemaking after the search for challenging work proved futile:

A: Becoming a teacher was sort of a little dream I had. When I did meet my husband, right after graduation, we just hit it off so perfect, I didn't want to jeopardize any relationship we might have by running off to go to school. [So] I went to the business school instead. [But] I didn't like typing and taking shorthand that well, so I ended up as a keypunch operator. I really didn't like that either, but I didn't know what I wanted to do. I just finished that, and I went to work as a keypunch operator for an insurance company. If I work again, I want it to be something I really like.

Second, decisions that built a committed relationship with a man also created a context in which childbearing became feasible and desirable. When the experience of intimacy was coupled with declining work opportunities, it sparked a new attitude toward children and motherhood. Work aspirations lessened, and children came to be seen as a natural expression of the relationship. Newly awakened desires for parenthood emerged to replace work goals, and old ambivalences toward childbearing subsided. A deepening commitment to her spouse nurtured a new desire for a child as this pregnant ex-saleswoman wearied of work at thirty-three:

Q: Have there ever been times when you seriously considered having children before now?

A: I think I'd make a good mother, but I've never yearned for motherhood per se. The only time I ever *really* felt a desire to have a baby was with my husband before we were married.

Q: So it's very tied up with the man?

A: With the loving. And the way it's going, because if it hadn't been going right and if it hadn't been unfolding as it was, we wouldn't have had children. There was a time when I felt I would never have children. Around five or six years ago I felt that way.

The desire for a child did not result from an abstract, generalized 'mothering need'. It arose in the context of a specific relationship and from the commitment, goals, and desires this relationship fostered. In this context, having a child became an expression of commitment and a means for establishing a permanent home, as this thirty-six-year-old ex-nurse and mother of two explained:

Q: Thinking back to when you first got pregnant, what were your main reasons for having a child at this time?

A: Because I wanted one [laughter]. I don't know. I guess after you live together so long, you just want more, and a baby really does fill it. It doesn't make your house a place where you stop in to sleep. It kind of brings you closer.

Although the stereotype that women leap hungrily into motherhood, dragging their reluctant husbands along, persists in theory as well as in popular culture, many mothers reported a reverse process. This thirty-four-year-old mother of three acquiesced to her husband's strong desire for children:

A: Jim was the person of primary importance, and he wanted kids. If I had married a man who didn't want children, fine. I would have gone along with that, too. I didn't think much about it. Motherhood was no big thing to me. I took it very casually. I had no great emotional interest in it. I didn't fight it or anything. [But I did it] to please my husband.

Indeed, some planned for or bore children despite their own reluctance. These reluctant mothers (most of whom are members of the non-domestic group) viewed childbearing not as an end in itself, but as a means of pleasing a valued partner and cementing a relationship that might not otherwise endure. This motivation also prevented some from pursuing more autonomous goals. Remarriage to a child-oriented man thus prompted this thirty-three-year-old, childless teacher to suppress her ambivalence toward motherhood and trade her emerging independence for the security of home and family:

A: After my divorce, I first became fully aware of the choices that I had. I liked not being responsible to anyone, just being in charge of myself. I realized the limits that a marriage places on that, that you can't always do what you want; you have to reach a compromise. But Peter is very understanding and willing to listen and willing to sacrifice in my behalf. So I'll probably have children. I don't know if freedom is worth the loneliness. You have to give up something to get something. I don't want to lose Peter, and children are very important to him. He has definitely made the difference in my decision.

Finally, for some, marriage itself was a package deal. The decision to marry automatically implied the decision to have children. For this part-time saleswoman and mother of two, the choice to bear children did not involve a conscious process:

Q: Why did you decide to have children?
A: I was very naïve. You get married; you get pregnant. We were only married a month, and I got pregnant. I guess I wouldn't have thought of getting married and *not* having children; put it that way. For me, the way my family grew was natural for us. It just was not a conscious decision-making thing.

The packaging of marriage and children had a greater impact on work aspirations than did marriage alone. The early arrival of children in a marriage placed immediate pressures on the new wife to withdraw from school or work. This robbed her of the time postponers had to be exposed to alternative options and opportunities.

Thus, the decision to marry, itself, was a crucial turning point when this thirty-five-year-old mother of two chose family over career:

A: I was twenty-one when I got married. I was not planning on marrying at that age. I was sort of starstruck. He was a hero from Vietnam, a green beret. He was also trying to decide if he was going to . . . go back to Vietnam. He was set for another tour then. I guess it was a big decision: Am I getting married, or am I going ahead with my career? We decided on marriage instead. At that time, I was very unsure about wanting to get married. My husband had strong feelings about having his own family. And I was at that point beginning to think I could financially put myself through school. There were a lot of mixed emotions at that time.
Q: Why did you get pregnant right away?
A: My husband wanted children because he was adopted. As he put it, either we get married and we start our family, or we just end our courtship and he goes back into the service. . . . That was a very strong factor [in having a child]. Like I said, I was starstruck at the time.

The packaging of marriage and childbearing thus led some previously ambitious women to forgo strong work commitments.

The structure of traditional (or patriarchal) marriage and the maintenance of a committed relationship within such a marriage promoted the choice of family over committed work. Over time, women in traditional relationships watched opportunities outside the home slip by and workplace aspirations erode. As this happened, mothering took on greater importance in their lives.

Even in the absence of marital pressure, however, the relatively flat mobility structure of 'women's work' promoted domesticity and the defusing of ambition. Blocked opportunities at the workplace not only reduced women's motivation to work; limited job mobility also changed their orientations toward mothering, childbearing, and homemaking. The push *out* of the workplace was thus as important as the attraction of a traditional marriage in encouraging initially ambitious women to veer toward domesticity.

BLOCKED MOBILITY AND THE LURE OF DOMESTICITY

In contrast to those whose exposure to expanded opportunities sparked increased commitment to work, blocked mobility promoted disaffection from work among those who experienced declining aspirations. Unlike their counterparts who veered away from domesticity, this group did not gain access to the widening job opportunities for women in male-dominated occupations that opened to some during the 1970s. Instead, they remained ghettoized in female-dominated, pink-collar occupations with limited chance for advancement (Howe 1977), often despite their fondest wishes and best efforts.[3]

Consigned to occupations that failed to provide significant upward mobility over their work careers, these respondents experienced declining work aspirations. Although their jobs often appeared promising at the outset, this initial glow tended toward monotony and frustration as blocks to upward movement were encountered. The resulting demoralization at the workplace dampened their initial enthusiasm for paid work, eased their ambivalence toward motherhood, and turned them toward the home in spite of their earlier aversion to domesticity.

Routes to Blocked Mobility
Most who experienced declining aspirations entered the workforce with high hopes, only to find that the opportunities available to them did not measure up to their expectations. A thirty-three-year-old, full-time mother of two took a secretarial position that seemed to promise initiative, responsibility, and eventual status, only to find that it rapidly degenerated into busywork:

A: In my early twenties, I knew I would get a job, and I knew what I needed. By this time, I was thinking career. I was on my own. I wanted a job that had responsibilities and no slack time. When I interviewed, I'd rather be adamant than get the wrong job.

Q: Why did you take the job as secretary at _____?

A: In the beginning, it was terrific. It was a brand-new plant; they had to hire two hundred people. I had the responsibility of setting up all the filing; the job of figuring out how to set up a lot of record-keeping systems was mine. They sent me back to Virginia to a seminar to pick up on that. The fact that they would send *me* to fly back instead of sending my boss—I thought that really showed promise. Then everybody *got* hired and all my systems were set up and worked very well, worked too well. I would finish my work on Tuesday morning and have to sit there until Friday afternoon. And that for me, personally, was as much agony as anyone could impose on me.

Others entered dead-end 'careers' not as the result of initial enthusiasm, but because they possessed no better alternative. These respondents were unable to break out of traditionally female occupations despite their own desire to do so. This thirty-three-year-old homemaker and mother of two found that even a college education did not open the door to occupational opportunities. Economic necessity and lack of parental and social support forced her to relinquish the hope of joining a male-dominated profession in favour of work in a female-dominated one—work she ultimately grew to detest:

Q: What did you do after college?

A: I was sort of ambitious at that point. I was thinking of law or business. It was pretty much put down by the family, who felt that was ridiculous; it was better to get the teaching credential, which was *their* thinking. It was woman's work, blah, blah, blah. I did *not* want to go into teaching. I was forced into that because I needed to get a job. So I went to get the credential to get a higher paying job than the secretarial shit. I wanted to get out of the house; I wanted independence. There were no other options for me at that point. I was desperately angry. I saw my brother get offered his job right from the placement centre and then they hired me to type.

Q: What happened after you got your credential?

A: Then the series of nightmares began. I can only think of teaching in terms of nightmares, I'm sorry to say. They gave me a permanent job teaching art. It was just gruesome. I made money, but it was awful. There was no way out. You can't go up in a job like that. You can't change it in any way. It's a war zone teaching in the public school system. I really didn't like it.

Thus, among both the high school and the college educated, the route to blocked mobility involved a process of channelling women with initially high work aspirations into female-dominated occupations. Some entered these occupations enthusiastically; others were forced to opt for work they had hoped to avoid. Whatever their initial feelings and motives, however, the structure of opportunity they encountered was the same. Nurses, librarians, primary school teachers, and other female professionals generally faced the same low pay, circumscribed discretion, and limited advancement opportunities that their clerical counterparts confronted. Whether clerical or professional, these workers encountered poor working conditions and blocked mobility. In addition, female-dominated professions tend to cluster among those 'helping professions' where the gap

between clients' needs and the limited resources available to help them leads to high rates of 'burnout' among workers (whom Lipsky 1980, calls 'street-level bureaucrats'). Low status and an erratic work schedule left this ex-nurse disillusioned:

A: I liked working, but I just couldn't stand working at nights or on weekends. Things were getting worse and worse, and I couldn't stand being put down.

The route to blocked mobility began with the choice of a traditional female occupation. This choice, whether forced under protest or embraced enthusiastically, held unforeseen and unintentional consequences for both working-class and middle-class women with initially high work aspirations. Unlike their peers who experienced rising work aspirations, these women encountered blocked advancement and a host of attendant frustrations. Limited movement upward combined with low pay, low status, circumscribed control, and a lack of challenge to encourage a downward spiral of work commitment among this group of initially aspiring women.

The choice of a female occupation, however, does not inevitably lead to this conclusion. Among those who veered away from domesticity, some were given unanticipated chances to advance and others were able to switch occupations rather than forsake work commitment. Whatever the route, women who veered away from domesticity were generally able to break out of the female labour ghetto. In the process, they improved their position at the workplace as well as the conditions of their work.

Unlike their more fortunate peers, however, women with declining aspirations did not meet unanticipated opportunities at work and were unable to break out of traditional female jobs. What distinguishes these women from those whose disenchantment with their jobs sparked an occupational change rather than a rejection of work altogether?

Just as the time was not 'right' among members of the first group to opt for domesticity when workplace dissatisfaction mounted, the time was never quite 'right' for those with declining aspirations to make an occupational change that would have improved their work situation. Both groups were constrained, but in different ways. The first group lacked the means to opt for domesticity (for example, a willing partner); the second lacked the means, and especially the economic means, to escape from unrewarding work to pursue a new occupation. Even though events triggered the desire for change, the means were not available. At such critical points, women with declining aspirations were forced to stay in a bad situation that ultimately led to work disaffection.

Constraints other than commitment to a heterosexual relationship, especially economic constraints, also served as powerful inhibitors to career development. Financial pressures prevented this discouraged primary school teacher from pursuing a profession that promised greater social and personal reward:

A: I was separated in 1974. That was kind of a turning point because teaching just wasn't very gratifying. I felt I really needed something more for myself. I signed up for the LSAT and went through all the red tape, but I never took it.

Q: Why?

A: I seem to be unable to leave what I'm doing, because of the financial risk of losing the income and taking a chance on that, maybe not finding something else. I have felt trapped. I didn't feel that I had a choice to stop and quit and find another job because I've always had financial obligations. So here I am eleven years later, doing something I don't like doing. I feel overall my life has been wasted.

Thus, financial need kept some in jobs they disliked, which led to waning self-confidence as well as work disaffection. Because there is usually a delicate balance between economic need and how much a woman is motivated to work, job commitment persisted only for those who found satisfying employment that fed their egos as well as their bank accounts. When this search proved futile, a woman's outlook turned toward other pursuits, as in the case of this disillusioned government bureaucrat approaching thirty:

Q: Has working affected your feelings about yourself in any way?

A: It has in terms of I'm really disappointed that I haven't changed before now, that it's taken me so long to get my rear end in motion and jolly well take the risk of change.

Q: Why do you think you haven't changed jobs?

A: Probably because it has been so economically unfeasible. But now I know the house will somehow get paid for. The relationship will go on; somehow we'll make it if I don't earn this many dollars. So if I don't like it, I'm really an unpleasant lady to live with, and I ought to be doing something else.

Q: So you think you'd prefer staying home and having children?

A: I think it would be better because the gratification I'm *not* getting from the job hopefully I would get from being a parent. I would get a lot more instant feedback and more control over the situation. My change in behaviour, attitude, activity, whatever, would have a direct effect, which I really don't feel now. The only reason I say that is that I have not achieved any goal in work.

As their hopes for work accomplishment dwindled in the face of blocked opportunities, these women veered toward the home. They looked to motherhood to provide the fulfillment work had failed to offer.

Consequences of Blocked Work Opportunities

The consequences of blocked work opportunities reached beyond the confines of the workplace itself into the most private spheres of these women's lives. As their work expectations turned to disappointment and disaffection, women with declining aspirations began to look elsewhere for meaningful 'work'.

Two additional changes in outlook accompanied declining work aspirations. Previous ambivalences toward motherhood subsided, and domesticity became more attractive than it had earlier appeared. These changes were closely related, and one enhanced the pull of the other.

First, the decision to have a child typically coincided with mounting frustration at work. This thirty-one-year-old, full-time mother of two decided to have her first child at twenty-seven, when her secretarial job hit a dead end:

Q: Was secretary as high as you could go?

A: Apparently. The company was good about using young men; they had a lot of young male executives. I didn't see any young female executives.

Q: What happened next?

A: By this time I had married Jim, and we were talking about having a family; so it became a case of waiting it out. I wanted to have a baby. So the last six months was an extremely frustrating waiting period until I got pregnant. The career went down the drain, and it was extreme boredom.

As the experience of working soured, motherhood provided an enticing alternative, and doubts about childbearing turned to curiosity and enthusiasm.

The experience of blocked work mobility, although not the only factor, was a major contributing factor in this group's decision to become mothers. It promoted declining work aspirations, which in turn lessened old ambivalences toward motherhood, gave childbearing a more fulfilling aura, and halted the strategy of postponement.

Although those who encountered unanticipated work opportunities found the childbearing decision increasingly problematic, those who faced blocked mobility found motherhood an increasingly attractive option.

A second consequence of blocked work mobility and the declining aspirations it fostered is that the decision to bear a child became linked to and reinforced by the decision to withdraw from the paid workforce to rear a child. In the context of dissatisfaction with work, the meaning of motherhood changed: bearing a child became not simply an end in itself; it also furnished an alternative occupation. In other words, motherhood provided an avenue—in most cases, the only avenue—toward domesticity.

The linking of childbearing with domesticity, which made childbearing problematic for women with rising aspirations, had the reverse impact on those with declining aspirations. These women came to define motherhood as full-time mothering. This disillusioned teacher, for example, let go of earlier aversions and embraced motherhood as the only acceptable escape from work conditions she defined as oppressive:

Q: What changed your feelings about having children?

A: To be honest, what changed is that I reached a point in the job where I was just hating it daily, plus we were also moving into a new house. It's almost as stupid as saying, 'What colour do I paint the room? Yellow. We'll have a baby in there. Let's get pregnant.' We went and got pregnant. The time seemed right. It was a relief not working, the relief of not having that pressure. I was doing something I wanted to do.

This ex-teacher's aide wanted more than a child; she wanted the chance to stay at home as well:

Q: What were the main reasons you got pregnant when you did?

A: I'll tell you the truth. I wanted an excuse to stay home. I wanted an excuse to do my own thing—not to be a housewife, but to do my own thing. I loved having my own time. Being a woman is the neatest role. You can choose what you do with your time, whereas men still have that pressure. I was glad I quit [work]; I hated the nine-to-five drag.

A would-be mother did not typically see the link between the development of disaffection from the workplace and the decision to have a child, but this process was all the more powerful because it was hidden. The birth of a child seemed natural and unforced in these cases. As this ex-clerk who could 'hardly wait to stop' working explained:

Q: Why did you decide to have a baby?
A: We really loved each other, and we wanted to share in creating one. . . . We decided the time was right.

This ex-secretary, for whom work was becoming 'terrible', agreed:

Q: Why do you think you decided to have a child at that time?
A: I don't know. I never really enjoyed children. I don't know what it is you feel. You just want one.

The 'right' time to have a child was consistently linked to job dissatisfaction. This ex-teacher came to view childbearing as a natural, inevitable choice, despite her earlier doubts:

A: I think there's a very ambivalent period, before you're married or just after when you *don't* have any children, and you look around and you see your friends and they are tied down and you say, 'Well, I'll put this off for a while.' And more and more of your friends do have children, and you

sort of join the crowd and have a couple, and that's what happened. I don't think *anybody* is *desperate* to have children. Maybe there are cases, but I wasn't that desperate. I just did it one day.

Although not apparent to the person making the choice, the movement toward motherhood was rooted in the structure and experience of work itself. Blocked mobility triggered a downward spiral of aspirations and gave childbearing a liberating aura by comparison. In this context, the choice to bear a child—and the choice to withdraw from the workplace to rear it—felt natural. In important respects, women's work is organized to promote this turn toward a home-centred life. The structure of blocked work opportunities thus encouraged a set of related responses in this group of initially aspiring women—the choice to bear a child, the choice of becoming a full-time mother, and the perception that both these choices were 'natural'. In some cases, blocked mobility and frustrating work were even judged to be good fortune. An ex-teacher and recent mother exclaimed:

A: If my career had really taken off, it's conceivable to me that I could have come to a decision not to have children. But I don't think that would have been a good idea. I think I was meant to have children.

DOMESTICITY AS A WAY OF LIFE

For women veering in a traditional direction, the decision to bear a child involved two closely linked and mutually reinforcing choices. Becoming a mother and becoming a homemaker came to be defined as the same act. Unlike those who veered away from domesticity, respondents with declining work aspirations found this 'package' of choices all the more inviting because these two acts were united: each aspect of the choice enhanced the pull of the other. An ex-nurse favourably compared her position as a homemaker to the alternative she would face if child-rearing did not consume her daytime hours:

A: [If I didn't have children,] I'd probably still be working at the health department, and I would feel just awful. I don't know whether the tension [I felt at work] was because of the health department. I shouldn't say that the children make me *not* tense. Just being home is much more relaxing.

Q: And you wouldn't be home if you didn't have children?

A: I don't think so. I would probably want to be, but with society the way it is, everybody thinks you should be working if you don't have children. I don't know if I'd be strong enough to buck it.

Thus, even when a return to work had been planned, unpleasant work experiences and blocked mobility sent these new mothers into the home. One day back on the job convinced this ex-secretary that mothering was far more rewarding and challenging than the work she was paid to do:

Q: How did you feel about the idea of quitting work to care for your child?

A: I loved it. I hated my job. I didn't quit right away. I took a leave and then went back after he was born and worked one day and quit. I had people tell me, 'After you're off for a few months, you're going to get so bored; you're going to want to come back to work.' What they didn't realize was that there was no way I could be as bored. [I wouldn't go back] unless somebody wants to make me the boss, but I have doubts that that's ever going to happen.

The realization that staying home was preferable to working came as a surprise to those who saw themselves as committed workers. They made the decision to mother full-time only after

the birth of the first child, when they were finally in a position to make a comparative assessment between the job of childrearing and paid work. An ex-clerk discovered unexpected pleasure in full-time mothering:

A: I thought I could work and have a child, too. I was totally prepared [to return to work], and the only thing I hadn't prepared myself for was how I was going to feel the day she was born about going back to work. I thought it would be easy; I thought I'd be able to do it. Then I realized that I couldn't stand being away from her. [And I was] frustrated on the job because I really didn't have the job I wanted. The best alternative seemed to be quit and stay home.

After a history of ill-rewarded jobs and thwarted aspirations these women chose domesticity as the better alternative, even though they could have pursued other avenues. They concluded that motherhood was the only occupation that did not threaten to disappoint. This ex-secretary decided to have a second child rather than return to work:

Q: What about the decision to have your second child?

A: I had intended to quit work when I got pregnant with Jenny, to wait until Jenny was in school, then go back to work. But when I went back, I wanted to go back as other than a secretary. I thought, would I like to be an electrician, a fireman? What is there in the world that I want to spend the rest of my life at? Then it came to me that I really enjoy what I'm doing now more than anything else I've done or anything I could think of doing. So I decided to have another baby. For a year I had been going back and forth. Yes, no, yes, no. Once I had eliminated the other [a career] and only that was left [a child], it sort of solved itself and then became a strong desire.

For these women, mothering became their 'career'. They concluded that domesticity offered them many of the things they had sought in the paid workforce and failed to find: self-control, self-expression, self-direction. An ex-clerical worker explained:

Q: And now you like staying home?
A: I don't have to have anybody bossing me around! I like being with my children most of the time. Sometimes I don't, but . . . I like taking care of my own house and being in charge of what goes on in my own household.

This choice of domesticity was not without its costs. The hardest cost to bear was the lurking fear that, by giving up earlier work aspirations, these women had disappointed themselves and others. Because many of their female friends and neighbours *did* work, they faced either overt or covert social disapproval as well as personal doubts. This ex-secretary absorbed the disapproval of her peers, but nevertheless contested its validity:

A: [Sometimes I think] 'What's wrong with you? You want to be home.' But I really don't have any need [to work] at this point in our lives.

For those whose work experiences were deflating and discouraging and whose future prospects at work promised more of the same, domesticity offered freedom from market work and its attendant ills. Motherhood provided the route out of the workplace and into a more fulfilling job. Like their nontraditional counterparts, these respondents did not greet the accompanying devaluing of homemaking with enthusiasm. Given their other alternatives, however, they saw these drawbacks as a necessary and acceptable

price to pay for the chance to engage in the more personally rewarding (if less socially rewarded) work of caring for children.

THE TRADITIONALLY SEXUAL DIVISION OF LABOUR

Implementing a domestic choice required more than motivation; it also required structural support. Domesticity depended on the presence of a breadwinner who was willing and able to provide the economic means for his partner's withdrawal from paid work.[4] Those who veered away from domesticity often lacked this structural support. In contrast, those who veered toward domesticity could do so only because their spouses' economic support allowed it to happen. This enabling circumstance was a necessary, if not sufficient, condition for domesticity. It was, however, a circumstance that many took for granted. This salesman's wife, for example, mentioned her spouse's financial support almost as an afterthought:

Q: Why did you decide not to return to work after your children were born?
A: It really wasn't a conscious decision to work or not to work. It was just my lifestyle. I never had any doubts about my husband's ability to support us; so I didn't look for work outside the home for financial reasons. We always had a place to live, and we enjoyed the way we lived; so there was no burning need to go out and work.

Remember, however, that assessment of need is a subjective process. It involves agreement between *both* spouses that the emotional benefits of female domesticity outweigh the economic costs. This homemaker, for example, looked to her husband, a trucker, for 'permission' to stay home:

Q: Did you consider working after your children were born?

A: I just knew when my babies were little that I wanted to be the one to take care of them, and I know my husband thought that was just fine. His mother worked a lot when he was growing up, but he didn't feel I had to work because he never depended on my income. We didn't have any money worries at all. My husband's job was adequate. He never made super big money, but we didn't have any bills.

This reliance on the male paycheque had important repercussions on the sexual division of labour within the home. Those who opted for domesticity 'earned' their economic security by performing the least desirable tasks associated with caring for a child. This homemaker took total responsibility for all-night vigils in order to avoid paid work:

Q: How did you make a decision about not working?
A: When Gail was born, it was sort of a joke. Charlie said, 'The first time I have to get up and change diapers in the middle of the night, you go back to work,' because he was working and I wasn't. If he had to get up in the middle of the night, there was something wrong with the arrangement. So I made sure I got up in the middle of the night.

The inequality in the income commanded by each partner reinforced this traditional exchange and made role reversal an option in name only. Trading places with her husband, a businessman, was unthinkable to this ex-nurse:

Q: Did you ever consider working and having your husband stay home to look after the baby?
A: That would have to be an economic question. Work is not a hobby. You work primarily to make money. It becomes a trade-off. If I could make more money than him, that's another thing.

In this context, it became difficult to distinguish preferences from real options. When a respondent realized that she would have to add paid employment to the work performed at home, her motivation to work outside the home decreased. Faced with the complications of combining home and market work, this ex-secretary concluded it was easier to stay home:

A: Our understanding was, if I wanted to work, I could work—as long as I made adequate provisions for the children. Well, the pieces didn't fit. It was a very strung-out kind of puzzle thing; it just didn't all fit right.

In the face of mounting duties at home, work for pay became increasingly less attractive, and the pride of earning a paycheque was replaced by the pride of caring for others in less strictly economic ways. This eased the acceptance of economic dependency, even among ex-workers, such as this thirty-three-year-old ex-secretary who had been accustomed to supporting herself for many years:

Q: Was it difficult for you to adjust to not earning money?
A: No. I liked it. My husband gives me money. It's not hard for me.

Once committed to domesticity, moreover, these women perceived events forcing others into the workplace as threats to a preferred way of life. Having relinquished occupational aspirations, this twenty-seven-year-old ex-clerk feared the loss, especially through divorce, of her construction worker husband's earnings and the way of life it permitted her to have:

Q: Has having a child changed your feelings about yourself in any way?

A: It made me very dependent, which is just the reverse of what I used to be. . . . I think [my husband] was attracted to me because I was very independent, and now I'm very dependent. I don't know what I would do if things didn't work out between him and me and we had to separate and I had to go to work to support my child. . . . I just don't know if I could handle that, taking her to some lady's house and saying, 'Here. Take care of my child while I'm at work.' It's scary to me.

In opting for motherhood, women with declining work aspirations traded what they had come to define as a bad job for what, in comparison, came to be seen as a good one. Disenchantment with work created the context that made mothering attractive; it also reinforced a traditional structure of marriage and parenting. This process involved gradual changes in orientation that were generally not experienced on a conscious level. Because breadwinning is a historic male responsibility and not working for pay a historical female 'right', the balance of male economic responsibility and female economic dependency was rarely noticed unless it was threatened or upset. For this group, disruptions in the traditional sexual division of labour did not occur. Rather, a set of interrelated and reinforcing circumstances made traditional arrangements the preferred alternative.

Notes

1. Gilligan (1982) argues that women tend to stress a morality of intimacy and interconnectedness over a morality of autonomy, objectivity, and independent accomplishment. This female morality, she suggests, contrasts with a male morality that affirms independence, rationality, and personal success at the expense of connectedness. She concludes that the male stress on accomplishment at the expense of intimacy is as skewed as, or even more skewed than, the female stress on interpersonal connection at the expense of individual autonomy.

   A morality that excludes connectedness is surely as suspect as a morality that excludes autonomy. Gilligan thus provides an important corrective to prevailing and one-sided theories of moral development. However, her characterization of the first perspective as distinctively male and the second as distinctively female is questionable. There is nothing inherently masculine or feminine about stressing independence versus interdependence. Many women place success before interpersonal commitment. Moreover, some women's concern with interpersonal relationships and some men's concern with success reflect and emerge from the structural constraints each group faces. The fundamental problem for both sexes stems from structural arrangements that force people to choose between the equally important pursuits of love and work.

2. Despite a dramatic rise in the ratio of employed women to employed men, large earnings differentials persist according to sex. According to Masnick and Bane (1980: 100), 'The mean earnings of female workers stand at about 56 per cent of those of males, a rate that has been surprisingly constant over time. In 1955, the median earnings of year-round, full-time female workers were about 64 per cent of males, 60 per cent in 1965, and 59 per cent in 1975. The ratio of female to male earnings has, if anything, declined slightly over time.' This earnings gap persists even when age, educational level, prior work experience, and number of hours worked are controlled (Barrett 1979).

3. Although unprecedented job opportunities in male-dominated occupations opened to women during the 1970s, most women workers remain in overwhelmingly female occupations with relatively blocked advancement ladders (Howe 1977). Clerical, service, and private household jobs account for almost 55 per cent of all women workers. These female-dominated occupations are rarely structured to provide significant upward mobility

over a work career. Moreover, whether an occupation is male-dominated or female-dominated, men tend to occupy a disproportionate share of the positions at the top. In sum, although growing, the percentage of female clerical workers, secretaries, bank tellers, saleswomen, nurses, and the like able to rise into the ranks of management or into the better rewarded occupations still dominated by men remains small.

4. Despite the rise of the dual-income family, a significant number of women retain the social and psychological option of economic dependency. In contrast, men who feel trapped at the workplace are rarely able to muster similar material, social, and emotional support for *not* earning a wage—for themselves and their families. Even among the nontraditional respondents in this sample, who placed great importance on their own economic self-sufficiency, few expressed a willingness to provide full economic support for their partners or to indulge male partners who might prefer total domesticity to paid work.

References

Barrett, N.S. 1979. 'Women in the Job Market: Occupations, Earnings, and Career Opportunities' in *The Subtle Revolution: Women at Work*, ed. Ralph E. Smith (Washington, DC: Urban Institute).

Blumstein, P., and P.W. Schwartz. 1983. *American Couples: Money, Work, Sex* (New York: Morrow).

Gilligan, C. 1982. *In a Different Voice: Psychological Theory and Women's Development* (Cambridge: Harvard University Press).

Horner, M. 1972. 'Toward an Understanding of Achievement-Related Conflicts in Women', *Journal of Social Issues* 28: 157–75.

Howe, L.K. 1977. *Pink Collar Workers: Inside the World of Women's Work* (New York: Putnam's).

Huber, J., and G. Spitze. 1980. 'Considering Divorce: An Expansion of Becker's Theory of Marital Instability', *American Journal of Sociology* 86 (July): 75–89.

Kanter, R.M. 1977a. *Men and Women of the Corporation* (New York: Basic Books).

———. 1977b. *Work and Family in the United States: A Critical Review and Agenda for Research and Policy* (New York: Russell Sage Foundation).

Lipsky, M. 1980. *Street Level Bureaucracy: Dilemmas of the Individual in Public Services* (New York: Russell Sage Foundation).

Masnick, G., and M. J. Bane. 1980. *The Nation's Families: 1960–1990* (Cambridge: Joint Center for Urban Studies of MIT and Harvard University).

Papanek, H. 1973. 'Men, Women, and Work: Reflections on the Two Person Career' in *Changing Women in a Changing Society*, ed. Joan Huber (Chicago: University of Chicago Press).

Section 2   **Sexuality and Love: Gendered Experiences**

*T*he social processes that create people as gendered are very closely connected to the processes that produce people's sexuality. Less explored by
sociologists than perhaps any other social interaction, sexuality is examined in interesting and provocative ways in the following two chapters.

Chapter 16

In this brief selection from her book, Sex, Power and Pleasure, *Mariana Valverde pushes us to question our assumptions about sexuality. She especially challenges all notions that heterosexuality is somehow* *natural rather than socially created—as an ideal at the level of culture, and as a set of desires on the part of the individual.*

Heterosexuality: Contested Ground

Mariana Valverde

It is not easy to write generally about heterosexuality. Relations between men and women have been subject to much scrutiny over the past twenty years and although traditional ideas and practices continue to hold sway in some quarters there are other circles in which little can be taken for granted any more. These different perspectives do not merely coexist in peaceful détente. Even if there are some 'islands' of both traditionalism and feminism where people live without many direct, personal challenges to their beliefs, by and large we are all living in an ideological battlefield. The combined effect of skyrocketing divorce rates and feminist ideas has produced a counterattack by the traditionalists, who have become increasingly shrill about the divine rights of husbands. This right-wing backlash is a desperate reaction to a situation in which the breadwinner husband/dependent wife model has become economically unfeasible for the vast majority of couples as well as emotionally unsatisfying for many women.

We live therefore in a very polarized situation, with different groups contending for the power to define heterosexuality and the family. Within each camp people strategize about how to strengthen their forces and how to improve their position on the field; they react to one another's ideology and on occasion are influenced by ideas from the 'enemy' camp. All this means that, reassurances of sex and family experts notwithstanding, we cannot speak confidently about heterosexuality in general. Both the ideas about it and the corresponding sexual and social practices are quite diverse and we are in a process of struggle and change.

Furthermore, we see many gaps between theory and practice. Some women have embraced the idea of an egalitarian heterosexuality that stresses choice and creativity, but in their own lives fall into traditional gender roles which they experience as 'natural'. On the other hand, many women who have sincerely believed in traditional concepts of marriage are finding themselves by design or by accident in unorthodox situations that are not part of the plan. Faced with such realities as an unwanted pregnancy, a daughter who comes out as a lesbian, or a divorce, women who have led 'traditional' lives sometimes show a remarkable degree of flexibility and inventiveness. So we cannot assume that all women with feminist beliefs have what one might describe as feminist relationships, or that women who are married and go to church on Sundays necessarily restrict themselves to monogamous heterosexuality in the missionary position.

It might be useful first to pause and consider one of the most prevalent myths used by the anti-feminists in the ideological struggle to define heterosexuality. It is a myth that often lingers in the hearts if not the minds of feminists, and so must be explicitly refuted if we are to make a fresh start. This myth comes in many guises but the common denominator is an appeal to Nature to legitimize a certain traditional definition of heterosexuality as 'natural' and therefore inevitable, good, and not to be argued about or criticized. Arguments for Nature try to remove heterosexuality from the realm of politics and history and put it safely away on a high shelf marked 'Mother Nature: things that just are'.

An influential exponent of this argument for Nature is 'America's number one counsellor', Dr Joyce Brothers. In her 1981 book entitled *What Every Woman Should Know About Men* she blithely 'deduces' the traditional nuclear family from her perception of 'primitive' human life. Appealing to our stereotype of 'cavemen', she writes:

> It is as if way back in prehistory Mother Nature had searched for the most effective way of protecting mothers and children. Without someone to provide food for and defend the mother and child, they were at the mercy of wild beasts and predatory males. . . . The obvious source of protection and provisions was the male. But how to keep him around?
>
> Mother Nature's solution was sex. Sex on tap, so to speak. The day-in, day-out sexual availability of the human female created what scientists call a pair bond and most of us call love. The nuclear family was born (Brothers 1981: 178).

Let us unpack the assumptions and values contained in this unfortunately typical piece of popular 'scientific' writing.

- 'Mother' Nature is portrayed as a manipulative mother-in-law. This is anthropomorphism at its worst, where Nature is not only a human female but an 'old hag' who manipulates people for her own purposes.

- Men are portrayed as naturally predatory and obsessed with sex. Dr Brothers is apparently relying here on some now-discredited anthropological studies that claimed to show it was the aggressiveness and sexual jealousy of the male that pushed us along the evolutionary path and made us into a civilized species. The myth of 'Man the Hunter' has been successfully challenged by feminist anthropologists and primatologists. Male anthropologists have tended to assume that for example a social system could be understood by looking at the *men* in the system, and that competition and aggression were 'natural' and beneficial to the species. Without going into details about how this traditional view was challenged, suffice it to say that now only the die-hards in the anthropological profession would see even a grain of truth in Dr Brother's description.[1]

- Further, even if her description were accurate there is a logical error in her argument. If males were so predatory, why would women turn to them as the 'obvious source' of protection? . . .

- The women in Dr Brothers's prehistory appear to have not sexual feelings but only sexual 'availability'. Now, given that many female primates show clear signs of sexual pleasure, and some species even exhibit what can be interpreted as female orgasms, one wonders why women in prehistory would have such a passive sexuality. But the myth is that women do not really want sex, and exchange sexual favours only for male protection, while men do not really want to nurture but will reluctantly provide protection for the sake of sex. There is a lapse here in the logic of how the nuclear family can emerge from this coming together of such vastly different beings with such completely different purposes in mind.

- Finally, it seems clear that according to Dr Brothers the only 'natural' expression of human sexuality is monogamous heterosexuality within a nuclear family. By trying to ground her view of heterosexuality in 'Mother Nature' she confines all other possibilities to the obscurity of non-natural or anti-natural human behaviour. In the rest of her book she downplays the family and does not insist on children the way the Pope does. But she certainly believes that real sex is heterosexual sex, and real love is heterosexual love.

This belief in the naturalness of heterosexuality is so commonly accepted that we do not even notice it. . . . These days it is seldom articulated in its most blatant forms. But in its more sophisticated and subtle versions, which de-emphasize reproduction and stress sex itself, it continues to exercise a great deal of influence not just over our thoughts but over our very feelings. We feel it is somehow right for men and women to be attracted to one another precisely because they are men or women. We smile on young happy heterosexual couples and we attend wedding celebrations regardless of the actual interactions of the two people in question. By contrast, we feel uncomfortable when rules about monogamy and exclusive heterosexuality are broken, and feel compelled to find explanations for why woman A has so many lovers or why man B is attracted to men. But if A and B join up as a stable, monogamous couple, then we cease to ask questions. Their relationship, like Dr Brothers's primitive society, simply is.

One of the most crucial building blocks of the traditional view of natural heterosexuality is the idea that penises and vaginas 'go together' or 'are meant for each', and that erotic attraction between men and women is only the psychological manifestation of the physiological urge to engage in intercourse. There are several problems with this view. First it portrays men and women as the dupes of their own physiology and considers eroticism as a mere cover-up for Nature's reproductive aims. People are thus dehumanized, first by being reduced to one sexual organ and

then by having those sexual organs reduced to the status of reproductive tools. Secondly, it ignores the specificity of sex by collapsing it into reproduction. This implicitly devalues not only homosexuality but all non-reproductive sexual practices. It is true that if one wants to have a child, intercourse is one of the best means. But sex research has shown that if female sexual pleasure is the aim then intercourse is a poor choice, since masturbation and lesbian sex are both much more effective. (Shere Hite [1976] for example found that only 30 per cent of a large sample of women regularly achieved orgasm from intercourse, while 99 per cent of the women could easily achieve orgasm by masturbating.) Men, for their part, often prefer fellatio to intercourse.

This sex research ought to have demolished once and for all the myth that sexual pleasure is maximized by intercourse. And the increasing availability of birth control ought also to have helped break the bond between sex and reproduction. But people still cling to the theory that the vagina is women's 'real' sex organ and the 'natural' receptacle for the penis and for sperm.

Why is this?

Well, perhaps the sexual revolution happened a bit too fast for us all. Despite our experiments in sexual practices we still keep alive the notion of intercourse as the most 'natural' kind of sex, providing ourselves with a fixed point or home to which we can return. It is genuinely unsettling to watch old ideas and values go out the window. We are more comfortable adding diversions and 'deserts' (as *The Joy of Sex* calls them) to our sexual repertoire than questioning the underlying assumptions of a hierarchy of sexual acts that puts regular intercourse in the role of 'main dish' and everything else in the role of hors d'oeuvre. It is very important to question the division of sexual acts into 'basic' or 'natural' and 'frills'. Only after we have shaken the foundations of the old edifice will we be able to look honestly at our own sexual desires and decide what really pleases us. *The Joy of Sex* approach appears very liberated, but the way sexual acts are classified suggests that one would not want to make a whole meal out of 'just' oral sex. The equation of intercourse with protein in a meal is simply an ideological construct. This argument for intercourse as the real thing is based on assumptions about penises and vaginas 'fitting' together. Indeed, if a woman has to be told she is 'infantile' and 'immature' if she doesn't experience intercourse as the most natural and pleasurable form of sex, or if her privileging of the vagina is achieved only after a lengthy process of indoctrination and internalization of what being an adult woman is all about, then one must wonder how well penises and vaginas do fit together. The tired clichés used to convince us that our sexuality can be reduced to the vagina (the 'lock' or the 'glove') and the vagina in turn to a place for the penis (the 'key' or the 'hand') reveal a crucial logical fallacy, a phallocentric fallacy. The lock was made so that a key would fit into it, and has no purpose in and of itself; ditto for gloves which make no sense if considered apart from hands. But vaginas have all sorts of purposes such as allowing menstrual blood out, and most importantly giving birth to children—that have nothing to do with the phallus. One is tempted to understand the clichés about the vagina as nothing but male jealousy and defensiveness around female reproduction.

The myth of intercourse is also sustained by the idea that all eroticism depends in an essential way on *difference*, and specifically *genital difference*. Now, this idea is not necessarily patriarchal in its form and intent, for difference does not necessarily imply subordination. There can be amiable, egalitarian difference, which is presumably what fuels eroticism among enlightened heterosexuals.

The idea of difference as erotic is so commonsense and commonplace that we do not usually pause to criticize it. We merrily proceed to examine our own erotic attraction to individual X or type Y and come up with the 'differences' that are significant. But we could just as well analyze our own attractions and non-attractions by reference to similarities.

Let me give an example. A friend of mine once said 'I like men because they're so different!' so I envisaged her with a tall, muscular hunk with a masculine beard and a masculine personality. But when I met her lover he turned out to be neither tall nor muscular nor aggressive; rather he was androgynous both in physique and personality. So where was the big difference? (My friend, incidentally, also looks more androgynous than feminine.) Was the difference that he had a penis? But other men who were much more 'different' than this guy also had penises, and my friend was not interested in them. Was it really difference that attracted her to him?

There are many criteria one could use to measure human differences: size, weight, skin colour, hair colour, race, language, age, intelligence, physical fitness, beliefs, talents, etc. If a heterosexual couple is composed of two individuals who are remarkable similar in for example their class backgrounds, interests, and ethnicity (as is usually the case), and who are different primarily in their gender, then one cannot claim with any certainty that the key to their erotic attraction is difference. In their case gender difference has been eroticized, but so have their much more numerous non-gender similarities.

It is not my intention to argue for the intrinsic erotic appeal of similarity or difference. Some people can only get interested in partners who are basically similar to them, while others need sharp differences in order to have their erotic interest sparked. To each her own, as far as I'm concerned. The point is that I do not see any valid reason for privileging gender above all else, and then *assuming* that gender difference is essentially erotic while other differences are not. In ancient Athenian culture for instance, adult men saw adult women primarily as reproductive partners and reserved their odes to eroticism for adolescent boys. There, age differences were eroticized as a matter of course, whereas the gender difference might or might not have been erotic.

By understanding eroticism as a force which pivots around sex and gender differences we separate the erotic realm from other aspects of human existence. Activities and relationships in which sex and gender are not major factors are perceived as non-erotic. Now, to some extent there is clearly something specific about erotic interaction that makes it distinct from the pleasure of working together with others, or of having shared family roots. However, to take this distinction for granted and to absolutize it is a mistake that reinforces certain philosophical beliefs that are simply myths. First, the separation of the erotic—as the sexual, the mysterious, the irrational, the dialectic of difference—from other aspects of human interaction fosters a view of the human self as essentially and eternally divided between Reason and Passion. Secondly, because eroticism is exiled beyond the pale of reason, the everyday life of rational interaction is de-eroticized. And finally, separating Reason from Passion constructs a realm of the instinctual to which women are largely confined.

Women have suffered from this ideological division of the passionate and the rational, as many feminists have noted and criticized. . . . Because erotic play is thought to depend on sexual difference and on the contrast between reason and passion, erotic relations have been largely confined to relations between unequals. Reason and Passion as the male and female principles are not simply different. They are unequal within the hierarchy that prevails between them. On the other hand, relations among equals as 'thinking persons' have been a priori de-eroticized, because they hinge not on difference but on a sameness in what the philosophers have called 'the common light of reason'. Western philosophers have argued that this commonality is the basis both of thinking itself and of democratic society. Most of them also believed women did not share fully in the light of reason and therefore could not enter into the world of politics or philosophy. But even those few who argued that women did indeed have the prerequisite rationality and personhood to enter into the realm and be participants in the social contract still left untouched the basic divi-

sion between the erotic and the rational. Even if women had an element of rationality, they still had to represent Mother Earth and the dark instincts. And much popular culture since the nineteenth century hinges on women's *internal* struggle between their personhood, as the desire for example to learn or succeed, and their womanhood. This struggle is often tragic because the claims of the feminine are considered to be contradictory to the claims of personhood.

Thus whether or not women were allowed some access to the realm of reason and public life, there was still a sharp separation between 'human' interactions (based on male-defined equality among rational human beings as conceived on the male model) and erotic interactions based on sexual difference. The equality prevailing in the intellectual world and the marketplace was considered to be inherently non-erotic, even anti-erotic, while the unequal struggle between Reason and Passion was understood as inherently sexy. Women's confinement to the realm of the semi-rational went hand in hand with a desexualization of the world of men, politics, work, and culture. One of the reasons for this was the age-old desire to use Reason as a tool to dominate Nature, subjugate the passions, and not coincidentally to put women, as those closest to Nature, in their place. But certainly another reason was that to admit sexuality and eroticism into the public world would have necessarily entailed recognizing homosexuality, or at the very least homoeroticism. Thus, insofar as men and women were defined as being divided by sexual difference and so fundamentally unequal, society could not afford to eroticize equality.

A further result of this has been to create a much larger gap than necessary between heterosexuality and homosexuality. Just as we have exaggerated the role of difference in heterosexuality eroticism, so too have we exaggerated the role of similarity in homosexuality. A gay man does not necessarily eroticize only his partner's masculinity. And two lesbians might have certain commonalities in bodily parts and psychological traits, but can otherwise be as different as night and day. So my point is not so much that one has to 'make room for' homosexuality as an eroticism of sameness, but more fundamentally to question the very separation of sameness and difference, and the process by which we overvalue difference when theorizing about sexual attraction.

Heterosexuality is too complicated and too unpredictable to be reduced to such a simple formula as 'boy meets girl', 'like meets unlike', 'opposites attract'. Men and women are clearly different, but their attraction to one another does not necessarily depend only on that difference. And in any case they are not *opposites*. Because there happen to be only two sexes, we absolutize this fact and assume that the two sexes are opposites. But why? What if there were three or four sexes created through some miracle of modern science? Or if we only had two senses instead of five, would we assume that those two—sight and hearing, let's say—were 'opposites'? If I have two daughters, or a daughter and a son, are they opposites of one another?

Heterosexuality cannot be free until we stop thinking in terms of 'opposites' that are 'drawn' to one another. Men and women are not like iron filings and magnets, keys and locks, or any object in those functionalist and fatalistic metaphors that try to legitimize heterosexuality as the norm by presenting it as a fate imposed on us by Nature. Heterosexuality is not our fate. It is a *choice* that we can make—or, more accurately, it *would be* a choice if our society were more pluralistic and less rigid in its construction of sexual choices. After all, choice implies the existence of several valid options, and as long as we continue to see eroticism between the sexes as fated by some inevitable sexiness inherent in genital differences, we will have a rather impoverished experience of heterosexuality. . . .

In all our erotic desires and activities there is an interplay of sameness and difference, of recognition and fascination, of familiarity and strangeness. Neither difference nor sameness are *per se* erotic; rather it is the playful movement of and between them which creates erotic exchange. . . . What we need to work toward and begin imagining is an eroticism where sameness and difference are both eroticized and valued. This can help us to both break down the walls of the ego and recognize the other as our equal while maintaining the 'admiration' for otherness and difference. Perhaps the most important thing to remember is that men and women were not made for heterosexuality but rather heterosexuality exists for men and women. . . .

Note

1. See for instance Ruth Bleier, *Science and Gender* (New York: Pergamon, 1984), especially Chapter 5 on human evolution. See also Eleanor Leacock, 'Women in Egalitarian Societies' in *Becoming Visible*, eds R. Bridenthal and C. Koonz (Boston: Houghton Mifflin, 1977).

References

Brothers, J. 1981. *What Every Woman Should Know About Men* (New York: Ballantine).

Hite, S. 1976. *The Hite Report* (New York: Dell).

Chapter 17

*That gender inequality might seriously erode the pos-
sibility of pleasure in sexual relations between men
and women is pretty obvious. Less clear is that sexual desire itself can reproduce gender inequality—*
*because of the different experiences boys and girls go
through as they acquire gender identity, in this gen-
der-divided world. Wendy Hollway fills out this argument, in a provocative and insightful article.*

Heterosexual Sex: Power and Desire for the Other

Wendy Hollway

A curious thing has been happening to me with
various men lately; they don't want to have a sexual relationship when I do. But men are supposed
'not to be able to get enough of it', so the common
assumption goes. The most obvious explanation
would be that they're just not attracted to me. Well,
they are! It's curious precisely because of the strong
mutual attraction. Unfortunately, I don't think it's
because these are feminist-influenced, anti-sexist
men throwing off their conditioning about sex; and
I'd probably think it was my fault if a couple of my
friends weren't experiencing the same problem—
for reasons that are strikingly similar.

In this chapter, I am going to give an account
of the relation between sex and power in heterosexual relationships which explains why men in
certain circumstances choose to avoid sex. It has
very different implications for a theory of men's
power from an 'all heterosexual sex is violence'
position. It does not deny men's power in heterosexual relationships. But it doesn't deny women's
either; it specifies how they differ.

$$*\qquad*\qquad*$$

The question of women's desire for men is a
huge one. I want to focus on sex because it is such
an important definer of all those intense feelings.
More particularly, I want to look at why *men* feel
similarly intense, irrational, and vulnerable, and
what effects it has on their relationships with
women.[1] Feminists do a lot of talking and thinking and writing about our gender and sexuality. If
we're not careful, it ends up looking as if all this
desire and contradiction is part of being a
woman. And that can get read back through old
sexist assumptions as further 'proof' of how irrational and needy we are: women as pathology,
man as normality. It's perfectly clear to me that it's
not like that at all.

What does 'sex' mean that it produces all
these strong feelings of desire, jealousy, dependence, dedication, and fear? How do these affect
the power relations between men and women
who are involved with (or potentially attracted to)
each other? How is it the same and different for
men and women?

The sections (of this chapter) run as follows:
the 'greatest need' (1) indicates the intensity of
feeling that is underneath men's sexual attraction
to women. In (2), I show how these feelings have
been assumed to be a part of women's, not men's
sexuality. By referring to several coexisting sets of
assumptions about sexuality, I show how women
and men's sexuality is differentiated in such a way
that men's vulnerability is protected by displacing
those feelings on to women. In (3) I use the psychoanalytic concept of defence mechanisms to
explain this. In (4) I indicate an answer to why
men feel so vulnerable by showing the link
between men's desire for the mother and the
desire for a woman. Men's power can then be seen
as something not inherent, but at least in part as a

resistance (5). The perception of men as powerful is also promoted by women's desire for the Other and subsequent misrecognition of men as a result of their own vulnerability and also their assumptions about gender difference. In (6) I show how men's desire for the Other/mother is particularly felt in heterosexual sex, and how they thus experience the woman involved as powerful. When in other respects a woman and man occupy equal positions (and where the man cannot compensate in other arenas, as he has been able to do traditionally), the woman may well be experienced as 'too powerful' (7). I conclude by pointing out some of the implications of the argument (8).

The 'greatest need'

What do men feel like when they are attracted to a woman? Is it just an urge as society would have us believe, located in their anatomy (in their erections, to be precise)? One man I talked to put it as follows. He generalizes, but as men are wont to do that to protect themselves I was pretty convinced that he was talking about himself. Besides where else would he have got such knowledge? Certainly not from how men are supposed to feel:

> Martin: 'People's needs for others are systematically *denied* in ordinary relationships. And in a love relationship you make the most *fundamental* admission about yourself—that you want somebody else. It seems to me that that is the *greatest* need. And the need which, in relation to its power, is most strongly hidden and repressed. Once you've opened yourself, once you've shown the other person that you *need* them, then you've made yourself *incredibly* vulnerable.'[2]

Because I knew Martin quite well—indeed, I'd been in the position of being very attracted to him and had experienced him as astonishingly strong, self-sufficient and independent of women—I wanted to find out more about this question of vulnerability.

Wendy: 'Yes, I agree. But I think there's a question about how much you show yourself to be vulnerable.'

Martin: 'But you *do*, just by showing that you're *soft* on somebody. When you're not *admitting* it and when you're going around looking very self-sufficient. But it seems to me when you've revealed that need, you put yourself in an *incredibly* insecure state. You've shown someone what you're like. Before you've managed by showing them only what is *publicly* acceptable. And as soon as you've shown that there is this terrible *hole* in you—that you want somebody else—then you're in this absolute state of insecurity. And you need much *more* than the empirical evidence that somebody likes you, or whatever. You become neurotically worried by the possibility that you're not accepted, now you've let them see a little bit that's you, that it'll be rejected. The insecurity gives someone else power. I don't mean any viable self-exposure, or anything like that. I just mean any little indication that you *like* the other person.'

The intensity with which Martin speaks, the implications of the terms 'love relationship', 'wants', 'incredible vulnerability'; all these suggest that he is talking about a once-in-a-lifetime love. It comes as a surprise, then, when he explains that he's not talking about a 'viable self-exposure' (a wholesale declaration of life-long love perhaps?), but rather 'any little indication that you like the other person'. And this liking is bound up with attraction: he also refers to it as 'showing you're soft on somebody'.

For me, this example—and it is by no means unique—raises two questions: First, why are the feelings—the wants and needs resulting from being attracted to someone else (in Martin's case, it was to women)—so strong, so non-rational? In other words, where do they come from? Secondly what effects do those feelings have on men's relationships with women whom they're attracted to (or have a sexual relationship with)? The following two sections address these questions.

The Sexism in Assumptions about Difference in Women's and Men's Sexuality

'Sex' does not just mean one thing. In fact the significance of sexual practices is that they stand in for so much which can go unsaid or misrepresented as a result. It's rare for two people to be explicit about what they want and mean when they make love/have sex for the first time. The needs and fantasies expressed through sex make us feel too vulnerable, or too guilty maybe. Yet people assume that 'sex' is simply about bodily pleasure and doesn't *mean* anything else. This comes from the assumption which sees sexual urges as natural and direct, unmediated by social meanings. Although more recently in Western culture the idea of sex as a biological urge has been applied to women's sexuality too, it is still more characteristic of views of men's sexuality.[3] So the meanings of 'sex' are different for women and men. For example, the curious phenomenon that I described at the beginning of this chapter—men refusing sex with women where there was a mutual attraction—would not have seemed so curious in the case of a woman. Men are assumed to want sex anywhere for its own sake. Traditional assumptions place women as wanting sex within the security of married life and motherhood. For contemporary feminists it is not as clear-cut as that, but for some it's still very much about relationships:

> Dot: 'The one time I did fuck with Charles, it felt really *good*, like there was an awful lot that was important going on. But I didn't have an orgasm . . . I had lots of highs . . . maybe the tension between us was too great, or something. I don't know, but I was very *turned* on. When I think about that, I get a kind of quiver which is not about how successful it was sexually—if you can separate out these things. It was . . . it was the idea of fucking

with *him*, rather than with someone else. If I'm caught off my guard thinking about it, the image I get makes me physically shudder with excitement. . . . It grabs me at an *uncontrolled* level. That reinforces my hunch that it's the *idea*—that it's what's invested in the *idea*. I was in love with him. It's not fucking itself, it's something to do with the rights it gave me to see myself as having a relationship with him. I didn't have any of course.'

Despite the teachings of a permissive era that sex without a relationship was fine because women could be into sexual pleasure too, Dot's sexual responses, even at the level of her physical arousal, were a product of 'being in love'. What sex meant in that case was that it gave her 'rights to a relationship'. She reflects the obsolescence of this assumption in her final comment 'I didn't have any of course'.

Despite this recognition, and her participation in 'permissive' sex while growing up, her feelings and fantasies about wanting a relationship were still aroused by having sex. Men often see women's involvement through the same lens. One man described it in the following way:

> Jim: 'I remember I had a strong thing for many years that you shouldn't actually sleep with someone unless you were actually in love with them in some way. And if you did it to someone you weren't in love with it was somehow pretty horrid and pretty nasty. One reason was feeling that sex was kind of dangerous. If you had sex, it meant that you were committed in some way and I didn't want that. Also that it said something—if you *just* had sex without a relationship it was letting them down because you somehow thought that they'd expect a relationship and it was a pretty shitty thing to do to have one part of it without the other. I still feel that to some extent—that somehow it was cheapening sex. It was very prissy—that this thing was so beautiful that you couldn't actually spread it around too much.'

Despite feeling that it is prissy (and indeed it is not consistent with men's claims about sex), Jim feels that the beauty of sex had to do with it being in a relationship. He's not explicit about it, but it's fairly obvious that many men (and most likely Jim) do desperately want and need relationships with women. Yet despite sideways references to his own experience of the specialness of sex within a relationship; he implies that it's *women* who want the relationship; that it's because of *women's* needs that he didn't indulge in sex without a relationship; it was *women* who wanted commitment. Why did he not want commitment? His explanation below situates the sexual relationship where it belongs for him—in the realm of 'strong emotions'. However, there too his account avoids his own strong feelings by projecting them on to the woman:

Jim: 'I was frightened of strong emotions, that's basically it. Because I remember, again a person at school, the tremendous relief when I ended the relationship, of not actually having to carry that—of not actually having to be responsible for those things.'

Wendy: 'And was it that the girls wanted to be more intimate?'

Jim: 'Yeah—that really frightened me, because I was frightened of making that kind of commitment, that kind of involvement, I thought I'd be let down, because of what happened the first time, when I was so unreserved about how I felt. I think that really affected my life incredibly, that first time when I fell in love.'

Wendy: 'Why was having a relationship with this girl such a burden?'

Jim: 'She was very strong and very emotional—that's pejorative—but I mean she had strong reactions, so that I didn't actually feel safe that I wasn't going to be knocked out, or sucked in, by her.'

'Responsibility' turns in to 'commitment' and 'commitment' turns into 'involvement'. Her

involvement turns out to be his involvement. His fear of involvement is linked to the first sexual relationship he'd had, before he'd learned any defences against the strength of his feeling towards women he fell in love with/made love with. With a woman who was strong and emotional the fear was greatest, because he could not be sure of his defences, his own ego boundaries. During a different conversation, Jim used the same term 'sucked in' to refer to the pleasure, intensity, and danger he felt when he made love with the woman he was in a relationship with at that time. 'Sex' is capable of meaning the same things for men as it does for women: intense feelings of involvement and need, the danger to one's separate identity; wanting to have somebody forever and fearing that they will let you down.

However, gender makes a difference to the recognition of what 'sex' means. Men can represent themselves according to a set of assumptions in which they are not in need of a relationship—in fact, not in need of anything that would make them vulnerable. After all, according to the idea that male sexuality is a 'natural drive', men are only in need of sex and they can, supposedly, get it anywhere.

'Permissive' sexuality gave new legitimacy to men's wish to have uncommitted sex with women without feeling irresponsible. In the following extract, Sam illustrates the points that I have made above—the same slippage and projection, the fear of feeling strongly. His principle that it is all right not to feel any responsibility is legitimated by permissiveness. It is motivated by his fears of his own 'sentimentality':

Sam: 'I'll tell you something—I don't know what it means, but I'll say it anyway. When I say to somebody, who I'm making love to, I'm close to, when I say 'I love you, I love you', it's a word that symbolizes letting go. The night before Carol went away, she was saying it, and then I started saying it to her, when we were making love and um, what frightened me in that word is . . . it's an act of commitment.

Somebody suddenly *expects* something of me. They've said something that's somehow . . . the first word in a long rotten line towards marriage. That when you fall in *love* you're caught up in the institution. And it's been an act of principle for me, that I can love somebody and feel *loved*, without feeling any responsibility. That I can be free to say that I love somebody if I love them. Be free to feel. I can feel it quite unpredictably. It can hit me quite unexpectedly. And I think I worry about it because I can be quite sentimental.'

To the extent that this is possible in practice, Sam can eat his cake *and* have it, so to speak. His feelings, which can hit him unexpectedly, particularly when making love, are worrying. So his wish to say 'I love you' gets projected onto her declaration, where it can be comfortably located as somebody *else* expecting something of *him*. Of course, he still wants to feel loved—isn't that the crux of the matter?—but with no strings attached.

I have referred to three different assumptions concerning sexuality in the course of commenting on the meaning in the accounts that I have used. These are (i) that men's sexuality is a natural drive with any women as its object; (ii) that women want sex within a relationship and men can get caught in commitment; (iii) (characteristic of 1960s 'permissiveness'), both women and men just want physical pleasure from sex and neither wants a relationship.

The point that I want to emphasize is that women and men occupy different positions in these 'discourses'.[4] In the first case men are subjects, the possessors of biological urges whose 'natural' object is women. In contrast, women are subjects of the second. According to this, they are subjects of the wants and needs for relationships, rather than one-off sexual encounters. Men experience themselves as objects of this wanting and fear being 'hooked' when they sleep with women. According to 'permissive' ideas, in principle women and men are equally subjects; that is, the assumptions are 'gender blind', they are suppos-

edly subject to the same sexual urges and wishes not to commit themselves. In the previous analyses, I have shown how men position women as wanting commitment rather than position themselves there.

Defence Mechanisms

Gender difference thus means that women and men experience their sexuality differently. I have shown, in the case of Jim, why he was motivated to take up this position. He was enabled to defend himself against his own strong emotions by displacing them on to the woman. This is best understood through a psychoanalytic perspective.

According to Freud, material is repressed through defence mechanisms. These do not operate only within a person, but between people. The clearest example of a relational defence mechanism is projection: the feelings which a person is uncomfortable with, and therefore cannot recognize in her/himself, are projected onto another. Jim is motivated to suppress his strong emotions and sees the woman as being the one who feels strongly, wants commitment, and so on. This makes sense of his fear of involvement (which is actually to do with getting too involved) in terms of her needs. He is thus purged of his own—they have been externalized.

However, a psychoanalytic account does not draw the implications about the power differences which result from these dynamics.[5] Gender difference means that women are suitable vehicles for men's projections: they have already been constructed in such a way that they manifest the characteristics that men are suppressing. Likewise they experience themselves as wanting commitment and materially are more likely to be in the position of needing it, because this is how they have been positioned historically. Thus women's and men's positions are complementary, in the sense that these gender differences make it likely that both men and women will see men as wanting uncommitted sex and women needing committed relationships. The way that gender produces different identities leads to a collusion between women and men which makes change in these areas difficult. Nonetheless, the effect is consistently oppressive to women: it reproduces a power difference where men are supposedly free of needs and invulnerable. Women are left carrying this for both. No wonder we sometimes feel powerless! Despite collusion, the resultant contradictions have created a significant space for change.

If men's sexuality were wholly accountable through these gender positions (subject of natural drives, object of women's wishes for commitment), why would they ever stay with women, need women, feel strong emotions, and feel lost and desperate when women leave them? The answer is that 'sex' does mean more than natural urges for men too, but their subject position in that discourse offers them the possibility of repressing their strong needs of women. They take up this position unconsciously, as the slippage from one meaning to another in Jim's account illustrated. As psychoanalytic theory would insist, the slippage of meanings, the inconsistencies and illogicalities, are not arbitrary; they are motivated. As Martin's account illustrates, they are motivated by the extreme vulnerability which is the consequence of needing a woman that much—a consequence which is not eradicated when the feelings are projected onto her.

Desire for the Other Is Desire for the Mother

We want to feel loved. Sex is just about the only practice permitted to adults where wishes for comfort, support, loving can be expressed. Lacan summed up the origin in each person's history of this desire in his phrase 'desire for the Other is desire for the mother'. It may sound a little farfetched. In the following extract, Jim's account of what he wants from a relationship with a woman makes the same point in a way which is recognizable to most of us:

Wendy: 'What was it that you wanted out of your relationship with Jeanette?'

Jim: 'Well I think support, actually. Knowing that there was somebody who was going to be on my side. That I could talk about things that were affecting me and they would automatically be important to her. And that she would be able to give me strength in that way. Very classic. Like my parents' relationship in a way. But it was me who set the agenda, set the whole thing up. I remember her saying—well I was into classical music, so Jeanette pretended she was until she got confident enough. She wouldn't actually challenge me. There's a gaze of uncritical, totally accepting love that I find really attractive. 'I'll love you forever whatever' is a really powerful gaze. And that's a mother's gaze.'

Wendy: 'Is that how your mother relates to you?'

Jim: 'Absolutely. Whatever I do, she'll support me, she has supported me. It's quite incredible. And that makes my relationship with her very easy.'

Wendy: 'And did you get that from your father?'

Jim: 'No, that was very different. Well, I always felt he loved me, definitely. But he was much more—well he got annoyed with me when I didn't do it right.'

There is no reason to suppose that this 'desire for the mother' is not the historical origin of desire for the Other in both men and women. However, according to Freudian theory, the passages of boys' and girls' entry into culture and to gender create a difference not only in the object of that desire but in the intensity of that desire. Girls supposedly transfer their desire onto the father, and in doing so displace their desire for the mother, who nonetheless remains the primary giver of love and caring. Boys repress their desire for the mother but do not normally displace it from one gender to the other,[6] it is usually relocated with full force in the first sexual relationship that a boy has.[7] As Jim's comments illustrate, sex is the most powerful expression of this desire—the site where men want and need most and therefore feel most vulnerable. It is not arbitrary that Jim uses the same term—'sucked in'—to refer to his relation to women's emotionality and his feelings while making love with the woman he loved. Men 'enter' women when they make love. There is a metaphorical slippage between the womb of the mother (the ultimate in protection and security and the antithesis of separation) and the vagina, wherein they can feel engulfed in the love of the Other/mother. Women's vaginas thus can be dangerous places—dangerous because men's identity depends on separation from the mother; a maintenance of fragile ego boundaries which are most vulnerable, as Martin testified, when 'attraction' to a woman heralds desire for the Other/mother.

Men's Power as Resistance to Women's Power as the Mother/Other

The link of meaning between the mother and the woman with whom a man has sex (or is attracted to) is significant only insofar as it has political effects. It is a mixed blessing to understand that women do in fact have power over men. One of the puzzling things about feminists' analyses is that they stress men's power and women's lack of power as if they were immutable principles. I am astonished when my mother, in her matter-of-fact, apolitical way, talks about men in terms which leave me in no doubt that she feels more powerful, competent, and in control than they are. Why is it so elusive to many of the women I know? In this section, I want to suggest some answers to this question. First, men's strategies of resistance to the vulnerability they feel through 'needing' a woman are precisely ways of exercising power: a power conferred on them by the positions available to men through the system of

gender difference. Secondly, women misrecognize men and women because we too are subject to (sexist) assumptions in which men are produced as 'strong' and women as 'weak'.

Martin's comment in the first extract I used indicates that his way of coping with his extreme vulnerability to women he is attracted to is to put on a front in which he is strong and self-sufficient. Yet because he feels so vulnerable, he cannot believe it doesn't show ('but you do show yourself to be vulnerable, just by showing that you're soft on somebody'). As a result, he cannot see himself as others see him. However strong he appears to women, he experiences himself as dreadfully vulnerable. The meanings attached to his identity are inextricable from his desire for the Other. It is ironical that Martin is one of those men who is systematically most recognized by women as the ideal in dependability, strength, resourcefulness, and so on! Women see the façade and do not see what it is covering up, particularly if they are attracted to him. How does this misrecognition come about? In the following extract, Clare gives graphic description of her misrecognition of Phil, the man she lived with for many years.

Clare: 'That guy! I didn't even know he was so dependent on me—I had no idea, not a clue.'

Wendy: 'That's so often the way men play it. But it's also often the way women *read* it.'

Clare: 'Oh, exactly. It's two-way. His behaviour was very stereotypical, really. He was very . . . I thought he was a *competent* person, but he didn't think he was at all. He was outwardly confident—domineering—which actually made me feel incredibly oppressed.'

Wendy: 'How long did it take you to realize that?'

Clare: 'Oh a long time. I didn't realize he was dependent on me till I left him—literally, I had no *idea*. And when I look back on it, I realized that I *should* have known. I realized that all the signs were there, and I hadn't read them. I felt him as—dominant, and domineering, and confident. And he felt *lacking* in confidence. The very signs that I took to signify confidence were actually exactly the signs of his *lack* of confidence—like talking too much, being opinionated . . . and things that I couldn't *bear*. And when I read it back as lack of confidence, I could see. But when I was in a situation, reading it as confidence, I could never get that. Quite a lot of things changed in our relationship. When I first met him, he had a degree and he encouraged me but I got far higher qualifications than he did. So that also made him feel unconfident. And I hadn't realized that either. We did things like—both applying for Open University teaching. I got it, he didn't. It didn't occur to *me* it was a problem. Of course it was a problem for him.'

Phil's displays are equivalent to Martin's public acceptability. True, masculinity is meant to involve being confident, dominating, self-sufficient (all signs that Clare systematically misreads).

What is interesting is that Clare knew in retrospect that she had misrecognized Phil. However, she goes on to say that she falls into exactly the same patterns with her present man. Learning about men is not a process of rational acquisition of experience. She misrecognizes the men she is attracted to (just like men misrecognize those women whom they desire). For both, recognition of their own power disappears at the advent of desire.

> Clare: 'Why is it, then, that I can't get hold of that knowledge about Ken? Why can't I see it?—because I can't. I still don't feel as if I know it—I don't, not in my gut. It's very silly. It's obviously that I don't want to see it. But I am extremely powerful, when I stand back and think about it, I know that. I know where my power lies. If I were somebody else, I could see it. But I have great resistance to recognising it in myself.'

Desire produces misrecognition. Through the sense of vulnerability that it inspires, the other is seen as relatively strong. The fantasy is that he/she can fulfill those needs which, though so long repressed, go back to the infant-mother relationship. The sense of vulnerability may not itself be a sign of misrecognition of oneself, but in the way that it floods other feelings about oneself, and evidence of realistic capabilities, it creates a distortion. However, the *content* of these misrecognitions depends on gender. The way that vulnerability is a product of desire for the Other may well be the same for women and men, but the positions that can be taken up in order to resist the Other's power must be different because of gender. It is for this reason that men's and women's power in sexual relationships cannot be said to be equivalent. It is not a question of 'equal but different'.

Women's power as the Other/mother in sexual and couple relationships is politically contradictory because it motivates men's resistance. Men's experience of women's power is not equivalent to women exercising it. Ironically, it is a power that women do not necessarily recognize because of our misrecognition of ourselves and men (although unawares we may use it in the way we 'mother' men in order to keep them needing us).

'Frightened of Getting in Deep'

Broadly speaking, the sites of men's resistance to women's power are twofold. First, traditionally, men have used the same site—sexuality—to resist the women of their desire. By having multiple or serial sexual relationships, men dilute the power that they experience one woman having over them.[8] But it's not entirely satisfactory. As Sam said:

> Sam: 'The thing that has caused me the most pain and the most hope is the idea of actually living with Jane, and that's in the context of having tried to live with three other women before. And each time the relationship's been full of possibility. I don't want to live on my

own. There's too many *things* all wrapped up in coupling. There's too many needs it potentially meets, and there are too many things it frustrates. I *do* want to have a *close, central-person* relationship, but in the past, the negative aspects outweighed the positive aspects dramatically. Or my inability to work through them has led me to run.'

He then specifies further what led him to run:

Sam: 'I'm very frightened of getting in *deep*—and then not being able to cope with the demands the relationship's making. You see a lot of these things aren't really to do with sexuality. They're to do with responsibility.'

Whose? Isn't it the same slippage again? From responsibility to commitment to involvement to fear of being let down. Multiple or serial relationships enable men (and women) to avoid facing the fear.

Secondly, in juxtaposition to the private world of the home, which is also the site of women's sexual/mothering practices, men have asserted the superiority of their position in the public world. If they depend on women at home it is not so bad if there is always work to do which comes first, or meetings to go to, or buddies to meet in the pub. The woman's sexual power can be countered through her material dependence, or her emotional dependence, or her incompetence/unconfidence in the 'real' world. When men are attracted to women who occupy all the same positions in the world as men do, women end up having a 'double power': there is no site of resistance for men, no place where they are uncontestably in power.

'Too Powerful'

So let me return to my original question and summarize my conclusions as to why (some) men avoid sex even when they are attracted to a woman. Put simply, the feelings that they are keyed into by having sex in those circumstances makes a man feel extremely vulnerable. I want to emphasize that it's not the 'power' of a woman's sexuality as such. That would be to naturalize it in much the same way as many oppressive cultures do. It would also be to carry over the sexist rationalizations that men have used to claim the power of their own sexual 'drives' or their penises as natural. Rather a woman becomes the 'object' onto which older desires are hooked. The power of women's sexuality is as 'psychic' object not as real object. But in practice the two cannot be separated (until a man has either done some hard work on those feelings, or displaced them into a different object).

There are an infinite number of strategies whereby men can deal with their vulnerability. I don't want to generalize to 'all men'. Most men don't resist sex: they are too driven by their desire for the Other. Usually, as I have argued above, the power is balanced by all the other arenas in which men can so easily operate. Men's power is as 'real' objects as well as 'psychic' objects for women.

However, when none of the usual inequalities operates to produce a power which counterbalances their vulnerability, they may have to refuse a sexual relationship. The boundary is drawn to exclude sex because it is there that desire is strongest and therefore there where vulnerability and the threat of losing a separate identity is greatest. Emotional involvement is not necessarily banished with sex however. He phones up because he cannot bear to lose contact. He might need me after all. But instead, he asked me if I'm all right. Displacement of his needs onto the 'needy' woman convinces him he's fine and it's me who's suffering. He wants to carry on being friends (because I'm the only one 'who really understands'). Another will stand on the doorstep for half an hour (after midnight) saying 'I'm going now', but never quite bringing himself to leave. Another will reach out physically to touch me (before he's censored the spontaneous gesture), then, when I respond, he withdraws.

What is it like to be on the receiving end of these contradictions? Women have often felt that it was our madness, or paranoia, or confusion, or our failure to reach the right standards of femininity. Now at last I recognize these double messages when I receive them straight in the gut. I see it clearly: it is not that he doesn't like me or doesn't want me. But, yes, it is that he will not have a relationship with me. One tells me quite openly that it would be a disaster because he'd need me too much and then I'd go. For another, it was too good. For a third it would change everything and so he's safer with his present part-time relationship.

We must also be scrupulous in recognizing how these double messages, power plays, contradictions, fears are used by us in relationships too. Desire for the Other is not only men's bane. However, there are two differences. One is that women have taken on the need to change these harmful practices more seriously than men have and can often be very honest and courageous about them. The second is that we have never been exonerated from these needs anyway. It is only the sexism of assumptions—the way that established 'truths' about sexuality are gender-differentiated—that have provided a cover for men's actions and feelings.

It is not impossible to change these dynamics. Just because women have a head-start doesn't mean men can avoid them. Some men are strong enough in themselves not to feel engulfed by their desire for the Other/mother. I think what it takes is that every man has to 'separate' from this mother. Most don't. Rather, they displace the desire onto a safe woman 'object'. If he can make it feel that she's needier than him (not so difficult, given patriarchy) he won't even know that he's vulnerable. Well, hopefully, it won't escape us so easily.

*   *   *

Conclusions

I want to stress that there is a relation between knowledge and power. It is relevant for feminist politics to theorize men's sexuality as well as our own. Most particularly, it is important to understand power in such a way that our own powers become apparent to us and we are not trapped in a discourse which sees power as being solely the property of men—a possession which we can never acquire by virtue of our sex. In this chapter, I have used a notion of power which sees it as being part of all social relations. It is produced not only through differences in material resources, but in the meanings through which we understand our relationships, and in the effects of gender difference in conferring power on men. However, these meanings are multiple and contradictory. By recognizing these contradictions, we are not stuck with a political analysis which sees men's power as monolithic and unchangeable and which keeps women in the victim role. Power is productive, and wherever there is power, there is resistance. Heterosexuality is a site of power and of resistance for men and for women. As women we can share and analyze our relations with men in such a way as to challenge the sexist assumptions whose effects I have shown here.

Notes

1. Much more has been said about women's sexuality in relationships. My focus here is on men's. This means that there is a danger of implying that only men are subject to those feelings in relationships, and the resistances that result. I know that's not true. What is true is that their needs and desires in relationships have been camouflaged by 'knowledge' about men's sexuality and what is underneath their sexual relationship has not been scrutinized.

2. All the quotations come from my research (Wendy Hollway, *Identity and Gender Difference in Adult Social Relations*, unpublished Ph.D. thesis, University of London, 1982). Italics indicate emphasis used by the speaker. In this article I have altered the transcript slightly where it has made the meaning more clear or shortened the quote. This has meant editing out pauses and repetitions but not changing the meaning.

3. Lucy Bland and Wendy Hollway, 'What's Natural About Sexuality? The Problem for Feminism of Biological Accounts of Sexuality and Sexual Desire', *Feminist Review* 13.

4. By the term 'discourse', I mean a system of statements which cohere around common meanings and values. The meaning of the term is similar to a 'set of assumptions' but the way 'discourse' has been theorized (most importantly by Michel Foucault, *The Order of Things: An Archaeology of the Human Sciences*, Tavistock, London, 1970 and *The History of Sexuality*, v. 1, *An Introduction*, Allen Lane, London,1979) emphasizes how these meanings and values are a product of social factors, of powers and practices, rather than an individual's set of ideas. My use of the term here also enables me to make the link with language and grammar where people are positioned (and position others) by the use of personal pronouns in sentences. For an extended discussion of these theoretical issues see J. Henriques, W. Hollway, C. Venn, and V. Walkerdine, *Changing the Subject of Psychology* (London: Methuen, 1983).

5. This tendency in psychoanalysis theory is exacerbated by the way it reduces content to process. For example, Freud emphasized that the object to which desires attach themselves or around which fantasies develop was displaced from the real object and therefore of little significance. This view fails to see the systematicity in what is projected onto whom. I believe that it is here that gender (or race or class) as a *social* system of differences is necessary for the analysis.

6. This would suggest that a heterosexual man's desire for the Other is even stronger, and therefore even more threatening, than a heterosexual woman's (displaced) desire. Men's greater repression, and more driven resistance to women's powerfulness (as they experience it through their vulnerability) would make sense in this light.

7. Several men have described to me the same phenomenon when they were young, particularly when they fell in love with older women. But there's also a danger of overgeneralizing. I think many men get into relationships with women who are less experienced and less confident (apparently) than they are and, by retaining this power inequality, never experience the vulnerability. Yet they don't feel entirely satisfied and will be the ones who pull away from the relationship.

8. Women do too, though the opportunity has not been equally available.

Section 3 | Becoming a Mother, Becoming a Father, Doing Motherwork

*P*arenthood is at the heart of family and of gender. Historically, the social construction of motherhood as we know it was closely entangled with the evolution of current ideas about differences between women and men. Today, parenthood is the most engendering experience most people will have.

Chapter 18

Many couples feel that they are a family only after they become parents. For these people, childbirth constitutes the transition to family life. More broadly, as an exclusively woman's experience, childbirth warrants serious attention: how women are treated as they become mothers should tell us much about gen- *der in this society. This essay reports the findings of a study conducted in the early and mid-1990s. It gives a sense of the types of childbirth experiences typical in downtown Toronto hospitals, and develops a critical analysis of medicalized childbirth which highlights women's agency.*

Making Labour Work:
Women Negotiating Medicalized Childbirth

Diana Worts and Bonnie Fox

Giving Birth: Two Women's Stories

Meredith gripped the edges of her hospital bed, every muscle in her body tightened in defence. Another contraction. This was more than she could bear. For hours now, they had been coming one on top of another. And they hurt. They hurt more than she had ever imagined possible. She wanted an epidural to take away the pain.[1] But the nurse had told her to be patient; the anesthesiologist was tied up in surgery. Meredith was indignant. This was inhumane! Surely she should not have to endure more.

Hugh stood by the bed, uncertain how to help. 'Try to slow down your breathing; look at me,' he offered. The room was tiny and airless. There was barely space for the bed and intravenous pole, and even less room for the couple to maneuver. And now a resident had come in, wanting to take a medical history. It was all too much. Where *was* that anesthesiologist?

Meredith had been in labour for twelve hours. The first contractions had wakened her at 2 a.m. that morning. At 7 a.m. she and Hugh had left for the hospital. But shortly after their arrival things had taken a wrong turn. Tests had indi-

cated the baby might be too large for Meredith's pelvis; and this raised concerns about its well-being. Although the hospital staff had not seemed overly concerned, Meredith's anxiety levels had shot up. The doctor on call had broken the 'bag of waters' surrounding the baby to assess the situation.[2] To everyone's relief, the fluid had been clear; the baby was not in serious trouble. However, the procedure had almost immediately accelerated the pace of the labour, producing very strong contractions with little space between them. Meredith had been unprepared for any of this. It had left her feeling drained, both physically and emotionally. Now, all she wanted was something to take away the pain.

After what seemed an eternity, the anesthesiologist arrived. The epidural was set up with some difficulty; but it was not all Meredith had hoped. Almost immediately she found she was numb—and immobilized—from her upper chest to her toes.[3] She felt cold, and began to shake uncontrollably. Although she knew that many women experience some trembling immediately after receiving epidural anesthesia, her reaction was more violent than most. The nurse brought her a warm blanket, but still the shaking wouldn't stop.

By 10 p.m. that evening Meredith had progressed little more than halfway through her labour.[4] She was suffering from heartburn and nausea.[5] Her legs were immobilized, one arm was completely numb, and the other was hampered by a blood pressure cuff. She felt helpless. By 3 a.m. Meredith and Hugh had seen three shifts of nurses. A couple from their prenatal classes had come and gone, baby in hand. And still, Meredith was not ready to deliver.

Finally, at 5 a.m. in the morning, Meredith was examined and told it was time to start pushing her baby out into the world. Still attached to a monitor and intravenous pole, and with an epidural catheter taped to her back, she found it extremely difficult to co-ordinate the massive effort needed. After an hour and a half with no progress she was exhausted and declared she could go no further. She was moved to a delivery room where, disoriented and panicky, she hauled herself awkwardly onto the table. The doctor informed her that the baby was still too high in her pelvis for a forceps delivery; the only option remaining was a cesarean section.[6] Meredith lost whatever shreds of composure remained. All that work, all that pain, all that worrying, and now the baby was to be born by surgery after all. What had it all been for?

The medical staff prepared Meredith for the cesarean, with Hugh standing by. Eight-pound, three-ounce Laura was born about half an hour later. The baby was in perfect health; Meredith, however, did not fare as well. She was left with pain in her neck and jaw from the uncontrollable shaking, an infection that required treatment with antibiotics, an incision that caused her pain for several weeks, and a legacy of anger over the way things had gone that took months to heal. In the postpartum ward she had difficulty holding Laura, and could not get the baby to nurse properly. From Meredith's perspective, this was, quite simply, a birth in which 'everything that could possibly go wrong did go wrong'.

In a nearby hospital, Celia stood in the shower adjoining her labour room, her husband Paul waiting patiently outside the door. For two hours she let the water run over her, breathing deeply, relaxing her muscles, and calming her fears. Celia wanted very much to give birth without medical intervention. She knew that where such procedures are concerned 'one thing often leads to another', in a cascade of interventions that may ultimately compromise the well-being of mother and/or baby. She felt prepared to work with her body, and to trust that her labour would follow its own course safely.

It was nearly two weeks past Celia's due date. The previous day her doctor had recommended the topical application of a hormonal preparation to 'get things started'.[7] But on examining her and finding that dilation was already underway, he had decided this was no longer appropriate. There had been some worrying signs, though. The baby was big and its head was high (meaning the labour might be long); and the length of time that had passed since Celia's due date meant the baby's health might be at risk.[8] A full-scale induction—the stimulation of labour using intravenous chemical hormones—had been scheduled for the following day.

Celia had not looked forward to the possibility of an induced labour. She wanted to be in control of her mental and physical capacities. She did not relish the thought of being confined to bed by monitoring equipment and/or an epidural, or of being held to a strict time line.[9] But all these interventions were likely to accompany an induced labour.

Much to her relief, Celia had gone into labour on her own at midnight the night before the scheduled induction. The contractions had been strong from the start, but walking and deep breathing had helped. After a few hours at home, Celia and Paul had headed to the hospital. The contractions, however, had stopped on their arrival. Celia had been disappointed, thinking her labour would be induced after all. But the attending physician had been sympathetic; knowing Celia's feelings about induction, he had suggested she take a long shower to 'think it over'.

Now, at 8 a.m., Celia stepped out of the shower. As she did so, the 'bag of waters' surrounding the baby ruptured spontaneously, and contractions began again. Over the next four hours, as the labour increased in intensity, Celia moved from pacing the floor of the labour room to sitting in a lazy-boy chair. All the while she did deep breathing through her contractions, and kept her eyes closed to help maintain her concentration. It took a great deal of energy to stay with the contractions, but she felt up to the task. Paul stayed in the room with her, waiting, watching, and comforting by his presence.

At midday, the labour moved into high gear. Celia began to use shallow breathing to get through the contractions. Paul massaged her hands and feet to help her relax. The contractions were extremely painful, but Celia maintained her focus and took each one as it came. The nursing staff entered the room from time to time. Seeing the couple working together, they left quietly. No doctors examined Celia internally. No one told her how far she had (or had not) progressed. As Celia worked with the contractions, she felt her labour was progressing just as it should.

By 3 p.m. in the afternoon the contractions were strong enough that Celia felt 'about ready to jump off a bridge'. The doctor arrived and found she was fully dilated. However, as the baby's head was still high, he suggested Celia have an epidural and get some rest, and that they reassess the situation in a couple of hours. Celia was reluctant, having come this far without medical assistance. So the doctor suggested, once again, that she take a shower and give it some thought. This time Celia stood not more than ten minutes under the running water before she began to feel an urge to push with each contraction. This, she knew, was a sign that the baby had moved down.

Celia got out of the shower and was examined. This time, her baby was indeed ready to be born. She moved to the labour bed and, squeezing Paul's hand hard, pushed with every ounce of strength she possessed. The baby inched its way down. The doctor applied warm compresses to avoid a tear or the need for a cut to enlarge the opening.[10] After forty-five minutes, Melissa—a healthy 8 lbs, 15 oz.—emerged with a wail. She was placed on Celia's belly for a few minutes, then wrapped and placed in her arms. Admiring her daughter, Celia felt both proud and fortunate. Three times she had faced the prospect of a medicalized birth and three times she had been able to work with her body to avoid it. She felt strong and ready to go forward into the future.

The Critique of Medicalized Childbirth

Celia and Meredith are both participants in a study of first-time parents.[11] Their stories chronicle their passage into motherhood—an event that many have argued has major social implications for women (Oakley 1980a, 1980b; Martin 1987; Davis-Floyd 1992). But the implications of Meredith's and Celia's birth stories are very different. Meredith felt both physically injured and emotionally shattered by her experience; Celia felt energized and empowered. For Meredith, labour was simply impossibly hard work; for Celia it was much, much more. Labour 'worked' for Celia, but not for Meredith.

Observers have drawn on just this kind of contrast to develop a critique of medicalized childbirth in Western societies. Writers from various academic disciplines—from medicine (Tew 1985; Chalmers, Enkin, and Keirse 1989) and public health (Brown et al. 1994), to psychology (Ball 1987; Collins et al. 1993), sociology (Oakley 1980a, 1980b; Graham and Oakley 1981; Katz Rothman 1982, 1989), and anthropology (Jordan 1978; Romalis 1981; Kay 1982; MacCormack 1982; Martin 1987; Michaelson 1988; Sargent and Stark 1989; Davis-Floyd 1990, 1992, 1994)—have contributed to the critique. They have been joined by childbirth educators (Kitzinger, 1972; Barclay, Andre, and Glover 1989; Chamberlain et al. 1991; Priya 1992), policy analysts (Eakins 1986), and the popular press (Arms 1981; Mitford 1992). Despite differing backgrounds and orientations, these authors unanimously criticize the extent to which, and the manner in which, medical professionals exercise control over the birth process—and not incidentally, over women—in Western society. Medicalized childbirth, they suggest, is both evidence of, and a contributing factor to, women's subordinate position in society.

In general, the critics argue that medicalization decreases the birthing woman's control over her own body and its functions, and alienates her from a potentially empowering experience. They suggest that medical professionals, acting on a definition of childbirth as hazardous, intervene in what is essentially a natural process. They argue, further, that childbirth in a hospital setting separates the physical from the emotional, social, psychological, and spiritual dimensions of the process, and hence addresses only one facet of what should be a holistic event. Finally, they point out that medicalization has led to a shift in the focus of concerns from the woman to the unborn baby: success is equated with the birth of a healthy baby, and the woman's well-being has come to be seen as relatively unimportant.

All this might be well and good if it clearly improved physical outcomes for mothers and babies. However, the critics also cite evidence that modern medicine often falls short of its claims in this regard: improvements in maternal and infant health, they argue, can be traced primarily to more general advances in public health and living standards, while medical interventions are often associated with unnecessary risks to the health and well-being of mother and child (Tew 1995).

Among sociologists, Ann Oakley's (1980a, 1980b, 1984) work has been especially important in developing the critique of medicalized birth. Using postpartum depression as a measure of women's well-being (or lack thereof), Oakley effectively criticizes standard physiological explanations, and relates the condition instead to the amount of medical intervention (i.e., drugs and technology) used during labour and delivery (Oakley 1980b). The problems associated with

medically managed births are further elaborated in a more rigorous study by Entwisle and Doering (1981), who find that the most critical aspect of medical intervention, with respect to the woman's feelings about the birth, is whether or not she retains consciousness—and thus a sense of control—through the birthing process.

The issue of women's control over what happens to them during labour and delivery has been at the heart of the critique. Thus, for example, anthropologist Emily Martin (1987) argues that social relations in childbirth increasingly mimic the class relations of industrial production under capitalism: women's bodies are seen as more or less efficient machines, women as unskilled workers, and doctors as managers. The significance of the analogy between birthing women and waged workers lies in the fact that both have little or no control over the production process for which they labour.

The History of Medicalization, Part I: Medical Control

Critical historians expand on this analysis by demonstrating that current practices have not always been the preferred way of managing childbirth. They chronicle how a formerly woman-centred event—occurring in the woman's home and attended by a midwife and female friends and relatives—was transformed into an occasion for hospitalization and medical management and control. These writers argue that male medical practitioners wrested control from women, and later secured their position by instituting near-universal hospitalization.

In the United States and Canada, the process by which male doctors displaced female midwives was part and parcel of a campaign to attract patients. Because they were unorganized in the early part of the nineteenth century, doctors had to compete in an unregulated marketplace populated by a variety of medical practioners. Childbirth offered advantages in the struggle to build a clientele: it gave the doctor access to an entire family of potential patients, and entailed the management of a process whose outcome was usually positive regardless of the skills of the attendant (Wertz and Wertz 1979).

As the status of doctors as a group rose over the course of the nineteenth century, these 'male midwives' increasingly drew their reputations from their medical training (Donegan 1978; Wertz and Wertz 1979). Their patients' heightened expectations pushed them to 'do something' while attending a birth. Intervention typically involved the use of instruments aimed at speeding up the delivery and, later in the century, anesthesia for pain relief (Wertz and Wertz 1979). Unfortunately, strong Victorian norms about modesty prevented doctors from gaining clinical experience in medical school, so the range of their skills was tremendous, and their intervention during birth was often harmful to the woman, the baby, or both (Leavitt 1986).

In Canada, doctors also secured their position by lobbying persistently against the training and registration of midwives through the nineteenth and twentieth centuries (Biggs 1990; LaForce 1990; Arnup 1994: 76). Their campaign was an ideological one that played on prejudices about social class as well as gender: midwives were portrayed as dirty, ignorant, and dangerous, in contrast with the gentlemanly doctors and their 'scientific' knowledge (Biggs 1990). In addition, childbirth was increasingly defined as 'dangerous', thus requiring a doctor's presence (Biggs 1990; LaForce 1990).[12] Hospitalization followed from this redefinition of birth: in 1926 (the first year statistics were gathered on the subject), less than 20 per cent of births took place in hospital, but by 1960 nearly 95 per cent were occurring there (Arnup 1994: 74). Childbirth had become almost exclusively a medical matter, with midwives practising only on the fringes.

During the 1990s, however, pregnant women's options had broadened somewhat. By the end of the decade, midwives were being licensed and funded by the provincial health-care systems in Ontario, B.C., and Quebec; other provinces were licensing midwives (Bourgeault 1999).[13]

Childbirth in Toronto Today

How typical of childbirth today, then, is Celia's non-medicalized birth? And how typical is Meredith's highly medicalized one? Our in-depth interviews with forty Toronto-area women suggest that medically managed births are the norm for first-time mothers. Births like Celia's, on the other hand, are rare.[14] Well over half the women interviewed had their labour artificially stimulated with oral or intravenous medication, and/or by artifical rupture of the membranes. These techniques—however useful—bring with them constant monitoring, restricted mobility, and very strong contractions, usually requiring the use of epidural anesthesia.

For the vast majority of the women in the study, the baby's heart rate and their own contractions were monitored electronically as long as the woman laboured in the hospital. Most were monitored using belts around their abdomen. In a few cases, an internal clip was attached directly to the baby's scalp.[15] Either way, continuous electronic monitoring—in contrast to intermittent ultrasonic or manual techniques—restricted the woman's movements and often meant she was confined to bed.

The vast majority of these first-time mothers were also given epidural anesthesia—likewise associated with constant monitoring and restricted or complete loss of mobility. A few were given Demerol, a narcotic used to manage pain in early labour. And a couple were given sleeping pills to allow them rest in early labour.

Most women in the study were happy with their decision to use pain medication. Some, however, suffered adverse reactions, particularly to epidural anesthesia (e.g., shaking, vomiting, difficulty breathing), and/or got more than they bargained for (e.g., immobility and numbness, and difficulty co-ordinating pushing during the actual birth). In a few cases women got less than they bargained for: the procedure gave them little in the way of pain relief. Some women—those who were discovered immediately *after* the administration of an epidural to be ready or nearly ready to deliver—felt in retrospect that if they had been assessed more carefully they would have refused the medication.

About a quarter of the women gave birth with the help of forceps or a vacuum extractor—both mechanical aids to delivery. Births by these methods were preceded by an episiotomy, or incision to enlarge the outlet of the birth canal. A couple of women with episiotomies also tore (in one case, a third-degree tear required forty stitches). Among those who did not require mechanical assistance delivering their babies, a similar number either sustained a small tear (usually requiring minimal repair and healing with little difficulty) or were given an episiotomy. At least one woman felt the episiotomy was 'the worst part' of giving birth. In several cases the procedure was carried out without consulting the woman. For most, the episiotomy was a source of considerable pain—and occasionally infection, and/or subsequent restitching—for several weeks postpartum.

Fifteen per cent of the women in the study gave birth by cesarean section. In one case this was planned in advance because the baby was in a breech (head-up) position. In the remaining cases the decision was made after many hours of labour, either because the baby was in trouble (rare), or because the baby did not descend through the birth canal after an extended period of pushing.

'Natural' births—those not involving the use of pain medication, artificial stimulation, assisted delivery, or surgery—were rare among the women interviewed. Only four women gave birth this way. In addition, one woman had a straightforward labour in which the only intervention was a low-level form of induction—the topical application of a hormonal preparation to initiate contractions.

And for another woman the only form of medical management was electronic fetal monitoring—which she appreciated for the information it gave her on the strength of the contractions and the baby's condition. One woman had no intervention until the last moments, when a vacuum extractor was used to speed up the delivery. A couple of women had only epidural anesthesia administered very near the end of their labours.

The general picture, then, is one in which some form of medical intervention/assistance is the norm for first-time mothers. This picture contrasts with the stated hopes and expectations of the participants in the first-time parenting study, prior to giving birth. During pregnancy, ten of the women interviewed expressed a strong desire for a 'natural' birth. Only two wanted medically managed births, in both cases to manage pain. The remainder of the women in the study anticipated being flexible in the face of the unknown—though most hoped for minimal intervention. The disjuncture between what is hoped for and what is delivered suggests that the contrast between stories like Meredith's and Celia's captures something real, and that the critics do indeed raise important questions about the medical management of childbirth today.

At the same time, though, the results of some empirical research suggest that the critique needs further development. For example, apparently only middle-class women desire a sense of control over what happens during the birth. For working-class women, control means a variety of things—control over pain according to one study (Nelson 1983) and control over their own behaviour according to another (McIntosh 1989). Other research shows that, although some women are alienated by their experience of medicalized birth, many women across social classes welcome medical intervention, if not management, and are quite satisfied with their hospital deliveries (Gordon 1988; McIntosh 1989; Sargent and Stark 1989; Davis-Floyd 1992; Lazarus 1994).

Women's Responses to Medicalized Birth

How did the women in the first-time parenting study react to the medical management they encountered? Many were, in contrast to Meredith, quite satisfied with their medicalized births—even when they had hoped to give birth 'naturally'. One reason for a shift in attitude was that all these women identified very closely with their babies' interests. This was especially evident where monitoring procedures indicated that the baby might be at risk. Judy, who sought and received pain relief during labour, and who ultimately gave birth by cesarean section, reflected afterward on her experience, 'There's nothing wrong with him, so it's perfect for me. That's all I wanted. I didn't care how he came out.' Joanne also gave birth by cesarean section, after a lengthy struggle to avoid medical intervention. Her concern for the well-being of her baby—despite her own strong desires for a non-medicalized birth—prompted her to comment, 'You just want to have your baby. And it's like, "well, do what you have to do."' Sue, who welcomed an epidural during labour, but wound up with a forceps delivery as a result, also understood her experience in terms of the baby's needs: 'To be honest, I don't think at the time I really cared. I think it was just, "make sure the baby's okay, and get her out."'

Negative reactions to medicalized births tended to occur some days or weeks later, in women with healthy babies. Just over half of the women in the study were angry, upset, or had other negative feelings about their experience of labour and delivery. (Two-fifths of the women felt positive, and for two women feelings about the birth were overshadowed by subsequent medical emergencies involving the mother or child.) Some of the negative reactions centred around reasons that were consistent with the critique of medicalized childbirth: loss of control (even among women for whom staying in control had not been a high priority) or negative reactions to specific forms of medical intervention (e.g., epidurals that numbed all sensation, monitoring that restricted movement, or augmentation that made the contractions intolerable). Natalie, who had an epidural despite her desire to avoid intervention, said afterward that 'I don't really feel like I had a vaginal birth because it was nothing . . . I feel like I missed something.' Zoe, who had no firm birth-related goals beforehand, reflected afterward that 'I think being hooked up to all this equipment and not being able to walk or get up made me feel very vulnerable and very frustrated.'

On the other hand, several women reacted negatively to events not necessarily caused by medical management (e.g., long labours or a poorly positioned baby). And more important, nearly a quarter complained that medical staff had *failed* to intervene soon enough (or at all) to help them manage their pain. Carla felt abandoned by hospital staff who 'totally lose the fact that there's actually some pain involved here'. She 'didn't like the experience at all because I felt like I was at their mercy.' Similarly, Esther felt that medical personnel were unresponsive during her long and painful labour: 'My experience at the hospital has been that they do things which cause you pain, and then they wait a very long time to give you pain relief.' Trish gave birth without medical intervention (having gone into the experience with a flexible attitude); however, in the weeks afterward she appeared to be suffering from depression, which she attributed to the pain she had endured in labour.

Women who reacted positively to their birth experience sometimes did so for reasons consistent with the critique of medicalization—for example, those who cited the absense of pharmaceutical or technological intervention, or the ability to stay in control. Nora, who had planned a home birth, found her hospital birth 'great' because 'I really felt a lot of control all the way through, and I think one of my biggest fears about hospitals was not being in control . . . I felt like I was making the decisions.'

Some, however, reacted positively for altogether different reasons. Among these were women who highlighted the absence of pain, and the tremendous support they received from those around them, even where there was medical intervention. Marie, whose primary goal during labour was to avoid pain, said afterward that because her birth was 'pain-free', 'it was wonderful; it was great.' Karen had wanted to avoid intervention, but wound up with an epidural. She commented afterwards that, 'I now pray to the epidural god.' Nora, who had a positive experience despite hospitalization and medical intervention in what was to have been a home birth, attributed her response not only to the feeling that she had 'done everything I could' to avoid intervention, but also to having been surrounded throughout her long labour by a 'wonderful circle of friends'.

Thus, the women in this study reacted in a variety of ways to the experience of giving birth. Moreover, many of their reactions suggest that the critical understanding of medicalized birth as alienated and alienating may be an oversimplification. Their stories suggest that the absence of medical intervention does not necessarily make for a positive and empowering experience; neither does medical intervention necessarily leave women feeling alienated and disempowered. The question we must ask, then, is what factors beyond the absence of medical control *per se* might make labour 'work' for women.

The History of Medicalization, Part II: Women's Agency

While the majority of histories of the medicalization of childbirth argue that current arrangements have been forced on women—that male doctors systematically took over control of the process from birthing women and their female attendants—the work of Judith Leavitt (1986) presents a somewhat different view. Leavitt argues that women's agency was central to the process of medicalization, and that in fact many of the changes addressed women's needs and desires at the time.

Moreover, according to Leavitt, doctors gained control over childbirth only gradually, and not until it moved into the hospital setting. Prior to that time, there is evidence that many doctors were critical of unnecessary intervention, and that when they did intervene it was primarily out of concern for the woman they were attending, rather than for mercenary reasons. In short, Leavitt suggests that the dynamics of medicalization are not reducible to a collective desire on the part of medical men to control access to birthing women.

Instead, a number of factors appear to have been at work in the transformation of childbirth. First, the nineteenth-century reality was that women approached the event with apprehension and fear because it was indeed hazardous. One in thirty women died from complications arising during the birth, and many others were left permanently disabled (Leavitt 1986: 25).[16] Women coped with the threat of childbearing by surrounding themselves with women friends and relatives, who provided support and assistance, and by engaging the services of an experienced female midwife for information and help. In the process, new mothers were 'brought to bed' for three to four weeks—sometimes more—by women who assumed responsibility for the household throughout the period of confinement (Leavitt 1986). Wertz and Wertz (1979) use the term 'social childbirth' to describe this way of handling the event.

During the nineteenth century, however, women's attitudes toward the risks associated with childbearing began changing. Instead of simply accepting 'fate' with respect to life and death, they increasingly believed people could shape and even control their destinies (Wertz and Wertz 1979). Thus they searched for ways to improve outcomes in childbirth. According to Leavitt (1986: 38),

> Women garnered support from their networks of companions, but they continued to fear childbirth because of the possibilities of death or disability. It was precisely these fears that led women away from traditional

birthing patterns to a long search for safer and less painful childbirths.

As a result, women invited male doctors to attend their births. They believed that these men's training had taught them more about handling problems than the training of female midwives (Donegan 1978; Wertz and Wertz 1979; Leavitt, 1986). Nevertheless, when a male doctor attended a birth, the woman giving birth and the women surrounding her retained control over the doctor's actions: he could intervene only with their consent, and the procedures used (e.g., anesthesia or forceps) were subject to the women's approval (Wertz and Wertz 1979; Leavitt 1986). Doctors who did not accommodate women's wishes during childbirth 'risked losing patients and damaging their reputations among a whole community of women' (Leavitt 1986: 59).[17]

Another key reason women chose medical attendants was that they offered the promise of pain relief. Physicians increasingly used chloroform and ether through the latter half of the nineteenth century and into the twentieth century. But women themselves were instrumental in defining their goal as a painless birth (Leavitt 1986). This is clearest in the struggle that took place early in this century around 'twilight sleep' (the use of scopolamine to permit women to labour and deliver 'asleep', and to wake with no memory of the pain). Upper- and middle-class women fought for this kind of birth, while doctors resisted. Advocates of twilight sleep were often feminists seeking some measure of control over their labours and deliveries (Leavitt 1986). Because doctors were dependent upon women's invitations to attend births, they could ignore women's wishes 'only at great risk to their own practice' (Leavitt, 1986: 140).

A major consequence of the demand for physician assistance, however, was to change the definition of birth: once a normal physiological process, childbirth was now an illness requiring a doctor, hospitalization, and medical procedures. This change ultimately shifted control from the birthing woman to the doctor in attendance (Leavitt 1986).

Although women initially sought medical care during labour and delivery in an attempt to reduce the risks to their lives and health, those who gave birth in hospital during the latter part of the nineteenth century were in fact more likely to die or suffer injury as a result. Doctors understood the iatrogenic (i.e., doctor-caused) nature of the infections that often took women's lives (Wertz and Wertz, 1979). By the 1880s the campaign to prevent puerperal fever included recognition of the need for better sterilization methods and increased control over the whole process: 'doctors had to regard each woman as diseased, because birth provided the occasion and medicine the cause for infection' (Wertz and Wertz 1979: 128).[18] Birthing women were therefore subjected to a regimen of procedures that were ultimately controlling and dehumanizing. Thus, certain aspects of medical management arose primarily out of a desire to improve outcomes for childbearing women.

As well—and often overlooked in the literature—postpartum hospital stays early in the century involved 'social care' as well as medical care. Women typically had two to three weeks of care and help with their babies while they were in the hospital (Wertz and Wertz 1979). It could be argued that with the demise of a world in which women and men lived segregated lives—in 'separate spheres'—and the corresponding erosion of women's tight personal networks, 'social childbirth' at home became less and less feasible (Rapp and Ross 1986; Strong-Boag 1988). The extended hospital stays that replaced care in the home remained common until recently.

Giving Birth in Social Context: One Final Story

The risk that critics take in emphasizing the issue of control is that of implicitly condemning women who welcome medicalized birth as contributing to their own powerlessness and alienation. It may be more useful, instead, to direct attention to the *context* within which women's choices during childbirth are made. In her discussion of home birth, sociologist Barbara Katz Rothman (1982) argues that *a dignified transition to motherhood depends upon the receipt of adequate social support*. Perhaps, then, women who approach childbirth without much social support welcome the support of medical intervention instead, while those with strong support systems find themselves less in need of medical assistance. The story that follows—also that of a participant in the first-time parents study—shows how social support may be important on many levels during labour, delivery, and the early postpartum period.

Nora sat in her living room, along with her partner Glen and midwife Ellen, and contemplated the options now before her. She wanted very much to give birth at home—with Glen, Ellen, and friend Barb in attendance—and had made all her plans accordingly. She was well informed and in good health, and all signs during her pregnancy had indicated this would be a 'low-risk' birth. But as events were now unfolding, it seemed her plans might have to be revised. The prospect of a hospital birth frightened Nora and filled her with a deep sense of loss. She needed Ellen's guidance. Through long discussions during her pregnancy, she knew the midwife's philosophical approach matched her own, and that her skills and knowledge would help keep medical intervention at bay. Nora needed to feel certain she was making the right decision.

It was sixteen days past Nora's due date, and there were signs the baby's health might be compromised if the birth did not take place soon. Nora had tried to initiate labour with vigorous daily walks, but to no avail. Her doctor had advised an induction, and booked it for the following day—leaving the decision as to whether to follow through in the hands of Nora, Glen, and Ellen.

In the hours before the scheduled induction, Nora and Glen had tried more intensive means of inducing labour at home. Still there were no con-tractions. Now it was time for a decision. With Ellen's help they worked out a compromise. They would seek the lowest level of medical assistance—the topical application of a chemical hormone—to try to get contractions started. Afterwards they would return home in the hopes that labour would proceed uneventfully.

But once more, they were disappointed. Three times that day they went in for the treatment. By midnight Nora was having mild contractions, only to have them stop when she fell asleep. The next morning Ellen advised Nora that a full-scale induction was probably necessary to sustain her labour. Nora knew that meant the birth would take place in hospital.

By 9:30 a.m. that morning Nora, Glen, Ellen, and Barb were settled in a labour room. Much to her surprise, Nora found the hospital setting less alienating than she had anticipated. Ellen's presence was crucial in that regard. She provided trusted continuity of care, reassurance, advice, and help with comfort measures. She negotiated on Nora's behalf, kept her informed, and made her feel a part of each decision. And she handled all the necessary paper work, freeing Glen to devote his attention to his partner. For Nora, this kind of support turned an experience she had dreaded into one she later described as 'just wonderful'.

Labour progressed very slowly. At 2:30 p.m. in the afternoon the doctor advised rupturing the membranes to speed up progress. After consultation with Ellen, Nora agreed. However, within thirty seconds of the procedure, Nora went into what she later described as 'hyperactive labour'. The abruptness of the onset was overwhelming. Nora felt shocked and afraid. She doubted her ability to handle the contractions, and worried that something had gone terribly wrong with her labour. But once again her support team came through for her. Ellen reassured her that what she was experiencing was normal and helped her cope; Glen provided emotional support and grounding; and Barb offered practical help with comfort measures. The fear subsided and Nora was able to handle the contractions in spite of their strength.

After three hours of very high-intensity labour, dilation had progressed somewhat, but Nora was still nowhere near ready to deliver her baby. Feeling she could not continue for what promised to be several more hours, Nora requested an epidural. She later recalled the administration of the epidural as 'the worst part of the whole labour'. Having to stay motionless through contractions while the needle and catheter were inserted into her back felt to her like 'torture'. And in the end the medication proved effective for only about ten minutes.

But there was a good reason for the intensity of the labour at this point. Within twenty minutes Nora was ready to deliver her baby. She pushed for a little under an hour, with Ellen, Glen, and Barb acting as a 'cheering team'. This part of the labour was hard work and a bit overwhelming. But as Nora later explained, the excitement of her support team took away her fear. Baby Luke was born at 7:20 p.m., into the hands of the midwife. Nora, exhausted but proud, was grateful to be surrounded by three people she trusted to hold and comfort her newborn.

Nora, Glen, and Luke left the hospital three hours later. They felt confident, knowing they had round-the-clock access to advice and follow-up care from Ellen. Glen's mother and Nora's sister would do the housework for the first two weeks. And a strong network of friends (one of whom was also a midwife) would be close at hand to offer emotional support and practical advice on parenting—and when the time came, to share childcare.

Glen, whose work allowed him some flexibility, and who planned to be as much a part of his son's care as Nora, would be at home for the first two months of his child's life. The family's departure from the hospital immediately after the birth meant that Glen was never separated from Luke in the early days of learning how to parent. The strong bond that developed between father and son continued at least into Luke's third year, when the study ended.

Glen's involvement affected Nora's experience of the postpartum period as well. In contrast to nearly all the other mothers interviewed for this study, Nora felt there was someone else in her child's life whom she could trust absolutely with his care. Two months after Luke's birth—a point at which most mothers were struggling with lack of sleep, isolation, and overwork—Nora responded without hesitation to a question about how her life had changed, with 'I'm in *heaven*— just *heaven*'.

The Significance of the Immediate Social Context

Nora's story highlights the importance of the immediate social context within which women give birth. This context can shape decisions made during labour and delivery, and the woman's subjective experience of childbirth and early parenting. Key to the social context are the quality of the support received during labour and delivery, and more importantly, the *degree to which the responsibility for childrearing is shared* rather than falling on the shoulders of the mother alone. Nora was fortunate. She felt surrounded by supportive individuals on all counts. Another participant in the study, Karen, was more representative of the new mothers interviewed. She was very much alone in her responsibility for her daughter—both during and after labour. She and her husband Jerry had struck a traditional-style 'bargain' upon marriage: although Karen earned the higher income, enjoyed her work, and had the more stable employment history, she would care for their home and family while Jerry would take primary responsibility for their financial needs. In addition, Karen could not count on support from her family, who were busy with their own lives, or Jerry's family, with whom she was not close. Her close friends did not have children, and the activities she shared with them did not encompass her new role as a mother. Karen (quoted earlier as 'now pray[ing] to the epidural god') was more than happy to accept medical assistance during the birth of her child.

Labour in Social Context

In fact, a sensitivity to social context can shed light on women's responses to childbirth that appear anomalous from the perspective of the critique of medicalization. In general, the interviews with the forty first-time mothers and their partners indicate that women who could count on solid support from their partner and/or other relatives after they gave birth were more likely to resist medical management. Those whose support was weak or non-existent were more likely to find medical management acceptable, perhaps even desirable.

This was particularly evident where pain medication was concerned. Pain, or its avoidance, was clearly a major component of these women's experience; it was a central theme in two-thirds of their birth stories. Nearly all of the happiest, most empowered women reported having experienced very little pain—or very little that they could not handle—during labour. Nancy gave birth to twins with the help of an epidural. She recalled the experience as 'really, really terrific 'cause I didn't have the pain.' In contrast, the most distressed women often spoke at great length about the pain they experienced in labour. Jeanne recalled her labour as 'gruesome', and involving 'sheer and utter panic' because of the amount of pain she experienced.

Ironically, some women chose pain medication for reasons that appear consistent with the critique of medicalized childbirth—the desire to 'stay in control', to think and make decisions, and to act in a 'rational' manner, during labour and delivery. For these women, staying in control was premised on being able to manage pain. As Joanne described it,

> I didn't feel in control when I was feeling the contractions. But I could really concentrate with the epidural. That's what I liked about

it. I could really *think about what I was doing*. . . . [Otherwise], it was too much, I think, to comprehend.

Despite a long struggle to avoid medical intervention, Joanne felt that 'the fact that the epidural takes the pain away makes such a big difference 'cause . . . you use your head.' Several others found that they became 'human again' once they had obtained some measure of pain relief.

Indeed, staying in control meant different things to different women. Some defined it in a way that was consistent with the critique of medicalization: the ability to influence the course of their labours and deliveries through their input into decisions. But a few women defined control in a more limited way: simply remaining conscious, rational, and aware of what was happening. Both of these definitions suggest that women may experience labour as being 'out of control' for reasons other than the use of medical intervention per se. In fact, more important than control (in the sense of not being subjected to medical procedures) seems to be whether or not the woman's needs—as she defines them—are addressed during labour.

In addition, many of the women's comments suggest that pain management is connected to larger social factors. In a context where childcare is the personal responsibility of the parents, especially the mother, pain relief during labour can leave a woman feeling more able to assume the work of parenting immediately afterwards. Judy had these thoughts on the matter:

> Yeah, it was hard. I mean, being up for that many hours and then right away having to function again. Yeah it's hard, so . . . I can't imagine. Next time I'm just going to ask for the epidural and cesarean. Forget the labour.

The promise of pain relief, then, is that it gets women through a physically taxing experience in better shape to take on the heavy responsibilities of parenting. Women may seek pharmaceutical pain relief in a social context where this kind of assistance is readily available and commonly accepted, and where ongoing support for new parents is weak.[19]

In fact, strong social support does seem to reduce the need for pain medication in labour. Among the participants in the first-time parenting study, this kind of support was generally provided by the woman's partner. There was a strong relationship between whether or not the partner was generally supportive and whether or not (or how quickly) the woman sought pain medication in labour. Supportive partners were generally empathic to the woman, and as a result shared experiences and responsibilities related to the care of home and family (measured by their ongoing involvement in, and responsibility for, housework). Women whose partners were supportive in this way felt they could expect responsibility for the baby to be shared in the days, weeks, and years following the birth of their child.

Women whose partners offered little ongoing support generally requested pain relief early in their labours. Just over half of the women in the study fit this profile. On the other hand, women with solid support from their partners—a quarter of those in the study—most often went to great lengths to avoid medical intervention in labour. Two of these women gave birth without medical intervention, despite having very long and painful labours.[20]

Some women found that the support of those around them was fundamental to their ability to manage anxiety as well. Nearly all of the women in the study experienced anxiety during labour—in many cases directly connected to their anticipation of mounting pain. As Sally explained, 'I wasn't frightened of what was happening. I was more frightened of the pain. I didn't want to be left alone.' She found that as long as her partner stayed with her she could manage her anxiety. Likewise, Nora (in the third story) found that during her delivery 'They [her partner, friend,

and midwife] were all screaming [with excitement]. . . . And maybe that took away the fear. It was kind of their excitement.' Thus, in the case of both pain and anxiety, social support had a significant impact on decision-making about intervention in labour.

The Immediate Postpartum Period in Social Context

In addition, women's support networks seemed to protect them from experiencing the brief periods of emotional volatility commonly known as 'baby blues', which often occur a few days after giving birth. Women themselves made the connection between emotional volatility and lack of support. Those who experienced periods of tearfulness often hesitated to label their feelings baby blues, but saw them, instead, as responses to isolation and the overwhelming responsibilities they now faced. Erica referred to this condition as 'the shock of everything coming on'. Carla spoke more specifically about the enormity of the responsibilities and the lack of support systems encountered by new parents.

> It was so scary the first few days, you know. You don't know what you're supposed to do. . . . The awesome amount of responsibility sort of just hits you, and it was like, 'oh my God', you know, 'we're responsible for this little person now; nobody is going to help us.' Not that they helped us much in the hospital, but still you had that sort of fall-back position.

More than half of the women in the study had relatively little support beyond the first few days postpartum. All of these women experienced one or more episodes of baby blues. In several cases the episode occurred upon discharge from the hospital or upon the partner's return to work. In contrast, half of the women with substantial support had no baby blues—including two women with the most difficult births.[21]

In addition, social support seemed to offer some protection against the onset of more serious forms of emotional upset following the birth. Thus, for example, Margaret, who had a history of depression, insisted that the strong support of her mother-in-law kept her from suffering a relapse during this vulnerable time.

Being a Patient in Social Context

Personal responsibility for childrearing was not only a part of the broader social context within which these women gave birth; it was also actively produced by the medical institutions they attended. The postpartum hospital stays of many women in the study were affected by recently established 'early release' policies. These policies stipulated that women giving birth vaginally were released after twenty-four hours, and those giving birth by cesarean section were released after three days. This meant that there was little opportunity to attend any classes in breastfeeding or babycare that may have been offered. In addition, the vast majority of women in the study were given little or no individual instruction in, or assistance with, babycare by the nurses on the floor—even when they specifically requested it. Instead, they were left to figure out how to feed, change, and bathe their babies on their own. Sara's and Leslie's comments were typical: 'Once you're up there, you're on your own; you sink or swim'; 'You feel like you're left on your own right away.' Similarly, Robin was told, after repeated requests for instruction in bathing her baby, 'Just do the best you can. . . . It's your baby.' Worse still, when she asked the nurse on duty about the possibility of dehydration (her baby was admitted to the emergency ward two days after his release 'as dehydrated as a baby can be and still be alive'), she was told, 'What do you want me to do about it?' Occasionally advice was offered on breastfeeding; however, several women complained that the instructions they received were contradictory.[22]

Medicalized birth, then, 'gives birth' to a mother who typically has just had her own vulnerability underlined, at a time when she is about to undertake what may be the most demanding task of her life. It offers support at arms length—to the body and nothing more—and withdraws it abruptly following the delivery of a healthy baby. Because medicalized childbirth offers only strictly delimited assistance, it communicates the message that the woman is alone (with perhaps the help of a partner) in her long-term responsibility for the care of the new child. That motherhood is a private responsibility may be the most important message conveyed.

A few women, however, had very different experiences on the maternity wards in these same hospitals. These women were very appreciative of the care they received during their postpartum stay. Judy commented that, 'Everyone there [on the ward] was just *so* amazing. They were great.' Irene felt that, 'Everybody [on the ward] was just so wonderful and supportive.' Both Judy and Irene were recovering from cesarean sections. In fact, all of the women who felt positive about their post-partum hospital stay had medical problems known to the hospital staff. These women were 'patients' in a way that healthy new mothers were not. As such, they received both personal care and instruction in babycare—services not generally available to women without obvious medical need.

In addition, new mothers were more likely to elicit the support of partners when they were clearly suffering from a medical condition or recovering from surgery. Men whose wives were ill were far more likely than others to be doing the full range of housework and babycare. Their partners' medical problems seemed to facilitate their own involvement in babycare, making it both necessary and socially acceptable that they be active parents from the start. Although this was especially true for fathers who had expressed a strong desire to be involved in babycare before-hand, even men who had resisted their partners' earlier attempts to get them to share housework took on a much larger share when their wives were undeniably in need of recovery.

Ironically, then, becoming a patient—that is, having a highly medicalized birth—may enable new mothers to elicit various forms of help and support to which they would not otherwise have access. It may be, then, that the problem with medical management is not only that it alienates by supplanting a woman-centred process, but also that it substitutes for more general social support of women and their children, and offers instead only a limited kind of help. This suggests one possible reason for women's 'accommodation' to the medical model during labour and delivery: a realistic assessment of available options. Where general social supports for childbearing and parenting are in short supply, women's apparent acquiescence to medical control may be understood, despite its obvious limitations, as one means of strengthening personal resources to meet the enormous challenges ahead—of making labour 'work' for women.

Conclusion: Making Labour Work

It appears, then, that one way to reconcile the disjuncture between the critique of medicalized birth and women's subjective experiences and personal choices is to pay more attention to the social context within which childbirth takes place. Although women have played, and continue to play, a major role in determining how birth is managed, the choices they make cannot be understood in isolation from the social context in which they give birth. The circumstances shaping women's lives affect how they approach and experience childbirth.

Key to those circumstances is the extent to which responsibility for the work of childrearing falls to the mother. Our society offers remarkably few collectively organized social supports to new mothers. As a result, the support women receive—or do not receive—through personal networks can be critical to their experience of labour and the immediate postpartum period, and the actions they take to cope with that experience.

When we understand women's choices during birth in this light, we avoid the trap of blaming women for their 'acquiescence' to medical control. No less importantly, though, we broaden the focus of our efforts to change the situation: it becomes clear that, for women to be strengthened by their experience of childbearing, a variety of resources may need to be channelled in support of parenting.

Giving birth has the potential to work for women by empowering them to meet new challenges. But, as we have seen, making labour work in this way means paying attention to the more concrete meaning of 'work'—the labour involved in childrearing. By spreading this workload more evenly—that is, by providing ongoing social support for the tasks involved in raising a child—we may succeed in making labour work for women. Conversely, we should perhaps not be surprised, in the current era of cutbacks to social services, to see women making labour work for them by turning increasingly to the pharmaceutical and technical supports offered by modern obstetrics.

Notes

The research reported here was supported by the Social Science and Humanities Research Council of Canada (grant no. 410–94–0453) and the University of Toronto. We wish to thank Sherry Bartram for excellent research assistance; Liz Walker, Ann Bernardo, and Rebecca Fulton for timely transcribing; Emily Worts for helpful comments on an earlier draft of the chapter; and the forty women who shared their stories with us.

1. This is a type of anesthesia used in labour.

2. This procedure is known as artificial rupture of the membranes, or ARM. It may be performed to speed up a long labour, but in Meredith's case the doctor was looking for meconium (the contents of the unborn baby's intestines), which is often released into the waters when the baby is under stress during labour.

3. Epidural anesthesia involves the administration of a drug, similar to dental anesthesia, into the space between the membranes surrounding the spinal cord. The drug is administered through a needle and catheter in the lower back. The catheter is then taped securely to the woman's back to hold it in place. Some women experience non-life-threatening side effects like Meredith's.

4. Progress during the first stage of labour is measured in terms of the dilation (i.e., the diameter of the opening of the cervix, or neck of the womb). The cervix is generally closed prior to labour. As the labour progresses it gradually opens to a diameter of 10 centimetres, or full dilation. At this point the woman begins to actively work with the contractions to push the baby down through the birth canal. This is known as the second stage of labour.

5. Some women experience these sensations near the end of the first stage of labour. Meredith had them longer than most.

6. Forceps resemble a large set of salad servers. They fit around the baby's head, and may be used to accomplish delivery when the baby has moved partway through the birth canal. An alternative method involves the use of a vacuum extractor—a device not unlike a large suction cup that attaches to the baby's head to speed up the last stages of the delivery. Assisted deliveries are fairly common— but by no means universal—with first babies.

   A cesarean section is a surgical birth, in which the baby is delivered through an incision in the woman's lower abdomen. Except in dire emergencies (or at the woman's request) it is generally performed using epidural anesthesia, so the woman remains conscious. A shield is placed between her head and abdomen to block her view of the surgery.

7. The treatment referred to here is the application of prostaglandin gel to the woman's cervix. Prostaglandin helps soften the cervix to prepare it for dilation, and may initiate contractions as well.

8. The reason for this is that the placenta (the temporary organ that supplies the baby with nutrients and oxygen during pregnancy) may function less effectively as it 'ages'.

9. The electronic fetal monitor is a device used to continuously monitor the baby's heart rate and the length, strength, and spacing of the woman's contractions. External monitoring uses two belts around the woman's abdomen to attach the monitoring devices. Internal monitoring replaces one of the belts with a clip attached to the baby's scalp.

10. This type of incision is known as an episiotomy. It is performed to speed up the delivery or avoid a tear (both controversial reasons), or to permit the use of forceps or a vacuum extractor to assist in the delivery.

11. All names used are pseudonyms. The interviews with these women were part of a larger study of first-time parents, involving both members of the couple making this transition. All the couples who participated in the study had taken childbirth education classes, and were, in fact, recruited through these courses. All gave birth in a hospital.

    Interviews were conducted for a pilot study in 1991 and 1992, and for the main study in 1995 and 1996. Each member of the couple was interviewed separately, during pregnancy, when their child was two months old, around the child's first birthday, and around the child's second birthday. The man and woman were interviewed together when their child was six months old. Among other things, these interviews provided detailed information on the couple's division of household labour, and the support they received from friends and relatives. In addition, the woman was interviewed alone a few days after giving birth. Most of the material for this chapter is based on the latter set of interviews; however, background material is also drawn from the former set.

12. Because this latter shift occurred at a time when women were excluded from medical schools, medical management continued to mean management by men.

13. While midwives were being licensed and funded in Ontario by late 1993, only one of the women in the study of first-time parents had a midwife at her side.

14. This general observation is consistent with hundreds of stories gathered during Diana Worts's eight years as a childbirth educator and birth attendant.

15. This is a more accurate, but also more invasive, way to assess fetal well-being.

16. This was at a time when women had far more pregnancies than they do today.

17. Wealthy women were the first to invite doctors to attend their births, and their class status undoubtedly reinforced their power in the situation.

18. Puerperal fever is an 'infection of the genital tract after delivery'. It was eventually discovered to have been caused during the latter part of the nineteenth century by doctors who went directly from dissecting corpses to attending women in labour without washing their hands (Pritchard and MacDonald 1976: 757).

19. Interestingly, Leavitt (1986: 128) quotes turn-of-the-century discussion that links painless birth to the move toward women assuming individual responsibility for their babies: 'In scopolamine deliveries, the woman went to sleep, delivered her baby and woke up feeling vigorous: "so free from fatigue that she could leave her bed at once and care for her own baby".'

20. Some of these women also had daily help from their mother or mother-in-law. A small number of women in the study with very supportive partners faced unexpected circumstances, such as serious concerns about the baby's well-being, that necessitated the use of medical procedures despite the support they received.

21. All the remaining women with strong support experienced very disturbing events in the postpartum period, such as serious health problems or the presence of extremely disruptive in-laws, which complicated their reactions.

22. This general picture of dissatisfaction contrasts with most women's experience during labour and delivery. Many volunteered comments on how 'wonderful' the care on the labour floor had been. Again, this distinction is consistent with that found in stories collected during Diana Worts's eight years as a childbirth educator and birth attendant.

References

Arms, S. 1981. *Immaculate Deception: A New Look at Women and Childbirth in America* (Boston: Houghton Mifflin).

Arnup, K. 1994. *Education for Motherhood: Advice for Mothers in Twentieth-Century Canada* (Toronto: University of Toronto Press).

Ball, J. 1987. *Reactions to Motherhood: The Role of Postnatal Care* (Cambridge: Cambridge University Press).

Barclay, L., C. Andre, and P. Glover. 1989. 'Women's Business: The Challenge of Childbirth', *Midwifery* 5: 122–33.

Biggs, C.L. 1990. '"The Case of the Missing Midwives": A History of Midwifery in Ontario from 1795–1900' in *Delivering Motherhood: Maternal Ideologies and Practices in the 19th and 20th Centuries*, eds K. Arnup, A. Levesque, and R.R. Pierson (London: Routledge), 20–35.

Bourgeault, I. 1999. Personal communication.

Brown, S., J. Lumley, R. Small, and J. Astbury. 1994. *Missing Voices: The Experience of Motherhood* (Melbourne: Oxford University Press).

Chalmers, I., M. Enkin, and M. Keirse. 1989. *Effective Care in Pregnancy and Childbirth*, v. 1 and 2 (Toronto: Oxford University Press).

Chamberlain, M., B. Soderstrom, C. Kaitell, and P. Stewart. 1991. 'Consumer Interest in Alternatives to Physician-Centred Hospital Birth in Ottawa', *Midwifery* 7: 74–81.

Collins, N., C. Dunkel-Schetter, M. Lobel, and S. Scrimshaw. 1993. 'Social Support in Pregnancy: Psychosocial Correlates of Birth Outcomes and Postpartum Depression', *Journal of Personality and Social Psychology* 65 (6): 1243–58.

Davis-Floyd, R. 1990. 'The Role of Obstetrical Rituals in the Resolution of Cultural Anomaly', *Social Science and Medicine* 31 (2): 175–89.

———. 1992. *Birth as an American Rite of Passage.* (Berkeley: University of California Press).

———. 1994. 'The Technocratic Body: American Childbirth as Cultural Expression', *Social Science and Medicine* 38 (8): 1125–40.

Donegan, J. 1978. *Women and Men Midwives* (Westport, CT: Greenwood).

Eakins, P. 1986. *The American Way of Birth* (Philadelphia: Temple University Press).

Entwisle, B., and S. Doering. 1981. *The First Birth: An American Turning Point* (Baltimore: Johns Hopkins University).

Gordon, J. 1988. 'Childbirth: The Mother's Perspective' in *Feminist Research: Prospect and Retrospect*, ed. P. Tancred-Sheriff (Kingston and Montreal: McGill-Queen's University Press).

Graham, H., and A. Oakley. 1981. 'Competing Ideologies of Reproduction: Medical and Maternal Perspectives on Pregnancy' in *Women, Health and Reproduction*, ed. H. Roberts (London: Routledge & Kegan Paul).

Jordan, B. 1978. *Birth in Four Cultures: A Cross-Cultural Investigation of Childbirth in Yucatan, Holland, Sweden and the U.S.* (St Albans, VT: Eden Press).

Katz Rothman, B. 1982. *Giving Birth: Alternatives in Childbirth* (Harmondsworth: Penguin).

———. 1989. *Recreating Motherhood: Ideology and Technology in a Patriarchal Society* (New York: Norton).

Kay, M.A. 1982. *Anthropology of Human Birth* (Philadelphia: F.A. Davis).

Kitzinger, S. 1972. *The Experience of Childbirth* (Harmondsworth, UK: Penguin).

LaForce, H. 1990. 'The Different Stages of the Elimination of Midwives in Quebec' in *Delivering Motherhood: Maternal Ideologies and Practices in the 19th and 20th Centuries*, eds K. Arnup, A. Levesque, and R. Roach Pierson (London: Routledge), 36–50.

Lazurus, E. 1994. 'What Do Women Want?: Issues of Choice, Control and Class in Pregnancy and Childbirth', *Medical Anthropology Quarterly* 8 (1): 25–46.

Leavitt, J.W. 1986. *Brought to Bed: Childbearing in America, 1750 to 1950* (New York: Oxford).

MacCormack, C. 1982. *Ethnography of Fertility and Birth* (London: Academic Press).

Martin. E. 1987. *The Woman in the Body: A Cultural Analysis of Reproduction* (Boston: Beacon).

McIntosh, J. 1989. 'Models of Childbirth and Social Class: A Study of Eighty Working-Class Primagravidae', *Midwives, Research and Childbirth* 1: 189–214.

Michaelson, K. ed. 1988. *Childbirth in America: Anthropological Perspectives* (Westport, CT: Bergin & Garvey).

Mitford, J. 1992. *The American Way of Birth* (London: Victoria Golancz).

Nelson, M. 1983. 'Working-Class Women, Middle-Class Women and Models of Childbirth', *Social Problems* 30 (3): 284–97.

Oakley, A. 1980a. *Becoming a Mother* (New York: Schocken).

———. 1980b. *Women Confined: Towards a Sociology of Childbirth* (Oxford: Martin Robertson).

———. 1984. *The Captured Womb: A History of the Medical Care of Pregnant Women* (Oxford: Basil Blackwell).

Pritchard, J.A., and P.C. MacDonald. 1976. *Williams Obstetrics*, 15th edn (New York: Appleton-Century-Crofts).

Priya, J. 1992. *Birth Traditions and Modern Pregnancy Care* (Shaftesbury, Dorset: Element Books).

Rapp, R., and E. Ross. 1986. 'The 1920s: Feminism, Consumerism, and Political Backlash in the United States' in *Women in Culture and Politics: A Century of Change*, eds J. Friedlander, B.W. Cook, A. Kessler-Harris, and C. Smith-Rosenberg (Bloomington: Indiana University Press), 52–61.

Romalis, S. 1981. *Childbirth: Alternatives to Medical Control* (Austin: University of Texas Press).

Sargent, C., and N. Stark. 1989. 'Childbirth Education and Childbirth Models: Parental Perspectives on Control, Anesthesia, and Technological Intervention in the Birth Process', *Medical Anthropology Quarterly* 3 (1): 36–51.

Strong-Boag, V. 1988. *The New Day Recalled: Lives of Girls and Women in English Canada, 1919–1939* (Markham, ON: Penguin).

Tew, M. 1995. *Safer Childbirth?* (London: Chapman & Hall).

Wertz, R., and D. Wertz. 1979. *Lying In: A History of Childbirth in America* (New York: Schocken).

Chapter 19

For many Canadians, becoming parents means becoming much more conventional in terms of gender roles. This essay reports the findings of a small study consisting of in-depth interviews of women and men as they made the transition from preg- *nancy to parenthood, and as they negotiated the challenges of the first year of their baby's life. What emerges is a summary of the variety of factors that move men and women to specialize their family work and responsibilities.*

Reproducing Difference: Changes in the Lives of Partners Becoming Parents

Bonnie Fox

It has long been assumed by feminists that women's subordination is produced in large part in 'the family' (Gilman 1898; Friedan 1963; Firestone 1970; Mitchell 1971; Rowbotham 1973). Such an assumption seems to contradict many women's experiences of family as a 'haven in a heartless world', the place where they find love, support, and personal fulfillment. Indeed, for many women of colour, family has constituted protection from and resistance to the oppressive cultures in which they live (Caulfield 1975; Gutman 1976; Davis 1981).

Perhaps it is because feminist analysis is often about the organization of society as a whole that our arguments seem to contradict women's experience. An important feminist argument is that in heterosexual nuclear families the sexual division of labour—whereby women are responsible for the domestic sphere and men for breadwinning—channel resources, power, and privilege to men and away from women (see Luxton 1980). Whether individual women in relationships that are characterized by conventional divisions of labour feel oppressed as wives, housewives, and mothers is another matter, however.

Yet, on the matter of the division of household work, women's experiences and feminist analyses have converged over time. Largely because of the women's liberation movement women have come to expect more of their male partners. Consequently, the sexual division of labour is not only at the heart of gender inequality, it is also more and more perceived as such by individual women.

Despite the importance of the sexual division of household labour to the perpetuation of gender inequality, there has been relatively little attempt empirically to examine its development in the daily lives of women and men. Theoretical discussions have tended to imply that the division of household work is static, and determined largely by the separation of public and private production and gendering of these arenas—the fact that certain work is seen as 'men's' and other work is seen as 'women's'. That the division of responsibilities and work evolves, that it is 'negotiated' as a relationship or family develops, has scarcely been explored.

What is also interesting about discussions of the sexual division of labour is how rarely motherhood is the centre of attention. Empirical examinations of household work—whether or not by feminists—often fail to distinguish motherwork from housework (except Luxton 1980).[1] More important, the significance of the transition to parenthood in the negotiation of a division of labour and responsibility is often overlooked.[2]

In fact, parenthood may be the most important experience producing gender differences in this society. These days, some women are able to carve out daily lives that bear a strong resemblance to those of their male partners—labour-market earnings and opportunity differentials aside. It is when partners become parents that difficult choices must be made that often force differences in women's and men's lives.

Aside from its significance for gender inequality, parenthood also holds the promise of change towards gender equality. Men who take on more housework give up obvious privilege, but those who develop close relationships with their children by caring for them daily gain something very precious. Indeed, sociological research shows that in instances where men take on more domestic labour, they do more childcare than housework (Goldscheider and Waite 1991; Gerson 1994). In short, in order to understand both the origins of inequality between men and women in intimate relationships, and where changes in gender inequality are most likely to occur, a focus on parenthood is long overdue.

Mothering and Gender Inequality

Feminist theorists have developed a number of important insights about the ways in which motherhood reproduces gender inequality. Perhaps most influential is Nancy Chodorow's (1978) argument, which focuses on the future generations mothers create, and not on mothers themselves. Asserting that boys and girls develop differently as they acquire gender identity in a society where women alone mother, Chodorow attempts to show how men and women acquire different 'relational capacities'. Accordingly, she perpetuates a tradition common to social scientists—namely, a focus on parents' influence on their children (LaRossa and LaRossa 1981). The

other half of the story remains unexplored. As Amy Rossiter (1988: 15) has noted,

> the relationship between mothering and patriarchy can only be understood if we look not only at how women reproduce Mothering, but at how Mothering reproduces Women. Nancy Chodorow may well have answered the question of why women want to mother; but she neglected to inquire how the enactment of that desire produces Woman.

Research by feminist social scientists on the daily experiences of mothers of young children shows clearly how privatized childcare oppresses women, inducing stress and constraining their lives in a variety of ways (Gavron 1966; Rosenberg 1987; Boulton 1983).[3] Jessie Bernard's (1974) claim that the way mothering is organized is bad for both mothers and children is substantiated by a number of studies that document how mothers suffer from a dearth of social supports and from social isolation (Gavron 1966; Boulton 1983; Rosenberg 1987). Indeed, depression and stress are likely accompaniments to full-time mothering, especially of babies, since the absence of control over time makes for a high-demand, low-control work situation (Rosenberg 1987 and Chapter 20 this text). If there are parallel but different stresses for new fathers, however, they remain largely uncovered since these insightful studies only examine women's experience (except Lewis 1986).

Research by sociologists indicates that becoming a parent—in a world organized as ours is—may be the most significant experience producing gender differences today. The anticipation of mothering, more than anything else, seems to distinguish girls from boys. That is, while the psychological evidence on gender differences in personality shows no significant differences (Maccoby and Jacklin 1974; Tavris 1992), evidence on high-school students' expectations about their future family roles does show major differences.

For example, Baker's (1985) study of Canadian high-school students found that girls planned to prioritize domestic responsibilities while boys did not. Gaskell's (1983 and Chapter 20 this text) study of working-class Vancouver girls leaving high school in the late 1970s showed the same thing. More important, Gaskell found that family, children, and relationships took priority for girls not because they were attracted to domesticity, but partly because they assumed that babies needed full-time mothers. Popular beliefs about motherhood are clearly important in shaping women's lives.

A number of researchers—mostly psychologists—have examined the transition to parenthood. The most thorough of these studies, which examines both fathers and mothers, is by psychologists Cowan and Cowan (1992). While they followed a large number of couples over several years, Cowan and Cowan focused on children's development and adjustment, which were assumed to be affected tremendously by the quality of their parents' relationship. Findings about the nature of parents' experiences constitute almost a backdrop to this issue. Nevertheless, Cowan and Cowan found that among the differences in the experiences of mothers and fathers was an increase in the sexual division of housework and an increased devotion to paid work by men. Research by sociologists, usually involving survey data, has also reported a relationship between a traditional division of labour and parenthood (LaRossa and LaRossa 1981).

Research shows that mothers spend far more time providing care for their children than fathers do—twice as much when employed and, of course, far more when at home full time (LaRossa and LaRossa 1981). Studies of fathers indicate that they tend to assume the roles of mother's helper and baby's playmate, rather than primary caregiver (Lewis 1986), and that they rarely assume primary responsibility for their children. Overall, while there is evidence from a variety of studies that parenthood creates gender differences, those differences and their creation are seldom the objects of inquiry.

Recent work by Canadian feminists has begun to address this neglected issue. Blain (1991) has examined the ways in which class and gender, and especially discourses about gender, affect the ways people fulfill the responsibilities of parenthood, and she argues that parenthood 'constitutes' gender. More than any other researcher, McMahon (1995) has developed an argument that parenthood 'engenders' people. Her argument focuses on how the experience of mothering shapes women's identities. Her insightful work calls for complementary examinations of how parenting creates gender differences in more material ways.

The Study

To pursue the question of parenthood and gender difference, I interviewed ten white heterosexual couples over the course of the last trimester of the women's pregnancies and the first year in which they were parents.[4] Five couples were middle-class, one was middle-class but low-income, another involved a professional women and a working-class man, and three were working class.

The interviews were structured, but the questions open-ended. Interviews took place separately, with the women in the latter part of the pregnancy, shortly after the birth, and at two months, six months, and a year after the birth. The men were interviewed late in the pregnancy, at two months of parenthood, and at a year of parenthood; half of the men were also interviewed at the six-month period.

Becoming a Mother, Becoming a Father

Gender differences were exacerbated and often created as these people became parents. Even couples who had never before divided the domestic work quickly developed a pattern where each person specialized with respect to responsibilities and, to a lesser extent, work. All of the women became primary caregivers, and, as mothers, the people most responsible for their babies' well-being. At the same time, seven of the ten men became noticeably more serious, even aggressive, about their jobs or careers. Indeed, the role of breadwinner seemed more salient to all of the men when they became fathers.

Studying the way mothers and fathers divide responsibility and work between them is not easy. The most influential decision—that the woman stay home with her baby—is often so automatic that it is hard to distinguish the factors responsible for that outcome. The first factor in the decision is the conviction that a baby is best cared for at home by one of its parents, at least during the first year of its life (unless the economic situation precludes it). All of these first-time parents believed it was important to care for their baby at home. Second, all of these mothers wanted to breastfeed their babies. The decision to breastfeed virtually precluded a decision not to stay home—given the organization of paid work. At the same time, these women's commitment to breastfeeding was affected by their decision to stay home. That decisions about breastfeeding were shaped by other decisions is clear in the patterns that developed over the year. All three babies who were breastfed through the entire year had mothers who stayed home with them full-time. Three women (Nancy, Jennifer, and Sophia[5]) weaned their babies in order to go back to paid work; two women who were home all year (Jane and Susan) weaned their babies in an effort to gain some autonomy (especially since weaning made it easier to leave them with sitters or relatives). (See Appendix.)

The gender gap in earnings potential was also very important in determining that the mother stay home—and thus take on the bulk of childcare and assume primary responsibility for the baby. While all of the women had contributed some earnings to the household income the year of their pregnancy, only one of them (Jennifer, a career woman) was the primary earner in her household, and another (Sally) earned about as much as her partner (doing the same kind of

work). In contrast, at the time of their pregnancy, three of the women (Susan, Ruth, and Mary) were adding very little to household finances: they were either primarily studying or taking occasional freelance jobs. The five other women earned between one-fifth and one-third of the household income. Three women (Jane, Jennifer, and Sophia) were in jobs that allowed them to take paid maternity leaves.

At the time of the pregnancy, then, in all but two of the households, the man was the primary earner. In one household, the man left freelance work and took a regular, full-time job while his wife was pregnant—putting him also in the position of chief breadwinner. So, for nine of the ten couples, by the time the baby was born there were significant gender differences with respect to financial contributions. Decisions about who was to do what work in the home must be considered in light of this difference. In the one household where the man was not the primary breadwinner, Jennifer was home on maternity leave while Joe continued working outside the home—again setting up a situation where it was easiest for the mother to become the primary parent, at least initially.

Economic considerations also shaped the couples' decisions about how long the women remained at home full-time. Six women stayed home virtually all year; one of them (Jane) even quit paid employment to do so. Only one of the women (Susan) stayed away from paid employment and school all year, however. Her husband made considerably more money than the other men, and the gap between his and her potential and actual incomes was the largest in the group—Susan had been doing only occasional freelance jobs before getting pregnant.

What distinguished Susan and the five other women who virtually stayed home all year—occasionally earning money or attending classes—was the absence either of dire need or a high 'opportunity cost' to staying home (i.e., foregoing high wages/salaries). In all but one case (Mary's), their partners had good careers or jobs. In Mary's case, where money was very tight, there were two babies to care for—Mary and Greg had twins. Two of the women (Ruth and Mary) were still students, who resumed their studies part-time before the year ended. Two other women (Lisa and Sally) were artists—and motivated to make the kind of investment necessary for financial success.

Of the four couples where the woman returned to paid employment before the year's end (in three cases, full-time), two were low-income and clearly struggling (Nancy and Simon, and Claire and Stephen) and another was a working-class couple (Sophia and Max) whose income was 'adequate' only because the man worked very long hours (a strategy seen as problematic). In the fourth case, Jennifer earned considerably more than Joe, and indeed had a successful career: she returned to paid employment at the end of her maternity/parental leave. Without Jennifer's paycheque this family would have had a very low income.

Economics aside, staying home with a baby has its attractions. Nearly all of the babies had been planned, and all were very welcome by the time of their birth. In fact, about half of the mothers were absolutely awed by their babies from the very beginning of the babies' lives; for them the possibility of missing any of their babies' daily experiences was a huge cost they attached to reentry to paid employment. Moreover, for women who had held paid jobs for years, pregnancy and even motherhood presented the opportunity to take 'time out', to give up anxieties about appearance and weight, and temporarily abandon the need to accomplish things (in market terms). For some, pregnancy was even a time to indulge themselves by taking care of themselves.

For other women, motherhood represented a clear role or life's occupation when they had not succeeded in marketplace terms. In other words, staying home was more than an economic decision: for some women it solved a kind of identity problem.

As for the men, becoming a parent commonly meant becoming more serious about breadwin-

ning. One man (Charles) always answered my inquiries about 'what life is like these days' with reference to success at work (despite my purpose of studying parenthood). While Charles was very involved in providing care for his baby when he was at home, fatherhood for him seemed to be equated first and foremost with breadwinning. Simon, who was a skilled tradesman, reported that since becoming a father he had a 'totally' different stance vis-à-vis his boss: he had become more aggressive. Jake switched from contract work at home to a regular full-time job when Sally was pregnant. Max, who worked on an assembly line, put in very long hours, taking all the overtime he could get long after his baby was born, despite intentions of cutting back. Sam took a job out of town four days a week when his baby was about six months old, for the sake of a higher salary. Greg changed jobs to earn more money before the year was up, and Joe was looking for a second job by the end of the first year.

At minimum, becoming a father increased the men's concern about money—especially since all of the women had earned at least some money before the birth and then stayed home several months afterwards. More than money was at issue, though. The huge sense of responsibility that the women felt upon the arrival of their babies was shared by the men. And fatherhood translated, in varying degrees, into the responsibility to provide financial support. Stephen, who seemed the least driven to succeed financially, said 'I never used to worry about money. Now I feel much more responsible.'

Overall, every couple experienced a shift in their division of labour, such that the women became responsible for most of the childcare and the men concentrated on breadwinning. By no means, though, was that division of work absolute. All fathers did childcare, though in varying amounts, and even the women who stayed home typically continued to earn some money or take courses. Jane quit her job, but did some freelance work at home; Ruth, Lisa, and

Mary all resumed their courses or training during their year at home; Susan did briefly, but then decided to wait.

While none of the couple divided the work completely, the responsibility for the babies' daily needs was exclusively held by the women. Mothers nursed their babies and later decided what solid foods to feed them and when, they decided when and whether their sleeping should be put on a schedule, they made the doctors appointments, etc.

The sense of responsibility was a constant in these women's experiences of parenthood, and it was usually their largest concern about motherhood. That this responsibility is the product of a society that privatizes childcare must be recognized. In turn, as the literature has made clear, this responsibility can result in considerable stress for women (see Rosenberg 1987 and Chapter 20 this text). At the same time, the responsibility entailed some rights over the child. In several cases, parents had disagreements about some aspect of parenting; in every such case the woman's preference prevailed.

For instance, Nancy persuaded Simon that their two month old should remain in bed when put there at night, even when he was crying and Simon felt he should be picked up. Similarly, Stephen wanted their baby fed immediately when he cried, but Claire sometimes waited until she had finished what she was doing. Both cases show very responsive fathers with less power in the situation than the women who bore the chief consequences of whatever course of action was taken.[6] More common, though, were cases where the woman defined how to care for the baby because her partner was not doing the job according to her standards. Joe, for example, was not patient enough with his baby when he fed him, so Jennifer regularly did the feeding—and thus got more time with her baby who, once she went back to work, spent most of his day (Monday through Friday) at a babysitter's. In short, there were some advantages to being primarily respon-

sible for the baby. Yet, whether experienced positively or negatively, or a bit of both, for all the couples this was the woman's responsibility.

From Motherwork to Housework

One of the chief consequences of the increased division of labour these couples experienced as they became parents was a tendency for the burden of housework to shift more solidly onto the women's shoulders, despite the demanding nature of babycare. In half the couples, the woman was doing more of the housework at the end of the first year of parenthood than before becoming a parent. The shift is especially significant given that most of these women reported doing more housework in their last trimester of pregnancy, because they were home, than they had before. That is, they began parenthood already bearing an increased amount of housework. For a sixth couple (Susan and Charles), the division of housework was very conventional before the birth and remained so afterwards— Susan did nearly all the necessary daily tasks except some after-dinner clean-up. For the four other couples, the women's share of the housework had increased, but towards the end of the first year it shifted back towards the men. So, by the year's end, these four women were doing relatively less than at the beginning.

The processes by which the division of labour shifted between the women and the men were very complex. The most dramatic shift involved a couple (Jane and Tom) who had shared the housework nearly equally in the past, though Jane had borne the ultimate responsibility for running the household. Jane described a progressive reduction over time in the amount of housework Tom did, first with marriage, then with her pregnancy and then when they became parents. Similarly, her life had changed from being like her partner's—in that she had worked long hours away from home, often eaten out at night with women friends or with him, and scarcely was home—to increasing home-centredness. Motherhood, in fact, 'domesticated' Jane. When she stayed home late in her pregnancy, she began to pay more attention to the state of her home (i.e., its appearance and cleanliness). Being home itself had an effect on Jane's orientation, and she stayed home the first year of motherhood.

Jane also encouraged Tom to be with the baby rather than do housework when he was home. She did so for two reasons. First, she experienced housework as a 'break' from the baby because it allowed her to be alone—even though that solitude came at the cost of standing over a kitchen sink. Second, the father-child relationship took precedence over the issue of Tom's contribution to the housework, for Jane and, I suspect, for other women. She and other women in the study worked at ensuring that a relationship developed between their partners and the baby—if the men were not actively doing so themselves.

More was going on in this case, however. When pregnant (and apparently without thinking), Jane had prefaced a statement with, 'Now that I'm a woman. . . .' And at the end of the year, looking back, she explained that she had taken on the responsibility for the baby and all the housework because that was what she thought 'women were supposed to do'. Jane's mother had done so, and such a strong role model (in Jane's words) had confirmed the validity of that gender ideology.

For four other couples—including Susan and Charles, who began and ended the first year of parenthood with Susan doing much of the work in the home—the main reason why the woman did so much of the housework was that she was home and her partner was away much of the time. In two of these cases (Lisa and Sam, and Sally and Jake), the men had done at least as much housework as the women before parenthood, but these were the only couples where this was true. Sam did most of it because Lisa's back problems prevented her from doing many household chores, and Jake was a 'neat freak' who 'saw what needed doing' before Sally did. For both couples, things changed with parenthood because of the importance of the men's breadwinning: Sam took a much more lucrative job out of town before the year ended, leaving Lisa alone four days each week, and Jake began a regular full-time job outside the home during Sally's pregnancy. Both men did housework on weekends, and apparently as much as they could, but their wives ended up with considerably more housework than before they became parents.

In another of these four cases (that of Nancy and Simon), the burden of housework dramatically shifted towards the woman by the second month of parenthood. But it shifted back to near sharing when she went out to paid work full-time. Thereafter, Nancy did more housework only because she was home earlier than Simon and thus did most of the cooking. Simon began the housecleaning on Saturdays before Nancy got out of bed.

In the one household where the woman did nearly all of the housework before and during the first year of parenthood, Susan had battled with Charles about sharing housework for years. Reluctantly and gradually she had accepted most of the daily household responsibilities well before the pregnancy, and only after she began doing freelance work at home. In this case, pregnancy and parenthood reinforced a very conventional pattern which had developed earlier in connection with the woman being home.

The final case in which housework shifted towards the woman illustrates yet another pattern. For this couple (Claire and Stephen), time at home was not the issue: Stephen was home as much as Claire was. The key dynamic for them was that Claire seemed driven to keep the household organized and clean—and Stephen did not. In addition to this gender difference, Stephen had a Ph.D. but had not yet found a permanent job. His need to do research and write was continually pulling him away from domestic concerns (and Claire encouraged the prioritization of his writing). This pattern was present in other couples as well, however. Many women were similarly driven; only the rare man noticed dust and disorder.

Overall, four of the six women who were at home all year took on a greater share of the housework. So, simply being home was an important factor in the increased division of household work. At the same time, it should be noted that all of these ten mothers had been responsible for the running of the home before becoming parents, even when they worked outside the home as much as their partners. In some cases the workload was nearly balanced, in terms of time, but always the woman bore the ultimate responsibility—as evidenced by the fact that she made the grocery lists, and typically had to push her partner to do housework. The gender difference in household workload was only enhanced by parenthood and the fact that the women stayed home. In turn, part of what occurred was that because paid work so absorbed the men's time, the women were motivated to trade off men's share of the housework against their relationship with their children.

In four of the ten couples the woman was doing somewhat less housework at the end of the year than before becoming a parent. For all of these women, the improvement came towards the end of the year, and either because the women simply could not do all the work that was required or because they persistently pushed their partners to do more. In the case of the career woman, Jennifer, who returned to her paid employment at the end of her maternity leave, a cleaning woman was hired to do most of the cleaning, so mainly cooking remained. That became Joe's duty because Jennifer's employment kept her at the office until late in the day, while he was home much of the afternoon. On balance, then, Joe did more of the housework by the end of the year than at the start.

For two couples (Ruth and David, and Mary and Greg), the women—both students whose studies were mostly suspended—stayed home all year, and had periodic 'showdowns' with their partners that moved the men to take on more

housework. In the final couple, Sophia had always done the bulk of the housework. After she returned to her full-time paid job she found she simply could not do as much as she had. Max began doing laundry when she fell so far behind he was regularly without clean clothes.

Motherwork, Fatherwork

As in other studies, the men in this study were more likely to do childcare than housework. While only four men (Simon, David, Sam, and Jake) tried to share the housework—that is, do nearly half of it—seven of these new fathers were doing around half the childcare (and sometimes more) when they were home (which, from Monday to Friday, was usually a very small portion of the day).

It is not clear what factors accounted for how involved fathers were with their babies. Neither the amount of time spent breadwinning nor the seriousness attached to that responsibility explained how much care these men gave their babies. Some of the men working extremely long hours outside the home were the fathers who did half the basic babycare when they were home. On the other hand, men who had lots of time to spend with their babies did not necessarily do so. Tom was home the first two months of parenthood but failed to alter his usual schedule of daily workouts and sports during those early months of parenthood; he provided very little babycare.

The men more likely to assume responsibility for housework were also more likely to do childcare, although there were cases where the women were doing the vast majority of household tasks and the men were doing half the childcare or more when home. All the fathers clearly loved their babies. Yet what seemed to move some of them to take on childcare duties when at home was empathy with and concern about their partner. When asked what a baby needs from its father (at two months), Charles said, 'I think what the father can do is take a bit of pressure off the mother. . . . I see guys go on with their sports, etc.

But it's not fair. I just can't do that to [Susan].' And Sam explained, 'I'm just trying to share the load, and be fair about it.'

So, there was a considerably more even division of childcare than housework. At the same time, however, men frequently were involved in babycare while the women were doing housework: they did childcare instead of housework (in part, as we saw, with their partner's encouragement). Their involvement with the baby did not free up the women's time.

Time Deprivation and Other Stresses

While other studies have found sleep deprivation to be the main difficulty in adjusting to life with a baby, the women here (after the first two months) found the absence of time for themselves to be the hardest aspect of motherhood. Uniformly positive about motherhood, and apparently increasingly confident about their abilities over the course of the year, these women's faces typically clouded over only when they talked about the issue of time. In turn, the degree to which they had time seemed to summarize something more fundamental: that the daily lives of these women had 'totally changed', while that was obviously true for only a couple of the men (Greg and Jake).[7] As Jennifer stated, Joe's life had 'an addition; mine is totally changed'.

There was a gender difference in the amount of time people had, in consequence of the gendered division of work and responsibility. Of the ten couples in the study, five couples demonstrated a sizeable difference between his and her time, and at least one more couple showed a subtle difference. That is, five of the women reported having absolutely no spare time 'for myself' while their male partners clearly had at least some time to do as they wanted. In the extreme case, Tom reported (after his wife had pointed it out shortly before the interview) that his life 'had not changed at all' since the birth of this baby. Other men had discretionary time as well, though—one

man to continue his involvement in sports, another to remain active in a study group, and another to spend much of the afternoons at home while his wife was at work and his baby was with a sitter. A fifth man, Stephen, an unemployed Ph.D., was continually encouraged by his partner, Claire, to be in his study in front of the computer while she did the housework and childcare. All the partners of these men admitted to an absence of any time for themselves.

At the same time, half of the fathers seemed nearly as consumed by their responsibilities as their partners. These men had no discretionary time in the sense that all of their usual social activities had been dropped, they came directly home after work and did either childcare or housework for the rest of the day. Their sleep deprivation in the early months was as apparent as their partners'.

Even for these five couples, though, there was a significant difference between the pace of the women's daily lives and those of the men. Several of the men commented that although their time at their paid job was hectic it was nothing in comparison with their wives' time at home. Even in a pressured job there is usually time for oneself during the day or at lunch, and some of the men were quite aware of these small luxuries.

The stresses on these new mothers were clear. For the first two months, a couple of them reported 'having no life', and later more of the women talked about 'feeling trapped'. The problem was feeling socially isolated and particularly of being relatively alone in the midst of what seemed like a huge, undefined responsibility. Feeling overwhelmed and therefore anxious was most common when the baby was very young, but some mothers found their one year olds to be even more demanding than newborns. Both isolation and anxiety in the face of their responsibility were relieved tremendously for women who had the frequent company of other new mothers. Jane had many old friends with babies, and both Jennifer and Mary found participation in a new mothers' group organized by the city's public health department 'made all the difference in the world'. The friends they made there they saw many times a week.

An important aspect of the isolation of full-time mothers is the invisibility and lack of social recognition of their work. Several of these mothers were caught up in a struggle to 'accomplish something' in their endless days at home—that is, something in addition to keeping the baby satisfied. Socially unrewarded by their motherwork, this drive in part explained why some of the women did so much housework and met such high standards of housekeeping.

The stresses on the men were different, and in some cases less heavy than those faced by the women. The biggest source of stress for the new fathers was the feeling of being pulled in two directions, between their paid work and their family responsibilities. Half of the men suffered from this tension—a tension usually seen as unique to women who work outside the home. For the two working-class men, earning what they felt was a decent amount of money required about 60 hours of work a week. Little time was left for family. In Max's case, time spent with family often meant he could not return to work on time. But three of the other fathers experienced this contradictory pull, and tore themselves away from their paid work only out of concern for their partners and their relationship.

Income and class differences made for stunning differences in men's experiences of early fatherhood. The four low-income earners felt money worries were the hardest adjustment they had to make to parenthood. Money worries had become a perpetual source of stress for them. The middle-class men with comfortable earnings complained instead of a shortage of time for themselves and their leisure pursuits.

These new fathers experienced another stress which involved the tension generated by the disparity between their partners' and their own expectations and standards about parenthood. In three cases, the women defined how to carry out

babycare tasks in a way that left the men feeling inadequate. These men's relationships with their babies and with their partners suffered as a result.

Strains in the adults' relationship are a common outcome of becoming parents. Six couples experienced a persistent strain in their relationship, and not only because they had no time for each other. The main difficulty seemed to be that the women needed a tremendous amount of support from their partners, both emotional and practical. If the response was not forthcoming there was tension. And for the men who were also under stress, that response came with difficulty. The women also did not welcome demands from their partners for the satisfaction of their own needs. As Jennifer said, 'I need [Joe] to let me devote all my time to this baby.' Joe reported that fathers 'sort of get displaced'.

Sex was especially problematic for many of the couples. All the women were less interested in sex, especially during the period they were breastfeeding their babies. Fatigue, the overwhelming sense of responsibility for the baby, and hormonal changes add to the 'love affair' between women and their babies to diminish women's desire for sex. That new parents spend so much of their time doing different kinds of work makes sexual intimacy even more difficult.

Accounting for the Differences

For these couples parenthood has meant increased differences between the lives of the women and the men with respect to responsibility, work, and time. There were several reasons why the women's and men's lives tended to diverge in this first year of parenthood.

First and most obvious was the effect of women's disadvantage in the labour market relative to men. Nine of the ten women were in worse positions in the labour market than their male partners. In turn, those women without a clear alternative to homemaking and full-time mothering—or the pressing need to return to paid work—seemed to be more absorbed in mother-hood than the other women. Their identity was more wrapped up with being a mother,[8] and they subordinated their own needs to those of their babies more than the other women did. Of course, in turn, this stance meant a reduced like-lihood of returning to paid work or school.[9]

There were two cases in which full-time homemaking—at least over the next few years—seemed the likely future of these new mothers. Susan (who had a BA) had never developed a clear direction in her work history, had moved from one contract job to another, and was tentatively plan-ning to acquire more educational credentials at the time she got pregnant. Ruth, who was an appar-ently very talented young artist/performer, was still studying and training a few hours a week but very unsure about whether she could have a career. Their partners both had well-paid careers. Susan reported a continuing dilemma about whether to 'go back to work' or not; she read 'everything she could get her hands on' about the decision to stay home or not. Ruth waivered tremendously throughout the year in her determi-nation to pursue a career—in the face of David's active discouragement and hindrance. Both were pregnant again before that first year of mother-hood was over; only one other woman was.

At minimum, the fact that they were home all year, had an obviously large responsibility and nothing to pull them away from it contributed to differences between their and their partners' ori-entations to household responsibilities. Their cir-cumstances did not simply shape their lives, though: these were also two of the four women who continually and persistently pushed their partners to share the household work—with good results, at least in the case of childcare.

Second, simple male power and privilege influenced the division of labour and responsi-bility, in at least one case. David, a professional, simply refused to relinquish all of his discre-tionary time despite a concerted protest by his partner. Ruth described him as 'selfish' (with

agony and disbelief in her voice). David's posi-tion was that he would be 'unhappy' if he had to do any more housework or childcare than he was already doing—despite his wife's periodic 'explo-sions' (in her words) about how unhappy she was with his failure to share the load. Tom—whose life 'didn't change' with parenthood—failed to participate in the work much, but did so when asked (the few times he was): Jane allowed him his time, and in fact worked to ensure his life did not change with parenthood.

A third factor was also at work in many of the cases. Gender ideology, which equates woman-hood with meeting people's needs, and the popu-lar discourse about motherhood, which under-lines mothers' responsibilities, were clearly influential for all the women. Jane illustrated these effects clearly. At the end of the year—act-ing as if she had emerged from a deep sleep—Jane said that she had 'spent the whole year trying to make his [Tom's] life easy'. As previously men-tioned, her explanation was that she thought that was what women did.

This obviously influential gender ideology was reinforced by common-sense ideas about motherhood. This couple and all the others felt strongly that babies were best cared for at home by their parents (though not necessarily by their mothers; fathers would also do). As well, Tom firmly believed in the 'naturalness' of mother-hood—women's natural maternal instincts. Some of the other men also referred to their partners' greater 'natural' affinity for mothering. Again, though, life is not simple: at the year's end, Jane had refused to move to a small town where Tom had just gotten the job offer he had been seeking for over a year, and she was about to begin a new full-time paid job.

There is another dimension of gender ideol-ogy at work in the growing differences between mothers' and fathers' lives. Gender subjectivity showed up in a difference in attitude about dust and disorder. Some of the men (indeed the major-ity) were able to be 'laid back' about housework and childcare because they were not, in the end, responsible for either. Not easily captured in subjects' responses on lists of domestic chores, this is a difference in attitude or stance as much as behaviour. As Lisa explained it (speaking about Sam who clearly tried to share the housework and childcare), 'he can lie down on the sofa and fall asleep *during the day*, when there's stuff to be done, or he's got the baby; I would never think of doing that.' This is the most complicated dynamic to explain; at the same time, it is an important cause of the gender differences in work and time discussed here. Its importance was clear: all of the women reported this difference. That is, while they felt there was always something that needed to be done, their partners could sit down and do nothing.

Motherhood is not behind what drives women to feel they must attend to the dust, disorder, and daily needs of family. Singlehandedly assuming the responsibility for a helpless child, and being home alone much of the time, do seem to reinforce the impulse, however. A house needs to be clean when a baby is crawling around.

Friends, Family, and the Issue of Support

Mothers' lives do not diverge only from their partners' lives. The privacy of the domestic sphere and tremendous social distance between life organized around the needs of babies and that led by adults in the world of paid work also separates mothers from other adults. Many studies of full-time mothers of young children report the feeling of isolation to be one of women's key complaints about staying home (Oakley 1974; Boulton 1983; Rosenberg 1987). When I began this study I wondered whether increasing social isolation is common for most women as they move through the stages typical of women's lives which end in motherhood.

In seven of the ten cases in this study the woman's social life and network of active friendships constricted significantly as she became a mother. Generally, these new mothers lost contact with friends who did not have young children. So luck and demographics played an important role in how likely women were to lose touch with friends. Nine of the ten women saw their old women friends considerably less often during this first year of parenthood than they had before; most went out with friends scarcely more than once over the course of the entire year. At the same time, half of the men seemed to see friends as much as before they became parents although, like the women, several of the men also 'lost' former friends. There were age and class differences at work here too: the young working-class couples, whose social lives had revolved around going out to dance and drink, were more likely to have completely lost that former way of socializing.

Luck and demographics determined which women had former friends going through the same experiences. Countering those factors, though, were state-provided social services. Two of the new mothers met women in the local 'mothers' groups' they attended, and spent many days each week in the company of these women. Both reported that these new friendships 'made all the difference in the world [to their experience of motherhood]'. While their involvement with old friends declined, these two women were neither isolated socially nor without people to share anxieties and information. In a time of cutbacks to social services, programs like these, which represent lifelines to new mothers, must be protected.

The other major change in people's social networks and social lives was a stunning shift toward more socializing as a couple, and with extended family rather than friends. All of these couples felt they had become 'a family', and a focus around socializing as a nuclear unit seemed to underlie that feeling. There is, then, an interesting connection between the evolution of 'family' and gender differences.

Meanwhile, every woman whose mother lived in the city saw her more than she had before. All of these grandmothers lent their daughters considerable help. One working-class mother who returned to paid employment full-time relied on her mother to care for her child not only during the day, but often at night as well. Another woman who came to rely on her mother for help and advice, and in the process began to see her as her 'best friend', felt more comfortable with her parents and siblings than with her friends (even those with babies). She felt she could trouble her family with her moods, the baby's needs, etc., while these might strain friendships.

For these new mothers, the world divided into an inner circle of 'family' centred on the baby, and everyone else. Even women who didn't rely on their larger family network appeared to feel separated from everyone in the world not connected to their own baby. Only friends with babies were part of this 'mother zone' the women seemed to inhabit.[10]

Reproducing Difference

The experiences of these couples indicate that the way parenthood is organized creates profound differences between women's and men's lives. Privatized parenthood strongly encourages couples to specialize their roles and divide their work. Interestingly, the experience of becoming 'family' served to obscure the growing difference between men's and women's lives for many of these couples. Accordingly, many of the women were reluctant to conclude that their lives had grown separate from their partners'. Uppermost in the women's minds was the common interest in the baby they shared with their partner, and often their increased time together. Though their lives took different paths daily, they were on a joint venture in a world that leaves parents on their own.

Let me be clear about the gender differences I saw developing. Most of the men were very involved in the care and love given their babies. They were profoundly affected by becoming parents. Nevertheless, all these men felt pressured to concentrate on financial support. Given the way paid work is structured, this typically took them away from their babies for most of the week. So, the responsibility for the baby became the woman's. It is with respect to this responsibility

that the sexual division of labour was so stark.

The division of household work was less so, as was the division of childcare tasks. Indeed, in most cases the division of the work was quite fluid—whole tasks sometimes changed hands suddenly. Certainly the distribution of work established by the end of the first year of parenthood was not immutable: in some cases it had changed significantly over the course of the year. Nevertheless, all of the women did more housework than the men, and many had taken on a larger portion of it with parenthood.

Since responsibility is the essence of motherhood, it is important to try to understand how women come to assume it. My initial assessment is that here too there seemed to be different patterns. In some cases, the responsibility automatically came to the woman in that it was assumed to be hers 'naturally' (by both parents); these women actively and aggressively shouldered it from the start. In other cases, the feminization of the responsibility was contingent: the fathers saw themselves as equally responsible and attempted to be as active as the mothers, at least with respect to making decisions about the child. The women were apparently not eager to take on the entire task, but they increasingly assumed responsibility for the child because of the way their daily lives were organized (i.e., the men were gone and they were home). So in some cases even this clear gender difference evolved slowly over time, and was wholly contingent upon circumstances.

The coincidence of a developing gender difference in roles and people's sense of becoming 'family' is interesting when we consider the ideological weight carried by the concept of 'family' in this society. Moreover, the way motherhood seems to draw women into housewifery also warrants some attention. Women's increased social isolation as they become mothers plays a large role in those dynamics. Any attempt to understand both the slowness of change in the division of household work and the perpetuation of gender differences and inequalities must consider the dynamics of parenthood.

Appendix

Fictitious Names	Social Class	Woman's Employment: Before Pregnancy	During First Year	Weaning of Baby
Jane and Tom	middle-class	employed full-time (paid maternity leave)	home all year	at 5 months
Susan and Charles	middle-class	some freelance	home all year	at 6 months
Nancy and Simon	working-class	employed full-time; just laid off	job, full-time at 3 months	at 6 months
Jennifer and Joe	middle-class woman, working-class man	full-time career (paid maternity leave)	back at 6 months	at 6 months
Ruth and David	middle-class	just laid off; studying	home all year	not by a year
Lisa and Sam	middle-class	self-employed	home all year	not by a year
Claire and Stephen	middle-class but low-income	employed full-time	back part-time at 2 months	at 10 months
Mary and Greg	working-class	in college	home all year with twins	at 4 months
Sophia and Max	working-class	employed full-time (paid maternity leave)	back at 6 months	at 6 months
Sally and Jake	middle-class	full-time freelance	home all year	not by a year

Notes

Financial support for the pilot study reported here was received in a General Research Grant from the University of Toronto. Many people made this research possible. Sincere thanks go to Jodi Pemberton, Barbara Chalifoux, Diane Chopping, Dr Donna Steele, Sheila Martineau, Evangeline Davis, Sandra Badin, Women's College Hospital, St Michael's Hospital, and the Toronto Public Health Department. I thank Meg Luxton and Jane Springer for their enthusiasm and their helpful comments. Of course, I extend very special thanks to the couples who so generously talked to me about their lives.

1. The General Social Survey carried out by Statistics Canada did, however, distinguish them.

2. For example, Arlie Hochschild's *The Second Shift* (1989) highlights children and the issue of motherwork when explaining the many different consequences of the tension between women's paid and unpaid work, but ignores them in her conclusions. Children remain almost invisible in scholarly work.

3. The privatization of mothering is a privilege as well as a source of problems: women of colour have often cared for their children only by recruiting their kin and friends to share the responsibility (Stack 1975). Domestic workers, especially nannies, typically are forced to leave their children behind them when they come to Canada, leaving someone else to shoulder the daily responsibilities while they care for the children of the wealthy. As Glen (1992) has shown so carefully, motherwork is not only gendered; it is also characterized by a racial division of labour, with women of colour carrying out the least satisfying of the tasks.

4. All but one volunteered in response to appeals I made in person at two Toronto hospitals' childbirth classes and at several lamaze classes, or in writing to people taking classes organized by the city; one couple was acquainted with a graduate student who knew me.

5. The names are fictitious. See Appendix.

6. These cases of less responsive mothers were the minority, but indicate clearly some of the negative consequences of the privatized care of babies. The women tired out by their round-the-clock responsibility.

7. Of course the other men may simply have failed to indicate to me how overwhelmed they were with the responsibilities of parenthood. Three of them (Charles, Simon, and Max) were spending very long hours at their paid jobs—largely in response to the financial pressures of parenthood.

8. Each woman filled in a pie chart indicating her various identities and the relative importance of each. Aside from this measure, I am basing the statement mostly on impression.

9. I am not making a value judgment here. My own experience leads me to favour the mother staying home the first year, for her sake and that of the baby. The women in the study also felt it would be better for the baby at least if they stayed home. But income needs, and sometimes the man's insistence, led some of the women to go back to work outside the home.

   All the women were very identified as mothers, and seemed to put their babies' needs before their own regularly (whenever the two conflicted). What varied, then, was whether or not they were forced to spend some of their time away from home, and thus to change the baby's routine (e.g., even to wean him or her) to fit their schedule. Women who worked outside the home could not let their babies' demands shape their days, while women at home had that option—and were more likely to pursue it.

10. This is writer Marni Jackson's (1992) phrase. Her book is full of insight about what it means to become a mother in our society.

References

Baker, M. 1985. 'What Will Tomorrow Bring? A Study of the Aspirations of Adolescent Women' (Ottawa: Canadian Advisory Council on the Status of Women).

Bernard, J. 1974. *The Future of Motherhood* (New Haven: Yale University Press).

Blain, J. 1991. 'Gender, Class and Family', Ph.D. diss., Dalhousie University, Halifax, Nova Scotia.

Boulton, M. 1983. *On Becoming a Mother* (London: Tavistock).

Caulfield, M. 1975. 'The Family and Cultures of Resistance', *Socialist Revolution* 20: 67–85.

Chodorow, N. 1978. *The Reproduction of Mothering* (Berkeley: University of California).

Cowan, C., and P. Cowan. 1992. *When Partners Become Parents* (New York: Basic Books).

Davis, A. 1981. *Women, Race & Class* (New York: Vintage).

Firestone, S. 1970. *The Dialectic of Sex* (New York: Morrow).

Friedan, B. 1963. *The Feminine Mystique* (New York: Dell).

Gaskell, J. 1983. 'The Reproduction of Family Life', *British Journal of Sociology of Education* 4.

Gavron, H. 1966. *The Captive Wife* (Harmondsworth, UK: Penguin).

Gerson, K. 1994. *No Man's Land* (New York: Basic Books).

Gilman, C.P. 1898. *Women and Economics* (Boston: Small, Maynard and Company).

Glen, E.N. 1992. 'From Servitude to Service Work: Historical Continuities in the Racial Division of Paid Reproductive Labor', *Signs* 18 (1): 1–42.

Goldscheider, F., and L. Waite. 1991. *New Families, No Families?* (Berkeley: University of California).

Gutman, H. 1976. *The Black Family: Slavery and Freedom, 1750–1925* (New York: Pantheon).

Hochschild, A. 1989. *The Second Shift* (New York: Viking).

Jackson, M. 1992. *The Mother Zone* (New York: Henry Holt and Company).

LaRossa, R., and M. LaRossa. 1981. *Transition to Parenthood* (Beverly Hills: Sage).

Lewis, C. 1986. *Becoming a Father* (London: Milton Keynes, Open University Press).

Luxton, M. 1980. *More Than a Labour of Love: Three Generations of Women's Work in the Home* (Toronto: Women's Press).

Maccoby, E., and C. Jacklin. 1974. *The Psychology of Sex Differences* (Stanford: Stanford University Press).

McMahon, M. 1995. *Engendering Motherhood* (New York: The Guildford Press).

Mitchell, J. 1971. *Woman's Estate* (New York: Vintage Books).

Oakley, A. 1974. *The Sociology of Housework* (New York: Pantheon).

Rosenberg, H. 1987. 'Motherwork, Stress and Depression: The Costs of Privatized Social Reproduction' in *Feminism and Political Economy: Women's Work, Women's Struggles*, eds H.J. Maroney and M. Luxton (Toronto: Methuen).

Rossiter, A. 1988. *From Private to Public* (Toronto: Women's Press).

Rowbotham, S. 1973. *Woman's Consciousness, Man's World* (Harmondsworth, UK: Penguin).

Stack, C. 1975. *All Our Kin: Strategies for Survival in a Black Community* (New York: Harper & Row).

Tavris, C. 1992. *The Mismeasure of Woman* (New York: Simon & Schuster).

Chapter 20

Harriet Rosenberg discusses new mothers' common responses to their experience of early motherhood. Focusing on the problems women encounter as mothers, Rosenberg analyzes the social relations in which mothering occurs, and its general social organization.

She discusses the isolation of 'motherwork' from other work, and the lack of social supports for mothers. She also carefully considers the nature of this very important work as it is done in our society.

Motherwork, Stress, and Depression: The Costs of Privatized Social Reproduction

Harriet Rosenberg

The Political Economy of Pain

'Mother who killed two sons says she's paid price,' announced a front-page headline. In 1970 a woman smothered her six-week-old son; two years later she smothered a second infant. Both deaths were recorded at the time as crib deaths. In 1984, 'frayed for more than a decade of struggling for her sanity', she said that she wanted to warn other women about the postpartum depression that led to the killings. 'At the first sign of that, don't hesitate to. . . . For God's sake, ask for help,' she said. 'I just wouldn't want any woman to go through what I went through' (Toronto *Star*, 3 March 1984).

Why did this happen? Such violence is usually explained in individual psychological terms: people go crazy and do violent things. Yet other violent crimes such as rape, murder, and suicide have been linked to underlying social causes. The correlation between increases in suicide rates, for example, and rising levels of unemployment (Brenner 1973, 1977, 1979) established a link between crisis in individual lives and crisis in an economic system. But, because childbirth and childrearing are widely considered to be a 'natural' female condition, the possibility of social structural origins of 'postpartum depression' has rarely been investigated

(Friedan 1963; Oakley 1972). Rather, the dominant contemporary explanatory model, constructed and maintained by a powerful medical establishment, is explicitly asocial. It defines the emotional distress of mothers as an exclusively individual problem called 'postpartum depression' and has developed a variety of individual therapies including psychoanalysis, drugs, and vitamins to deal with it. To combat the tendencies which constantly push analysis of motherhood and depression in a personalistic direction we must start with a fresh perspective—one that has both feminist and political economy underpinnings.

Producing or not producing human beings is part of the political discourse of most societies. Historically, as nation-states developed, debates about population grew with them. From the mercantilists to Malthus, demography, taxation, and militarization all became intertwined problematics (Davin 1978; Seccombe 1983). Furthermore, the institutions which turned children into soldiers, taxpayers, and workers have always been part of the public debate on how societies organize to reproduce themselves. Public funds are now seen as being legitimately allocated to these tasks, through school systems and the armed forces, for example. It is the proportions which are debated, not the appropriateness of the undertaking.

And yet the daily work of childrearing within the household/family is almost entirely eclipsed from political discussion and considered to be a private matter. The fact that the motherwork is integral to social reproduction and not a personal pastime is obscured. In the public domain debates rage about sexuality, abortion, and birth control, but not about the social condition of motherwork.

This radical separation of motherwork from social reproduction has a variety of consequences, including depression, anxiety, and violence. But if we start with the premise that the personal is political and that political economy is a significant component of even the most seemingly personal experience, we can analyze motherwork as an integral part of social reproduction. Such an approach enables us to view postpartum depression not just as an issue of private medicine but as one of public health, and to explore the consequences of the denial of parenting as a form of social labour under capitalism. . . .

Emotional Pain After Birth or Adoption

When they say to me, 'Oh, what a wonderful baby. How lucky you are,' I look around in a daze to see who they're talking to. I'm in a fog all the time. I'm so tired I can't think straight. I hate it. I want my life back.

In Western societies between 60 per cent and 80 per cent of mothers have emotional problems after childbirth (Hamilton 1962; Yalom 1968; Dalton 1971; Davidson 1972; Balchin 1975; Kruckman 1980). Depression and anxiety are also experienced by women who adopt[1] and by men (Bucove 1964). About 20 per cent of women continue to experience depression for many months after birth or adoption, or even occasionally throughout life (Kruckman 1980; Welburn 1980; Rosenberg 1980).

In the medical and popular literature the terms 'postpartum depression', 'baby blues', and 'postpartum psychosis' are often used interchangeably. 'Baby blues' is frequently applied to all forms of postnatal psychological problems. Ideologically dismissive, it is akin to the blame-the-victim connotation of 'blue-collar blues'. However, more precise medical usage distinguishes different forms of the depressed experience. More carefully defined, the term 'blues' is restricted to a depressed mood and transitory tearfulness that is experienced by about 80 per cent of mothers on the third or fourth day after birth. This mild postpartum depression lasts for a few hours only. Although some explanations have associated it with hormonal changes at the onset of lactation (Dalton 1971), others have pointed out that there is little cross-cultural evidence for such a claim and have argued that there is a historical link in North America between the medicalization of birth and the appearance of mild postpartum depression (Catano and Catano 1981).

At the other extreme, 'postpartum psychosis' is also frequently conflated with postpartum depression, especially in medical literature. This confusion results from the fact that medical studies are frequently based on hospitalized populations. Actual psychosis is relatively rare, occurring in one in a thousand cases. It is treated by psychiatric intervention, hospitalization, and electroconvulsive therapy (ECT).

There is also a 'mid-range' depression which may be expressed as slow, tired, hopeless behaviour, eyes filling with unshed tears or a constant crying, or by intense anxiety and frantic behaviour. In this form, feeling of anger and conflict with children or mates is common. About 65 per cent of the 1,000 women who sought the services of the Post-Partum Counselling Services (see note 1) expressed fears of harming their children, although very few actually did so. Physiological symptoms like constant colds and rashes, as well as frequent accidents and alcohol and drug abuse, are all associated with this form of postpartum depression (PPCS files). It is a terrifying and debilitating experience, made all the more frightening by the fact that it is rarely mentioned. 'You never hear about this,' said one woman. 'No one ever talks about it. Are they all lying?'

It is this mid-range form of postpartum depression which will be discussed in this paper. It is this type of depression which can be clearly seen to have social structural causes. . . .

Treatment: Medical Models, Feminist Models

> My doctor is very squelching. He says 'It's just cabin fever, dearie. Don't worry.'

> Sometimes I think my volunteer [at Post-Partum Counselling Services] is the only person in the world who puts the mother first.

There are two competing general models for the treatment of postpartum depression. The medical model stems from an analysis of depression as an individual problem; the feminist model identifies it as a problem related to the oppressed social position of women.

Although there have been different explanations of the etiology of postpartum depression and consequently different fashions in its treatment, the medical model has consistently tried to 'cure' the individual. Treatment has included the use of drugs, sleep cures, and prolonged hospitalization in the nineteenth century and electroconvulsive, insulin shock, and psychoanalytic therapies in the twentieth century (Kruckman 1980). One practitioner in the 1940s was so fond of shock therapy that he claimed a 75 per cent recovery rate and was not at all alarmed by the 5 per cent death rate resulting from it (Kruckman 1980). By the mid-1950s, a new psychopharmacological approach had come to dominate in research and treatment. Psychoactive drugs, often coupled with hormonal injections, were widely used by doctors claiming phenomenal success rates.

The psychoanalytic theories of postpartum depression which developed in the 1930s rested upon the normative conception that biological mothering was the essential mark of femininity. A pioneer of this approach, Zilboorg, stated that depression after childbirth was related to 'symbolic castration' and was common 'in narcissistic, frigid, latent homosexual women' (cited in Kruckman 1980: 8). The psychiatric literature still characterizes women with postpartum depression as infantile, immature, having unresolved conflicts with their mothers, failing to adjust to the feminine role, and having penis envy. And contemporary medical analyses continue to rely heavily on theories of biological causality (Karacan and Williams 1970; Seltzer 1980).

> Therapy is usually directed at the conflictual areas—helping the patient accept the feminine role or express jealous feelings toward the child, occasioned by thwarted dependency needs. . . . (Seltzer 1980: 2549).

However, the studies of hormonal and genetic causes of depression tend to be poorly designed and yield insufficient and even contradictory results (Livingston 1976; Weissman and Klerman 1977; Parlee 1980). The poor quality of research on the physiological causes of postpartum depression should not cause us to discount this line of inquiry, but should alert us to the inadequacy of relying on the simplistic, unicausal models which medical research tends to favour.

A path-breaking alternative feminist model has been developed by the Vancouver Post-Partum Counselling Services (PPCS) after over a decade of experience in working with more than a thousand women (Robertson 1980; Robertson with Howard 1980). The PPCS model is explicitly woman-centred, and looks to find the causes of depression in the structure of society rather than solely in individual pathology or hormonal imbalance. This perspective has informed the PPCS definition of depression, the population at risk, and the organization of treatment.

Basically we redefine the term. We invented a definition separate from blues and psychosis.

A social perspective has enabled them to identify situations likely to generate postpartum depression. Since they do not see the causes of postpartum depression to be either exclusively physiological or a manifestation of failed femininity, the counsellors and volunteers at PPCS are able to respond to symptoms of depression in all new parents, including men and adoptive parents. It has also enabled them to draw a profile of the person who is most likely to get postpartum depression. The most striking feature of the profile is that the woman who is expected to make the most trouble-free transition to motherhood is the one who is most at risk.

The average woman seen by PPCS is twenty-seven, married, middle-class (in terms of occupation and income),[2] and has had at least two years of postsecondary education. She has held responsible paying jobs (e.g., nurse, teller, social worker, hairdresser, secretary, teacher). The pregnancy was planned. Both parents attended prenatal classes. The father was present at the delivery. The woman chose to breastfeed. No significant prior incidents of depression were found among these women. PPCS also found that there was no significant correlation between caesarean sections and depression, although many of the mothers had negative hospital experiences.[3] Nor have they found that the supposed closeness or bonding said to be inherent in non-medical childbirth and in breastfeeding has been a mitigating factor (Robertson 1976; Arney 1980).

The societal model used by PPCS has identified loss, isolation, and lack of social support as significant factors contributing to depression. Women who have lost their connection with their paid workplace are particularly vulnerable to depression. Some women keenly feel the loss of status as a 'girl' in this youth-oriented culture, an ironic situation when we consider that many societies count motherhood to be the resolution of a crisis period and the onset of social adulthood for women (Silverman 1975). Other feelings of loss stem from the very real experience of many women who report feeling deserted by their friends and family members after the first few weeks of their child's life (Saulnier 1988). They have few sources of reassurance, advice, or assistance in their work as mothers. They feel their husbands do not understand the pressures of 'full-time mothering'. And even men who 'help' can be undermining because they define the problem solely as the woman's. They do not seem to be able to offer emotional support ('I want a hug and he vacuums the living room'). Past miscarriages, the recent or past death of a parent, or loss of emotional contact with a significant person because of illness or alcoholism can also contribute to feelings of depression.

In an overall sense, postpartum depression is an expression of social isolation accompanied by loss of personal identity, loss of confidence in one's ability to cope. To understand why this should be so, we need to look at how motherhood and motherwork are structured in our society.

Mothering as Social and Personal Work

Defining mothering as work is crucial to the PPCS strategy for postpartum depression.

It is very important for women to realize that what they are doing is work. When I talk to women, I consciously change the language I use. I talk about the job and the fact that the woman is the manager. That's one of the hardest parts about the job and it usually isn't even recognized as work—even by husbands who are 'nice guys' and 'help' [with housework and childcare]. They don't seem to realize that helping is not the same thing as carrying the weight of responsibility that mothers carry.

This redefinition is also a prerequisite for a feminist analysis of the political economic determinants of mothering as an aspect of social reproduction under capitalism. The overlapping organization of gender relations and the division between what are called 'the public' and 'the private' (or the domestic household and the economy) effectively assigns the major responsibility for the social work of reproduction to women without any social recognition or social support. Geographical mobility and segmented households, combined with the ideology of family privacy, mean that women with babies get very little on-the-job training from experienced workers.

For many women, becoming a parent is often devastating and confusing because they suddenly find themselves in unfamiliar work situations. Although they have prepared for childbirth by taking classes and reading books, they suddenly find that they have not just given birth to a baby but to an endlessly demanding human being. The care of that human being is not defined as work: it is seen as a private, natural, and essentialist enterprise. When women complain or despair they are frequently told, 'Well, you were the one who wanted this baby. . . .' But raising a baby is not a personal hobby like raising begonias; it is an undertaking which reproduces society as well as expressing the individual need to love and cherish children.

Examples from kin-ordered societies demonstrate that childrearing is usually viewed as being both social and personal, and most cultures have provided very rich systems of social support to new parents (Dawson 1929; Bettelheim 1954; Lewis 1958; Mead 1962; Metraux 1963; Kupferer 1965; Newman 1966; Oakley 1976). While postpartum customs and rituals may seem obscure or unusual to Western eyes, they serve the very concrete social function of making a public statement that a new birth is significant to the community as a whole and that social attention must be focused on care for the new child. In industrial capitalist societies the spotlight tends to be on the fetus, the

doctor, and the technology of hospital births (Arms 1977; Jordan 1978). After a mother leaves the hospital, the thousands and thousands of socially approved dollars and hours and hours of work energy crystallized in the hospital setting evaporate. The woman is on her own: she moves from the public realm of hospital medicine to the private world of her household.

In contrast, in kin-based communities mothers can usually command social support as their right in custom and ritual. Mothers can expect kin to cook, clean, protect, and advise. A new mother may be ritually prohibited from preparing food, thus placing the onus of meal preparation on her kin (Solway 1984). In such settings new mothers are not expected to know or do everything for themselves. They are seen to be at the centre of a social drama and are understood to be entitled to help with caregiving and household tasks. The existence of amulets, special foods, and behavioural taboos constantly reinforce the sensibility that mothering is a public concern and not a private pastime.

In part these social concerns reflect fears for the health of mother and child in societies with high rates of infant and maternal mortality. Postpartum ritual is at one level of a communal attempt to deal with a time of real danger for babies and mothers. But such cultural supports can persist and have other effects even when mortality rates are not obviously at issue. By maintaining these rituals communities symbolically testify to their collective responsibility for children and mothers. In one study, Mexican-American women in Chicago who adhered to customary rituals in the postpartum period had no incidence of depression (Kruckman 1980). The confidence these mothers had in the social importance of childrearing was revealed in their attitude toward the evil eye. Mothers felt that if a stranger were to look at a baby he or she must immediately touch the child to ward off the evil eye. One woman recounted how when she spied a man looking at her baby, she crossed a crowded restaurant and insisted that he touch the infant. This belief, which defines uninvolved onlookers as dangerous, presses encorporating claims which prohibit looking without touching. What may look like 'superstition' to those outside the culture is actually a cultural safety-net which asserts community responsibility for infant and maternal well-being. The women in this study, unlike those that PPCS found to be vulnerable in their isolation, did not find that they had to solve all problems by themselves.

For most women in North American and Western Europe, however, the capacity to override claims of social non-involvement in childcare is quite limited. Unwaged caregiving in the household is rarely recognized as either a contribution to social reproduction or as real work; rather, it is seen in essentialist biological terms for women and as a private and personal reward for waged work for men. Mothers are not supposed to need, nor have the right to need, social services or social funds. Public funding for social services to alleviate the work done by mothers in households is identified as a 'frill'—an unnecessary expenditure which is unwarranted, especially in times of economic decline.

Furthermore, for women who do the work of caregiving there are contradictions between the low status of the work they do and the seemingly high status of the role.[4] 'Mother', 'motherhood', and 'mothering' are words that bring forth flamboyant, extravagant, romantic images. In contrast, the work itself includes many tasks which are not socially respected. Motherwork involves dealing with infant bodily functions: people who clean up human wastes have low status (Luxton 1983). Few jobs have this contradiction so deeply ingrained.

Equally significant to the stress of mothering tasks is the fact that many women do not really know what motherwork involves until they are faced with doing it. They have only a series of

platitudes to go on, about it being 'the most important job in the world'. It is as if one were hired for a new job with the understanding that the job description would be so vast and so vague as to be undoable, that little assistance would be provided, and that any errors would be the employee's sole responsibility. Motherwork, like any other job, must be learned. Books and courses have become the major means of learning: for most it is an inadequate method, because it is not based on experience. There is no apprenticeship period in our society as there is in small-scale kin-ordered societies where young girls learn the ropes as caregivers to younger children. In industrialized societies, a falling birthrate has resulted in small families in which girls (and boys) grow up playing in peer-oriented, age-segregated groups. Many leave home having experienced little or no contact with newborns and infants. Said one North American mother, 'When the baby was born, I knew I wasn't ready. I hadn't got through the reading list.'

One should add that the experts, the writers of childrearing guides, are often men who in fact rarely do the daily work of caregiving themselves.[5] ('Provide a stimulating environment for the infant but don't overstimulate him,' says one TV advice-giver.) Advice-givers define the job goals, and they judge the outcome. They garner wealth, prestige, and status by explaining three-month colic, thumbsucking, and toilet training, without experiencing the day-to-day working conditions of mothers. This separation between expert and worker can lead to condescending attitudes on the part of the expert. For example, Dr Frederick W. Rutherford, in *You and Your Baby*, has some inkling that all may not go well for mothers. He had no index entry under depression but does mention 'baby blues'. His advice:

If you are feeling blue, pour out your troubles to someone who will make no moral judgments, someone who will understand that *no matter how little real basis there is for your depression* you nevertheless feel it strongly, but who also knows that with a little help you will manage nicely before very long. Try not to wallow in the blues, but don't be ashamed to express your feelings. You don't have to act like a cheerful cherub when you feel like Pitiful Pearl (Rutherford 1971: 167, emphasis added).

To the non-worker, the pain of the worker is not quite real.

Contradictory, guilt-inducing 'how-to' books, magazines, and TV talk shows cater to the isolated model of caregiving and miss the social context—people with whom to talk, ask questions, share experiences. Some doctors fill this role, but the medicalization of parenting has been a risky business for mothers. Visits to the doctor can further reinforce the isolated and individuated nature of childrearing. Medical consultations are usually brief and centre on the health of the child, not the work of childrearing or the mental health of the mother. Simple-minded measures like weight gain can become an index for whether the mother is doing a good job. The fact that the child may be gaining and the mother falling apart may not be perceived by the doctor. Furthermore, family doctors may be reluctant to raise the issue of postpartum depression because they feel that women are suggestible and will get the symptoms if the issue is discussed.

Yet women are very dependent on advice from the medical establishment. Mothers may be labelled overinvolved or hysterical, but since they so rarely have alternative methods of assessing health and nutrition matters, they must rely on their doctors. If they go outside the doctor-patient dyad, women risk criticism for listening to 'old wives' tales' (i.e., other women) or for negligence (e.g., attacks on home birth). Thus the privatized, asocial model of childrearing is constantly reinforced.

Stress, Depression, Burnout

This is a very scattered job. I can't think any thoughts more than halfway. At least when my husband goes to work he gets silences.

I work 24 hours a day. He [her husband] doesn't. At night when the baby cries, he never wakes up first. I have to wake him and he goes to the baby. Then he's so proud because he let me sleep!

I wish I could remember what it felt like not to have a knot in my stomach.

If we step back from the issue of mothers learning a new job, to the larger context of workplace stress, we gain some useful insights into the predicament in which many women find themselves.

The effects of stress (Selye 1956, 1974, 1980; Holmes and Rahe 1967; Lumsden 1981) on mental health are now being widely studied. Unions representing police, firefighters, public employees, and teachers in Canada and the USA have become very concerned with psychosocial stress in the workplace. Unions, employers, and courts are increasingly reading symptoms like chronic anxiety, depression, fatigue, and substance abuse (alcohol, drugs, overeating) as signals of strain produced on the job (Ellison and Genz 1978).

Some extreme forms of mental strain and emotional exhaustion have been called 'burn-out' (Freudenberger and Richelson 1980). It has been argued that 'any kind of frontline person—teacher, social worker, therapist, nurse—who is at the beck and call of needy individuals is prone to burn-out' (Murdoch 1981: 6). The literature on burn-out among professionals offers some important insights into what unwaged mothers experience in the home. Burned-out front-line workers complain of unrelenting demands, little time away from intense personal interaction with clients or patients, shift work, and constant responsibility for two or more things at once (Maslach and Pines 1977). Burned-out professional childcare workers are reported to experience feelings of 'inarticulated personal distress' and fatigue as do lawyers, psychiatrists, nurses, and clinical psychologists when faced with the tense conditions of their jobs (Maslach 1976; Mattingly 1977; Maslach and Pines 1977; Pines and Kafry 1978).

If they are not alerted to burn-out as a potential response to these stressors, professionals may respond by blaming themselves and seeking psychiatric help for what they perceive to be personal deficiencies. Those who have studied this process among daycare workers, for example, argue that it is the structure and intensity of the job, and not personal idiosyncrasies, that cause some workers to develop feelings of worthlessness. Psychiatric intervention, according to this research, rarely succeeds unless the work situation is taken into account (Maslach and Pines 1977).

These stressful job conditions are also true of motherwork. Most of the psychological and physical symptoms associated with burn-out are the same as those reported by mothers diagnosed as having postpartum depression. Thus I would argue that postpartum depression, like burn-out, is actually a syndrome in response to the organization of work.

Not all professionals have emotional problems; nor do all mothers. But there are times in any worker's life when job demands deplete, exhaust, and undermine. Motherwork, especially in relation to an infant, is a job of high demands. For many women it is a job of perpetual shift work—of always being on call (see Stellman and Daum 1973 on health and shift work). In that respect it is like policing or nursing, with the exception that in motherwork there are rarely shifts off. Furthermore, unlike other workers, mothers are not encouraged to separate home and work life. Since mothering is seen as a role, and not as work, mothers are supposed to always remain in character. They rarely get restorative 'time outs', let alone extended vacations or sick leave. The disorientation caused by lack of sleep and the disappearance

of predictable routines of eating, sleeping, and waking contribute to a 'twilight zone' atmosphere. In addition, women who do motherwork also do housework and frequently must combine both jobs in a space like the kitchen that can be unsafe for infants and young children (Rosenberg 1984). Time-budget studies (Meissner et al. 1975; Proulx 1978) and case studies (Luxton 1980, 1983) tell us just how unrelenting these jobs are.

Low Control and High Demands

Those who study industrial workers argue that the most stressful job situations are not caused by high demand levels alone. Multiple demands, under the right circumstances, can create positive work experiences. It is situations of high demand combined with low levels of control in decision making that cause the highest levels of worker stress, measured in terms of exhaustion and depression (Karasek 1979). Daycare workers who feel that they have high levels of participation in their centres, or social workers who feel they participate in agency decision making, express high levels of job satisfaction (Maslach and Pines 1977; Pines and Kafry 1978).

Mental strain from high demands and low control occurs more commonly among assembly-line workers, whose movements are often rigidly contained, than it does among executives, who can set hours and control working conditions (Karasek 1979). Mothering is usually thought to be more similar to an executive job than to assembly-line work. But for many women,

> It's a myth that we are our bosses or that we can have a cigarette and a coffee when we want. You can't plan a thing, especially when they are young. You are lucky if you can find time to go to the bathroom. And even then, you don't go alone.

Women as mothers are like women in many other work situations: they have the appearance of wide 'decision-making latitude' or control, but in reality they have little power to define their work situations.[6] Typically, women's waged work (nursing, teaching, social work, working as bank tellers, as well as pink-collar jobs) is structured by institutionalized gender hierarchies. Female teachers have responsibilities within classrooms, but major decisions are usually made by predominantly male administrators. Men supervise women in social service agencies, banks, department stores, and beauty shops (Howe 1975; Tepperman 1976; Bank Book Collective 1979; Armstrong and Armstrong 1984). Women who quit underpaid, undervalued jobs for the 'freedom' of domestic work and childrearing may find themselves escaping into more of the same. They may make trivial consumer choices between brands of detergent, but ultimately they can be very dependent. Women who give up waged work become financially dependent on mates; they become dependent on 'expert' advice-givers; and they are tied to infant-defined schedules, the schedules of other children, and the schedule of the wage-earner.

In motherwork, one of the most devastating aspects of lack of control is the absence of feedback. The isolation of the job severely limits the feedback which is so essential to decision making. Daycare workers who work with under-two year olds argued that isolation from adult company is what they felt most distinguished motherwork form daycare work. As one teacher said,

Even though the job description is sometimes vague, I know I will get support and feedback from other [teachers] on how I am doing and how a child is doing. That's the big difference between us and mothers.

Some mothers have compared their isolation to being a prisoner of war. Said the nursing mother of a two month old whose mate was frequently absent because of job commitments,

It's pure torture. Your street clothes are taken away and you wear a bathrobe, since all you do all day is [breast]feed the baby. Just as you fall asleep, you are woken again. You're afraid to fall asleep anyway. What's the point? But God, the worst is that there is no one to talk to.

Strategies for Job Redesign

Occupational health and safety research on stress and social science studies of burn-out situate the problems of exhaustion and depression in the workplace. They argue that solutions are social and structural, and lie in redesigning the job to lessen demands and increase control.[7] This is also true for motherwork stress and burn-out, and is a solution that was first suggested by nineteenth-century feminists.

Over one hundred years ago, feminist economist Charlotte Perkins Gilman wrote a short story called 'The Yellow Wallpaper' ([1899] 1973). It is a nightmarish account of postpartum depression based on Gilman's own experience. Gilman's pioneering economic and architectural writings go further. They outline plans for job redesign which take up the whole question of how housework and motherwork should be socially structured, albeit from a somewhat élitist perspective (Hayden 1979). Other thinkers and activists struggled to bring housework and motherwork overtly into the public sphere through daycares and producers' and consumers' co-operatives (Hayden 1981). But by the 1930s these movements were defeated. Housework and motherwork became thoroughly identified as women's individual, private projects and as 'natural' expressions of femininity.

The reawakened women's movement of the 1960s once again introduced housework and mothering as social issues. Such a task is not easy and has led to reassessments of stereotyped patterns of the division of labour. With the exception of breastfeeding, motherwork is not sex-typed labour. Caregiving can be performed by other adults, including men, or by older children, within and outside the nuclear-family unit. This work is not 'help', which still pins organizational responsibility on a supposedly all-knowing mother, but rather inclines toward the development of strategies for sharing responsibility, which may require women to relinquish some of the pleasures of feeling indispensable. Said one woman:

> When it was his shift with the baby, I had to leave the house. Otherwise, I just hovered over him the whole time. He got anxious and insecure and then I'd take over. It took me a long time to let go and let him be really in charge.

Such a restructuring of jobs and responsibilities forces women and men to face very deep currents of internalized socialization about what mothers and fathers should do and how they should act. It may require constant struggle with previously unacknowledged feelings and fears. At times it may seem that the struggle to assign tasks fairly is just too difficult. But discussions within the household and actions which aim to deliberately involve community members (e.g., drop-in centres, paid maternity/paternity leave or paid leave for a designated caregiver, flexible work hours, choice of workplace or community daycare, babysitting exchanges, co-operative non-profit daycare, and political pressure groups that lobby for the maintenance and enhancement of locally controlled social services for parents) all ultimately serve to create dense networks of involvement which can lessen the ambivalences, stresses, and burn-out of motherwork.

At the level of political practice, the women's movement has provided the context for this kind of debate. Local self-help groups, such as the Vancouver Post-Partum Counselling Service, have provided immediate crisis support and have helped to reduce women's dependency on experts, enhanced self-perceptions of competence, and enabled women to break down the tendency to personalize domestic problems. Since the 1960s, the lesson of consciousness-raising groups has always been that groups of women who have shared experiences begin to see that their private pain has social roots. This type of collective experience has often served as a prelude to the formation of a variety of helping organizations, from rape crisis centres to shelters for battered wives to groups like PPCS.

However, attempts to socialize childcare outside the household—a project crucial to the redesign of motherwork and parenting—continue to meet with enormous resistance. In North America there is still much popular and official hostility to 'institutionalized' daycare. While it may be tolerated for 'working mothers', the idea that women who do not work for wages should have access to publicly funded childcare arrangements raises even stronger negative reactions.[8] The intensity of the 'fight for good daycare', defined as top-quality, universally accessible, twenty-four-hour-a-day and community controlled (Ross 1979), illustrates that redesigning the job of parenting is deeply ideological, because it challenges the essentialist ideologies of 'the nuclear family' and 'motherhood', and the allocation of resources and funds. But such struggles—economic, ideological, and political—are necessary to dismantle the crazy-making structure of privatized motherwork and in its place to create the social job of caregiving.

Notes

Data for this paper were collected during visits to the Post-Partum Counselling Service (PPCS), Ministry of Human Resources, Vancouver, British Columbia, in 1980, 1981, and 1982. PPCS was founded in 1971 and has served over 1,000 women. Despite the efforts of hundreds of people, PPCS was closed by the Social Credit government of British Columbia in 1983. This paper is dedicated to Joann, Jim, Penny, Allison, and Fran, former counsellors who truly fought the good fight.

I would like to thank the men, women, and children whom I interviewed in New York, Toronto, and Vancouver for their time and the effort they made to share their understanding of parenting with me.

Thanks, too, to Gloria Gordon, Jeanne Stellman, Lawrence Kruckman, Jan Schneider, Rayna Rapp, Joan Jacobson, Don Hale, Meg Luxton, and Richard Lee for their encouragement and suggestions.

1. Based on interviews with Post-Partum Counselling Service (PPCS) counsellors and interviews with adoptive parents in Toronto.

2. Most of the women who went to PPCS are middle class in terms of income level, lifestyle, and education. The counsellors have assumed that this self-selection was an artifact of a class-based society in which middle-class people have better access to services. However, some poor women do come to PPCS. They tend to be young (late teens or early twenties) single parents on welfare. PPCS counsellors concluded that their depressions were so concretely rooted in economic and social deprivation ('Dealing with the welfare system is automatically depression') that their situation was not technically postpartum depression.

   Over the years PPCS has received letters from women across Canada in response to various radio and television broadcasts they have done. This admittedly informal and unscientific survey seems to indicate that postnatal depression does cut across geographic, occupational, and ethnic lines.

   Since so little research has been done on the question of postpartum depression and class, we cannot make any assumptions about differential rates between working-class, upper-class, and middle-class women. One community study in London on depression and marriage (i.e., not specifically the postnatal period) found that, subject to equivalent levels of stress, working-class women were five times more likely to become depressed than middle-class women. Working-class married women with young children living at home had the highest rate of depression (Rice 1937; Brown, Bhrolchain, and Harris 1975).

   This data should caution one against assuming that working-class women are automatically plugged into networks of support that mitigate the effects of stress and depression.

3. J. Croke, *Postpartum Depression* (Master's thesis, School of Social Work, Carleton University, Ottawa, 1982) shows that women who have had home births are less likely to experience depression after birth. However, her sample is small and further research is needed to obtain more significant data.

4. There exists a body of literature (reviewed by Parlee 1980) which links postpartum depression to a woman's difficulty in her *role* as a mother. With the exception of Luxton (1980), however, there has been little discussion of the actual work that women do as mothers on a day-to-day basis.

   Since mothering is constantly defined as a role, women who don't like to do some parts of the job may be considered crazy. See Boszormenyi-Nagy and Spark (1973) for family therapists who criticize women who do not fulfill the female domestic role, and Ehrenreich and English (1979) for criticism of the experts.

5. See Bloom (1976) for a short summary of the vagaries of childcare advice from the mid-nineteenth century to the late 1960s, as well as Ehrenreich and English (1979).

6. The terms 'control', 'decision-making latitude', and 'discretion' as used in Karasek's study deserve a closer look. Karasek based his data on male labour force statistics in the USA and Sweden. 'Control' was defined through the questions in the questionnaire that received a yes answer to whether the job was at a high skill level; one learned new things; the job was non-repetitious, creative; allowed freedom; permitted one to make decisions; and to have a say on the job. These were collapsed into the definition of 'control' over tasks and conduct during the day. Two measures—'decision authority' and 'intellectual discretion'—were selected for the study because of their similarity to other measures in the literature. Karasek argues that the literature shows that 'decision authority' and 'intellectual discretion' are highly correlated. He argued that highly skilled work rarely combined with low decision-making authority.

   This combination may be rare in male jobs, but it is more common in female jobs, where the contradiction of high skill but low authority is built into a sex-segregated labour force. Thus female nurses, teachers, tellers, and social workers are usually in the position of knowing that male authority can override their decisions. This sexist structure, coupled with the fact that women are more vulnerable to lay-offs than men, argues for more sensitive measures in aggregate data studies to pick up the special stressors to which women are subject. Furthermore, in relation to (unwaged) domestic labour like motherwork, we find the contradiction between high skill levels and low authority levels to be important. The popular myth that housewives/mothers are autonomous and have high degrees of decision-making power in their jobs is belied by their economic dependence on a male breadwinner (Smith 1973; Zaretsky 1976; Luxton 1980).

7. Karasek (1979) argues for work teams rather than single-task assembly lines. Maslach and Pines (1977), Pines and Kafry (1978), Freudenberger and Richelson (1980), and Mattingly (1977) all include mention of techniques which can give professionals more control in their workplace, including rotations and times off from constant face-to-face patient or client contact. Collegial support, awareness sessions, and variation in tasks are considered useful ways of restructuring work situations.

Other stress-reducing techniques operate on an individual level. They include strenuous exercise (Freudenberger 1977) and biofeedback (Greenspan 1978). These individual solutions are frequently difficult for mothers of new infants, who may be overwhelmed by lack of energy, time, and money, and by the difficulty of finding babysitters to take over while they go out.

The mother of an infant said in this regard, 'I know exactly why I didn't get postpartum depression. I bought my way out. We hired a housekeeper to come in five days a week, make meals, clean, and babysit. I went out and just sat in the library. Eventually, I got a job and felt less guilty about the housekeeper.'

8. When I proposed this solution to a group of previously quite sympathetic upper-middle-class women, they balked. Said one woman, 'Sure, it sounds like a good idea, but our husbands would never give us the money. It'll never work.'

References

Arms, S. 1977. *Immaculate Deception* (New York: Bantam).

Armstrong, P., and H. Armstrong. 1984. *The Double Ghetto: Canadian Women and Their Segregated Work*, rev. edn (Toronto: McClelland & Stewart).

Arney, W.R. 1980. 'Maternal Infant Bonding: The Politics of Falling in Love with Your Child', *Feminist Studies*, 6 (3).

Balchin, P. 1975. 'The Midwife and Puerperal Psychosis', *Midwife Health Visitor* 11 (2).

Bank Book Collective. 1979. *An Account to Settle: The Story of the United Bank Workers (SORWUC)* (Vancouver: Press Gang).

Bettelheim, B. 1954. *Symbolic Wounds: Puberty Rites and the Envious Male* (New York: Free Press).

Bloom, L.Z. 1976. 'It's All for Your Own Good: Parent-Child Relationships in Popular American Child Rearing Literature, 1820–1970', *Journal of Popular Culture* 10.

Boszormenyi-Nagy, I., and G.M. Spark. 1973. *Invisible Loyalties: Intergenerational Family Therapy* (New York: Harper & Row).

Brenner, M.H. 1973. *Mental Illness and the Economy* (Cambridge, MA: Harvard University Press).

———. 1977 'Health Costs and Benefits of Economic Policy', *International Journal of Health Services* 7 (4).

———. 1979. 'Unemployment and Economic Growth and Mortality', *Lancet*, 24 (March).

Brown, G., M. Bhrolchain, and T. Harris. 1975. 'Social Class and Psychiatric Disturbances among Women in an Urban Population', *Sociology* 9.

Bucove, A. 1964. 'Postpartum Psychosis in the Male', *Bulletin of the New York Academy of Medicine* 40.

Catano, J., and V. Catano. 1981. 'Mild Post-partum Depression: Learned Helplessness and the Medicalization of Obstetrics', unpublished manuscript (St Mary's University, Halifax).

Dalton, K. 1971. 'Puerperal and Premenstrual Depression', *Proceedings of the Royal Society of Medicine* 64 (12): 1249–52.

Davidson, J.R. 1972. 'Postpartum Mood Change in Jamaican Women: A Description and Discussion of Its Significance', *British Journal of Psychiatry* 121: 659–63.

Davin, A. 1978. 'Imperialism and Motherhood', *History Workshop* 5 (Spring): 9–65.

Dawson, W.R. 1929. *The Custom of Couvade* (Manchester: Manchester University Press).

Ehrenreich, B., and D. English. 1979. *For Her Own Good: 150 Years of Experts' Advice to Women* (Garden City, NY: Anchor/Doubleday).

Ellison, K., and J.L. Genz. 1978. 'The Police Officer as Burned Out Samaritan', *FBI Law Enforcement Bulletin* 47 (3) (March).

Freudenberger, H.J. 1977. 'Burn-Out: Occupational Hazard of Child Care Workers', *Child Care Quarterly* 6 (2).

———, and G. Richelson. 1980. *Burn-Out* (New York: Doubleday).

Friedan, B. 1963. *The Feminine Mystique* (New York: Dell).

Gilman, C.P. [1899] 1973. *The Yellow Wallpaper* (Old Westbury, NY: Feminist Press).

Greenspan, K. 1978. 'Biologic Feedback and Cardiovascular Disease', *Psychosomatics* 19 (11).

Hamilton, J.A. 1962. *Postpartum Psychiatric Problems* (St Louis, MO: C.V. Mosby).

Hayden, D. 1979. 'Charlotte Perkins Gilman and the Kitchenless House', *Radical History Review* 21: 225–47.

———. 1981. *The Grand Domestic Revolution: A History of Feminist Designs for American Homes, Neighbourhoods and Cities* (Cambridge, MA: MIT Press).

Holmes, T., and R. Rahe. 1967. 'The Social Adjustment Rating Scale', *Journal of Psychosomatic Research* 1 (2).

Howe, L.K. 1975. *Pink Collar Workers* (New York: Avon Books).

Jordan, B. 1978. *Birth in Four Cultures: A Cross-Cultural Investigation of Childbirth in Yucatan, Holland, Sweden, and the United States* (Montreal: Eden Press).

Karacan, I., and R.L. Williams. 1970. 'Current Advances in Theory and Practice Relating to Postpartum Syndromes', *Psychiatry in Medicine* 1: 307–28.

Karasek, R.A. 1979. 'Job Demands, Job Decision Latitude, and Mental Strain: Implication for Job Redesign', *Administration Science Quarterly* 24:285–308.

Kruckman, L. 1980. 'From Institutionalization to Self-Help: A Review of Postpartum Depression Treatment' (Chicago: School of Public Health, University of Illinois Medical Center).

Kupferer, H.J.K. 1965. 'Couvade: Ritual or Illness?' *American Anthropologist* 67d: 99–102.

Lewis, O. 1958. *Village Life in North India* (Urbana: University of Illinois Press).

Livingston, J.E. 1976. 'An Assessment of Vitamin B_6 Status in Women with Postpartum Depression', MSc thesis, Department of Medical Generics, University of British Columbia.

Lumsden, D.P. 1981. 'Is the Concept of "Stress" of Any Use, Anymore?' in *Contributions to Primary Prevention in Mental Health*, ed. D. Randall (Toronto: Canadian Mental Health Association).

Luxton, M. 1980. *More Than a Labour of Love: Three Generations of Women's Work in the Home* (Toronto: The Women's Press).

———. 1983. 'Two Hands for the Clock: Changing Patterns in the Domestic Division of Labour', *Studies in Political Economy* 12.

Maslach, C. 1976. 'Burned-Out', *Human Behaviour* (Sept.).

———, and A. Pines. 1977. 'The Burn-Out Syndrome in the Day Care Setting', *Child Care Quarterly* 6 (2) (Summer): 100–13.

Mattingly, M.A. 1977. 'Sources of Stress and Burnout in Professional Child Care Work', *Child Care Quarterly* 6 (2).

Mead, M. 1962. 'A Cultural Anthropological Approach to Maternal Deprivation' in *Deprivation of Maternal Health Care: A Reassessment of its Effects*, ed. World Health Organization (Geneva: WHO).

Meissner, M. et al. 1975. 'No Exit for Wives: Sexual Division Labour and the Cumulation of Household Demands', University of British Columbia. *Canadian Review of Sociology and Anthropology* 125, (4) Part 1 (Nov.).

Metraux, A. 1963. 'The Couvade' in *Handbook of South American Indians* v. 5, ed. J.H. Stewart (New York: Cooper Square).

Newman, L. 1966. 'The Couvade: A Reply to Kupferer', *American Anthropologist* 68.

Oakley, A. 1972. *Sex, Gender and Society* (London: Temple-Smith).

———. 1976. *Housewife* (Harmondsworth, UK: Penguin).

Parlee, M.B. 1980. 'Psychological Aspects of Menstruation, Childbirth, and Menopause' in *Psychology of Women: Future Directions Research*, eds J.A. Sherman and F.L. Denmark (New York: Psychological Dimensions).

Pines, A., and B. Kafry. 1978. 'Occupational Tedium in the Social Services', *Social Work* (Nov.): 499–508.

Proulx, M. 1978. *Five Million Women: A Study of the Canadian Housewife* (Ottawa: Advisory Council on the Status of Women).

Rice, M.S. 1937. *Working Class Wives: Their Health and Conditions* (Harmondsworth, UK: Penguin).

Robertson, J. 1976. 'The Abusive Parent: A Different Perspective', *Canada's Mental Health* 24, 4 (Dec.): 18–19.

———. 1980. 'A Treatment Model for Post-Partum Depression', *Canada's Mental Health* (Summer).

———, with A. Howard. 1980. *The Post-Partum Counselling Service Manual* (British Columbia: Ministry of Human Resources).

Rosenberg, H. 1980. 'After Birth Blues', *Healthsharing* (Winter): 18–20.

———. 1984. 'The Home is the Workplace' in *Double Exposure: Women's Health Hazards on the Job and at Home*, ed. W. Chavkin (New York: Monthly Review Press).

Ross, K.G. 1979. *Good Day Care: Fighting for It, Getting It, Keeping It* (Toronto: The Women's Press).

Rutherford, F.W. 1971. *You and Your Baby: From Conception Through to the First Year* (New York: Signet).

Saulnier, K.M. 1988. 'Social Networks and the Transition to Motherhood' in *Families and Social Networks*, ed. R. Milardo.

Seccombe, W. 1983. 'Marxism and Demography', *New Left Review* 137.

Seltzer, A. 1980. 'Postpartum Mental Syndrome', *Canadian Family Physician* 26 (November): 1546–50.

Selye, H. 1956. *The Stress of Life* (New York: McGraw-Hill).

———. 1974. *Stress Without Distress* (Toronto: McClelland & Stewart).

———. 1980. Preface to Selye's Guide to Stress Research, v. 1 (New York: McGraw-Hill).

Silverman, S. 1975. 'The Life Crisis as a Social Function' in *Toward an Anthropology of Women*, ed. R. Reiter (New York: Monthly Review Press).

Smith, D.E. 1973. 'Women, the Family, and Corporate Capitalism' in *Women in Canada*, ed. M. Stephenson (Toronto: New Press).

Solway, J. 1984. 'Women and Work among the Bakgalagiadi of Botswana', paper presented at the Canadian Ethnology Society, Montreal.

Stellman, J.M., and S. Daum. 1973. *Work Is Dangerous to Your Health* (New York: Vintage).

Tepperman, J. 1976. *Not Servants, Not Machines* (Boston: Beacon Press).

Weissman, M.M., and G. Klerman. 1977. 'Sex Differences and the Epidemiology of Depression', *Archives of General Psychiatry* 34 (Jan.): 98–111.

Welburn, V. 1980. *Postnatal Depression* (Glasgow: Fontana).

Yalom, D.I. 1968. 'Postpartum Blues Syndrome' *Archives of General Psychiatry*, 18: 16–27.

Zaretsky, E. 1976. *Capitalism, the Family and Personal Life* (New York: Harper & Row).

Section 4 | The Gendered Division of Household Work

*F*or decades, many social researchers have focused their energy on determining whether men's involvement in the responsibilities of the home has increased, given that most women now share the role of income earning. Their answer continues to be that the gendered division of household work has not significantly changed. Understanding why that is so requires a thorough understanding of the gender relations at the heart of heterosexual families.

Chapter 21

The incompatibility of paid employment and family responsibilities is something with which most Canadian women, and many men, must struggle daily. Meg Luxton reviews recent evidence on how Canadian couples are allocating paid and unpaid work. Based on recent interviews of Toronto family members, she describes the dilemmas common in many households. Then she examines the various strategies that may be pursued in solving the problem of the 'double day' of work.

Family Coping Strategies:
Balancing Paid Employment and Domestic Labour

Meg Luxton

Since the early twentieth century, the majority of families in Canada have made a living by combining paid employment and unpaid domestic labour.[1] To ensure an income, one or more family members sell their capacity to work, or their labour power, to an employer. On the job their labour power is consumed and they earn its monetary recompense, a wage or salary. In consumer markets and in their homes, people use those earnings and their unpaid labour to obtain and produce the goods and services that make up the means of subsistence for themselves and their families. Each day, the means of subsistence are prepared and consumed and family subsistence, including the capacity to work again, is produced. This labour of social reproduction ensures the survival of both individuals and the society as a whole (Fox and Luxton, Chapter 3 this text). A man explained how this cycle of production and consumption played out in his daily life:[2]

> I like my job. It's interesting and it pays pretty good. I go to work every day, come home, and you know how it is, some of the money you make has to go to food and the mortgage and stuff you need for everyday. So you have to keep working just to have

enough money to live on. And you hope that maybe you can make a bit more than you need for everyday. If you're lucky, maybe you do (M A#27 1/00).

This particular form of family economy imposes conflicting demands on people whose livelihood depends on it. A young mother with two preschool children described her situation:

> I have to work and so does my husband. Without both incomes we wouldn't get by. But we have two little kids. So who is supposed to look after them? If I quit work, I could stay home with them, but we wouldn't be able to pay the bills. If we pay someone else to look after the kids, it takes almost all of my pay. Like it's almost impossible! I think maybe people won't be able to have families soon, unless something changes (F A#26 1/00).

As her description implies, while such family livelihoods depend on both paid employment and domestic labour, the organization of the two different labour processes mean that the demands of one are at odds with the demands of the other. An office worker explained how she saw the issue:

At my workplace they call it 'family friendly' policies and talk a lot about helping us employees 'balance work and family'. Mostly it just means you can come in a bit earlier and leave earlier, or it's okay to take unpaid time off occasionally if your kids are sick or that it's okay to have your kids call you at work. And though they call it 'family', they really mean women 'cause the guys never have to worry about that stuff. And it doesn't really help with the fact that if you're at work, you can't be at home looking after things. And if you stay home, you don't get paid (F A#30 1/00).

As the comments of these two women indicate, the massive entry of women into the paid labour force has made it harder for individual families to manage their domestic responsibilities. As people struggled to find ways of improving the conditions of their lives, a range of social policies and practices have developed, some of which have made paid work and domestic labour a bit more compatible. These include universal services such as education and health care and a range of policies designed to ensure minimum income and employment standards, access to housing, childcare, and care of dependent adults (Ursel 1992). However, most social policies assume that individuals and their families are primarily responsible for personal caregiving and that women remain primarily responsible for managing the competing demands of the two labours necessary for family subsistence (Eichler 1988, 1997). A woman explained how this worked:

My husband was injured at work. He was in hospital for weeks and we thought he was going to die. So I took time off work to stay with him. Then I had to go back to work. When he got out of hospital, he needed full-time care. Everyone—the doctors, the social workers, the nurses—they all assumed I would take care of him. When I said I couldn't, they acted like I was a monster! Surely if I was a good wife I would do anything for him. Like who was going to pay the bills? I said, he needs care, he should get it. That's what health care is for. Or, he was injured at work, the company should pay someone to care for him. It was a big struggle. I spent hours fighting to get him the care he needed. They really tried to make me do everything but I said I can't, I have to work. I felt terrible, but he understood (F M#16 12/99).

Changing Patterns of Paid Employment

In the early twentieth century, the tensions between the two labours were mediated by the predominant family form, a heterosexual nuclear family, and its conventional divisions of labour based on gender and age. According to prevailing norms, adult men were 'breadwinners' whose primary responsibility was to earn an income for the family while adult women were 'housewives' whose primary responsibility was running the family home and caring for its members.[3] In practice, the higher the man's income and the more secure his employment, the less income other family members had to provide. Whether income-earning men were available or not, women were primarily responsible for domestic labour, and their participation in paid employment was always negotiated in relation to the needs of family members, especially when children were young or when there were family members who needed regular care related to illness, disability, or aging. Where necessary, many women augmented family incomes by intensifying domestic labour—making preserves, clothing, and other items for household use or engaging in a variety of home-based income-generating activities such as taking in laundry or sewing or renting rooms to boarders. Children were typically expected either to attend school as part of a strategy to strengthen their future employment chances or to get paid employment and contribute to the family economy by either contributing their earnings to the family household or reducing its expenses by moving away to set up their own household. Where necessary, older girls were expected to contribute to domestic labour, especially where there were a number of younger children or where their mother had income-generating work that made it difficult for her to handle all the domestic labour (Bradbury 1993 and Chapter 8, this text).

This strategy, widely accepted as the norm, was idealized as the appropriate way to organize family life and naturalized in economic and social policies as diverse as wage rates and welfare regulations (Ursel 1992; Armstrong and Armstrong 1994). From the early twentieth century until the 1970s it was the dominant family form and division of labour (Armstrong and Armstrong 1994: 84–5). However, as Dionne Brand (1994) and Linda Carty (1994) have shown, African Canadian woman have a history of higher than average labour-force participation rates. Indigenous or aboriginal women have had lower than average labour-force participation rates but have worked in mixed economies since colonization (Abele 1997). Immigration policies have permitted particular categories of women workers to enter Canada to fill certain types of labour needs (Stasiulis 1997; Preston and Giles 1997). Patterns of class, race, ethnicity, national origin, region, religion, and other cultural differences shaped the ways in which different populations both were located in the labour market and related to prevailing norms and the economic and social policies that presumed specific family forms and divisions of labour. A woman described her mother's experience as an immigrant:

> She came here in the fifties, as a domestic worker. She came because she had two daughters and in Jamaica she couldn't make enough to support us. The Canadian government wouldn't let her bring us so for years she sent money home and our grandmother raised us (F A#13 11/99).

Another woman described how the prevailing norm of the income-earning husband and the homemaker wife created problems for her family in the 1960s:

> I remember how ashamed I used to feel because my father was unemployed—for years—and my mother went out to work. The worst was when teachers would tell me my mother should come to help at some school event, and I would have to explain that she couldn't. They would look at me and I always felt like scum of the earth. In those days, fathers worked and mothers stayed home and anyone who didn't conform was obviously of a lesser sort (F A#15 1/00).

Never a satisfactory resolution, this strategy excluded those who did not live in heterosexual nuclear families and created pressures on people to marry. It depended on the man's ability to earn enough money to support a dependent wife and children, something few men actually achieved. It put pressure on men as the sole income providers while isolating women in a demanding low status and unpaid job. It made women economically dependent on their husbands which left them vulnerable, especially if the relationship broke down (Luxton 1980). While it encouraged economic independence on the part of young-adult children, in low-income households it easily pitted parents and young-adult children against each other in struggles over family unity versus individual independence.[4] Parents might urge children to leave school to earn a living and contribute to the family household whereas children often preferred to stay in school or set up their own households. Parental demands often undercut girls' chances for staying in school by expecting them to help out at home.[5] This strategy also depended on families' capacities to make ends meet by expanding unpaid labour in the home to reduce expenses, something that became difficult as household expenses were increasingly monetary, such as mortgage payments and taxes—demanding income rather than useable goods (Parr 1999: 101–18).

Throughout the century, the participation rates of women in the formal labour force steadily increased, dramatically changing family economics and divisions of labour (see Table 1). Among cohabiting male-female couples in 1961, almost 70 per cent relied on the man as the single income provider. By 1991 only 19 per cent did so, a number that has remained fairly constant since. In the majority of cohabiting male-female families (61 per cent), both adults had paid employment and, in 5 per cent, women were the sole income providers (Oderkirk, Silver, and Prud'homme 1994). By 1997 women were the higher income earner in 23 per cent of couples and the sole income provider in about 20 per cent of couples (Globe and Mail 21 Feb. 2000: A2). Most dramatically, the labour-force participation rates of married women with young preschool children increased from 49.4 per cent in 1981 to 69.0 per cent in 1991. By 2000, the vast majority of mothers with young children remained in the labour force.

There were many reasons for such changes. The growth of the service sector in the 1960s and 1970s created a particular demand for women workers (Marchak 1987). Birthrates have declined as women had fewer children, and as a result women spent less of their adult lives in active child care. In 1961 the average number of children born per woman was 3.84 (Grindstaff 1995); by 1997 it was 1.6 (Statistics Canada 2000: 7). Changing gender ideologies, fuelled by the revitalization of the feminist movement, reflected women's interest in paid employment, as protection from the vulnerability of dependency on men, to augment their families' incomes, and because they liked the income, sociability, and

Table 1: Canadian Labour Force Participation Rates of All Men, All Women, and Married Women 1901–1995

Year	All Men	All Women	Married Women	Women as a % of the Total Labour Force
1901	78.3	14.4	n.a.	13.3
1911	82.0	16.6	n.a.	13.3
1921	80.3	17.7	2.16	15.4
1931	78.4	19.4	3.45	16.9
1941	85.6*	22.9*	3.74	24.8
1951	84.4	24.4	9.56	22.0
1961	81.1	29.3	20.7	29.6
1971	77.3	39.4	33.0	34.4
1981	78.7	52.3	51.4	40.8
1991	75.1	58.5	61.7	45.4
1995	72.5	57.4	61.4	45.1

*includes those in active service
Population 15 years of age and over

Sources: Leacy, F.H., ed. in *Historical Statistics of Canada*, 2nd edn, eds M.C. Urquhart and K.A.H. Buckley (Toronto: Macmillan, 1965), 107–23; Statistics Canada, *Historical Labour Force Statistics, 1995*, cat. no. 71–201; *Labour Force Annual Averages*, cat. no. 71–529; *Women in Canada*, cat. no. 89503E, p.78; 1961 Census 94–536.

status that paid employment secures. The potential consequences of women's economic dependency on men were revealed by a 1997 study which showed that men gained financially when their marriages ended; their incomes went up 10 per cent. In contrast, women and children did poorly; women lost about 23 per cent of their incomes. The only way women could regain their former financial status was by remarrying (*Toronto Star* 10 April 1997).

Men's earnings since the 1980s typically have been insufficient to support a family. The average earnings of men over 35 years of age have remained relatively unchanged while younger men's earnings have declined (Best 1995; Morissette 1997). The importance of women's earnings to total family income is reflected in the percentage of families whose income would fall below the Low Income Cut-off if women's earning were not available.[6] In 1992, the average family had to work 77 weeks per year just to pay the bills. Since there are only 52 weeks in a year that meant either families had to go deeply into debt, or they had to rely on more than one income (*Toronto Star* 7 Feb. 1998). In the same year, 4 per cent of dual-earner families had low incomes; if wives' earnings were deducted, this number would have increased to 16 per cent (Statistics Canada 1995b: 88). Between 1991 and 1996, average family incomes for all husband-wife families in Canada declined. Where the wife had no income, family income declined by 6.9 per cent, compared to families where the wife was employed whose incomes declined by 1.9 per cent (Statistics Canada 1998b: 3).

But, like men, most women seek paid employment for more than just financial benefits. A 1995 Statistics Canada survey found that 64 per cent of adult women said that having a paid job was important for their personal happiness and 55 per cent agreed that having a paid job was the best way for a woman to be an independent person (Ghalam 1997: 16). A mother who had stayed home for two years after her first child was born, refused to do so again. She explained why:

When I stayed home, I hated it. I only did it because I really thought it was the best thing for the baby. I missed going to work, I was bored at home and I don't think it was so great for the baby to have me moping around. With what we're paying for childcare, it isn't financially worth our while me working, but a job is more than money (F A#19).

By the early twenty-first century, women had become an integral part of the paid labour force and women's paid employment was an essential part of their household's livelihood. Employers depended on women's labour force participation. In 2000, 54.8 per cent of women twenty-four years of age and over had paid employment and women were about 45 per cent of all paid workers (*Globe and Mail* 21 Feb. 2000).

However, while women are increasingly in the paid labour force for most of their adult lives, their relationship to paid work continues to be quite different from men's. Jobs remain significantly sex segregated with women clustered in jobs that are typically low paid. Even when they do the same work, women often get paid less than men. In 1996 the top ten jobs for men were (in descending order) truck drivers, retail sales, janitors, retail trade managers, farmers, sales reps, and wholesale trade, motor vehicle mechanics, material handlers, carpenters, construction trade helpers. For women they were retail sales, secretaries, cashiers, registered nurses, accounting clerks, elementary teachers, food servers, general office clerks, babysitters, receptionists (*Toronto Star* 18 March 1998). Women's attachment to the labour force continues to be shaped by their responsibilities for domestic labour. Under pressure to manage things at home, they often take part-time or home-based employment. They are about 70 per cent of all part-time workers, 47 per cent of home-based employment (Ghalam 1993) and 29 per cent of all self-employed workers (Nadwodny 1996: 17). They are far more likely (62 per cent) than men (27 per cent) to have employment interruptions 'stopping working for pay for a period of six months or more' (Fast and Da Pont 1997: 3). The combination of job ghettos, reduced work time, work interruptions, and discriminatory pay rates means that women continue to earn less than men (Drolet 1999).

But just as domestic labour responsibilities shape women's attachment to paid employment, paid employment shapes men's and women's relationship to domestic labour. The assumption that men are income earners and do not have responsibility for domestic labour is central to the way most paid work is organized and fundamental to most male-dominated occupations (Luxton and Corman forthcoming). While employers need workers, they have no immediate interest in how their workers live, whether they support anyone else with their earnings, nor whether their workers have children or are responsible for caring for other people. Some employers have implemented 'family friendly' policies, and the labour and women's movements have won important policies such as paid maternity and parental leaves or unpaid personal leaves, but, for the most part, paid employment is organized on the principle that during working hours, workers are available for work and undistracted by other concerns. Typical male occupations usually assume that workers can do eight-hour shifts or longer, can be counted on to do overtime or travel, and don't expect time off for the birth of a child or to care for people who are sick or elderly. Many men assume that if they provide their family's main income, they have met their familial responsibilities and cannot be expected to take full responsibility for domestic labour as well.

As more women with young children and other pressing domestic responsibilities entered the paid labour force, they confronted directly the problems arising from the way paid employment fails to accommodate domestic labour. Caregiving to children, elderly, ill, or disabled people requires attention and energy, often unpredictably. The more dependent the person, the more likely their lives may depend on immediate care, regardless of the paid work responsibilities of the caregiver. A mother described how this played out in her life:

> I got a phone call at work. My supervisor came to tell me and he was pissed off. He said I was not ever to get calls at work again but he let me go. We're paid piece work so I don't know why he was so mad. He wasn't paying me when I stopped working. It was my daughter's teacher. She'd fallen and hurt her head and the ambulance was taking her to the hospital. I told the supervisor I had to go to the hospital. He said if I didn't go straight back to work I was fired! Well, I had no choice did I? (F M#14 12/99).

Changing Strategies for Managing Domestic Labour and Paid Employment

As the homemaker wife/income-earner husband strategy became increasingly less of an option, families developed a variety of other strategies to cope with the competing demands of domestic labour and paid employment. Where both partners have paid work, the responsibility for income generating is shared, providing the household with some protection from the insecurities of the labour market. A man explained:

> I got laid off with no warning. We showed up for work one night and the place was padlocked. They'd gone bankrupt and the owners had disappeared. Well, if it had happened two years earlier, we would have been in deep trouble, but as it was, my wife was working so we managed (M A#19 12/99).

This arrangement not only reduces the onus on men to provide incomes for their families, it also reduces women's dependence on their husbands:

> I never thought about it before, but after I started working, I realized how much it meant

to me not to have to ask him for every penny.
I love having my own money (F A#22 1/00).

However, with no one available to do domestic labour full-time, it is harder to get it done, caregivers for dependants have to be found and the relationships managed. There are additional expenses as well as complications arising from scheduling, coordinating, and planning. A woman with two school-aged children described her arrangements:

> I work 11–3 Mondays to Wednesdays and 3–9 on Thursdays and Fridays. My husband works rotating shifts so one week he's on days 7–3, then afternoons 3–11, then nights 11–7. So the way we do it is, if one of us is home, no problem. If it's a Thursday and my husband can't be there, the kids can go to a neighbour's after school and she will keep them til I get home. It's a bit late. They don't get to bed til 10 p.m. which means it's a struggle to get them up in time to go to school the next morning. If it's a Friday, either my girlfriend comes over to stay with them or I hire a babysitter—one of the kids from the local high school. Well, you can imagine how many phone calls it takes each week to make sure everything works! (F A#17 12/99).

WOMEN'S STRATEGIES FOR COPING WITH THE DOUBLE DAY

Women who make the transition from being either childless employees or full-time mothers at home to being employed mothers often begin their new double day by trying to do both jobs so that neither deflects from the other. A women with two preschool children described how she presented herself at work:

> When I came back to work after my maternity leave, I knew I had to act like I did before I had children, as if I had no kids. My workplace had been really good to me—no

fuss about maternity leave either time. They gave me really nice showers for both babies. But I knew enough was enough. They expected me to leave anything to do with the kids at home and I couldn't let it come up at work. Occasionally my boss will ask how my children are, but he does it to be friendly. He doesn't really want to know. So I make sure, no matter what is happening, no one at work ever sees me dealing with family stuff (F M#16 11/99).

Many women try to continue their domestic labour as if they had no other demands on their time and energy (Luxton 1990: 43). A woman recalled her efforts, when she first started her job, to maintain what she considered appropriate standards at home:

> I was running from morning til night, and late into the night at that. My house was spotless, my kids took home baking to parents' night, I made their Hallowe'en costumes myself, and I made sure we ate home-cooked meals every night. That lasted for about a year. Then I collapsed. I just couldn't keep it up and I stopped feeling like I should (F M#18 1/00).

Few women can keep up such intensity for very long. While some maintain reduced involvement in paid employment, working part-time or trying to work from home, most end up relinquishing their exacting standards for domestic labour in order to reduce the amount of time they have to spend. The more hours women spend in paid employment, the more they cut back on household labour (Frederick 1995; Luxton and Corman forthcoming). They tolerate lower standards of cleanliness and tidiness, rely more on take-out foods, and as one woman put it:

> . . . just focus on what's important and let the rest go hang. What matters is spending time

with the kids. If we do it in a messy house, so what? If I buy the snacks when it's my time to contribute to school lunches, so what? (F A#22 1/00).

It is much more difficult for most women to cut back on the amount of time and energy they put into caregiving. A mother described the difficult changes she had to make when her employer changed the time she had to start work:

My shift used to start at 10 a.m. That was very good. I got the children up and took them to the daycare. We had a lot of time. We could sing and tell stories and I didn't have to rush them. Mornings were a very good time. Now I have to be at work at 7 a.m. I let the children sleep until 5:30. Then I must wake them. It is very hard. They are so tired and do not want to get up and then I have to rush, rush, rush. My employer, he says if we are late three times we get fired so I am very mean to my children in the morning now. It makes me very sad (F A#28 1/00).

The less time and energy mothers have available to them, the less they can attend to their children. One mother captured an important effect of time constraints and stress on her parenting:

Mostly for me it isn't the time per se. My kids know I am busy and they're fine with it. It's when I am so stretched and stressed that I lose my sense of delight in their lives. I get snappy. I'm short with them. My [15-year-old] son said the other day, 'Mom, when you're not here or you're upstairs working, and I don't see you, it's okay because I know you love me. But when you scream at me, I don't feel loved.' He's right. But sometimes I just lose it. I can't cope (F M#18 11/99).

Women who are already stretched by employment and childcare responsibilities may find it impossible to care for others, imposing cruel choices on them. A single mother, struggling to manage on two part-time jobs, felt she had too little time for her three children, when her mother was suddenly taken ill:

I just cry all the time. I am too tired. I can't give my kids the attention they need. I am terrified I will lose my job and now this! My mama's in hospital and she needs me. Yesterday I didn't even get to visit her! But my youngest didn't come home from school so I went looking for him. I felt like God was making me choose between my mama and my son! (F M#25 3/00).

This strategy imposes serious strains on women. A national survey found that more than 28 per cent of women and slightly less than 16 per cent of men in relationships where both were employed full-time felt severely time crunched (Frederick 1993: 8). 'Nearly 50 per cent of full-time . . . mothers reported they would like to spend more time alone. The proportion for men never rises much above 25 per cent' (Frederick 1995: 58).

SHARING DOMESTIC LABOUR WITH MEN

As more and more women took on paid employment, there was a widespread assumption that their male partners would take on more domestic labour. Since the 1970s, popular media and academic studies alike have proliferated, claiming that men are beginning to increase their involvement in household labour, especially childcare (McMahon 1999). Public opinion polls in Canada show that since the 1970s there has been an increase from about 50 per cent to over 80 per cent of adults who agree that husbands should share domestic labour (Luxton 1990; Wilson 1991: 56). However, extensive studies of the impact of women's employment on domestic labour actually show that household labour remains sex segregated and that women do the bulk of it (Nakhaie 1995). As McMahon (1999: 13) documents, hundreds of studies from Australia, Europe, the United States, and Canada reveal that women's employment has a minimal impact on men's involvement in domestic labour, and men's domestic-labour participation rates remain consistent, regardless of race or social class differences across various countries: 'there are no significant cross-cultural and cross-class differences in men's performance of domestic labour'.[7]

A 1983 Canadian study of a national sample of 2,577 people investigated the extent to which men were taking on more traditionally female household tasks. In dual-earner couples, on average, women performed over 76 per cent of feminine-typed tasks, while men did less than 30 per cent (Brayfield 1992: 25). The 1992 General Social Survey found that even among young people 'young women did more unpaid work than young men and spent more time on the "traditionally female" chores such as cooking and housekeeping' (Frederick 1995: 14).[8] Only 10 per cent of men in dual-earner households claimed to have primary responsibility for domestic labour and an additional 10 per cent said they fully shared responsibilities (Marshall 1993). Since October 1990, fathers in Canada have been entitled to take a paid ten-week parental leave for a new baby. Of the 31,000 parents who have taken leave at the birth or adoption of a new baby, about 1,000 were fathers. Fathers as a percentage of all parents on leave have been about 3 per cent annually since 1991 (*Globe and Mail* 29 March 2000).

The 1996 census in Canada, which included questions on unpaid work for the first time, confirmed that there continued to be significant gender differences in the amount of time spent on unpaid work. Asked if they had spent time in the previous week doing housework or home maintenance, 25 per cent of women and 8 per cent of men said they spent thirty hours or more. Among those with full-time employment (thirty hours or more), 51 per cent of wives reported spending fifteen hours or more doing unpaid

housework, compared with 23 per cent of husbands. Among men and women with full-time employment and children, 64 per cent of women and 39 per cent of men spent at least fifteen hours a week on childcare. If at least one child was a preschooler, the numbers increased: 80 per cent of women and 49 per cent of men spent at least fifteen hours a week on childcare. For those with no children under 6, the proportion dropped to 51 per cent of women and 29 per cent of men (Statistics Canada 1998a: 17–18).

While survey research demonstrates general trends by comparing women and men, it does not investigate intrahousehold divisions of labour. Case studies based on interviews with both partners in a household, and especially longitudinal studies which trace domestic patterns over time reveal the interpersonal dynamics behind the time-use patterns. Typically, where households can afford to pay for services, they do so. Where household income is insufficient, men are drawn into domestic labour in limited ways, usually filling in while their wives are at their paid work (Luxton and Corman forthcoming). A majority of parents have organized their childcare by ensuring that parents work different shifts so that one of them can always be home. But while men may be providing care for their children, parenting is not gender-neutral, so the type of care fathers and mothers provide continues to be different. Women often talk about having to do additional work to compensate for men's approach to childcare. One couple's comments about their divisions of labour illustrate such gender differences at work. The man described his after- work routines:

> I get home before she does so I pick the kids up from the sitter and bring them home. I usually start dinner, then when she gets home we finish getting it ready together. We both put the kids to bed (M A#16 11/99).

His wife elaborated:

We both look after the kids. He picks them up and they usually get home about half an hour before I do. When I get in, it's crazy. The kids are hungry and squabbling so we rush to get dinner ready. Then we play a bit and do homework and read stories, then it's bath time and to bed (F A#16 11/99).

She went on to explain the difficulties she had with their arrangement:

He's great with the kids. He really is, but I wish he would be a bit more on top of things. Like, he never thinks to give them a snack when he comes home. He says it's too much bother and makes a mess and it will spoil their appetite for dinner. He'd rather just concentrate on getting dinner ready. But it means they are so cranky and strung out. I always have to break up fights and calm them down when I come in. And he never will get them doing their homework before dinner. He says they need time to play but it ends up I have to be the heavy saying 'homework now!' (F A#16 11/99).

He offered a different assessment:

She's always fussing. She thinks I should make them do their homework after school but I don't like to pressure them. They need time to relax and I don't want to be always nagging them. Then she thinks I should give them snacks and play with them, but if I did that, dinner would be late. I don't like to eat late (M A #16 11/99).

In effect, while he spent more time than she did, and both did the evening cooking and childcare together, he was ensuring that the basic work got done, while leaving the responsibility for emotional well-being and discipline to her.

There are a variety of explanations for why men have not taken on more responsibility for

domestic labour. Prevailing cultural norms about and representations of domesticity, ranging from gender-specific toys such as dolls and play kitchens to ads for household products, typically assume that men are not involved in domestic labour. Men get little public validation or support for their involvement in domestic labour and may be subject to ridicule for doing 'women's work' (Luxton 1990: 50). A man described the reaction of his employer when he asked for reduced working hours to allow him to care for his elderly father:

The request obviously threw him for a loop. He didn't want to say no outright but it made him uncomfortable, even though several women in the office have taken time off or reduced time to look after families and he had no problem with that. In fact, he is proud to say he is an enlightened employer. When I asked for the same thing, he hesitated, then he asked if my wife couldn't get time off her job. I said I wanted to look after my father. He was almost squirming but he finally agreed I could work four days and leave early two of those days. But he kept asking me if I really wanted to be doing it. It was like he couldn't believe I really wanted to do it. It was hard not to feel like a freak (M M#23 1/00).

Even fewer men than women have paid jobs that in any way help workers accommodate family responsibilities, and in workplaces that are predominantly male, work practices typically have evolved to seriously preclude any such possibilities (Luxton and Corman forthcoming).

Existing sex-based differences in income reinforce sexual divisions in the home. In most households where both partners are employed, men are still typically the higher income-earners. If the woman's paid time is worth substantially less than her husband's, it makes sense financially for her to quit work in order to take care of a newborn or an elderly relative while her partner keeps his job. This apparently sensible coping strategy increases the pay gap between them, for in moving in and out of the labour force more frequently, her earning potential is diminished. The more continuous employment record of the man is rewarded with promotions, seniority, training opportunities, and so on. This strategy also reproduces gender differences because it reinforces women's involvement in caregiving while undermining men's possibilities of increasing theirs:

> Before the baby was born we agreed we both wanted to share childcare. But after she was born, I was home all the time so I just got better at caring for her and she knew me. He helps out a lot but it's not like what I do (F A#24 1/00).

When men are the higher income-earners, both women and men can readily justify subordinating domestic demands to the requirements of his employment. Whether this means moving to accommodate his transfer and promotion, keeping the children quiet during the day while a shift worker sleeps or a professional works at home on the weekend, or accepting men's prolonged absence from the home as they work overtime to meet their job's expectations, most women accept the demands of men's paid employment as a legitimate reason for men's lack of domestic labour:

> He often stays late at work so how can I expect him to come home after such a long day and start housework. That's just too much (F M#18 1/00).

The importance of economic earnings in shaping domestic divisions of labour is underscored by evidence that suggests that men's participation in domestic labour may increase in relation to the strength of their wives' labour force attachment. The longer women are in paid employment and the greater the women's income is as a proportion of total household income, the more likely men

are to do domestic labour (Luxton 1981; Marshall 1993).

But the power that accrues to most men who are income-earners plays out in other ways as well. When so few men do domestic labour, those who do are often highly praised for even minimal contributions, a practice that can easily reinforce the notion that domestic labour is not expected of men. A woman conveyed her confusion about how to assess her husband's contributions:

> Everyone tells me that he is so terrific around the house. They tell me I am so lucky to have a husband who does so much. All my friends are forever telling me they wish their husbands were half as helpful. So then, I feel so mean when I want to say he doesn't do nearly enough. Maybe I expect too much? And sometimes when we fight over it, he says, 'Well all your friends say I do more than my share. So what's your problem?' I don't know (F M#19 1/00).

In the context of marriage and a commitment to making it work, many women hesitate to escalate their demands that men do more. They risk undermining their important and valued sense that their relationship is based on love and mutual caring if they challenge their partners to do more, and lose. If they force a serious confrontation about the distribution of domestic labour, they run the risk of provoking a major fight. In the interests of domestic harmony and of maintaining their sense of the value of their marriage, many women concede. Conversely, some women decide that struggles over the redistribution of household labour and responsibilities are not worth it. Growing numbers of young women and men are not marrying, more women are choosing to remain childless, and more women are having children without marrying (Oderkirk 1994: 5). Married women who are frustrated by their husbands' resistance may opt to leave the marriage. Charles Hobart (1996:

171) argues that one explanation for contemporary divorce rates is that:

> paid employment has greatly reduced the time available to wives for domestic work, and having paycheques has empowered them, giving them increased influence and independence. Conflict has resulted, over (1) husbands' reluctance to share the domestic work fairly and (2) wives' refusal to be traditionally subservient.

The strategy of redistributing domestic labour between women and men is thus difficult to implement, both because the material conditions of social life work against it, and because, typically, men have the power in their own households to resist. It is not in their interests to take on more, unpaid, work, especially if their wives continue to do it if they refuse. Women's efforts to encourage men to do more are hampered by the private nature of family life. Their struggles are rarely understood as part of major changes in social divisions of labour; instead they are experienced as private conflicts between the individuals involved. Unlike struggles to change the occupational segregation of the paid labour force, where collective action by unions, legal challenges and public campaigns have provided support for the workers involved, efforts to change household divisions of labour remain private, the interpersonal struggles of the couple involved.

Finally, systemic sexism means that not only do most men resist changing domestic divisions of labour, but there is little social recognition of the problem and widespread resistance to feminist efforts to make a political issue of the inequality. As McMahon (1999: vi) has argued, 'the central role men's material interests play in their motivation to defend the gendered status quo' has been 'systematically obscured or marginalised in both popular and academic discussion' because men have deeply vested interests in keeping the discussion of the existing inequalities in

the gendered division of labour in the home 'blandly apolitical'.

PAYING FOR DOMESTIC LABOUR

One solution, for those who can afford it, is to hire replacement labour such as cleaners, babysitters, nannies, or nursing care or to pay for services such as restaurant meals, nursery schools, or nursing homes. A wife's sole responsibility for housework and a husband's 'propensity for doing housework' both decline as each individual's income increases (Marshall 1993). The more money people have available to them, the more they are able, and inclined, to purchase services and labour instead of doing the work themselves (Brayfield 1992: 28). A lawyer described what she did when her mother was released from hospital needing full-time care:

> For the first few days, she came to my home and I hired round-the-clock nursing care. But it was very unsatisfactory. I couldn't rely on them. They kept phoning me to ask questions and I didn't really trust them around the house. So I contacted one of these services and got them to locate a good nursing home. It costs the earth, but I don't have to worry (F M#15 11/99).

There are at least four problems with this solution. The first was identified by the same lawyer who was satisfied with the care her mother received but regretted her lack of personal involvement, a lack imposed by her need to work long hours in order to make enough money to pay for the care:

> I could afford it. That wasn't the problem. But I felt terrible. I want to be more involved, you know. If she could have stayed at home I could have seen her more often and been much more involved in her care every day. As it is, I go to visit early in the morning on the way to work and I pop in briefly at night. But it's not the same (F M#15 11/99).

The second problem is that it makes no economic sense for families to pay more for services than the earnings of their lower earner. That means in effect that relatively low-earning women hire other women at even lower earnings or pay for services that are affordable only because the employees are paid low wages. Such dynamics perpetuate low-wage employment and trap immigrant women who come to Canada under government foreign domestic worker plans in terrible working conditions (Giles and Arat-Koc 1994; Bakan and Stasiulus 1997). As Sedef Arat-Koc notes (1990: 97–8), they also pit women against each other:

> Current domestic service arrangements bring the interests of employers and employees into conflict. Given the pressures on their budget and time that some middle-class working couples do indeed face, a domestic service relationship may turn into a zero-sum game in which improvements in the pay and working conditions of domestic workers mean losses for the employers. As a relationship between female employers and workers, domestic service emphasizes, most clearly, the class, racial/ethnic and citizenship differences among women at the expense of their gender unity.

A woman who had hired a foreign nanny described how such differences had a devastating effect on her children:

> At first we got along fine and the children loved her. She was always terrific with them. Gradually things got tense. If I was late getting home, she would be mad. Then she wanted more money and I just couldn't afford it. It was too uncomfortable and I was so relieved when she left but the children were devastated. They cried for months for their 'other mother' (F M#13 12/99).

Strategies that involve purchasing services are attractive to many people because they are relatively straightforward and do not require people to engage in lengthy and complicated political negotiations to change legal and social policies. However, as they depend on maximizing individual family incomes, they encourage competition among people in a society. They generate tendencies for individuals to want higher pay and lower taxes even when reductions to government revenues mean cuts to the social services available to everyone. A unionized worker described the impact such views had on collective bargaining in her local:

> Up to now, we have always had a commitment to ensuring those at the lowest pay got the most. But recently, more and more members are saying they don't care about making pay rates more fair. They just want more money for themselves. It's very divisive (F M#25 2/00).

A parent involved in his daughter's daycare centre made a similar point, showing how such practices increase inequalities:

> I'm on the board at our daycare centre. We are part of a large coalition of groups who have been fighting for a national childcare plan for Canada. We want the federal and provincial governments to fund great childcare centres everywhere. Economists have done the calculations. We could afford it. But so many people are calling for tax cuts. If governments have less money, they won't fund childcare. But the tax cuts won't give individual people enough money to buy childcare. They will just mean the rich get richer and the poor get less money and no services (M A#25 2/00).

The most important problem with hiring or purchasing alternatives is that most households simply cannot afford to do so. The costs of childcare in a regulated centre, for example, were in 2000 about $9,000 a year for infants (*Toronto Star* 11 Sept. 1999: A1, A30), a hefty chunk out of the average full-year full-time earnings for women of $31,506 per year (Drolet 1999: 25). The majority of households cannot sustain such expenditures over any length of time.

CHANGING PAID EMPLOYMENT —'FAMILY FRIENDLY' WORKPLACES

Another strategy for coping with the conflicting demands of paid employment and unpaid domestic labour has focused on changing the organization of paid work. As individuals, community activists and union members, employees have struggled to make workplaces more accommodating of employees' personal lives (de Wolff 1994). They have fought for maternity, parental, and caregiving leaves (Heitlinger 1993; Mishra 1996). They have argued for flexible working hours that allow workers to coordinate their time more effectively with family demands. Employers have responded unevenly to such demands (Duxbury et al. 1992). Most are reluctant to implement such policies unless they see an obvious advantage to the success of their enterprise. Policy analyst Judith Maxwell (2000) argues that even though there is a tension between short-term goals of immediate growth in earnings and long-term goals of the viability of the enterprise and future productivity, business leaders have an interest in promoting more effective policies:

> Employers also have an immediate role to play in the way they support today's employees in their role as parents. Employers should ask these parents what working conditions they need to be the best that they can be at work, and still do their best for their children.

Workers who have access to such policies readily acknowledge that even limited programs help. However, they do not always work in ways that policy analysts expect. A study by Statistics Canada found that while such policies were originally intended to support women workers, typically men have benefited more from them (Frederick 1997). And the limits to such policies

leave many people in crisis. A woman whose husband was hospitalized for three weeks said that her employer allowed her to have one week paid 'emergency' leave and two weeks unpaid leave. She was deeply grateful and made full use of both:

> It was so wonderful. I could just stay at the hospital and not have to even think about work. My company was really good to me (F M#21 1/00).

However, her husband's illness lasted more than the time allowed her. She had to go back to work just when he was sent home, still too ill to care for himself. Like so many others in her situation, she found that existing policies are insufficient:

> I was in a state of panic for weeks. It was so difficult. I went to work, but how could I concentrate? I was frantic with worry about what was happening at home (F M#21 1/00).

The more a workplace relies on women workers and the more skilled those workers are (and therefore harder to replace), the more likely the employer is to implement and permit workers to make use of such policies. Unionized workers have been more successful than non-unionized employees in winning such benefits. In a study of eleven workplaces that implemented policies intended to help employees mediate their paid employment and family responsibilities, Laura Johnson (1995: 63) concluded that: 'Employers and employees have provided ample opinion that they benefit from family friendly programs.'

CHANGING STATE POLICIES

Closely tied to efforts to reorganize working conditions in the paid labour force are struggles over government policies. Throughout much of the twentieth century, most government policies were based on the premise that women were wives and mothers with husbands to support them (Eichler 1988, 1997). A range of social policies provided some modest support for families in general, such as the family allowance, initiated in 1945 as a universal benefit to assist families with the costs of childrearing (Baker 1995: 128). Policies were developed for women, especially mothers, who did not have income-earning husbands to support them (Ursel 1992; Baker 1995). However, from the 1980s on, governments turned to neo-liberal economic policies aimed at reducing government provision of social services while fostering private for-profit businesses. The resulting government policies increasingly embodied a major ambivalence about the role of women in families and the labour market. In all areas of policy—from taxes, social assistance, legislated maternity and parental leaves to the absence of a national system of early childcare—governments reluctantly recognized that caregivers could not participate in the labour force without some government support. The policies that were developed, however, put pressure on individuals to provide as much care for themselves and others as possible (Armstrong 1996; Brodie 1996). As Chow, Freiler, and McQuaig (1999: 1) note: 'Not knowing whether to support women as mothers, workers or both has led to a form of policy paralysis and an under-developed system of support to families with children.'

In the current context of limited assistance from certain policies and haphazard access to other services, families develop coping strategies that enable them to manage the competing demands of paid employment and domestic labour as best they can. A man described the decision-making process he and his wife went through after the birth of their first child. His comments indicate how vital even the limited support available was for them:

> My job wasn't very secure. I was afraid if I asked for time off I would get fired, so we weren't going to mess around there. My wife really liked her job. She could get maternity leave paid and even take some unpaid time too. So we did that. But then when it came time for her to go back, we weren't sure we could find childcare that wouldn't cost more

than she was making. And we weren't sure what we thought about her being home with the baby—people say sitters or childcare are okay but how do you know? But she liked her job and didn't want to give it up. Once we found this daycare centre—it's great! Then we were set (Values A#23).

What's at Stake? The Politics of Social Reproduction

A mother of two preschoolers tried to understand why unpaid domestic labour is such a problem:

> I really don't understand why it's so difficult to get men to do their fair share in their own homes or why employers and governments don't just see that it's in everyone's interests to ensure children get good care and parents can go to work secure in knowing their kids are having a wonderful time at daycare. It's almost like a conspiracy—it's just cheaper to get women to do everything for free. Do you think they just want women to carry the burden? (F M#17 12/99).

The United Nations (1991) estimates that women's unpaid work internationally is worth about $4 trillion annually. The General Social Survey indicates that in 1992 people in Canada performed at least 25 billion hours of unpaid work, 95 per cent of which was domestic labour —looking after children and caring for the home. Statistics Canada estimates that this labour is equivalent to about 13 million full-time jobs, is worth about $234 billion, and equals about 40 per cent of Canada's gross domestic product and that women did two thirds of it (Statistics Canada 1992; Chandler 1994; Statistics Canada 1995a).[9]

More importantly, this labour is the main source of caregiving for all children and for many dependent adults. As the labour that ensures households' livelihoods, it is critical for the personal well-being and daily survival of most people in Canada. If women were actually paid for all that work (especially at good wage rates), the wage bill would be enormous.[10] Conversely, if men had to take on even half of the work women do, they would add enormously to their workload; their leisure time would be seriously eroded. Employers and governments understand that provision of universal quality services by well-paid employees is expensive. They are typically resistant to reducing profits or spending public revenues unless there is widespread public support for doing so.

In countries where there has been a demand both for women's participation in the paid labour force and for increased birthrates, there have been well-developed policies to mediate the demands of both labours. Women have benefited by having long paid maternity leaves, as well as the right to have their former job back and retraining when they return to the job (Heitlinger 1979). In countries where there are public commitments to reduce wealth inequalities, and to ensure that all people have adequate care and decent standards of living, there are welfare state provisions available to all. Women and men have benefited from a range of policies and services that relieve the pressure on individuals and particularly women, such as lengthy parental leaves, free or low-cost high-quality childcare centres, or home care for the ill and elderly (see Mahon and Phipps, Chapters 32 and 33 this text).

Canada has never had a strong welfare state and since the late 1970s, the neo-liberal economic policies that federal, provincial, and territorial governments have implemented dramatically cut government provisions of social services and other measures that foster greater equality among people and between women and men (Brodie 1996). Jane Jensen and Sharon Stroick (1999: 3) describe what such changes have meant for parents and children:

> As Canada has done in the past, many countries pay family allowances or allow tax exemptions or credits for all children, whatever their parents' incomes may be. In

Canada, recognition of this universal dimension of family life began to disappear in the 1970s, when targeting of social programs became popular. . . . [H]aving and raising a child was, in effect, treated as a 'private consumption decision' of adults, as if parents did not have legal or moral obligations to spend money on childcare.

A woman described the impact of such changes on her life as an employee:

> I used to work for a government agency as a homecare provider. They privatized the agency, so I lost my job. Later I got another job in a private agency but it wasn't unionized and I make about half what I made before. And all they care about is making their money so we actually don't provide care to people any more. We go in and get out as fast as we can. I feel terrible about it (F A#13 11/99).

Another woman described the impact on her unpaid domestic responsibilities when her husband was injured:

> So on top of my regular job I now have almost a second job, at home, looking after him. I have to get up with him at night, sometimes three or four times. I have to make sure he gets his medication at the right time. Sometimes if I get stuck in traffic on the way home I get so scared because he has to get his injections right on time and if I'm late, it's just so much a problem (F M#16 12/99).

What these examples illustrate is the way most women, as the main people responsible for the work of social reproduction, maintain the standards of living for their household through their unpaid labour. When neo-liberal economic policies impose even more unpaid work on private family households, they rely on women's ability to increase their unpaid work, and in effect, force women to absorb the social costs.

While individual women and men engage in whatever strategies they can to get by, organized groups in the women's movement and the labour movement continue to struggle for policies that will redistribute more of the wealth in society to the majority of families, reduce the conflicts between paid employment and domestic labour, reduce the burdens on women and improve the quality of caregiving and the standards of living for the majority of the population. In 1995 at the United Nations fourth International NGO conference on women at Beijing China, Canadian delegates were among the 30,000 women from over 185 countries at the NGO Forum who identified prevailing neo-liberal policies as detrimental to most women around the world. Instead, they called for a new political orientation that took account of the needs of the majority of the world's people. In the years since then, Canadian feminist and labour groups have identified a range of policies that would help families secure their standards of living and improve the conditions of women's unpaid domestic labour.

In 2000, as part of an international campaign to eliminate women's poverty and violence against women, the main national labour organization, the Canadian Labour Congress (CLC), and the largest national women's organization, the National Action Committee on the Status of Women (NAC) demanded (among other things) a right to social security, equality at work, childcare, and an end to violence against women:

> We demand full access to welfare and income security, fully-funded public health care and education, social housing, and adequate pensions. Working women demand improved labour standards, including a minimum wage above the poverty line—$10 an hour; the right to unionize; we want effective and enforceable pay and employment equity legislation; we need sexual, racial, sexual orientation and personal harassment protection; and we demand the restoration of unemployment insurance to 1996 levels at a minimum. Women demand access to nonprofit, state funded childcare, paid maternity leave, parental leave, family leave, dependent care leave (Canadian Women's March Committee 2000).

These demands illustrate what is at stake in the politics of social reproduction and show that negotiations between individuals in family households over how to balance paid employment and domestic labour are part of much larger struggles over standards of living, allocations of social resources and, ultimately, over the kind of society Canada will become.

Notes

1. This focus on the majority pattern tends to obscure the fact that capitalist class households acquire their income from investments and can hire workers to do all their domestic labour for them. Some households based on farming, fishing, arts and crafts, or other kinds of self-employment generate incomes by selling the products of their labour. Those who receive government transfer payments such as employment insurance, workers' compensation, or other forms of social assistance have to fight to ensure they receive enough to get by while those who have no secure sources of income typically live in precarious poverty.

2. The quotes cited in this paper come from interviews that are part of a study 'Care Giving and Support Among Family, Friends, Neighbours and Communities,' a subproject of a larger project funded by the Social Sciences and Humanities Research Council grant # 410-94-1502 'Rethinking Families: Canadian Social Policy and International Commitments to Conceptualize, Measure and Value Women's Family Work.' The interviews were conducted between September 1999 and January 2000. The identification in brackets indicates the sex (F or M), the situation they were interviewed about—either A for adult children living with their

parents or M for people who had experienced an unexpected medical emergency, ID number of the speaker, and the date of the interview. The people interviewed lived in the greater Toronto area.

3. The term *breadwinner* with its assumption that bread is the main dietary staple illustrates the cultural specificity of this norm. Although it remains a popular term, I have used the culturally neutral term *income-earner* instead.

4. Bettina Bradbury (1993: 119–27) documents for the late nineteenth century how parents and children negotiated and struggled over the competing dynamics of schooling, household needs for additional incomes, and children's commitment to contributing to their parental household or establishing their own. Similar struggles continued for working-class and low-income households throughout the twentieth century.

5. For poignant personal accounts of the impact on their lives of taking on family responsibilities when parents either needed help or were unavailable see Campbell (1973), Crean (1995: 11), Joe (1996).

6. Statistics Canada identifies families or individuals as 'low income' if they spend on average at least 20 per cent more of their pre-tax income than the

Canadian average on food, shelter, and clothing (Statistics Canada 1995b: 86).

7. As McMahon points out: 'Men's performance of domestic labour is one of the few sociological phenomena of which this can be said' (1999: 12).

8. The 1992 General Social Survey done by Statistics Canada (1992) was based on interviews with more than 9,000 people and was designed to find out about the amount and range of unpaid work done in Canada.

9. There are several different ways of calculating the economic value of unpaid work: replacement costs (what it costs to pay someone to do the work), opportunity costs (what the worker would earn if she or he were employed instead of doing domestic labour) or input/output costs (calculating the market equivalents to determine the price of household output)(Goldschmidt-Clermont 1993; INSTRAW 1995).

10. A 1992 study based on Statistics Canada data and using very low rates of pay as comparators calculated that the average annual cost of unpaid household work was between about $12,000 to $16,000 per year per household. (Chandler 1994; Luxton 1997: 437).

References

Abele, F. 1997. 'Understanding What Happened Here: The Political Economy of Indigenous Peoples' in *Understanding Canada Building on the New Canadian Political Economy*, ed. W. Clement (Montreal and Kingston: McGill-Queen's University Press).

Arat-Koc, S. 1990. 'Importing Housewives Non-Citizen Domestic Workers and the Crisis of the Domestic Sphere in Canada' in *Through the Kitchen Window: The Politics of Home and Family*, 2nd edn, eds M. Luxton, H. Rosenberg, and S. Arat-Koc (Toronto: Garamond Press).

Armstrong, P. 1996. 'Unravelling The Safety Net: Transformations in Health Care and Their Impact on Women' in *Women and Canadian Public Policy*, ed. J. Brodie (Toronto: Harcourt Brace and Co.), 129–49.

———, and H. Armstrong. [1978] 1994. *The Double Ghetto: Canadian Women and Their Segregated Work*, 3rd edn (Toronto: McClelland & Stewart).

Bakan, A., and D. Stasiulis, eds. 1997. *Not One of the Family Foreign Domestic Workers in Canada* (Toronto: University of Toronto Press).

Baker, M. 1995. *Canadian Family Policies: Cross-National Comparisons* (Toronto: University of Toronto Press).

Bradbury, B. 1993. *Working Families: Age, Gender, and Daily Survival in Industrializing Montreal* (Toronto: McClelland & Stewart).

Brand, D. 1994. '"We weren't allowed to go into factory work until Hitler started the war": The 1920s to the 1940s' in *We're Rooted Here and They Can't Pull Us Up Essays in African Canadian Women's History*, eds P. Bristow et al. (Toronto: University of Toronto Press).

Brayfield, A. 1992. 'Employment Resources and Housework in Canada', *Journal of Marriage and the Family* 54: 19–30.

Brodie, J. 1996. 'Canadian Women, Changing State Forms, and Public Policy' in *Women and Canadian Public Policy*, ed. J. Brodie (Toronto: Harcourt Brace and Co.), 1–28.

Best, P. 1995. 'Women, Men and Work', *Canadian Social Tends* 36 (Spring): 30–3.

Campbell, M. 1973. *Halfbreed*. (Halifax: Goodread Biographies).

Canadian Women's March Committee 2000. 2000. *An Open Letter to Canadian Women*, 24 Jan. 2000.

Carty, L. 1994. 'African Canadian Women and the State: "Labour Only, Please"' in *We're Rooted Here and They Can't Pull Us Up Essays in African Canadian Women's History*, eds P. Bristow et al. (Toronto: University of Toronto Press).

Chandler, W. 1994. 'The Value of Household Work in Canada', *1992 Canadian Economic Observer*, Statistics Canada, cat. no. 11–010 (April).

Chow, O., C. Freiler, and K. McQuaig. 1999. 'A National Agenda for All Families: Reframing the Debate about Tax Fairness', paper submitted to the Finance Sub-Committee, Federal Government, 12 May.

Crean, S.G.H. 1995. *A Woman for Her Time* (Vancouver: New Star Books).

de Wolff, A. 1994. *Strategies for Working Families* (Toronto: Ontario Coalition for Better Child Care).

Drolet, M. 1999. 'The Persistent Gap: New Evidence on the Canadian Gender Wage Gap', Statistics Canada, *Income Statistics Division* (Ottawa: Industry).

Duxbury, L., C. Lee, C. Higgins, and S. Mills. 1992. *Balancing Work and Family: A Study of Canadian Private Sector Employees* (Ottawa: Carleton University).

Eichler, M. 1988. *Families in Canada Today: Recent Changes and their Policy Consequences*, 2nd edn (Toronto: Gage Educational Publications).

———. 1997. *Family Shifts: Families, Policies, and Gender Equality* (Don Mills, ON: Oxford University Press).

Fast, J., and M. Da Pont. 1997. 'Changes in Women's Work Continuity', *Canadian Social Trends* 46 (Autumn): 2–7.

Frederick, J. 1993. 'Tempus Fugit . . . Are You Time Crunched?', *Canadian Social Trends* 31 (Winter): 6–9.

———. 1995. *As Time Goes By . . . Time Use of Canadians* (Ottawa: Industry).

———. 1997. Statistics Canada (Ottawa: Industry).

Ghalam, N. 1993. 'Women in the Workplace', *Canadian Social Trends* 28 (Spring).

———. 1997. 'Attitudes Toward Women, Work and Family', *Canadian Social Trends* 46 (Autumn) 13–17.

Giles, W., and S. Arat-Koc, eds. 1994. *Maid in the Market: Women's Paid Domestic Labour* (Halifax: Fernwood).

Goldschmidt-Clermont, L. 1993. 'Monetary Valuation of Unpaid Work', paper presented at the International Conference on the Measurement and Valuation of Unpaid Work, Statistics Canada, April.

Grindstaff, C.F. 1995. 'Canadian Fertility, 1951 to 1993', *Canadian Social Trends* 39 (Winter): 12–16.

Heitlinger, A. 1979. *Women and State Socialism: Sex Inequality in the Soviet Union* (Montreal: McGill-Queen's University Press).

———. 1993. *Women's Equality, Demography and Public Policy: A Comparative Perspective* (London: Macmillan Press).

Hobart, C. 1996. 'Intimacy and Family Life: Sexuality, Cohabitation, and Marriage' in *Families Changing Trends in Canada*, 3rd edn, ed. M. Baker (Toronto: McGraw-Hill Ryerson), 143–73.

INSTRAW (International Research and Training Institute for the Advancement of Women). 1995. Measurement and Valuation of Unpaid Contribution Accounting Through Time and Output, Santo Domingo, Dominican Republic.

Jensen, J., and S. Stroick. 1999. 'Finding the Best Policy Mix for Canada's Kids', *Perception* 23 (3) (Dec.): 3–5.

Joe, R. 1996. *Song of Rita Joe: Autobiography of a Mi'kmaq Poet* (Charlottetown, PEI: Ragweed Press).

Johnson, L. 1995. *Changing Families, Changing Workplaces Case Studies of Policies and Programs in Canadian Workplaces* for the Women's Bureau, Human Resources Development Canada (Ottawa: Supply and Services).

Luxton, M. 1980. *More Than a Labour of Love: Three Generations of Women's Work in the Home* (Toronto: The Women's Press).

———. 1981. 'Taking on the Double Day: Housewives as a Reserve Army of Labour', *Atlantis* 7 (1) (Fall): 12–22.

———. 1990. 'Two Hands for the Clock: Changing Patterns in the Gendered Division of Labour in the Home' in *Through the Kitchen Window: The Politics of Home and Family*, 2nd edn, eds M. Luxton, H. Rosenberg, and S. Arat-Koc (Toronto: Garamond Press).

———. 1997. 'The UN, Women, and Household Labour: Measuring and Valuing Unpaid Work', *Women's Studies International Forum* 20 (3): 431–9.

———, and J. Corman. Forthcoming. *Getting By in Hard Times: Restructuring Class and Gender in Hamilton, Ontario 1980–1996* (Toronto: University of Toronto Press).

Marchak, P. 1987. 'Rational Capitalism and Women as Labour' in *Feminism and Political Economy: Women's Work, Women's Struggles*, eds H.J. Maroney and M. Luxton (Toronto: Methuen).

Marshall, K. 1993. 'Dual Earners: Who's Responsible for Housework?', *Canadian Social Trends*, cat. no. 11–008E (Spring/Winter): 11–14.

Maxwell, J. 2000. 'We must invest in our kids', *The Globe and Mail* 24 Feb. 2000: A21.

McMahon, A. 1999. *Taking Care of Men: Sexual Politics in the Public Mind* (Cambridge: Cambridge University Press).

Mishra, R. 1996. 'The Welfare of Nation' in *States Against Markets: The Limits of Globalization*, eds R. Boyer and D. Drache (London: Routledge), 316–33.

Morissette, R. 1997. 'Declining Earnings of Young Men', *Canadian Social Trends* 46 (Autumn): 8–12.

Nadwodny, R. 1996. 'Working at Home', *Canadian Social Trends* 40 (Spring): 16–20.

Nakhaie, M.R. 1995. 'Housework in Canada: The National Picture', *Journal of Comparative Family Studies* 26 (3) (Autumn): 409–25.

Oderkirk, J.C. 1994. 'Marriage in Canada: Changing Beliefs and Behaviours 1600–1990', *Canadian Social Trends* (Summer): 2–7.

———, C. Silver, and M. Prud'homme. 1994. 'Traditional-Earner Families', *Canadian Social Trends* 32 (Spring): 19–25.

Parr, J. 1999. *Domestic Goods: The Material, Moral, and the Economic in the Postwar Years* (Toronto: University of Toronto).

Preston, V., and W. Giles. 1997. 'Ethnicity, Gender and Labour Markets in Canada: A Case Study of Immigrant Women in Toronto', *The Canadian Journal of Urban Research* 6 (2) (Dec.): 135–59.

Stasiulis, D. 1997. 'The Political Economy of Race, Ethnicity, and Migration' in *Understanding Canada: Building on the New Canadian Political Economy* ed. W. Clement (Montreal and Kingston: McGill-Queen's University Press).

Statistics Canada. 1992. Initial Data Release from the 1992 General Social Survey on Time Use (Ottawa: Author).

———. 1995a. 'Unpaid Work of Households', *The Daily* (20 Dec.).

———. 1995b. *Women in Canada: A Statistical Report* (Ottawa: Industry).

———. 1998a. *The Daily*, cat. no. 11–001E (17 March).

———. 1998b. *The Daily*, cat. no. 11–001E (12 May).

———. 2000. *Canadian Social Trends*, cat. no. 11–008, 56 (Spring).

United Nations. 1991. *The World's Women, 1970–1990: Trends and Statistics* (New York: United Nations Social Statistics and Indicator, series K, no. 8).

Ursel, J. 1992. *Private Lives, Public Policy: One Hundred Years of State Intervention in the Family* (Toronto: The Women's Press).

Wilson, S. 1991. *Women, Families, and Work*, 3rd edn (Toronto: McGraw-Hill Ryerson).

Chapter 22

In the late 1980s and early 1990s, Arlie Hochschild interviewed and observed a large number of people working—in all kinds of jobs—for a large company with 'family-friendly policies'. What she learned about the relationship between their life at work and their life at home should sound an alarm for everyone concerned about family and personal life. The devastating effects that corporate America is having on the family lives of the Americans Hochschild observed are summarized in this chapter taken from her book Time Bind. *The controversial argument developed in the book is that work has become like home, and home has become like work (in an industrial-capitalist workplace, that is). While the former is highly debatable, for most Canadians, the latter should give us all cause for concern.*

The Third Shift

Arlie Hochschild

Amerco, a highly profitable, innovative company, had the budget and the will to experiment with new ways to organize its employees' lives. Its Work-Life Balance program could have become a model, demonstrating to other corporations that workforce talents can be used effectively without wearing down workers and their families. But that did not happen. The question I have asked is: Why not? The answer . . . is complex. Some working parents, especially on the factory floor, were disinclined to work shorter hours because they needed the money or feared losing their jobs. Though not yet an issue at Amerco, in some companies workers may also fear that 'good' shorter-hour jobs could at any moment be converted into 'bad' ones, stripped of benefits or job security. Even when such worries were absent, pressure from peers or supervisors to be a 'serious player' could cancel out any desire to cut back on work hours. But all these sources of inhibition did not fully account for the lack of resistance Amerco's working parents showed to the encroachments of work time on family life.

Much of the solution to the puzzle of work-family balance appeared to be present at Amerco—the pieces were there, but they remained unassembled. Many of those pieces lay in the hands of the powerful men at the top of the company hierarchy, who had the authority and skill to engineer a new family-friendly work culture but lacked any deep interest in doing so. Other pieces were held by the advocates of family-friendly policies lower down the corporate ladder, who had a strong interest in such changes but little authority to implement them. And the departmental supervisors and managers, whose assent was crucial to solving the puzzle, were sometimes overtly hostile of anything that smacked of work-family balance. So even if the workers who could have benefited from such programs had demanded them, resistance from above would still have stymied their efforts.

But why *weren't* Amerco working parents putting up a bigger fight for family time, given the fact that most said they needed more? Many of them may have been responding to a powerful process that is devaluing what was once the essence of family life. The more women and men do what they do in exchange for money and the more their work in the public realm is valued or honoured, the more, almost by definition, private life is devalued and its boundaries shrink. For women as well as men, work in the marketplace is less often a simple economic fact than a complex cultural value. If in the early part of the century it was considered unfortunate that a woman had to work, it is now thought surprising when she doesn't.

People generally have the urge to spend more time on what they value most and on what they are most valued for. This tendency may help explain the historic decline in time devoted to private social relations,[1] a decline that has taken on a distinctive cultural form at Amerco. The valued realm of work is registering its gains in part by incorporating the best aspects of home. The devalued realm, the home, is meanwhile taking on what were once considered the most alienating attributes of work. However one explains the failure of Amerco to create a good program of work-family balance, though, the fact is that in a cultural contest between work and home, working parents are voting with their feet, and the workplace is winning.

In this respect, we may ask, are working parents at Amerco an anomaly or are they typical of working parents nationwide? In search of an answer, I contacted a company called Bright Horizons, which runs 125 company-based childcare centres associated with corporations, hospitals, real estate developers, and federal agencies in nineteen states.[2] Bright Horizons allowed me to add a series of new questions to a questionnaire the company was sending out to seven thousand parents whose children were attending Bright Horizons Children's Centers. A third of the parents who received questionnaires filled them out. The resulting 1,446 responses came from mainly middle- or upper-middle-class parents in their early thirties.[3] Since many of them worked for Fortune 500 companies—including IBM, American Express, Sears Roebuck, Eastman Kodak, Xerox, Bausch and Lomb, and Dunkin' Donuts—this study offers us a highly suggestive picture of what is happening among managers and professional working parents at Amerco's counterparts nationwide.

These parents reported time pressures similar to those Amerco parents complained about. As at Amerco, the longest hours at work were logged by the most highly educated professionals and managers, among whom six out of ten regularly averaged over forty hours a week. A third of the parents in this sample had their children in childcare forty hours a week or more.[4] As at Amerco, the higher the income of their parents, the longer the children's shifts in childcare.

When asked, 'Do you ever consider yourself a workaholic?' a third of fathers and a fifth of mothers answered yes. One out of three said their *partner* was a workaholic. In response to the question 'Do you experience a problem of "time famine"?' 89 per cent responded yes. Half reported that they typically brought work home from the office.[5] Of those who complained of a time famine, half agreed with the statement 'I feel guilty that I don't spend enough time with my child.' Forty-three per cent agreed that they 'very often' felt 'too much of the time I'm tired when I'm with my child'. When asked, 'Overall, how well do you feel you can balance the demands of your work and family?' only 9 per cent said 'very well'.

If many of these Bright Horizons working parents were experiencing a time bind of the sort I heard about from Amerco employees, were they living with it because they felt work was more rewarding than family life? To find out, I asked, 'Does it sometimes feel to you like home is a "workplace"?' Eighty-five per cent said yes (57 per cent 'very often'; 28 per cent 'fairly often'). Women were far more likely to agree than men. I asked this question the other way around as well: 'Is it sometimes true that work feels like home should feel?' Twenty-five per cent answered 'very often' or 'quite often', and 33 per cent answered 'occasionally'. Only 37 per cent answered 'very rarely'.

One reason some workers may feel more 'at home' at work is that they feel more appreciated and more competent there. Certainly, this was true for many Amerco workers I interviewed, and little wonder, for Amerco put great effort into making its workers feel appreciated. In a large-scale nationwide study, sociologists Diane Burden and Bradley Googins found that 59 per cent of employees rated their family performances 'good or unusually good', while 86 per cent gave that rating to their performances on the job—that is, workers appreciated *themselves* more at work than at home.[6] In the Bright Horizon national survey, only 29 per cent felt appreciated 'mainly at home', and 52 per cent 'equally' at home and work. Surprisingly, women were not more likely than men to say they felt more appreciated at home.

Often, working parents feel more at home at work because they come to expect that emotional support will be more readily available there. As at Amerco, work can be where their closest friends are, a pattern the Bright Horizons survey reflected. When asked, 'Where do you have the most friends?' 47 per cent answered 'at my work'; 16 per cent, 'in the neighborhood'; and 6 per cent, 'at my church or temple'. Women were far more likely than men to have the most friends at work.[7]

Some workers at Amerco felt more at home at work because work was where they felt most relaxed. To the question 'Where do you feel the most relaxed?' only a slight majority in the Bright Horizons survey, 51 per cent, said 'home'. To the question 'Do you feel as if your life circumstances or relationships are more secure at work or at home?' a similarly slim majority answered 'home'. I also asked, 'How many times have you changed jobs since you started working?' The average was between one and two times. Though I didn't ask how many times a person had changed primary loved ones, the national picture suggests that by the early thirties, one or two such changes is not unusual. Work may not 'always be there' for the employee, but then home may not be either.

I should have asked what arena of life—work or family—was most engrossing. Amerco parents loved their children but nonetheless often found life at work more interesting than life at home. The workplace, after all, offered a natural theatre in which one could follow the progress of jealousies, sexual attractions, simmering angers. Home, on the other hand, offered fewer actors on an increasingly cramped stage. Sometimes, the main, stress-free, 'exciting' events at home came during the time Americans spend watching television. (According to one study, Americans spend about 30 per cent of their free time in front of the television.)[8]

For this sample, then, we find some evidence that a cultural reversal of workplace and home is present at least as a theme. Unsurprisingly, more people in the survey agreed that home felt like work than that work felt like home. Still, only to half of them was home a main source of relaxation or security. For many, work seemed to function as a backup system to a destabilizing family. For women, in particular, to take a job is often today to take out an emotional insurance policy on the uncertainties of home life.

The Bright Horizons parents—middle- and upper-middle-class employees of large corporations who had children in childcare—are a good match for many Amerco parents, and the results of the survey confirm that much of what we have seen in Spotted Deer is in fact happening across the nation. Obviously, however, many working parents do not resemble those in the Bright Horizons group. What kinds of families might be omitted from this sample, and what are *their* experiences of work and home and the relation between the two? As a start, we need to recognize at least four other models of family and work life, each based on the relative emotional magnetism of home and work. Most real families, of course, blend aspects of more than one of them.

There would be a 'haven model', for instance, in which work *is* a heartless world and family still a haven. Amerco workers who fit this traditional 'haven model' to any extent tended to be factory hands, who did jobs that were relatively unpleasant and lacked on-the-job community. For many blue-collar men and even more women, home is still often far more of a haven than work. When I asked women whether they would continue to work if they did not need the money, the proportion who answered 'no' rose as occupational level fell. This, in part, may reflect the fact that, over the last decade as the rich have become richer and the poor poorer, those with 'desirable' jobs have generally found their jobs to be ever more inviting (with more carefully engineered workplace cultures and more impressive corporate perks). Those with 'undesirable' jobs, on the other hand, have generally found them ever less welcoming (with little cultural engineering, growing vulnerability to technological displacement, greater insecurity, and declining pay). Many of these 'have-nots' may still look to home as a haven, no matter what the realities of their actual home lives.

Bill and Emily Denton fit another 'traditional' model, in which home and work each exhibit gender-specific pulls. Bill, and men like him at the top of the corporate ladder, flee neither a dismal workplace or a stressful home. They make pleasurable 'homes' for themselves at the office to which they devote most of their waking hours, while their real homes become like summer cottage retreats. Wives like Emily are then left to manage home and children. For them, home is not a refuge from the workday world, but a potentially fulfilling world in its own right. This old-style model of work-family balance in which each sphere of life is given to one gender is on the decline even among top executives at corporations like Amerco. The magnetic pull of work is drawing some executive wives out of the house; while for those who remain the appeal of housewifely and motherly duties and pleasures has probably diminished.

There is also a 'no-job, weak-family' model, in which neither work nor home has any strong attraction for the individual. Poor people who can't find work and to whom a job may be the economic and emotional prerequisite for a reasonable family life would fit this model. In his book *When Work Disappears*, focusing on the plight of African Americans, the sociologist William Julius Wilson has argued that without a New Deal–style national public works program many blacks will find themselves living in a spreading economic desert.[9] Inner city street corner and gang life, buoyed by an underground economy, loom ever larger as substitute sources of appreciation, relaxation, and security, while drugs help provide the temporary illusion that these ideals are really within one's grasp.

Finally, there is the 'work-family balance' model in which parents take advantage of family-friendly options at work and do not crave time on the job so much that they are tempted to steal it from time allotted to their children. Such parents might begin to break the time-deficit cycle and so escape the need for a third shift at home. This model was a reality for a small minority at Amerco, and probably a larger minority nationwide.

If families matching the 'haven' and 'traditional' models are on the decline, and families matching the 'no-job, weak-family' model fluctuate with the economic times, families that fall in to the reversal model in which home is work and work is home have been on the increase over the last thirty years. But what social conditions have been fostering this change? The takeover of the home by the workplace is certainly an unacknowledged but fundamental part of our changing cultural landscape.

Behind Reversing Worlds

Although work can complement—and, indeed, improve—family life, in recent decades it has largely competed with the family, and won. While the mass media so often point to global competition as the major business story of the age, it is easy to miss the fact that corporate America's fiercest struggle has been with its local rival—the family. Amerco company officials worry about their battles for market share with companies in Asia and Europe. But they take for granted their company's expanding share of domestic time. For where the workplace invests in its employees, as at Amerco, it often wins the emotional allegiance of its workers—and so ever more of its workers' time.

The ascendancy of the corporation in its battle with the family has been aided in recent years by the rise of company cultural engineering and, in particular, the shift from Frederick Taylor's principles of scientific management to the Total Quality principles originally set out by Charles Deming.[10] Under the influence of a Taylorist worldview, the manager's job was to coerce the worker's mind and body, not to appeal to his heart. The Taylorized worker was deskilled, replaceable, cheap, and as a consequence felt bored, demeaned, and unappreciated.

Using more modern participative management techniques, companies now invest in training workers to 'make decisions' and then set before their newly 'empowered' workers moral as well as financial incentives. Under Taylor's system, managers assumed that workers lacked the basic impulse to do a good job. Under Total Quality, managers assume workers possess such an impulse. Under Taylorism, the worker was given no autonomy. Under Total Quality, the worker has a certain amount of autonomy and is drawn further into the world of work by the promise of more.

As the Amerco work environment illustrates, the Total Quality worker is invited to feel recognized for job accomplishments. The company publishes a quarterly magazine, *Amerco World*, that features photos of smiling workers credited with solving problems, anticipating bottlenecks, inventing new products, reducing errors, and otherwise 'delighting the customer'. In describing its application of the Total Quality system before the House Subcommittee on Science, Research, and Technology, an Amerco vice president noted that the company preferred to reward quality work with personal recognition rather than money. Personal recognition, he pointed out, has proved an extremely effective motivational tool, one far less likely to create the jealousies that often result from giving financial rewards to some workers and not others. Company surveys confirm this.

At Amerco, employees are invited to feel relaxed while on the job. Frequent recognition events reward work but also provide the context for a kind of play. Amerco's management has, in fact, put thought and effort into blurring the dis-

tinction between work and play (just as that distinction is so often blurred at home). Fridays during the summer, for instance, are 'dress down' days on which employees are urged to dress 'as though' they are at home; and the regular rounds of company picnics, holiday parties, and ceremonies are meant to invest work with celebratory good feeling. For white-collar workers at Amerco headquarters, there are even free Cokes, just as at home, stashed in refrigerators placed near coffee machines on every floor.

Amerco has also made a calculated attempt to take on the role of helpful relative in relation to employee problems at work and at home. The Education and Training Division offers employees free courses (on company time) in 'Dealing with Anger', 'How to Give and Accept Criticism', 'How to Cope with Difficult People', 'Stress Management', 'Taking Control of Your Work Day', and 'Using the Myers-Briggs Personality Test to Improve Team Effectiveness'. There are workshops in 'Work-Life Balance for Two-Career Couples' and 'Work-Life Balance for Single Adults'. At home, people seldom receive anything like this much help on issues so basic to family life. At home, there were no courses on 'Coping with Your Child's Anger over the Time Famine' or 'Dealing with Your Child's Disappointment in You or Yours in Him'.

As a result, many Amerco managers and professionals earnestly confessed to me that the company had helped them grow as human beings in ways that improved their ability to cope with problems at home. Even in the plants, training in team building sometimes instills similar feelings in the workers. One Amerco handout for its managers lists a series of 'qualities for excellence at work' that would be useful at home—an employee would be judged on whether he or she 'seeks feedback on personal behaviors', 'senses changes in attention level and mood', or 'adapts personality to the situation and the people involved'. Amerco is also one of about a hundred companies that enrolls its top executives in classes at the Corporate Learning Institute. There, managers learn how to motivate and influence others and manage conflict. The Institute offers an open-ended 'personal focus program designed for people from all walks of life who have a genuine desire to explore and expand their unique possibilities'. One can, at company expense, attend a course on 'Self-Awareness and Being: The Importance of Self in the Influence Process'.[11]

The Total Quality worker is invited to feel committed to his company. When, in *Modern Times*, a speedup finally drives the Taylorized Charlie Chaplin crazy, he climbs into a giant complex of cogs and belts and is wound around a huge wheel. He has become part of the machine itself. How could he feel committed to a company that had turned him into a machine part?

Under Total Quality at Amerco, the worker is not a machine; he's a believer. This became clear to me when I witnessed a 'Large Group Change Event', held in a high school cafeteria one summer morning in 1992. The event, Amerco's response to losing customers to a growing competitor, was staged somewhat like a revival meeting. Its purpose was to convince each worker to renew his commitment not to his spouse or church but to his workplace. It was one of a series of such events held at underproducing plants in the valley. Two banners hanging at the entrance said, 'Show Our Commitment'. Four hundred workers, most of them white men between the ages of twenty and forty, were assembled eight to a table. They tended to sport tee-shirts, blue jeans, and baseball caps worn back to front. One young man in sunglasses casually lifted his leg over the back of his chair as if mounting a horse and sat down to join his group. 'What's frustrating about your job?' the group leader asked.

'A few supervisors don't have anything to do but watch for you to make a mistake,' one man responded. 'Why don't they just get to work themselves?'

Talk soon turned to the effect the morning's proceedings might have on life at home. George, twenty-two, his hair in a Mohawk, volunteered,

'Me and my wife just got back together. We were going down to New Orleans for a trip; but now this event comes along.'

'If we keep this plant open,' another worker replied wryly, 'that will help keep your family together more than going on some trip.'

The organizer of the event then introduced three people, a plant manager, an investor, and a union representative, each emphasizing the need to improve production in the next six months. As a revivalist minister might plumb the depths of sin, the plant manager described how 'low down' plant production had sunk, how many fewer defects per million parts Amerco's competitors had, and how many more employee-initiated ideas (or, as they were calling them, Corrective Action Requests) their plants were generating each year. He went on to bemoan Amerco's declining share of the market.

The union representative, who had been a mold maker at another company for twenty-six years, told how his plant had merged with another, then closed. 'We lost over 400 jobs in a town of 2,000,' he said. 'This is what American industry and labor face today.' To think up good ideas, to concentrate harder, to be more careful, to cooperate with the coworkers on your team—these were, he suggested, patriotic as well as pro-labour acts.

Workers were then handed pads of Post-its and asked to write down good ideas, which would be stuck on a large wall in the cafeteria under the heading, 'Action Ideas'. Typical Post-its read: 'Don't throw safety goggles away.' 'Recycle the water.' 'Don't need to wax the floor three times a day—save money.' Each eight-person group was then given twenty-one adhesive gold stars and asked to vote for the best suggestions by sticking stars on the wall next to the action ideas of which they most approved. Back at their tables, workers discussed the stars their groups, now renamed 'Worker-Management Improvement Teams', had given out.

Each team was then asked to consider the question 'What am I willing to commit to?' Men at one table talked about quitting their horseplay, their back talk, their slowdowns. They vowed to 'cast out the devil' of taking petty revenge on the company for the tediousness of their jobs.

The event organizer then asked all the workers to take a Myers-Briggs Personality Test using pamphlets and pencils set out on the tables.[12] This test focuses on one's capacity for teamwork, one's tendency to lead or follow, to stand up or hide, to work fast or slow. 'Who here is an introvert? Who is an extrovert?' People volunteered and were then asked, 'Is your personality getting in the way of committing yourself to improvement?' As was the intent of the whole meeting, the test tacitly invited these blue-collar workers to take on a managerial viewpoint in which people skills matter more than brawn, in which you and the company both should care about what type of personality you have and how it best suits the workplace. They were invited to leave their individual fates behind and try, like any executive, to envision, care about, and plan for the fate of the company.[13]

At the end of the event, to signify their new 'commitment', workers inscribed their names on one of the immense red banners that hung at the cafeteria entrance. They signed with fancy long g's and tall t's, with lines under their names, and curlicued s's. Under some names they bracketed nicknames, others as in a high school yearbook were cleverly written inside one of the banner's larger letters that corresponded to the beginning letter of a name.

The event had climaxed with a promise of redemption. Workers had offered themselves up, name by name, to be 'saved' from unemployment, and to save the company from falling profits. Amerco, too, wanted these workers to be saved, not laid off. It had already spent four million dollars to get the 'mission' of Total Quality out of the plants—and now it was spending even more to save plants and jobs. That said something in itself, the workers felt: Amerco cared.

This sense of being cared for encouraged workers to adopt a more personal orientation toward work time. If, in *Modern Times*, Chaplin,

like millions of real factory workers of his era, found himself the victim of a company-initiated speedup, Amerco's professionals, managers, and even factory workers were being asked to envision themselves as their own time strategists, their own efficiency experts. They were to improve their own production, to manage their own intensified work pace at their own plants, even in their own lives. Under the moral mantle of Total Quality, however, workers weren't being asked to consider the speed of their work—not directly anyway— only its 'quality'. Meanwhile at home, the same workers were finding that quality was exactly what they had to let go of in order to do a certain quantity of chores in the few hours left to them.

The Taylorized Family

If Total Quality called for 'reskilling' the worker in an 'enriched' job environment, capitalism and technological developments have long been gradually deskilling parents at home. Over time, store-bought goods have replaced homespun cloth, homemade soap and candles, home-cured meats, and home-baked foods. Instant mixes, frozen dinners, and take-out meals have replaced Mother's recipes. Daycare for children, retirement homes for the elderly, wilderness camps for delinquent children, even psychotherapy are, in a way, commercial substitutes for jobs a mother once did at home. If, under Total Quality, 'enriched' jobs call for more skill at work, household chores have over the years become fewer and easier to do.

Even family-generated entertainment has its own mechanical replacement—primarily the television, but also the video game, VCR, computer, and CD player. In the Amerco families I observed, TV cartoons often went on early in the morning as a way to ease children into dressing and eating breakfast. For some families in the evening, CNN or network news lent an aura of seriousness to the mundane task of preparing dinner. After dinner, some families would sit together, mute but cozy, watching sitcoms in which *television* mothers, fathers, and children talked energetically to one another. TV characters did the joking and bantering for them while the family itself engaged in 'relational loafing'. What the family used to produce—entertainment—it now consumes. Ironically, this entertainment may even show viewers a 'family life' that, as in the sitcoms *Murphy Brown* and *Ink*, has moved to work.[14]

The main 'skill' still required of family members is the hardest one of all—the ability to forge, deepen, and repair family relationships. Under normal circumstances the work of tending to relationships calls for noticing, acknowledging, and empathizing with the feelings of family members, patching up quarrels, and soothing hurt feelings.

In the wake of the 'divorce revolution', this sort of emotional work, always delicate, has become even more complicated and difficult. Two-thirds of the marriages that end in divorce involve children. In *Second Chances*, Judith Wallerstein and Sandra Blakeslee report on a fifteen-year study of sixty middle-class parents and children. Within ten years, half of the children whose parents had divorced had gone through a parent's second divorce; typically, one parent happily remarried and the other did not. Only one child in eight saw both parents remarry happily. Half the women and a third of the men were still intensely angry at their ex-spouses a decade later.

The study provided other insights as well. For one thing, parents and children often saw divorce differently. Two-thirds of the women and half of the men claimed they felt more content with the quality of their lives after divorce, but only one in ten children felt the same way. Three out of four children felt rejected by their fathers. Yet Wallerstein and Blakeslee found, poignantly enough, that these 'rejecting' fathers often maintained phantom relations with the children they didn't see or support, keeping their photographs near at hand. One national study found that half of children aged eleven to sixteen living with a divorced mother had not seen their fathers during the entire previous year.[15]

Family life can be baffling under the best of circumstances. But in a society based on the nuclear family, divorce creates extra strains. Blending and reblending people into remarriage 'chains' can be much harder than the word 'blend' implies. Stepsiblings in such families are rarely as close as biological siblings—and that's only one of many problems such new families face. One divorced Amerco employee complained that his stepchildren refused to obey him and instead confronted him with the challenge 'You're not my *real* Dad!' On the other hand, many divorced mothers also deeply resented the ways their remarried ex-husbands favoured their new families. One divorced wife, for instance, observed bitterly that her ex-husband had managed to buy a new car and boat while remaining in arrears on his child support payments. Faced with such issues and in need of emotional 'reskilling' few parents at home have the faintest idea where to look for 'retraining'.

At Amerco, successful completion of on-the-job training is rewarded with a recognition ceremony, a Total Quality pin, and possibly even a mention in the company magazine. At Amerco, large sums of money are spent to stage 'commitment ceremonies' between the company and its workers whenever a 'divorce' seems to threaten. But who rewards a difficult new kind of emotional work or watches for declining profit margins at home?[16] Who calls for renewed vows of commitment there?

The Hydro-Compressed Sterilized Mouth Wiper

Working parents often face difficult problems at home without much outside support or help in resolving them. In itself time is, of course, no cure-all. But having time together is an important precondition for building family relations. What, then, is happening to family time?

Working parents exhibit an understandable desire to build sanctuaries of family time, free from pressure, in which they can devote themselves to only one activity or one relationship. So, for instance, the time between 8 and 8:45 p.m. may be cordoned off as 'quality time' for parents and child, and that between 9:15 and 10 p.m. as quality time for a couple (once the children are in bed). Such time boundaries must then be guarded against other time demands—calls from the office, from a neighbour to arrange tomorrow's car pool, from a child's friend about homework. Yet these brief respites of 'relaxed time' themselves come to look more and more like little segments of job time, with parents punching in and out as it on a time clock. When Denise Hampton read *The Narnia Chronicles* to her two sons at night, for instance, she made a special effort not to think about the e-mail piling up for her in cyberspace and the memos she might soon have to compose and e-mail back. Thus, for her, 'relaxed' quality time actually took special discipline, focus, and energy, just like work. Even when Denise was at home, even when her mind was on domestic matters, she often found herself approaching time in a quasi-industrial way.

Paradoxically, what may seem to harried working parents like a solution to their time bind—efficiency and time segmentation—can later feel like a problem in itself. To be efficient with whatever time they do have at home, many working parents try to go faster if for no other reason than to clear off some space in which to go slowly. They do two or three things at once. They plan ahead. They delegate. They separate home events into categories and try to outsource some of them. In their efficiency, they may inadvertently trample on the emotion-laden symbols associated with particular times of day or particular days of the week. They pack one activity closer to the next and disregard the 'framing' around each of them, those moments of looking forward to or looking back on an experience, which heighten its emotional impact. They ignore the contribution that a leisurely pace can make to fulfillment, so that a rapid dinner, followed by a speedy bath and bed-

time story for a child—if part of 'quality time'—is counted as 'worth the same' as a slower version of the same events. As time becomes something to 'save' at home as much as or even more than at work, domestic life becomes quite literally a second shift; a cult of efficiency, once centred in the workplace, is allowed to set up shop and make itself comfortable at home. Efficiency has become both a means to an end—more home time—and a way of life, an end in itself.

A surprising amount of family life has become a matter of efficiently assembling people into prefabricated activity slots. Perhaps the best way to see this is to return to a classic scene in the film *Modern Times*. A team of salesmen is trying to persuade the president of Electro Steel, where Charlie Chaplin works on an assembly line, to install a J. Willicomb Billows Feeding Machine, which, as the mad inventor explains, 'automatically feeds your men at work'. The sales pitch, an automated recording, continues: 'Don't stop for lunch. Be ahead of your competition. The Billows Feeding Machine will eliminate the lunch hour, increase your production, and decrease your overhead.' In scientific-looking white lab coats, two sales demonstrators—with the muted smiles and slightly raised eyebrows of French waiters—point to the 'automatic soup plate with the compressed air blower' ('no energy is required to cool the soup'); to the 'revolving plate with automatic food pusher'; to the 'double knee-action corn feeder with its syncro-mesh transition, which enables you to shift from high to low gear by the mere tip of the tongue'; and finally to the 'hydro-compressed sterilized mouth wiper', which offers 'control against spots on the shirt front'.

The hapless Chaplin is chosen to test the machine, and a salesman straps him into it, his arms immobilized. The machine begins to pour soup into his mouth, and, of course, finally down his shirt. Chaplin keeps a doubtful eye on the automatic mouth wiper, which periodically spins in to roll over his lips and, if he doesn't stretch up, his nose. Buttered corn on the cob appears, moving automatically back and forth across his mouth. As a deskilled eater, his only job is to bite and chew. However, the corn, like the factory's conveyor belt, soon begins to speed up, moving back and forth so fast that he has no time to chew. The machine breaks. Impassive white-coated salesmen try to fix it, but it only malfunctions again, feeding Chaplin bolts with morsels of sandwich and splashing a cream pie in his face. The mouth wiper leaps out widely to make a small, clean stripe across his smeared face, and Chaplin drops away from the machine in a faint.

The CEO of Amerco didn't have to introduce a Billows Automatic Feeding Machine. Many of his employees quite voluntarily ate lunch quickly at their desks to save time. This pattern is by no means unique to Amerco. A recent report commissioned by the National Restaurant Association found that these days business lunches are faster and fewer in number. Only 38 per cent of adults polled in 1993 said they ate lunch out at least once a week, compared with 60 per cent in the mid-1980s. According to Wendy Tanaka, an observer of San Francisco's business district, people take less and less time out for lunch, and many restaurants are being turned into take-out businesses to make ends meet. Customers who do sit down to lunch are more likely to bring work with them. As Tanaka observes, it is no longer unusual for someone to walk in with a laptop computer and have lunch opposite a project not a partner.[17]

Perhaps more significant, though, a feeding-machine atmosphere has entered the home. *Working Mother* magazine, for example, carries ads that invite the working mother to cook 'two-minute rice', a 'five-minute chicken casserole', a 'seven-minute Chinese feast'. One ad features a portable phone to show that the working mother can make business calls while baking cookies with her daughter.

Another typical ad promotes cinnamon oatmeal cereal for breakfast by showing a smiling mother ready for the office in her square-shouldered suit, hugging her happy son. A caption reads, 'In the morning, we are in such a rush, and my son eats so slowly. But with cinnamon oatmeal cereal, I don't even have to coax him to hurry up!' Here, the modern mother seems to have absorbed the lessons of Frederick Taylor as she presses for efficiency at home because she is in a hurry to get to work. In a sense, though, Taylor's role has been turned over to her son who, eager for his delicious meal, speeds *himself* up. What induces the son to do this is the sugar in the cereal. For this child, the rewards of efficiency have jumped inside the cereal box and become a lump of sugar.

A Third Shift: Time Work

As the first shift (at the workplace) takes more time, the second shift (at home) becomes more hurried and rationalized. The longer the workday at the office or plant, the more we feel pressed at home to hurry, to delegate, to delay, to forgo, to segment, to hyperorganize the precious remains of family time. Both their time deficit and what seem like solutions to it (hurrying, segmenting, and organizing) force parents to engage in a third shift—noticing, understanding, and coping with the emotional consequences of the compressed second shift.

Children respond to the domestic work-bred cult of efficiency in their own ways. Many, as they get older, learn to protest it. Parents at Amerco and elsewhere have to deal with their children, as they act out their feelings about the sheer scarcity of family time. For example, Dennis Long, an engineer at Amerco, told me about what happened with his son from a previous marriage when he faced a project deadline at work. Whenever Dennis got home later than usual, four-year-old Joshua greeted him with a tantrum. As Dennis ruefully explained,

> Josh gets really upset when I'm not home. He's got it in his head that the first and third weeks of every month, he's with me, not his mom. He hasn't seen me for a while, and I'm

supposed to be there. When a project deadline like this one comes up and I come home later, he gets to the end of his rope. He gives me hell. I understand it. He's frustrated. He doesn't know what he can rely on.

This father did his 'third shift' by patiently sitting down on the floor to 'receive' Josh's tantrum, hearing him out, soothing him, and giving him some time. For a period of six months, Joshua became upset at almost any unexpected delay or rapid shift in the pace at which events were, as he saw it, supposed to happen. Figuring out what such delays or shifts in pace meant to Joshua became another part of Dennis Long's third shift.

Such episodes raise various questions: if Josh's dad keeps putting off their dates to play together, does it mean he doesn't care about Josh? Does Josh translate the language of time the same way his father does? What if time symbolizes quite different things to the two of them? Whose understanding counts the most? Sorting out such emotional tangles is also part of the third shift.

Ironically, many Amerco parents were challenged to do a third-shift work by their children's reactions to 'quality time'. As one mother explained,

> Quality time is seven-thirty to eight-thirty at night, and then it's time for bed. I'm ready at seven-thirty, but Melinda has other ideas. As soon as quality time comes she wants to have her bath or watch TV; *no way* is she going to play with Mommy. Later, when I'm ready to drop, *then* she's ready for quality time.

A busy doctor married to an Amerco executive offered a similar description of the disruption of her well-laid plan to have 'special time' with her children:

> Normally, we pay our neighbour to drop Sam and Grace off at childcare at eight in the morning. Wednesday mornings I give the kids a supposed special treat. I drive them

myself and stay and watch them for half an hour. I think of it as a great treat, but usually it's a disaster. Normally, they're pretty happy to be dropped off. But when I do it, they cry. They cling. They get hysterical. And here I am, thinking, 'Isn't this great? "Quality time".'

In such situations, pressed parents often don't have time to sort through their children's responses. They have no space to wonder what their gift of time means. Or whether a parent's visit to daycare might seem to a child like a painfully prolonged departure. Is a gift of time what a parent wants to give, or what a child wants to receive? Such questions are often left unresolved.

Time-deficit 'paybacks' lead to another kind of difficult emotional work. For example, like many salespeople at Amerco, Phyllis Ramey spent about a fifth of her work time travelling. She always kept in touch by phone with her husband and their two children—Ben, three, and Pete, five—and at each sales stop, she bought the boys gifts. Ben enjoyed them but thought little about them; Pete, on the other hand, fixated anxiously on 'what mommy's bringing me'—a Tonka truck, a Batman cape, a bubble-making set. As Phyllis put it,

> When I call home and Pete gets on the phone, that's the first thing he'll ask me, 'What are you bringing me?' Then he'll tell me what he wants, and he gets disappointed or mad if I don't bring just the right toy. I don't like Pete to care that much about toys. I don't like him to *demand* toys.

Phyllis believed that Pete 'really needed more time' with her, and she sensed that she was buying him things out of guilt. Indeed, she talked and joked about guilt-shopping with coworkers. But in Pete's presence she had a hard time separating his anxiety about gifts from his relationship with her.

Amerco parents like Phyllis are not alone, of course. Spending on toys has soared from

$6.7 billion in 1980 to $17.5 billion in 1995. According to psychologist Marilyn Bradford, preschoolers looking forward to Christmas ask for an average of 3.4 toys but receive on average 11.6.[18] As employers buy growing amounts of time from employees, parents half-consciously 'buy' this time from their children. But children rarely enter into these 'trades' voluntarily, and parents are tempted to avoid the 'time work' it takes to cope with their children's frustration.

Part of modern parenthood now includes coping with children's resistance to the tight-fitting temporal uniforms required when home becomes work and work becomes home. Even the best of parents in such situations find themselves passing a systemwide speedup along to the most vulnerable workers on the line. It is children like Josh and Pete who signal most clearly the strains in the Taylorized home. Just as a company that is good to its workers need not worry about strikes, so a family without speedups could be less concerned about time-tantrums and might find little need for third-shift work. Of course, some children adapt quietly to the reversal of home and work, as do adults. But many children want more time with their parents than they get, and they protest the pace, the deadlines, the irrationality of 'efficient' family life. Parents are then obliged to hear their children's protests. To experience their resentment, resistance, passive acquiescence, to try to assuage their frustrations, to respond to their stubborn demands or whining requests, and in general to control the damage done by a reversal of worlds. This unacknowledged third shift only adds to the feeling that life at home is hard work. Parents are becoming supervisors with stopwatches, monitoring meals at bedtimes and putting real effort into eliminating 'wasted' time. If Charlie Chaplin's mechanized dance evoked a speedup in the Taylorized workplace, it is Janey King's interrupted dance that reveals the strains of the Taylorized home.

Children dawdle. Children refuse to leave places when it's time to go, or they insist on leaving places when it's still time to stay. Surely, this is part of the stop and go of childhood itself, but is it also a plea for more control over family time?

Notes

1. Those whose time is not compensated by money—housewives, children, the elderly—are held in lower regard than those whose time is compensated by money, everything else held equal. (This holds true only for jobs that are not subject to moral censure; a prostitute is not more highly valued than a housewife because she has a paying job in public life.) For many paid workers themselves, the trade of time for money can take on very different cultural meanings depending on the societal context. (Thanks to Deborah Davis for clarification on the relation between work for money and time.) See Nowotny, H. 1994. *Time: The Modern and the Postmodern Experience* (Cambridge, Polity); and Linder, S. 1974. *The Harried Leisure Class* (New York: Columbia University Press).

2. Founded in 1986, Bright Horizons was named the nation's leading work-site childcare organization in 1991 by the Child Care Information Exchange. The company offers a range of services: drop-in care, weekend programs, and programs for infants, toddlers, preschoolers, and school-age children. Bright Horizons pays its teachers 10 per cent more than whatever the going rate may be at nearby childcare centres and has a rate of teacher turnover that averages only half of the industry-wide 40 to 50 per cent a year.

3. Thirty-five per cent of parents responded (9 per cent were male and 90 per cent female; 92 per cent were married and 7 per cent single). Percentages may not add up to 100 for some questions either because some respondents didn't answer that question or because the percentages that are reported were rounded to the nearest whole number.

4. Twenty per cent of parents reported that their children were in childcare 41–45 hours a week; 13

per cent, 46–50 hours; 2 per cent, 51–60 hours. In the lowest income group in the study ($45,000 or less), 25 per cent of parents had children in child-care 41 hours a week or longer. In the highest income group ($140,000 or higher), 39 per cent did.

5. Parents were asked how many hours they spent doing work they brought home from the office 'on a typical weekday'. Eighteen per cent didn't answer. Of those remaining, half said they did bring work home. The largest proportion—19 per cent—brought home 'between six and ten hours of work [per week]'. They estimated even longer hours for their partners.

6. Sue Burden, D. and B.K. Googins 1987. 'Boston University Balancing Job and Homelife Study' (Boston: Boston University School of Social Work), 30.

7. Yet friends may not be a working parent's main source of social support. When asked which were the 'three most important sources of support in your life', nine out of ten men and women mentioned their spouses or partners. Second came their mothers, and third 'other relatives'. So people turned for support to kin first. Among *friendships*, however, those at work proved more significant than those around home. As sources of emotional support, 10 per cent of the respondents also mentioned 'books and magazines', the same percentage as mentioned 'church or temple'; only 5 per cent mentioned neighbours. Thirteen per cent turned for support first to friends at work—as many as turned to their own fathers.

8. Jim Spring, 'Seven Days of Play', *American Demography* 15 (Mar. 1993): 50–4. According to another study, in the average American home, a television is on for almost half of all waking hours. Teenagers watch approximately twenty-two hours of television each week (Anne Walling, 'Teenagers and Television', *American Family Physician* 42 [1990]: 638–41), and children watch an average of two to three hours each day (Althea Huston, John Wright, Mabel Rice, and Dennis Kerkman, 'Developmental Perspective of Television Viewing Patterns', *Development Psychology* 26 [1990]: 409–21).

9. See William Julius Wilson, *When Work Disappears: The World of the New Urban Poor* (New York: Knopf, 1996).

10. W. Edwards Deming, 'Improvement of Quality and Productivity through Action by Management', *National Productivity Review* (Winter 1981–2): 2–12. See Mary Walton, *The Deming Management Method* (New York: Dodd, Mead & Co., 1986); Frederick Taylor, *The Principles of Scientific Management* (New York: Harper, 1911). While the Total Quality movement has come to many corporations, the influence of Frederick Taylor is hardly dead. Many low-skill workers are vulnerable to Taylorization of their jobs. In her book *The Electronic Sweatshop* (New York: Simon & Schuster, 1988), Barbara Garson describes a McDonald's hamburger cook whose every motion is simplified, preset, and monitored.

11. Hugh Mulligan, 'Employers Foster Friendly Workplaces [Associated Press release]', *Louisville Courier Journal*, 1991. In some companies, such as Hudson Food Inc.'s processing plant in Noel, Missouri, the company hires chaplains as company counsellors. As Barnaby Feder describes in his *New York Times* article,

> As the workers chop and package the birds' carcasses, others talk about their battles with drinking or drugs, marital tensions, sick parents, runaway children and housing crises. Such chats (with the chaplain) frequently lead to private counseling sessions, hospital visits and other forms of pastoral ministry.

Companies hiring chaplains are, in a sense, offering themselves as sources of the spiritual help that workers need to cope with problems at home (Barnaby J. Feder, 'Ministers Who Work around the Flock', *New York Times*, 3 Oct. 1996).

12. The Myers-Briggs Type Indicator (MBTI) is a 'self-report questionnaire designed to make Carl Jung's theory of psychological types understandable and useful in everyday life.' An Amerco manual states that, among many uses, understanding your type on the MBTI 'enhances cooperation and productivity'. Types are based on various dimensions of personality—extroversion, introversion, sensing, intuition, thinking, feeling, judging, and perceiving.

Each type is assumed to make a different kind of contribution to a work team and to need a different kind of support. See Isabel Myers-Briggs, *Introduction to "Type": A Guide to Understanding Your Results on the Myers-Briggs Type Indicator* (Palo Alto, CA: Consulting Psychologists Press, 1993), 1.

13. Just as the Total Quality *expands* workers' authority at work, the declining size of the family and, for men, pressure to share the second shift at home *diminish* their authority at home. On the other hand, women who already have a low degree of authority in marriages with traditional men sometimes relish jobs where they can at last speak up and be heard. For very different reasons, then, both men and women can feel that their authority is curtailed at home and enhanced at work.

14. As Ella Taylor observes, over the years many television situation comedies have centred on 'fun' family-like relationships between coworkers at a workplace. *The Mary Tyler Moore Show* featured a work-family that ran a television news operation; *M*A*S*H* depicted a work-family that operated an army medical unit during the Korean War; and the 'familial' coworkers in *Taxi* worked at a cab company. See Ella Taylor, *Prime-Time Families: Television Culture in Postwar America* (Berkeley: University of California Press, 1989); see also Gerard Jones, *Honey, I'm Home! Sitcoms: Selling the American Dream* (New York: St Martin's Press, 1992).

15. Andrew J. Cherlin, ed., *The Changing American Family and Public Policy* (Washington, DC: Urban Institute Press). See Judith Wallerstein and Sandra Blakeslee, *Second Chances: Men, Women, and Children a Decade after Divorce* (New York: Tichnor and Fields, 1989). The authors, unfortunately, do not compare the children from divorced families with those from intact marriages, so we do not know to what degree the children of intact families have comparable experiences. See also P. Bohannon, *Divorce and After: An Analysis of the Emotional and Social Problems of Divorce* (New York: Anchor Books, 1971); and William Goode, *World Revolution and Divorce* (New York: Free Press, 1956).

16. One partial sign of the devaluation of home life is the low status of the homemaker. A national 1981 Harris poll asked, 'If you had to place a dollar value on the job of a homemaker, what do you feel fair wages for a year's work would be?' Men said $12,700, women $13,800. Those women who did *paid* work gave homemaking a higher dollar value ($24,000) than homemakers themselves ($13,400), and feminists gave it a higher value ($21,500) than traditionalist women ($19,600). In particular, the value of caring for children seems to have declined. A Harris poll asked adults and teenagers whether they agreed that 'parents today don't seem as willing to sacrifice for their children as parents did in the past'. Two-thirds of men and women forty years old and over agreed, as did half of those aged eighteen to thirty-nine (Louis Harris and Associates, *The General Mills American Family Report 1980–81*, conducted by Louis Harris and Associates, Inc., Minneapolis, 1981).

17. Wendy Tanaka, ''90s Trends Bite into Business Lunch', *San Francisco Examiner*, 9 Oct. 1994, A4.

18. Gary Cross, 'If Not the Gift of Time, At Least Toys', *New York Times*, 3 Dec. 1995.

Chapter 23

While much of the discussion of housework and childcare centres on the question whether men do their share, it is clear to most researchers that domestic labour must be de-privatized to the extent that is possible and desirable: two adults simply cannot satisfy the demands of two full-time jobs, *family, and their own needs. Unfortunately, a common response to these demands by middle-class and upper-class Canadians has been to employ a nanny to care for their children and do most of the housework. Sedef Arat-Koc explores the significance of this phenomenon.*

The Politics of Family and Immigration in the Subordination of Domestic Workers in Canada

Sedef Arat-Koc

Despite marked increases in the participation of women in the labour force, neither the availability and the quality of socialized childcare arrangements nor the division of housework between men and women appear to have changed radically. The structure, demands, and pressures of the labour market in Canada allow for less flexibility in the accommodation of family needs and responsibilities. Under these circumstances, housework and childcare remain private problems to be shouldered mainly by women, who must either work double and triple days or find substitutes.

In this context, the employment of live-in domestic workers, a long-abandoned practice in North America, is once again being presented as a solution to the burdens of housework and childcare among high- and middle-income groups. Yet the way domestic service is organized in capitalist society in general, and the specific conditions of the majority of live-in domestic workers (98 per cent of whom are women) make this type of work particularly oppressive. This 'solution' therefore presents a 'problem' for 'women's liberation' as a collective ideal.

In discussing the implications of the domestic service 'solution' to the housework and childcare problem, I will document and analyze the structural and historical conditions of live-in domestic workers in Canada. My primary focus is on foreign domestic workers with temporary work permits. The conditions of this group best demonstrate the complex articulation of gender issues with those of class, race, and citizenship.

The Crisis of the Domestic Sphere

There has been a very significant increase in women's participation in the labour force in Canada since the 1960s. By the late 1980s, around 44.3 per cent of the labour force comprised women (Statistics Canada 1989: B-2), and the percentage of couples in the man-the-breadwinner/woman-the-homemaker category was reduced to less than 16 per cent from around 65 per cent in 1961 (The Task Force on Child Care 1986: 7). What is more interesting, however, is that the change has been most dramatic among women with family responsibilities. In 1997, the employment rate of women with children under 16 rose to 66 per cent, from 39 per cent in 1976 (National Council of Welfare 1999: 12). When statistics take account of women who are actively looking for work, as well as those employed, the figures are even higher, even for mothers with very young children. In 1998, 64 per cent of all mothers with children under the age of three, and 70 per cent of all women whose youngest children were between three and five years of age were in the labour force. Once the youngest child reached school age, the participation rates for mothers (of children 6 to 16) went up to 78 per cent (Childcare Resource and Research Unit 1999).

The response of society and the state to these changes in women's employment has been negligible. First, the behaviour of men in the home has changed very little in terms of their contributions to housework and parenting responsibilities (Luxton, Chapter 21 this text). Although attitudes among men have changed positively (Luxton 1986: 20), the actual numbers of men regularly doing a considerable share of housework have not changed significantly. Moreover, even when men regularly contribute to domestic labour, the sex-typing of duties continues, with men only taking on certain defined tasks and rarely doing any pre-task planning. Overall, the contribution of most men who do some housework does not very often go beyond 'helping out' (Vanek 1983; Luxton 1986).

Second, the childcare situation in Canada is in a state of crisis. Rather than keeping up with the need for adequate, affordable, and quality spaces, childcare in Canada in the 1990s has become, as Susan Prentice puts it, 'less, worse and more expensive' (Prentice 1999). A very large percentage of children receiving non-parental care are in unlicensed arrangements, the quality and dependability of which are unknown. In 1998, regulated childcare spaces were available for only 10 per cent of all Canadian children under 13 years of age. In some provinces, the percentage of children served by regulated childcare locations was even lower: 3.9 per cent in Saskatchewan and 5 per cent in Newfoundland and Labrador (Childcare Resource and Research Unit 2000: 122). Even among children whose parents work or study more than twenty hours a week, access to licensed care is quite limited. In 1996, among children in this category, only 16 per cent of infants, 19 per cent of children eighteen to thirty-six months old, 45 per cent of those three to six years of age, and 9 per cent of those between six and thirteen years of age were served by regulated childcare (Human Resources and Development Canada 1997: 12–13).

A third factor that contributes to a crisis of the domestic sphere has to do with the inflexibility of work arrangements. Canadian employers and the state have provided little accommodation for the family responsibilities of working people. Except for an inadequate parental leave system (which has only recently been extended to fathers, only replaces a relatively small portion of regular income, and covers a relatively short period of time) Canada lacks official recognition of recent changes in the labour force. In stark contrast to most European countries, there are no systems of extended childcare leave, leave for care of sick children or other types of family responsibility leave in Canada. Without the rights to refuse shift work and overtime and to work reduced hours or flexible work weeks (rights that are almost commonplace in Europe), working parents in Canada find that even privatized solutions fail to meet their needs (The Task Force on Child Care 1986: chs 11, 12).

As a result of the squeeze on working couples from pressures in the public and private spheres, there are signs that employment of domestic servants, a rare practice since the 1920s, is becoming widespread again. Several governmental and mass media sources have mentioned the employment of domestic workers as a solution (Royal Commission on the Status of Women 1970; Hook 1978; Vanstone 1986). Indeed, there is evidence to suggest that employers of live-in domestic workers are now overwhelmingly dual-career couples with small children. For 71.4 per cent of the employers the major reason for hiring a domestic has been to 'free both spouses for the labour market' (The Task Force on Immigration Practices and Procedures 1981: 35–45). While the majority of employers are in upper-middle to upper-income categories, there is a possibility that the demand for live-in domestic servants among middle-income families may rise. An important reason for this is that user fees—as opposed to municipal, provincial, or national government financing—constitute a high proportion of childcare costs and middle-class families cannot get subsidies for such services in Canada. In 1995, the average parent fee for a three-year-old child was $753 per month (Prentice 1999: 139). In addition, user fees in childcare have been going up substantially in recent years. Between 1989 and 1995, for example, monthly daycare fees for preschoolers increased by 11 to 40 per cent in different Canadian provinces (National Council of Welfare 1999: 50). It has been suggested that especially for parents with two or more preschool children, employment of a live-in nanny costs significantly less than sending children to a daycare centre or hiring live-out help (Vanstone 1986: 51; Walmsley 1989: 129).

While the demand for domestic workers rises, the conditions of domestic service in general and live-in service in particular are so undesirable that it is very difficult to find Canadians willing to do the job. As a result, the Canadian Department of Immigration has devised mechanisms to bring in domestic workers, usually from the Third World, on temporary status. Since the mid-1970s, between 10,000 to 16,000 foreign workers a year have been issued temporary work permits. Almost all (96 per cent) of these workers are in live-in service (The Task Force on Immigration Practices and Procedures 1981: 53).

Although foreign domestic workers have certainly provided some solution to the pressures their employers face in meeting the demands of work and family, this solution is very questionable when one considers the working and living conditions of the workers involved. If these conditions are not changed radically, this solution also has serious implications for the women's movement. With the employment of domestic workers, work in the domestic sphere becomes a source of division, rather than unity and 'sisterhood' among women.[1]

This paper starts with a short history of domestic service. The discussion of the conditions of domestic workers is divided into three parts. The first part examines the labour process in domestic service and analyzes what the domestic worker shares with the housewife. The second part focuses on the ambiguous status of the domestic as a special type of worker who is neither a member of the family nor an employee in the public sphere, enjoying some advantages of socialized work. Finally, the citizenship status of foreign domestic workers in Canada is analyzed as a major factor contributing to, as well as perpetuating, the oppressiveness of their conditions.

History of Domestic Service

The emergence of domestic service, as service provided by non-family members in the domestic sphere, is relatively recent, corresponding to the public/private split that came about with industrialization. Although servants were very widely employed in feudal Europe, the nature of their work and their status differed significantly from those of later domestic servants.

In feudal Europe, the labour requirements of most households—including those of most peasants and artisans—necessitated, at least during certain phases of their family cycle, the employment of servants. Servants were the children of poorer families and/or the children of families in different phases of their family life cycle. Social historians like Flandrin (1979) and Mitterauer and Sieder (1982) have clearly demonstrated that in an era when 'family' was synonymous with household, servants were very much a part of the patriarchal family, owing the same obedience to, and expecting the same protection and guidance as would, any family member, especially a child. In households that combined productive and reproductive work, servants performed unspecialized work alongside other family members, little of which had to do with the creation and maintenance of a comfortable domestic environment (Fairchilds 1984: 23–4).

With industrialization, the types of work performed by the family were divided and assigned to separate and gendered spheres. As the middle-class home sought to become a 'haven' in the competitive and harsh environment of early industrial society, the very purposes and nature of servant-keeping were transformed to serve the new emphasis on domestic comfort. Changes in the structure of society and the family in this period affected domestic service in more ways than one. Parallel to servants' work becoming exclusively 'domestic' for the first time was the 'feminization' of the occupation. As the home was defined to be women's sphere and housework to be women's work, domestic servants as well as their employers became predominantly female.

Another change that characterized this period of transformation was the increased social distance between master and servant. Two factors contributed to this. One was the increased privatization of the family, which defined it as a nuclear unit of parents and children and excluded servants as 'strangers' (Fairchilds 1984: 13–17; Rollins 1985: 33–6). Second, unlike the situation in feudal peasant and artisan households, where masters were direct producers, some of the bourgeois mistresses of the new domestic servants began to separate themselves from manual work. While the majority of middle-class women who could only afford one servant had to work side by side with them to keep up with highly demanding housework, upper-class women, committed to an ideology of domesticity, nevertheless began to maintain a clear distinction between their own managerial and supervisory roles in the home and the physical drudgery that servants undertook (Dudden 1983: ch. 5).

The history of domestic work in both Canada and the United States has been closely connected to histories of racial and ethnic relations and immigration, as well as to industrialization and urbanization. During the colonial period in the United States, domestic service was performed mainly by convicts, indentured servants, and black slaves. In this period, the low status and indignities that servants suffered were common in both the South and the North (Rollins 1985: 49).

From the American Revolution until about mid-nineteenth century, the exploitative and degrading treatment of black slaves in the American South coincided with relatively egalitarian master/servant relationships in the northern United States and Canada. The term *help* was used for the native-born whites in the American North, who partially replaced the foreign or black servants of the colonial period (Rollins 1985). Generally employed by farmers and small shopkeepers, the 'help' co-operated with the employer in the hard work of the household economy. The relationship of 'help' to their employers was quite egalitarian in the sense that they shared the conditions and the tables of the families for whom they worked. Also distinguishing the 'help' from past and future groups of domestic workers was the fact that theirs was less an occupation and lifelong status than an activity that allowed casual, temporary, and/or part-time employment (Dudden 1983). These conditions contrasted sharply with relations in bourgeois households in the cities, where the social distance between employers and employees was growing.[2]

From around the middle of the nineteenth century to the 1920s, the kinds of changes in domestic service that occurred in Europe as a result of industrialization and urbanization also prevailed in North America. As the urban middle-class family became more privatized, its emphasis on domestic comforts and luxury increased and therefore it became more dependent than ever on outsiders to actualize its standard of a private haven. While this substantially increased the demand for domestic workers, changes such as the decline in the general status of the domestic sphere, the 'bourgeoisification' of servant employers, and the distinction drawn between the family and non-family members precluded better working and living conditions for domestic workers.

Further contributing to a decline in the status of servants—or, in certain regions, the persistence of their low status—was the availability of groups of vulnerable workers. In the northeastern United States, immigrants like the Irish—many of them single women—were fleeing economic desperation in their own countries. Finding almost no alternatives to domestic work, they were particularly vulnerable. The term *servant*, which was rarely used in the democratic atmosphere of the postrevolution era in the American North, was re-introduced in this period (Steinberg 1981: 159; Rollins 1985: 51–2). In regions where there were large concentrations of people of colour, it was usually the women of the oppressed racial/ethnic groups who had to take domestic service positions.

> Despite differences in the composition of the populations and the mix of industries in the regions, there were important similarities in the situation of Mexicans in the Southwest, African Americans in the South, and Japanese people in northern California and Hawaii. Each of these groups was placed in a separate legal category from whites, excluded from rights and protections accorded to full citizens (Glenn 1992: 8).

Since the turn of the twentieth century, changes in the labour market as well as changes in the household have led to a decline in domestic service. First, alternative avenues of female employment opened up, as industrialization proceeded and some white-collar occupations were feminized. So, women rejected domestic service in favour of better working conditions elsewhere. Even when net wages from clerical, shop, or factory work were lower, women left domestic work to enjoy the relative independence of private life after work (Barber 1985). The demand for domestic workers also began to fall with improve-

ments in household technology, falling birth rates, and the market production of goods previously produced in the household (Leslie 1974: 74). Since the beginning of the twentieth century, increased access to electricity, running water, and sewage systems; mechanization of heating, refrigeration, laundry; the development of food processing; and increased use of ready-made clothing meant for middle- and upper-class women that one person alone (in this case, the housewife) could do all the housework (Fox 1980; Luxton 1980). To the extent that domestic service survived, living-out became more widespread (Rollins 1985: 54).

In Canada, despite women's unwillingness to enter domestic service, employers were remarkably successful in maintaining a large supply of servants until World War II. Organized around church groups, YWCA, and other women's clubs and organizations, women seeking domestics were greatly helped by the Immigration Department (Leslie 1974; Roberts 1979). As domestic service in urban Canada became so undesirable that no native-born whites would do it, and as industrialization diverted women into other occupations, the Immigration Department became increasingly and more directly involved in ensuring a supply of domestics.

Although the demand for domestic workers decreased from the early part of the twentieth century until the late 1960s, it has always exceeded the supply. This has especially been the case for live-in jobs. As a result, the Department of Immigration developed new schemes in the postwar period to bring domestic workers to Canada, and to keep them doing domestic work.

The Material Conditions of Privatized Household Work

The geographic, economic, social, and ideological separation of the public work sphere from the home, which developed with socialized commodity production under capitalism, has led to a decline in the status of domestic labour—whether done by a housewife or a servant. One of the causes of this decline is the physical, economic, and ideological invisibility of domestic labour. Physically, what makes domestic labour 'invisible' is the service or maintenance nature of the work whose products are either intangible or consumed very quickly. The domestic labourer is at a disadvantage compared to the factory worker in this regard:

> The appropriate symbol for housework (and for housework alone) is not the interminable conveyor belt but a compulsive circle like a pet mouse in its cage spinning round on its exercise wheel unable to get off . . . (Williams, Twart, and Bachelli 1980: 114).

Also, domestic labour is performed in private, and perhaps is more isolated than ever before in human history. As the production of goods as well as services (such as education and health care) moved out of the home, as the husband and children left, and as the development of household technology made collaboration in certain tasks with other women less necessary, the household worker faced increased isolation, loneliness, and invisibility.

Economically, domestic labour is invisible because it is not part of capitalist production that utilizes wage labour to produce commodities (for the market) and profit. When performed by the housewife, domestic labour is unpaid; it produces use value and no profit. The work is more visible when carried out by a domestic servant because it is paid. As one domestic servant stated, however, it still can remain invisible, even in the eyes of the female employer:

> You know how housework is; you could tidy up the house and wash the dishes twenty times a day. At the end of each day, especially with three growing boy child, the house look

like a hurricane pass through it, so when she is in a bad mood she wants to know what I do all day (Noreen in Silvera 1983: 25).

Domestic labour involves physical and mental work, which goes into the reproduction of labour power and of the labour force. This is indispensable for the economy. Intertwined as it is with intimate, personal relations, however, domestic labour is considered a private matter, a 'labour of love'. As such, it is ideologically invisible as a form of real and hard work, a status that is hard to change even when it is paid.

Domestic labour generally does not appear on paycheques or in GNP figures; it is not considered 'real work', and is defined as 'non-productive'. Yet it involves very long working hours.[3] It is work that never ends. Especially for caregivers of young children who must be always on call, there is no clear boundary between work and leisure. For the housewife and the live-in domestic servant, the place of work is also the place of leisure. A domestic does not go to work, but wakes up to it. This makes her 'leisure' vulnerable to interventions and her work hours stretchable to twenty-four hours a day, seven days a week.

Contrary to its image as a place of comfort and safety, the home is a hazardous and stressful workplace for the domestic labourer. Besides working with dangerous chemicals and being involved in several activities that are accident prone, the domestic worker also experiences stress. Stress is typical for occupations that involve high demand and low control (Rosenberg 1986, 1987). In domestic work, the need to adjust the work to the different schedules of family members, and to juggle conflicting demands of housework and childcare, create stressful conditions. Being her own boss is largely a myth for the housewife. It is probably more so for the domestic worker whose schedule and standards of work are controlled by the employer.

Unlike wage labour which is—at least theoretically—changeable, the labour of the housewife is a lifelong, or at least marriage-long commitment. Compared to the housewife, the domestic servant should fare better in this respect. This is only the case when we consider the free labourer, however. Domestic servants in Canada have very often been restricted in their ability to change employers, or even to decide whether or not to sell their labour power.

Although domestic labour under capitalism assumes several universal characteristics such as invisibility, isolation, and low status, the way these are experienced by individuals performing domestic labour may vary significantly by class, race, and citizenship. In the case of foreign domestic workers, the isolation and resulting loneliness imposed by the privatized nature of housework and childcare are perpetuated by racial, cultural, and linguistic barriers. Likewise, the invisibility of domestic labour and the low status attached to it are further reinforced by the powerlessness of domestic labourers when they are visible-minority women from the Third World on temporary work permits, who lack basic political rights.

Neither a Wife Nor a Worker: The Contradictions of the Domestic Worker's Status

While sharing with the housewife many of the material conditions of privatized housework and childcare, the domestic worker also has an ambiguous status: she is neither a wife nor a full-fledged worker with corresponding rights and privileges. Squeezed between the private and public spheres, she belongs to neither one nor the other, and probably experiences the worst aspects of both.

With the historical privatization of the family, the domestic worker has been excluded from membership in, or close bonding with, the employing family. Lost are the co-operation and companionship apparently characteristic of relations between 'help' and employers in rural America. The domestic worker today is like a stranger, 'being *in* the family, but not *of* it' (Leslie

1974: 87). She is involved in the work of a *house*, but not the pleasures and intimacies of a *home*. Positive aspects that are rightly or wrongly attributed to the private sphere—love, intimacy, nurturance, companionship—are not even part of her realistic expectations.

> I feel as if this is my home. It is my home, this is where I live. It's not like I come to work for them and then eveningtime I leave and go home. When you are living with them, they make you feel as if you really don't belong, and where the devil do you really belong? It's a funny thing to happen to us, because it make us feel like we don't know if we coming or going. This live-in thing really puts us in a funny situation (Gail in Silvera 1983: 113).

Potentially, lack of intimacy with the employing family is liberating. Since class differences turn close employer-employee relationships into paternalistic ones, many domestic workers actually prefer maintaining a business-like professionalism. Professionalism in relations, however, is not possible for the domestic worker, since it requires relative power in social, political, and legal terms. Historically, the social construction of domestic work in Canada has deprived domestic workers from these forms of power.

In losing the close relationship to the family and becoming an employee, the domestic worker has not been compensated by the advantages other employees enjoy. The isolation of domestic service makes the organization of workers, as well as the standardization and regulation of working conditions, very difficult. This difficulty is greater for live-in workers for whom there is no separation between home and work. The result is generally a vulnerable and often exploited worker whose conditions are at the mercy of the employer:

> Wages are too often regulated by the employer's bank account, hours of service by his personal caprice, and moral questions by

his personal convenience (Salmon cited in Leslie 1974: 112).

Labour standards legislation—which is under provincial jurisdiction in Canada and therefore not uniform—either does not apply or only partially applies to domestic workers. As of the mid-1980s, domestic employees in private homes were totally excluded from labour standards legislation in Alberta, New Brunswick, Nova Scotia, the Northwest Territories, and the Yukon. In other provinces they were only partially covered—in many, only with provisions providing lower than the general minimum wage, longer than the forty-hour work week and rarely any overtime pay (The Task Force on Immigration Practices and Procedures 1981: 74–8; Estable 1986: 51–3).

In Ontario, which has about two-thirds of all domestic workers in Canada, the Employment Standards Act was extended finally to domestics in 1984. It set daily and weekly rates of pay based on a standard work week of forty-four hours. This change, however, was almost meaningless for live-in domestic workers because they were not covered by the hours of work and overtime pay provisions of the Act. Since it is not uncommon for live-in domestic workers to work or be on call sixty to eighty or more hours per week, the actual hourly wage can in many cases fall substantially below the minimum wage. Working very long hours and having little or no time off are actually some of the most common complaints of live-in domestic workers:

> I want something where I can go home to my house at night, close my door and pray to my God in peace. I want to know that when I go to bed at night, I don't have to listen out for people shouting at me to come and look after their food or come and change diapers (Noreen in Silvera 1983: 26).

It took two years of negotiations with the Ontario government, and a Charter of Rights case against it (filed by the Toronto Organization for Domestic Workers' Rights, INTERCEDE) before Ontario acquired labour regulations (in October 1987) that gave live-in domestic workers the right to claim overtime pay after a forty-four hour work week.[4] Whether or not this provision is enforced depends on how much *de facto* bargaining power domestics have in relation to their employers. So far, even when protective legislation exists, governments have generally failed to enforce it. In practice, especially when they are dealing with vulnerable workers who have no choice but to remain in their jobs, employers are free to set work hours, duties, and pay rates.

In Ontario, provincial governments have not only failed to enforce existing legislation, but also have prevented domestic workers from defending their rights in an organized, collective way. The Ontario Labour Relations Act denies the domestics employed in private homes the right to unionize. The same Act also denies domestics access to an impartial tribunal for unfair practices (Estable 1986: 51).[5] In some cases, existing regulations may even sanction abuse. One serious problem domestic workers face is the lack of clear job definitions. The Canadian Classification and Dictionary of Occupations (which the Immigration Department uses in connection with employment authorizations) may add to the problem. In this system *baby sitter* is defined as someone who, besides doing other work, 'keeps children's quarters clean and tidy' and 'cleans other parts of home'. The definition of *maid/domestic*, on the other hand, includes, 'may look after children' (The Task Force on Immigration Practices and Procedures, 1981: 76). The specific combination of the class status of the domestic worker and the fact that domestic service takes place in the private sphere creates the potential for a very peculiar relation of domination between the employer and the domestic worker, especially if there is a live-in arrangement—which is compulsory for foreign domestic workers on temporary work permits.

There are social-psychological dimensions to the subordination of a domestic worker that make it different from the subordination of housewives (who also do domestic work) and workers (who also stand in an unequal class relation to their employers). While a factory worker experiences subordination and control during work, when she leaves her job at the end of the day she is a free person in relation to her employer. The live-in domestic worker, on the other hand, cannot leave her workplace and her employer's supervision. Sharing private space with the employers, and yet not being part of their family, the domestic finds it difficult to create her own private space and private life:

> Some domestics have to share a room with the children in the household or have their room used as a family room, TV room, sewing room, etc. One woman had to keep her door open at all times in case the children started to cry; others say their employers do not respect their privacy and walk in without knocking. In one case the piano was moved into the domestic's room for the children to practice on! (Epstein 1983: 26).

Living in the employer's home, it is also difficult to invite friends over. Other specific complaints about lack of privacy refer in certain cases to the domestic's mail and phones being watched, personal belongings searched, and inquiries into her activities after days off (Silvera 1981; Silvera 1983). Because live-in domestic service creates the possibilities of total scrutiny over both the work and the lives of domestic workers, it probably is not an exaggeration to call it a 'total institution' (Cock 1980: 58–60; Fairchilds 1984: 102–4).

Clearly, during its historical development, domestic service lost only some of the elements of the child-like status it had in earlier patriarchal households. Gone are the protection, security, and bonding to the family that were typical of service in feudal society. Remaining are the supervision and the personal nature of the authority relationship that strip the domestic worker of full adult status. Linguistic practices are often reflec-

tive of this. For example, it is very common for both employers and domestics themselves to refer to domestics as 'girls', regardless of their age. It is also common for domestic workers to be called by their first names while they are expected to address their employers as Mr or Mrs (Hook 1978: 63; Rollins 1985: 158).

Besides heavy physical work, domestic service involves a personal relationship with the employer. Unlike factory work, which requires completion of clearly defined tasks in clearly defined ways, domestic service is very unstructured. Especially in live-in arrangements, a domestic is not just hired for specific tasks, 'but for general availability; above all, a servant ha(s) to take orders as well' (Leslie 1974: 83). Consequently, the deference, obedience, and submissiveness that the domestic is supposed to display can sometimes be as important or a more important part of her job than the actual physical work.[6] The domestic worker, therefore, is hired not for her labour alone but also for her personality traits.

Also unique to the employer-employee relationship in domestic service is that both the domestic and the mistress are designated, on the basis of gender, as responsible for domestic work. In different studies, all the female employers interviewed have indicated that they needed the domestic worker to help them because their husbands would not (Kaplan 1985; Rollins 1985). Employment of a domestic worker has enabled these women to avoid a confrontation with their husbands about sharing domestic work. In this sense, the presence of the domestic worker 'emphasizes the fact that women—all women—are responsible for cleaning the house, at the same time that it releases the housewife to become a lady of leisure or a career woman' (Kaplan 1985: 17). Given the gendered division of labour in the household, the labour of the housewife and the domestic worker are interchangeable: the domestic worker is employed to replace an absent full-time housewife; but when the domestic worker can't work, the housewife must. Given social degradation of domestic work and the class inequality between the domestic worker and the mistress, however, their shared subordination does not often lead to solidarity:

> the domestic represents the employer in the most devalued area of the employer's activities. . . . Any identification the employer has with the domestic is a negative identification (Rollins 1985: 185).

Rather than solidarity, shared subordination can lead to 'housewife power strategies' through which 'many housewives seek to maintain class and race privileges vis-à-vis their domestics' (Kaplan 1985). Often, what characterizes servant-mistress relationships is deference from the worker and maternalism from the employer.

Good Enough to Work, Not Good Enough to Stay: Implications of Citizenship Status for Foreign Domestic Worker

From the nineteenth century on, the Canadian state has been very active in recruiting and controlling a domestic labour force (Leslie 1974; Barber 1986; Lindstrom-Best 1986). The amount of planning and energy that has gone into these activities tells us a great deal about the importance of domestic service for the Canadian economy and society. The low status and unfavourable conditions of the workers involved, however, stand in stark contrast to the attention their recruitment and control have received. In fact, the conditions have been so undesirable that not only has it been difficult to find Canadians interested in the job, but the only way of keeping immigrant domestics in domestic work has sometimes been through indenturing them.

Active state involvement in recruitment and control of domestic workers started in late nineteenth century when industrialization diverted women into other occupations and it became difficult to find enough Canadian-born women interested in domestic service. This involvement

ranged from making the immigration of domestics easier by sending immigration employees to England and Scotland to select domestics, to encouraging and even enforcing the so-called 'assisted passage' agreements that bonded servants to their employers for a certain period of time (Leslie 1974: 95–105). Bonding became such a necessary part of controlling the domestic labour force that the Department of Immigration sometimes evaded legislation in order to fulfill its policing function. For example, around the turn of the century, most provinces enacted master and servant legislation aimed to protect servants from an exploitative contract that they might have signed in order to immigrate. According to this legislation, contracts signed outside the province were not legally binding. The Immigration Department, however, in order to enforce bonded status, avoided this legislation by having immigrant domestics re-sign their contracts upon arrival in Canada (Leslie 1974: 122, ff. 79).

Immigration of British and Scottish domestic workers in the late nineteenth and early twentieth centuries shared with later domestic immigration the practice of bonding. What made immigration practices in this period different from later periods, however, was that recruitment of domestics from abroad was closely linked to Canada's nation-building efforts. Until the 1920s, the middle-class women and social reformers involved in female immigration work voiced racist, nationalist, and moralistic concerns that went beyond a simple interest in meeting demands for the domestic labour force. Through their efforts in selecting, protecting, and supervising domestics, the organizations involved in female immigration wanted to make sure that the recruits would become more than servants—that these women of the 'right' national and racial stock and character would, in the long run, constitute the 'pure and virtuous mothers of the ideal Canadian home and the foundation of the moral Canadian nation' (Roberts 1979: 188–9). While these expectations were certainly restrictive for domestic workers, they also conveyed the message that these women 'belonged' in Canadian society, a message that would be missing in later immigration practices.

THE WEST INDIAN DOMESTIC SCHEME

Although the demand for domestic servants has decreased since the early part of the twentieth century, it has still exceeded the supply. This has especially been the case for live-in jobs. As a result, the Department of Immigration has developed new schemes in the postwar period to bring domestic workers to Canada and to keep them doing domestic work. In 1955, for example, the Domestic Worker Program was started to import domestic workers from the Caribbean region (primarily from Jamaica). Under this scheme single women of good health, between eighteen and forty years of age, with no dependants and of at least Grade 8 education, were allowed into Canada as landed immigrants on the condition that they would spend at least one year as domestic servants before being free to choose other types of work (Arnopoulos 1979: 26). Through this program, between 1955 and 1960, an average of 300, and between 1960 and 1965 around 1,000 domestic workers, were admitted per year (Bolaria and Li 1985: 178).

Even though the West Indian Domestic Scheme brought in domestics as landed immigrants, it involved special 'administrative controls' which were missing in previous immigration schemes involving white European domestics. Any domestic who broke her contract or was found 'undesirable' (e.g., upon becoming pregnant in her first year) would be deported to her country of origin at the expense of the Caribbean government. Also, unlike preferred domestics from western and northern Europe, West Indian domestics were not eligible to apply for interest-free travel loans from the Canadian government under the Assisted Passage Loan Scheme (Calliste 1989: 143).

THE INTRODUCTION OF TEMPORARY STATUS

In the late 1960s, the demand for domestic workers started to increase in Canada. This was due to women's increasing participation in the labour force and the underdeveloped childcare system they faced. In this period, the Department of Immigration started to see the Domestic Worker Program as an inadequate solution to the labour shortage in domestic service because most women who came as domestics found their working conditions unacceptable and left service for other work once they fulfilled their one-year obligation. Rather than providing the mechanisms to improve the conditions of domestic work and make it attractive for people to stay in—by extending and effectively enforcing labour standards and human rights legislation to domestic workers, for example—the Canadian state opted for a solution that would force people to stay in domestic work.

In the 1960s and the early 1970s—in spite of the high and rising demand for domestic workers—immigration authorities arbitrarily lowered the rating for domestic work within the occupational demand category (Bakan and Stasiulis 1992a). In 1973, the government started issuing temporary work permits that would only let these workers stay in the country for a specified period of time (usually a year), doing a specific type of work, for a specific employer. The temporary employment authorization system is a new version of indenture. From 1973 to 1981, foreign domestic workers could only come to Canada as 'guest workers'—instead of immigrants. As guest workers they had no rights to stay in Canada or claim social security benefits. Although foreign domestics could be allowed to change employers with special permission from immigration authorities, they could not leave domestic service without also having to leave Canada. Extension of the employment visa beyond the first year was possible and common, but the foreign worker inevitably had to leave Canada. Under this new scheme, increasing numbers of domestic workers were brought into Canada every year. The numbers of employment visas issued to domestics rose consistently from around 1,800 in 1973 to more than 16,000 in 1982 (Silvera 1983: 15; Bolaria and Li 1985: 178).

The official purpose of the employment visa system was to meet the urgent and temporary needs of Canadian employers to fill jobs that cannot be filled domestically without threatening the employment opportunities of Canadian residents (Wong 1984: 86). When we consider the case of domestic service, however, both the unwillingness of Canadians to take live-in work, as well as the century-long efforts of the Canadian state to import domestic workers from abroad, suggest that neither the need nor the solution has been temporary. Despite the persistence of a high-demand/low-supply situation, domestic workers have, since the 1970s, only been accepted to Canada with temporary status. Except for foreign agricultural workers—who do seasonal work—domestic workers have been the *only* occupational group to whom temporary work permits apply on a permanent basis.

When we look into Canada's immigration practices since the mid-1970s, we see an increasing tendency to resort to temporary employment visas as opposed to permanent immigration to meet labour demands not only in domestic service but also in several other job categories. Since 1975, the annual number of people entering Canada on temporary employment visas has consistently exceeded the number of landed immigrants destined for the labour force (Epstein 1983: 237; Wong 1984: 92). Migration to Canada, therefore, has changed in part from a movement of people to a movement of labour power. The benefits of this to Canada as a labour-importing country are enormous. As the literature on migrant workers in Western Europe, South Africa, and California has demonstrated, recipient countries benefit not only by avoiding the costs of developing a young and healthy labour force, but also by avoiding a commitment to supporting them during old age, sickness, and unemployment (Gorz 1970; Castles and Kosack 1980; Burawoy 1980).

Behind the term 'guestworker' (is) a belief that such workers (are) like replaceable parts. Like cogs in a machine, for every part that

breaks down, there (is) a seemingly endless supply of replacements (Rist 1979: 51).

There are also significant political advantages to employing workers without citizenship rights. Lacking electoral and political rights and freedoms, and dependent on their employers not only for wages but also for their continued stay in the country, workers on employment visas are expected to create a docile and acquiescent labour force. Historically, the presence of migrant workers has also frequently been associated with racist and xenophobic divisions in the working class.

Canadians have the feeling that we are coming here to rob them, to take away their jobs, yet we are the ones who clean up their mess, pick up after them. We take the jobs they wouldn't take and yet they hate us so much (Primrose in Silvera 1983: 100).

One significant ideological implication of temporary work permits is that designation of a group of workers as temporary and foreign encourages a desensitized attitude towards their conditions. Hannah Arendt argues that with the development of nation-states and national sovereignty, basic human rights and freedoms were throughly implicated with the rights of citizenship (1966: ch. 9). In liberal democratic societies, where emphasis on formal equality has become a part of popular political discourse, separation of people into 'citizen' and 'non-citizen' categories, into 'insiders' (to whom rights apply) and 'outsiders', serves to legitimize inferior conditions and lesser rights for the latter group.[7]

The major effect of Canada's employment visa system on domestic workers has been the creation of a captive labour force, which has guaranteed that the turnover in domestic service would remain low no matter how bad the working and living conditions. Unable to leave domestic service without losing their rights to stay in Canada, foreign domestics have also found it difficult, in practice, to change employers. A foreign worker's status in Canada changes to that of visitor if she leaves or loses her job. While in practice workers are generally given a period of two weeks to find a new employer, the decision to issue a new employment visa is at the discretion of the individual immigration officer who judges whether the working conditions with the previous employer have in fact been intolerable (The Task Force on Immigration Practices and Procedures 1981: 26–7).[8] Besides the hassle given by individual immigration officers, there is a regulation that requires workers on employment visas to have a 'release letter' from the former employer before changing employers (Toughill 1986).[9]

Unlike other workers who enjoy the basic freedom to leave a particular job or employer, the only freedom that the foreign worker on an employment visa has is to return to her country of origin. In the case of many Third World women who come to Canada out of conditions of economic desperation, there is no choice but to stay in Canada. As Nancy Hook reported, compared to Canadian workers, foreign domestic workers on employment visas were more likely to live in the homes of their employer, to work more days per week more overtime without pay, and receive a smaller hourly wage (Hook 1978: 107–8).[10]

Even though their status in Canada was by definition temporary, domestic workers on employment visas have been required to pay Canada Pension Plan, Unemployment Insurance premiums, and income tax (about one month's earnings a year) without being able to claim benefits.[11] The nature of the employment visa has made access to unemployment insurance benefits impossible because the worker either has to find a new employer or leave the country if she loses a job. Benefits from Canada Pension Plan have also been inaccessible because the 'guest worker' is expected to retire in the country of origin (The Task Force on Child Care 1986: 121). For services that they do not expect to receive, foreign domestics have paid a very high price. Revenue Canada has calculated the total of revenues from

CPP and UIC premiums collected from foreign domestics between 1973–9 to be more than 11 million dollars (The Task Force on Immigration Practices and Procedures, 1981: 70).[12]

THE FOREIGN DOMESTIC MOVEMENT (FDM) PROGRAM

In 1981, a federal task force was established to study the conditions of domestic workers on temporary work permits. Its report recommended that the Temporary Employment Authorization system be continued provided that opportunities for landing be broadened (The Task Force on Immigration Policies and Procedures 1981). The Foreign Domestic Movement (FDM) program which came into effect in November 1981 has enabled foreign domestics who have worked in Canada continuously for two years to apply for landed immigrant status without having to leave the country. While this was a progressive step, it failed to solve the problem of foreign domestic workers in Canada. First, the FDM continued to impose a two-year period of bonded service that the domestic had to fulfill before applying. In some ways, the practice of indenturing was strengthened by the entrenchment in the FDM of a mandatory live-in requirement for all participants in the program. Domestic workers who insisted on live-out arrangements would not only lose their rights to apply for landed immigrant status but would not even receive extensions on their employment authorization (Employment and Immigration Canada 1988: 17–18).[13]

Another problem with the FDM program has been that it gave no guarantee that landed immigrant status would be granted. Applicants needed to meet Immigration assessment criteria and demonstrate a 'potential for self-sufficiency'.[14] Reflecting societal notions about domestic labour in general, these women continued to get very low points for both the Specific Vocational Preparation category and, ironically, the Occupational Demand category (The Task Force on Immigration Practices and Procedures 1981: 18–21).[15] As a result, immigration officers required domestic applicants (again without any guarantees to grant them landing) to take upgrading courses (with high foreign student fees), to demonstrate adaptation and integration into Canadian society (through volunteer work in the community), and to prove financial management skills (through showing evidence of savings, etc.)—all special requirements applying to domestic workers only. For live-in foreign domestics, it has been difficult to afford both the time and the money to meet these requirements. Another problem has been that domestics with children (in the home country) and older domestics have faced special discrimination during assessment for immigrant status.[16]

> They say Immigration say any woman over 45 soon can't clean house and will be just a burden on the government, and woman with over two children will bring them into the country and take away the opportunities other Canadian children have (Noreen in Silvera 1983: 29).

So-called 'rationalized' immigration policies, oriented towards the demands of the market, aim to import labour power rather than people. It is not, therefore, surprising to see dependants being treated as 'superflous appendages' of the labour market (as they are called in South Africa).

The overall effect of the 1981 changes in the Temporary Employment Authorization Program has been to create the possibility for *individual* upward mobility of some domestic workers while providing no *structural* solution to the problems of domestic service or foreign domestic workers in general. Indeed, it is ironic that to accumulate enough points to get landed immigrant status, a domestic has had to move out of domestic service altogether. The implicit message that immigration policies and practices give is that domestic workers, as domestic workers, are 'good enough to

work, but not good enough to stay' in this country. This message surely tells us a great deal about the status of domestic labour in general.

Furthermore, it is interesting to note the parallel between the modern attitude of the Canadian government and the historical treatment of domestic workers. Domestic servants did not receive legal equality and citizenship rights until the late nineteenth or early twentieth century. In France and England, for example, because they were considered to be too dependent on their masters to be recognized as civil persons, domestics (together with women) were the last groups to be enfranchised. Many of the basic workers' rights and freedoms we take for granted and often associate with capitalist society are, in fact, connected to citizenship rights. With the alleged attempt to meet the temporary labour requirements of the Canadian economy without threatening the jobs of Canadians, the Employment Visa system has created a *permanent* temporary workforce without citizenship rights.

By treating both the need and the presence of foreign workers as *temporary* the Canadian government has done nothing *permanent* either to improve significantly the conditions of workers or to find other solutions to problems of housework and childcare. As long as it has been able to maintain a captive labour force without citizenship rights to do live-in domestic service, the Canadian government has found little incentive for improving conditions for domestic work. Changes in immigration policy since the early 1990s also demonstrate this point.

THE LIVE-IN CAREGIVER PROGRAM (LCP)

In April, 1992, the Ministry of Employment and Immigration introduced several changes to the previous FDM program and renamed it the 'Live-in Caregiver Program' (LCP). According to the new policy, women intending to do domestic work will be admitted to Canada on the basis of the education and training they have related to the care of children, seniors, and the disabled.

Specifically, this would involve the successful completion of the equivalent of Canadian Grade 12 education plus proof of six months of full-time formal training in areas such as early childhood education, geriatric care, and pediatric nursing (CEIC 1992, *Domestics' Cross Cultural News*, June 1992). The introduction of these new criteria has raised concerns for domestic workers' advocacy organizations who fear that many potential applicants from Third World countries will not qualify under the new program. In many countries, basic schooling only goes to Grade 10 or Grade 11 and formal training in areas of child, elderly, and disabled care does not exist (DeMara 1992; *Domestics' Cross-Cultural News*, June 1992).

The new program lifts some of the extra requirements the earlier FDM placed on foreign domestics for landed status (i.e., doing skills upgrading, demonstrating successful adaptation by doing volunteer community work, and demonstrating financial management skills by having to show savings). To become a landed immigrant, a foreign domestic worker must now only demonstrate a minimum of two years employment as a full-time live-in domestic worker. Also, domestic workers no longer need to obtain a 'release letter' from their employer in order to change employers. To receive a new employment authorization from immigration officers, domestic workers will now have to get a 'record of employment' from their employers showing how long they were employed and a statement of their earnings (CEIC 1992).

Despite limited improvements on freedom of movement and the conditions for landed status, the LCP continues in the tradition of immigration policies regarding domestic workers by imposing the kind of status and conditions on workers that lead to abuse and an unfavourable working environment. Under the LCP, the temporary work permit system and the mandatory live-in requirement still prevail, while women have to prove higher qualifications to work as domestic workers. The new program 'enables Canadian employers to obtain higher qualified labour for less pay' (*Domestics' Cross Cultural News*, June 1992) while doing little to help domestic workers to improve their conditions.

POTENTIAL DIRECTIONS IN IMMIGRATION POLICY

Currently, LCP is still under effect. There is, however, a possibility that policies regarding domestic workers might change along with an expected overhaul of the Immigration Act of 1976. In 1998, a report commissioned by the Liberal government (the Immigration Legislative Review Advisory Group) unveiled a detailed review of many aspects of immigration which included drastic proposals for change. Although it is not clear what aspects of the report will be adopted by the government in the formulation of new policy and legislation, the report has been influential enough to set the agenda and shape the discourse of a public debate on immigration.

The report, titled *Not Just Numbers: A Canadian Framework for Future Immigration*, does not promise a positive improvement in the status and conditions of foreign domestic workers in Canada (Arat-Koc 1999). While the report seems to use a more liberal language in relation to domestic workers, on close examination, this seems to be a deception. One of the recommendations suggests that there should be no excluded occupations under the point system—which should, at least theoretically, remove one of the obstacles in the way of permanent status for domestic workers—other parts of the report automatically categorize domestic workers as part of the Foreign Worker Program, once again reinstating the temporary status of domestic workers in Canada (in ways akin to the infamous policies of the 1970s). One of the recommendations suggests that domestic workers would come to Canada as temporary workers, but could apply for landed immigrant status if they could get a valid, permanent job offer. What would constitute a permanent job offer in the caregiving occupations is not clearly defined. Also, there is reason for concern that caregivers' dependency upon a specific employer, for a permanent job offer, can easily lead to abusive employer/employee relationships. Another contradictory recommendation regarding domestic workers has to do with the living-in requirement. The report argues for the elimination of this as a government requirement. It does, however, (once again) defer to 'the arrangement they make with the employer'. In a relationship where the employee is dependent on the employer for the possibility of permanent status in Canada, it is hard to be optimistic about the freedom and power domestic workers would enjoy in their negotiations with employers (Arat-Koc 1999: 20–1).

CONDITIONS OF DOMESTIC WORK AND THE ROLE OF THE STATE

In Canada, the state has played a contradictory role in the organization of domestic work. It has underregulated working conditions while over-regulating the workers. While the provincial labour standards laws, respecting 'the sanctity of the home', have either completely ignored or at best unequally treated the home as a workplace, the federal government, which has jurisdiction over immigration, has overregulated the workers (Luxton, Rosenberg, and Arat-Koc 1990: 15). In Canada, therefore, it has not simply been the generally low status of housework, or even the availability of a supply of foreign workers, that have created the conditions of domestic workers' vulnerability. As Castells (1975: 54) put it:

> immigrant workers do not exist because there are 'arduous and badly paid' jobs to be done, but, rather, arduous and badly paid jobs exist because immigrant workers are present or can be sent for to do them.

It is ironic that the consistently high and increasing demand for domestic work has corresponded with a deterioration of workers' conditions. This is due to the active role the state has played in structuring and controlling not only the volume but also the conditions of these workers.

There is a striking contrast between the laissez-faire approach the liberal state has taken that favours private solutions to problems in the domestic sphere and its rigid intervention in the provision, organization, and control of 'help' for that sphere. Given the specific combination of state policies in areas of childcare provision, labour legislation and immigration, domestic service is not simply a private but a politically constructed solution to the crisis of the domestic sphere.

In the last two decades, the positions put forward by both the federal and provincial governments in policy debates on childcare indicate the persistence of a clear preference for privatized solutions—with little concern about the quality and conditions for either children or caregivers. The federal childcare plan proposed in 1987, for example, emphasized a tax-credit approach to childcare, with no commitments to providing universal access to dependable and affordable licensed care spaces. In 1993, the federal government promised a commitment to the expansion of regulated spaces, but the promise has not been realized. In 1996, in line with a general process of downloading responsibilities, the federal government identified childcare as a provincial responsibility (Childcare Resource and Research Unit 1997: i). While federal and provincial governments claim to have recognized the plurality of parental preferences for childcare arrangements, the lack of socialized childcare spaces means that parents are left with no choice but to make private arrangements.

In the 1980s, in Ontario, during a struggle for amendments in the Employment Standards Act to provide set hours and overtime pay for domestic workers, the government fought against the change, claiming concerns that the potential increase in costs would 'upset the childcare arrangements of parents some of whom may already be in a financial squeeze' (Fruman 1987). Even the Labour Ministry report, which proposed the amendment, expressed reservations about its extension to all live-out domestic workers, including babysitters, on the grounds that it would jeopardize the inexpensive informal care arrangements which included 400,000 children in Ontario (Rauhala 1987). In the early 1990s, the NDP government in Ontario symbolically recognized the right of domestic workers, along with other groups of previously non-unionized workers, to unionize—but did not provide solutions for the practical difficulties of organizing from the private sphere. After the Conservative Party came to power in 1995, however, even this symbolic right was taken away (Fudge 1997). While the financial squeeze that many parents face in relation to childcare needs is a real and serious problem, the assumption in these legislative debates and proposals has been that domestic workers should subsidize the inadequacy of the social childcare system through their underpaid and overworked conditions.

Current domestic-service arrangements bring the interests of employers and employees into conflict. Given the pressures on budget and time that many middle-class working couples face, a domestic-service relationship may turn into a zero-sum game in which the improvements in the pay and working conditions of domestic workers mean losses for the employers. As a relationship between female employers and workers, domestic service emphasizes, most clearly, the class, racial/ethnic and citizenship differences among women which stand in the way of gender unity.

Feminism and Domestic Service

The domestic-service question is a feminist question, not just because 98 per cent of domestic workers are women, or because it potentially may create divisions among women that feminism needs to solve to make 'sisterhood' a reality. It is also a feminist question because it is so closely implicated in the privatized nature of domestic labour in our society. Domestic service, as it is organized in Canada, is not just a question of human and workers' rights. It is a question of women's oppression and liberation. Women's liberation has been defined by some as the upward

mobility of individual women *out of* some subordinate positions and occupations. According to this definition, 'women's liberation' can be compatible with a general devaluation of the subordinate positions and occupations many women hold.[17] If we choose, instead, to define women's liberation as a collective and transformative struggle—in addition to being one of individual liberation—that deals with class and racial inequalities and aims to re-structure society to eliminate subordinate positions, live-in domestic service becomes a very conservative solution for the crisis of the domestic sphere.

Domestic service leaves housework and childcare as women's work—still isolating, of low status and low value. Rather than solving the problem of gender inequality, it adds class and racial dimensions to it. Instead of housework and childcare being the responsibility of *all* women, it becomes the responsibility of *some* with subordinate class, racial and citizenship status, who are employed and supervised by those they liberate from direct physical burdens.[18] Reinforcing divisions of mental and manual labour, this may perpetuate low status and pay for domestic service.

The domestic-service solution is also conservative because it does not solve the problems posed by the separation of spheres. Given the availability of a cheap source of vulnerable workers, it discourages a struggle for socialized services and more flexible work arrangements.[19] Rather than easing the public/private split in society, therefore, this solution polarizes and deepens it with added class and racial dimensions.

The structural approach used in this paper has so far treated domestic workers as victims of unfavourable conditions that have shaped their work and lives. The history of domestic service has shown, however, that domestic workers can and have been able to act as subjects. Full of attempts to unionize and to standardize and improve working conditions, the history of domestic service and the political practice of domestic workers have a lot to offer the women's movement. First, domestic workers help to 'denaturalize' housework and childcare by doing domestic work for a wage rather than as a labour of love, and doing it as outsiders to the family. Second, the struggles of domestic workers can help to decrease the invisibility of the domestic sphere and contribute to making the personal political. While politicization of all domestic relations, including those between women, would not be a comfortable task, it promises to enrich, deepen, and extend the equality principle that feminism upholds.

While the issues raised and goals set by domestic workers' organizations can contribute to feminist theory and practice, these organizations and workers also need feminist support in their struggle. There are limits to how much can be achieved by domestic workers alone. Besides the obstacles domestic isolation places on organization and unionization, there are the legal restrictions imposed by provincial labour relations acts and the employment visa program. In addition, the temporary, outsider status sustained by the employment visa system serves to increase the invisibility and marginality of foreign domestic workers and desensitize others to their conditions. Domestic workers need the wider women's movement to help overcome these obstacles and to liberate their struggle from its corporate boundaries.

The women's movement also has to address the larger domestic labour question. In the nineteenth and early twentieth century, during the first wave of feminism, there were some efforts to transform domestic labour through collectivizing it. Feminists like Charlotte Perkins Gilman, Melusina Fay Pierce, and Mary Livermore developed radically creative and elaborate proposals for changed architecture, collective kitchens, and cooperative housekeeping schemes (Hayden 1981). While the theory and practice of these feminists have been extremely useful in offering alternatives to privatized domestic labour, they did not deal adequately with the gender and class aspects of the issue. These feminists not only failed to demand increased male participation in domestic labour, but they also generally disregarded the interests of domestics as women and workers. They articulated their concerns as finding efficient and rational solutions to the 'waste', 'annoyance', 'unreliability', and 'laziness' of servants through rigid supervision and factory-like discipline imposed by collective housework schemes (Hayden 1981). Domestic workers were neither agents nor the intended beneficiaries, but rather the basis of change in these projects which seemed to prioritize extension of the principles of industrialization over concerns for equality.

The contributions of the new wave of feminism have been indispensable in terms of the critique that has been developed about the sexual division of labour in society and in the family. The domestic-labour debate of the 1970s and radical-feminist analyses have, in different ways, also provided a critique of the privatized home. As Dolores Hayden (1981: 303) has pointed out, however, the second wave of feminism still lacks a clear vision of positive alternatives to privatized and gendered home life. In the absence of an honest, open debate around each solution and its gender, class, and racial implications, and a vision of concrete, constructive alternatives that would emerge from these debates, individualized ad hoc solutions may bring more harm than good to both individual women and to the struggle for the emancipation of all women.

Notes

This is a revised and updated version of a paper originally published in *Studies in Political Economy* 28 (Spring 1989) and M. Luxton, H. Rosenberg, and S. Arat-Koc, *Through the Kitchen Window*, 2nd edn (Toronto: Garamond, 1990). I am grateful to Pramila Aggarwal, Michal Bodemann, Bonnie Fox, Charlene Gannage, Roberta Hamilton, Mustafa Koc, Meg Luxton, Barb Neis, Lynne Phillips, Ester

Reiter, Harriet Rosenberg, Jane Ursel, and Fely Villasin for ideas and useful comments on different version of the paper.

1. Christine Delphy (1984) suggests that the appropriation of women's labour power in housework by men in the 'family mode of production' constitutes the major form of women's oppression and the material basis for 'sisterhood'.

2. *The Canadian Settler's Handbook* advised immigrant domestics that they would enjoy 'social amenities' in rural Canada and that 'no lady should dream of going as a home-help in the cities, for there class distinctions (were) as rampant as in England' (cited in Lenkyj, 1981: 10).

3. According to one study, in Sweden, 2,340 million hours are spent in housework annually, as compared to 1,290 million hours in industry (cited in Rowbotham 1973: 68).

4. Although these regulations may be a progressive step in recognizing the principle of overtime for domestic workers, they do not necessarily provide standard overtime protection since it is the employers who are given the option to negotiate with their employees to take the overtime in time off rather than in money for actual overtime worked. In this respect, regulations covering domestic workers still deviate from provisions of the provincial Employment Standards Act.

5. There is also the 'Subversive Activities' provision in the 1977 federal Immigration Act which, through its vague wording, provides an intimidating message to all non-citizen residents in Canada that engaging in union activities may become grounds for deportation (see Arnopoulos 1979: 41–5).

6. It is wrong, however, to confuse this appearance with real thoughts and feelings of the worker. Responding to Lockwood who referred to the domestic worker as the 'most socially acquiescent and conservative element' of the working class, Jacklyn Cock emphasizes the need to differentiate between deference and dependence. While the domestic recognizes her dependence on and powerlessness in relation to her employer, her deference is only 'a mask which is deliberately cultivated to conform to employer expectations, and shield the workers' real feelings' (Cock 1980: 104–6).

7. Here I have drawn on an argument made by Gerda Lerner in a different context. Commenting on the origins of slavery, Lerner has suggested that the process of marking a group of people as an out-group and 'designating th(is) group to be dominated as entirely different from the group exerting dominance', have been essential to the mental constructs involved in the institutionalization of slavery (see Lerner 1986: 76–7).

8. The criteria for tolerability used by immigration officers could sometimes be very flexible. Silvera reports the case of a domestic from the Caribbean who wanted to leave her employer for reasons of sexual assault. Because the assault was less than sexual intercourse, her complaint was not found legitimate and she was deported from Canada (see Silvera 1981: 58).

9. Although Employment and Immigration spokespersons have on a number of occasions announced that the practice of requiring release letters would be ended, a survey conducted among foreign domestic workers in Toronto suggests that it is very common (Arat-Koc and Villasin 1990: 12).

10. Research also shows that there is a very strong relationship between living-in (a requirement for foreign domestic workers) and working very long hours. According to a survey among 576 domestic workers in Toronto, only 35 per cent said they worked a standard work week of forty-four hours. Forty per cent worked for an average of forty-five to fifty hours a week. Eighteen per cent worked fifty to sixty hours and 6 per cent worked more than sixty hours a week. Among the live-in domestics who did overtime work, only 34 per cent received the legal compensation. Twenty-two per cent said they received some, but less than the legal rates of compensation. An overwhelming 44 per cent of those doing overtime work stated that they received no compensation whatsoever! (Arat-Koc and Villasin 1990: 6).

11. In 1987 Canada had international agreements with only six countries (the United States, Jamaica, Italy, Greece, Portugal, and France) whose nationals

could combine CPP contributions in Canada with pension contributions in their own countries (INTERCEDE 1987: 12).

12. Since 1986 the immigration department has been imposing fees for issuing, extending, and renewing employment authorizations. In addition to being underpaid and overtaxed in a society that offers them no privileges and freedoms of citizenship, domestic workers are now being asked to 'take the burden off the Canadian taxpayer' and pay the costs of their own processing and policing.

13. The enforcement of the live-in requirement has been so strict that some domestics who lived-out have been threatened by deportation—even if their employer didn't have room and agreed with the arrangement (see 'Patriarch of the Month' 1992).

14. Many domestic workers who have had years of experience supporting themselves (and others) find it very offensive to have to prove such potential:

> I supported five children *before* I came here, and I've supported five children *since* I came here, and they want to know if I can manage on my own? (Mary Dabreo, cited in Ramirez [1983/1984]).

15. A point needs to be made about conceptions of the value of different occupations that immigration partly borrows from Canadian Classification and Dictionary of Occupations. CCDO has a rigid and static conception of skill as a 'thing' that is largely determined 'objectively' by the time spent in formal education. As Gaskell (1986) has argued, however, 'skill', far from being 'a fixed attribute of a job or a worker which will explain higher wages or unemployment', is a result of a political process determined by the relative power (through supply/demand advantages, organizational capabilities, etc.) of different groups of workers.

16. The 1978 case of 'seven Jamaican women' was fought on the basis that discrimination against women with children was discrimination on the basis of gender. Seven Jamaican women filed a complaint with the Canadian Human Rights Commission after being ordered deported for having failed to list their minor children in their applications to come to Canada. They won their case on the ruling that no married man had ever been deported for having to list his children (cited in Timoll 1989: 57).

Although explicit and direct discrimination against women with dependent children has been eliminated, the practice still survives because those women who express their intention to stay in domestic service and also sponsor their dependants to Canada often fail to meet Immigration criteria on the grounds that they would not make enough income to make their families 'self-sufficient'.

17. This is Betty Friedan's position on housework. She approvingly cites others in *The Feminine Mystique* who think housework can be done by 'anyone with a strong enough back (and a small enough brain)' and find it 'peculiarly suited to the capacities of feeble-minded girls' (Friedan 1963: 206, 244).

18. With the emergence of surrogate motherhood, the same potential also applies to childbearing. The employment of surrogate mothers of working-class backgrounds may indeed become the solution upper-class and career women opt for to avoid the time and inconvenience a pregnancy would cost.

19. During the 1920s, in southern United States where there were more servants, the growth of commercial bakeries and laundries lagged behind such developments in the North and West (see Katzman 1978: 275).

References

Arat-Koc, S. 1999. 'NAC's Response to the Immigration Legislative Review Report "Not Just Numbers: A Canadian Framework for Future Immigration"', *Canadian Woman Studies* 19, (3) (Fall).

———, and F. Villasin. 1990. 'Report and Recommendations on the Foreign Domestic Movement Program' (prepared for INTERCEDE, Toronto Organization for Domestic Workers' Rights).

Arendt, H. 1966. *The Origins of Totalitarianism* (New York: Harcourt, Brace and World).

Arnopoulos, S.M. 1979. *Problems of Immigrant Women in the Canadian Labour Force* (Ottawa: Canadian Advisory Council on the Status of Women).

Bakan, A., and D. Stasiulis. 1992a. 'Foreign Domestic Worker Policy in Canada and the Social Boundaries of Citizenship', unpublished paper.

———. 1992b. 'Making the Match: Domestic Placement Agencies and the Racialization of Women's Household Work', paper presented at the 16th Annual CRIAW Conference: Making the Links: Anti-Racism and Feminism', Nov. 13–15, Toronto.

Barber, M. 1985. 'The Women Ontario Welcomed: Immigrant Domestics for Ontario Homes, 1870–1930', in *The Neglected Majority: Essays in Canadian Women's History*, eds A. Prentice and S.M. Trofimenkoff (Toronto: McClelland & Stewart).

———. 1986. 'Sunny Ontario for British Girls, 1900–30' in *Looking into My Sister's Eyes: An Exploration in Women's History*, ed. J. Burnet (Toronto: The Multicultural History Society of Ontario).

Bolaria, B.S., and P.S. Li. 1985. *Racial Oppression in Canada* (Toronto: Garamond Press).

Burawoy, M. 1980. 'Migrant Labour in South Africa and the United States' in *Capital and Labour*, ed. T. Nichols (Glasgow: Fontana).

Calliste, A. 1989. 'Canada's Immigration Policy and Domestics from the Caribbean: The Second Domestic Scheme' *Socialist Studies* 5.

Castells, M. 1975. 'Immigrant Workers and Class Struggles in Advanced Capitalism: The Western European Experience', *Politics and Society* 15 (1): 33–66.

Castles, S., and G. Koscack. 1980. 'The Function of Labour Immigration in Western European Capitalism' in *Capital and Labour*, ed. T. Nichols (Glasgow: Fontana).

CEIC. 1992. *Immigration Regulations, 1978* as amended by SOR/92–214, P.C. 1992–685 (9 April).

Childcare Resource and Research Unit. 1997. *Childcare in Canada: Provinces and Territories 1995* (Toronto: Childcare Resource and Research Unit, University of Toronto).

———. 1999. *Statistics Summary: Canadian Early Childhood Care and Education in the 1990s* (Toronto: Childcare Resource and Research Unit, University of Toronto).

———. 2000. *Early Childhood Care and Education in Canada: Provinces and Territories 1998* (Toronto: Childcare Resource and Research Unit, University of Toronto).

Cock, J. 1980. *Maids and Madams: A Study in the Politics of Exploitation* (Johannesburg: Ravan Press).

Delphy, C. 1984. 'The Main Enemy' in *Close to Home: A Materialist Analysis of Women's Oppression* (Amherst: University of Massachusetts Press).

DeMara, B. 1992. 'New Immigration Rules Racist Domestic Workers Rally Told', *Toronto Star,* 3 Feb.

Domestics' Cross-Cultural News. 1992. (Monthly newsletter of the Toronto Organization for Domestic Workers' Rights), June.

Dudden, F.E. 1983. *Serving Women: Household Service in Nineteenth-Century America* (Middleton: Wesleyan University Press).

Employment and Immigration Canada. 1986. *Foreign Domestic Workers in Canada. Facts for Domestics and Employers* (pamphlet), (Ottawa: Supply and Services, cat. no. MP23–61/1986).

Epstein, R. 1983. 'Domestic Workers: The Experience in B.C.' in *Union Sisters: Women in the Labour Force*, eds L. Briskin and L. Yanz (Toronto: The Women's Press).

Estable, A. 1986. *Immigrant Women in Canada: Current Issues*, a Background Paper for the Canadian Advisory Council on the Status of Women, March. (Ottawa: Supply and Services).

Fairchilds, C. 1984. *Domestic Enemies: Servants and Their Masters in Old Regime France* (Baltimore: The Johns Hopkins University Press).

Flandrin, J.L. 1979. *Families in Former Times* (Cambridge: Cambridge University Press).

Fox, B. 1980. 'Women's Double Work Day: Twentieth Century Changes in the Reproduction of Daily Life' in

Hidden in the Household: Women's Domestic Labour Under Capitalism, ed. B. Fox (Toronto: The Women's Press).

Friedan, B. 1963. *The Feminine Mystique* (New York: Dell Publishing).

Fruman, L. 1987. 'Ontario's Domestics: The Fight for Basic Rights', *The Toronto Star*, 30 March: C1.

Fudge, J. 1997. 'Little Victories and Big Defeats: The Rise and Fall of Collective Bargaining Rights for Domestic Workers in Ontario', in *Not One of the Family: Foreign Domestic Workers in Canada*, eds A.B. Bakan and D. Stasiulis (Toronto: University of Toronto Press).

Gaskell, J. 1986. 'Conceptions of Skill and the Work of Women: Some Historical and Political Issues', in *The Politics of Diversity*, eds R. Hamilton and M. Barrett (Montreal: Book Center).

Glenn, E.N. 1992. 'From Servitude to Service Work: Historical Continuities in the Racial Division of Paid Reproductive Work', *Signs* 18 (1).

Gorz, A. 1970. 'Immigrant Labour', *New Left Review* (61).

Hayden, D. 1981. *The Grand Domestic Revolution: A History of Feminist Designs for American Homes, Neighbourhoods, and Cities* (Cambridge: MIT Press).

Hook, N.D. 1978. *Domestic Service Occupation Study: Final Report*. Submitted to Canada Manpower and Immigration, January.

Human Resources and Development Canada. 1997. *Status of Daycare in Canada 1995 and 1996: A Review of the Major Findings of the National Day Care Study 1995 and 1996* (Ottawa: Author).

INTERCEDE. 1981. 'Domestics Sweep the World', *Wages for Housework Campaign Bulletin* 5 (1) (Spring).

———. 1987. *Know Your Rights (A Guide for Domestic Workers in Ontario)* (Toronto: October).

Kaplan, E.B. 1985. '"I Don't Do No Windows"' *Sojourner*, 10 (10), (Aug.).

Katzman, D.M. 1978. *Seven Days a Week: Women and Domestic Service in Industrializing America* (New York: Oxford University Press).

Lenkyj, H. 1981. 'A "Servant Problem" or a "Servant-Mistress Problem"? Domestic Services in Canada, 1890–1930', *Atlantis* 7 (1) (Fall).

Lerner, G. 1986. *The Creation of Patriarchy* (Oxford University Press).

Leslie, G. 1974. 'Domestic Service in Canada, 1880–1920' in *Women at Work, Ontario, 1850–1930* (Toronto: The Women's Press).

Lindstrom-Best, V. 1986. '"I Won't Be a Slave!"—Finnish Domestics in Canada, 1911–30' in *Looking into My Sister's Eyes: An Exploration in Women's History*, ed. J. Burnet (Toronto: The Multicultural History Society of Ontario).

Luxton, M. 1980. *More Than a Labour of Love* (Toronto: The Women's Press).

———. 1986. 'Two Hands for the Clock: Changing Patterns in the Gendered Division of Labour in the Home' in *Through the Kitchen Window: The Politics of Home and Family*, eds M. Luxton and H. Rosenberg (Toronto: Garamond Press).

———, H. Rosenberg, and S. Arat-Koc. 1990. *Through the Kitchen Window: The Politics of Home and Family*, 2nd edn (Toronto: Garamond Press).

Malos, E., ed. 1980. *The Politics of Housework* (London: Allison & Busby).

Mitterauer, M., and R. Sieder. 1982. *The European Family* (Chicago: University of Chicago Press).

National Council of Welfare. 1999. *Preschool Children: Promises to Keep: A Report by the National Council of Welfare* (Ottawa: Author).

'Patriarch of the Month'. 1992. *Herizons* 6 (3) (Fall).

Prentice, S. 1999. 'Less, Worse and More Expensive: Childcare in an Era of Deficit Reduction', *Journal of Canadian Studies* 34 (2) (Summer).

Ramirez, J. 1983/1984. 'Good Enough to Stay', *Currents* 1, 4.

Rauhala, A. 1987. 'Amended Labor Law Would Give Domestics Overtime, Set Hours', *The Globe and Mail*, 27 Jan. 1987: A1, 12.

Rist, R. 1979. 'Guestworkers and Post-World War II European Migrations', *Studies in Comparative International Development* 15 (2): 28–53.

Roberts, B. 1979. '"A Work of Empire": Canadian Reformers and British Female Immigration', in *A Not Unreasonable Claim: Women and Reform in Canada, 1880s–1920s*, ed. L. Kealey (Toronto: The Women's Press).

Rollins, J. 1985. *Between Women: Domestics and Their Employers* (Philadelphia: Temple University Press).

Rosenberg, H. 1986. 'The Home is the Workplace: Hazards, Stress and Pollutants in the Household' in *Through the Kitchen Window: The Politics of Home and Family* (Toronto: Garamond Press).

————. 1987. 'Motherwork, Stress, and Depression: The Costs of Privatized Social Reproduction' in *Feminism and Political Economy*, eds H.J. Maroney and M. Luxton (Toronto: Methuen).

Rowbotham, S. 1973. *Women's Consciousness, Man's World* (Harmondsworth, UK: Penguin).

Royal Commission on the Status of Women. 1970. *Report of the Royal Commission on the Status of Women* (Ottawa: Supply and Services).

Silvera, M. 1981. 'Immigrant Domestic Workers. Whose Dirty Laundry?', *Fireweed* 9.

————. 1983. *Silenced*. Talks with Working Class West Indian Women about Their Lives and Struggles as Domestic Workers in Canada (Toronto: Williams-Wallace Publishers).

Statistics Canada. 1989. *The Labour Force, October 1989* (Ottawa: Supply and Services).

Steinberg, S. 1981. *The Ethnic Myth: Race, Ethnicity, and Class in America* (Boston: Beacon Press).

The Task Force on Child Care. 1986. *Report of the Task Force on Child Care* (Ottawa: Supply and Services).

The Task Force on Immigration Practices and Procedures. 1981. *Domestic Workers on Employment Authorizations*. Report. April.

Timoll, A.L. 1989. 'Foreign Domestic Servants in Canada', unpublished research essay, Department of Political Science, Carleton University, Ottawa.

Toughill, K. 1986. 'Domestic Workers Praise Rule Change', *The Toronto Star*, 22 Sept.: C2.

Vanek, J. 1983. 'Household Work, Wage Work, and Sexual Equality' in *Family in Transition*, 4th edn, eds A.S. Skolnick and J.H. Skolnick (Little Brown and Company).

Vanstone, E. 1986. 'The Heaven-Sent Nanny', *Toronto Life* (April).

Walmsley, A. 1989. 'Can a Working Mother Afford to Stay Home?', *Chatelaine* (Nov.).

Williams, J., H. Twart, and A. Bachelli. 1980. 'Women and the Family' in *The Politics of Housework*, ed. E. Malos (London: Allison & Busby).

Wong, L.T. 1984. 'Canada's Guestworkers: Some Comparisons of Temporary Workers in Europe and North America', *International Migration Review* 18 (1): 85–97.

Part Five **Ethnic/Racial Diversity in Families**

Chapter 24

Race and ethnicity provide critical sources of diversity in family patterns today. This section first presents description and analysis of African-American family patterns. Because the research on African Americans addresses broad questions about the effects on families of different cultural traditions, racism (in the past, as extreme as slavery, and also in the present), and economic marginality, it is relevant to Canadians as well as Americans. Certainly the American 'culture of poverty' arguments, which blame African Americans for their poverty, and more

recent discussions of 'welfare dependency', are not foreign to Canada.

This chapter gives a concise description of the West African family patterns and traditions that slaves drew on in their struggle to survive and resist slavery. Sudarkasa gives some indication of the impact on family of slavery and also of the current economic and political conditions in which African Americans live. And she provides a very useful interpretation of how and why she thinks African-American families are changing.

African-American Families and Family Values

Niara Sudarkasa

All over the United States, families are changing. The American ideal of the nuclear family, composed of two parents and their children, is only one of many different types of family groupings occupying single households today. Various permutations of the stepfamily, resulting from the marriages of couples with children from previous marriages, are commonplace. The numbers of households composed of single mothers and their children have increased dramatically over the past twenty-five years. Single parenting by men is also on the rise, as is the incidence of parenting by couples of the same gender.

Public policy discussions and debate over these changes have not focused on the economic, demographic, and sociological forces underlying them. Rather, these discussions have tended to portray changes in family structure as moral failures that signal the breakdown in the fabric of our society. Thus, instead of seeking to understand and assess these emerging forms of the family in order to influence their development, the public is warned against (a) the 'alarming disintegration'

of the nuclear family and (b) the 'loss of traditional family values'.

No fewer than three US presidents have identified the disintegration of the family and the loss of family values as issues of national concern. Former presidents Ronald Reagan and George Bush (along with former vice president Dan Quayle) exhorted the country to 'return to traditional family values'. President Bill Clinton is focusing efforts on restoring and strengthening the nuclear family. An attentive observer will recognize right away that these different emphases are actually two stanzas of the same lament for the 'demise' of the American family.

And no matter what particular 'spin' is given to this theme, the stated or unstated premise is the same: something is 'wrong' with families throughout America, but there is 'more wrong' with black families than with any others. Although families in various ethnic groups and at various income levels are recognized as undergoing change, only the African-American family is consistently described as being 'in crisis'. Other families are 'in transition'.

African-American families are portrayed as being 'on the brink of collapse'.

Starting from this premise, a number of journalists, scholars, and public officials have gone on to lay the blame for the relatively high incidence of crime that occurs in certain Black neighbourhoods on the 'disintegration of the Black family' and the 'absence of family values'. Despite the persuasive evidence and arguments presented by William Julius Wilson in his book *The Truly Disadvantaged* (1987), that poverty and unemployment are the fundamental causes and predictors of high crime rates among African Americans, we still hear that the Black family is the 'root cause' of these social problems. This notion of the 'pathological' Black family, traceable to the work of Daniel Patrick Moynihan (1965) and others, still dominates thinking about the form and function of African-American families, and still misinforms public policies supposedly designed to assist those families.

My primary goal in the present essay is to place the recent changes in African-American family structures in their historical context, to promote a better understanding and more accurate interpretation of these changes. I ask: What do we know about the earliest African-American families, and what do we know about the changes these families have undergone from the period of slavery to the present day? The discussion begins with an overview of West African family structure, because most of the enslaved population brought to America came from West Africa. Understanding the family structure brought with them by the Africans who came to America in chains is essential to an understanding of what happened to these families as they adapted and evolved during slavery and afterward.

Obviously, we cannot explain African-American families only by reference to their West African cultural antecedents. By the same token, we cannot understand African-American families without taking into account the West African family structures out of which they evolved.

Scholars from E. Franklin Frazier ([1939] 1966) to Andrew Billingsley (1992) have emphasized the adaptive nature of African-American families. Indeed, African-American families, like all families, are adaptive institutions. Thus, in analyzing the changing structure of African-American families, one must examine the contexts and conditions that influenced those changes. Slavery, segregation, urbanization, changing economic conditions, changing educational opportunities, changing demographics, housing options, welfare restrictions, and other public policies must all be taken into account. Yet one cannot begin to speak of the adaptation of any structure to any condition unless one knows what the structure was to begin with. In the case of African-American families, we first must understand the African family structures that were brought to America in order to analyze, appreciate, and assess how those structures adapted and changed over time. In that way, we can better interpret what we see today.

In the first part of this essay, I provide an overview of the African extended family out of which African-American families evolved and discuss some aspects of the transformation of African families into African-American families during the period of slavery and beyond. Given space constraints, in reviewing African family structure and in seeking to interpret some of the changes that occurred in America, I must greatly simplify many complex aspects of family organization, and I can only allude to or abbreviate certain lengthy scholarly debates. Readers are encouraged, therefore, to trace the various arguments back to the publications in which they were first set forth.

In the second and third sections of this essay, I call attention to special aspects of African-American household and family organization and outline the changes that have occurred in these structures in the past thirty years. Drawing on data found in Billingsley's recent book *Climbing Jacob's Ladder* (1992), I highlight the extraordinary decline in two-parent households, the phenomenal increase in female-headed households, and the increase in households with individuals living by themselves. In this connection, I cite K. Sue Jewell's *Survival of the Black Family: The Institutional Impact of U.S. Social Policy* (1988) to support the view that many of the changes in African-American family structure that have occurred in the past thirty years are linked directly to welfare policies and programs, especially the program known as Aid to Families with Dependent Children. The central argument in Jewell's copiously documented and cogently argued book is that female-headed households have proliferated as a result of welfare policies that discourage or disallow the presence of males in the home (see also Sudarkasa 1981: 46, 1993).

Of the various changes in family structure documented by Billingsley and Jewell, the most far-reaching is the proliferation of female-headed households, especially two-generational households in which women are living alone with their children. Most writers, including Billingsley and Jewell, attribute the phenomenal increase in this type of household to the breakdown of the nuclear family. I suggest that this is also the result of the breakup of the multigenerational female-headed household that was common before the welfare system encouraged and enabled young mothers to live alone with their children (Sudarkasa 1993). The implications of this point are very important. Instead of focusing solely on strengthening and rebuilding nuclear families, we should also acknowledge the benefit of reconnecting and strengthening multigenerational female-headed households, which have proven in the past that they, too, can be a source of stability and upward mobility within the African-American community. . . .

The final point I would like to make is that all social ills in the Black community cannot and should not be laid at the doorstep of the African-American family. As many persons have said, and as Andrew Billingsley puts it in *Climbing Jacob's*

Ladder (1992), 'Societies make families' just as 'families make societies'. Billingsley goes on: 'The so-called black family crisis is not of their own making; nor is it the worst crisis they ever faced and survived' (p. 79). In my judgment, this is both a justifiable conclusion from the evidence on the history of Black families in America and an appropriate starting point for analyses and action designed to address the problems they face.

African Roots of the African-American Family

To understand African-American families today, one must understand their evolution over time. Fundamentally, they grew out of African institutions brought to the Americas by enslaved populations over a period of centuries. Over time, the transplanted African families evolved into African-American families, Afro-Caribbean families, Afro-Brazilian families, and so forth. In the various countries or regions where the enslaved Africans were settled, they were forced to accommodate and adapt to whatever European laws and traditions prevailed. Nevertheless, the similarities evident in family life among people of African descent throughout the Americas are a testament to the strength and viability of the extended family, which is one of the two most important bases for kinship groupings throughout sub-Saharan Africa (the other being the lineage).

Not surprisingly, throughout the Americas, surviving features of African family structure tend to be strongest among the lower-income segments of the Black population. The greater the income and the higher the formal education of Africa's descendants, the more their family organization and other sociocultural attributes are intentionally or unintentionally patterned after those of the European-derived dominant group. There is no question that, everywhere, formal education and exposure to the dominant group have tended to validate and reinforce the culture and lifestyle of that group.

African extended families were (and are) large multigenerational groupings of relatives built around a core group known as a *lineage*. Members of this group of 'blood relatives' trace their descent from a common male ancestor through a line of males in some societies, such as the Yoruba of Nigeria, or from a female ancestor through a line of females, in societies such as the Ashanti of Ghana (see Figures 1 and 2). Those lineages that trace descent through the father line are termed *patrilineages*, and those that trace descent through the mother line are termed *matrilineages*.

Because lineage members were and are prohibited from marrying one another, they must take their spouses from other lineages. In this way, extended families are created. The adult members of an extended family consist of the lineage members who form the core group and their spouses, who 'marry in' from different lineages. According to whether the rule of descent is patrilineal or matrilineal, the children (both male and female) are considered to be born into the lineage of their father (in patrilineal societies such as the Yoruba) or their mother (in matrilineal societies such as the Ashanti).

Traditionally, extended families lived together in residential units we term *compounds*. In the countryside, a compound might be a collection of small, conically shaped, one-room mud-brick (that is, adobe) houses facing inward around a large circular courtyard. To visualize a compound within a town, imagine a series of one-story or two-story houses built adjacent to one another and enclosed by a large fence or wall. Alternatively, a compound could take the form of a one-story structure built around a large inner courtyard. Each side of this square-shaped building would be divided up into adjacent rooms facing a veranda or corridor that opens onto the courtyard. Members living in the compound might use the courtyard for recreation, outdoor cooking, meetings, and so forth. The back walls of such compounds would have small, highly sit-

Figure 1: Schematic View of a Matrilineage

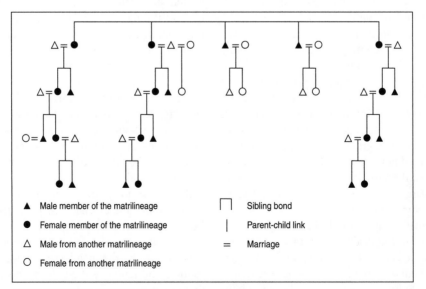

▲ Male member of the matrilineage
● Female member of the matrilineage
△ Male from another matrilineage
○ Female from another matrilineage

⊓ Sibling bond
| Parent-child link
= Marriage

Source: Adapted from Sudarkasa (1980).

Figure 2: Schematic View of a Patrilineage

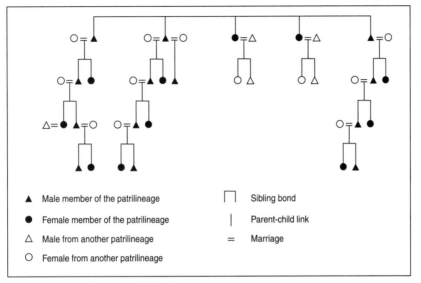

▲	Male member of the patrilineage	⊓ Sibling bond
●	Female member of the patrilineage	│ Parent-child link
△	Male from another patrilineage	= Marriage
○	Female from another patrilineage	

Source: Adapted from Sudarkasa (1980).

uated windows, forming a continuous barrier to the outside. One would enter the compound through centrally located gates or large, heavy doors (see Figure 3).

Many families were (and are) so large that their compounds consisted of not just one but several such square buildings, and the entire cluster of dwellings might be enclosed by a wall. A compound might house thirty or forty people, or its residents could number in the hundreds. Royal compounds might have thousands of members. Each compound, whether made up of one large dwelling or several such dwellings, was named after the lineage that formed the core of the extended family occupying the compound. The land on which a compound was built was collectively owned by a lineage, and lineage members built and owned the houses themselves. The oldest member of the lineage was its head, and all important decisions concerning the lineage or the compound were made or approved by the lineage head and the other elders.

From this brief description of the living patterns of West African extended families, it may be deduced that each extended family occupying a compound could be looked at from two perspectives. From the perspective of the lineage, the extended family consisted of its own lineage members, as one component, and in-marrying spouses as the other component (see Figure 3). Lineage members were related by 'blood' ties conceived as existing in perpetuity. Spouses were 'in-laws' whose relations could be broken 'by law', and hence they were portrayed as an 'outsider group' on certain ceremonial occasions (Marshall 1968; Sudarkasa 1980).

From the perspective of the individual families created by marriage, the extended family in a compound could be viewed as a group of related conjugal families (see Figure 3). Each of these conjugal families would consist of a man and his wife or wives and their children. These conjugally based families differed from typical 'nuclear families' in several respects (Sudarkasa 1981, 1988).

Figure 3: An Extended Family Occupying a Single Compound

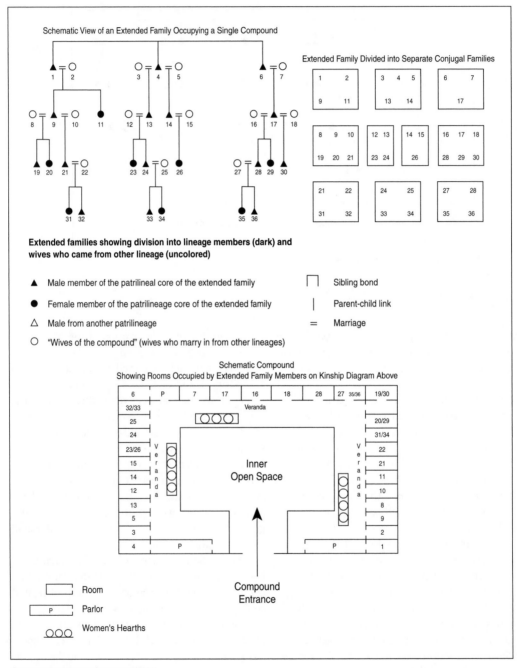

First, even when a man had only one wife, the possibility of plural wives was always there. Second, because of the lineage principle that linked members of the various conjugal families, children in the same generation grew up more or less like sisters and brothers, rather than strictly separating themselves into siblings versus cousins. In some languages, such as that of the Yoruba, there was and is no word equivalent to the English word *cousin*, only words for *older sibling* and *younger sibling* (*egbon* and *aburo*, respectively), used for both males and females. Thus the strength of the lineage principle made the boundaries of African conjugal families far less rigid than those that delineate nuclear families. For example, 'uncles' might raise their 'nephews' as their 'sons' without any mechanism such as formal adoption. Usually, only in legal matters would questions of precise kinship relationships arise.

In describing what happened to African family structure when Africans were captured and enslaved in America, we must acknowledge that the family structures on plantations, as reconstructed from written records and oral history, cannot be viewed as examples of direct institutional transfer from Africa to America, but rather as examples of institutional transformation that took place from Africa to America (Sudarkasa 1981: 39). As I have stated previously:

> The extended family networks that were formed during slavery by Africans and their descendants were based on the institutional heritage which the Africans had brought with them to this continent, and the specific forms [these families] took reflected the influence of European-derived institutions as well as the political and economic circumstances in which the enslaved population found itself (Sudarkasa 1981: 45).

The conditions of slavery did not allow the enslaved Africans to replicate or re-create the compounds and extended families they had left behind on the African continent. Yet, even in cramped quarters, one could find multigenerational families comprising couples, their children, some grandchildren, other relatives, and even non-kin. The influence of European norms as well as the demographics of the plantations meant that marriage was usually monogamous. Yet several historians have noted instances of polygamy (the commonly used term) where wives lived in separate houses (Blassingame 1972: 171; Gutman 1977: 59, 158; Perdue, Barden, and Phillips 1980: 209).

Despite the fact that Africans enslaved in America were forced to compartmentalize their extended families, the importance of their kinship networks on the plantations and across plantations has been noted by many historians. Moreover, the continuing strength of the lineage principle was manifest through the strong sense of obligation to consanguineal ('blood') relatives. Gutman (1977) puts it this way: 'The pull between ties to an immediate family and to an enlarged kin network sometimes strained husbands and wives' (p. 202) (see also Frazier [1939] 1966, part 2).

After slavery, wherever African Americans had access to large parcels of land, they re-created kin networks that resembled African extended families and compounds. Parents and their married children lived in houses built in close proximity to one another, and three or four generations of kin typically resided together in these houses. Two of my former students, Dr Mary Faith Mitchell and Mr Bamidele Agbasegbe Demerson, studied such compounds in the Sea Islands off the coast of South Carolina in the early 1970s (Demerson 1991).

Even where relatives did not live in spatial proximity, the extended family ties linked people across households and even across states, so that relatives could turn to one another for assistance, not only in childrearing but also in caring for the sick and the aged, in providing accommodations for those who migrated from one state to another, and in rendering financial support in times of need. Such patterns of transresidential extended family cooperation and support have been reported by contemporary writers (for example, Stack 1974; Aschenbrenner 1975; Billingsley 1992) as well as by many historians and sociologists writing about earlier periods.

To summarize, enslaved Africans living on plantations could not replicate African compounds, but their households were often 'extended' beyond the nuclear family. Most important, they maintained transresidential kinship networks with many of the features of extended families that had resided together in single compounds in West Africa. When we speak of extended families among African Americans, we must always recognize that these are kin groups that transcend individual households. Billingsley (1968, 1992) uses the term *extended family* to refer to households in which family members such as grandparents reside with nuclear families. Such households do not in and of themselves constitute entire extended families. African-American extended families embrace many households, some with two generations, some with three or more, and some of these households are headed by women, some by men, and some by both.

Household Formation Among African Americans

Several points concerning household formation among African Americans must be made before I present an examination of recent trends in Black family organization. The first and most general observation is that family and household are not the same thing. Indeed, in all societies, the notion of family embraces more than a single household. In the contemporary United States, however, there is a tendency to treat the concepts of family and household as if they are one and the same. This tendency stems from the fact that the majority culture in the United States views the nuclear family formed at marriage as the most important family (some would say the 'real' family, in comparison to other relatives), and one that ideally should occupy a household separate and apart from that of others. Thus, in many instances, the words *family* and *household* are used interchangeably. For example, the concepts of 'two-parent families' and 'two-parent households' tend to be used interchangeably. So, too, are the concepts of 'single-parent families' and 'single-parent households'.

Historically, among the African Americans it has always been important to recognize that the term *family* refers not only to family members resident in particular households but to extended family members living in other households as well. Because of the strength of consanguineal ties, particularly those between mother and children, but sometimes also among siblings, one cannot conclude that the nuclear family built around the marital relationship is conceived of as 'the' primary family. For many African Americans, marriage does not mean that the husband-wife relationship will 'replace' the mother-daughter or mother-son relationship as the primary relationship in the newly married person's life. In the best of circumstances, as Gutman (1977) points out, the consanguineal ties may place a 'strain' on the husband-wife relationship. In any case, where these consanguineal ties are very strong, in order to understand the form and functioning of the 'immediate' family among African Americans, one would have to study a cluster of related households, not simply any single isolated nuclear family household.

A second general observation to be made concerning household formation among African Americans is that, historically, although female-headed households were a minority of the households in the Black community, they were an accepted form of household organization. In fact, because of the general acceptance of female-headed households during slavery and afterward, some writers erroneously proclaimed this to be the typical or normative form of the African-American family. Frazier's ([1939] 1966) characterization of *some* Black families as 'matriarchal' was generalized by others to refer to 'most' Black families.

The publication of Herbert Gutman's monumental book *The Black Family in Slavery and Freedom, 1750–1925* (1977) dispelled the myth of the Black family as predominantly 'matriarchal' (or 'matrifocal', which was the newer and more descriptive characterization). Gutman reported that from the mid-1700s through the mid-1920s, less than one-fourth of African-American households were headed by single women. As recently as 1960, only 22 per cent of African-American families were female-headed (Jewell 1988: 17; Billingsley 1992: 36). Thus the incidence of female-headed households did not change much in 200 years. These data show that, contrary to popular belief, historically, African-American women, like their African foremothers, typically gave birth to children within the context of marriage.

The point must be made, however, that a rate of 20 per cent to 25 per cent female-headed households within the African-American population was still high compared with that of the Euro-American population. Billingsley (1968: 14) reports that in 1960 only 6 per cent of White families with children were headed by women. To understand why a larger percentage of African-American women were single heads of household, one must take into consideration a number of cultural, demographic, and economic factors.

First, it must be understood that, historically, African-American women, like their African ancestors, placed a very high value on having children, and most of them wanted to have their own children even if they adopted or reared others (Sudarkasa 1975). Although this has changed somewhat under the influence of 'radical feminism', even today very few African-American women want to be childless throughout their lives.

Second, it has to be understood that because polygamy (or, more accurately, polygyny—the term for plural wives)—was not and is not a legal form of marriage in the United States, unequal gender ratios among African Americans living in many areas meant that not all marriageable women would be able to find husbands during their prime childbearing years. Some of the factors that contributed (and still contribute) to the preponderance of African-American women over African-American men in many localities included the death or incarceration of males in their prime reproductive years; the migration of males in search of work; high male unemployment rates, which reduced the number of men available for, or interested in, the responsibilities of marriage; the overall higher birthrate of females; and the shorter lifespan of males. Given these factors and the high value placed on children, it is not surprising that historically nearly one-fourth of all African-American families were headed by single women (Sudarkasa 1993).

This does not mean that the incidence of female-headed households was or is solely due to the birth of children out of wedlock. Some of the same factors mentioned above as contributing to the gender imbalance between males and females in some localities also contributed to a relatively high incidence of divorce, separation, and widowhood among African Americans. Thus, now and in the past, many mature, previously married women are among those heading single-parent households (Billingsley 1968, 1992; Jewell 1988; Sudarkasa 1993).

Turning from the issues surrounding the formation of female-headed households, the third point I want to make concerning household formation among African Americans relates to the notion of the 'household head' itself. In the sociological literature and in the media in this country, considerable emphasis is placed on the question of who heads a household or family. In fact, the way the question is asked presumes that the position of household or family head is a straightforward, easily discernible status.

In the case of African-American households, several points of caution need to be raised concerning the concept of household headship. First, the answer to the question of who heads a household may differ depending on whether the respondent is thinking about the primary decision maker or the primary provider. Second, key decision makers for a given household may not even reside in that household. This is especially true today, when households are headed by young single mothers who are dependent on other adults for advice and various forms of support. Third, in order to understand the functioning of a household, it is sometimes more important to understand who are the core adults in the household, rather than who 'heads' it. Historically, this was particularly the case in multigenerational female-headed households. The oldest adults in the house (who might be two or three sisters, a sister and a brother, or an older woman and her mature daughters) might share the responsibilities of headship, in terms of both decision making and financial support.

The fourth and final point I wish to make concerning household formation among African Americans is that, historically, households headed by married couples (like those headed by women) typically included relatives other than parents and children (see, for example, Billingsley 1968; Stack 1974; Aschenbrenner 1975). Many of these two-parent households were multigenerational through the inclusion of grandchildren or a parent or parents of one of the spouses. Many of them were also 'extended' laterally to include an uncle, aunt, cousin, niece, or nephew. In other words, even these two-parent families were not typical nuclear families. In the section that follows, I observe that the breakup of multigenerational households, headed by women and by married couples, subsumes and accounts for all the major trends that have been identified in Black family and household organization over the past few decades.

Recent Changes in African-American Family and Household Organization

Without question, the major change that has occurred in Black family organization in the past three decades has been the rise in the number of female-headed households. The percentage has almost tripled in thirty years, a phenomenal increase that we are only now beginning to understand. Billingsley (1992) notes:

> The incidence of one of the alternatives to the traditional family, the female-headed single-parent family, has escalated enormously over the past generation. Consisting of a minority of 20 percent [actually 22 percent] of families with children in 1960, this family form had increased to 33 percent by 1970, to 49 percent by 1980, and to a whopping 57 percent by 1990. Over the same period single fathers bringing up their own children increased from 2 percent to 4 percent (pp. 36–7).

He goes on to make the very interesting point that the change in household headship is mainly a reflection of changing marriage patterns rather than an indication of a diminishing commitment to family or to family living.

> The major observation here is that both black men and women have been avoiding or abandoning marriage in record numbers during recent years. *But this is more a shift in the marriage relation than in the family*. Marriage . . . is only one of several bases for family formulation and endurance. The allegiance to families is still so strong that on any given day the overwhelming majority of African-American people will be found living in families of one type or another. In 1990, for example, 70 percent of the 10.5 million African-American households were family households with persons related by blood, marriage, or adoption (p. 37, emphasis added).

This observation supports a point that cannot be overemphasized—namely, that marital stability and family stability are not one and the same. More than twenty years ago, I noted:

Black families are not necessarily centered around conjugal unions, which are the sine qua non of the nuclear family. Among blacks, households centered around consanguineal relatives have as much legitimacy (and for most people, as much respectability) as family units as do households centered around conjugal unions. When this fact is understood, it becomes clear that the instability of conjugal relations cannot be taken as the sole measure of the instability of the family. That black families exhibit considerable stability over time and space is evidence by the enduring linkages and bonds of mutual obligation found among networks of consanguineal kin (Sudarkasa 1975: 238).

In the case of nuclear families, divorce signals the 'breakdown' of at least one family, but where consanguineal relationships form the core of the family, the failure of a marriage or a companionate relationship does not necessarily have a disruptive effect on the unit, although it might have emotional effects on the individuals concerned.

As I stated earlier, in my view, the African-American commitment to consanguineal relatives is traceable to Africa, where lineage ties based on descent, rather than marital ties based in law, provided the primary source of stability within extended families living together in compounds (Sudarkasa 1980: 47–8; 1981: 43–4). In the United States, the dependence on blood relatives as sources of support and stability in the family remained strong among African Americans, even in the face of the White American idea that the primary source of family stability is the marriage bond that forms the core of the nuclear family.

The strength and stability of consanguineal ties, as Gutman (1977) suggests, could be one cause of the fragility of marriage bonds noted among African Americans. Obligations to the extended family could be a source of dissension between spouses, particularly when these obligations appear to consume resources and time that

could be devoted to their home and their nuclear family. Moreover, because the extended family is there as a source of support when a divorce or separation does occur, marital dissolution is less threatening and less traumatic for the partners involved (Sudarkasa 1981: 49–50).

In the 1990s, we are facing a situation in which the great increase in the percentage of African-American female-headed households, particularly among the working and non-working poor (almost 70 per cent of all African-American households), means that these single parents must depend on their blood relatives for stability and support if there is to be any family stability at all. Yet one of the most alarming changes that has occurred since 1960 renders this support less readily available to them than it was in the past. I refer to the fact that many young single mothers are living alone with their children, whereas in the past most of them would have been living in households with other adult relatives who could provide economic assistance, emotional support, and, most important, advice and assistance in the rearing of their children.

It is very important to point out that the pattern of single mothers living alone with their children is a recent phenomenon among African Americans. As a teenager in the 1950s, I witnessed a relatively high dropout rate among girls in junior high school and high school, who left school because they became pregnant. These young mothers never set up households of their own. They lived with their mothers, with both parents, grandmothers, grandparents, or other senior relatives. And the younger the mother, the longer she probably would reside with other adults. Households headed by mature mothers and grandmothers were usually as stable as two-parent families in terms of their longevity and their ability to provide adequately for the needs of the adults and children within them.

Most of the discussion concerning the rise in the number of female-headed households among African Americans has focused on the breakdown of the nuclear family. In *Survival of the Black Family* (1988), Jewell is especially detailed in attributing the increase in divorce, separation, and births out of wedlock to welfare policies that started in the 1950s and began to show serious effects in the 1960s, 1970s, and 1980s. She also points out that from the 1950s onward, as more Black males shifted their occupations from farm worker to unskilled labourer, more of the Black elderly became eligible for social security benefits and therefore were less dependent on their children. With this came 'the establishment of [more] independent living arrangements', as indicated by the decrease in the number of 'subfamilies' living in the one household between 1950 and 1960 (p. 24).

Jewell (1988) summarizes the effects of social welfare policy on the structure of African-American families as follows:

> Although liberal social welfare legislation created economic independence for the elderly, conservative administration of social welfare programs, especially in the Aid to Families with Dependent Children program, promoted marital conflict, as welfare policies and practices required male absence as a condition for eligibility. Hence, through overt and covert practices, social welfare agencies, not black wives, forced men out of the home. Thus, the black female-headed household, created through separation, divorce, or non-marriage, has been system-precipitated. Thus, one could expect an escalation in the dissolution of marriages among blacks and an increase in the number of black women with children who choose to permanently forego marriage. The trend in both of these areas was initiated in the 1950s and became firmly established by 1980s. By excluding black males through the institution of the 'man-in-the-house' policy in the 1950s and maintaining this policy in the 1960s and 1970s and by systematically entitling women, and not their husbands, to benefits,

black two-parent families were undermined (pp. 24–5).

Even though Billingsley and Jewell emphasize the 'breakdown' in the nuclear family as a result of economic, demographic, and policy factors previously mentioned, the data presented by both authors demonstrate that another important trend is in evidence. I am referring to the breakup of multigenerational female-headed households, formerly the most common type of household headed by women. In the past, female-headed households usually included at least three generations, sometimes four. Women normally started having children at an early age (in their teens or early twenties) and might continue having them into their late thirties or forties. Thus it was not uncommon for women to be rearing their own children while assisting their daughters with the upbringing of theirs.

Not only were these female-headed households extended lineally (that is, by including a woman, her children, grandchildren, and possibly great-grandchildren), but they often were also extended laterally to include never-married, widowed, or divorced sisters or brothers of the household head. For example, such households might include a woman, her adult sister or brother, her adult daughter(s), her adult unmarried son(s), and the dependent children of any or all of the women in the house, including any minor children the woman herself might have.

Today, owing to the effects of social welfare policies as delineated by Jewell (1988), and as a result of the skyrocketing unemployment of Black males since the late 1970s and 1980s, what might have been a single multigenerational female-headed household of the 1950s or early 1960s is likely to be several separate female-headed households. For example, a woman's unmarried daughters would probably be living alone with their dependent children, making three or four female-headed households where previously there would have been one.

After reflecting on the data presented by Billingsley, Jewell, and others, I have concluded that the major trend among African-American families over the past thirty years has been the increasing *disaggregation of households*, whether headed by married couples or by women. In other words, we see more separate households in relation to population size than ever before. It is not surprising that the majority of these households are female-headed, given that many Black males are incarcerated, unemployed, and 'on the streets', unemployed and living in dependent relationships with their mothers or girlfriends, or otherwise unable to assume the responsibility of household headship.

The trend toward the disaggregation (and hence diminishing size) of households is evidenced not only by the proliferation of two-generational female-headed households, but by the increase in the number of elderly persons living alone or in couples, as noted by Jewell (1988), and by the substantial increase in the number and percentage of single persons living alone (Billingsley 1992: 37–8, 47–8). As of 1990, 25 per cent of all African-American households were occupied by single adults, and most of these were single women.

Historically, for economic reasons as well as for reasons related to cultural traditions, unmarried African-American adults lived with their parents or other relatives. In 1975, I cited this as one of the 'fundamental structural differences' between Black families and traditional nuclear families:

> Adulthood for Black people does not necessarily entail the establishment of new households; therefore one finds many single adults living with married and unmarried relatives. In fact, in some places it is considered highly preferable for unmarried adults to live with relatives than to live alone or to live outside the family with 'roommates' (Sudarkasa 1975: 238).

The rise in the number of households occupied by persons living alone represents a dramatic shift in patterns of residence over a twenty-year period.

Implications of the Recent Changes

What are some of the consequences of the disaggregation of African-American family households? In particular, does the proliferation of female-headed households signal a 'crisis' in the Black family?

I have stressed above that most young single mothers used to live in multigenerational households that provided a wide range of mutual support. Such households were particularly important for the rearing of children—that is, looking after them on a day-to-day basis, sharing the expense of their food and clothing, and providing for all their other needs. The breakup of these units has left many poor, inexperienced mothers alone to cope with childrearing, and this has created serious problems.

One of the often cited signs of 'crisis' in the Black family is the inability of some single mothers to 'control' their children, particularly their sons. When single mothers lived with their adult relatives, they could rely on these adults (male as well as female) to assist them in establishing and enforcing the rules by which children were brought up. The effect of a father's absence could be compensated for by the presence of a maternal grandfather, mother's brothers, and other male figures living in, or frequenting, a household. Today, even when these relatives play supporting roles in the life of a single mother and her children, the fact that they live in different residences, sometimes great distances apart, means that they cannot have the continuous influence on the children that they would have had in the past.

Adults as well as children are inevitably affected by the disaggregation of African-American family households. On a very practical level, the economic support and sharing of resources that were features of the multigenerational households are unavailable to the same degree as in the past. In addition to gifts and in-kind services to one another, borrowing among relatives was a major feature of African-American households of the past. Without other adults in the house today, single mothers have no one from whom to borrow small amounts of cash, personal items (such as toiletries, clothing, or jewellery), housewares, or food items. In the past, different members of the household would buy different appliances for the house, or they might all chip in to purchase what was needed. The loss of such material support cannot be underestimated, and it no doubt explains why single parents may 'look the other way' when their children become involved in illegal activities that bring much-needed cash into the home.

The absence of the adult companionship provided by African-American households of the past makes the life of the single mother today harder to bear. In the past, when a woman did not have a husband or 'boyfriend', she could turn to her relatives in the household for companionship and support. Today, without the presence of adult relatives in the home, the burden of rearing children alone may be compounded by loneliness or, worse, by despair.

Even if we agree with Billingsley (1992) that the 'so-called black family crisis is not of their own making' and that it is not 'the worst crisis they ever faced and survived' (p. 79), we have to acknowledge that this is the first time since the breakup of families during slavery that external factors have had such a profound effect on African-American family structure. To overcome what could become a crisis, it is necessary to consciously strengthen and augment the extended family networks that have been the key to the survival of Blacks in the United States and to which many people still turn for support (see, e.g., McAdoo 1978, 1983; Hatchett and Jackson 1993).

The changes discussed here have already sent an alarm through the African-American community nationwide. Various initiatives to rekindle the commitment to kin and provide support to female-headed households are being undertaken by churches and other religious groups as well as by civic and service organizations, such as the National Council of Negro Women (NCNW), the Coalition of 100 Black Men, and national sororities and fraternities. Support is given to children and young adults in the form of tutoring, mentoring, and guided recreational activities, and help is also given directly to single mothers to enable them to better cope with their responsibilities. The NCNW's annual Black Family Reunion Day serves as an occasion to rededicate to family-hood and to demonstrate to the nation that the Black family is in much better condition than the media would have us believe.

In a recent paper on female-headed households, I have suggested that we also need to call for the building of public and private housing units that are large enough to accommodate multigenerational kinship and friendship groupings, which can provide single mothers with the help they need to be able to go to work to support themselves and their children. One way in which the government could assist welfare mothers to become working mothers would be through support to elderly women who now live alone, but who might be persuaded to live with or near young working mothers, helping them with their children, as African-American grandmothers did in the past. In short, we need to strengthen and expand existing transresidential kinship and friendship networks and develop new types of extended residential arrangements in order to reverse the debilitating effects of the breakup of the multigenerational households of the past (Sudarkasa 1993: 89).

One thing is certain—we must be realistic about the trends we are seeing and about the best ways to respond to them. It is futile to think that the 'salvation' of the Black family lies in the revival of the nuclear family, when the nuclear family per se has never been the dominant pattern in the African-American community. It is true that most households were headed by married couples, but, as I have noted, at various phases in their domestic cycles they took in grandchildren, elderly parents, and other relatives. In other words, both two-parent and single-parent households among African Americans have usually been more inclusive than the typical nuclear family. It was such multigenerational households and the extended families that linked them together that enabled African Americans to survive and thrive in this country.

Rather than look to the nuclear family, with its ideology of isolationism and self-centredness, as the building block for African-American communities of the future, we need to look to the inclusive, mutually supportive household and family structures that proved their effectiveness in the past. We know that some of these households were successfully headed by women. As we seek to reconnect the disaggregated households that have become the reality of the 1990s, we need to accept the fact that in the twenty-first century many if not most of the African-American households that will emerge will still be headed by women. As in the past, women will have to rely on male relatives and friends, wherever they reside, to play the supportive roles that will enable these households to thrive and succeed, just as they did in the past.

References

Aschenbrenner, J. 1975. *Lifelines: Black Families in Chicago* (New York: Holt, Rinehart & Winston).

Billingsley, A. 1968. *Black Families in White America* (Englewood Cliffs, NJ: Prentice Hall).

———. 1992. *Climbing Jacob's Ladder* (New York: Simon & Schuster).

Blassingame, J.W. 1972. *The Slave Community* (New York: Oxford University Press).

Demerson, B.A. 1991. 'Family Life on Wadmalaw Island' in *Sea Island Roots*, eds M.S. Twining and K. Baird (Trenton, NJ: Africa World Press).

Frazier, E.F. [1939] 1966. *The Negro Family in the United States* (Chicago: University of Chicago Press).

Gutman, H. 1977. *The Black Family in Slavery and Freedom, 1750–1925* (New York: Vintage).

Hatchett, S., and J.S. Jackson. 1993. 'African American Extended Kin Systems' in *Family Ethnicity: Strength in Diversity*, ed. H.P. McAdoo (Newbury Park, CA: Sage).

Jewell, K.S. 1988. *Survival of the Black Family: The Institutional Impact of U.S. Social Policy* (New York: Praeger).

Marshall, G.A. [Niara Sudarkasa]. 1968. 'Marriage: Comparative Analysis' in *International Encyclopedia of the Social Sciences*, v. 9 (New York: Macmillan), 8–19.

McAdoo, H.P. 1978. 'Factors Related to Stability in Upwardly Mobile Black Families', *Journal of Marriage and the Family* 40 (4): 761–76.

———. 1983. *Extended Family Support of Single Black Mothers*. DHSS Research Report No. NIMH 5701, MH32159 (Washington: Government Printing Office).

Moynihan, D.P. 1965. *The Negro Family: The Case for National Action* (Washington: US Department of Labor, Office of Policy Planning and Research).

Perdue, C.L., Jr, T.E. Barden, and R.K. Phillips. 1980. *Weevils in the Wheat: Interviews with Virginia Ex-Slaves* (Bloomington: Indiana University Press).

Stack, C.B. 1974. *All Our Kin: Strategies for Survival in the Black Community* (New York: Harper & Row).

Sudarkasa, N. 1975. 'An Exposition on the Value Premises Underlying Black Family Studies', *Journal of the National Medical Association* 67 (May): 235–9.

———. 1980. 'African and Afro-American Family Structure', *Black Scholar* 11 (8): 37–60.

———. 1981. 'Interpreting the African Heritage in Afro-American Family Organization' in *Black Families*, ed. H.P. McAdoo (Beverly Hills, CA: Sage).

———. 1988. 'Interpreting the African Heritage in Afro-American Family Organization' in *Black Families*, 2nd edn, ed. H.P. McAdoo (Newbury Park, CA: Sage).

———. 1993. 'Female-Headed African American Households: Some Neglected Dimensions' in *Family Ethnicity: Strength in Diversity*, ed. H.P. McAdoo (Newbury Park, CA: Sage).

Wilson, W.J. 1987. *The Truly Disadvantaged: The Inner City, the Underclass, and Public Policy* (Chicago: University of Chicago Press).

Chapter 25

That poor African-American families are different from white and black middle-class families has long been recognized. In fact, the characteristics of these families—that they are often headed by women, that the children in them are frequently born to unwed parents, etc.—typically have been seen as the source of this community's poverty and related problems. In the late 1960s, anthropologist Carol Stack studied a poor African-American community in order to explore family patterns.

Sudarkasa's discussion of extended family represents one corrective to white commentators' descriptions of black families: men are likely to be present in the lives of children whose mothers are not married. Stack moves us beyond the focus on household composition, however, in her examination of the relationships that ensure people's daily livelihood (or subsistence). She finds that 'family' in this community consists of networks of women—who are often relatives but may be just friends—which extend across households. She argues that the daily exchange that goes on within these networks ensures children's and adults' survival, and thus represents a very strong adaptation to poverty. Below is the selection from Stack's book All Our Kin *that describes the exchange at the heart of this family pattern.*

Swapping: 'What Goes Round Comes Round'

Carol Stack

Ruby Banks took a cab to visit Virginia Thomas, her baby's aunt, and they swapped some hot corn bread and greens for diapers and milk. In the cab going home Ruby said to me, 'I don't believe in putting myself on nobody, but I know I need help every day. You can't get help just by sitting at home, laying around, house-nasty and everything. You got to get up and go out and meet people, because the very day you go out, that first person you meet may be the person that can help you get the things you want. I don't believe in begging, but I believe that people should help one another. I used to wish for lots of things like a living room suite, clothes, nice clothes, stylish clothes—I'm sick of wearing the same pieces. But I can't, I can't help myself because I have my children and I love them and I have my mother and all our kin. Sometimes I don't have a damn dime in my pocket, not a crying penny to get a box of paper diapers, milk, a loaf of bread. But you have to have help from everybody and anybody, so don't turn no one down when they come round for help.'

Black families living in The Flats need a steady source of cooperative support to survive. They share with one another because of the urgency of their needs. Alliances between individuals are created around the clock as kin and friends exchange and give and obligate one another. They trade food stamps, rent money, a TV, hats, dice, a car, a nickel here, a cigarette there, food, milk, grits, and children.

Few if any black families living on welfare for the second generation are able to accumulate a surplus of the basic necessities to be able to remove themselves from poverty or from the collective demands of kin. Without the help of kin, fluctuations in the meager flow of available goods could easily destroy a family's ability to survive (Lombardi 1973). Kin and close friends who fall into similar economic crises know that they may share the food, dwelling, and even the few scarce luxuries of those individuals in their kin network. Despite the relatively high cost of rent and food in urban black communities, the collective power within kin-based exchange networks keeps people from going hungry.

As low-skilled workers, the urban poor in The Flats cannot earn sufficient wages and cannot produce goods. Consequently, they cannot legitimately draw desired scarce goods into the community. Welfare benefits which barely provide the necessities of life—a bed, rent, and food—are allocated to households of women and children and are channelled into domestic networks of men, women, and children. All essential resources flow from families into kin networks.

Whether one's source of income is a welfare cheque or wages from labour, people in The Flats borrow and trade with others in order to obtain daily necessities. The most important form of distribution and exchange of the limited resources available to the poor in The Flats is by means of trading, or what people usually call 'swapping'. As people swap, the limited supply of finished material goods in the community is perpetually redistributed among networks of kinsmen and throughout the community.

The resources, possessions, and services exchanged between individuals residing in The Flats are intricately interwoven. People exchange various objects generously: new things, treasured items, furniture, cars, goods that are perishable, and services which are exchanged for childcare, residence, or shared meals. Individuals enlarge their web of social relations through repetitive and seemingly habitual instances of swapping. Lily Jones, a resident in The Flats, had this to say about swapping, 'That's just everyday life, swapping. You not really getting ahead of nobody, you just get better things as they go back and forth.'

The Obligation to Give

'Trading' in The Flats generally refers to any object or service offered with the intent of obligating. An object given or traded represents a possession, a pledge, a loan, a trust, a bank account—given on the condition that something will be returned, that the giver can draw on the account, and that the initiator of the trade gains prerogatives in taking what he or she needs from the receiver.

Mauss's (1954) classic interpretation of gift exchange in primitive societies stresses the essence of obligation in gift giving, receiving, and repaying. A gift received is not owned and sometimes can be reclaimed by the initiator of the swap. A person who gives something which the receiver needs or desires, gives under a voluntary guise. But the offering is essentially obligatory, and in The Flats, the obligation to repay carries kin and community sanctions.

An individual's reputation as a potential partner in exchange is created by the opinions others have about him (Bailey 1971). Individuals who fail to reciprocate in swapping relationships are judged harshly. Julia Rose, a twenty-five-year-old mother of three, critically evaluated her cousin Mae's reputation, 'If someone who takes things from me ain't giving me anything in return, she can't get nothing else. When someone like that, like my cousin Mae, comes to my house and says, 'Ooo, you should give me that chair, honey. I can use it in my living room, and my old man would just love to sit on it,' well, if she's like my cousin, you don't care what her old man wants, you satisfied with what yours wants. Some people like my cousin don't mind borrowing from anybody, but she don't loan you no money, her clothes, nothing. Well, she ain't shit. She don't believe in helping nobody and lots of folks gossip about her. I'll never give her nothing again. One time I went over there after I had given her all these things and I asked her, 'How about loaning me an outfit to wear?' She told me, 'Girl, I ain't got nothing. I ain't got nothing clean. I just put my clothes in the cleaners, and what I do have you can't wear 'cause it's too small for you.' Well, lots of people talk about someone who acts that way.'

Degrees of entanglement among kinsmen and friends involved in networks of exchange differ in kind from casual swapping. Those actively involved in domestic networks swap goods and services on a daily, practically an hourly, basis. Ruby Banks, Magnolia Waters' twenty-three-year-old daughter, portrays her powerful sense of obligation to her mother in her words, 'She's my mother and I don't want to turn her down.' Ruby has a conflicting sense of obligation and of sacrifice toward her mother and her kinsmen.

'I swap back and forth with my mother's family. She wouldn't want nobody else to know how much I'm doing for her, but hell, that's money out of my pocket. We swap back and forth, food stamps, kids, clothes, money, and everything else. Last month the AFDC people had sent me forty dollars to get a couch. Instead of me getting a couch, I took my money over to Mama's and divided with her. I gave her fifteen dollars of it and went on to wash because my kids didn't have a piece clean. I was washing with my hands and a bar of face soap before the money come. I took all the clothes I had, most of the dirty ones I could find, and washed them. It ran me up to six dollars and something with the cab that my sister took back home. I was sitting over at the laundry worrying that Mama didn't have nothing to eat. I took a cab over there and gave her ten more dollars. All I had left to my name was ten dollars to pay on my couch, get food, wash, and everything. But I ignored my problems and gave Mama the money I had. She didn't really have nothing after she paid some bills. She was over there black and blue from not eating—stomach growling. The craziest thing was that she wouldn't touch the rent money. I gave the last five dollars out of the rent money. She paid her sister her five and gave me five to get the kids something to eat. I said, 'What about my other ten?', but she put me off. She paid everybody else and I'm the one who's helping her the most. I could have most everything I needed if I didn't have to divide with my people. But they be just as poor as me, and I don't want to turn them down.'

Close kin who have relied upon one another over the years often complain about the sacrifices they have made and the deprivation they have endured for one another. Statements similar to Ruby's were made by men and women describing the sense of obligation and sacrifice they feel toward female kin: their mothers, grandmothers, or 'mamas'. Commitment to mutual aid among close kin is sometimes characterized as if they were practically 'possessed' or controlled by the relationship. Eloise, captured by the incessant demands of her mother, says, 'A mother should realize that you have your own life to lead and your own family. You can't come when she calls all the time, although you might want to and feel bad if you can't. I'm all worn out from running from my house to her house like a pinball machine. That's the way I do. I'm doing it 'cause she's my mother and 'cause I don't want to hurt her. Yet, she's killing me.'

When Magnolia and Calvin Waters inherited a sum of money, the information spread quickly to every member of their domestic network. Within a month and a half all of the money was absorbed by participants in their network whose demands and needs could not be refused.

The ebb and flow of goods and services among kinsmen is illustrated in the following example of economic and social transactions during one month in 1970 between participants in a kin-based cooperative network in The Flats. As I wrote in my field notes:

Cecil (35) lives in The Flats with his mother Willie Mae, his older sister and her two children, and his younger brother. Cecil's younger sister Lily lives with their mother's sister Bessie. Bessie has three children and Lily has two. Cecil and his mother have part-time jobs in a café and Lily's children are on aid. In July of 1970 Cecil and his mother had just put together enough money to cover their rent. Lily paid her utilities, but she did not have enough money to buy food stamps for herself and her children. Cecil and Willie Mae knew that after they paid their rent they would not have any money for food for the family. They helped out Lily by buying her food stamps, and then the two households shared meals together until Willie Mae was paid two weeks later. A week later Lily received her second ADC check and Bessie got some spending money from her boyfriend. They gave some of this money to Cecil and Willie May to pay their rent, and gave Willie Mae money to cover her insurance and pay a small sum on a living room suite at the local furniture store. Willie Mae reciprocated later on by buying dresses for Bessie and Lily's daughters and by caring for all the children when Bessie got a temporary job.

The people living in The Flats cannot keep their resources and their needs a secret. Everyone knows who is working, when welfare cheques arrive, and when additional resources are available. Members of the middle class in America can cherish privacy concerning their income and resources, but the daily intimacy created by exchange transactions in The Flats insures that any change in a poor family's resources becomes 'news'. If a participant in an exchange network acquires a new car, new clothes, or a sum of money, this information is immediately circulated through gossip. People are able to calculate on a weekly basis the total sum of money available to their kin network. This information is necessary to their own solvency and stability.

Social relationships between kin who have consistently traded material and cultural support over the years reveal feelings of both generosity and martyrdom. Long-term social interactions, especially between female kin, sometimes become highly competitive and aggressive. At family gatherings or at a family picnic it is not unusual to see an exaggerated performance by someone, bragging about how much he has done for a particular relative, or boasting that he provided all the food and labour for the picnic himself. The performer often combines statements of his generosity with great claims of sacrifice. In the presence of other kin the performer displays loyalty and superiority to others. Even though these routines come to be expected from some individuals, they cause hurt feelings and prolonged arguments. Everyone wants to create the impression that he is generous and manipulative, but no one wants to admit how much he depends upon others.

The trading goods and services among the poor in complex industrial societies bears a striking resemblance to patterns of exchange organized around reciprocal gift giving in non-Western societies. The famous examples of reciprocal gift giving first described by Malinowski (1922), Mauss (1925), and Lévi-Strauss (1969) provided a basis for comparison. Patterns of exchange among people living in poverty and reciprocal exchanges in cultures lacking a political state are both embedded in well-defined kinship obligations. In each type of social system strategic resources are distributed from a family base to domestic groups, and exchange transactions pervade the whole social-economic life of participants. Neither industrial poor nor participants in nonindustrial economies have the opportunity to control their environment or to acquire a surplus of scarce goods (Dalton 1961; Harris 1971; Lee 1969; Sahlins 1965). In both of these systems a limited supply of goods is perpetually redistributed through the community.

The themes expressed by boasting female performers and gossiping kin and friends resemble themes which have emerged from black myth, fiction, and lore (Abrahams 1963; Dorson 1956, 1958). Conflicting values of trust and distrust, exploitation and friendship, the 'trickster' and the 'fool', have typically characterized patterns of social interaction between Blacks and Whites; notions of trust and distrust also suffuse interpersonal relations within the black community. These themes become daily utterances between cooperating kinsmen who find themselves trapped in a web of obligations. But the feelings of distrust are more conspicuous among friends than among kin.

Many students of social relations within the black community have concluded that friendships are embedded in an atmosphere of distrust. However, intense exchange behaviour would not be possible if distrust predominated over all other attitudes toward personal relations. Distrust is offset by improvisation: an adaptive style of behaviour acquired by persons using each situation to control, manipulate, and exploit others. Wherever there are friendships, exploitation possibilities exist (Abrahams 1970, p. 125). Friends exploit one another in the game of swapping, and they expect to be exploited in return. There is a precarious line between acceptable and unacceptable returns on a swap. Individuals risk trusting others because they want to change their lives. Swapping offers a variety of goods and something to anticipate. Michael Lee, a twenty-eight-year-old Flats resident, talks about his need to trust others, 'They say you shouldn't trust nobody, but that's wrong. You have to try to trust somebody, and somebody has to try to trust you, 'cause everybody need help in this world.'

A person who gives and obligates a large number of individuals stands a better chance of receiving returns than a person who limits his circle of friends. In addition, repayments from a large number of individuals are returned intermittently: people can anticipate receiving a more-or-less continuous flow of goods. From this perspective, swapping involves both calculation and planning.

Obtaining returns on a trade necessarily takes time. During this process, stable friendships are formed. Individuals attempt to surpass one another's displays of generosity; the extent to which these acts are mutually satisfying determines the duration of friendship bonds. Non-kin who live up to one another's expectations express elaborate vows of friendship and conduct their social relations within the idiom of kinship. Exchange behaviour between those friends 'going for kin' is identical to exchange behaviour between close kin.

The Rhythm of Exchange

'These days you ain't got nothing to be really giving, only to your true friends, but most people trade,' Ruby Banks told me. 'Trading is a part of everybody's life. When I'm over at a girl friend's house, and I see something I want, I say, 'You gotta give me this; you don't need it no way.' I act the fool with them. If they say no, I need that, then they keep it and give me something else. Whatever I see that I want I usually get. If a friend lets me wear something of theirs, I let them wear something of mine. I even let some of my new clothes out. If my friend has on a new dress that I want, she might tell me to wait till she wear it first and then she'll give it to me, or she might say, well take it on.' Exchange transactions are easily found and create special bonds between friends. They initiate a social relationship and agreed upon reciprocal obligations (Gouldner 1960; Foster 1963; Sahlins 1965).[1]

Reciprocal obligations last as long as both participants are mutually satisfied. Individuals remain involved in exchange relationships by adequately drawing upon the credit they accumulate with others through swapping. Ruby Banks' description of the swapping relationship that developed between us illustrates this notion. 'When I first met you, I didn't know you, did I? But I liked what you had on about the second time you seen me, and you gave it to me. All right, that started us swapping back and forth. You ain't really giving nothing away because everything that goes round comes round in my book. It's just like at stores where people give you credit. They have to trust you to pay them back, and if you pay them you can get more things.'

Since an object swapped is offered with the intent of obligating the receiver over a period of time, two individuals rarely simultaneously exchange things. Little or no premium is placed upon immediate compensation; time has to pass before a counter-gift or a series of gifts can be repaid. While waiting for repayments, participants in exchange are compelled to trust one another. As the need arises, reciprocity occurs. Opal Jones described the powerful obligation to give that pervades interpersonal relationships. 'My girl friend Alice gave me a dress about a month ago, and last time I went over to her house, she gave me sheets and towels for the kids, 'cause she knew I needed them. Every time I go over there, she always gives me something. When she comes over to my house, I give her whatever she asks for. We might not see each other in two or three months. But if she comes over after that, and I got something, I give it to her if she want it. If I go over to her house and she got something, I take it—canned goods, food, milk—it don't make no difference.

'My TV's been over to my cousin's house for seven or eight months now. I had a fine couch that she wanted and I gave it to her too. It don't make no difference with me what it is or what I have. I feel free knowing that I done my part in this world. I don't ever expect nothing back right away, but when I've given something to kin or friend, whenever they think about me they'll bring something on around. Even if we don't see each other for two or three months. Soon enough they'll come around and say, 'Come over my house, I got something to give you.' When I get over there and they say, 'You want this?', if I don't want it my kin will say, 'Well, find something else you like and take it on.'

When people in The Flats swap goods, a value is placed upon the goods given away, but the value is not determined by the price or market value of the object. Some goods have been acquired through stealing rings, or previous trades, and they cost very little compared to their monetary value. The value of an object given away is based upon its retaining power over the receiver; that is, how much and over how long a time period the giver can expect returns of the gift. The value of commodities in systems of reciprocal gift giving is characterized by Lévi-Strauss

(1969, p. 54), 'Goods are not only economic commodities, but vehicles and instruments for realities of another order, such as power, influence, sympathy, status and emotion. . . .'

Gifts exchanged through swapping in The Flats are exchanged at irregular intervals, although sometimes the gifts exchanged are of exactly the same kind. Despite the necessity to exchange, on the average no one is significantly better off. Ruby Banks captured the pendulous rhythm of exchange when she said, 'You ain't really giving nothing away because everything that goes round comes round in my book.'

These cooperating networks share many goals constituting a group identity—goals so interrelated that the gains and losses of any of them are felt by all participants. The folk model of reciprocity is characterized by recognized and urgent reciprocal dependencies and mutual needs. These dependencies are recognized collectively and carry collective sanctions. Members of second-generation welfare families have calculated the risk of giving. As people say, 'The poorer you are, the more likely you are to pay back.' This criterion often determines which kin and friends are actively recruited into exchange networks.

Gift exchange is a style of interpersonal relationship by which local coalitions of cooperating kinsmen distinguish themselves from other Blacks—those low-income or working-class Blacks who have access to steady employment. In contrast to the middle-class ethic of individualism and competition, the poor living in The Flats do not turn anyone down when they need help. The cooperative life style and the bonds created by the vast mass of moment-to-moment exchanges constitute an underlying element of black identity in The Flats. This powerful obligation to exchange is a profoundly creative adaptation to poverty.

Social Networks

The most typical way people involve others in their daily domestic lives is by entering with them into an exchange relationship. Through exchange transactions, an individual personally mobilizes others as participants in his social network. Those engaged in reciprocal gift giving are recruited primarily from relatives and from those friends who come to be defined as kin. The process of exchange joins individuals in personal relationships (Boissevain 1966). These interpersonal links effectively define the web of social relationships in The Flats.

Kinsmen and others activated into one another's networks share reciprocal obligations toward one another. They are referred to as 'essential kin' in this study.[2] Strings of exchanges which actively link participants in an individual's network define that individual's personal kindred. The personal kindreds described . . . are ego-centred networks. Even the personal kindreds of half siblings differ slightly; each half sibling shares some kin, but relates uniquely to others. Personal kindreds are not a category from which individuals are recruited, but a selection of individuals mobilized for specific ends (Goodenough 1970; Keesing 1966).

In the process of exchange, people become immersed in a domestic web of a large number of kinfolk who can be called upon for help and who can bring others into the network. Domestic networks comprise the network of cooperating kinsmen activated from participants' overlapping personal kindreds. Domestic networks are not ego-centred; several participants in the network can recruit kin and friends to participate in domestic exchanges. Similar to personal kindreds, domestic networks are a selection of individuals mobilized for specific ends and they can be mobilized for extended periods of time.

Many descriptions of black American domestic life by both Blacks and Whites (Frazier 1939; Drake and Cayton 1945; Abrahams 1963; Moynihan 1965; Rainwater 1966) have overlooked the interdependence and cooperation of kinsmen in black communities. The underlying assumptions of these studies seem to imply that female-headed households and illegitimacy are symptomatic of broken homes and family disorganization. These studies fail to account for the great variety of domestic strategies in urban black communities.

Notes

1. Foster's (1963) model of the dyadic contract includes two types of dyadic contractual ties: colleague ties between individuals of approximately equal socio-economic positions and patron-client ties between individuals of unequal social position. The underlying principles of exchange transactions discussed in this chapter approximate features of the dyadic model of colleague ties. According to Foster's model, colleague ties are expressed by repeated exchanges; they are informal and exist as long as participants are satisfied; they are usually of long duration; and exact or perfectly balanced reciprocity between partners is never achieved.

2. 'Essential kin' refers to members of the culturally specific system of kinship categories and others who activate and validate their jural rights by helping one another, thereby creating reciprocal obligations toward one another. Firth et al. (1970) distinguish between 'effective kin' (those kin with whom one maintains social contact) and 'intimate kin' (those kin with whom contact is purposeful, close, and frequent—members of the immediate family circle).

References

Abrahams, R. 1963. *Deep Down in the Jungle: Negro Narrative Folklore from the Streets of Philadelphia* (Hatboro, PA: Folklore Associates).

———. 1970. *Positively Black* (Englewood Cliffs, NJ: Prentice-Hall).

Bailey, F.G. 1971. *Gifts and Poison: The Politics of Reputation* (New York: Schocken Books).

Boissevain, J. 1966. 'Patronage in Sicily', *Man,* Journal of the Royal Anthropological Institute of Great Britain and Ireland 1 (1): 18–33.

Dalton, G. 1961. 'Economic Theory and Primitive Society', *American Anthropologist* 63: 1–25.

Dorson, R. 1956. *Negro Folktales in Michigan* (Cambridge, MA: Harvard University Press).

———. 1958. *Negro Tales from Pine Bluff, Arkansas, and Calvin, Michigan* (Bloomington: Indiana University Press).

Drake, St. Clair, and Cayton, Horace R. 1945. *Black Metropolis: A Study of Negro Life in a Northern City* (New York: Harcourt, Brace).

Firth, R., J. Hubert, and A. Forge. 1970. *Families and Their Relatives: Kinship in a Middle-Class Sector of London* (New York: Humanities Press).

Foster, G. 1963. 'The Dyadic Contract in Tzintzuntzan II: Patron-Client Relationships', *American Anthropologist* 65: 1280–94.

Frazier, E.F. 1939. *The Negro Family in the United States* (Chicago: University of Chicago Press).

———. 1970. *Description and Comparison in Cultural Anthropology* (Chicago: Aldine).

Goodenough, W.H. 1970. *Description and Comparison in Cultural Anthropology* (Chicago: Aldine).

Gouldner, A.W. 1960. 'The Norm of Reciprocity: A Preliminary Statement', *American Sociological Review* 24: 161–78.

Harris, M. 1971. *Culture, Man, and Nature: An Introduction to General Anthropology* (New York: Thomas Y. Crowell).

Keesing, R.M. 1966. 'Kwaio Kindreds', *Southwestern Journal of Anthropology* 22: 346–55.

Lee, R.B. 1969. 'Kung Bushman Subsistence: An Input-Output Analysis', in *Environment and Culture Behavior: Ecological Studies in Cultural Anthropology*, ed. A.P. Vayda (New York: Natural History Press), 47–79.

Lévi-Strauss, C. 1969. *The Elementary Structures of Kinship* (Boston: Beacon Press [first published 1949]).

Lombardi, J.R. 1973. 'Exchange and Survival', preprint (Boston: Boston University).

Malinowski, B. 1922. *Argonauts of the Western Pacific* (New York: Dutton).

Mauss, M. 1925. 'Essai sur le don: Forme et raison de l'échange dans les sociétés archaïques', *Année Sociologique*, n.s., 1: 30–186.

———. 1954. *The Gift* (New York: Free Press).

Moynihan, D.P. 1965. 'The Negro Family: The Case for National Action' (Washington, DC: U.S. Government Printing Office. Prepared for the Office of Policy Planning and Research of the Department of Labor).

Rainwater, L. 1966. 'Crucible of Identity: The Negro Lower-Class Family', *Daedalus* 95 (2): 172–216.

Sahlins, M.D. 1965. 'On the Sociology of Primitive Exchange', in *The Relevance of Models for Social Anthropology*, ed. M. Banton. A.S.A. Monograph I. (London: Publications; New York: Praeger).

Chapter 26

Agnes Calliste's overview of some of the patterns of African-Canadian families indicates similarities with black Americans. This should not be surprising given the racism and economic marginality of minorities which are common to both countries. The article also describes some African-Canadian history.

Black Families in Canada: Exploring the Interconnections of Race, Class, and Gender

Agnes Calliste

Blacks have been in Canada for over 300 years. However, the study of black families, their most basic institution, has been largely ignored in social science research. The few studies (Tyszko 1959; Chambers 1977; Christensen and Weinfeld 1993; Henry 1994) that exist are preliminary and exploratory. Moreover, Chambers (1977) and Tyszko (1959) focus on common-law relationships, family instability, and out-of-wedlock births among working-class blacks from a deficit perspective (Moynihan 1967), while ignoring middle-class families and stable poor black families. This focus on the deviation of black families from white middle-class norms gives the impression that black families are pathological. However, some researchers (Clarke 1957; Blackwell 1991; Collins 1991) suggest that some black family lifestyles in the Caribbean and the United States are adaptive responses to the social structure. For instance, Edith Clarke (1957) argues that the matrifocal black family organization (revolving around the mother) in Jamaica resulted from the migrant labour system that developed after slavery ended.

This essay discusses the effects of the intersection of race, gender, and class on black families in Canada, focusing on black families in Nova Scotia and Caribbean families in Toronto, from a political economy perspective. It also examines the role of culture and cultural retention in black families' adaptations as they cope with unequal power relations. The research methods used in this study include analysis of the 1991 census, thirty in-depth interviews of black families in Nova Scotia and Toronto, archival research, and review of the literature. All names of interviewees have been changed to maintain confidentiality.

Blacks in Canada have always occupied a subordinate position in economic, political, and ideological relations. This has had a distinct impact on black families. They migrated to Canada as slaves, refugees, and cheap labour to do mostly unskilled work—working, for example, as domestics, miners, and railway porters (Winks 1971; Walker 1976a; Calliste 1987, 1991, 1993–4). They provided a reserve army of labour and were employed in the split labour market (Bonacich 1972, 1976) where they were paid less than white workers for doing the same work. For example, in the early 1960s, Caribbean domestics earned about $150 a month less than white domestics, though employers reported favourably on their performances (*New Nation*, 31 May 1964). Blacks, particularly in Nova Scotia, are still disproportionately concentrated in the lower tier of the secondary labour market (Gordon, Edwards, and Reich 1982; Shadd 1987) where they earn low wages and have little or no job security. Segmented labour-market theory (Piore 1971; Edwards 1979; Gordon, Edwards, and Reich 1982) argues that jobs and industries are readily divided into primary and secondary sectors, and this division is reinforced by barriers that make it difficult for workers to move from one sector to another. In the *primary sector*, jobs are characterized by higher wages and fringe benefits, greater employment stability, a high degree of unionization, superior working conditions, and due process in negotiating job rights. In contrast, the *secondary sector* includes work in marginal industries (e.g., wood-work, roofing, the lower levels of healthcare such as nursing assistants and nurses' aides, and domestic services). These jobs are low-paying, often seasonal or sporadic, less likely to be unionized, and offer little protection against the vagaries of either the individual employer or the ups and downs of the marketplace. Allocations to these labour markets follow existing divisions of race and gender. The secondary sector uses the groups with little bargaining power such as racial minorities, women, and youth.

Racism interacts with *sexism* and class *inequality* in the labour market. Racially constructed gender ideologies and images portrayed black women as 'naturally' suited for jobs in the lowest stratum of a labour market segmented along gender lines. Harold Potter (1949) estimates that in 1941, 80 per cent of black women in Montreal's labour force worked as domestics. Recent research indicates that because of racial and gender segmentation of the Canadian labour force, blacks, particularly women, experience more employment and income inequality than other minority groups despite above-average education (Reitz, Calzavara, and Dasko 1981; Li 1988; Richmond 1989).

The educational system produced and reproduced racial, gender, and class inequality through segregated schools in Nova Scotia and Ontario, a Eurocentric, sexist, and class-biased curriculum that bred low academic achievement and high dropout rates in high school (BLAC [Black Learners Advisory Committee] 1994; Dei 1994).[1] For example, the 1991 census indicates that among African Nova Scotians aged twenty to twenty-four, less than 30 per cent have graduated from Grade 12 (BLAC 1994, 60). The completion rate is much lower for the older age groups (p. 64). Racism and sexism in education and employment lead to high rates of unemployment and poverty. In 1994, the estimated unemployment rate among black adults in Nova Scotia aged twenty to twenty-nine exceeded 40 per cent. For those aged thirty to thirty-nine, unemployment was as high as 30 per cent; for those aged thirty to forty-five who are in the prime of their working careers, unemployment averaged 25 per cent (BLAC 1994: 85).[2] Such economic conditions are highly correlated with family structure and family instability (Hill 1981; Canadian Mental Health Association 1983).

As mentioned previously, systemic racism, sexism, and class bias in education, employment, and Canadian immigration policy affected black families. Many black families did not fit the model of separate *private* and *public spheres* (Kerber 1988; Morton 1993) developed from the experiences of white middle-class nuclear families. Such families are characterized by a male breadwinner (active in the public sphere) and a financially dependent full-time housewife (confined to the private sphere). Given that many black men could not earn family wages, black women often had to work outside the home to maintain the financial survival of their families. Similarly, women, men, and the extended family shared in childrearing to ensure the family's survival. Thus, there has been a fluid public/private sphere in black families, offering opportunities for egalitarian relationships. For example, given the lack of employment opportunities for African–Nova Scotian men in the early 1800s, many families practised gender interdependence and reversals of traditional gender roles in the division of labour. Some women worked in the paid labour force as domestics, laundresses, and seamstresses, or became market vendors, while their husbands took care of the children, made brooms, or gathered items such as berries and bouquets of fern, which the women sold in the Halifax market. As Seth Coleman (1815) reported to the Legislative Assembly about African–Nova Scotian families:

> I found a disposition in them to labour, and to help themselves but the fact is they have nothing to do, I found but four men that had families that had employment, others were making brooms or taking care of the family, while the mother was out to seek a day's work at washing or sewing; on their scanty pittance depended the subsistence of perhaps themselves and 4 or 5 children.

African–Nova Scotian women's active economic role in their families' subsistence, their relative sexual autonomy, and the importance of the extended family in black communities partly reflect a West African cultural tradition (Sudarkasa 1981) as well as survival strategies. Given the pressures of the Canadian political economy (for example, poverty, and children orphaned by sale or death of their parents), taking on childcare responsibilities for each other's children served a critical function in the black community.

Canada's racialized, gendered, and class-oriented immigration regulations and policy reinforced the subordinate status of black workers and hindered the proper formation and reunification of black families. Before the late 1960s, blacks were imported to Canada solely for their labour power, not as future permanent citizens. They were stigmatized as inferior and a potential social problem in Canada. Immigration officials sought to avoid the problem by restricting the entry of black settlers and their families (Calliste 1987, 1991, 1993–4; Satzewich 1991). The cases of American railway porters' and Caribbean domestics' families serve as illustrations.

Before 1943, Canadian immigration officials barred black migrant porters' wives and families from visiting them in order to discourage any increase in Canada's black population while making Canadian Pacific Railway (CPR) porters more dependent and controllable by their employers. As the District Superintendent of Immigration, Winnipeg, wrote in 1943:

> For obvious reasons I do not think we would want to add to our coloured population and I do not believe that the arrangement with the Canadian Pacific Railway for the admission of these coloured porters contemplated the entry of their families. We have been discouraging their admission as visitors or otherwise, by every means possible here on this assumption.

This policy also had economic benefits for the state (for example, it helped to reduce costs for social services such as childrearing and education). It was modified in 1943 to accommodate labour-force needs. The Immigration Department decided to deal with each case on its own merits and ruled that exceptions would be made only where the CPR was certain that the porter in question would resign to return to the United States and his family. In these exceptional cases, his wife would be allowed to visit him for a maximum of thirty days (Smith 1943).

To return to the case of domestics, between 1910 and 1966 Canadian immigration regulations stipulated that Caribbean domestics were to be single and without children. Some domestics who had children in Canada were deported as likely to become a public charge (Calliste 1991, 1993–4). Moreover, in the 1950s and 1960s, immigration officials attempted to obstruct domestic workers' sponsorship of their relatives and fiancés. For example, if a fiancé was admitted, the couple had to be married within thirty days; otherwise, the fiancé was to be deported to the Caribbean. A woman also had to prove to immigration officials that the man sponsored really was her fiancé by providing personal letters to substantiate the relationship. Neither of these practices was applied to white fiancés of white immigrants (Winks 1971: 440–1). This policy demonstrated the devaluation of black women and men as parents and a denial of black women's reproductive freedom. Caribbean blacks, particularly those in the lower class, were stereotyped as promiscuous and likely to become single parents. The dominant ideology of parenthood (making and caring for children within the context of the 'ideal' nuclear and patriarchal family) constructed some locations within social relations of race, class, and citizenship that were more appropriate for parenthood than others. That is, some racial groups or classes were defined as less appropriate parents. The devaluation of black motherhood is demonstrated by some Canadians' opposition to the immigration of Caribbean domestics to Quebec in 1911. As C. Godsal (1911) wrote to C.A. Magrath, MP:

> Are there many negro women who are desirable immigrants, they will certainly all be mothers some day? We may not be able to forbid negroes from entering Canada, though we do stop Chinese, Japs and E. Indians, but importing them wholesale, paying their passages, finding places for them is another matter.

This portrayal of blacks as promiscuous, undesirable immigrants and less deserving of parenthood (Godsal 1911; Deputy Minister of Citizenship 1964) further rationalized and reinforced their subordination in Canada. Godsal's opinion on the undesirability of black women as immigrants and unfit mothers was still current in the mid-1960s (Deputy Minister of Citizenship 1964).

The Immigration and History of Black Families in Nova Scotia

The history of black families in Canada began with slavery, which was given its legal foundation in New France between 1689 and 1709 to help solve the chronic shortage of unskilled labour. By 1759, of the 3,604 slaves in New France, 1,132 were black (Winks 1971: 9). A small number of slaves and free blacks also were brought to Nova Scotia between 1686 and 1750 by British families from New England. By the 1770s, there were several hundred slaves living in Nova Scotia (Oliver 1968; Walker 1976b).

Slavery undermined the family as the most fundamental unit of the social order blacks had known in West Africa, even though it never completely destroyed marriage and the family as important social institutions. Slaves had no marital or parental rights. They were allowed to marry with their owners' consent (Winks 1971); however, the children born of slaves became the property of the mother's owner, irrespective of the status of the father. Thus female slaves were commercially valuable to their masters not only for their labour, but also for their capacity to reproduce more slaves. Controlling black women's reproduction and denying blacks parental rights were essential to the creation and perpetuation of capitalist class relations. They were also manifestations of a systematic and institutionalized devaluation of black women and men as parents. Working-class black families have been stigmatized as deviant (for example, the 'bad' promiscuous mother and ineffectual father). Slavery distorted black gender relations and shaped black gender roles, since black women generally performed the same work as men.

During slavery, many family units were destroyed by the practice of selling fathers, mothers, and children separately. Even free black families were not safe from slave owners who sold them illegally. For example, Edna Wilson (1976) reports that William Castels pretended to send Randon, a black Loyalist, from Birchtown to Barrington, but actually sent him to the Caribbean and sold him, leaving his wife, Mary Randon, aged twenty, destitute. Similarly, Binah Frost's husband also was taken to Jamaica and sold. However, black parents struggled to regain and protect their families. Free black parents sued those who enslaved their children or sold them without holding the properly authorized documents of indenture. In 1791, Mary Postell sued Jesse Gray of Argyle for taking away her children (Shelburne Records 1791).

The majority of indigenous African–Nova Scotian families are descendants of black Loyalists and refugees of the War of 1812. In 1783–4, over 3,500 free black Loyalists, 1 per cent of all Loyalists, and 1,200 slaves owned by white Loyalists arrived in Nova Scotia (Winks 1971; Walker 1976a). Unlike white Loyalists, few black Loyalists received land, and even when they did their farms were too small to maintain their families and were usually located in the most isolated and infertile regions of the province, such as Preston, Sunnyville, and Lincolnville.[3] Thus the state marginalized black families and helped to reinforce and maintain their subordination. The unequal distribution of land and the exploitation of black labour (for example, through the split labour market) contributed to the poverty and oppression of generations of Nova Scotian blacks. Some impoverished black Loyalists, unable to sustain their families, unwillingly indentured or apprenticed themselves and their children (Wilson 1976). Moreover, some black communities (such as Upper Big Tracadie in Guysborough County and Rear Monastery in Antigonish County) are still located on dirt roads on the fringe of white communities.

Black Loyalist families, dissatisfied with broken promises, denial of their democratic rights, and visions of a bleak future for their children, petitioned the British government for redress of their grievances. As a result, 1,196 black Loyalists migrated to Sierra Leone in 1792 (Fergusson 1971; Winks 1971; Walker 1976a).

During the War of 1812, approximately 2,000 black refugees were brought to Nova Scotia (Fergusson 1948; Grant 1990). Initially, they were welcome as a source of cheap labour. However, with the postwar depression and the arrival of 40,000 Scots labourers who tended to drive blacks out of the labouring and semiskilled jobs upon which they had come to rely, the black workers became dependent on the state (Walker 1976a: 101–2). In 1815, since blacks no longer had a valid economic role, white Nova Scotians began to oppose further black immigration.

The survival of black families against extreme oppression and hardship reflects their strength and resilience. One of their strengths was their strong kinship bonds. They took relatives and fictive or symbolic kin (often, older people who were treated as 'uncles', 'aunts', or 'grandparents') into their households more frequently than did white families, partly because it was a West African tradition and partly because their survival depended on their ability to help one another (Hill 1971; Sudarkasa 1981). Research on African-American history (Foster 1983) reveals that the earliest forms of family organization recreated in America by enslaved blacks represented both a syncretization (a fusion or combination) of African patterns and an adaptation of certain universal features of the realities and demands of slave life. Among the African patterns that were transplanted and transformed by African-American slaves were kin networks, husband-wife relations, sibling bonds, socialization practices, relationships between alternate generations (grandparents and grandchildren), and the extension of kinship terminology to elders throughout the community.

With specific reference to black families in Nova Scotia, James Walker (1976a: 85) reports that a Halifax official in the 1790s commented on blacks' strong attachment to their families, which impelled them 'always to act together'. Similarly, John Clarkson (Fergusson 1971; Walker 1976a) noted in 1791 that black Loyalist families went beyond the British definition of family to include godchildren, orphans, widows, neighbours, people from the same church, or simply people in the same black community. Moreover, African–Nova Scotian parents brought up other people's children as if they were their own, without distinction between biological and adopted children. The extended-family system and the practice of sharing childcare reflects a survival strategy as well as a West African cultural tradition that is found in many black communities, including the Caribbean (Bryan, Dodzie, and Scafe 1985; Collins 1991).

Commenting on black Loyalist family structure, Walker (1976a: 85) points to the common stereotype that there was 'a casual attitude towards sexual relationships, or at least towards the sacrament of marriage.' He argues that common-law relationships and 'illegitimacy' were frequent even among professed Christians. However, Herbert Gutman (1977) argues that slaves had their own ideas of morality. Though prenuptial intercourse was common among slaves in Virginia and Carolina (from which many black Loyalists and refugees migrated), there was hardly any indiscriminate mating. Prenuptial intercourse was viewed as a prelude to settled marriage, and marriage followed most prenuptial slave pregnancies. This practice was not peculiar to slave populations. It was also found in diverse 'premodern' populations. Moreover, giving birth to a child at a relatively early age diminished the probability of the physical separation of its mother from her family of origin and made the future of a new slave family much more secure, since slave owners were less likely to sell a fecund than a 'barren' woman. The relative frequency of common-law relationships and 'illegitimacy' among some black Loyalists in Nova Scotia may be attributed partly to the lack of legal recognition given to marriages performed by black preachers and to slaves' marriage rituals such as jumping over a broomstick.

Though the baptismal records of the Anglican Church in Shelburne (1783–1869) indicate that some black children came from single-parent families, marriage records for the same period show that many black Loyalists were married in that church. In the period 1785–90 there were twenty-three weddings of black Loyalists.

The baptismal records of the Anglican Christ Church in Guysborough (1785–1879) indicate that twenty-four out of twenty-five black children who were baptized in the years 1785 and 1786 had parents who were married.

The 1871 and 1881 censuses for Halifax County indicate that though there were some common-law relationships among African–Nova Scotians, most households included a married male and female. For example, the 1871 census for Halifax County lists 48 female-headed households and 208 households with a married couple with children under twelve. What seems to be most distinct about African–Nova Scotians' family structure in the late nineteenth century was the number of extended families, including households with children with different surnames from the household head, and/or the number of households in which third-generation children were residing. This probably also included neighbours' children. For example, the 1871 census lists forty-five extended families for Halifax and thirty-two for Guysborough. The evidence suggests, however, that the role of the extended family and black community in socializing and disciplining children weakened considerably after World War II with the emergence of the state's social programs, migration of African–Nova Scotians to cities such as Toronto and Montreal, industrialization, and societal emphasis on competition and individualism (S. Jones, HERO tapes, 24 June 1971; D. Brown, personal communication, 18 Aug. 1993; Jones 1993).[4] Some programs, such as social development and welfare, weakened black families and communities by assuming roles and responsibilities traditionally held by parents, neighbours, and church leaders. Thus, the communities began to rely on the state for solutions to their problems such as economic survival and family conflict.

African–Nova Scotian family structure varied by location according to adaptive responses to the social structure. In 1970, Clairmont and Magill (1970: 50–1) found that while rural non-farm

African–Nova Scotian households had a tendency to include 'other' (non-nuclear family) relatives and boarders as an adaptive response to racism and poverty, they tended, along with urban fringe families, to have fewer female lone-parent households. Blacks in Halifax mid-city had 28 per cent female-headed households compared to 11 per cent in the urban fringe and 12 per cent in rural non-farm communities. For Halifax as a whole, 10 per cent of the families had female heads in 1961. Thus, the urban fringe and rural non-farm black families were similar to the general Halifax population, while blacks in Halifax appeared 'to have a family structure similar to that found in Black ghettoes in the United States' (p. 52). Literature on ethnicity and single parenting in the United States supports Clairmont and Magill's finding. Laosa (1988: 27) found that there is a dramatic increase in the incidence of single parenting as one moves away from rural areas and into urbanized settings. In addition to the impact of more intense racism and poverty in rural areas of Nova Scotia such as Guysborough and Preston, the low proportion of female-headed households could be attributed to the role of the church and pressure from the community to conform to societal norms. Oldtimers in Guysborough recall that

families tended to exert pressure on pregnant single women and their partners to marry before the child's birth (D. Brown, personal communication, 18 Aug. 1993; D. Smith, personal communication, 2 Aug. 1993). In Halifax one can live in comparative anonymity, and the church and community had less social control. Recently, however, black family structures in rural communities have changed dramatically from mostly married families to some common-law relationships and female lone-parent households. In many of the latter families, the fathers moved out as a family survival strategy for the mothers to be eligible for social programs such as the family allowance and welfare (I. James, personal communication, 29 July 1994).

Black Family Structures in Canada and Nova Scotia

The 1991 census indicates that nearly three-fifths (58.2 per cent) of black families compared to four-fifths (78.0 per cent) of Canadian families of all ethnic groups involve a married couple (Table 1). However, there is a slight tendency for proportionately more Canadian families than black families (except African–Nova Scotians) to

---

Table 1: Comparison of Family Structure of Blacks and Canadians of All Ethnic Groups, 1991

	Blacks			Canada
	Nova Scotia	Metro Toronto	Canada	All Ethnic Groups
Family Structure				
Married	48.4	55.6	58.2	78.0
Common-law	12.2	6.0	7.2	9.9
Male lone parent	3.8	3.7	3.6	2.1
Female lone parent	35.6	34.7	31.0	10.0
Total	100.0	100.0	100.0	100.0
	(3,515)	(37,545)	(77,825)	(7,146,825)

Calculated from Statistics Canada, 1991 census based on a 20 per cent sample.

live in common-law relationships (9.9 per cent versus 7.2 per cent versus 12.2 per cent respectively). African–Nova Scotian families are even less likely to be married than blacks in Metropolitan Toronto and Canada in general (48.4 per cent versus 55.6 per cent versus 58.2 per cent respectively). This lower proportion of married families among blacks is mostly a result of socioeconomic forces—high unemployment rates and low wages.

These factors place added strains on marriages or keep them from forming in the first place. A significantly larger percentage of black than non-black households are headed by a woman. While 10 per cent of non-black families have a woman head, 31 per cent of black families in Canada and 35.6 per cent of African–Nova Scotian families are headed by a woman. Black family structure reflects the interaction of race, class, and gender. Blacks, particularly in Nova Scotia, are more likely to be confined to the lower tier of the secondary sector of the dual labour market, where they earn low wages and have little or no job security.

Table 2 presents data indicating that family structure varies by income. Controlling for geo-graphical location and race, married families earn the highest income, followed by those in common-law relationships. Female-headed single-parent (lone-parent) households earn the lowest income—about half the income of married families. Male lone-parent households, on the other hand, earn about three-fourths the income of married families. These great differences in income reflect the feminization of poverty—both female gender and single parenthood influence the likelihood of poverty (Goldberg and Kremen 1990). Table 2 also shows that black families, particularly in Nova Scotia, earned lower average incomes in 1990 than the Canadian population. Blacks in Nova Scotia earned the lowest income partly because they reside in a poor region and partly because of more intense racism due to the 'greater competition for jobs, particularly in the high wage, monopoly sector of the economy' (Shadd 1987: 109).

As levels of education and income rise, so does the number of male-headed households. Marriage is as much the *result* of economic security, well-being, and upward mobility as it is the *cause* of economic well-being among families. Black household heads with postsecondary edu-

Table 2: Comparison of Family Structure of Blacks and Canadians of All Ethnic Groups by 1990 Average Income for Selected Geographical Locations

	Locations					
	Nova Scotia		Metro Toronto		Canada	
Groups	Blacks	All Ethnic Groups	Blacks	All Ethnic Groups	Blacks	All Ethnic Groups
Family Structure						
Married	$44,823	$49,322	$58,698	$72,967	$54,177	$57,410
Common-law	34,428	39,538	48,013	65,036	44,736	48,287
Male lone parent	30,985	38,650	43,159	57,630	40,360	46,400
Female lone parent	20,143	24,201	29,192	38,006	26,170	28,972

Calculated from Statistics Canada, 1991 census based on a 20 per cent sample.

Table 3: Canadian Black Family Structure by Education

	Education					
	Less than Grade 9	Grades 9–13	Trades Certificate or Diploma	Other Non-University	Some University	University Degree or Higher
Family Structure						
Married	53.2	53.0	67.6	54.7	61.9	78.5
Common-law	5.8	7.7	6.0	7.4	8.4	5.5
Male lone parent	5.1	3.6	3.9	3.3	3.6	3.5
Female lone parent	35.9	35.7	22.5	34.6	26.1	12.5
Total	100.0	100.0	100.0	100.0	100.0	100.0
	(6,495)	(24,150)	(26,350)	(8,235)	(3,320)	(9,285)

Calculated from Statistics Canada, 1991 census based on a 20 per cent sample.

cation are more likely than those with less education to be married (Table 3). For example, about 78 per cent of those with a university degree or higher compared with about 53 per cent of those with high-school certificate or lower are married. Conversely, about 12 per cent of household heads with a university degree or higher compared to about 36 per cent with a high-school certificate or lower are female single parents. At the highest level of education, the percentage of black families that is married is comparable to that for the Canadian population.

The percentages of African–Nova Scotian married families whose household heads obtained either less than a Grade 9 education or a university degree or higher are comparable to those for other blacks in Canada with similar levels of education. However, at other levels of education, the effect of education on family structure is weaker for blacks in Nova Scotia than for other blacks. This is due largely to the greater economic marginalization of African–Nova Scotians. For example, 54.1 per cent of African–Nova Scotian household heads with a trades certificate or diploma are married. The percentage for all

Canadian blacks at that education level is 67.6 per cent (Table 3).

Family structure fluctuates by education, however, given employment and income inequities, occupation and income might be better predictors of family structure among African–Nova Scotians. The interaction of age and income also has an effect on family structure. A plausible assumption is that the relatively high proportion of married families among those with less than Grade 9 education is attributable to age and income. Older people are more likely to be married and less likely to be single parents. Controlling for education and occupation, older people earn more than younger people. Generally, older people also tend to have more resources than younger people.

Table 4 allows us to discount the effect of education. Controlling for education, the higher the income of African–Nova Scotian families, the more likely they are to be married. For example, among those with some secondary education, almost nine out of ten families (87.5 per cent) who earn $50,000 and over are married, compared to four out of ten (39.1 per cent) of those

Table 4: African–Nova Scotian Family Structures by Income, Controlling for Education

	Education			
	Less than Grade 9			
Income	<$20,000	$20,000–$34,999	$35,000–$49,999	$50,000 and Over
Family Structure				
Married	47.1	66.0	63.6	64.7
Common-law	6.9	6.0	15.1	0.0
Male lone parent	3.5	8.0	6.1	11.8
Female lone parent	42.5	20.0	15.1	23.5
Total	100.0	100.0	99.9	100.0
	(435)	(250)	(165)	(85)
	Grades 9–13			
Income	<$20,000	$20,000–$34,999	$35,000–$49,999	$50,000 and Over
Family Structure				
Married	14.5	39.1	78.4	87.5
Common-law	12.0	20.3	8.1	0.0
Male lone parent	3.6	6.2	0.0	0.0
Female lone parent	69.9	34.4	13.5	12.5
Total	100.0	100.0	100.0	100.0
	(415)	(320)	(185)	(80)
	Postsecondary			
Income	<$20,000	$20,000–$34,999	$35,000–$49,999	$50,000 and Over
Family Structure				
Married	7.5	34.6	62.0	81.7
Common-law	5.7	19.2	22.0	12.7
Male lone parent	0.0	3.9	4.0	2.8
Female lone parent	86.8	42.3	12.0	2.8
Total	100.0	100.0	100.0	100.0
	(530)	(260)	(250)	(355)

Calculated from Statistics Canada, 1991 census based on a 20 per cent sample.

who earn \$20,000–\$34,999. Conversely, also controlling for education, the lower the income the more likely a family is to be headed by a female lone parent. For example, among families whose household head has some postsecondary education, 86.8 per cent of those who earn less than \$20,000, compared to 12 per cent of those who earn \$35,000–\$49,999, are female lone-parent families.

Other factors that account for racial differences in family structure are the shortage of black men of marriageable age,[5] the tendency for more black men than women to be involved in interracial marriages, and a cultural tradition that is partly a legacy of colonialism and slavery. Though marriage is the most common form of family structure in the Caribbean, less emphasis is placed on marriage as a context for childbearing, particularly among the lower class (Smith 1988). The higher rate of single-parent families among blacks also is related to high separation and divorce rates (Richmond 1989; Christensen and Weinfeld 1993; Henry 1994) which result partly from the economic and social stress experienced by blacks across all social lines. Some black women have reacted to the black male shortage by parenting outside of marriage. Another factor

that has contributed to the growth of black single-parent homes is the high ratio of out-of-wedlock births. Many of these children are born to teenagers and young adults.

Table 5 indicates that more than half (56.3 per cent) of black families in the fifteen to twenty-four age group are headed by female lone parents. The corresponding proportion for African–Nova Scotians is 66.7 per cent, compared to 20.4 per cent in the general Canadian population (Table 6). Moreover, the 1991 census indicates that 85 per cent of these young black female lone parents in Canada and 91 per cent in Nova Scotia earned less than \$20,000 in 1990. These statistics reflect the multiple jeopardy of race, class, gender, and age.

Though being a single parent causes poverty, the widespread poverty among young blacks and their slim prospects of future economic stability are important causes for the formation of single-parent households among blacks. This feminization of poverty has serious consequences for young black families. It also has serious policy implications; for example, it suggests the need for programs in education and employment equity and sex education, and the need for better communication between parents and children. Many parents, particularly blacks, do not talk frankly

Table 5: Canadian Black Family Structure by Age

	Age					
	15–24	25–34	35–44	45–54	55–64	65+
Family Structure						
Married	23.5	53.1	58.8	63.4	69.6	71.9
Common-law	18.8	11.3	5.7	5.2	2.5	1.8
Male lone parent	1.4	2.4	3.9	4.9	3.6	5.2
Female lone parent	56.3	33.2	31.6	26.5	24.3	21.1
Total	100.0	100.0	100.0	100.0	100.0	100.0
	(3,895)	(19,670)	(25,720)	(18,170)	(6,965)	(3,380)

Calculated from Statistics Canada, 1991 census based on a 20 per cent sample.

Table 6: Family Structure by Age for Canadians of All Ethnic Groups

	Age					
	15–24	25–34	35–44	45–54	55–64	65+
Family Structure						
Married	34.7	69.6	77.1	81.6	87.3	89.2
Common-law	44.4	18.3	8.9	6.0	3.5	1.8
Male lone parent	0.5	1.1	2.5	3.1	2.1	1.9
Female lone parent	20.4	11.0	11.5	9.3	7.1	7.1
Total	100.0	100.0	100.0	100.0	100.0	100.0
	(229,280)	(1,606,725)	(1,942,460)	(1,359,260)	(1,014,165)	(994,920)

Calculated from Statistics Canada, 1991 census based on a 20 per cent sample.

about human sexuality with their children (J. Brown, personal communication, 29 June 1993; G. Williams, personal communication, 22 July 1994). Some Caribbean parents, for example, told children that babies came from the airplane or were brought by friends. Thus, many teenagers rely on their peers for sex education that is sometimes inaccurate.

In addition to high percentages of female lone-parent families among the youngest age groups (fifteen to thirty-four), African–Nova Scotian families aged fifteen to twenty-four are four times more likely to live in common-law relationships than to be married (27.3 per cent versus 6.0 per cent). The corresponding percentages for other blacks in the same age group are 18.8 per cent common-law and 23.5 per cent married (Table 5). The low proportion of marriages in the youngest age groups (fifteen to thirty-four) suggests that African–Nova Scotians marry at a later age than other blacks and the general Canadian population.

About one-third (34.7 per cent) of young heads of households in the fifteen to twenty-four age group in the Canadian population are married (Table 6). Conversely, one in five (20.4 per cent) families in this same age group is headed by a single woman. Surprisingly, four out of ten (44.4 per cent) Canadian families in this age group live in common-law relationships. While this reflects economic instability, it also indicates the increasing tendency of young people to live in a trial marital arrangement. Common-law relationships are becoming acceptable in Canada, especially with the high separation and divorce rates.

Racial differences in births to single women could be attributed to differences in the frequent and effective use of contraceptives and abortion; as well as differences in legitimation (or 'shotgun') weddings (Cutright and Smith 1988). Less-educated and poorer people are less likely to use contraceptives. Also, abortion has never been as popular in the black community as in the white community; moreover, many black youths cannot afford abortions. Thus, race intersects with class. Blacks are also less likely than whites to put their children up for adoption, which affects the relative proportions of single-mother households. Historically, black women were substantially more inclined to incorporate the child of an unwed mother into the basic family structure or the extended family, occasionally explaining the newborn as the child of its grandmother or as a relative's child. Thus, children resulting from 'unplanned' pregnancies were not referred to as 'unwanted' (Clarke 1975).

Gender Role Identities, Gender Division of Labour, and Gender Relations

Black women have needed to be strong in order for the family to survive, and since most black women have been forced to work outside the home, they tend to be relatively independent. However, black women often have not had the resources to impose their authority on black men in this society. Given patriarchy and gender ideologies, there is a *gendered division of labour* in black households. Generally, women perform the domestic labour *inside* the house while men tend to do the tasks *outside* (such as barn and yard work). In farm families in rural Nova Scotia both men and women work on the farm during planting and harvesting time (D. Jones, personal communication, 24 Aug. 1993; M. Payne, personal communication, 27 July 1993; P. Sam, personal communication, 22 July 1993). In some families, men and women share in the making of family decisions as well as the housework and childcare, but it is still assumed that women are primarily responsible for domestic labour and that men are 'helping' their wives. In exceptional cases, there are exchanges or role reversals, which sometimes are structured by the social situation and sometimes take place when family members prefer to perform a favourite task. For example, in one Caribbean family interviewed, the husband does most of the cooking, especially when the family is entertaining, and particularly on special occasions such as Christmas, because he enjoys cooking (I. Hobson, personal communication, 30 June 1993). In another family, since the wife's job requires a great deal of travelling, the husband does most of the domestic labour except cooking, because he is not a good cook. The wife also performs some tasks outside (such as painting and gardening) because she prefers to do them (J. Brown, personal communication, 29 June 1993). In both cases, the women described their relationship with their husband as egalitarian. The literature on families (Eichler 1983; Blackwell 1991; Collins 1991) suggests that role exchanges or fully developed role sharing are characteristic of egalitarian families.

Black women, like other women (Luxton 1983), have developed a variety of strategies and tactics with which to get the men to take on more work. These range from appeals to fairness to militant demands for greater or equal participation (P. Sam, personal communication, 22 July 1993; Group interviews, personal communication, 26 June 1993). However, some men perceive these attempts as a challenge to their power and their traditional notions of masculinity and femininity. Thus, they resist their wives' attempts to be assertive and to change some gender roles. This sometimes results in power struggles and marital problems, including separation and divorce. For example, Mendoza (1990: 324) reports that the militancy of one woman, Edith, resulted in a separation for one year. Edith explains her experience:

> My husband was the breadwinner and made decisions [in the Caribbean and in their earlier years in Canada]. When we moved to Brampton [Ontario] I started to change some roles and become aggressive. I started to gain my freedom. Before I listened and did what he said. We had a lot of problems because of this.

Edith's husband abused her physically and emotionally for challenging his power. Their conflict also resulted in other familial problems such as disputes within the extended family, because her husband's relatives commended her behaviour.

Despite black men's resistance to changing gender roles, some are adapting and learning to accept women as 'equals', partly as a survival strategy (P. Sam, personal communication, 22 July 1993; Focus Group, personal communication, 26 June 1993). As one Caribbean woman points out:

> A number of them have changed. They have to change. I think it's a change of survival, and not of understanding—understanding that women are people too. Because it's a superficial change in a sense, our children are coming up in homes where they are not see-

ing black men respecting black women and vice versa and teaching our sons that black women are to be respected and got a lot going for them. It's an accommodation by black men, not a change. There's no illumination on their parts. No genuine awakening. I don't see too many black men walking with their children (Mendoza 1990: 329).

Some women who still internalize traditional notions of masculinity and femininity also resist men's efforts to change gender roles and patterns of domestic labour. A Caribbean man explained that his attempt to perform childcare functions and some of the domestic labour was interpreted as feminine and resulted in family conflict and separation. In his words:

> My wife was in nursing school. So I decided to stick by her and support her. I took care of the children, made her breakfast and lunch. After she left for school, I took the children to the daycare before I went job hunting. . . . She told me that I was acting like a woman and that her mother said I looked like the type of man who would stay at home and let the woman work (P. Peters, personal communication, 26 June 1993).

His behaviour challenged the two women's notions of gender roles. In the Caribbean, men generally did not participate in childcare and domestic labour (Smith 1988). The two women also perceived him as not performing his role as provider.

Though many black women acknowledge that black families simultaneously oppress them and act as a site for shelter and resistance against racism, most black men tend to deny or downplay sexism. They argue that racism and class exploitation are the major problems affecting black families and communities. They also claim that black men's oppression of their families is largely a result of the frustrations and powerlessness they experience in society and its major institutions ('Sexism

in Our Community' 1987; 'A Woman Is Killed' 1987). For example, at the Black Family Strategy conference in Halifax in 1993, some women pointed out the need to discuss gender relations in black families and for black men to accept financial and social responsibility as fathers. Some black men responded that discussing sexism would be divisive and that they experienced more difficulties in the labour force than black women since they present a threat to the white male dominant group. In other words, they maintained that racial subordination of black men negates their advantages as males. An effective strategy, however, requires that both women and men address sexism in black families and communities in order to foster egalitarian relationships.

Most black families are very reluctant to speak about domestic violence. They fear that such disclosure will reinforce stereotypes of the violence of black men and increase the criminalization of the black community. This conspiracy of silence is also encouraged by the church, community leaders, and the police. For example, one woman's pastor blamed her for leaving her husband after five years of physical, mental, and emotional abuse because, as he said, marriage is intended to be for good and bad (Douglas 1986; 'A Woman Is Killed' 1987). This supports Aldridge's (1991) argument that the ideology of sexism and the Judaeo-Christian ethic have an interactive effect on black male-female relations since these ideologies support the inequalities that exist in these relations. As Wells (1986: 7) points out:

> Given the racism and sexism in Toronto, when Black women are battered it is treated lightly by the police and general community. . . . There are countless cases of Black women being battered and the police treat our complaints with mocking disrespect.

The failure of the police to charge Lesline Senior's husband despite repeated beatings and the

Toronto black community's silence after he murdered her illustrate Wells's point. The evidence suggests that, as in other communities, 'woman abuse is common behaviour in the Black community' ('A Woman Is Killed' 1987).

Socialization in Black Families

Black parents face an extraordinary challenge in raising children who will be able to survive in a racist, sexist, and capitalist society. They have to socialize children to develop a high self-concept and positive racial identity in a society in which being black has negative connotations. Black children must learn to achieve in a school system in which the curriculum negates their lived experiences and the contributions of people of African descent. They also must learn to cope with deterrents and roadblocks that inhibit their access to mainstream Canadian life. Simply put, black children must be socialized to deal with the racism that they will encounter daily. Black girls and women must be encouraged to be independent because many of them will carry family and economic responsibilities alone.

Peters (1985: 161) defines racial socialization as 'raising physically and emotionally healthy' black children in a society with anti-black racism. Many black families in Canada develop racial socialization strategies to develop positive self-concepts and racial identity to prepare their children to deal with racism. In addition to teaching Black Heritage, some parents emphasize to their children that they are as good as other people: beautiful, intelligent, and so forth. Given the importance of education for upward social mobility, parents emphasize the value of education. Some parents also instil in their children that given racism, they have to be 'twice as good' as whites to compete, and black women have to be 'ten times better'. However, some parents argue that this strategy puts too much pressure on children. Thus, they simply encourage them to do their best (Focus Group, personal communication, 4 Aug. 1993).

Another racial socialization technique that some black parents use in preparing children to deal with racism is the teaching of folklore and telling of anecdotes about their experiences with racism and how they resisted. Thus some children learn about oppression and resistance very early. Black families and churches have also taught blacks to be strong and to stand up for their rights by emphasizing spiritual values such as equality and justice (D. Barnes, personal communication, 31 Aug. 1993).

Some black parents claim that they are socializing their daughters and sons to be non-sexist. For example, some parents assign domestic chores by casting lots or ensuring that their sons learn to cook and clean (S. Paul, personal communication, 11 Aug. 1993; Focus Group, personal communication, 4 Aug. 1993). This does not guarantee that black males treat women as equals, particularly given other socialization agents such as the media and peers, and role modelling by some parents. Black youths regard their mother as the mainstay of the family. They claim that though their father may provide financial support, it is usually their mother who supervises the homework and encourages them to pursue higher education (C. James, personal communication, 16 Jan. 1994).

Ironically, some feminists are socializing their sons for traditional male roles such as not sharing most domestic labour. One feminist has stated that she would socialize her children in traditional parenting patterns as she was socialized. For example, she would be more protective of her daughter than her son and teach her to do domestic labour. She says that feminism is an ideology that we strive for, but it is not reality (L. Bain, personal communication, 24 June 1994). Research is needed on the interaction effects of race/ethnicity and class on gender socialization.

Caribbean parents tend to be strict disciplinarians. They believe that they should not 'spare the rod and spoil the child' (Wills 1987). Since they have not been trained to make the transition from the traditional parenting in the Caribbean to the Canadian pattern, they tend to socialize their children in traditional parenting patterns. They emphasize values such as respecting older people (for example, not calling them by their first names) and obeying parents (Mendoza 1990; L. Bain, personal communication, 24 June 1993). They argue that the Canadian tradition of parenting gives children too much freedom and that they do not want their young daughters or sons to act 'womanish' or 'mannish'. For example, an eight-year-old girl was scolded for being womanish because she wanted a particular hair style and decided what outfit she should wear. Her parents felt that it was her mother's right to decide, not hers. Some parents regret that they cannot scold their children as they would like to, since children are knowledgeable about Canadian abuse laws. This difference in Caribbean and Canadian parenting patterns accounts for some allegations of child abuse (Wills 1987). However, some parents have incorporated elements of their traditional Caribbean socialization patterns into the more liberal Canadian patterns. This syncretization has assisted them in providing their children with a more rounded upbringing.

Caribbean parents tend to direct their children and are protective of them much longer than Canadian parents (L. Bain, personal communication, 24 June 1993; James 1981; Mendoza 1990). For example, Caribbean parents do not approve of their children leaving home in their late teens. This delayed protection tends to delay the maturation process and results in intergenerational conflict.

Another source of conflict in some Caribbean families is the effect of their migration patterns. Parents, particularly single mothers and those from low-income groups, tend to leave their small children in the care of relatives when they emigrate. Sometimes it takes several years before the parents have the money to sponsor their children's entry into Canada. Years of separation tend to strain parent-child relations. Some children see their stepfather and siblings for the first time when they arrive. They are expected to simultaneously fulfill their parents' aspirations and expectations, adjust to their stepfather, siblings, and an unfamiliar child role, and adapt to the new society.

Undoubtedly, the circumstances under which some Caribbean families 'reunite' and the drastic social changes that the children experience result in psychological problems and intense family conflict. DaCosta (1976: 63–9) found that over 75 per cent of Caribbean students seen in therapy were depressed and that their depression stemmed largely from the migration pattern of their families. Most of the children in his study had been separated from the parent or parents and had rejoined them up to twelve years later; in many cases they came into new family constellations. Some of the problems involved the children's distorted perception of their place among their siblings and in the family; fear of stepparents, particularly stepfathers; and parental shame when their newly arrived children failed to establish an immediate and harmonious relationship with them. In addition to the negative effect of migration patterns on parent-child relationships, there may also be stresses on the marriage.

Conclusion

This study of the interconnected effects of race, class, and gender on black families in Canada supports the view that blacks' subordinate position in economic, political, and ideological relations has an impact on black families. Though working-class blacks are less likely to be married than their Canadian counterparts, middle-class black family structure is similar to that of the Canadian population. Similarly, while there are proportionately more black female lone-parent families than in the general Canadian population, contrary to the popular stereotype, blacks are less likely to live in common-law relationships then other young Canadians. The high rate of teenage pregnancy and the feminization of poverty among blacks, particularly in Nova Scotia, deserve serious attention by the state and the black community, including programs in education and employment equity and sex education, and parenting sessions. The black community must also address sexism and male-female relationships, strengthen black families, and continue to struggle for justice and equity.

Notes

The author would like to thank the men and women whom she interviewed, five anonymous reviewers, and Akua Benjamin for their helpful comments. Funding from the Centre for Regional Studies and the University Council for Research, St Francis Xavier University is gratefully acknowledged.

1. Schools were officially desegregated in 1954. However, in Nova Scotia segregated schools continued to exist in isolated black communities.

2. The comparable unemployment rates for all Nova Scotians from Statistics Canada's Labour Force Survey ranged from a high of 27 per cent for those aged twenty to twenty-four to a low of 10.7 per cent for those aged forty-five to fifty-four (BLAC 1994: 85).

3. During the American War of Independence, the British offered freedom, security, and self-sufficiency through land acquisitions and provisions to rebel-owned slaves who joined the British army (Winks 1971; Walker 1976a).

4. The transcript for S. Jones's (1971) interview is in the Black Historical and Educational Research Organization collection, Black Educators Association, Halifax.

5. Research (Calliste 1991; Simmons and Turner 1991; Christensen and Weinfeld 1993) indicates that black women in Canada experience a sex-ratio imbalance largely as a result of Canada's immigration policy of recruiting domestic workers and nurses from the Caribbean.

References

'A Woman Is Killed, Community Silent'. 1987. Editorial. *Our Lives* (July/September): 2.

Acting Director of Immigration. 1943. Letter to C. Smith, 10 August. Public Archives of Canada, RG 76, v. 557, file 816222.

Aldridge, D. 1991. *Focusing: Black Male-Female Relationships* (Chicago: Third World Press).

Anglican Christ Church, Guysborough. 1785–1879. *Records*. Guysborough Museum, Guysborough, NS.

BLAC. 1994. *BLAC Report on Education*, v. 3 (Halifax: BLAC).

Blackwell, J. 1991. *The Black Community* (New York: HarperCollins).

Bonacich, E. 1972. 'A Theory of Ethnic Antagonism: The Split Labour Market', *American Sociological Review* 37: 547–59.

———. 1976. 'Advanced Capitalism and Black/White Relations in the United States', *American Sociological Review* 41: 34–51.

Bryan, B., S. Dodzie, and S. Scafe. 1985. *The Heart of The Race* (London: Virago Press).

Calliste, A. 1987. 'Sleeping Car Porters in Canada', *Canadian Ethnic Studies* 20 (2): 1–20.

———. 1991. 'Canadian Immigration Policy and Domestics from the Caribbean', *Socialist Studies* 5: 136–68.

———. 1993–4. 'Race, Gender and Canadian Immigration Policy', *Journal of Canadian Studies* 28 (4): 131–48.

Canadian Mental Health Association. 1983. *Unemployment: Its Impact on Body and Soul* (Toronto: Canadian Mental Health Association).

Chambers, G. 1977. 'An Analysis of the Lower-Class West Indian Family Pattern in Toronto', Master's thesis, University of Windsor.

Christensen, C., and M. Weinfeld. 1993. 'The Black Family in Canada: A Preliminary Exploration of Family Patterns and Inequality', *Canadian Ethnic Studies* 24 (3): 26–44.

Clairmont, D., and D. Magill. 1970. *Nova Scotia Blacks* (Halifax: Institute of Public Affairs, Dalhousie University).

Clarke, A. 1975. *The Bigger Light* (Boston: Little, Brown).

Clarke, E. 1957. *My Mother Who Fathered Me* (London: George Allen and Unwin).

Coleman, Seth. 1815. *Assembly papers*, v. 22 (March). (Public Archives of Nova Scotia).

Collins, P. 1991. *Black Feminist Thought* (New York: Routledge).

Cutright, P., and H. Smith. 1988. 'Intermediate Determinants of Racial Differences in 1980 U.S. Nonmarital Fertility Rates', *Family Planning Perspectives* 20 (2): 119–23.

DaCosta, G. 1976. 'Counselling and the Black Child' in *Black Students in Urban Canada*, ed. V. D'Oyley (Toronto: Citizenship Branch, Ministry of Culture and Recreation).

Dei, G. 1994. 'Beware of False Dichotomies: Examining the Case for "Black Focused" Schools in Canada' (Toronto: Department of Sociology in Education, Ontario Institute for Studies in Education).

Deputy Minister of Citizenship. 1964. Memorandum, 10 Dec. Public Archives of Canada, RG 26, v. 124, file 3–33–6, part 2.

District Superintendent of Immigration, Winnipeg. 1943. Letter to C. Magrath, 4 Aug. Public Archives of Canada, RG 76, v. 475, file 731832.

Douglas, D. 1986. 'Danger At Home: One Woman's Voice', *Our Lives* (May/June): 3.

Edwards, R. 1979. *Contested Terrain* (New York: Basic Books).

Eichler, M. 1983. *Families in Canada* (Toronto: Gage).

Fergusson, C. 1948. *A Documentary Study of the Establishment of Negroes in Nova Scotia* (Halifax: Public Archives of Nova Scotia).

———. 1971. *Clarkson's Mission to America, 1791–1792* (Halifax: Public Archives of Nova Scotia).

Foster, H. 1983. 'African Patterns in the Afro-American Family', *Journal of Black Studies* 14 (Dec.): 201–32.

Godsal, C. 1911. Letter to C. Magrath (10 April). Public Archives of Canada, RG 76, v. 475, file 731832.

Goldberg, G., and E. Kremen, eds. 1990. *The Feminization of Poverty* (New York: Greenwood Press).

Gordon, D., R. Edwards, and M. Reich. 1982. *Segmented Work, Divided Workers* (London: Cambridge University Press).

Grant, J. 1990. *The Immigration and Settlement of the Black Refugees of the War of 1812 in Nova Scotia and New Brunswick* (Halifax: The Black Cultural Centre).

Gutman, H. 1977. *The Black Family in Slavery and Freedom, 1750–1925* (New York: Vintage).

Henry, F. 1994. *The Caribbean Diaspora in Toronto* (Toronto: University of Toronto Press).

Hill, R. 1971. *The Strengths of Black Families* (New York: Emerson Hall).

———. 1981. *Economic Policies and Black Progress* (Washington, DC: National Urban League Research Department).

James, C. 1981. *Working with Immigrant Adolescents. The Family: Interventive Strategies in a Multicultural Context* (Toronto: The Multicultural Workers Network).

Jones, R. 1993. 'The Conspiracy to Destroy the Black Community', address delivered at the Black Family Conference, Halifax, Aug. 28.

Kerber, L. 1988. 'Separate Spheres, Female Worlds, Woman's Place', *Journal of American History* 75 (1): 26.

Laosa, L. 1988. 'Ethnicity and Single Parenting in the United States' in *Impact of Divorce, Single Parenting and Stepparenting on Children*, eds M. Hetherington and J. Arasteh (Hillsdale, NJ: Erlbaum).

Li, P. 1988. *Ethnic Inequality in a Class Society* (Toronto: Wall and Thompson).

Luxton, M. 1983. 'Two Hands for the Clock', *Studies in Political Economy* 12: 27–44.

Mendoza, A. 1990. 'An Exploratory Study on the Socioeconomic, Cultural and Sociopsychological Experiences of Caribbean-Born Women in Ontario, Canada', Ph.D. diss., York University.

Morton, S. 1993. 'Separate Spheres in a Separate World', *Acadiensis* 22 (2): 61–83.

Moynihan, D. 1967. 'The Negro Family: The Case for National Action' in *The Moynihan Report and the Politics of Controversy*, eds L. Rainwater and W. Yancey (Cambridge, MA: MIT Press), 39–124.

Oliver, W.P. 1968. *The Negro in Nova Scotia, 1668 to 1967*. Public Archives of Nova Scotia, v. 42, document 111.

Peters, M. 1985. 'Racial Socialization of Young Black Children', in *Black Children*, eds H. McAdoo and J. McAdoo (Beverly Hills: Sage).

Piore, M. 1971. *The Dual Labor Market: Problems in Political Economy* (Lexington, MA: D.C. Heath).

Potter, H. 1949. 'The Occupational Adjustment of Montreal Negroes, 1941–48', Master's thesis, McGill University.

Public Archives of Nova Scotia. 1815. Assembly Papers, v. 22, March (Halifax).

Reitz, J., L. Calzavara, and D. Dasko. 1981. *Ethnic Inequality and Segregation in Jobs* (Toronto: Centre for Urban Community Studies, University of Toronto).

Richmond, A. 1989. *Caribbean Immigrants* (Ottawa: Statistics Canada).

Satzewich, V. 1991. *Racism and the Incorporation of Foreign Labour* (London: Routledge).

'Sexism in Our Community'. 1987. Editorial. *Our Lives* (March/April): 2.

Shadd, A. 1987. 'Dual Labour Markets in "Core" and "Periphery" Regions of Canada', *Canada Ethnic Studies* 19 (2): 91–109.

Shelburne Records. 1791. *General Sessions*. Public Archives of Nova Scotia.

Simmons, A., and J. Turner. 1991. 'Caribbean Immigration to Canada, 1967–1987' (Toronto: York University).

Smith, C. 1943. Letter to A. Joliffe. Public Archives of Canada. 7 Aug. Immigration Branch Records, RG 76, v. 577, file 816222.

Smith, R.T. 1988. *Kinship and Class in the West Indies: A Genealogical Study of Jamaica and Guyana* (Cambridge: Cambridge University Press).

Sudarkasa, N. 1981. 'Female Employment and Family Organization in West Africa' in *The Black Woman Cross-Culturally*, ed. F. Steady (Cambridge, MA: Schenkman).

Tyszko, L. 1959. 'Family Life and Family Stability of Negroes in Halifax', Diploma in Social Work thesis, Dalhousie University.

Walker, J. 1976a. *The Black Loyalists* (New York: Africana Publishing).

———. 1976b. 'The Establishment of a Free Black Community in Nova Scotia, 1783–1840' in *The African Diaspora*, eds M. Kilson and R. Rotberg (Cambridge: Harvard University Press).

———. 1980. *Blacks in Canada* (Hull, PQ: Minister of State for Multiculturalism).

Wells, J. 1986. 'Shelter Whitewash', *Our Lives* (November/December): 7.

Wills, D. 1987. 'Future of the Indigenous, Migrant and Immigrant Family', Mimeo (Montreal).

Wilson, E. 1976. *The Loyal Blacks* (New York: Putnam's Sons).

Winks, R. 1971. *Blacks in Canada* (Montreal: McGill-Queen's University Press).

Chapter 27

In this article, Guida Man summarizes what she has learned of the changes women from Hong Kong have experienced in their move to Canada. In explaining those changes, Man makes clear how profoundly family and gender relations are shaped by the orga- *nization of the communities in which people live. Far from 'liberating' women, Canada seems to have imposed constraints on these middle-class Asian women which may promote gender inequality in their families.*

From Hong Kong to Canada: Immigration and the Changing Family Lives of Middle-Class Women from Hong Kong

Guida Man

The Canadian government has historically adopted an approach characterized by pragmatism and economic self-interest in regard to immigration. Its immigration policies toward the Chinese have in the past been discriminatory in terms of race, gender, and class and continue to be partial to people from middle- and upper-class backgrounds. Hence, the entry of Chinese women and consequently the formation of Chinese families in Canada have been hampered by these restrictions.

The Canadian government's expansionist economic strategy toward immigration, and the way in which race, gender, and class operate as social relations, determine at any historical moment whether the Chinese are allowed into Canada and what category of Chinese are permitted. During the early periods of Chinese immigration, many racially discriminatory measures such as the head tax and the Chinese Exclusionary Act were imposed on the Chinese, but not on Western European immigrants (see Abella and Troper 1982; Baureiss 1987; Hawkins 1988; Li 1988). And although some Chinese labourers were admitted into Canada to work on the railroad and the mines, the Canadian government prohibited Chinese women from entering Canada.[1] This measure effectively reduced the reproductive activities of the Chinese, and hence the formation of Chinese families.

While the head tax was imposed from 1885 to 1923, to prohibit Chinese labourers and their wives from entering Canada, affluent Chinese merchants and their wives were permitted entrance and an exemption from the head tax during the period 1911 to 1923 (Sedgewick 1973: 129; Wickberg 1982: 94, Man 1998: 120).[2] These wealthy merchants were useful in procuring trade for Canada, and therefore were accorded preferential treatment vis à vis their poor counterparts. Even during the exclusionary period between 1923 and 1947, when no Chinese was officially admitted, special privileges were granted to an elite class of Chinese who would otherwise have been prevented from entering Canada due to their race.[3] But the number of women who belonged to the elite class was minuscule, hence the population of Chinese women in Canada remained very small.[4] Consequently, the number of Chinese families was low even as late as 1951.[5]

The pivotal shift occurred in 1967, when the Canadian government adopted a universal point system to select immigrants. The point system allowed the Chinese to be admitted under the same conditions as other groups (Hawkins 1988).

The new initiative supposedly eliminated the racial and gender discriminatory elements of the Immigration Act, but the class discriminatory measures remained. The 1967 point system (and its subsequent revisions in 1978 and 1985) inevitably privileges people from middle- and upper-class backgrounds who have the opportunity to acquire the 'appropriate' educational, vocational, and language skills required by the Canadian government.

The 1967 revision of the Canadian immigration policy, coinciding with riots in Hong Kong triggered by skirmishes on the Chinese border, resulted in a large influx of Chinese immigrants from Hong Kong. Many of the Chinese who were admitted were middle-class professionals such as physicians and engineers. They were highly educated, cosmopolitan, with professional or technical skills, and proficient in either French or English. Many of the Chinese women who came into Canada at the time were sponsored by their husbands and relatives. But the selection policy also attracted some middle-class Chinese women professionals who had the educational and occupational skills to come in as independent applicants. By 1971, 83 per cent of the Chinese in Canada were recorded as belonging to a census family household (Statistics Canada 1971).

The universal point system of the 1967 immigration policy emphasized the educational and vocational skills of the new immigrants. Consequently, the 1986 Census data gave a very positive picture of Chinese immigrant women's educational level (see Table 1) and their participation in the labour market (see Table 2), in comparison with their male counterparts and other Canadians. The data show that a higher percentage (12.8 per cent) of Chinese immigrant women ('foreign-born') have obtained a university degree than other immigrants, both female and male (7.9 per cent and 11.2 per cent respectively). However, fewer Chinese immigrant women than immigrant

Table 1: Level of Schooling for Foreign-born and Native-born Chinese Canadians and Other Canadians by Sex, 15 Years of Age and Over, 1986

Level of Schooling	% Chinese Canadians				% Other Canadians	
	Foreign-born		Native-born			
	Female	Male	Female	Male	Female	Male
Some High School or Less	50.4	38.8	26.7	30.8	45.5	43.1
Completed High School	11.6	10.0	15.0	10.0	14.3	11.3
Trade Certification or Diploma	0.6	0.9	0.5	0.8	2.1	4.2
Non-university without Diploma	5.3	6.0	7.4	6.2	7.0	6.6
Non-university with Trade or Diploma	9.2	9.4	17.2	9.5	14.5	14.6
Some University	10.1	12.7	13.9	22.1	8.7	9.0
University with Degree	12.8	22.2	19.3	20.6	7.9	11.2
TOTAL %	100	100	100	100	100	100
TOTAL SAMPLE	2,520	2,401	367	389	198,139	188,864

Source: Compiled from 1986 Public Use Microdata File on Individuals, a product of the 1986 Census of Canada. These data are based on a sample of 500,000 individuals, representing approximately 2 per cent of the population.

Table 2: Occupations by Foreign-born and Native-born Chinese Canadians and Other Canadians by Sex, 1986

| Occupations | % Chinese Canadians | | | | % Other Canadians | |
| | Foreign-born | | Native-born | | | |
	Female	Male	Female	Male	Female	Male
Managerial, Administrative, and Related	4.5	9.0	7.4	12.1	4.5	10.1
Professional and Technical	9.9	16.4	17.8	14.6	12.4	10.3
Clerical and Related	17.3	6.0	31.3	12.6	20.1	5.5
Sales	4.7	6.4	8.2	10.3	5.8	7.1
Transport: Equipment Operating	0.0	1.7	0.3	2.8	0.4	4.8
Processing, Machining, and Construction	2.3	15.4	1.3	6.9	4.1	22.7
Service	13.7	21.4	10.1	12.3	10.2	8.2
Farming and Other Primary	0.6	0.4	0.5	1.8	1.7	6.8
Other	2.2	3.7	1.1	4.1	1.5	5.6
Not applicable	34.8	19.6	22.0	22.5	39.3	18.9
TOTAL %	100	100	100	100	100	100
TOTAL SAMPLE	2,520	2,401	367	389	198,139	188,864

Source: Compiled from 1986 Public Use Microdata File on Individuals, a product of the 1986 Census of Canada. These data are based on a sample of 500,000 individuals, representing approximately 2 per cent of the population.

men and native-born women were able to enter the highly coveted managerial and professional occupations (14.4 per cent, as opposed to 25.4 per cent and 25.2 per cent respectively). At the same time, native-born Chinese Canadians are more likely to hold university degrees than other Canadians, both female and male (19.3 per cent and 20.6 per cent respectively), and also have higher participation rates in managerial and professional occupations (25.2 per cent and 26.7 per cent respectively).

In response to the transfer of government from British to Chinese sovereignty in Hong Kong in 1997, and the anticipated political, social, and economic uncertainty under Chinese rule, the 1980s saw a second wave of Chinese immigrants from Hong Kong to Canada. The Canadian media responded to the new immigrants by focusing on

the wealthiest of the business immigrants. They are dubbed 'Gucci Chinese' (Cannon 1989) or 'yacht people' (*Calgary Herald*, 14 Feb. 1988: D3) by the media—in contrast with their poor Vietnamese cousins, the 'boat people'. Hence, a particular image of the immigrants has been created: that of affluent businessmen, driving Mercedes-Benzes and living in monster homes (*Halifax Chronicle Herald*, 25 Jan. 1988: 15; *Vancouver Sun*, 26 May 1989: B4; *Maclean's*, 7 Feb. 1994: 30). In fact, this image typifies only a small minority, and is far from the actual 'lived experiences' of most Chinese immigrants, particularly Chinese immigrant women.

Although the media image of the Hong Kong Chinese immigrants does not include women, since 1987 the number of Chinese immigrant women from Hong Kong has exceeded that of their male counterparts. For example, in 1992, 20,102 females versus 18,829 males immigrated to Canada from Hong Kong, and in 1993 the numbers of females and males were 18,800 and 17,685 respectively (EIC 1992, 1993). Despite their numbers and their contributions, Chinese women's experiences have remained invisible. This is congruent with the fact that the study of women was not legitimized as a topic of discourse, and that women's perspective has largely been ignored in academic research until fairly recently (Eichler 1985). Moreover, women's labour has almost always been incorporated into the family, or into their husbands' work (Luxton 1980). Consequently, their experience is seen to be either subsumed under that of men (Jacobson 1979), or tied to that of their male counterparts, and therefore they are perceived as not having a separate reality.

Theoretical Framework and Methodology

More recently, feminist theorists have ruptured the silence of women's experience. Hence since the 1980s, we have seen the emergence of studies on immigrant women in general (see, for example, Ng and Estable 1987; Boyd 1990; Ng 1998; Thobani 1998; Lee 1999), and on Chinese women in particular (see, for example, Nipp 1983; Adilman 1984; Yee 1987). Nipp's and Adilman's studies shed light on the historical accounts of Chinese immigrant women in Canada, while May Yee and the Chinese Canadian National Council's (1992) book project illuminated Chinese women's lives by making space for Chinese women to voice their stories from their own perspectives. These studies have found Chinese women to be actors who toiled and laboured alongside their male counterparts, and who were involved actively in political and community organizing.

Research on immigrants has typically derived its theoretical perspectives from work centred around the concepts of 'adaptation' and 'adjust-ment'. Such analyses assume that the onus is on the individual immigrant to adjust. The immigrant's failure to assimilate is seen to be her or his own fault. Studies based on these theoretical perspectives often focus only on microstructural processes, (i.e., on the individual and the immediate family). Their analyses seldom go beyond the individual to investigate the interaction between her or him and the macrostructure, to look at how socially constructed opportunities and limitations rooted in institutional and organizational processes shape individual immigrants' lives. In my research, I have adopted a feminist methodology (Ng 1982; Hartsock 1983; Haraway 1985; Smith 1987; Hill-Collins 2000) which places women as 'subjects' of the study and takes into account both structural processes and individual negotiations. This methodology has enabled me to investigate how individual Chinese immigrant women as subjects account for their situations, and how their stories are as much their subjective experiences as they are shaped by objective structures in the form of organizational and institutional processes. Organizational and institutional processes are in fact interconnected. I have delineated them in order to obtain clarity in my exploration.

As mentioned previously, the Chinese come from diverse backgrounds and locations. I will focus on exploring the experiences of middle-class women in Chinese families that have recently immigrated from Hong Kong, and I will attempt to explain how their experiences in Canada have been transformed as a result of the difference in the social organization of the two societies. I have artificially categorized their experiences into topics: employment opportunities, housework and childcare, relationships with husbands and children, and social life. In actuality, people's everyday lives are not neatly delineated into categories. Human experiences and interactions with others occur in dialectical, rather than in linear relations. Events and feelings diverge and converge. Similarly, these categories overlap each other.

The Sample

The data for this study were generated through in-depth interviews with thirty recent middle-class Chinese immigrant women from Hong Kong. The women were all married, with at least one child. They had immigrated to Canada between 1986 and 1990. The majority of them (twenty-six out of thirty) came as dependants of their husbands. Five of them were living in Vancouver at the time of the interview, and the rest were living in Toronto. A snowball sampling method was used to locate the interviewees. In other words, friends and colleagues were asked to refer women with the requisite characteristics. Women who were interviewed were then asked to suggest other women for inclusion in the study.

Each interview lasted between one and a half hours to three hours. An interview schedule was used as a guideline. All questions were open-ended. Interviewees were encouraged to talk freely about their experiences in Canada and in Hong Kong. Most of the interviews were conducted in Cantonese (a Chinese dialect spoken by most people in Hong Kong), interspersed with some English phrases—a mode of speaking favoured by most 'Chyuppies'.[6] Two interviewees preferred using the English language, and the interviews were conducted in English interspersed with Chinese phrases.

Institutional Processes

Institutional processes here refer to those processes and practices that are embedded in government, law, education, and professional systems. Such processes can engender and perpetuate social injustice in our society. In the previous section, I described how the institutionalized discriminatory process and practice of the Canadian immigration policies regulated the entrance of Chinese women into Canada. In this section, I will show how their opportunities for employment were restricted by institutonalized processes.

EMPLOYMENT OPPORTUNITIES

Most of the women in this study came to Canada as dependants of their husbands who were the principal applicants under the 'Independant Class'[7] as 'business' or 'other independent' (professionals such as engineers, accountants, etc.) immigrants. These women therefore need not have high educational levels to score entry points. Due to their middle-class background, however, on the whole, their education is quite high. The majority have university degrees or postsecondary education. Their qualification is even higher than that of the average immigrant from Hong Kong. Despite the fact that these women were classified as 'dependants' by the immigration policy, and were therefore supposedly not destined for the labour market, many of these women had worked as professionals in Hong Kong. Although not all of these women actively sought employment when they first arrived, those who did were either underemployed or unemployed. Institutionalized practices in the form of the requirement of 'Canadian experience', and the lack of an accreditation system to calibrate their qualifications, have made it difficult for them to obtain employment commensurate with their qualifications. Consequently, some women found themselves economically dependent on their husbands for the first time in their lives. At the same time, immigrant men are subjugated to the same institutionalized discrimination.

The experiences of the husbands of these women were not unlike the experiences of other Chinese immigrants from Hong Kong. A study conducted in 1991 by the Alberta Career Development and Employment Policy and Research Division, the Hong Kong Institute of Personnel Management, and the Canadian Employment and Immigration Commission found that of 512 Hong Kong immigrants between the ages of thirty and thirty-nine who entered Canada after 1980, 23 per cent reported no change in income, 46 per cent recorded a drop, and 31 per cent reported a rise in income. The majority

(62 per cent) also experienced a drop in occupational status, 25 per cent experienced no change, and only 13 per cent had acquired a higher status (*Canada and Hong Kong Update* 1992: 7).

Another survey conducted in 1989, which focused specifically on Chinese immigrant women's needs in Richmond, B.C. (SUCCESS 1991), found that whereas 70 per cent of the women surveyed had worked prior to immigrating to Canada, fewer than 50 per cent were employed when surveyed. Of those who were employed, there was a significant degree of frustration and loss of self-esteem as a result of underemployment, low salaries, and limited opportunities for advancement. Nearly one-quarter of the respondents stated that their foreign education was not recognized in Canada. Over 46 per cent of these women had completed secondary education, and 41.2 per cent had postsecondary education which included college/university or professional training.

Chinese Canadians are concerned about the upsurge in racism. They feel that they are disadvantaged when it comes to getting jobs and being promoted—a 'glass ceiling' keeps them from advancing to management ranks. In a survey conducted for the Chinese Canadian National Council, 63 per cent of survey respondents from Chinese-Canadian organizations and 59 per cent from non–Chinese-Canadian social service organizations reported their belief that Chinese Canadians are being discriminated against (*Globe and Mail*, 26 April 1991: A7).

These findings concur with my interview data. One of the women I interviewed, who has a postgraduate degree, and has worked as a translator and teacher in Hong Kong, got so exasperated with her job search that she gave up the idea of entering the labour force altogether. She lamented,

> It's a catch-22. I cannot get a job because I don't have Canadian experience, and yet I don't see how I can possibly get Canadian experience without being hired in the first place!

Her frustration is echoed by other Chinese immigrant women.

A common strategy many immigrant women I interviewed adopted is what Warren (1986) terms a 'positive and pragmatic bridge' attitude toward their new positions. As one woman who worked as a Chief Executive Officer supervising over three hundred employees when she was in Hong Kong rationalized:

> In terms of my employment here when I first arrived, I couldn't work as a manager as I didn't have Canadian experience; I couldn't work as a secretary because I was told I was over-qualified. I was lucky to get a job with this company. They wanted to do business with Hong Kong. . . . That's why they hired me. They wanted someone to start the H.K. market. I was hired as an assistant. . . . They paid the B.Com. graduates $1,200 a month. They paid me $1,500 a month. So they really respected me. . . . Either you don't work for someone, but if you work for them, you have to do your best, doesn't matter what the pay is. I kept telling myself that they were paying me to learn. I was in a new country. I didn't have a choice. I was paving my way for the future.

These women are cognizant of the futility of hoping for changes in processes that are institutionalized and embedded in the social system. Since they could not transform the macrostructure, they therefore resolved to change their own attitude toward their situations.

Organizational Processes

Organizational processes refer to the differences in the way societies are organized. Immigrants are often judged by their ability to 'adjust' to the host society. What is neglected, however, is an investigation into the differences between the social organization of the society from which the immigrant has come and the one to which she or he has immigrated. By uncovering how the individual woman's experience is shaped by the larger socioeconomic structure, we can begin to understand the problems which seemingly dwell only on the micro level. The differences in the ways societies are organized determine the different ways people get their work done, conduct their lives, and relate to other people. In the following, I have attempted to demonstrate how Chinese immigrant women's everyday lives have been transformed because of the different organization of Hong Kong and Canadian societies.

RELATIONSHIPS WITH HUSBANDS AND CHILDREN

Being in a new country may change the relationships these women have with family members. The effects of their transformed relationships with husbands and family members vary depending on their labour-market participation and that of their husbands. Apart from the institutional processes that hamper immigrants' opportunities to enter the Canadian labour market, the differences between the social and organizational structures of Hong Kong and Canadian societies also contribute to new immigrants' unemployment and underemployment.

Under British colonial rule, Hong Kong adopted what economists consider a pure capitalist system. With an industrious workforce, this system created, on the one hand, a very low unemployment rate (around 3 per cent); on the other hand, it engendered a wide disparity between the rich and the poor, between professionals and low-level blue-collar workers. As well, unions have a relatively low profile, and workers enjoy few benefits. Although the Hong Kong economy has always been robust, the absence of a guaranteed minimum wage and the lack of an adequate social safety net (Cheng and Kwong 1992) makes life extremely difficult for the poor and the unemployed. For the middle-class citizens, however, the situation is promising. The low unemployment rate, coupled with the

brain drain due to emigration, allows professionals, whether men or women, to enjoy good salaries and excellent benefits.

In Canada, the situation is quite different. The relative strength of unions means that many workers, whether white or blue collar, are protected. The wage gap between blue-collar workers and mid-level professionals is relatively narrow. Compared to Hong Kong, the average low-level worker in Canada fares better. Workers generally enjoy fairly good employee benefits, and comparable wages. But while there is a guaranteed minimum wage, the high cost of living has kept some people on welfare. And while the government strives to provide a social safety net for its citizens, the unemployment rate has remained high (hovering around 10 per cent). The continuing economic recession further exacerbates the situation. Competition for jobs is keen, and employers can be discriminatory about whom they hire. This does not provide an ideal situation for a new immigrant looking for work.

The changes these couples experience in their economic situation either improve or worsen their relationships. Some middle-class immigrant women professionals, who became unemployed or underemployed as a result of immigration, have found themselves economically dependent on their husbands for the first time in their lives. Such dependency has put some Chinese women in relatively powerless relationships with their husbands. Other women, however, have more positive experiences. They have found that their relationships with their husbands have improved because of their husbands' diminished career demands in Canada, which allows more time with their spouses. Their husbands have become underemployed or have reduced their business activities because of the lack of business connections and opportunities in a country with a less favourable economic environment. These women reported greater intimacy with their husbands. Spouses were drawn closer to each other by their common struggle to overcome obstacles in the new country, and to comfort each other when they were overwhelmed by feelings of isolation and alienation. As one woman whose husband used to be part owner of a manufacturing business in Hong Kong told me:

> My relationship with my husband has improved since we've emigrated. We are now much closer to each other. . . . In Hong Kong, my husband needed to entertain his clients, so he was out in the evenings a lot. He also used to travel back and forth to China quite often. So, even though we were living together, we led separate lives. Here, we only have a small business. He doesn't need to entertain any clients. Also he doesn't know that many business contacts, so he's home every evening. And because we are still struggling with the new business, I now help out in the store quite a bit, so we are together a lot. I'm really enjoying this togetherness. It's brought a new dimension to our marriage. We've discovered a renewed intimacy in our relationship. Now that we are together a lot, he really appreciates my help. He consults everything he does with me, something which he had never done when we were in Hong Kong. He used to consult with his mother, but not with me. They have a very close relationship, you see.

There were others, however, who found the isolation of being new immigrants and the stress of unemployment heightened their incompatibility and lack of communication, leading to marriage breakdown. One of the women I interviewed complained about her situation:

> My husband has been unemployed for over a year now. He had a very good position as an administrator with lots of benefits when he was in Hong Kong. The first year we were here, he found a job as a clerk. He was get-ting less than half of what he was making before. . . . But then the company went bankrupt, and he was unemployed. He's so depressed now that he is making me down too. He also kept blaming me for making him come here. We've had a lot of fights, and I'm not sure what will happen next. We talked about separating. I'm just living day-to-day at the moment.

Some of the husbands of the interviewed women who were either unable to complete the transfer of their businesses from Hong Kong to Toronto in time for their departure, or were afraid of relinquishing all their business contacts in Hong Kong, ended up spending half of the year in Hong Kong and away from their families in Toronto. These men are known among the Hong Kong immigrants as 'astronauts'.[8] This phenomenon also occurs among other immigrants who are reluctant to forgo their high-status, lucrative professional jobs in Hong Kong to face possible unemployment in Canada.[9] This long-distance arrangement has varying consequences for the wives. One astronaut's wife lamented the burden and the loneliness of maintaining the household on her own. She confided, 'I can't wait for the time when my husband can stop travelling back and forth. I'm tired of being here alone with the kids.' Her dissatisfaction is like that of women in the same situation in another study who expressed considerable worries stemming from their husbands' absence (SUCCESS 1991).

Another astronaut's wife in my study, in contrast, marvelled at her newfound independence, and attributed her heightened communication with her husband to his frequent absences. Interestingly, her positive reaction was similar to the findings of studies on dual-career commuting couples, which showed that some couples' relationships improved because of their time apart (Gerstel 1984; Man 1991, 1995). Here is what she told me:

The first year when he [the husband] was still spending a lot of time in Hong Kong, he used to call me long distance all the time. We also wrote love letters to each other regularly. We were missing each other very much. We hadn't been that close together since we were married. And every time he came back to visit, it is like reliving our honeymoon again. It was really the sweetest year we have had for a long time.

One women reported that she had been having problems with her two teenage children since they immigrated to Canada. What appear at first to be this family's adjustment problems due to immigration in fact have a concrete, material base. As this women confided to me:

Mothering is of course a lot easier in Hong Kong than here. There, the kids can be a lot more independent. My kids usually just hop on a cab right after school, and go to their respective tennis or music lessons. Afterwards, they just hop on a cab to go home. By the way, cabs are really cheap in Hong Kong. Also, Hong Kong is such a small place, you can go to any place within half an hour. I never had to worry about my children's transportation. The situation here is very different. It is too expensive for my kids to take cabs everyday, and the public transportation in my area is not very good. I have to dovetail my work schedule with that of my children.

This woman now works late every night, so she can go straight after work to pick up her teenage son from his extracurricular activities. By the time she gets home, finishes making dinner, and cleans up, she is usually so exhausted that she just goes straight to bed. Her relationship with her children has become strained. Her son resents his loss of independence because he now has to wait for his mother to pick him up; and her daughter is annoyed that her mother cannot

spend quality time with her. It is clear that what seem to be this women's private, personal problems with her children in fact originate from external factors. The differences in social organization in Canada and the home country, such as the size of the city, the transportation system, and the high cost of living, have tremendous impact on the individual woman, affecting her everyday life, and the relationships of family members.

HOUSEWORK AND CHILDCARE

In advanced capitalist societies such as Canada and Hong Kong, housework and childcare are privatized. Rather than acknowledging childcare as a public issue and allocating funds to establish childcare facilities, these governments have shifted the responsiblity onto private households—that is, onto women (see Arat-Koc, Chapter 23 this text). Despite the fact that economic demands have pushed many married women into the labour market, the unequal division of labour in the home has relegated women to primary responsibility for housework and childcare.

Feminist debates have located the family as the site of oppression for women, creating for housewives 'the problem with no name' (Friedan 1963); and housework as 'more than a labour of love' (Luxton 1980). Feminist research has also focused on the interconnectedness of housework and paid work (Connelly 1978; Armstrong and Armstrong 1984; Luxton and Reiter 1997; Man 1997; Hill-Collins 2000), and on how women must negotiate the conflicting demands of paid work and family responsibilities (Duffy, Mandell, and Pupo 1989).

Many upper-class women, and increasingly some middle-class women, try to 'resolve' the demands and pressures of juggling paid work, housework and childcare by employing paid domestic help. Such a solution, however, inevitably creates a division among women along class lines, and threatens to undermine the collectivism within the feminist movement.

Although the gendered division of household labour is in some ways similar in Hong Kong and

Canada, the differences in family structures and the social organization of these societies transform the situation of Chinese immigrant women, making their day-to-day living vastly different in Canada than in Hong Kong.

While the nuclear-family structure is prevalent in Hong Kong, many Chinese families (whether in Canada, Hong Kong, or elsewhere) retain vestiges of the extended-family form.[10] In such cases, three generations typically reside in the same residence. This extended-family arrangement is as much an adherence to the Confucian ideal (which stresses one's duty to care for the old), as a pragmatic arrangement in response to the high cost of housing and the shortage of state-subsidized homes for the aged. Very often, the arrangement is mutually beneficial for all parties. The grandparent (typically the grandmother) or the unmarried aunt is provided for; in return, they are able to help with housework and childcare. In cases where families adopt the nuclear-family structure, the small geographical area of the colony enables relatives to live in close proximity to each other, and thus promotes the development of close-knit support networks.

Regardless of whether the household in Hong Kong consists of a nuclear family or extended family (i.e., whether members of the extended family live together under one roof), the organization of the society enables members of the extended family to interact regularly and to lend support to each other if they so wish. The definition of family advocated by Fox and Luxton (Chapter 3 this text) urges ignoring household and focusing on personal support networks. It is evident that for Hong Kong Chinese families, who is in the household is less important than who interacts and helps each other to meet the needs of family members (see also Eichler 1988: 8–18). As one woman described her situation in Hong Kong:

> When we were in Hong Kong, my mother-in-law used to live with us. She did the cooking and the cleaning. She also picked up my oldest son after school so I didn't have to rush home right after work. My mother, on the other hand, lives close to my youngest son's school, so she used to pick him up after school and looked after him until I got to her place to pick him up after work. That's why my oldest son is very close to his maj-maj (paternal grandmother), and my youngest one is attached to his paw-paw (maternal grandmother)! You see, I had a lot of support in Hong Kong. Here, I have to do everything myself.

Beyond assistance in housework and childcare from members of the extended family, the class privilege of these middle-class Chinese women permitted some of them the luxury of hired help when they were in Hong Kong. This support system enabled them to pursue their career interests and allowed them free time for recreational or creative activities. Many of these women have taken this support system for granted.

Transplanted to Toronto, these women experience, first, a loss of support from the extended family (since many older parents are reluctant or unable to emigrate); and second, a decrease in their earning power due to the women's under-employment or unemployment, making it no longer economically feasible for them to have hired help. The extra burden of domestic labour is almost always assumed by the woman as her sole responsibility. Those women who tried to cope with a dual workload of housework and paid work often felt exhausted at the end of the day. Their predicaments are echoed by Chinese immigrant women in another study who described problems in childcare, household maintenance, and transportation (SUCCESS 1991). One woman described to me her typical day:

> I usually get up at seven, prepare breakfast for my kids and my husband, then take the TTC to go to work. It takes me at least one hour to get to work by public transit. We're a one car family. I don't usually get to drive the

car except when my husband is not around. Depending on where I work, I don't usually get home until six-thirty or seven, make dinner, clean up, and if I'm lucky, I get to watch a bit of television before going to bed. But usually, I need to do the ironing, washing, and mending, etc. I really don't have time to do much else. My husband and kids, though, they watch a lot of television.

A few women managed to recreate in Canada the support system they had in Hong Kong. Unlike other women, these women did not experience a drastic change in household duties, and were therefore able to maintain the balance of work and family responsibilities. Lily, whose parents had immigrated to Canada a few years prior, described how she maintained this mutually supportive network with her parents:[11]

When I came here in 1987, I told my parents that I've brought money with me to buy a house. But I promised them that we'll live close by. . . . So we bought a house very close to theirs, so close that my younger daughter could go there after school. And we now eat dinner at my parents' place every night. . . . It's not only because of the fact that I don't know how to cook, but my mother felt that since my husband and I had to work, it would be better that we eat at their place. She told me that it's the same cooking for two people as cooking for six. At least this way, we get to see them every day. If we weren't eating there, I don't think we'd be driving there to see them every day. Also, because my younger daughter's school is very close to my parents' house, it's very convenient for my daughter as well. . . . So this is how my parents help us out. My mother cooks for us Monday to Friday, and on the weekends, I take them out for dinners. This way, my mother gets to have the weekends off. So, we take care of each other. . . . Also, it gives my

mother something to look forward to every night when we go over there.

While in Hong Kong, many of these middle-class women did not actually engage in the physical labour of doing housework (cooking and cleaning), but rather the management of it. But since they clearly identified the management and control of the household as domestic labour, and as such an important task, they were proud to define themselves as capable housewives, in addition to being successful career women. For these women, power lies very much in the management and control of every aspect of family life. Nor is this image contradictory to their commitment to participation in the labour market in Hong Kong. These women were able to juggle the dual or triple workload of housework, paid work, and childcare because of the household support system they had when they were in Hong Kong. There, many Chinese husbands took for granted that their wives would share the breadwinner role, as well as managing the household. Domestic harmony was maintained even though wives went out to work, because the husbands' daily substance was provided. Dinner still appeared on the table on time (although not prepared by the wife); shirts and pants were washed and ironed, ready to be worn the next morning (compliments of the mother or the hired help); and household maintenance chores were taken care of (by the hired workman). All this, however, did require skillful management by the wives. Husbands were relieved of virtually all of these tasks when they were in Hong Kong.

When asked whether her husband shared the housework in Canada or not, one of my interviewees laughed,

No way! He had never lifted a finger all his life. Before we got married, he used to live at home, and his mother did everything for him. I would never dream of asking him to help me with housework. Besides, Chinese women don't do that. To ask your husband to help you with housework is to admit that you are incapable of being a good wife! It is a loss of face on the woman's part!

Since many of the husbands had never done housework before, they did not offer to help their wives after they immigrated to Canada. Nor do these women seek their help. As one woman explained:

> I feel that if I can manage it myself, I wouldn't ask. Furthermore, if my husband really wants to do it, he can offer to help. But he hasn't! As for my children, I would rather they spend their time studying or having fun. I don't really want them to waste their time on housework.

Some women, however, did get help from other family members, particularly with cleaning and grocery shopping:

> There's a lot of work. Fortunately, my husband and sons do help me with vacuuming. They also do the yard work and cut the grass. Grocery shopping is very convenient here. There are also many Chinese supermarkets close to where we live. My husband loves to go grocery shopping. Usually, we just pick up some grocery on our way home from work. We shop several times a week because it's so convenient.

For some women, galvanizing the help of family members, with lots of planning and organization, were the keys to 'getting things done' in Canada:

> First of all, domestically, I have a lot of help. But I also have to be organized. My daughters are now older, so it's not like they would dirty up the walls, etc. Also being daughters they are much tidier than boys. I plan my schedule carefully. We only do laundry once

a week. Every Friday night, we do the laundry. We also take turns ironing, me and my daughters usually. Sometimes my husband would offer to help. . . . Actually, there aren't too many things we buy that need ironing. I do everything the easy way; e.g., in terms of flowers, I buy pots of cactus. I change them only once every one or two months. . . . Also, there's not much dust here, so we only dust once a month. Once in a blue moon, we'll do a spring cleaning. Vacuum cleaning is my husband's responsibility. So is changing light bulbs, fixing the water faucet, gardening. He really enjoys gardening. We call him 'the gardener'.

Although cheaper housing costs allowed families to have bigger residences in Canada, these increase the amount of housework for women. Here is a comment from an interviewee:

> There seems to be more housework here. One reason could be that our house here is more than twice as big as our apartment in Hong Kong, so there's a lot more space to clean. As well, in Hong Kong, people usually have parquet floors, or tiled floors. Here, we have carpeting, which needs vacuuming more often.

In regard to doing other, more 'male-oriented' types of housework, Mabel revealed her and her husband's ignorance about this kind of work:

> Oh, he (husband) had never even used a hammer . . . and I'm definitely not handy myself either. I don't know how to fix a lock, or even to put up a nail. Most Canadians know how to do these things, but I never had to do it, so I didn't know how to do it at all. In the winter, I didn't know that I had to put caulking on my window. All these are little things, but they all add up. . . . In Hong Kong, services are so easily available people never think of doing anything themselves.

You call up a handyman even just to put up a picture, or screw on a light bulb. It sounds ridiculous, but that's the reality there.

Both Mabel and her husband are highly educated professionals. They are capable and motivated people. However, they felt totally inadequate when they first came to Canada because they were not able to do small household maintenance chores like 'other Canadians'. This is due to the fact that the way in which the labour market is organized in Hong Kong is quite different from Canada. Until 1980, because of a constant flow of legal and illegal immigrants from China (Wong 1992), there had been a stable supply of cheap labour in Hong Kong, and services were relatively inexpensive. This in turn alleviates maintenance chores in middle-class households where both spouses participate full-time in the paid labour force. In Canada, because of the high cost of services, people are compelled to learn to do many household maintenance chores out of necessity.

In cases where the children are young, or when they participate in extracurricular activities which require the wife to chauffeur them back and forth, the women carry a triple burden of paid work, housework, and childcare. The way in which a society organizes its childcare facilities can have a tremendous impact on women who work full-time for pay. Kathy, a social worker, voiced her criticism of the inadequacy of daycare in Canada:

> I have a five year old and a two year old. I'm finding that daycare is a serious problem. Daycare is not flexible enough to accommodate working parents. Their hours of operation doesn't fill our gaps. We have to choose between quality or service. Sure, there are a few daycare centres now which run from 7 a.m. to 6 p.m. They are all privately run. They offer the service, but not necessarily the quality. So sometimes you don't want to put your child at risk. I have to choose very care-

fully. I have now found a very good quality daycare, and I can trust them very much . . . they have a lot of educational activities, lots of good materials which enable my children to learn a lot. On the other hand, they don't provide the service—i.e., their hours of operation are limited. So I have to juggle with my time to put my kids there. I am always dashing about like a mad woman. . . . I have no social life at all.

Most of the women I interviewed choose to live in areas within close proximity of friends and relatives, and which have easy access to Chinese grocery stores. However, the actual location of the houses is almost always determined by their children's schools and husbands' workplaces. Their own work location was not a determining factor in their initial decision. This can be attributed to the fact that children are considered the wives' responsibility. In order not to cause the women any more time loss in chauffeuring the children to and from school, it makes perfect good sense that homes be located close to schools.

Social Life

The immigrant women I interviewed have frequent interactions with other Hong Kong immigrants. Socializing with people who have common backgrounds and experiences creates for them a sense of continuity and is a stabilizing force in their new country (Warren 1986). Agnes, a secretary turned housewife, commented,

> I feel we have more in common with each other. We often get together and reminisce about our lives in Hong Kong. We also laugh about our ignorance of Canadian culture, and the little faux pas that we get ourselves into. Other times, we exchange information about schools, dentists, and other practical knowledge. Or we marvel at the high price we now pay for little things such as cooking wares and stockings. I have a feeling of solidarity when I

talk to these people. They understand where I'm coming from.

Some women, however, also have friends from different ethnic groups. Usually, these friends are neighbours or parents of their children's friends, and occasionally friends they have met at work. This is in contrast to their lives in Hong Kong, where most working women customarily socialize with their colleagues. As well, social life there is more spontaneous. As one woman puts it succinctly, 'We usually just get together after work for movies and dinners; it's never planned.'

Although it is common and economically feasible for most people to organize frequent dinner parties at restaurants in Hong Kong, the astronomical cost of dinner parties at restaurants in Canada forces many to have small dinner parties at home, and only occasionally. This kind of change is seen by some as having positive effects. One woman expressed it this way:

> Life is comparatively quieter here. On the other hand, I now feel closer to my few friends. Our conversation is more personal and more meaningful, whereas before, I was always with a big crowd, and the conversation was usually superficial.

Nevertheless, women who have to juggle paid work, housework, and childcare typically are too exhausted at the end of the day to have much social life (Bernardo, Shehan, and Leslie 1987; Duffy, Mandell, and Pupo 1989). A mother of two who has a demanding career explained:

> I don't have any time for social life at all. Even if someone invites me for dinner on the weekend, I find it tiring to go. I don't know how everybody else does it here. There's no time for social life here at all. I have a lot of friends here, but I never have time to see them.

In Hong Kong, her situation was quite different:

> I was a member of a pottery club, caligraphy club, and an alumni choir. Here, I don't have any extracurricular activities. I simply don't have the time or energy. It seems foolhardy to drive an hour to go to a class when I don't even have enough time to manage my household chores. On the other hand, I really need this kind of outlet. But I don't have the kind of time and energy.

It is clear that the differences in social organization between Hong Kong and Canada, in terms of the household support system and the size and spread of the city, transform this woman's everyday experience.

Conclusion

Many migration studies have previously assumed that migration involves moving from a less developed to a more developed country, and from a rural to an urban area. It is further assumed that the entry of female migrants into the host labour market will lead to a rejection of their traditional roles and subjugated positions. These studies argue that the economic independence migrant women acquire through their engagement in waged work will assure them a higher status and a more equitable position in the family. Hence, migration has the positive effect of engendering equality of the sexes, as well as generating beneficial changes in domestic relations (Schwartz-Seller 1981; Morokvasic 1981).

I found that these migration theories are not applicable to middle-class Chinese immigrant women. Many of these highly educated, urbanized women do not necessarily enjoy a 'liberating' or 'less oppressive' experience when they settle in Canada. Because of the differences in the social organization of Hong Kong and Canada, these women's daily experiences have been transformed. While in Hong Kong, many of these middle-class women had help with their housework and childcare from either members of the extended family such as mothers or mothers-in-law, or hired help. This kind of support system enabled the women to pursue their career interests, and allowed them free time for social life and recreational activities.

Transplanted to Canada, these middle-class women lost the support system they had in Hong Kong. The lack of a support system exacerbated the workload of these middle-class women, making their struggle to negotiate the conflicting demands of family and career even more difficult. Furthermore, the physical spread of Canadian cities, and the lack of transportation systems in suburbia—where most of the Hong Kong immigrants reside—heighten children's dependency on their mothers, intensifying women's workloads. Consequently, some of them experience an intensification of traditional roles, unequal distribution of household labour, and gender and sexual oppression in the home. This, compounded with institutionalized discrimination which renders their previous work experience obsolete and the absence of an adequate accreditation system, has subjected some of them to unemployment and underemployment. These states, in turn, force them to become economically dependent on their husbands, who are themselves subject to the same discrimination.

Although some of the women I interviewed experienced improved family relations with their husbands after immigration, there were others who suffered communication problems, and marriage breakdowns. For some women, their power and status inside and outside the home deteriorated after they emigrated to Canada. Moreover, those who had professional careers in their home country experienced a loss of economic power through unemployment or underemployment (although some of their husbands also experienced such losses). They also experienced diminished buying power, and a general lack of opportunity.

Notes

1. Adilman (1984) made reference to the discussions of the immigration of Chinese women found in the Debates of the House of Commons (1923, v. 3, pp. 2310, 2311, 2314, 2318, 2384, and 2385); and in the Debates of the Senate (1923, pp. 1121–4). It is evident from these debates that the central concern in regard to the immigration of Chinese women into Canada was the proliferation of the Chinese population in Canada. In prohibiting Chinese women from coming into Canada, the government intended to effectively prevent the Chinese from settling permanently in Canada.

2. According to Sedgewick (1973), Immigration Policy at the time 'allowed merchants and their families exemption from the head tax and freedom to move in and out of the country' (p. 136). However, the qualifications for 'merchant' status were not clearly defined. Hence, some labourers were able to immigrate in the guise of merchants.

3. According to Wickberg (1982: 141), the Chinese Immigration Act of 1923 contained the following provisions: abolition of the head tax; students below university age were no longer admitted; and only four groups of immigrants could enter Canada. All were categorized as temporary settlers. They were

   (i) university students

   (ii) merchants—(term was changed so as to exclude operators of laundries and restaurants, retail produce dealers, and the like). Merchant status was defined as 'one who devotes his undivided attention to mercantile pursuits, dealing exclusively in Chinese manufactures or produce or in exporting to China goods of Canadian produce or manufacture, who has been in such business for at least three years, and who has not less than $2,500 invested in it. It does not include any merchant's clerk, tailor, mechanic, huckster, peddler, drier or curer of fish, or anyone having any connection with a restaurant, laundry or rooming-house.'

(iii) diplomatic personnel

(iv) native-borns returning from several years of education in China

4. For example, in 1911, the ratio of Chinese men to Chinese women in Canada was approximately 28:1; in 1921, it was 15:1; and in 1931, it was still 12:1. Even as late as 1951, the ratio was 3.7:1 (see Li 1988: 61, Table 4.2).

5. As late as 1941, there were 20,141 'separated' families in the Chinese community, whereby the husbands resided in Canada, while the wives remained in their home country. In the same year, there were only 1,177 'intact' Chinese families in Canada in which both the husbands and wives resided in Canada. By 1951, the situation only improved slightly, and the discrepancy still remained very high: 12,882 'separated' families versus 2,842 'intact' families (see Li 1988: 67, Table 4.4).

6. Chinese yuppies.

7. 'Independent Class' immigrants are immigrants that are selected on criteria which are tied to the economic needs of Canada. They include skilled workers, also known as 'other independents', and 'business immigrants', which include entrepreneurs, investors, and the self-employed (see Margaret Young, *Canada's Immigration Program*. Library of Parliament, Research Branch, July, 1992).

8. Some immigrants took advantage of an immigration clause (Immigration Part III, Chap. I–2, p.17, 24(2)) which allowed a permanent resident to be outside of Canada for one hundred and eighty-three days in any one twelve-month period without losing their permanent residency status, by continuing to conduct business between Hong Kong and Toronto. In fact, one husband I interviewed started his first year of immigration by conducting his business this way; and another husband was still commuting between Hong Kong and Toronto at the time of the interview.

9. For an in-depth study of the astronaut phenomenon, see Guida Man, 'The Astronaut Phenomenon: Examining Consequences of the Diaspora of the Hong Kong Chinese', in *Managing Change in Southeast Asia: Local Identities, Global Connections, Proceedings of the 21st Annual Conference of the Canadian Council for Southeast Asian Studies*, University of Alberta, 1995.

10. This, however, is not to be collapsed with the popularized stereotypical image of Chinese families being largely patriarchal extended families with several generations living under the same roof. Ho et al. (1991) has reported empirical evidence which shows that the average size of the Chinese households has always been small, even prior to industrialization. The average size ranged from less than six from AD 755 to approximately five for the first half of the twentieth century. This is as much because of economic reasons as to the social customs of the time. The majority of the Chinese were poor peasants who subsisted on meager means, and could not afford to support more than their immediate family members. Poverty and hunger governed the lives of these peasants. The idealistic Confucius conception of extended families were the entitlement of the few aristocratic gentry who numbered fewer than 10 per cent of the Chinese population.

11. The names mentioned here are pseudonyms, since the interviewees were assured anonymity. Most Chinese (especially the baby boomers and post-baby boomer generation) who were brought up in the British educational system in colonized Hong Kong find themselves adopting English names over and above their Chinese names. Many Chinese in Hong Kong use their English names at school, at work, and for everyday use, but kept their Chinese names for official documents. In Canada, most Chinese maintain the same practice.

References

Abella, I., and H. Troper. 1982. *None Is Too Many: Canada and the Jews of Europe* (Toronto: Lester & Orpen Dennys).

Adilman, T. 1984. 'Chinese Women and Work in British Columbia', BA thesis, University of Victoria, April.

Arat-Koc, S. 1990. 'Importing Housewives: Non-Citizen Domestic Workers and the Crisis of the Domestic Sphere in Canada' in *Through the Kitchen Window: The Politics of Home and Family*, eds M. Luxton, H. Rosenberg, and S. Arat-Koc (Toronto: Garamond Press).

Armstrong, P., and H. Armstrong. 1984. *The Double Ghetto: Canadian Women and Their Segregated Work* (Toronto: McClelland & Stewart).

Baureiss, G. 1987. 'Chinese Immigration, Chinese Stereotypes, and Chinese Labour', *Canadian Ethnic Studies* 19 (3): 15–34.

Bernardo, D.H., C.L. Shehan, and G.R. Leslie. 1987. 'A Resident of Tradition: Jobs, Careers and Spouses' Time in Housework', *Journal of Marriage and the Family* 49: 381–90.

Boyd, M. 1990. 'Immigrant Women: Language, Socioeconomic Inequalities and Policy Issues' in *Ethnic Demography: Canadian Immigrant Racial and Cultural Variations*, eds S. Halli, F. Trovata, and L. Driedger (Ottawa: Carleton University Press).

Canada and Hong Kong Update. 1992. No. 7 (Summer).

Cannon, M. 1989. *China Tide* (Toronto: Harper & Collins).

Cheng, J.Y.S., and P.C.K. Kwong, eds. 1992. *The Other Hong Kong Report* (Hong Kong: The Chinese University Press).

Chinese Canadian National Council (CCNC). 1992. The Women's Book Committee. *Jin Guo: Voices of Chinese Canadian Women* (Toronto: The Women's Press).

Connelly, P. 1978. *Last Hired, First Fired: Women and the Canadian Work Force* (Toronto: The Women's Press).

Duffy, A., N. Mandell, and N. Pupo. 1989. *Few Choices: Women, Work and Family* (Toronto: Garamond Press).

Eichler, M. 1985. *On the Treatment of the Sexes in Research* (Ottawa: Social Sciences and Humanities Research Council of Canada).

———. 1988. *Families in Canada Today: Recent Changes and Their Policy Consequences* (Toronto: Gage).

Employment and Immigration Commissions (EIC). 1985. Immigration Act.

———. 1992, 1993. Immigration Statistics. Quarterly Statistics.

Estable, A. 1986. *Immigrant Women in Canada: Current Issues.* (Ottawa: Canadian Advisory Council on the Status of Women).

Finch, J. 1983. *Married to the Job: Wives' Incorporion in Men's Work* (London: George Allen & Unwin).

Friedan, B. 1963. *The Feminine Mystique* (New York: Dell Books).

Gerstel, N. 1984. 'Commuter Marriage', Ph.D. diss., Columbia University.

Haraway, D. 1985. 'A Manifesto for Cyborgs: Science, Technology, and Socialist Feminism in the 1980's', *Socialist Review* 80.

Harding, S. 1986. *The Science Question in Feminism* (Ithaca: Cornell University Press).

Hartsock, N. 1983. 'The Feminist Standport: Developing the Ground for a Specifically Feminist Historical Materialism' in *Discovering Reality*, eds S. Harding and M.B. Hintikka (Boston: D. Reidel), 293–310.

Hawkins, F. 1988. *Canada and Immigration: Public Policy and Public Concern*, 2nd edn (Kingston and Montreal: McGill-Queen's University Press).

Hill-Collins, P. 2000. *Black Feminist Thought* (New York: Routledge).

Ho, Lok-sang et al. 1991. *International Labour Migration: The Case of Hong Kong* (Hong Kong: Hong Kong Institute of Asia-Pacific Studies, The Chinese University of Hong Kong).

hooks, b. 1984. *Feminist Theory: From Margin to Center* (Boston: South End Press).

Jacobson, H. 1979. 'Immigrant Women and The Community: A Perspective for Research', *Resources for Feminist Research* 8 (3) (Nov.): 17–21.

Kanter, R. 1977. *Men and Women of the Corporation* (New York: Basic Books).

Lee, J. 1999. 'Immigrant Women Workers in the Immigrant Settlement Sector', *Canadian Women Studies*, 19 (3).

Li, P.S. 1988. *The Chinese in Canada* (Toronto: Oxford University Press).

Luxton, M. 1980. *More Than A Labour of Love: Three Generations of Women's Work in the Home* (Toronto: Women's Educational Press).

———. 1990. 'Two Hands for the Clock: Changing Patterns in the Gendered Division of Labour in the Home' in *Through the Kitchen Window: The Politics of Home and Family* (Toronto: Garamond Press), 39–55.

———, and E. Reiter. 1997. 'Double, Double, Toil and Trouble. . . , Women's Experience of Work and Family in Canada 1980–1995' in *Women and the Canadian Welfare State: Challenges and Change*, eds P.M. Evans and G.K. Werkele (Toronto: University of Toronto Press).

Man, G. 1991. 'Commuter Families in Canada: A Research Report', report presented to the Demographic Review Secretariat, Health and Welfare Canada, September.

———. 1995. 'The Astronaut Phenomenon: Examining Consequences of the Diaspora of the Hong Kong Chinese' in *Managing Change in Southeast Asia: Local Identities, Global Connections* (Edmonton: University of Alberta), 269–81.

———. 1997. 'Women's Work Is Never Done: Social Organization of Work and the Experience of Women in Middle-Class Hong Kong Chinese Immigrant Families in Canada' in *Advances in Gender Research* v. 2 (Greenwich: JAI Press), 183–226.

———. 1998. 'Effects of Canadian Immigration Policies on Chinese Immigrant Women (1858–1986)' in *Asia-Pacific and Canada: Images and Perspectives* (Tokyo: The Japanese Association for Canadian Studies), 118–33.

Morokvasic, M. 1981. 'The Invisible Ones: A Double Role of Women in the Current European Migrations' in *Strangers in the World*, eds L. Eitinger and D. Schwarz (Bern, Stuggart, Vienna: Hans Huber).

Ng, R. 1982. 'Immigrant Housewives in Canada', *Atlantis* 8: 111–17.

———. 1993. 'Racism, Sexism, and Nation Building in Canada' in *Race, Identity and Representation in Education*, eds C. McCarthy and W. Crichlow (New York: Routledge).

———. 1998. 'Work Restructuring and Recognizing Third World Women: An Example from the Garment Industry in Toronto', *Canadian Women Studies* 18 (1): 21–5.

———, and A. Estable. 1987. 'Immigrant Women in the Labour Force: An Overview of Present Knowledge and Research Gaps', *RFR/DRF* 16 (1) (March).

Nipp, D. 1983. 'Canada Bound: An Exporatory Study of Pioneer Chinese Women in Western Canada', MA thesis, University of Toronto.

Schwartz-Seller, M. 1981. *Immigrant Women* (Philadelphia: Temple University Press).

Sedgewick, C.P. 1973. 'The Context of Economic Change Continuity in an Urban Overseas Chinese Community', Ph.D. diss., University of Victoria.

Smith, D. 1987. *The Everyday World as Problematic: A Feminist Sociology* (Toronto: University of Toronto Press).

Statistics Canada. 1971. Census of Canada.

———. 1986. Census of Canada, Public Use Sample Tape, Individual File.

SUCCESS, Women's Committee Research Group. 1991. Chinese Immigrant Women's Needs Survey in Richmond (Vancouver: SUCCESS).

Thobani, S. 1998. 'Nationalizing Citizens, Bordering Immigrant Women: Globalization and the Racialization of Women's Citizenship in Late 20th Century Canada', Ph.D. diss., Simon Fraser University.

Warren, C.E. 1986. *Vignettes of Life* (Calgary: Detselig Enterprises).

Wickberg, E., ed. 1982. *From China to Canada: A History of the Chinese Communities in Canada* (Toronto: McClelland & Stewart).

Wong, S.L. 1992. 'Emigration and Stability in Hong Kong', *Asian Survey* 32 (10) (Oct.).

Yee, M. 1987. 'Out of the Silence: Voices of Chinese Canadian Women', *RFR/DRF*, 16 (1) (March).

Young, M. 1992. 'Canada's Immigration Program', background paper, Library of Parliament, Research Branch, July (Ottawa: Supply and Services).

Part Six   **Families That Challenge Conventional Patterns**

Chapter 28

Largely in response to heterosexist assumptions, and questions raised in court (during custody battles) about children's well-being, considerable research has been carried out on lesbian and gay families—mostly by psychologists. With respect to psychological variables, researchers generally find no differences between lesbian and heterosexual mothers and their children in terms of how well they do in the years following divorce (the most researched topic) with respect to adjustment and functioning, and with respect to children's gender and sexual identity.

What follows is Fiona Nelson's study of thirty lesbian mothers—both donor-inseminated (DI) mothers and their partners, and 'blended' families (those that follow divorce)—done in 1991 in Alberta. As a sociologist, Nelson has different concerns than the psychologists. What she finds is that because they violate strong heterosexual norms about parenthood, lesbian mothers must negotiate everything as they create their families. And the results involve very interesting similarities with, and differences from, heterosexual families.

Lesbian Families

Fiona Nelson

There are characteristics that are unique to lesbian families, and there are issues that only lesbian (and probably sometimes gay male) families have to face. This chapter begins with an exploration of the process whereby lesbian couples come to identify themselves, and be identified by others, as 'families'. The discussion continues with an examination of what it is like to live in a lesbian family.

Becoming a Family

Each DI couple reported that the addition of a child changed how they perceived themselves. They were no longer a couple—they were a family. For Tina and her partner, this transition occurred almost immediately after the birth of the child:

> It was an instant sense of family. It was like before it had been Rose and me, and the baby was an unknown quantity. We had no idea what he was going to look like. We didn't know what the father looked like . . . [When the baby was born] it was just instant family. There was instant bonding.

Iris was among the women who echoed this sentiment:

> *Now* we're a family. We have, we're a family of five now instead of a family of four, including the [two] animals, of course. Now we're different. I mean Blaire's and my relationship isn't different. We still treat each other the same way, with the same respect, but now we have a little person around too who makes us a family.

Blaire described what was involved in the transition from couple to family:

> It's, um, it's not like something new that we don't know, but it *is* something new that we don't know. I mean we're learning all the time how we have to change how we relate to each other, how we have to know that not only do we just talk about caring for Steven—what did he have for lunch today, you know, what we're doing for each other, what we're doing for ourselves, and how we

can't do what we used to do as much, or not at all, um, our expectations for each other, our changing and need to change and being able to give up things that we could do before willingly and, I don't know, regretfully, to mourn them for a minute and then say, 'Okay, we can't do them any more, but it doesn't mean we won't be doing them again.' You know, Iris's new favourite word is 'family'. She comes in the door and it's 'hello, family'. You know, it's changed everything, you know, and, we don't resist the change too much, but we can't predict it and so we sort of learn it as it comes along.

Although most of the women experienced an 'instant bond' with the baby, the transition to 'family' was not always so immediate. Elly described the process she and Nancy went through:

I don't think it [having the baby] did [immediately transform us into a family], although I wanted it to and it has now. I think it took a long time for that to take, and I think that's because we struggled with a lot of issues surrounding whose baby is it, you know. . . . Like just all that stuff [ideas about what a 'real' family is] came and it's all there and it's internalized within us and so it, I mean we wanted it to be, and in my head, I mean it was partly that way. It was partly a family, but I don't think it was at the beginning. I think it is now. I really feel like we're a family now. We're definitely not a couple, and that's from sharing the responsibilities of having a child for a year and a half has made us into a family, but I don't think we automatically were.

Feeling like a family is one thing—being perceived as such is sometimes quite another. As Elly's experiences demonstrate, people's reluctance or inability to acknowledge a lesbian couple and their children as a family can make it difficult for the couple to see themselves as one. For friends, family, and acquaintances who have not accepted that the couple are unequivocally a couple (which can be seen as a type of family itself), it can be difficult to acknowledge that the 'couple' are now a childed family. The biological mother's parents are often able and willing to accept the child as their grandchild, but they sometimes hesitate to acknowledge that the partner has any relationship to them, their daughter, or their grandchild. Many women found that their close friends and members of the lesbian community were most likely to acknowledge their family status. Blaire described how perceptions varied depending on the source:

Well, in the [lesbian] community definitely we're perceived as a family. Iris's family perceives us as a family. My family is learning how to perceive us as a family. You know, just because we're lesbians they have some difficulty. They can't see us as a heterosexual family, so there's some resistance. . . . Anybody who knows us as a family treats us as a family.

As we shall see later, many of the challenges lesbian families face can be traced to the lack of social acknowledgment that they are families.

The process of becoming families and coming to perceive themselves as such was different for the blended families in that the biological mothers tended to feel that they and their children already constituted families. Thus the transition was generally not that of *becoming* a family—it was *changing* from one kind of family to another. Like the DI families, the blended families found that a lesbian family was not widely acknowledged or supported except by close friends and sometimes by family members. However, some women did find that people's perceptions changed. Laura, the biological mother in a blended family, described how perceptions of her personal status changed once she regained custody of her children:

Actually, when I was just with a partner, people saw me as single. Even those members of my family who I was most out with and who were most comfortable would tend to see me as a single person . . . and I probably saw myself that way anyhow. But with kids, yeah, I'm a family, we're a unit . . . and I'm not single. But my guess is my family would see me as a single person with a lover if it weren't for the kids. They do tend to view us as a family unit with the kids.

Many of the stepmothers in blended families faced the same problem outside the home that they did inside: they were not acknowledged as mothers. If people (including the biological mother) are unwilling to give the stepmother a parental role or label, it is difficult for them to see the group as a family; instead, they see a mother, her children, and her lover. This tendency became even more evident when I asked the respondents to identify the people that they believed constituted their families. Women in blended families sometimes said that their families consisted of their partners and their own biological children. Ellis was among the stepmothers who excluded their partner's children from their conception of the family unit:

I would see Nanette and my kids as being my family. And at this point I don't include her kids in that. That actually is a real area of tension for us, um, I find her kids really difficult to deal with.

This was not always the case, however, and some stepmothers—always ones with no biological children of their own—found it much easier to feel that their partners' children were family to them.

Some of the women in blended families made a conscious effort not to label themselves as a 'family'. Nanette explained that she, her children, Ellis, and Ellis's daughter actually composed three families. She and Ellis were one family, she and her children the second, and Ellis and Ellis's daughter were the third. She explained how this arrangement was to everyone's advantage.

We don't presume that we are a family. And I think that has created a closer, ah, an opportunity for closeness that would not have been there if I had just assumed that we were a family and dammit behave like one! Because it gives choice. You know there's always a choice. She can choose to share with me or she can choose not to, and there's no hurt feelings, you know, there's no assumption. And vice versa.

In contrast, the DI mothers, whether biological or non-biological, always included their partners and their children in their conception of 'family'.

Another unique aspect of lesbian family life was revealed when I asked the respondents to identify the members of their extended families. Almost all the women in both the DI and blended families said that their friends were their extended family. Although consanguineous family members such as parents or (more frequently) siblings were sometimes included, they were almost always secondary. For most women, the primary and most actively involved extended families were composed of friends, both homosexual and heterosexual.

Support Networks

Although emotional and material support was generally more forthcoming from friends than from relatives, it should be noted that many of the women in the sample lived some distance from their parents and siblings. Very few had relatives in Alberta. (This is not merely a coincidence; often the friction between lesbian women and their families is an impetus for the former to move away.) Some women did believe, however, that their parents and siblings would be more involved in their newly formed families if they were geographically closer.

The parents of the biological mothers often considered themselves grandparents and more or less behaved as such, by providing emotional and material support. It was not uncommon, for example, for the biological mother's parents to purchase the crib or clothing for the baby. Very often the grandparents restricted their interest to their grandchild, largely ignoring their daughter's other 'family'.

Some grandparents were discomforted less by the fact that their daughter was part of a lesbian couple than by the fact that the child would be 'illegitimate'. The parents of both biological and non-biological mothers expressed this concern.

Sometimes the stigma of having an 'illegitimate' grandchild put even more emotional distance between the woman and her parents. This was especially true for the biological mothers. Yet the reverse was sometimes true for the parents of the non-biological mothers. Because it was not *their* illegitimate grandchild, they were more likely to be involved with him or her than had their own daughter given birth to it. Tina described her father's attitude towards her non-biological son, Tim:

> My sister once said that she was jealous and hurt because my father treated Tim better [than the sister's illegitimate children]. And it's because of that distance. It's not a bloodline; it's not illegitimate in *his* family. Whereas my sister has given birth to illegitimate children—that's his problem.

Because the women in the blended families had, for the most part, much older children, their relatives were not called upon for the same sorts of assistance often requested by parents of babies. And, because the children were older and had been born into a heterosexual relationship, the parents of the biological mothers had a history of being grandparents to them. Thus they did not have to struggle with becoming grandparents under unusual circumstances. It was, however, extremely unlikely that a stepmother's parents would regard some other woman's children as their grandchildren.

A few of the couples, from both DI and blended families, said that they received no support from their relatives. Many more women in the two sample groups said that, although they received a degree of acknowledgment or emotional support from their parents, they received very little material support from them. As Noreen explained:

> You know, basically, we did it on our own, and I think that's how we've done it all along pretty well. You know, it's always nice if you get something from somewhere, but basically you know you're going to do it on your own. . . . Of course, when you don't have the big marriage where you get all the gifts, you know, that's always a good start for some people.

Kim expressed a similar sentiment:

> I think lesbian couples do more of it for themselves. I mean look at, nobody gets wedding presents. . . . Like how do heterosexual couples start? . . . I mean anniversaries—my parents buy all my brothers and sisters anniversary presents. They don't even recognize that we might have one.

I do not want to give the impression that these women spent their time moping about the presents lesbian women never receive. I specifically asked them to comment on the types of *material* support they received. When I did not make this specification, and just asked them about the 'support' they received, they always talked about emotional support. The material aspect of the support was something I had to draw out.

Some women felt that their relatives offered support because it was proper and not necessarily because they had warm feelings for the lesbian family. Evelyn said that her relatives and Kim's relatives 'went through the motions. They know the motions to go through [when someone has a baby].' Kim believed that because her sister Sally had a baby shortly before she did, her parents were obligated to treat Evelyn and Kim better than they might have otherwise.

Many of the women in the overall sample found that their siblings were far more enthusiastic and involved than their parents. Nancy described relations with her siblings:

> They [brothers] are really great, and my sister is a little bit more—she's not as willing to accept that we're actually lesbians. But that we can have a really great relationship together and stuff is okay with her, and that we're raising a kid together, that's fine. She can see Astrid as pretty close to like a niece, but I don't know if she's quite made that connection. It's pretty good with my siblings. They were great when we were there [visiting] and stuff.

As mentioned earlier, the greatest amount of support, acknowledgment, and assistance generally came from friends, who as a result were often considered closer members of the families than were relatives. Lesbian friends did not always start out with an understanding of why these couples wanted to have children, but with a little education, they usually came around. Each couple had a circle of friends, both lesbian and heterosexual, who offered enthusiastic support through the entire family-making process. Tina noted how important friends can be:

> In our case both our families live some distance away, so we're not in regular contact with them. So really our circle of friends *is* the immediate family in that respect. And they probably are more important in our lives than if we were a heterosexual couple, because your whole lifestyle is, um, under attack—that's too strong a term—but is in question from the rest of society. [Whereas] everything you do as a heterosexual cou-

ple—as long as you don't put on a rubber suit and run around the neighbourhood—is fine. There's no question that almost everything you do, because you are a lesbian, is called into question. So yeah, I think you're always looking to be, you know, bolstered by people who have the same kind of lifestyle or the same values you do.

The support network described by Elly was fairly typical of many of the families:

> I think I get as much support from my family as I would if I was in a heterosexual relationship. I get quite a bit. I mean my mom bought the crib, which is sort of the classic grandmother thing to do. And I had a house full of baby clothes before Astrid was even born from my sister and my sister-in-law, my mom. I guess I get half as much as I would if Nancy's family was as supportive as well. I try to imagine what that would be like—that would be Christmas, it would be great. So we don't get any support from her side of the family, so that's different, I guess, than it would be. I don't, I don't feel I get nearly the same amount of support from the community at large, like the people at work that I'm out to. . . . They don't understand my family. They somehow think I'm a single parent, but I have this friend, you know. Like it's confusing to them so they don't have a box to put me in, so I don't think I get as much support from them. But my close lesbian community [friends] I get quite a bit of support from. I had two years of diaper service paid for from all our friends, which is extraordinary. It's a large amount of money. It's like $1,800 for two years of diaper service. People went together and paid for it. And I've had, I mean I happen to have a couple of more well-off friends and that, I mean they've bought tons of things for Astrid. Single lesbians without children, you know. Astrid loves them; they

bring goodies all the time. So I have that, but that's sort of financial and some forms of other support but I don't . . . I don't feel like I have the support of any kind of community as much as I would if I was straight. In terms of just sort of lifestyle support, you know, like young mothers with children getting together to do this. And I mean I have straight friends that have kids, but it's not the same as it would be if I had lesbian friends that had kids.

It should be noted that the children had their own support networks. Most of the children who were older than infants had friends to whom they had 'come out'. None of the friends seemed bothered by the family 'situation'; indeed, many thought it was 'neat'. Nor did the friends' parents appear concerned about the lesbian families. Whether this was an example of what Stebbins (1988: 13) calls 'habitual tolerance' (a superficial tolerance of something that does not seem threatening), or whether it was indicative of 'enlightened tolerance' (meaning that the parents had a deeper understanding and appreciation of the family form) is impossible to tell. Whatever the parents' attitudes, they did not impede friendship. The children of lesbian families did, however, carefully select their confidants. None revealed their family situation to all of their classmates, for example. Nonetheless, each was able to maintain what appeared to be a 'normal' friendship network.

Domestic Roles

Contrary to the stereotype that lesbian couples sort themselves into traditionally feminine and masculine roles and behaviours, *every* woman in my sample said that domestic tasks were shared equally in terms of quantity and divided in terms of each partner's area of ability and enjoyment. Most couples shared fairly evenly tasks such as housecleaning and cooking. In homes with older children, the children were expected to help with housework, do their own laundry, and sometimes cook one supper a week.

In the DI families, whoever was home and available would usually perform the bulk of the housecleaning. Because the partners tended to take turns staying at home, there was no permanent division of labour. The following responses were typical of the DI mothers:

> We lead really hectic lives. We both have shift jobs, and so we get weeks of total shutdown where neither of us [is] doing anything. And then we get weeks where one of us is working but the house is a pigsty, so someone's got to do it, right. We don't really split the roles. It's just whatever gets done, whoever does it does it.

> With Steven [baby] now it's whoever is home does most of the housekeeping and cooking and things like that. And so, you know, I mean Iris is a far better cook than me, but I'm cooking so it's a bit of a struggle, but it's okay. And we're really really conscious of gender stereotypical roles.

None of the blended families had preschool-age children, so no partner stayed home for this reason. All the women were employed or in school. Two of the couples had occasional housekeepers to 'keep things under control', while the rest divided housework between them (again, according to 'abilities and availabilities').

Each woman said that she and her partner performed the tasks they most preferred and then divided equally the less pleasant ones. I asked the respondents to specify what tasks were divided according to employment. It became clear that not one of these women was stereotypically 'feminine' or 'masculine' in terms of their interests or abilities. The woman who enjoyed cooking and sewing might also be the one who kept the family cars running and built the shed in the backyard.

By sharing equally in the domestic labour, these women managed to overcome the gender-typed role playing in which they had seen their parents participate. Iris said that she and Blaire made a conscious effort not to get trapped in rigid roles:

[We are] really sensitive to roles in the house because, as far as domestic roles go, I'm more handy than Blaire is and she's more particular about cleanliness than I am, and so it's really easy for us to fall into those roles. But we've challenged each other to accept those roles for ourselves. Like if Blaire was hanging a mirror or something, there was a time I would have just stepped in and said, 'Here, let me do that.' But now we're at the point where we expect each other to do it for ourselves. Because I would always step in and Blaire would never be able to hang a picture or whatever. And the same goes for things around the house, you know, if Blaire let me get away with it, she'd do the laundry all the time. So we really force each other to do what has to be done and not depend so much on roles.

These women's lives point out the erroneous-ness of notions about the biological bases of domestic and social roles. They also belie the stereotype that lesbian couples emulate hetero-sexual roles by playing 'butch' and 'femme' roles (although individuals or couples may *choose* to do so). Just as there is no necessary link between biology and sexual orientation, there is no neces-sary link between biology or sexual orientation and domestic or parenting roles.

The key roles in these lesbian families are the parenting roles. Parenting roles were not divided the same in DI and blended families. The DI moth-ers tried to divide mothering evenly, with each partner performing the same tasks with identical frequency. Many said that the only difference in the mothering roles they played was that some of the biological mothers breastfed, which, of course, the non-biological mothers could not do. In the blended families, the biological mothers often performed the bulk of the mothering tasks for their children, leaving the stepmothers to try to establish themselves in the home in general and in some type of parenting role in particular.

Once a couple decided if and how they would co-parent within the home, they had to decide if and how they would present themselves as co-parents outside the home. Having children brings people into greater contact with such pub-lic institutions as schools, daycare centres, clinics, and hospitals. Each couple had to decide whether to be 'out' in these places. All the DI couples felt strongly that they should clearly present them-selves as co-parents. On school records and hos-pital documentation, for example, they scratched out 'name of father' and wrote in 'co-parent'. Four of the six DI couples had infants, and so their con-tact with some of these institutions was limited. The other two couples, however, had presented themselves as co-parents throughout their chil-dren's lives. One of these couples had two grown children, the other a four year old. Not only did both couples present themselves as co-parents on paper, but they were also equally and openly involved as parents in their children's public lives. Almost never had they encountered openly dis-criminatory attitudes or behaviour on the part of teachers or parents of their children's friends.

Each of the DI couples had decided that it would be wrong to tell the child that they were his or her parents inside the home and then pre-sent themselves in some other relationship out-side the home. Tina's description of how she and Rose approached this issue was typical of all the DI mothers:

We had decided from the beginning that when Tim was born we would be upfront and open about it [their relationship to each other and to him]. His daycare knows. When he goes to elementary school, they'll know because we feel that, I mean it will be [at] his discretion whether to disclose or not to his peers. But we are not going to make our lifestyle something that he should see as something to be ashamed of. We'll be positive about it, and hopefully he'll gain security from that [and be able] to deal with it in whatever manner he wants. We would hope that he would feel comfortable about it—you know, not to have to hide it—but we wouldn't condemn him if he felt the need to do that.

Although each of the DI couples had decided that it was important that significant parties be made aware of their relationship and of the fact that they were co-mothering, it was sometimes difficult to determine *which* parties were significant. They had to decide who was worth telling and who was not. Denise described such a situation:

> Once we started getting babysitters in—fourteen-year-old girls—I kept thinking, 'Oh my God', you know. One of the girls, she brought her mother over, and they came in the house and I could just see the mother going, 'Is this girl a sister? How does she fit into the picture?' You know, you can just see the questions going through their mind, and you think, 'Well now, should we just plain go ahead and say, you know, we're gay?' But then it's like people don't walk around going 'well, you know, we're heterosexual'. . . . You just don't know quite how to deal with nonpermanent relationships—that's the place that it gets a little tough. So you come up with the answers as you need to.

For Noreen, one of the problems with being out as lesbian parents is that people tend to think of lesbian families as different or not quite 'real':

> People perceive them [lesbian families] to be different, but they're not. You know, it's just two people parenting that are loving their

kids. And that's it, you know, and there shouldn't be any discussion beyond that except acceptance. You know, like if you just accept the family then that's all you need.

Fear of rejection was one of the factors that kept many of the blended family couples from presenting themselves publicly as co-parents. Another crucial factor was that these couples very often were *not* co-parents in the sense of sharing parenting tasks and authority. Almost all the biological mothers in these families had decided against listing their partners as 'co-parent' on school documents and the like. While the stepmothers were sometimes invited to school plays and baseball games, they were rarely invited to parent-teacher interviews. This was often an area of contention between the women, resulting in the stepmothers' feeling even more excluded from the lives of the children they often cared deeply about and had some considerable hand in raising.

Challenges and Benefits: Blended Families

Because of the social stigma attached to lesbianism, many blended-family couples kept their family lives closeted—usually, as we have seen, out of concern for the children. Although one family, including the children, was completely 'out' (and had never suffered negative repercussions because of it), none of the other women was willing to assume the risks associated with coming out.

Related to concerns about being out was the realization by previously childless women that having children put them in much greater contact with the public world. Dealing with children's schools, friends, and leisure activities put the relationship under much greater public scrutiny than generally happens for childless couples. This made staying in the closet for the sake of the children all the more difficult—but also, many women believed, all the more necessary.

The public gaze was not the only gaze to which the couples were subject. Whereas biological mothers were used to sharing their lives with their children, previously childless women were surprised by the extent to which the relationship had to accommodate itself to the presence of children. 'It's sometimes really frustrating,' Laura said, 'but you can only do your arguing or your intimate kinds of discussing or have sex together at certain times in certain contexts.'

Lack of acknowledgment in the heterosexual world was often exacerbated by relatives who could not accept a family member's lesbianism. What emerges is a picture of families living in varying degrees of isolation and 'closetedness', and sometimes receiving minimal social support. As Carol explained:

> We're [not] necessarily acknowledged as a family needing support and that sort of thing. I think probably quite the contrary. . . . If Laura and I were mixed-gender parents I think it would be different.

One might assume that if recognition and support were not forthcoming from the heterosexual world, then these families would rely more heavily upon their lesbian friends for support. Although most tried to find support within the lesbian community, a few encountered total incomprehension on the part of their lesbian friends as to why they (especially the previously childless women) would become part of a blended family. Although lesbian friends might have been willing to acknowledge that a family had been formed, and that there were difficulties maintaining it, they were sometimes hesitant to offer real assistance. Carol elaborated:

> One thing too that we've noticed is people are quite willing to acknowledge how hard it is, you know, because we don't have enough money really to support our household, and that sort of thing. But nobody's really willing

to get involved in that. You know, like, they're, they're very much *our* children. . . . Although they acknowledged how hard it must be for us, it was *our* problem. It was very much ours.

Nonetheless, as we have seen, many couples reported that their friends, lesbian and heterosexual, were the closest they came to having an extended family.

Some stepmothers were uncomfortable with the primacy of the children in the lives of the biological mothers. Often the biological mother had to struggle to balance the needs of the lesbian relationship with the needs of the relationship with the children. Laura, a biological mother, stated that one of the biggest challenges she and Carol faced was

> spontaneity and setting priorities and remembering to leave enough time for the relationship. . . . I think when Carol and I first got involved . . . my relationship with the kids and the kids' needs had to come first, at the expense of everything else. And really, I've had to learn to honour the relationship too, [and to realize] that it is important and it isn't going to just be there because I wish it would be. It needs time and it's just as important. That's probably been the biggest thing, juggling all of that. It got a lot easier once I figured out you have to kind of just do it.

Although the need to juggle priorities can exist in any blended-family situation, the women in my sample attributed certain compromises that they had to make to the fact that they were two women—and often two *mothers*—trying to co-exist. These women were faced with the difficult task of trying to reconcile two different approaches to mothering. In some cases, the result was a lack of co-parenting, which some women felt was to their child's detriment. Daphne said:

[Nanette and I] see our kids, both sets of kids, as losers in this relationship. That the kids aren't gaining anything from the relationship. Financially, her kids have gained. But that's the only way in which they have gained really . . . because I don't have a relationship with [Nanette's children]. So they have this person in the house, um, who they're not really relating to. Basically, there's very little communication between the children and I.

Some of the challenges faced by these families were related to the women's lesbianism, and some were not.

Christine offered a general overview of the drawbacks to lesbian family life:

I think the primary thing is that children eat up a great deal of your life and your soul, and there isn't as much left over as we perhaps would like. We said we dream about the day they're finally gone. There's always inherent issues of disclosure, protecting the kids from disclosure. The secretness. Lack of community acknowledgment as parents.

Despite the many challenges and issues they faced, the women derived from their membership in a blended family benefits that they did not feel would otherwise have come their way. Many women said that life in a blended family contributed to their personal growth and development. Several women who had been previously childless found that parenting, whatever form it assumed, required them to be less self-involved. Daphne said:

[I'm] glad I didn't have any kids 'cause I really learned a lot by not having kids. I didn't give up myself to meet a bunch of other people's needs, and I feel good about that. And I know now that living with [Sharon's kids] that I'm perfectly capable of giving up and compromising, and I feel really good about that too.

Carol described how the presence of children had affected her own development:

It has helped me not take myself so seriously, not take my relationship so seriously. It's helped me to not be so selfish, I think. I think it's really good, but part of me kind of goes, 'Why would you think that?' you know. But yeah, I think it has been *exceptionally* good for me to have these kids in my life.

Many women felt that having children diluted the emotional intensity of the lesbian relationship, or, at the very least, made it impossible for the partners to be involved only with each other. The presence of children forced an emotional balance they had seldom experienced in earlier lesbian relationships where there had been a real possibility of 'mergence'. As Barbara put it:

Maybe it [being in a childed family] normalizes the relationship. It doesn't become this awe-inspiring unique little thing that the two of you have, right, it's just part of relating. You're part of a family instead, or part of the world instead of two people off in isolation.

For some women—especially the biological mothers—it was not the contact with children that was especially new and important to them; it was claiming a lesbian identity and sharing their parenting within a lesbian relationship. 'I'm more me now,' Nanette said. 'I can be who I wish to be now that I'm in this relationship.' Several women expressed their relief that they did not have to deal with men as partners or co-parents. One of the most appealing features of lesbian co-parenting, for many women, was that it allowed them unprecedented equality in a relationship with another adult.

Many of the previously childless women found that being part of a family brought stability to their lives. Marda said:

It [involvement with a woman who had a child] was kind of like a bonus, or a kind of adding a bit of stability to my life that I had not had for a long time, or really in actuality before.

Similarly, Barbara revealed:

I get stability because, um, I'm a real workaholic and I was not, um, it's really nice to have people to come home and share things with. That's what I get out of it. Frustration too, but I get satisfaction, you know, sharing things with other people. I have a family now, and it's something that's very important to have. . . . It's stable and it's allowing me to be happy, more aware of myself, to discover myself more as a person.

Andrea was among those women who genuinely enjoyed being with children and being able to play a role in their lives:

I get a lot of enjoyment out of watching people grow, whether they're adults or whether they're kids. You know, just hearing about how far Charlene [stepdaughter] is coming in school . . . I mean it's just really neat to me to watch that . . . being able to appreciate the gifts in her . . . I don't know where it comes from, but I feel proud to be walking around the grocery store [with Charlene] or wherever we happen to be. It's just kind of a neat feeling for me . . . I don't know if it's because I think other people think that she's my daughter and that's something that I want, and so that's a way that I can do it.

The benefits of life in a blended lesbian family were experienced by the children as well. Some women believed that the new family status energized a family situation that had grown somewhat stagnant. Others felt that a female co-parent was better for the children than a male co-parent would have been. Sharon stated:

It's better that it's a woman because my kids were used to having, their parent *was* a woman. Now they have two, so it's twice as good. It probably made it easier.

The vast majority of respondents believed that it was a very positive thing for children to grow up in such 'alternative' families. The view that life in a blended lesbian family would expose the children to options, and thereby open their minds, was expressed by several women:

Inadvertently, children—both male and female—begin to see a more androgynous gender as opposed to it always being dad things and mom things. But moms can do things that they thought only dads did and vice versa.

Because they can accept us, then they can accept all kinds of differences in other kids, in other people. So I think growing up in a 'non-normal' family will teach the kids more acceptance.

I think that homosexuals, whether they're lesbian or gay men, because they've had to go through a process and have had to challenge society, to say 'I'm different', and if they have come to the acceptance of their sexuality, they're more, um, they're better adjusted people than the average Joe on the street. And they're less limited because they've gone through—I mean that's a major struggle, right. So because of that they can transfer that to their kids, so their kids will be better adjusted and will have less limitations, limiting beliefs, or whatever.

Challenges and Benefits: DI Families

As one might expect with new parents, DI mothers were often surprised by the considerable labour involved in meeting a baby's needs. Their social lives were profoundly changed as they gave up many old social activities and sought out new ones in which babies could be included. The baby became the centre of the couple's attention, and they sometimes had to remind themselves to spend some time and energy on each other and on themselves. These challenges are not unique to lesbian parents. Almost all the difficulties that are unique to lesbian families can be traced to the social perceptions of this family form.

Nearly every woman said that once she had a baby, 'spontaneity' became impossible. Every aspect of her life had to be planned around the baby. Again, this is not unusual for any young couple with a baby. But the frustrations that the women in my sample sometimes felt with respect to parental responsibilities were exacerbated by the frequent lack of understanding within their lesbian social milieu. Lesbian couples having babies is a relatively new practice in the lesbian community, and that community very often simply fails to understand all that having a baby entails. Many women said that friends would continue to phone them with such questions as 'Do you want to go to the dance tonight?' They did not seem to comprehend that parents of young children cannot 'pick up and go out' at a moment's notice. Several women said that, instead of trying to plan events in advance, some friends simply stopped calling. Fortunately, close lesbian friends were often amenable to being educated about the demands of parenthood, and thereby became important support figures for the family.

The greatest challenges faced by DI families came from outside the lesbian community. Living in a world where the common assumption is that everyone is heterosexual sometimes places these families in awkward situations. As Iris explained:

> I always feel like when we're [Iris and Blaire] out walking together, unless we're holding hands, I always feel like people look at us like we're sisters or something, and I just

kind of laugh at it myself, although I do think about it when I do get that look of recognition in people's eyes. It's obvious that not many people assume we're lesbians, because we have a baby. . . . I think we'd be flattered if somebody assumed that we were lesbians, you know. It would be like 'Wow, society has taken a leap forward.'

The assumption of universal heterosexuality puts lesbian mothers in the position of having to repeatedly 'come out' if they want their family arrangement to be at all comprehensible to outsiders. We have already seen that many of these couples present themselves as 'mother' and 'co-parent' on all documentation regarding the child, and that one of the greatest difficulties they face is determining who is worth coming out to and who is not. Coming out is never easy, even without children, because people's responses cannot usually be anticipated. Each of the women believed, however, that it was important that the children not feel that there was anything wrong with their families. Thus it became a challenge for the women to become comfortable about coming out. Iris said:

> My big thing now is saying to people that I was artificially inseminated. And really, you know, what it is for me right now is having to say that and telling myself that I can cope with that, admitting to people that Steven doesn't have a father, but that I was artificially inseminated. And I feel it's really important for me to be able to say that if I want him to be able to cope with it when he's older.

Elly expressed similar feelings about the issue of coming out:

> One of my biggest concerns is that Astrid not be shamed or not feel shame about her family, and so that requires us to be brave and strong, and sometimes I'm not brave and

strong. My sort of ultimate worry is that one day someone will say to Astrid, 'Is Nancy your mother?' and she'll say no, or Nancy will say no, or I'll say, 'no, I am,' because we're in a threatening situation or it's not safe. What will that do to Astrid? 'Well, this was my mother. I thought she was my mother. Now you tell me she's not my mother'. . . . I think we've made the commitment that when Astrid is involved and aware of what is going on that we be clear that we are co-parenting her, that I'm her biological mother, Nancy is her other mother or her co-parent. And we've made a commitment to co-parent. Doing that, not necessarily expecting that that reveals the sexual relationship or just our relationship, but that reveals our relationship to Astrid and that's what's important to Astrid and whoever is asking.

Related to concerns about coming out was the need to prepare the child for discrimination that he or she might face as a result of the family's composition. All the women believed in the importance of taking measures to ensure that the children felt secure in their families and confident in themselves. Many women said there was a fine line between sensitizing a child to possible problems and scaring him or her. 'I think that all we can really do is tell him [son] what to expect,' Iris said, 'and tell him about our experiences, and be honest and let him know that he can talk to us about anything that happens.' Blaire added, 'The big thing is, we don't want to instil a sense of fear in him [such] that people are going to hate him.'

Because lesbianism is stigmatized in Canadian society, all the women found themselves, at one time or another, having to defend their right to have children and their ability to raise them. Evelyn said that she and Kim got tired of

having our right to be parents constantly questioned. Constantly, like no matter who you mention it to—'oh, Kim is going to have a baby'—[they say], 'Well do you think that's right?' So you've got to [go through] your whole political spiel with anybody you give this information to as if they have a right to decide whether you should be a parent or not.

The DI mothers said that not only did they have to defend the 'normalcy' of their families to friends, relatives, and complete strangers, but they also had to challenge institutions that conceived of 'family' only in terms of the traditional heterosexual nuclear family. Many places and events that offer 'family' admission rates do not regard lesbian families as families. As a result of the efforts of some of the women in my sample, a few establishments in Calgary, such as leisure centres and swimming pools, have modified their definition of family from 'a man and woman and their children' to 'two adults and children'. Many places, however, have yet to make this change.

What this means for lesbian families is that to live a 'normal' family life, they must constantly tell people that they *are* a normal family. Educating others proved to be a fatiguing process for some of the women, including Tina:

I think the hardest part is always educating [people], you know. And sometimes you get tired of saying, 'This is my family, and this is why we are the way we are, and this is what we do,' you know. And sometimes you sit back and go, 'Well, I don't get why you don't get it.' And we just keep slogging away, and it's for Tim's benefit mainly, but I mean it's for the benefit of anyone really that comes in contact with our family. But you do, you get tired educating people all the time.

Other women, however, enjoyed playing the role of educator and shaking up people's preconceptions.

Lack of social recognition of lesbian families means that there is no recognition of the role played by the non-biological mother. As we have seen, DI couples often have to inform their friends and relatives that they are *both* mothers to the child. The absence of social recognition presents an ongoing battle for these families.

Like the blended-family mothers, however, the DI mothers also believed that the benefits of this family form outweighed the challenges. Several said that the presence of two mothers meant that parenting could be divided more equally than they had seen it divided in many heterosexual households. Moreover, the sharing of mothering duties gave each woman an understanding of motherhood that she would not have received under a less equitable division of labour. Iris explained:

> Blaire's home with him [baby] in the summer, and then in the fall. I'll be home with him all winter. And it's been beneficial for us because now we both know what it's like to stay home with a baby, and there's no way we can take each other for granted now. I think, you know, in heterosexual couples when the husband comes home and goes, 'Oh the dishes aren't done. What have you been doing, watching soap operas?' You know, there's no way that we could say that because we know.

Several women were convinced that having two mothers made for greater consistency in the parenting the child received. Again, Iris explained:

> I think it's really hard not to generalize because I see us as having female qualities, and when you consider traditional female qualities—nurturing and gentleness and caring—then I include that as an asset. You know, as opposed to raising a child with a man. You know, I think that there's some consistency because we both have those qualities. And I'm not saying that men don't have those qualities, but I don't know many

who do. And I think there's more consistency in the way we raise him, between the two of us, because we both have those qualities.

Most of the respondents also believed that they were able to have an equitable division of labour because they were two women sharing the tasks.

Some couples observed that one advantage the DI family had over the blended family was that the former did not have to deal with the stepparenting issues; both women had been mothers to the children since birth. As Noreen explained:

> That's one of the good things [about] having children within your relationship. The kids have never yelled, 'Well, you're not my mother' or 'Who are you' or anything like that, which would be very hurtful to her [Melanie] I think. She's mature and I mean she could take it, but still for a non-biological parent sometimes it can be very hurtful when kids do that sort of thing. But we haven't [encountered it], and in discipline, that kind of thing, they listen to her the same as they do me.

For women like Blaire, the challenges that accompanied lesbian DI parenting were inextricably linked to its rewards:

> The benefits are the challenge of everything, you know. I mean if I was with a man I wouldn't explore it as I am with a woman. The sense of freedom that we can sort of be anything we want to Steven. It's more sort of if I could say proactive. Or it's thinking instead of reacting. I mean, you know, we think maybe more than we really need to, but we think about everything and we don't, we think about how things will affect Steven probably more than heterosexual people. But I think sometimes more than sexual orientation our actual personalities, who we are, has a lot more to do with parenting than being a lesbian.

Fighting for the Family

Being raised by two mothers is not identical to being raised by one mother, by a mother and a father, or by two fathers. Sharing mothering with another woman is not identical to mothering alone or mothering with a male partner. There are three dimensions along which these differences are meaningful for lesbian families in Canada:

1. both parents are women;
2. the parents are homosexual;
3. the family exists in a heterosexist, patriarchal, homophobic society.

The first two dimensions were not seen by my respondents to be problematic in and of themselves. Nor were they perceived to negatively affect the quality or type of life and upbringing the children experienced. Two women negotiating shared parenting roles may face different challenges and enjoy different rewards than might a man and a woman engaged in such negotiation, but this does not render lesbian families fundamentally different from, or alien to, other types of family. Often what distinguishes lesbian families, and life within them, from other types of families are the repercussions of the attitudinal and legal context within which they exist.

We have seen that lesbians, as lesbians, can be marginalized by their families of origin, by the society at large, and by other mothers. They are marginalized by their invisibility, which derives from the assumption of universal heterosexuality. As mothers they can be marginalized within the lesbian community due to a lack of recognition, respect, or understanding of their parenting choices. Lesbian families are marginalized by mainstream beliefs that families are, and should always be, created by heterosexuals; that parenting roles consist of 'mother' and 'father' or something closely analogous (such as stepmother and stepfather); that there is a correct way and time to become a mother (e.g., within a heterosexual marriage); and

that only certain women deserve to become mothers (generally, heterosexual married women).

Lesbian women, and lesbian family members, encounter on a daily basis the manifestations of heterosexist thinking, ranging from the attitudes of friends, family, acquaintances, co-workers, and strangers, through media portrayals of lesbian women and gay men, to discriminatory treatment within major social institutions such as education, medicine, and law. North America has seen dramatic increases in gay and lesbian rights activism over the last thirty years, especially since the Stonewall rebellion of 1969. It is striking that much of the opposition to gay and lesbian legal equality comes from those who claim that gays and lesbians are a threat to 'the family'. This perspective not only renders invisible healthy and functioning lesbian families, but it also implies that such a thing cannot and should not exist.

Such is the ideological milieu within which lesbian families exist in Canada. The legal system, informed by the dominant heterosexist ideology, serves to define and bolster 'the family' while often penalizing lesbian families and leaving them vulnerable to attack. Lesbians cannot be legally married in Canada, which means that partners are denied spousal benefits, pay more tax, and are left in a precarious legal situation regarding inheritances. The lack of legal recognition of the non-biological mother leaves her emotionally, legally, and financially vulnerable; in fact, it renders her completely powerless as a parent outside of the home.

It is little wonder, then, that lesbian women have banded together to fight not only for their own recognition and equal treatment under the law but also for the recognition and protection of their families. In 1985, the equality provision of the Canadian Charter of Rights and Freedoms (section 15) came into effect. Although 'sexual orientation' is not specified as a protected ground, it has been accepted as a ground analogous to those that *are* listed in the section. Canadian gays and lesbians have used section 15 to challenge discriminatory legislation. Herman (1994) points out that '[m]uch, although not all, of the resulting litigation turned on definitions of "family" or "spouse" within various federal and provincial statutes' (p. 27).

There is little consistency among the provinces in their responses to these challenges. For example, in May 1995 the Supreme Court of Canada reaffirmed that sexual orientation was a protected ground under the Charter, but ruled that the denial of spousal pension benefits to a BC couple did not constitute discrimination because the couple were not married.[1] Two weeks earlier, the Ontario Supreme Court had ruled that lesbians and gays could not be discriminated against in terms of adopting children.

Most major cities and many smaller communities in Canada have at least one lesbian and gay rights group. These groups fight for numerous changes, including coverage in human rights legislation, fair representation in the media, protection from discrimination and hate crimes, healthcare coverage for partners, spousal benefits, and legal recognition and protection of lesbian and gay partnerships. Although these groups often are not fighting explicitly for the sake of lesbian and gay *families*, it is no coincidence that much of the opposition to them arises from 'pro-family', anti-gay factions.

Anti-gay activists are always raising the spectres of paedophilia and the drafting of innocents into the 'homosexual lifestyle'. But these are not the threats that lesbians and gays pose to 'the family'. The threat is to heterosexual, patriarchal privilege, a large component of which is financial, and of which the traditional heterosexual, middle-class, white, nuclear family is the cornerstone. Legal marriage, legal status for parents, spousal benefits, pension benefits, spousal health-care coverage, and tax breaks for married and common-law couples are manifestations of the institutional ballast that surrounds 'the family'. These privileges not only protect families but also serve to define them.

Although legislation varies across Canada, for the most part lesbian and gay families are unrec-

ognized and unprotected. In response to this situation, some lesbian and gay parents have gone beyond the established political-action groups to create groups that specifically address the needs of lesbian and gay families. From 1978 to 1987, for example, the Lesbian Mothers' Defence Fund operated out of Toronto, with regional branches in some provinces. This group—which was established to 'improve the position of lesbian mothers in society' (Stone 1990: 199)—assisted lesbian mothers who were facing custody battles with their ex-spouses, and expanded its services to include social and educational activities. Although the group disbanded, other groups such as the Ontario-based Campaign for Equal Families and Foundation for Equal Families carry on the work of educating and litigating in the interests of gay and lesbian families.

It is beyond the scope of this discussion to explore the history of lesbian and gay political organizing in Canada. It is not even possible to give an overview of all the battles that are currently being fought. What is essential is that we understand that lesbian families exist in what is often either a hostile or complacently ignorant environment. In the face of ungrounded accusations that lesbians and gays are seeking special rights, lesbian mothers must struggle daily to protect and validate their families.

It is clear that life in a lesbian family is just as varied, challenging, comforting, amusing, frustrating, and rewarding as life in other kinds of families. More often than not, it is the stigma of lesbianism and lack of acknowledgment of lesbian families that make family life different for these women. Additionally, the fact of two women sharing parenting and domestic duties may have a greater influence on the tone of family life than the fact of their lesbianism ever could. It would appear that growing numbers of lesbian women are either using donor insemination or raising children conceived in prior heterosexual relationships. Popular, scientific, medical, and legal definitions of 'family' will have to acknowledge this reality.

Note

1. [Editor's note] Nevertheless, in May, 1999, the Supreme Court of Canada ruled that the Ontario Family Law Act was unconstitutional in distinguishing common-law heterosexual relationships from gay and lesbian relationships. Following the ruling, in Ontario gays and lesbians in common-law relationships have the same rights and obligations with respect to support—in the event their relationship dissolves—as do heterosexual common-law couples. The decision poses a challenge to all laws and practices that deny same-sex couples benefits that heterosexual couples are due.

References

Herman, D. 1994. *Rights of Passage: Struggles for Lesbian and Gay Legal Equality* (Toronto: University of Toronto Press).

Stebbins, R. 1988. *Deviance: Tolerable Differences* (Toronto: McGraw-Hill Ryerson).

Stone, S.D. 1990. 'Lesbian Mothers Organizing' in *Lesbians in Canada*, ed. S.D. Stone (Toronto: Between the Lines).

Chapter 29

In 1992, we conducted a series of interviews with people who had created unusual families—decidedly egalitarian families. We looked for such families in order to address student concerns that the obstacles *to living in an egalitarian way were enormous. We hope this essay generates discussion, but also inspires and even empowers.*

Pathbreakers: Some Unconventional Families of the Nineties

Bonnie J. Fox and Doreen Fumia

If the Cleaver family (of 'Leave It to Beaver' fame) resembled real 1950s families in basic structure alone, families like the Cleavers exist today only in our imaginations. Few men can achieve the role of exclusive breadwinner. Most women can neither afford nor tolerate the position of full-time homemaker.

In turn, because children and adults still need the nurturing and homemaking full-time housewives typically have provided, most families are experiencing considerable stress these days. In fact, the balancing act many women perform daily—juggling the opposing demands of family and employer—leaves them with less sleep and less time for friends, themselves, and probably their children than either their partners or full-time homemakers (Hochschild 1989).

The source of the stress on families is clear: economic changes have undercut the gendered division of labour on which nuclear families were built, while the social restructuring necessary to support the changes in women's work has not occurred. What is needed are a reorganization of employment to provide flexible schedules and decent part-time work, adequate provisions for parental leave from employment (involving years, not weeks), government and corporate assumption of responsibility for providing good childcare facilities for women who need them, and guaran-

teed annual incomes for lone-parent families. Instead, the government has cut back its support to parents (ending universal family allowances and federal transfer payments for daycare facilities, most obviously). Cutbacks in social services generally have increased families' (i.e., women's) responsibilities for providing care for dependants.

In the absence of a positive response by government, and amidst high rates of divorce and an apparent increase in violence against women, people are challenged to create new forms of family. In fact, given the lack of fit between the changes that have eroded the breadwinner and full-time homemaker roles and conventional nuclear-family arrangements, we are all challenged to do so. This is a difficult task, both because of the monopoly one idea of 'family' has on our minds and because various government policies still punish people who live outside heterosexual and nuclear families (see Eichler 1988). Nevertheless, the continuing vitality of the Women's Movement and feminist ideas means that we are not without any vision of different ways children, women, and men can live together. Indeed, there *are* people who are raising children, and living together quite happily, in ways that (in varying degrees) defy convention.

At this critical historical juncture, then, we thought it important to examine people who are attempting to create different kinds of families. We wanted to find role models, especially in light of the volumes of research reporting that despite women's paid employment the conventional gendered division of labour has not changed significantly—on *average*, that is (Hochschild 1989; Morris 1990; Frederick 1995; see Luxton, Chapter 21 this text). We all know that the social world consists of diversity (or variation) as well as typical patterns (or averages). We felt it was time for social scientists to turn to those people who have carved out lifestyles very different from the norm. Of course, many of these families would be seen as problematic by some—those involving one parent, those with men who have chosen to stay home, those with gay or lesbian parents, etc.

In order to learn about, and from, people who are creating new blueprints for gender and family life, we interviewed some people raising children and living in unconventional families. We interviewed eight Toronto families altogether. They are, in fact, the first eight families we found as we began a larger project to explore the diversity of family life. We found them in and through our personal networks, and via a few public notices. Not surprising, given that we are white and middle-class, all of them are white, although they consist of different classes, income groups, and ethnicities. In no way a sample, these people represent only themselves. But what they had to say we found very interesting.

Upon reflection, there is one theme woven through all of these interviews. The variations on this theme were what captured our attention with all these families. That theme has to do with the balance between individual autonomy and the needs of the family as a unit, but especially of the young children in it (and their seemingly infinite needs for caregivers' time). Nearly everyone we spoke to thought of family as a support base, promoting the welfare of its members and supporting their various endeavours. What was unusual about these families, though, was that a women's

personal needs were not being sacrificed to make possible everyone else's freedom to grow and thrive—as is so often the case in more conventional families (Rich 1976; Luxton 1980; Boulton 1983; Hochschild 1989).

What follows is a description of these families.

Our first interview took place in one of Toronto's middle-class neighbourhoods—in a backyard so lush with greenery that no buildings were in sight from where we sat on the patio. Tom and Barbara are in their early forties, and have a seven-year-old daughter, Dana. For both, this is their second marriage, and Tom has an adult daughter from his first marriage. Barbara is a well-paid professional who earns the main income doing contract work that sometimes takes her away from home for weeks and even months, and always involves days that are longer than nine-to-five. Tom is a freelance consultant who works in his home—but pretty intermittently. More important, he does the bulk of the childcare and housework. Together for over fourteen years, they settled on this pattern about three-and-a-half years ago.

Morning begins in this household when Tom gets up and makes breakfast for Dana, whose first word upon waking is 'Daddy . . .,' and for Barbara who gets breakfast in bed.[1] After getting Dana off to school, Tom is responsible for nearly all the housework, from laundry to meal preparation—although he has help, in the form of a cleaning woman who comes in every Friday. As well, Barbara often makes dinner on weekends, and even occasionally cooks in bulk and freezes meals; she also buys most of Dana's clothing.[2] Barbara also 'handles all the money': she pays the bills and does the bookkeeping. Finally, completing this reversal of conventional gender roles, Barbara does all minor household repairs, and arranges for the ones she cannot do herself. In short, the gender roles are reversed but Barbara does more housework than the typical man, despite Tom's shouldering of the bulk of the housework.

From Dana's perspective, both her mother and her father are active parents. Tom feeds her and gets her off to school; she looks to him for help, entertainment, and someone to listen; and he puts her to bed at night. Dana is apparently just as likely to go to her mother for help, entertainment, and someone to listen—when Barbara is home. Moreover, all major decisions about Dana, and planning (such as for birthday parties, or presents) involve both parents together. In short, Dana has two 'primary' parents.

Tom's active fathering allows Barbara to be gone from home for weeks and even months, when her work requires that. Despite occasional innuendoes about bad mothering from her colleagues, Barbara appears not to feel guilty about her absences. She and Tom both consider Dana to be a happy child. But Barbara's confident demeanour belies the tremendously hard choice she has made, and no doubt must grapple with daily: the decision to trust her partner to raise their daughter when Barbara is absorbed in her work. To compensate for her absences, Barbara has tried to spend special time together with her daughter. For example, the two of them have begun a pattern of taking trips together.

While the arrangements they have made seem to suit Barbara and Tom, the course they charted for themselves is not 'easy, or wonderful', according to Tom. He has minimized the problems associated with his situation: their friends are couples whose family patterns are like their own, so they avoid men who might criticize Tom; he walks his dog every day with four women neighbours (and their pets) to decrease his isolation; and he actively pursues contracts as a consultant in order to contribute to household income. Nevertheless, having assumed the position of 'househusband', Tom suffers most of the consequences inherent in the position of full-time homemaker. Although he would 'rather iron than do a press release', Tom experiences the isolation that full-time housewives complain of the most (Oakley 1974; Boulton 1983). His workplace is his home.

In addition, Tom has all the problems of the 'double day' of work: he is continually juggling the roles of father and consultant. The chief cause of the difficulty of the 'double day'—aside from the shortage of hours in a day, and the presence of only two adults in most households—is the fundamental incompatibility of market work and house work. Tom has taken on the handicap women acquire at birth: he argues that whenever he has made clear to employers that his family responsibilities come first (something assumed in the case of women), he has not been taken seriously. When working for someone else, his refusal to work weekends (like most other male employees) created problems. When interviewing for jobs, statements that family came first have (in Tom's estimation) disqualified him. Even working at home, he constantly must be vigilant to 'keep family out of work'. An advantage of working at home is that he can hide from clients the fact that his 'lunch date' is with his daughter. But hiding family responsibilities from work commitments is also harder *because* Tom is at home: his daughter may need him (noisily) while he is on the phone with a client.

That Tom and Barbara each have been, in a sense, forced to choose between family and career testifies further to the profound disjuncture between employment and family in this society. Fortunately for each of them, the choices that were easiest—the ones 'driven by economics', to use Tom's words—were those suited to their personal needs and desires, Tom to be at home with his daughter and Barbara to pursue her career as far as it takes her. So perhaps the main reason why Tom and Barbara have organized their family as they have is that Barbara's career was taking off, while Tom's was faltering; and the income Barbara could earn significantly higher than what Tom would. Unfortunately, Barbara's higher earning power underlines how unusual this family is. To quote Tom, they 'have the luxury to choose this kind of life'.

More than economic factors are involved in shaping this family, however. As is Barbara, Tom is an unusual man, whose life has featured several things that might seem sufficient to explain his decision to abandon traditional male roles, were they not present in the lives of many other men still in the hold of tradition. He grew up in a large family in which the mother was employed full-time, and all of the children—including the boys—were responsible for household chores. His father was a 'traditional' man, and emotion-ally absent from his children's lives. Tom's first marriage failed, and for a while his first daughter was estranged from him. What is interesting about much of this, though, is not so much the events as Tom's reactions to them. At the level of rational choice, he vowed not to be like his father; at the level of emotion, he distanced himself from 'men' and came to find women 'more interest-ing'.[3] The therapy he mentioned several times during the interview indicates a willingness to grapple with problems and work for personal change. Finally, it is clear that feminism has shaped his thinking: he has clearly rejected any equation of masculinity with occupational achievement. This is an unusual man.

So the multiplicity of causes that came together to promote Tom and Barbara's family arrangement underlines how rare it is. At the same time, this family is compellingly attractive. Each individual seems to have both support and personal space. There is a strong sense of the col-lective, of *family*, yet also strong evidence that this collective unit frees its members to explore emerging possibilities. Barbara's definition of 'family' is revealing, if not unusual:

> a family is a support system, where people help each other, and cooperate and work together to make room for everybody, so that everybody in a family can do what they want to do, what they need to do. . . . It doesn't have to be the same all the time. It can be one thing one year and another thing another time.

This family arrangement has been negotiated, and renegotiated, to suit the changing needs of its members.

While this family is very unusual in its near complete reversal of gender roles, it is not simply a mirror image of male breadwinner/female home-maker families. How it differs is in Barbara's level of involvement in her child's life: she is not in the role of 'father'; she *mothers* her daughter. Assuming women are unlikely to give up mothering, role reversal in household work may be a particularly effective means of drawing men into the daily care of children, and ensuring equal parenting.

The other role-reversed family we studied is a case in point. This couple, together (common-law) for only two years, had a baby nine months earlier because thirty-eight-year-old Colleen felt she could no longer wait to have a child, and because Charles (thirty-two years old) has 'always wanted a child' as well. Like Barbara, Colleen is a professional, with considerably greater earning potential than her partner, and the family breadwinner. But she is also older than Charles. And while Tom had pursued and given up on a career in the usual sense, Charles still looks forward to finishing university and, some day, teaching kindergarten.

For now, however, the baby's needs come first. So, Colleen works only part-time, in a job-sharing arrangement with another woman, and Charles works only occasionally. In short, they have decided, for now at least, to live on the small income that one part-time job brings in.

Colleen holds the responsibility both for sup-porting the household and for ensuring her child's well-being (i.e., when Reed is sick, she stays home from work). She admits that at times she is 'totally overwhelmed'. Nevertheless, the actual workload seems nearly even.

How is daily life organized? The needs of the baby dictate both adults' schedules—not just one person's, as in most homes. Charles usually gets up before the baby, around 8 a.m., and straight-ens up their modest apartment. He then cares for Reed until Colleen wakes up at around 11 a.m.

Either Colleen or Charles is in charge of Reed until Colleen goes to work (at 2:30)—and the person who is not doing childcare does housework. Charles and the baby visit Colleen at work around 6:30, so she can feed the baby. Charles, then, has the baby again until midnight, when Colleen returns and takes over. On Colleen's days off, she and Charles negotiate who takes Reed and who does housework.

In general, housework is about equally shared, though each adult does what he or she prefers—Charles most of the cooking and the laundry, Colleen more of the cleaning and all the shopping. Charles explains that he does more of the housework than Colleen—in the times when they are both home, and things are negotiable—because getting comfortable with the baby has been 'work' for him. Again, the difference from traditional couples (and even their mirror image) is striking: unlike most full-time housewives, Charles does not feel he should do all of the housework and the childcare, even though Colleen earns nearly all the money. In this case, role reversal promotes a sharing of parenting, but not necessarily an equalization of work responsibility.

This is a family in the making. In fact, only recently have they begun to consider themselves a family. Both products of 'very dysfunctional' families, the word 'family' does not resonate well with either Charles or Colleen. But one thing is clear: both adults are totally committed to meeting their child's needs. In the short term, that has meant that Charles postpones his education and career plans, while Colleen is employed for more hours than she would like.

Having so prioritized their child's needs, Colleen and Charles are both keenly aware that 'it's not a baby friendly society out there' (Colleen). Colleen talks about the lack of empathy and help from people on buses, when she is out alone with her baby. Charles seems to have special problems: 'The big disadvantage is . . . I don't get any respect [for caring for children] . . . men don't, that's for sure.' His brother continually asks him when he is going to get a 'job', his male friends stopped calling him long ago, elderly women on the street give him unwanted and presumptuous advice, and the mothers with babies in the park do not speak to him. His isolation seems worse than that of women at home. But he and Colleen are both still 'in love', and the baby obviously thriving and happy.

The second distinct pattern we saw is one of 'taking turns' at homemaking/parenting. The person not in the domestic role is in school. In this case, at this point in time, Carol (in her early thirties) is in university, working on a four-year BA, while Paul (also in his early thirties) does most of the housework and provides more than half the care for their eighteen-month-old son, Eli.

Together for nearly nine years, Carol and Paul have each spent much of their married lives in a quest for university degrees, and careers. As well, after intending to have five children, they have endured years of infertility treatment. They describe themselves as having 'big dreams'. Their relationship has enabled each of them to inch their way closer to personal goals, but it has also, simultaneously, slowed them down. They live with that contradiction, and indeed seem more conscious of it than most couples. For their journey has been a hard one.

When Paul and Carol met in 1983, neither of them had university educations. Carol was, however, doing well in a business career. They began to live together shortly after their first date and, over the course of the next three years, Paul got his three-year BA while Carol brought in most of the income. Then, because of Carol's boredom with her work, and out of a desire to get good infertility treatment, they moved to Toronto. For the next few years, their emotional and financial resources went primarily to several cycles of treatment—all unsuccessful, as is common. In 1989, Carol went back to school, to get her BA. Paul had plans for further education as well, but (he explains) Carol was 'more focused' about what she would do, so she went first.

Meanwhile, after seven cycles of infertility treatment, Carol got pregnant and had her child. While pregnant, she took a full load of courses, then dropped to a half-time schedule the term after Eli was born. But the next term, before the baby was a year of age, she was back to a full courseload; she explained that she could do it only because Paul was at home 'doing everything'. In fact, while working part-time at night, Paul was doing most of the housework and over half of the childcare.

Their long-term plan is that Carol will finish her BA, then wait to do the MA until Paul has finished his fourth year as an undergraduate. During Carol's wait, they hope to have a second child. After Carol's MA, Paul has very ambitious plans that involve considerable postgraduate schooling.

The risk, of course, is that once Carol settles into the career she wants, and especially if there is a second child, Paul's goals will never be realized. Paul admits to worrying about that, but argues that 'things always seem to fall into place for us'. The worry has not made him amend his 'big dreams'. Yet the crisis is already lurking: Paul assumes they will have to live separately for a while, as he pursues his training; Carol is very leery of that, claiming that family needs may interfere. The delicate balance between individual and family needs in this family will be hard to sustain as time passes.

The third non-traditional pattern we saw was that of egalitarian co-parenting. The pattern was clearest in the case of a lesbian couple with two children. Emily and Joy came together as a couple five years ago, when each was about to give birth. Once established, their relationship has sustained them both in their careers as (low-paid) health-care professionals, and as mothers. Both Emily and Joy work long and erratic hours, at emotionally intense and hard work. Meanwhile, although each child has a special relationship with his/her mother, each has another primary parent in the other woman—who can care for him/her while Mum may be gone for days and nights, or called away unexpectedly at night.

There is a very strong sense of family here. 'We have very strong convictions about the value of *stability* in families' (Emily). Both women are committed to co-parenting the children until they are old enough to be on their own (and have a legal agreement about parenting each other's child should one of them die). So, while they may be geographically separate for the sake of their work for some period in the future, the children would remain together, and move back and forth between their parents. Teaching and enabling their children to support each other is important to Joy and Emily: 'The bottom line [for "family"] is you support your brothers and sisters. It's all about nurturing' (Emily).

Caring for two children is hard for two adults with careers. Not surprisingly, then, the childcare provided by a gay male friend of Emily's has been essential from the start of this family. Also important have been the support and assistance of both sets of grandparents. And daycare was invaluable for a while, until it 'broke' them financially. Now arrangements are being made to exchange babysitting with another mother.

Meanwhile, housekeeping chores are divided equally, although Joy does all the cooking and Emily the aftermeal clean-up and laundry. Equal sharing is fundamental to this household: 'We both have a very strong sense that this thing just can't work if one of us is coasting.' But not coasting means hard work, long hours.

Nevertheless, this family is a strong support base. Despite long hours of work, a continuing financial squeeze and co-mothering two children, Emily has been able to go back to university and finish her BA. They have also saved some money for the cottage they are building (themselves), and Joy is entering a Ph.D. program in the fall.

The most stretched financially, nevertheless this family seemed the most egalitarian to us. That the adults are both women—that gender differences are not an issue—no doubt greatly facilitates the egalitarianism characterizing their relationship. So too may be the fact that each woman has a child. Our impression was of two self-sufficient people, with very clearly thought out ideas about how to conduct their lives and raise their children. Their combination of individual strength and total commitment to a collective enterprise—of childcare, primarily—provided compelling evidence that the two are not at odds, and indeed complement each other. Both women work incredibly hard, at their jobs and at being parents and sustaining their family life. Their biggest obstacle is a society that does not sufficiently pay them for what they do.

While lack of money is the biggest obstacle in Emily and Joy's lives, the other egalitarian couple we interviewed benefits from the wealth and generosity of one set of parents, who hold the mortgage on their house and occasionally bestow on them large cash gifts. This financial bounty has made their lives easier, but it also makes the choices on which they have built their relationship and their family doubly impressive. Their financial cushion allows them to make choices most people cannot make. But money also seduces many of us away from attentiveness to the needs of our intimate relationships. And it hasn't seduced these two.

We were interested in talking to Karen and Raymond initially because we heard that they regularly found time to spend with each other, despite two busy work schedules and parenting. This was a couple that had really figured something out, we thought: couples without a woman at home much of the time, nurturing the kids and her partner, but also organizing their social life, typically lose out on time together. As we found out, that is not true for this couple.

How do they do it? First, they carefully designed a life that gave them time together and demanded less work; they said 'no' to forces that took time from family life, and their relationship. Second, they got help with childcare. Third, Raymond does as much of the childcare and housework as Karen.

Karen and Raymond have been together for seven years. Karen is older than Raymond, and this is her second marriage; she also has greater earning potential than Raymond. Their twin boys were born five years ago. The egalitarian and people-centred organization of their lives has been in place for the last three years (since Karen decided to quit a corporate job). Now both adults work in their home, on a freelance basis. That home is a modest one, in a neighbourhood that is heterogeneous both in ethnicity and income.

The choices and decisions Karen and Raymond have made are reflected at two levels: first, in their daily and weekly schedules and second, in their housing and material possessions. With respect to scheduling, Karen describes it as 'a whole constellation, like arranging for an eclipse of the moon. You have to line up everything right.' Their arrangement involves a good, regular babysitter who comes every Saturday at 4:00; early bedtimes for the twins; nanny/daycare/school (according to age) during the day for the twins' and both adults always 'on duty' and at work (doing housework or childcare) when the boys are home. The work seems to be shared equally. Raymond is clearly an equal parent. For instance, while both adults bathe the boys and put them to bed, it is Raymond who reads to them at night (and chooses most of their books), and takes them to the doctor and to school.

Days typically go as follows: While Karen makes breakfast, Raymond gets the boys up and ready for their day; he takes them to school as well; Raymond cooks most dinners and does all the marketing; Karen buys the clothes and keeps them clean; they both clean up after meals, and straighten up the house. Raymond pays the bills and does the bookkeeping, but Karen earns more of the money. They also have a cleaning woman every second week.

As impressive as their careful scheduling of work, though, is the choice they made about lifestyle, which enabled such attention to detail and principles. They chose a 'low overhead . . . low stress . . . non-ambitious lifestyle'. The 'whole show' can be run on one income, if need be, according to Karen. They live in a modest, low-cost home, when they could afford more. They work at home rather than commute to jobs (and spend more money on wardrobes and transportation). They own a ten-year-old car they intend not to replace. They buy very little. Consequently, they can take on just enough work to support themselves—a tricky business, since they live from contract to contract, and the tendency in that situation is to say 'yes' to everything. Karen describes their standard of living as 'luxurious hand-to-mouth living'.

In short, they have deliberately avoided dedicating themselves to career, success, and making money, in order to prioritize their relationship and schedule their lives as they want. Because they work at home (though only half the time, in Karen's case, since her work takes her out), and because they limit their work, they can, for example, take time during the day to be together—for lunch or even an afternoon at the movies.

According to Karen, taking care of each other and promoting each other's well-being is the essence of 'family'. This is not an unusual definition. The question is, why are these two people able to put such ideals in to practice? Perhaps Karen's wealthy background, and the continuing support of her parents, made her strong enough to make the choices that now allow her to 'take the time' she wants with Raymond and the children. Her strong earning power in the marketplace—greater than Raymond's—also, no doubt, matters. In Raymond's case, the memory of missing his father, who worked two jobs and was home only on Sundays when Raymond was young, had a strong impact: he did not want to be absent from his boys' lives. Feminism too had an impact on Raymond. 'It was in the air' when he entered adulthood, and he thinks it shaped his thinking significantly. Finally, he likes to cook, and thinks this 'eased' him into other domestic chores.

In the end, there is a lot that makes this couple unusual. But none of their unusual traits or circumstances explains the egalitarian, person-centred family they have created. Only their own daily struggles and choices explain that.

For the heterosexual couples we interviewed, the most intriguing question was why the man assumed homemaking chores and responsibilities. That these men do was the chief reason why these families are unusual, even though they are structurally nuclear. We also came across two families that are decidedly non-nuclear, however. Because the privatization of nuclear arrangements often entails problems—from the isolation of full-time homemakers (see Rosenberg, Chapter 20 this text) and the scarcity of time for dual-earner couples, to violence against women (see Gartner et al., Chapter 30 this text)—we thought these families especially important.

The first non-nuclear pattern we found involved a lesbian mother. Jennifer had had to 'really struggle' with the difficulties involved in having a family when she 'came out' as a lesbian and also began her professional career, in her late twenties. The former posed obstacles to motherhood pretty easily overcome, but the latter meant a 'difficult lifestyle' that would be hard to combine with motherhood.

Years later, in her mid-thirties, Jennifer decided to try to solve both problems by finding a sperm donor and potential parent. She wanted a man to co-parent in the event her child was a boy—knowing little herself of the experiences of boys. She became committed to finding a gay man because 'they have so little opportunity to become parents'.

Years before, she had 'put out the word' that she was looking for a father, but this time she placed an ad in a gay magazine. She received thirty replies. Claude's letter was the most interesting and, when they met, 'it seemed so *right*' that they talked the entire night.

Lee was born a little over a year later. The first several months of her life, she lived with Jennifer, although Claude was there every day. When Lee was four months old, Claude began caring for her, for whole days, in his home. Shortly after, she began staying overnight, and for weekends. The plan was to work up to a schedule whereby Claude would have Lee two-and-a-half days per week. When Lee was seven months old, Claude took her for a week's visit to the small community he grew up in, and where his family still lives. All went well. At present, a year after her birth, Lee spends six of fourteen days with Claude. Her mother and father see each other, or at least talk on the phone, every day—and are becoming closer friends because of their co-parenting.

In addition to her two parents, Lee virtually has a 'second string' of parents: Jennifer's and Claude's lovers. Jennifer's partner of seven years, Sally, lives next door to her, with her teenage daughter. Claude's partner of three years, Jon, lives with him in a house they bought together. Both Sally and Jon are very attached to Lee. Both have agreed to step into the role of parent in the event of Jennifer's or Claude's death. Meanwhile, Lee has four sets of grandparents doting on her. She is, in fact, immersed in a number of immediate families—that made up of her parents and herself; that consisting of her mother, herself, Sally and Sally's daughter; and that involving her father, herself, and Jon. On special occasions, all merge into one big family.

The logistics of this arrangement are complicated. Most immediately, the hardest thing about it is when one parent leaves town with the baby (or even takes her for a few days)—hardest, that is, for the parent left behind. Jennifer describes her upset at these times, but is quick and careful to separate her own needs from her daughter's. She describes the things Claude has done for her to ease the pain of separation; Claude nods and says, 'we try to take care of each other as parents.' Because of their independence of each other, an issue all parents face is just more immediate: 'how to give each other freedom to discover *your* way of being with that child' (Jennifer).

The prospect of separation in the future poses a larger challenge. But there is an agreement that neither will leave the city until Lee is five

years old, and that she will spend a considerable amount of time with her father should Jennifer move out of Toronto. At least this is being thought about now: a lot of planning has occurred for year-old Lee.

Our other non-nuclear family is based on a long-term commitment made years ago by one woman to her sister, to co-parent her two children and help support them financially. A graduate student at the time the commitment was made, Sarah dropped her studies and quickly obtained a professional degree that opened the door to a career. She moved in with her sister, and has been as much a parent to the two children as their biological mother. In fact, these two children—Timothy (seven years old) and Jeremy (six years old)—have four mothers. Aside from Sarah and Estelle, their biological mother, a third sister, Gwen, and the sisters' mother, Yvonne, all live together.

It was Yvonne who brought them together. When Estelle's boyfriend left her shortly after the birth of their second child, Yvonne—who had raised six children—'unquestionably took her in'. At that point, Estelle had little education, no marketable skills, and no money. Sarah, who had lived in an apartment next door to Estelle, and been very close to the children from birth, was living alone at the time. When her mother decided to rent a house in the suburbs, several months later, Sarah felt 'it would have seemed weird not to have helped out . . . I'd have lost out too.' Having just ended a relationship with a man, and not intending to have her own children, Sarah made a commitment like that of a husband and father—indeed, beyond that made by many fathers, since she has done mothering (or primary parenting) as well as providing financial support. The difficulties involved in carrying through such an unusual and weighty commitment are evident even in Sarah's daily schedule.

Sarah gets up at 5:30 every morning to make people's lunches. She and her sisters leave for work at 7:30, when the boys are just getting up. Their grandmother, then, feeds them and gets them off to school. She then goes off to her part-time job, until she has to pick them up at 3:20. Her responsibilities for the boys end at 4:30, when Sarah and Estelle return home from work. Dinner is prepared by the person most inclined to cook that night, although Sarah does the shopping and plans most of the meals. Clean-up is on an *ad hoc* basis, although Yvonne does the dishes. Basically, everyone does their share of the housework: 'It *has* to be done.' As for money, Sarah's entire paycheque, and most of Estelle's and Gwen's, go into the household account which is managed by Yvonne.

While the adults work very hard, the family they have created clearly has been a support base for each of them, as well as the children. In the five years they have been living together, the sisters have gotten five degrees among themselves, and are now earning larger salaries than they ever did before. Meanwhile, the children have four mothers. While Sarah has the most time for them, at present—and reads to them and puts them to bed every night—they seek out whichever adult is free at the moment the rest of the time. And although their father is absent from the household, without the responsibility of financial support he has proven to be a very attentive parent, on the weekend days he spends with them. 'They see him at his best,' Sarah points out.

Clearly an unusual family, Sarah acknowledges that few families of grown-ups could *do* what she, her sisters, and her mother are doing: 'We really like each other,' she says; 'we also respect and *love* our mother.' The trust that underlies her commitment to the children is apparent: she has no fears that her sister, who is dating, will marry and move her children out of the household (and away from Sarah, who loves them as her own). Because the childrens' welfare comes first, for Estelle as for Sarah, she is sure the household will remain together. And while Sarah's career prospects probably were not improved by her decision to commit to this unusual family arrangement, she feels her gains have been tremendous. The two children love her

as a mother, and she lives with the people with whom she is most comfortable, who love her, and who give her emotional support.

Finally, we have a story about the past, and some people's determined attempts to create a different pattern of family, and especially of childcare. This is Liz's story about raising her son, Carl, who is now twenty-one.

When Liz became pregnant in the early 1970s, she set out to raise Carl outside what she saw as the limitations of nuclear-family living. Her negative assessment of 'the nuclear family' was a common one among people entering adulthood in the late 1960s: the families they had grown up in had seemed constraining, even stifling—no doubt, partly as a result of the frustrations their mothers had felt as full-time homemakers. Accordingly, a critique of the position of full-time homemaker was one of the grounds on which 1960s women—including Liz—built the Women's Liberation Movement.

Liz's personal reaction to nuclear families went even deeper than most women's, however. Her parents had both died when she was a teenager. In fact, she had had to deal with her father's death, and then her mother's illness and death, all alone: she was an only child. The liabilities attached to children's reliance on only two adults were painfully clear to her.

At the same time, Liz recalls that the early 1970s in Toronto constituted a 'charged political moment' for many people her age. Many in the Women's Movement had a 'really strong visionary sense of *transforming* society', creating an antisexist, anti-racist, socialist world. Necessary to that task was 'transforming our children': 'We had some notion that if you could construct people differently, you could make a better world,' Liz remembers. Accordingly, Liz and many others lived collectively—in Liz's case, with her male partner and twelve other adults, in a large old house in downtown Toronto.

Additionally, a group of students and faculty at the University of Toronto set out to create a daycare centre on campus that was not primarily a service to employed parents, but instead a way of raising children differently, as part of a community. They occupied a building on campus, in order to create a second campus daycare centre. It was during this period that Carl was born.

Carl spent his early months living, day and night, in the occupied daycare centre. Liz joined him at four o'clock every afternoon, where she helped cook dinner for the dozens of adults and children occupying the building; she stayed overnight there, and then left in the morning to go work on her Master's thesis. Since his father, John, was away at the time, Carl was left under the care of adults Liz trusted would do their best for him.

Carl remained in daycare, during the day, after the occupation of the building ended (and the University was 'persuaded' to turn it into a second childcare facility). Additionally, for much of his childhood, Carl lived with more adults than just Liz and John. Their landlord turned their first house—the co-op—into luxury offices when Carl was a year old, so Liz used her father's life-insurance money to buy them a house. For the next seven years, various adult friends, and often children, lived with Liz, John, and Carl. Some of these adults, as well as a woman friend of Liz's who took Carl one night a week for years, forged very strong emotional bonds with Carl. And there were other adults outside the household who cared for Carl: one family, with a child Carl's age, took Carl one night a week, and sent their child to stay with Carl on another night.

The relationships supporting Carl (and John) seemed strong enough that Liz was able to leave Carl for a year (with pretty frequent visits) when he was four and a half, to do research for her Ph.D. thesis. Arguing that Carl did not suffer from the separation, and in fact had a better experience while growing up than other children, Liz describes his reaction as a six year old to the possibility that his father—who was driving on the highway in a snowstorm that day—could have an accident. When asked what he

would do should both parents die, Carl replied that he would go to Susan's house (the woman who cared for him one night a week), or, if she were not home, to Deborah's, etc., until he found someone who would take care of him. Liz describes a self-confident child, whose confidence she attributes to his assurance 'that there were many people he *knew* could look after him because they had *done* it'.

What began out of political will, Liz now sees as having such benefits she is recreating collective living and childrearing in her life today. The benefits for her involve having children around, and the possibility of forging close relations with them, when she cannot handle having many children of her 'own'. Looking back, she argues that something more profound is gained through collective childcare:

> The other thing it gave us was . . . We all had a lot more space to *delight* in being together because it wasn't tied so strongly to this overpowering sense of responsibility. . . . When I was with him [Carl] I felt really delighted and happy to be there, which made me a better parent than I'd have been if I'd felt lumbered by the ongoing responsibility. I think in terms of the kids, it gave them more of a sense of their capacity to be autonomous people because they saw all these varieties of ways of doing things [including parenting] . . .

As final evidence that Carl was raised in a more liberating way, Liz asserts that there never was a contested period during Carl's teens, there were never fights over authority and autonomy.

Liz goes on to say that she thinks the children raised in this community

> somehow . . . had a sense of responsibility, but it was a responsibility to the community. You behave responsibly because that's your obligation to the group. Not because a person has said you must or love will be taken

away. . . . [There's] something about the way personality gets formed in that kind of context . . . more solid, more individualized and more collectivized at the same time.

In all of these families, defying the norm demanded making very careful choices about how to organize family and personal life. A great deal of thought, self-examination, and negotiation went into the creation of all these domestic arrangements. Nevertheless, for all the heterosexual couples—where the man's assumption of domestic responsibilities was the chief variation from the norm—the women had better money-earning potential than their partners. These cou-

ples were fairly rare to begin with, then. And they were without the main material source of women's subordination. What is important, though, is that the men who stayed home full-time were pleased with their lives—finding great satisfaction in the close relationships they have with their children (as well as having the problems all homemakers experience). Very far from 'dysfunctional', these families seem to work well, satisfying both individual and collective needs. Also far from 'dysfunctional' are the non-nuclear families here. In fact, they have an advantage over nuclear families, in that they are disposed to incorporate more than just two adults into the responsibilities of raising children.

Notes

Our thanks to Ester Reiter for very helpful comments on an earlier draft, and especially to all the people who took time out of very busy schedules to tell us about their lives.

1. This is unusual, in more ways than the obvious. Berk (1985) found that even in households where men do some household work, women almost universally get up earlier and do all the meal preparation, housework, and childcare that occurs before school and paid work begin.

2. It was interesting to us that while Tom seemed pleased with his domestic role, Barbara evidenced some guilt in the course of this discussion of who did what.

3. The men in Hochschild's (1989) study who shouldered much of the housework and childcare also had reacted negatively to their fathers.

References

Berk, S. 1985. *The Gender Factory* (New York: Plenum Press).

Boulton, M. 1983. *On Being a Mother* (London: Tavistock).

Eichler, M. 1988. *Families in Canada Today*, 2nd edn (Toronto: Gage).

Frederick, J. 1995. 'As Time Goes By . . . Time Use of Canadians', cat. no. 89–544 (Ottawa: Industry).

Hochschild, A. 1989. *The Second Shift* (New York: Viking).

Luxton, M. 1980. *More Than a Labour of Love* (Toronto: The Women's Press).

Michelson, W. 1983. *From Sun to Sun* (Totawa, NJ: Rowman & Allenheld).

Morris, L. 1990. *The Workings of the Household* (Cambridge: Polity).

Oakley, A. 1974. *The Sociology of Housework* (New York: Pantheon).

Rich, A. 1976. *Of Women Born* (New York: Norton).

Part Seven **Other Family Matters**

Chapter 30

Tragically, families may feature violence. This needs explaining. That this violence is not so rare suggests that some core features of intimate relations between women and men may themselves be at the heart of the problem. This article contains a review of the main findings of a large study of the women who *were killed in Ontario between 1974 and 1994. Rosemary Gartner and her colleagues review their findings, and draw on other researchers' findings, to conclude that gender is indeed central to men's violence against women.*

Confronting Violence in Women's Lives

Rosemary Gartner, Myrna Dawson, and Maria Crawford

Woman Killing: Intimate Femicide in Ontario, 1974–94

In March 1988, a young mother of two was killed by her estranged husband in a northern Ontario town. The killer had been visiting his wife who was staying in a shelter for abused women. Convinced that she was not going to return to him, he shot her twice at close range. Later that year, in a small town outside of Edmonton, a woman was shot dead in her home by her estranged husband who then shot and killed himself. Miraculously, the woman's three-year-old girl, whom she was holding in her arms when she was shot, was not wounded. These women were two of the 202 female victims of homicide in Canada in 1988. They shared with 68 other female victims a marital relationship with their killers. These two women also shared the experience of having been clients and friends of women who worked in shelters for abused women in Ontario.

In response to these and other killings of women they had worked with, eight women met in January 1989 to share their experiences and provide each other emotional support. Within a few months the group had named itself the Women We Honour Action Committee, setting itself the task of learning more about the phenomenon of women killed by their intimate part-ners. With the support of a grant from the Ontario Women's Directorate, they conducted a literature review on women killed by their intimate partners, or intimate femicide.

That literature review led to a number of conclusions about the then-existing state of knowledge about intimate femicide (Women We Honour and R. Gartner 1990). First, obtaining an accurate estimate of the number of such killings in Canada or in Ontario from statistics in official publications was not possible because official publications restricted their classifications to 'spouse killings', which excluded killings by estranged common-law partners and current or former boyfriends. Second, information on the nature of intimate femicide—its dynamics as well as its structural and cultural sources—was incomplete. In part this reflected researchers' reliance on small, highly select samples, on offenders' recollections of their crimes, and on traditional psychological and psychiatric concepts and classifications. Third, much of the research had been conducted in the United States which is atypical in both the quantity and quality of its homicides. That is, spousal homicides make up a much smaller proportion of total homicides in the United States compared to many other nations. Moreover, the ratio of female to male victims of spouse killings is more balanced in the United States than in other countries (about 1.3: 1, compared to about 3:1 in Canada, Australia, Denmark, the UK, and other countries) (Wilson and Daly 1992b; Regoeczi and Silverman 1997).

It was to address these limitations that the Women We Honour Action Committee approached the Ontario Women's Directorate for funding to conduct their study of intimate femicide in Ontario. The study had three goals: to document for Ontario the incidence of killings of women by intimate partners, including legal spouses, common-law partners and boyfriends, both current and estranged, to describe the characteristics of the people involved in and the circumstances surrounding these killings; and to present the stories of a small number of women who had been killed by their intimate partners. That study, completed in 1992, compiled and analyzed data on all intimate femicides known to authorities in Ontario from 1974 to 1990 (Crawford, Gartner, and the Women We Honour Action Committee 1992). A second study, designed to update the data through 1994, was completed in April 1997 (Crawford et al. 1997).

In this article, we describe the major findings of these two studies of intimate femicide. Our purpose is twofold: first, to provide an overview and statistical picture of intimate femicide in Ontario for the twenty-one years from 1974 to 1994; and, second, to locate this statistical picture in what is now a substantially larger and more sophisticated literature on violence against women by intimate partners. That literature encompasses studies similar in many ways to ours—that is, studies of the incidence and characteristics of relatively large numbers of femicides—as well as work designed to provide a theoretical and conceptual framework for understanding intimate femicide. We draw on that literature below in discussing our findings.

Framing the Issue of Intimate Femicide

After completing our literature review in 1989, we concluded that intimate femicide is a phe-nomenon distinct in important ways both from the killing of men by their intimate partners and from non-lethal violence against women; and, hence, that it requires analysis in its own right. This view was in contrast to much of the existing literature which treated 'spousal violence' as a relatively undifferentiated phenomenon arising out of the intense emotions, stresses, and conflicts that often characterize marital relations (Goode 1969; Boudoris 1971; Chimbos 1978; Blinder 1985). These analyses tended to locate the sources of 'spousal violence' in patterns of learning early in life, in the disinhibitory effects of alcohol consumption, and in dysfunctional patterns of communication between marital partners. Much of this early work also tended to devote limited attention and analysis to gender differences in spousal violence.

In response to this neglect of gender, a number of analysts have made gender a central feature of their accounts of spousal violence. Sex role theorists highlight gender differences in socialization which teach males to view toughness, power, and control as masculine attributes. Evolutionary theorists argue that violence is an adaptive strategy for males facing the loss of status and control over their partners. Resource theorists view violence as the ultimate resource available to men when other means of exerting control over their partners are exhausted. General systems theorists argue that for men the rewards of violence against their wives are greater than the costs, because of society's failure to adequately sanction such violence. The arguments of these more gender-sensitive analyses resonated with the experiences of members of the Women We Honour Action Committee. Power, control, and domination were themes that they encountered daily in talking with abused women and that they detected in relationships ending in intimate femicide.

In recent work specifically focused on women killed by their intimate partners, these themes have been elaborated and, in the case of feminist analyses, placed in a historical and institutional context (Campbell 1992; Kelkar 1992;

Marcus 1994; Maloney 1994). For example, Wilson and Daly (1992a) cite 'male sexual proprietariness' as the predominant motive in the killing of wives across cultures and historical epochs. 'Men exhibit a tendency to think of women as sexual and reproductive "property" that they can own and exchange. . . . Proprietary entitlements in people have been conceived and institutionalized as identical to proprietary entitlements in land, chattels, and other economic resources.' They go on to note, 'That men take a proprietary view of female sexuality and reproductive capacity is manifested in various cultural practices,' including claustration practices, asymmetrical adultery laws, and bride-prices. From this perspective, an extreme, if apparently incongruous manifestation of male proprietariness is intimate femicide. If unable to control or coerce his partner through other means, a man may exert the ultimate control over her by killing her.

Thus, male proprietariness, or male sexual jealousy, has been placed at the centre of many empirical and theoretical analyses of intimate femicide. For example, research on intimate femicide and spousal homicide in Canada, Australia, Great Britain, and the United States (Dobash and Dobash 1984; Wallace 1986; Daly and Wilson 1988; Polk 1994) has identified a common core in these killings of 'masculine control, where women become viewed as the possessions of men, and the violence reflects steps taken by males to assert their domination over "their" women' (Polk 1994). This empirical work challenges many of the popular notions about the characteristics of such crimes, for example, the belief that they are explosive, unplanned, and unpredictable acts of passion. At the same time, it contests the validity and coherence of the concept 'spousal homicide' with its connotations of sexual symmetry in violence by revealing distinct differences between intimate partner killings by men and those by women. As Dobash et al. (1992) note:

> Men often kill wives after lengthy periods of prolonged physical violence accompanied by

other forms of abuse and coercion; the roles in such cases are seldom if ever reversed. Men perpetrate familicidal massacres, killing spouses and children together; women do not. Men commonly hunt down and kill wives who have left them; women hardly ever behave similarly. Men kill wives as part of planned murder-suicides; analogous acts by women are almost unheard of. Men kill in response to revelations of wifely infidelity; women almost never respond similarly.

In sum, there have been significant advances in both empirical and conceptual analyses of lethal violence against women by their partners since the literature review that served as the impetus for our research. Those advances have not, however, filled all of the gaps identified in our earlier review. In particular, empirical research in Canada has continued to rely largely on official statistics from police sources, which exclude from their classification of spousal homicides killings by men of their estranged common-law partners and girlfriends. Relying on these official statistics also restricts analyses to the information and coding schemes employed by police agencies and personnel. Because of our concerns about the potential for lost information and for the introduction of unknown biases, we relied on a wider range of information sources than typically used in previous research. In this way, our study is unusual in the comprehensiveness of its data. As we see below, it is not however unique in its findings about the nature of intimate femicide.

Data Sources

We began our data collection by searching death records kept by the Office of the Chief Coroner for Ontario. Coroner's records provide a centralized source of information on all deaths in Ontario, and a means of identifying and assessing records for deaths identified by the Coroner's Office as homicides. These files frequently contain copies of police reports as well as medical reports on the condition of the body, the way in which the woman was killed and the violence suffered— details often not available from other sources. However, coroner's records, like all official sources of information on homicide, are imperfect measures of the actual number of deaths due to homicide. For example, cases of homicide in which no body has been found will not typically appear in coroner's records. As a consequence, we expect our estimates of the incidence of intimate femicide to undercount the true incidence, an issue we discuss in more depth below.[1]

We were able to cross-check and supplement data from coroner's records by reviewing police homicide investigation files for many of our cases.[2] In the second study, we were also able to review data from Crown Attorney files on many of the cases in which charges were laid between 1991 and 1994. In both studies, we supplemented our data from official sources with information from newspaper and magazine articles on some of the killings and on trials of some of the alleged offenders.

We compiled this information so that it could be used in both quantitative and qualitative analyses. Our final data collection instrument was designed to provide codes for approximately fifty-two variables, as well as space to record a narrative of the case where further information was available.[3]

The Incidence of Intimate Femicide in Ontario, 1974–94

Between 1974 and 1994, 1,206 women aged fifteen and older were killed in Ontario, according to official records.[4] In 1,120 (93 per cent) of these cases, the crimes were solved and the killers were identified. In 705 (63 per cent) of the solved cases, the killers were the current or former legal spouses, common-law partners, or boyfriends of their victims. Thus, in Ontario over this twenty-one-year period, intimate partners were responsi-

ble for the majority of all woman killings and an average of thirty-four women were victims of intimate femicide each year. These data indicate that the focus in official publications and some academic research on 'spousal homicides' of women provides an incomplete picture of the more general phenomenon of intimate femicide: excluding killings of women by their estranged common-law partners and current and former boyfriends underestimates the total number of intimate femicides by about 25 per cent.

The actual number of intimate femicides in Ontario during these years is undoubtedly higher than this. Intimate partners were certainly responsible for some portion of the cases in which no offender was identified or in which we had too little information to determine the precise nature of the relationship between victim and offender.[5] Adjusting for excluded cases, we estimate that intimate femicides may have accounted for as many as 76 per cent of all femicides in Ontario between 1974 and 1994. However, since it is impossible to know the number and characteristics of excluded cases, the analyses that follow focus only on those 705 cases in which the offender was officially identified as the current or former intimate partner of the victim.

TRENDS IN INTIMATE FEMICIDE

Between 1974 and 1994, the rate of intimate femicide (i.e., the number of victims of intimate femicide per 100,000 women in the general population) ranged from a low of .55 in 1978 to a high of 1.26 in 1991, but appears to follow no particular trend over time (see Figure 1).[6] Dividing the twenty-one-year period in half suggests otherwise, however: the average annual rate for the second half of the period (1.01 per 100,000) was slightly higher than the rate for the first half (.92 per 100,000).

On its own, this difference is insignificant statistically and, it might appear, substantively. However, when compared to the statistically significant decreases in other types of lethal violence, the slightly higher rate of intimate femicide in the latter period takes on greater importance. The annual rate at which women were killed by strangers or unknown assailants declined significantly from an average of .27 during 1974–83 to .16 during 1984–94. Moreover, the annual rate at which men were killed by their spouses also declined significantly, from an average rate of .31 during 1974–83 to .18 during 1984–94. In other words, during a period when women's risks from strangers and men's risks from spouses decreased, women's risks from their intimate partners increased slightly. Put another way, after 1984—a period of substantial expansion in services for abused women—men's risks of being killed by intimate partners decreased significantly whereas women's risks did not.

Without further analysis of these patterns—which is beyond the scope of this article—we can only speculate as to the reasons for this apparently counter-intuitive finding. One possible explanation is that while the expansion of services for abused women may have resulted in the protection of abusive men from defensive violence by their intimate partners, these same services did not necessarily protect women from their male partners' violence. Research shows that women are most likely to kill their intimate partners after prolonged abuse and when they fear continued or more serious violence against themselves or their children (Browne 1987). Where services for abused women are available, women in abusive relationships have an alternative to killing their partners. As Browne and Williams (1989) note, 'By offering threatened women protection, escape and aid, [legal and extra-legal] resources can engender an awareness that there are alternatives to remaining at risk' and thus prevent 'killings that occur in desperation.' Their analysis of US data lends support to this interpretation: states with higher levels of services to abused women had lower rates of spouse killings of males, but not lower rates of spouse killings for females.

Figure 1: **Trends in Rates of Lethal Violence, Ontario 1974–94**

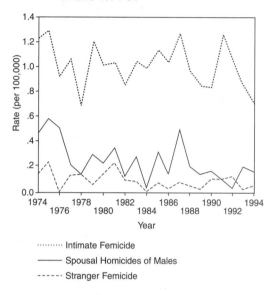

- ········· Intimate Femicide
- ——— Spousal Homicides of Males
- ------ Stranger Femicide

Characteristics of the Victims and Their Killers

In many respects, the women killed by their intimate partners and the men who killed them[7] are very similar to women and men in the general population of Ontario, as can be seen from the data in Table 1. For example, women killed by their intimate partners were, on average, about 37 years old; 51 per cent were employed; 80 per cent had children; and 76 per cent were born in Canada. These characteristics do not distinguish the victims from other women in Ontario.

In some other respect, however, victims of intimate femicide and their killers differed from women and men in the general population.[8] We can think of these differences as risk markers for intimate femicide because they tell us that some types of women and men face disproportionately high risks of intimate victimization or offending.[9] Each of the markers we discuss below has also been associated with increased risks of lethal violence against women in other research.

Table 1: Characteristics of Victims of Intimate Femicide and Their Killers, Ontario, 1974–94

Characteristics	Victims	Offenders
Total number	705	705
Average age	37	41
% born in Canada	76	70
% with children	80	77
Employment Status		
% employed	51	64
% unemployed	17	21
% homemakers	18	0
% students	5	2
% retired or on disability pension	9	13
Relationship of Victim to Offender		
% legal spouse, cohabiting	–	39
% legal spouse, separated	–	16
% common-law partner, cohabiting	–	18
% common-law partner, separated	–	7
% divorced spouse	–	<1
% current girlfriend	–	12
% estranged girlfriend	–	8
% Aboriginal	6	6

RELATIONSHIP STATUS

Research based on data on spouse killings from Great Britain, Australia, the United States, and Canada shows that two indicators of the status of the relationship—estrangement and common-law status—are associated with a higher risk of spouse killings of women (Wallace 1986; Campbell 1992; Wilson and Daly 1993; Johnson 1996). We find similar patterns in our intimate femicide data, although the limited availability of data on marital separation and common-law unions within the general population restricts our analysis somewhat.

Census Canada collects information on marital separations, but only for registered marriages. According to census figures, during the years of our study, 3 per cent of women in Ontario were separated from their legal spouses. According to our data, among the victims of intimate femicide, 16 per cent were separated from their legal spouses. Separation, then, appears to be a risk factor for intimate femicide, since women who were separated from their partners were greatly overrepresented among victims of intimate femicide. However, exactly how much greater the risks are for separated women cannot be determined from our data. This is because our measure of separation and the census measure of separation are not precisely compatible: the census measure captures largely long-term and relatively well-established separations, whereas our measure is more sensitive and captures short-term as well as long-term separations. Thus our measure will yield a higher estimate of separated couples. Nevertheless, we expect that even correcting for this difference, we would find separation to be associated with higher risks of intimate femicide.

Data on the prevalence of common-law unions in the general population have been collected only since 1991, so we can estimate the risks to women living in common-law relationships only for the most recent years of our research. According to census data, 4 per cent of women were living in common-law unions in 1991 in Ontario. According to our data, during 1991–4, 21 per cent of the victims of intimate femicide were killed by common-law partners with whom they were living. Based on our calculations, the rate of intimate femicide for women in common-law unions was approximately six times greater than the average rate of intimate femicide in Ontario in the early 1990s.[10] Clearly, then, women in common-law unions were greatly over-represented among victims of intimate femicide during the early 1990s, and perhaps in earlier years as well.

The higher risks associated with common-law status and estrangement have been interpreted in various ways. Compared to couples in registered marriages, common-law partners are more likely to be poor, young, unemployed, and childless—all factors associated with higher homicide rates. Compared to co-residing couples, estranged couples are more likely to have a history of domestic violence (Rodgers 1994; Johnson and Sacco 1995). This violence may be associated both with women's decisions to leave their relationships and with their greater risks of intimate femicide. In other words, 'the fact that separated couples constitute a subset of marriages with a history of discord could explain their higher homicide rates' (Wilson and Daly 1994).

Male sexual proprietariness could also play a role in the higher risks for common-law and estranged relationships. If, as some have speculated, 'husbands may be less secure in the proprietary claims over wives in common-law unions than in registered unions', they may be more likely to resort to serious violence to enforce those claims or to lethal violence when those claims are challenged (Wilson, Johnson, and Daly 1995: 343). Echoing a similar theme, several studies that have found elevated risks at separation have cited the male's inability to accept termination of the relationship and obsessional desires to maintain control over his sexual partner: 'He would destroy his intimate "possession" rather than let her fall into the hands of a competitor male' (Polk 1994: 29; see also Rasche 1989; Campbell 1992; Wilson and Daly 1993).

ETHNICITY

Women in certain ethnic groups have risks of intimate femicide disproportionate to their representation in the population, according to several studies. For example, in the United States African-American women face unusually high risks of intimate femicide. In Canada, such research is more difficult to do because of restrictions on the collection of crime statistics by race and ethnicity. However, Statistics Canada has collected data on Aboriginal victims of spousal homicides which indicate that Aboriginal women's rates of spousal homicide are between five and ten times higher than the rates for non-Aboriginal women (Kennedy, Forde, and Silverman 1989; Silverman and Kennedy 1993).

We had initially hoped to explore ethnic and cultural differences in the risk of intimate femicide in our research. Our community advisory group, which was composed of women from various ethnic backgrounds active in community organizations, encouraged us to do so.[11] However, our research agreement with the Ministry of the Solicitor General prevented us from compiling 'statistics based upon social, cultural, regional, linguistic, racial or ethnic group' from the coroners' records. Nevertheless, we were able to document the number of Aboriginal victims of intimate femicide during these years by relying on other sources of data.[12]

We estimate that at least 6 per cent of the victims of intimate femicide in Ontario between 1974 and 1994 were Aboriginal women. Census data for these years indicate that just under 1 per cent of all women living in Ontario classified themselves as Aboriginal. Thus, Aboriginal women in Ontario appear to be overrepresented among the victims of intimate femicide. Conversely, Aboriginal men are overrepresented as offenders, since all but four of the Aboriginal victims were killed by Aboriginal men.

A number of factors might explain the disproportionate risks of intimate femicide faced by Aboriginal women. Aboriginal Canadians, similar to African Americans, are an economically impoverished and politically disenfranchised ethnic minority. Considerable research has shown that economic, social, and political disadvantages are associated with higher homicide rates generally, as well as higher rates of serious spousal violence. In addition, Aboriginal Canadian heterosexual couples also have disproportionate rates of other risk markers for intimate partner violence, such as common-law marital status, low income, bouts of male unemployment, exposure to violence in childhood, alcohol abuse, overcrowded housing conditions, and social isolation—all of which have been cited as reasons for the higher rates of family violence in Aboriginal communities (Health and Welfare Canada 1990; Long 1995). Some analysts situate these risk factors within a structural approach that views them as consequences of internal colonialism: 'the conditions of colonialism [are] directly related to aboriginal acts of political violence as well as rates of suicide, homicide, and family violence among the aboriginal peoples' (Frank 1993; Bachmann 1993; Long 1995: 42).

EMPLOYMENT

Men's unemployment is commonly cited as a risk factor for wife assaults and is also associated with elevated risks of spousal homicide. Women's employment status, on the other hand, does not appear to be consistently associated with their risks of violence from their partners (Hotaling and Sugarman 1986; Brinkerhoff and Lupri 1988; Macmillan and Gartner 1996; Johnson 1996). The association between men's unemployment and violence against their female partners traditionally has been attributed to the stresses produced by unemployment and limited economic resources. But if this were the case, one would expect to find more evidence that women's unemployment is also associated with spousal violence, which is not the case. For those who see male violence against their partners as one resource for demonstrating power and control, the gender-specificity of the affects of unemployment is not surprising: men who lack more traditional resources (such as economic success) may 'forge a particular type of masculinity that centers on ultimate control of the domestic setting through the use of violence' (Messerschmidt 1993: 149).

Our data on intimate femicide are consistent with this interpretation. For women, employment status is not associated with differential risks of intimate femicide: 51 per cent of women in both the victim population and the general population were employed during the period of our study. For men, however, employment status is associated with differential risks. Among intimate femicide offenders, 64 per cent were employed, whereas among males in the general population, 73 per cent were employed. In Ontario, then, male unemployment appears to be associated with higher risks of intimate femicide offending.

OFFENDERS' VIOLENT HISTORIES

Several studies have shown that men who kill their spouses frequently have histories of violent behaviour, both in and outside their marital relationships (Johnson 1996: 183–6). As Johnson notes, '[a]lthough some wife killings are the result of sudden, unforeseeable attacks by depressed or mentally unstable husbands and are unrelated to a history of violence in the family, most do not seem to fit this description' (p. 183). Because of this, risk assessment tools designed to assess battered women's risk of lethal violence typically include measures of their partners' violence against their children and outside of the home, and threats of serious violence against their wives or others (Campbell 1995).

We also found evidence of unusual levels of violence in the backgrounds of the offenders in our sample. At least 31 per cent of them had an arrest record for a violent offence.[13] At least 53 per cent of them were known to have been violent in the past toward women they ultimately killed. This corresponds to data for Canada as a whole which indicates that in 52 per cent of spousal homicides of women between 1991 and 1993, police were aware of previous violent incidents between the spouses (Canadian Centre for Justice Statistics 1993). In addition, in at least 34 per cent of the cases of intimate femicide, the offenders were known to have previously threatened their victims with violence.[14] At least 10 per cent of the killings occurred while the offender was on probation or parole, or under a restraining order.

It is important to emphasize that these are *minimum* estimates of the number of offenders with violent and criminal histories. In over 200 of the 705 cases of intimate femicide we did not have enough information to determine if previous violence or police contact had occurred. Nevertheless, the information we were able to find clearly challenges the view that intimate femicides are typically momentary rages or heat-of-passion killings by otherwise non-violent men driven to act out of character by extreme circumstances.

A Summary of Risk Markers for Intimate Femicide

Women killed by their intimate male partners and the men who kill them are drawn from all classes, all age groups, all cultural and ethnic backgrounds. However, the victims of intimate femicide and their killers in our study did differ from other women and men in Ontario in some important respects: they were more likely than women and men in the general population to be separated from their partners, to be in common-law relationships, and to be Aboriginal. In addition, men who killed their intimate partners were also likely to be unemployed and to have histories of criminal violence. These risk markers for intimate femicide have been noted in other research on spousal homicides, and have been interpreted from within various theoretical frameworks. We suggest that they are perhaps most consistent with a framework which views intimate femicide as the manifestation of extreme (if ultimately self-defeating) controlling and proprietary attitudes and behaviours by men towards their female partners.

Characteristics of the Killings

An adequate understanding of the sources of intimate femicide will need to take account of the particular characteristics of these killings. Prior research has devoted much less attention to these characteristics than to the characteristics of the individuals involved in the killings.[15] As a consequence, we are limited in both the comparisons we can draw between our findings and the findings from other research and in the interpretations we can offer of these findings.

Intimate femicides are typically very private acts: three-quarters of the victims were killed in their own homes and, in almost half of these cases, in their own bedrooms. Less than 20 per cent occurred in public places, such as streets, parks, workplaces or public buildings. The most typical method was shooting: one-third of the victims were killed with firearms. Virtually all the other methods required direct and often prolonged physical contact between offenders and their victims: about two-thirds of the offenders stabbed, bludgeoned, beat, strangled, or slashed the throats of their victims.

One of the distinguishing features of intimate femicide is the extent and nature of violence done to the victim. Unlike killings by women of their intimate partners, intimate femicides often involve multiple methods of far more violence than is necessary to kill the victim.[16] For example, in over half of the stabbings, offenders inflicted four or more stab wounds. Beatings and bludgeonings typically involved prolonged violence—leading some coroners to use the term 'over-kill' to describe them. In about 20 per cent of the cases, offenders used multiple methods against their victims, such as stabbing and strangling or beating and slashing. In about 10 per cent of the cases, we also found evidence that the victim's body had been mutilated or dismembered.

The violence in these killings is much more likely to be sexualized than when women kill their intimate partners.[17] Records on approximately half of the cases in our study provided sufficient information for us to determine whether sexual violence was present. In 27 per cent of these cases we found evidence that the victims had been raped, sodomized, or sexually mutilated; in another 22 per cent of the cases the victim's body was found partially or completely unclothed.

Consumption of alcohol by offenders and/or victims was no more common in intimate femicides than in other killings: 39 per cent of the offenders and 32 per cent of the victims had been drinking immediately prior to the killing. In only 3 per cent of the cases was there evidence of drug use by offenders or victims immediately prior to the killing.

Establishing the motives in these killings is fraught with difficulties, as suggested earlier. We made our own determination of the motive after reviewing all the information available to us. In about one-fourth of the cases we felt we had insufficient information to make a judgment about the offender's motive. In the remaining cases, one motive clearly predominated: the offender's rage or despair over the actual or impending estrangement from his partner. This motive characterized 45 per cent of the killings in which we identified a motive. In contrast, women who kill their intimate partners only rarely kill out of anger over an estrangement (Browne 1987; Daly and Wilson 1988).

Suspected or actual infidelity of the victim was the motive in another 15 per cent of the intimate femicides. In 10 per cent of the cases the killing appears to have been the final act of violence in a relationship characterized by serial abuse.[18] In only 5 per cent of the cases did stressful life circumstances—such as bankruptcy, job loss, or serious illness—appear to motivate the killer;[19] and in only 3 per cent of the cases was there evidence that the killer was mentally ill.

Another feature that distinguishes intimate femicide from intimate partner killings by women is the number of people who die as a result of these crimes. The 705 cases of intimate femicide resulted in the deaths of 977 persons. Most of these additional deaths were suicides by the offenders: 31 per cent of the offenders killed themselves after killing their female partners.[20] But offenders killed an additional 75 persons,

most of whom were children of the victims. In addition, over 100 children witnessed their mothers' deaths; thus, while they may have escaped physical harm, they obviously suffered inestimable psychological harm.

Our documentation of these characteristics of intimate femicide cannot sufficiently convey the complexity and context surrounding these crimes. Nevertheless, it serves important purposes. Comparing characteristics of intimate partner killings by males and females shows the distinctiveness of these two types of killings—a distinctiveness that is obscured in studies that treat intimate partner killings by men and women as instances of a single phenomenon. Compared to killings of men by intimate female partners, intimate femicides are much more likely to involve extreme and sexualized violence, to be motivated by anger over separation, to be followed by the suicide of the offender, and to be accompanied by the killing of additional victims. These features highlight the gender-specificity of intimate partner killings and are consistent with a perspective on intimate femicide which views it as based in a larger system of gender[ed] inequality and stratification which perpetuates male control over women's sexuality, labour, and, at times, lives and deaths.

The Criminal Justice Response to Intimate Femicide

In our initial study of intimate femicide, we had not intended to collect and analyze data on the criminal justice responses to men who killed their intimate partners—in part because our primary interest was in the victims of intimate femicide and in part because we did not expect information on criminal justice responses to be consistently reported in coroners' and police records. However, contrary to our expectations, we were able to obtain information on charges laid, convictions, and sentencing in a substantial number of the cases. In 90 per cent of the 490 cases in which we were able to establish that offenders did not commit suicide, we found at least some information on criminal justice processing.

In 94 per cent of these cases, the offenders were charged with either first- or second-degree murder.[21] The proportion charged with first-degree murder increased over time, from 34 per cent of the cases in the first half of the period to 52 per cent in the second half. Of the 346 cases for which we found information on dispositions, 10 per cent were convicted of first-degree murder, 35 per cent of second-degree murder, and 38 per cent of manslaughter. Murder convictions increased over time: from 32 per cent of the dispositions in the first half of the period to 56 per cent in the second half. Acquittals accounted for a total of 13 per cent of the cases: 11 per cent were verdicts of not guilty by reason of insanity and 2 per cent were straight acquittals.

Sentencing information, available for 302 of the men convicted of killing their partners, also indicates that criminal justice responses to intimate femicide increased in severity over time. Prior to 1984, 7 per cent of convicted offenders received no jail time, 14 per cent were sent to secure mental institutions for indefinite periods, 25 per cent were sentenced to less than five years in prison, 38 per cent were sentenced to between five and ten years, and 15 per cent received sentences of more than ten years. After 1983, 4 per cent of convicted offenders received no jail time, 7 per cent were sent to secure mental institutions, 10 per cent received sentences of less than five years, 37 per cent received sentences of between five and ten years, and 41 per cent were sentenced to prison for more than ten years.

This evidence clearly shows that criminal justice responses to intimate femicide became increasingly punitive over the twenty-one years of our study. How much of this trend reflects increasing punitiveness towards all violent criminals and how much reflects growing public awareness and intolerance of violence against women is an issue requiring further research.[22]

The Gender-Specific Nature of Intimate Femicide

We have alluded to the gender-specific nature of intimate femicide at various points in our analysis. Here, we develop our ideas about this gender-specificity by considering what is known about gender differences in homicide more generally. We base this discussion on a large body of criminological research on homicide, as well as on data on over 7,000 homicides collected by Rosemary Gartner and Bill McCarthy as part of a separate research project.

Among those who study homicide, it is well known that women and men are killed in different numbers, by different types of people, and in different circumstances. Women are less likely to be victims of homicide than men in virtually all societies. Canada and Ontario are no different: men outnumbered women as victims of homicide by a ratio of approximately 2:1 in Canada and in Ontario between 1974 and 1994.

This may appear to indicate that women have a sort of protective advantage over men—that, at least in this sphere of social life, women are not disadvantaged relative to men. However, if we consider gender differences in offending, a different picture emerges. Men accounted for 87 per cent of all homicide offenders in Ontario during these years; and males outnumbered females as offenders by a ratio of almost 7:1. When women were involved in homicides, then, they were almost three times more likely to be victims than offenders; when men were involved in homicides they were more likely to be offenders than victims. In other words, women are overrepresented among victims and underrepresented among offenders; for men the opposite is true.

Women were also much more likely than men to be killed by someone of the opposite sex, as these figures imply. Fully 98 per cent of all women killed in Ontario between 1974 and 1994 were killed by men. Only 17 per cent of adult male victims were killed by women. Thus, man killing appears to be primarily a reflection of relations *within* a gender, whereas woman killing appears to be primarily a matter of relations *between* the genders. Because women are the majority of victims in opposite sex killings, such killings can be seen as one of the high costs to women of male dominance and desire for control in heterosexual relationships.

It is in intimate relationships between women and men that male dominance and control are most likely to erupt into physical violence. Women accounted for 75 per cent of all victims of spouse killings in Ontario during the last two decades.[23] So women outnumbered men among victims of spouse killings by a ratio of about 3:1. Moreover, spousal homicides accounted for over 50 per cent of all killings of women but less than 10 per cent of all killings of men.

If males, unlike females, are not killed primarily by their intimate partners, who are they killed by and under what circumstances? In Ontario, about 60 per cent of male victims are killed by acquaintances and strangers; another 20 per cent are killed by unknown assailants. Most male-male homicides are the result of arguments or disputes that escalate to killings. In many cases, both victim and offender have been drinking, and who becomes the victim and who the offender is a matter of happenstance.[24] One classic study of homicide (Wolfgang 1958) concluded that male-male homicides, as an instance of the more generally physically aggressive behaviour of males, converge with notions of masculine identity.

When males kill their intimate female partners, their methods of and motives for killing take on a character distinctive from male-male killings—a character that denotes the gender specificity of intimate femicide. As noted above, a substantial number of intimate femicides involved multiple methods, excessive force, and continued violence even after the women's death would have been apparent.[25] The violence in intimate femicides also frequently involves some form of sexual assault, a very rare occurrence in killings of men.

The motives in intimate femicide also point to its gender-specificity. The predominance of men's rage over separation as a motive in intimate femicides has no obvious counterpart in killings of men—even killings of men by their intimate female partners. We agree with others who see this motive as a reflection of the sexual proprietariness of males towards their intimate female partners.

In sum, our analysis of intimate femicide and our review of other research and data on gender differences in homicide suggest that women killing in general and intimate femicide in particular are uniquely gendered acts. By this we mean these killings reflect important dimensions of gender stratification, such as power differences in intimate relations and the construction of women as sexual objects generally, and as sexual property in particular contexts. Intimate femicide—indeed, probably most femicide—is not simply violence against a person who happens to be female. It is violence that occurs and takes particular forms because its target is a woman, a woman who has been intimately involved with her killer.

Conclusion

Our purpose in this article has been to document the incidence and provide a description of the phenomenon of intimate femicide. For some, our approach may be unsatisfying, because we have not proposed a systematic explanation of, nor outlined a detailed strategy for preventing, these killings. Obviously explaining and preventing intimate femicides are critical tasks, but both require comprehensive knowledge of the phenomenon. The statistical data we have gathered and analyzed are intended to contribute to this knowledge.

Nevertheless, we recognize that our overview of the extent and character of intimate femicide in Ontario between 1974 and 1994 has raised at least as many questions as it has answered. Why, for example, did women's risks of intimate femicide increase slightly when public concern over and resources available to abused women were also increasing; when other forms of lethal violence were decreasing; and when criminal justice responses to intimate femicide were becoming more punitive? Why did some women—such as those in common-law relationships and Aboriginal women—face disproportionately high risks of intimate femicide? Were there other types of women with elevated risks of intimate femicide—for example, immigrant women or women with disabilities—whom we couldn't identify because of the limitations of our data? Why are intimate partner killings by men and women so distinctively different? All of these questions deserve answers, but the answers will require research that goes beyond the data and analysis we have been able to present in this paper.

There are other types of questions raised by our research that are more immediately pressing, questions about how to prevent intimate femicides. Our research has shown that intimate femicides are not the isolated and unpredictable acts of passion they are often believed to be. Most of the killers in our study had acted violently toward their partners or other persons in the past and many had prior contact with the police as a consequence. Many of the victims had sought help from a variety of sources. In a substantial portion of these intimate femicides, then, there were clear signs of danger preceding the killing, signs that were available to people who might have been able to intervene to prevent the crime. We believe this information could be combined with what we know about the risk factors for intimate femicide—such as estrangement—to develop interventions that would save women's lives.

This is the question that has been at the core of our research and the recommendation that we tabled at the conclusion of both of our studies. We urged the establishment of a joint forces initiative that would include police, coroners, researchers, experts working in the field, as well as survivors of intimate violence, who would be charged with developing a system to respond more effectively to women when they are at greatest risk of intimate femicide. Such a response would need to be swift and focused on ensuring the victim's safety and deterring the offender from further violence or threats.

Of course, this kind of intervention must be coupled with efforts to address the underlying sources of intimate femicide. If, as we and others have argued, the sources lie at least in part in attitudes and behaviours that have been supported for centuries by patriarchal systems of power and privilege, those attitudes and behaviours, as well as the systems supporting them, must be confronted and contested. Some feminists argue that one means of doing this is through refining and reformulating law as a weapon against men's intimate violence against women. Isabel Marcus (1994), for example, argues for identifying domestic violence as terrorism and, as such, a violation of international human rights accords. Elizabeth Schneider (1994: 56) suggests redeploying the concept of privacy, not to keep the state out of intimate relationships as the concept has been used in the past, but to emphasize individual's autonomy and independence. She argues this affirmative aspect of privacy could frame a new feminist agenda against woman abuse.

As these and other analyses emphasize, preventing intimate femicides will require that the public as well as those working in fields relevant to the prevention of violence begin to see intimate femicide as a preventable crime. From our own and others' research on intimate violence, it should be apparent that these crimes are patterned and predictable. The danger lies in maintaining the view that violence is inevitable, unavoidable, and inherent in intimate relationships. Such fatalism must be challenged, so that women's safety in and outside their homes is seen as an achievable and preeminent goal.

Notes

Major funding for the studies described in this paper was provided by the Ontario Women's Directorate. The Ministry of Community and Social Services and the School of Graduate Studies at the University of Toronto each provided additional funding for one of the studies. The analyses and opinions in the paper are those of the authors and do not necessarily represent the views of any of these funders.

1. Coroner's records are limited in another obvious and unavoidable way: they are observations removed in time and space from the actual killing. As a consequence, the description in the records will be shaped by the interests and perspectives of the observer. A coroner's perspective is that of an investigator after the fact, and his/her primary interest is in determining the cause and means of death. Thus, the information recorded by coroners is intended to serve these purposes, not the interests of researchers.

2. Different procedures were used in the two studies to obtain access to municipal police and OPP records. These records are not centrally compiled and it was impossible to contact and obtain cooperation from all of the forces around Ontario which investigate and keep records on cases of homicide.

3. Obviously, the coded data provide only a partial and, in some respects, an incomplete portrayal of intimate femicide. The lives and deaths of the women represented in these statistics cannot be sufficiently understood from counts and categorizations. For this reason, we devoted a considerable portion of our first study to reconstructing the stories of some of the women who died through interviews with their family and friends.

4. Our research has looked only at killings of females aged fifteen and older because the killing of children differs in distinctive ways from the killing of adults.

5. The number of intimate femicides is undercounted in official records for other reasons as well. For example, in some cases of intimate femicide, the woman's death may be incorrectly classified as due to suicide, accident, or natural causes. Among the intimate femicides in our study, at least eight were not initially classified as homicides and only re-classified after further investigation. Another example of this occurred while this article was being written: the body of a southern Ontario woman who died by hanging was exhumed and an investigation revealed she had not killed herself, as originally determined, but had been killed by her boyfriend.

6. Although there are no statistics on the rate of intimate femicide for Canada as a whole, there are statistics on the rate of spousal killings of women. Since the mid-1970s, trends in Ontario's rate have paralleled those for Canada as a whole; and the mean rate for Ontario (.77) is very close to the mean rate for Canada (.83).

7. Of the cases of intimate femicide between 1974 and 1994, we found only three in which the offender was a woman.

8. Identifying differences between victims or offenders and women and men in the general population requires establishing the proportion of victims (or offenders) with the particular characteristic and comparing this to the proportion of women (or men) in the general population of Ontario during the years 1974–94 with the same characteristics. If the former proportion is larger than the latter proportion, this indicates that women with that particular characteristic are overrepresented among victims of intimate femicide. Tests for statistically significant differences are not appropriate here because the data are based on populations, not samples. Because we used information from census reports to determine the characteristics of women in the general population of Ontario, we were limited in our search for risk markers of intimate femicide to characteristics which are measured in the census.

9. By highlighting these characteristics, we do not mean to obscure the fact that women from all types of backgrounds and in all types of relationships are victims of intimate femicide; nor do we mean to imply that certain characteristics of women make them likely targets for intimate violence. Rather, we would suggest that certain groups of women may be more vulnerable to intimate violence because

they share characteristics that have isolated them, limited their access to resources for protection, or prevented them from obtaining a level of personal security that many Canadians take for granted.

10. The average annual rate of intimate femicide (per 100,000 women aged fifteen and older) for the years 1991–4 was calculated by: (1) dividing the number of victims during those years (159) by the number of women aged fifteen and older in the Ontario population in 1991 (4,130,450); (2) multiplying this figure by 100,000; and (3) dividing this figure by four (the number of years). This yields an average annual rate of .96 per 100,000 women aged fifteen and older.

    The average annual rate of intimate femicides of women living in common-law unions was calculated by: (1) dividing the number of victims living common-law during those years (45) by the number of women aged fifteen and older in Ontario living in common-law unions in 1991 (182,155); (2) multiplying this figure by 100,000; and (3) dividing this figure by four. This yields an annual average rate of 6.18 per 100,000 women aged fifteen and older living in common-law unions.

11. This group was formed at the beginning of our first study and met with the principal researchers regularly to review the research for cultural sensitivity and validity. At the completion of the first study, its members also reviewed and made contributions to the final report.

12. The final report for our first study (pp. 67–76) documents the problems with collecting information on race and cultural backgrounds of crime victims and offenders, as well as the procedures we followed to gather the data on Aboriginal victims.

13. Another 30 per cent had been arrested and charged with non-violent criminal offences.

14. In contrast, in only 6 per cent of the cases were the victims known to have been violent toward their killers in the past; and in only 2 per cent of the cases were the victims known to have previously threatened their partners with violence.

15. What researchers can describe about homicide and femicide is largely determined by the types of information officials collect. This means that many

details about the events leading up to the killing, the dynamics of the interaction immediately preceding the killing, or the states of mind of victim and offender are absent or at most only hinted at in official reports. Some characteristics of intimate femicide can be easily and reliably determined, such as where they occurred or whether weapons were involved. Other characteristics—such as the offender's motivation—are more susceptible to post hoc reconstructions that introduce the inevitable biases of observers and officials. When we collected and coded information, we reviewed all the information available to us and made our own best judgments about these characteristics. We recognize, however, that our judgments are necessarily based on limited information about extremely complex events. Our discussion of the characteristics of the killings therefore should be viewed with these limitations in mind.

16. We base this and other conclusions about the characteristics of intimate partner killings by women on data from an ongoing study by the first author of over 7,000 homicides in two Canadian cities and two U.S. cities over the twentieth century.

17. Indeed, none of the data or research with which we are familiar indicates that women who kill their intimate partners exact sexual violence against their victims.

18. This does not mean that offenders who appeared to act for other motives had not engaged in systematic abuse of the women they killed. Rather, it indicates that in 10 per cent of the cases, the only motive we could identify was systematic, serial abuse that ultimately led to the woman's death.

19. Typically, offenders who kill under these circumstances are characterized as extremely depressed, and are more likely than other offenders to commit or attempt suicide after the killing. Nevertheless, some have argued that sexual proprietariness can still be seen in killings apparently motivated by stressful life circumstances (e.g., Daly and Wilson 1988). According to this view, when men kill their wives (and often their children as well) because they feel they can no longer provide for them, their acts suggest that they see their wives as possessions to dispose of as they see fit and/or that they cannot

conceive of their wives having an existence separate from their own.

20. Other research has noted the high rates at which offenders suicide after intimate femicides, and has contrasted this to the rarity of suicides by women who kill their intimate partners (see, e.g., Carolyn R. Block and A. Christakos, 'Intimate Partner Homicide in Chicago over 29 Years', *Crime and Delinquency* 41 (1995): 496–526. Daly and Wilson (1988) have suggested that this pattern is grounded in males' feelings of possessiveness and ownership over their partners.

21. Murder is first-degree when the killing is planned and deliberate, when the victim is an officer of the law, or when a death is caused while committing or attempting to commit another offence, such as kidnapping. Any murder that does not fall within these categories is second-degree murder. According to the courts, the distinction between first- and second-degree murder is made solely for sentencing purposes. While anyone convicted of murder is sentenced to imprisonment for life, the parole ineligibility period varies between first- and second-degree murder.

22. Some analysts (e.g., Elizabeth Rapaport, 'The Death Penalty and the Domestic Discount' in *The Public Nature of Private Violence: The Discovery of Domestic Abuse*, eds M. Fineman and R. Mykitiuk [New York: Routledge, 1994], 224–51) have speculated that the killing of a woman by her intimate male partner is treated more leniently by the criminal justice system than other types of homicides, such as killings of men by female intimate partners. However, empirical evidence in this area is sparse and not conclusive.

23. We use the category 'spouse killings' here because we could find no statistics on the number of men killed by intimate partners, only statistics on men killed by spouses. To be comparable, we compare these figures to the number of women killed by spouses—a subset of all intimate femicides.

24. Marvin Wolfgang has noted in *Studies in Homicide* (New York: Harper & Row, 1967) that where males are victims of homicide, victim-precipitation of the violence is fairly common.

25. Wolfgang (1967) found a similar pattern in his study of homicides in Philadelphia.

References

Bachmann, R. 1993. *Death and Violence on the Reservation: Homicide, Family Violence, and Suicide in American Indian Populations* (New York: Auburn House).

Blinder, M. 1985. *Lovers, Killers, Husbands, and Wives* (New York: St Martin's Press).

Boudoris, J. 1971. 'Homicide and the Family', *Journal of Marriage and the Family* 32: 667–76.

Brinkerhoff, M., and E. Lupri. 1988. 'Interspousal Violence', *Canadian Journal of Sociology* 13: 407–34.

Browne, A. 1987. *When Battered Women Kill* (New York: The Free Press).

———, and K. Williams. 1989. 'Exploring the Effect of Resource Availability on the Likelihood of Female-perpetrated Homicides', *Law and Society Review* 23: 75–94.

Campbell, J. 1995. 'Prediction of Homicide of and by Battered Women' in *Assessing Dangerousness: Violence by Sexual Offenders, Batterers, and Child Abusers* (Thousand Oaks, CA: Sage), 96–113.

Campbell, J.C. 1992. 'If I Can't Have You No One Else Can': Power and Control in Homicide of Female Partners' in *Femicide: The Politics of Woman Killing*, eds J. Radford and D.E.H. Russell (New York: Twayne), 99–113.

Canadian Centre for Justice Statistics. 1993. *Homicide Survey*, unpublished statistics.

Chimbos, P.D. 1978. *Marital Violence: A Study of Interspousal Homicide* (San Francisco: R & E Associates).

Crawford, M., R. Gartner, and M. Dawson in collaboration with the Women We Honour Committee. 1997. *Women Killing: Intimate Femicide in Ontario,*

1991–1994 (Toronto: Women We Honour Action Committee).

Crawford, M., R. Gartner, and the Women We Honour Action Committee. 1992. *Woman Killing: Intimate Femicide in Ontario, 1974–1990* (Toronto: Women We Honour Action Committee).

Daly, M., and M. Wilson. 1988. *Homicide* (New York: Aldine de Gruyter).

Dobash, R.E., and R.P. Dobash. 1984. 'The Nature and Antecedents of Violent Events', *British Journal of Criminology* 24: 269–88.

Dobash, R.P., R.E. Dobash, M. Wilson, and M. Daly. 1992. 'The Myth of Sexual Symmetry in Marital Violence', *Social Problems* 39: 81.

Frank, S. 1993. *Family Violence in Aboriginal Communities: A First Nations Report* (British Columbia: Report to the Government of British Columbia).

Goode, W. 1969. 'Violence Among Intimates' in *Crimes of Violence,* v. 13, eds D. Mulvihill and M. Tumin (Washington, DC: USGPO), 941–77.

Health and Welfare Canada. 1990. *Reaching for Solutions: Report of the Special Advisor to the Minister of National Health & Welfare on Child Sexual Abuse in Canada* (Ottawa: Supply and Services).

Hotaling, G., and D. Sugarman. 1986. 'An Analysis of Risk Markers in Husband to Wife Violence: The Current State of Knowledge', *Violence and Victims* 1: 101–24.

Johnson, H. 1996. *Dangerous Domains: Violence Against Women in Canada* (Toronto: Nelson Canada).

———, and V. Sacco. 1995. 'Researching Violence Against Women: Statistics Canada's National Survey', *Canadian Journal of Criminology* 3: 281–304.

Kelkar, G. 1992. 'Women and Structural Violence in India' in *Femicide: The Politics of Women Killing*, eds J. Radford and D.E.H. Russell (New York: Twayne), 117–23.

Kennedy, L.W., D.R. Forde, and R.A. Silverman. 1989. 'Understanding Homicide Trends: Issues in Disaggregating for National and Cross-national Comparisons', *Canadian Journal of Sociology* 14: 479–86.

Long, D.A. 1995. 'On Violence and Healing: Aboriginal Experiences, 1960–1993' in *Violence in Canada: Sociopolitical Perspectives*, ed. J.I. Ross (Don Mills, ON: Oxford University Press), 40–77.

Macmillan, R., and R. Gartner. 1996. 'Labour Force Participation and the Risk of Spousal Violence Against Women', paper presented at the 1996 Annual Meetings of the American Society of Criminology.

Maloney, M.A. 1994 'Victimization or Oppression? Women's Lives, Violence, and Agency' in *The Public Nature of Private Violence: The Discovery of Domestic Abuse*, eds M.A. Fineman and R. Mykitiuk (New York: Routledge), 59–92.

Marcus, I. 1994. 'Reframing "Domestic Violence": Terrorism in the Home' in *The Public Nature of Private Violence: The Discovery of Domestic Abuse*, eds M.A. Fineman and R. Mykitiuk (New York: Routledge), 11–35.

Messerschmidt, J.W. 1993. *Masculinities and Crime: Critique and Conceptualization of Theory* (Lanham, MD: Rowman & Littlefield).

Polk, K. 1994. *When Men Kill: Scenarios of Masculine Violence* (Cambridge: Cambridge University Press).

Rasche, C. 1989. 'Stated and Attributed Motives for Lethal Violence in Intimate Relationships', paper presented at the 1989 Annual Meetings of the American Society of Criminology.

Regoeczi, W., and R. Silverman. 1997. 'Spousal Homicide in Canada: Exploring the Issue of Racial Variations in Risk', paper presented at the 1997 Annual Meetings of the American Society of Criminology.

Rodgers, K. 1994. *Wife Assault: The Findings of a National Survey* (Ottawa: Canadian Centre for Justice Statistics).

Schneider, E. 1994. 'The Violence of Privacy' in *The Public Nature of Private Violence: The Discovery of Domestic Abuse*, eds M. Fineman and R. Mykitiuk (New York: Routledge), 36–58.

Silverman, R., and L. Kennedy. 1993. *Deadly Deeds: Murder in Canada* (Toronto: Nelson Canada).

Wallace, A. 1986. *Homicide: The Social Reality* (New South Wales: NSW Bureau of Crime Statistics and Research).

Wilson, M., and M. Daly, 1992a. 'Til Death Do Us Part' in *Femicide: The Politics of Woman Killing*, eds J. Radford and D.E.H. Russell (New York: Twayne), 85.

———. 1992b. 'Who Kills Whom in Spouse Killings? On the Exceptional Sex Ratio of Spousal Homicides in the United States', *Criminology* 30: 189–215.

———. 1993. 'Spousal Homicide Risk and Estrangement', *Violence and Victims* 8: 3–16.

———. 1994. 'Spousal Homicide', *Juristat Service Bulletin* 14: 8.

———, H. Johnson, and M. Daly. 1995. 'Lethal and Nonlethal Violence against Wives', *Canadian Journal of Criminology* 37: 343.

Wolfgang, M. 1958. *Patterns in Criminal Homicide* (Philadelphia: University of Pennsylvania Press).

Women We Honour Action Committee and R. Gartner. 1990. *Annotated Bibliography of Works Reviewed for Project on Intimate Femicide* (Toronto: Women We Honour Action Committee).

Chapter 31

Divorce has different consequences for women than for men, since women often suffer a significant drop in standard of living and economic security. It is the children we worry about most when divorce occurs, however. Frank Furstenberg and Andrew Cherlin are American researchers who have studied the effects of *divorce on children, as well as many other issues in family life. This chapter from their book* Divided Families *presents an overview of the research findings on what most harms children, the extent of the damage, and how to prevent it.*

Children's Adjustment to Divorce

Frank F. Furstenberg and Andrew J. Cherlin

As Helen watched, Sally, then three, walked over to where her six-year-old brother was playing and picked up one of his toy robots. Mickey grabbed the robot out of her hand, shouted 'No!' and pushed her away. The little girl fell backward and began to cry. Helen had just finished another frustrating phone call with Herb, who had told her he could no longer afford to pay as much child support as they had agreed. She was grateful to her parents for allowing her and the kids to live with them temporarily, but the crowded household was beginning to strain everyone's patience. She rushed over to her daughter, picked her up, and shouted at her son, 'Don't you hit her like that!' 'But it was mine,' he said, whereupon he took another robot and threw it on the floor near his mother's feet. She grabbed his arm and dragged him to his room screaming at him all the way.

Then she sat down in the living room, with Sally in her lap, and reflected on how often scenes such as this were occurring. Ever since the separation eight months earlier, she had had a hard time controlling Mickey. He disobeyed her, was mean to his sister, and fought with friends at school. And when he talked back to her, she lost her temper. But that just made him behave worse, which in turn made her angrier, until he was sent to his room and she sat down, distraught.

Helen's problems with her son fit a pattern familiar to psychologists who study the effects of divorce on children, an escalating cycle of misbehaviour and harsh response between mothers and sons. But not all parents and children become caught up in these so-called coercive cycles after the breakup of a marriage. Studies show a wide range of responses to divorce. Some children do very well; others fare poorly. In this chapter we will examine these differences and inquire into why they occur.

We tend to think of divorce as an event that starts when a husband or wife moves out of their home. But it is often more useful to think of divorce as a process that unfolds slowly over time, beginning well before the separation actually occurs. In many cases it is preceded by a lengthy period of conflict between the spouses. It is reasonable to expect that this predisruption conflict, and the corresponding emotional upset on the part of the parents, may cause problems for children.

For example, when things began to heat up between Mickey and his mother, Helen naturally assumed that the problems between them were largely the result of the divorce. Perhaps she was right. But her guilty feelings made Helen conveniently forget that Mickey had had behavioural problems for several years—ever since the quarreling between his parents became severe. Almost two years before the separation, Mickey's preschool teacher had asked Helen if things were going all right at home. Mickey had displayed unusual fits of temper with his classmates and seemed distracted during play periods. If you had asked Mickey's teacher, she would have predicted that Mickey, although bright enough, was going to have adjustment problems in kindergarten. And so he did. True, Mickey's problems did get worse the year that his parents separated, but it is not obvious that his difficulties in school would have been avoided even if his parents had managed to remain together.

In fact, there is evidence that some children show signs of disturbance months, and sometimes even years, before their parents separate. In 1968 a team of psychologists began to study three year olds at two nursery schools in Berkeley, California. The psychologists followed these children and their families, conducting detailed personality assessments at ages four, five, seven, eleven, and fourteen. When the study started, eighty-eight children were living with two married parents. Twenty-nine of these children experienced the breakup of their parents' marriages by the time they were fourteen. Curious as to what the children were like before the breakup, the psychologists paged backward through their files until they found the descriptions of the children eleven years earlier, when they were age three.

The results were quite dramatic for boys. Years before the breakup, three-year-old boys whose families eventually would disrupt were more likely to have been described as having behavioural problems than were three-year-old boys whose families would remain intact. According to the researchers, Jeanne H. Block, Jack Block, and Per F. Gjerde, three-year-old boys who would eventually experience family disruption already were rated as more 'inconsiderate of other children, disorderly in dress and behavior', and 'impulsive' and more likely to 'take advantage of other children'. Moreover, their fathers

were more likely to characterize themselves as often angry with their sons, and both fathers and mothers reported more conflict with their sons. Much smaller differences were found among daughters.

Had the Berkeley researchers started their study when the children were age fourteen, they surely would have found some differences between the adolescents from the twenty-nine disrupted families and the adolescents from the fifty-nine intact families. And they probably would have attributed these differences to the aftermath of the disruption, as most other researchers do. But because they could look back eleven years, they saw that some portion of the presumed effects of divorce on children were present well before the families split up.

Why is this so? It is, of course, possible that some children have behavioural problems that put stress on their parents' marriages. In these instances divorce, rather than *causing* children's problems, may be the *result* of them. But it is doubtful that inherently difficult children cause most divorces. The Berkeley researchers suggest, rather, that conflict between parents is a fundamental factor that harms children's development and produces behavioural problems. In many families, this conflict—and the harm it engenders—may precede the separation by many years.

There are many other characteristics of divorce-prone families that might affect children. For example, people who divorce are more likely to have married as teenagers and to have begun their marriages after the wife was pregnant. They also are less religious. It is possible that these families may provide a less stable and secure environment and therefore cause children more problems even while the family is intact. But no researcher would suggest that all of the effects of divorces are determined before the actual separation. Much of the impact depends on how the process unfolds after the separation and how the children cope with it. Nearly all children are extremely upset when they learn of the breakup.

For most, it is an unwelcome shock. Judith Wallerstein and Joan Kelly found that young children seemed surprised even in families where the parents were openly quarreling and hostile. Although young children certainly recognize open conflict—and indeed may be drawn into it—they usually can't grasp the long-term significance and don't envisage the separation. Moreover, parents typically don't inform their children of the impending separation until shortly before it occurs.

When children do learn of the breakup, their reactions vary according to their ages. Preschool-age children, whose ability to understand the situation is limited, are usually frightened and bewildered to find that their father or mother has moved out of the house. Preschoolers see the world in a very self-centred way, and so they often assume that the separation must be their fault—that they must have done something terribly wrong to make their parent leave. Three-year-old Sally promised never to leave her room a mess again if only Daddy would come home. Older children comprehend the situation better and can understand that they are not at fault. But they still can be quite anxious about what the breakup will mean for their own lives. And adolescents, characteristically, are more often intensely angry at one or both of their parents for breaking up their families.

Short-term Adjustment

The psychologists P. Lindsay Chase-Lansdale and E. Mavis Hetherington have labelled the first two years following a separation as a 'crisis period' for adults and children. The crisis begins for children with shock, anxiety, and anger upon learning of the breakup. (But as was noted, the harmful effects on children of marital conflict may begin well before the breakup.) For adults, too, the immediate aftermath is a dismaying and difficult time. It is especially trying for mothers who retain custody of the children, as about nine in ten do.

Helen, for example, faced the task of raising her two children alone. Even when she was married, Helen had taken most of the responsibility for raising the children. But Herb had helped out some and had backed her up when the children were difficult. Now responsibility fell solely on her. What's more, she was working full-time in order to compensate for the loss of Herb's income. And all this was occurring at a time when she felt alternately angry at Herb, depressed about the end of her marriage, and anxious about her future. Harried and overburdened, she was sometimes overwhelmed by the task of keeping her family going from day to day. Dinner was frequently served late, and Sally and Mickey often stayed up past their bedtime as Helen tried to complete the household chores.

Children have two special needs during the crisis period. First, they need additional emotional support as they struggle to adapt to the breakup. Second, they need the structure provided by a reasonably predictable daily routine. Unfortunately, many single parents cannot meet both of these needs all the time. Depressed, anxious parents often lack the reserve to comfort emotionally needy children. Overburdened parents let daily schedules slip. As a result, their children lose some of the support they need.

A number of psychological studies suggest that the consequences of the crisis period are worse for boys than for girls; but it may be that boys and girls merely react to stress differently. Developmental psychologists distinguish two general types of behaviour problems among children. The first—externalizing disorders—refers to heightened levels of problem behaviour directed outward, such as aggression, disobedience, and lying. The second—internalizing disorders—refers to heightened levels of problem behaviours directed inward, such as depression, anxiety, or withdrawal. Boys in high-conflict families, whether disrupted or intact, tend to show more aggressive and antisocial behaviour. Hetherington studied a small group of middle-class families, disrupted and intact, for several years. She found coercive cycles between mothers and sons, like the ones between Helen and Mickey, to be prevalent. Distressed mothers responded irritably to the bad behaviour of their sons, thus aggravating the very behaviour they wished to quell. Even as long as six years after the separation, Hetherington observed this pattern among mothers who hadn't remarried and their sons.

The findings for girls are less consistent, but generally girls appear better behaved than boys in the immediate aftermath of a disruption. There are even reports of overcontrolled, self-consciously 'good' behaviour. But we should be cautious in concluding that girls are less affected. It may be that they internalize their distress in the form of depression or lowered self-esteem. And some observers suggest that the distress may produce problems that only appear years after the breakup.

It is also possible that boys do worse because they typically live with their opposite-sex parent, their mother. A number of studies report intriguing evidence that children may fare better if they reside with a same-sex parent after a marital disruption. Families in which single fathers become the custodial parent, however, are a small and select group who may be quite different from typical families. Until recently, sole custody was awarded to fathers mainly in cases in which the mother had abandoned the children or was an alcoholic, drug abuser, or otherwise clearly incompetent. Until there is more evidence from studies of broad groups of children, we think it would be premature to generalize about same-sex custody.

To sum up, researchers agree that almost all children are moderately or severely distressed when their parents separate and that most continue to experience confusion, sadness, or anger for a period of months and even years. Nevertheless, the most careful studies show a great deal of variation in the short-term reactions of children—including children in the same family. Most of this variation remains unexplained, although differences in age and gender account for some of it. Part of the explanation, no doubt, has to do with differences in children's temperaments. Some probably are more robust and better able to withstand deprivation and instability. They may be less affected by growing up in a one-parent family, and they may also cope better with a divorce. In addition, clinicians have speculated that some children draw strength from adults or even peers outside of the household, such as grandparents, aunts, or close friends. But we are far from certain just how important each of the sources of resiliency is to the child's ability to cope with divorce.

Long-term Adjustment

Even less is known about the long-term consequences of divorces than about the short-term consequences. Within two or three years, most single parents and their children recover substantially from the trauma of the crisis period. Parents are able to stabilize their lives as the wounds from the breakup heal. With the exception of some difficulties between single mothers and their sons, parent-child relationships generally improve. And the majority of children, it seems, return to normal development.

But over the long run there is still great variation in how the process of divorce plays out. Without doubt, some children suffer long-term harm. It is easy, however, to exaggerate the extent of these harmful effects. In their widely read book that reports on a clinical study of 60 recently divorced middle-class couples from the San Francisco suburbs and their 131 children, aged two to eighteen, Judith Wallerstein and Sandra Blakeslee paint a picture of a permanently scarred generation. 'Almost half of the children', they write, 'entered adulthood as worried, underachieving, self-deprecating, and sometimes angry young men and women.' Are these difficulties as widespread among children of divorce as the authors suggest? Despite their claim that the families were 'representative of the way normal people from a white, middle-class background cope with divorce', it is highly likely that the study exaggerates the prevalence of long-term problems. Its families had volunteered to come to a clinic for counselling, and many of the parents had extensive psychiatric histories. Moreover, there is no comparison group of intact families: instead, all of the problems that emerged after the breakup are blamed on the divorce.

We do not doubt that many young adults retain painful memories of their parents' divorce. But it doesn't necessarily follow that these feelings will impair their functioning as adults. Had their parents not divorced, they might have retained equally painful memories of a conflict-ridden marriage. Imagine that the more troubled families in the Wallerstein study had remained intact and had been observed ten years later. Would their children have fared any better? Certainly they would have been better off economically; but given the strains that would have been evident in the marriages, we doubt that most would have been better off psychologically.

Studies based on nationally representative samples that do include children from intact marriages suggest that the long-term harmful effects of divorce are worthy of concern but occur only to a minority. Evidence for this conclusion comes from the National Survey of Children (NSC), which interviewed parents and children in 1976 and again in 1981. For families in which a marital disruption had occurred, the average time elapsed since the disruption was eight years in 1981. James L. Peterson and Nicholas Zill examined parents' 1981 responses to the question, 'Since January 1977 . . . has [the child] had any behavior or discipline problems at school resulting in your receiving a note or being asked to come in and talk to the teacher or principal?' Peterson and Zill found that, other things being equal, 34 per cent of parents who had separated or divorced answered yes, compared with 20 per cent of parents of intact marriages.

Is this a big difference or a small difference? The figures can be interpreted in two ways. First, the percentage of children from maritally disrupted families who had behaviour or discipline problems at school is more than half-again as large as the percentage from intact families. That's a substantial difference, suggesting that children from disrupted families have a noticeably higher rate of misbehaving seriously in school. (Although some of these children might have misbehaved even if their parents had not separated.) Second, however, the figures also demonstrate that 66 per cent of all children from maritally disrupted homes *did not* misbehave seriously at school. So one also can conclude that most children of divorce don't have behaviour problems at school. Both conclusions are equally valid; the glass is either half full or half empty, depending on one's point of view. We think that in order to understand the broad picture of the long-term effects of divorce on children, it's necessary to keep both points of view in mind.

The same half-full and half-empty perspective can be applied to studies of the family histories of adults. Based on information from several national surveys of adults, Sara McLanahan and her colleagues found that persons who reported living as a child in a single-parent family were more likely subsequently to drop out of high school, marry during their teenage years, have a child before marrying, and experience the disruption of their own marriages. For example, the studies imply that, for whites, the probability of dropping out of high school could be as high as 22 per cent for those who lived with single parents, compared with about 11 per cent for those who lived with both parents, other things being equal. Again, the glass is half-empty; those who lived with a single parent are up to twice as likely to drop out of high school. And it is half-full: the overwhelming majority of those who lived with a single parent graduated from high school.

In addition, the NSC data demonstrate that children in intact families in which the parents fought continually were doing no better, and often worse, than the children of divorce. In 1976 and again in 1981, parents in intact marriages were asked whether they and their spouses ever had arguments about any of nine topics: chores and responsibilities, the children, money, sex, religion, leisure time, drinking, other women or men, and in-laws. Peterson and Zill classified an intact marriage as having 'high conflict' if arguments were reported on five or more topics or if the parent said that the marriage, taking things all together, was 'not too happy'. They found that in 1981, children whose parents had divorced or separated were doing no worse than children whose parents were in intact, high-conflict homes. And children whose parents' marriages were intact but highly conflicted in both 1976 and 1981 were doing the worst of all: these children were more depressed, impulsive, and hyperactive, and misbehaved more often.

To be sure, even if only a minority of children experience long-term negative effects, that is nothing to cheer about. But the more fundamental point—one that all experts agree upon—is that children's responses to the breakup of their parents' marriages vary greatly. There is no ineluctable path down which children of divorce progress. What becomes important, then, is to identify the circumstances under which children seem to do well.

What Makes a Difference?

A critical factor in both short-term and long-term adjustment is how effectively the custodial parent, who usually is the mother, functions as a parent. We have noted how difficult it can be for a recently separated mother to function well. The first year or two after the separation is a difficult time for many mothers, who may feel angry, depressed, irritable, or sad. Their own distress may make it more difficult to cope with their children's distress, leading in some cases to a disorganized household, lax supervision, inconsistent discipline, and the coercive cycles between mothers and preschool-aged sons that have been identified by Hetherington and others. Mothers who can cope better with the disruption can be more effective parents. They can keep their work and home lives going from day to day and can better provide love, nurturing, consistent discipline, and a predictable routine.

Quite often their distress is rooted in, or at least intensified by, financial problems. Loss of the father's income can cause a disruptive, downward spiral in which children must adjust to a declining standard of living, a mother who is less psychologically available and is home less often, an apartment in an unfamiliar neighbourhood, a different school, and new friends. This sequence of events occurs at a time when children are greatly upset about the separation and need love, support, and a familiar daily routine.

A second key factor in children's well-being is a low level of conflict between their mother and father. This principle applies, in fact, to intact as well as disrupted families. Recall the finding from the NSC that children who live with two parents who persistently quarrel over important areas of family life show higher levels of distress and behaviour problems than do children from disrupted marriages. Some observers take this finding to imply that children are better off if their parents divorce than if they remain in an unhappy marriage. We think this is true in some cases but not in others. It is probably true that most children who live in a household filled with continual conflict between angry, embittered spouses would be better off if their parents split up—assuming that the level of conflict is lowered by the separation. And there is no doubt that the rise in divorce has liberated some children (and their custodial parents) from families marked by physical abuse, alcoholism, drugs, and violence. But we doubt that such clearly pathological descriptions apply to most families that disrupt. Rather, we think there are many more cases in which there is little open conflict, but one or both partners finds the marriage personally unsatisfying. The unhappy partner may feel unfulfilled, distant from his or her spouse, bored, or constrained. Under these circumstances, the family may limp along from day to day without much holding it together or pulling it apart. A generation ago, when marriage was thought of as a moral and social obligation, most husbands and wives in families such as this stayed together. Today, when marriage is thought of increasingly as a means of achieving personal fulfillment, many more will divorce. Under these circumstances, divorce may well make one or both spouses happier; but we strongly doubt that it improves the psychological well-being of the children.

A possible third key factor in children's successful adjustment is the maintenance of a continuing relationship with the non-custodial parent, who is usually the father. But direct evidence that lack of contact with the father inhibits the adjustment of children to divorce is less than satisfactory. A number of experts have stressed the importance of a continuing relationship, yet research findings are inconsistent. The main evidence comes from both the Hetherington and Wallerstein studies, each of which found that children were better adjusted when they saw their fathers regularly. More recently, however, other observational studies have not found this relationship.

And in the NSC, the amount of contact that children had with their fathers seemed to make little difference for their well-being. Teenagers who saw their fathers regularly were just as likely as were those with infrequent contact to have problems in school or engage in delinquent acts and precocious sexual behaviour. Furthermore, the children's behavioural adjustment was also unrelated to the level of intimacy and identification with the non-residential father. No differences were observed even among the children who had both regular contact and close relations with their father outside the home. Moreover, when the children in the NSC were reinterviewed in 1987 at ages eighteen to twenty-three, those

who had retained stable, close ties to their fathers were neither more nor less successful than those who had had low or inconsistent levels of contact and intimacy with their fathers.

Another common argument is that fathers who maintain regular contact with their children also may keep paying child support to their children's mothers. Studies do show that fathers who visit more regularly pay more in child support. But it's not clear that they pay more *because* they visit more. Rather, it may be that fathers who have a greater commitment to their children both visit and pay more. If so, then the problem is to increase the level of commitment most fathers feel, not simply to increase the amount of visiting.

These puzzling findings make us cautious about drawing any firm conclusions about the psychological benefits of contact with non-custodial parents for children's adjustment in later life. Yet despite the mixed evidence, the idea that continuing contact with fathers makes a difference to a child's psychological well-being is so plausible and so seemingly grounded in theories of child development that one is reluctant to discount it. It may be that evidence is difficult to obtain because so few fathers living outside the home are intimately involved in childrearing. It is also likely that, even when fathers remain involved, most formerly married parents have difficulty establishing a collaborative style of childrearing. We remain convinced that when parents are able to cooperate in childrearing after a divorce and when fathers are able to maintain an active and supportive role, children will be better off in the long run. But we are certain that such families are rare at present and unlikely to become common in the near future.

Does Custody Make a Difference for Children?

The belief that the father's involvement is beneficial to children was an important reason why many states recently adopted joint-custody statutes.

Supporters argued that children adjust better when they maintain a continuing relationship with both parents. They also argued that fathers would be more likely to meet child-support obligations if they retained responsibility for the children's upbringing. Were they correct? Joint custody is so recent that no definitive evidence exists. But the information to date is disappointing.

Joint *legal* custody seems to be hardly distinguishable in practice from maternal sole custody. A recent study of court records in Wisconsin showed no difference in child-support payments in joint-legal-custody versus mother-sole-custody families, once income and other factors were taken into account. The Stanford study found little difference, three and one-half years after separation, between joint-legal custody (but not joint-physical custody) families and mother-sole-custody families. Once income and education were taken into account, fathers who had joint legal custody were no more likely to comply with court-ordered child-support awards than were fathers whose former wives had sole legal and physical custody. They did not visit their children more often; they did not cooperate and communicate more with their former wives; and they didn't even participate more in decisions about the children's lives. The investigators concluded that joint legal custody 'appears to mean very little in practice'.

The handful of other small-scale studies of joint legal custody show modest effects, at most. It appears that joint legal custody does not substantially increase the father's decision-making authority, his involvement in childrearing, or the amount of child support he pays. Why is it so hard to increase fathers' involvement after divorce? For one thing . . . many men don't seem to know how to relate to their children except through their wives. Typically, when married, they were present but passive—not much involved in childrearing. When they separate, they carry this pattern of limited involvement with them; and it is reinforced by the modest contact most have with their children.

Uncomfortable and unskilled at being an active parent, marginalized by infrequent contact, focused on building a new family life, many fathers fade from their children's lives.

Less is known about joint physical custody. But a few recent studies suggest that it isn't necessarily better for children's adjustment than the alternatives. Among all families in the Stanford study in which children still were seeing both parents about two years after the separation, parents in dual-residence families talked and coordinated rules more; but they quarreled about the children just as much as did parents in single-residence families. Several colleagues of Wallerstein followed fifty-eight mother-physical-custody families and thirty-five joint-physical-custody families for two years after the families had been referred to counseling centres in the San Francisco area. Many of the parents were disputing custody and visitation arrangements. Children from the joint-physical-custody families were no better adjusted than children from the mother-physical-custody families: their levels of behavioural problems, their self-esteem, their ease at making friends were very similar. What did make a difference for the children was the depression and anxiety levels of their parents and the amount of continuing verbal and physical aggression between them, regardless of the custody arrangement. The authors suggest that children whose parents are having serious disputes may have more behaviour problems, lower self-esteem, and less acceptance by friends if they shuttle between homes. They are exposed to more conflict, and their movement back and forth may even generate it.

The admittedly limited evidence so far suggests to us that custody arrangements may matter less for the well-being of children than had been thought. It is, of course, possible that when more evidence is available, joint custody will be shown to have important benefits from some families. As with father involvement, the rationale for joint custody is so plausible and attractive that one is tempted to disregard the disappointing evidence and support it anyway. But based on what is known now, we think custody and visitation matters less for children than the two factors we noted earlier: how much conflict there is between the parents and how effectively the parent (or parents) the child lives with functions. It is likely that a child who alternates between the homes of a distraught mother and an angry father will be more troubled than a child who lives with a mother who is coping well and who once a fortnight sees a father who has disengaged from his family. Even the frequency of visits with a father seems to matter less than the climate in which they take place.

For now, we would draw two conclusions. First, joint physical custody should be encouraged only in cases where both parents voluntarily agree to it. Among families in which both parents shared the childrearing while they were married, a voluntary agreement to maintain joint physical custody probably will work and benefit the children. Even among families in which one parent did most of the childrearing prior to the divorce, a voluntary agreement won't do any harm—although we think the agreement likely will break down to sole physical custody over time. But only very rarely should joint physical custody be imposed if one or both parents do not want it. There may be a few cases in which the father and mother truly shared the childrearing before the divorce but one of them won't agree to share physical custody afterward. These difficult cases call for mediation or counselling, and they may require special consideration. But among the vastly larger number of families in which little sharing occurred beforehand and one or both parents doesn't want to share physical custody afterward, imposing joint physical custody would invite continuing conflict without any clear benefits. Even joint legal custody may matter more as a symbol of fathers' ties to their children than in any concrete sense. But symbols can be important, and joint legal custody seems, at worst, to do no harm. A legal preference for it may send a message to fathers that society respects their rights and responsibilities for their children.

Our second conclusion is that in weighing alternative public policies concerning divorce, the thin empirical evidence of the benefits of joint custody and frequent visits with fathers must be acknowledged. All of the findings in this chapter have implications for the way in which we as a society confront the effects of divorce on children. A question to examine later is: Which public policies should have priority? What outcomes are the most important for society to encourage and support? In some cases, such as the economic slide of mothers and children, the problem is clear, and alternative remedies readily come to mind. In other cases, the problems are complex and the remedies unclear . . .

. . . [H]owever, we must note that a divorce does not necessarily mark the end of change in the family lives of children. A majority will see a new partner move into their home. A remarriage, or even a cohabiting relationship, brings with it the potential both to improve children's lives and to complicate further their adjustment.

Part Eight   **Toward Change: Social Policies for Families**

Chapter 32

The social policies that are clearly needed to support families seem to have only faint hope of becoming reality here. When social policies in Canada are compared to those that are common in Europe, however, it is clear that our stingy support of families is unusual. In this article, economist Shelley Phipps reviews European social policies affecting families.

Lessons from Europe: Policy Options to Enhance the Economic Security of Canadian Families

Shelley A. Phipps

As Canadians, we are used to thinking of ourselves as having social policies that are kinder and gentler than those of our neighbours in the United States. While this is partly true, it is essential for Canadians to realize that to European social policy experts, the similarities between Canada and the United States far outweigh the differences (Ringen 1987; Esping-Andersen 1990). European countries have policies that are very different from Canada's. More importantly, despite many similar macroeconomic and social trends, European policies have helped prevent the high levels of insecurity currently faced by many Canadian families. Hence, it makes sense to see what we might learn from the Europeans.

To explore new options for increasing the economic security of Canadian families with children, particularly young children, this chapter focuses on France, Germany, Finland, and Sweden. In all cases, these European countries offer more generous programs to assist families than we do, but the structure of available programs differs across the countries, providing a range of alternatives for Canadians to consider.

Policies in Sweden and Finland, two countries with social democratic histories, are most similar to one another. Programs in Germany and France look rather different. For example, German policy has been shaped by a strong belief that children are better off when cared for at home by their mothers until at least the age of three years. Swedish policy, on the other hand, has encouraged the labour force participation of mothers in an attempt to achieve equality between men and women, both in the home and in the marketplace.

In general terms, however, the European countries have more in common with each other than with Canada, since the goals that have guided the development of social policy in the European countries have been quite different from our own. For example, pro-natalism was one important reason for the creation of the generous child allowances still available in each of the European countries studied. Increasing the birthrate has not been such an important goal in Canada except in Quebec, where family policy has also responded to this concern with, for example, sizable birth allowances ($8,000) for third and subsequent children. All of the European countries studied regard children as a major societal resource and hence a public as well as a private responsibility (Kamerman 1980), while Canadian policy generally reflects the attitude that, except as a last resort, children are the private responsibility of their parents. Canadian policy makers worry about interfering with market outcomes; this has not been as important a consideration in the European countries.

Does it make any sense for Canadians to think about adopting policies developed elsewhere to meet possibly different goals? Yes. Regardless of why a policy idea appeared in the first place (e.g., to increase birthrates), if it seems likely to solve a problem we currently face (e.g., child poverty), we should consider using it, realizing, of course, that modifications may be required to use European ideas in the context of Canadian goals and institutions.

Socioeconomic Change in Canada and Europe

The availability of more extensive programs for families is an important explanation for the fact that, despite quite similar underlying socioeconomic trends, European families have avoided some of the problems Canadian families now face (Kamerman and Kahn 1988; Smeeding 1991; Jäntti and Danziger 1992; Wong et al. 1992). For example, rates of divorce or separation are high and single-parent families are increasingly common in all the countries, but extreme poverty among single-parent families is a Canadian and not a European phenomenon. Average family sizes have fallen and rates of labour force participation for mothers have increased in all countries, but the Europeans offer more policies to help ease the strain of meeting both home and workplace responsibilities. Unemployment rates are high and the job market for young people has deteriorated in all the countries, but poverty among families with children is far worse in Canada. These important socioeconomic patterns are outlined in more detail below.

First, Canada, Germany, and Sweden have almost identical and rather high divorce rates (Table 1); 44 per cent of marriages ended in divorce over the 1987 to 1990 period. Divorce rates are somewhat lower in Finland (38 per cent) and France (31 per cent). High rates of divorce can increase the economic vulnerability of women (if they had reasonable access to their husbands' incomes during marriage), since in all the countries studied, women have lower incomes than men. Canadian evidence indicates that men's standards of living typically rise by 30 per cent after separation (for the median non-custodial father who has not remarried). On the other hand, women's standards of living typically fall to 52 per cent of the predivorce level (for cus-

Table 1: Demographic Indicators: Canada vs. Selected European Countries

	Canada	Finland	France	Germany	Sweden
Divorces (as % of marriages contracted 1987–90)[a]	43	38	31	44	44
Single-parent families (as % of all families with children)[b]	18	15	9	7	18
Ratio (%) of 1991 fertility rate to 1960 fertility rate[a]	47	66	65	62	89
Crude live-birth rates[c]	15.2	13.1	13.3	10.4	14.4

Sources: [a]United Nations Development Program, *Human Development Report* (Oxford: University Press, 1993); [b]Luxembourg Income Study; [c]United Nations, *Demographic Yearbook (1992)* (New York: United Nations, 1994).

todial mothers who have not remarried) (Finnie et al. 1994). Of course, these figures assume that husbands and wives had equal standards of living while married, which is not always the case.

In all the countries, divorce and separation are the main routes to single parenthood (Lefaucheur and Martin 1993; Kahn and Kamerman 1994). In both Canada and Sweden, 18 per cent of all families with children are single-parent families; in Finland, 15 per cent of all families with children are single-parent families; in France (where divorce rates are lower) and Germany, only 9 per cent and 7 per cent of families with children are single-parent families (Table 1). Because Germany still puts a heavy emphasis on preserving the traditional family, divorces are less likely for couples with children, and births outside marriage are much less common than in other countries (Kahn and Kamerman 1994). In all cases, however, there has been significant growth in the number of single-parent families in recent years.

All countries studied have experienced a significant decline in fertility rates between 1960 and 1991. However, the drop in fertility over this period is most extreme in Canada, where 1960 marked the end of the postwar baby boom. The ratio of the 1991 fertility rate to the 1960 fertility rate is about 50 per cent in Canada; about 65 per cent in Finland, France and Germany; and about 90 per cent in Sweden. As of 1991, fertility rates were very similar in Canada and Sweden, slightly lower in Finland and France and significantly lower in Germany.

Smaller families have gone hand-in-hand with a second socioeconomic pattern: increases in female labour force participation rates in all countries (Table 2). Canada has experienced the sharpest increase of all countries studied. The ratio of 1990 female labour force participation to 1960 labour force participation is 2.4 in Canada, 1.9 in Sweden, 1.6 in France and 1.3 in Finland and Germany. Labour force participation is currently higher for Canadian women (69 per cent) than for

Table 2: Female Labour Force Participation: Canada vs. Selected European Countries

	Canada	Finland	France	Germany	Sweden
Female labour force participation rate (%) 1990[a]	69.0	72.9	57.7	55.9	83.5
Ratio of 1990 female labour force participation rate to 1960[a]	2.4	1.3	1.6	1.3	1.9
Married mothers with positive earnings (%)[b]	75	86	52	41	92
Single mothers with positive earnings (%)[b]	58	87	75	50	93
Female wages as a % of male wages 1990–1[a]	63	77	88	74	89

Sources: [a]United Nations Development Program, *Human Development Report* (Oxford University Press, 1993); [b]Luxembourg Income Study.

women in France and Germany (58 per cent and 56 per cent, respectively). However, despite the rapid changes observed in Canada, current levels of female labour force participation remain slightly lower than in Finland (73 per cent) and significantly lower than in Sweden (84 per cent). Swedish and Finnish women have a strong history of labour force participation from which we can learn. It is also worth noting that nearly 40 per cent of Swedish women who are in the labour force work part-time, whereas in Canada 24 per cent work part-time (Nordic Council 1994: 3). In part, this difference is a result of policies that help women in Sweden combine paid work and child-rearing (discussed later in this chapter).

Canada and the European countries can also be compared in terms of the percentage of mothers (married and single) with positive earnings.[1] In Sweden, 92 per cent of married mothers have paid employment; in Finland, 86 per cent; in Canada, 75 per cent; and in France and Germany, only 52 per cent and 41 per cent, respectively. In Germany, it is regarded as extremely important that a mother remain at home, particularly if she has children less than three years old. Percentages for single mothers with positive earnings are similar: 93 per cent in Sweden, 87 per cent in Finland, 75 per cent in France, 58 per cent in Canada, and 50 per cent in Germany. From the Canadian perspective, where much attention has recently focused on encouraging the labour force participation of single mothers, it is interesting to note that single mothers are more likely than married mothers to have paid employment in all of the European countries, but less likely to have paid employment in Canada.

These trends in labour force participation mean that, except in Germany, a majority of families do not have a 'stay-at-home mom' to take care of home and childcare responsibilities. Yet these responsibilities continue when mothers enter the labour force. For families without sufficient income to pay for help, the strain involved in balancing work and family is potentially significant. (Even when families have resources to pay for domestic help, there is still significant effort involved in coordination and in dealing with crises such as sickness.) Further, international evidence (Mikkola 1991; Wallace and Myles 1994) indicates that women still bear the greater share of family responsibilities even if they are full-time participants in the labour market. Thus, the strain of the double workday is felt by many women.

In addition, women earn less relative to men in Canada than in the European countries (Table 2). Female wages are 63 per cent of male wages in Canada, 89 per cent in Sweden, 88 per cent in France, 77 per cent in Finland, and 74 per cent in Germany. Thus, the potential vulnerability of families who rely on women's earnings is greatest in Canada. This includes families in which the husband's earnings are insufficient as well as families in which there is no man present.

A third socioeconomic pattern and a serious problem in all countries is unemployment (see Table 3). In 1994, unemployment in Canada (10.8 per cent) was roughly similar to unemployment in France (12.3 per cent) and Germany (10.0 per cent), lower than unemployment in Finland (18.5 per cent) and higher than unemployment in Sweden (7.6 per cent).

Youth unemployment rates are much higher than overall unemployment rates in all countries but Germany (where much-admired apprenticeship training programs for young people apparently ease school-to-work transitions). For anyone concerned with the economic security of families, the labour market difficulties faced by young people must be recognized. Unemployment today increases the likelihood of economic difficulties tomorrow, as skills deteriorate and experience is not acquired. Furthermore, economic difficulties for young adults must eventually translate into increases in child poverty as families are formed by people in their twenties and early thirties. In 1992, 60 per cent of Canadian children living with at least one parent aged less than 24 were poor (Sharif and Phipps 1994).

Since 1975, at least 30 per cent of new jobs created in most Canadian provinces have been

Table 3: Macroeconomic Indicators: Canada vs. Selected European Countries

	Canada	Finland	France	Germany	Sweden
Unemployment rate (%)					
Total (1983–91)[a]	9.5	5.0	9.7	7.3	2.1
Total (1994)[a]	10.8	18.5	12.3	10.0	7.6
Youth (15–24) unemployment rate/total unemployment rate (1992)[b]	1.6	1.8	1.9	1.2	2.4
Earnings per employee, annual growth rate (1980–9)[b]	0.1	2.7	2.0	1.8	0.9
GNP per capita, % annual growth rate (1980–91)[b]	2.0	2.5	1.8	2.2	1.7
Average annual rate of inflation (%) (1980–91)[b]	4.3	6.6	5.7	2.8	7.4
Overall budget deficit/surplus (1991)[b]	–2.7	0.1	–1.4	–2.5	0.7

Sources: [a]OECD, *Employment Outlook* (OECD, 1994); [b]United Nations Development Program, *Human Development Report* (Oxford: University Press, 1994).

part-time. A growing number of jobs are short-term (lasting less than six months), and an increasing number of individuals are self-employed without any employees of their own. Finally, temporary-help work tripled in the 1980s. These 'non-standard' forms of employment, which are especially likely to be experienced by youth and women, constitute nearly 30 per cent of total employment in Canada (Economic Council of Canada 1990). Similar trends are observable in the European countries studied here (OECD 1991, 1994).

Poverty or income inequality is a fourth socioeconomic pattern (Table 4). Here, Canada's performance is consistently the worst. In terms of income inequality, the richest 20 per cent of Canadian households (1986 to 1989) have 7.1 times the income of the poorest 20 per cent of households. In Sweden, on the other hand, the richest households have 4.6 times the income of the poorest, and in Germany the richest have 5.7 times the income of the poorest. A more stable distribution of income reduces economic insecurity.

The incidence of poverty among families with children is also significantly higher in Canada than in any of the European countries studied. Eighteen per cent of all Canadian families with children are poor, whereas in Finland and Sweden, only 5 per cent of all families with children are poor. Germany and France had intermediate records with 9 per cent and 12 per cent of families with children considered poor, respectively.

Single-parent families in Canada are particularly at risk of being poor. Forty-five per cent of Canadian single-parent families are poor, while only 9 per cent of Swedish single-parent families and 11 per cent of Finnish single-parent families are poor.[2] There are just as many single-parent

Table 4: Poverty and Inequality Indicators: Canada vs. Selected European Countries

	Canada	Finland	France	Germany	Sweden
Ratio of income of richest 20% of households to poorest 20% 1986–9[a]	7.1	6.0	6.5	5.7	4.6
Incidence of poverty among all families with children (%)[b]	18	5	12	9	5
Incidence of poverty among single-parent families (%)[b]	45	11	20	32	9

Sources: [a]United Nations Development Program, *Human Development Report* (Oxford: University Press, 1994); [b]Luxembourg Income Study.

families in Finland and Sweden as in Canada, so it is not small numbers that are enabling these countries to keep single parents out of poverty. France and Germany have intermediate records with 20 per cent and 32 per cent of single-parent families poor.

Of course, the poverty that is evident among single-parent families may have been hidden in households before separation if resources were not shared equally among all family members (Phipps and Burton 1995; Pulkingham 1995). Since women and children receive much smaller incomes, they may be poor within some families if men do not share. For example, traditional measures of poverty, which implicitly assume that wives have equal access to their husbands' incomes, indicate that 9 per cent of husbands and wives were poor in Canada in 1992. If, on the other hand, we assume that women have only very limited access to their husbands' incomes, poverty among wives increases to 25 per cent while poverty among husbands drops to 4 per cent (Phipps and Burton 1995).

To summarize, many of the same socioeconomic trends are apparent in Canada and the four European countries studied. In Canada, high rates of unemployment and deteriorating labour market conditions, especially for young adults, have left a large number of families in poverty or near-poverty. Many more families face the *risk* of deprivation and even families fortunate enough to have secure employment face significant strain in their attempts to juggle home and workplace responsibilities. In Europe, the same trends have not always resulted in the same problems.

Cash Transfers for Children in Canada and Europe

In the European countries, there has been 'a long history of acknowledging that children are a major societal resource and that the whole society should share in the costs of rearing them' (Kamerman 1980: 24). Universal cash transfers providing social support for all children are thus regarded as the core of family policy in these countries. In contrast, the Canadian attitude has increasingly been that children are the private responsibility of their parents, requiring state support only in the case of serious deprivation; therefore, Canada aims child benefits toward lower-income families.

PROGRAM COMPARISONS

France

Family allowances first appeared in France at the end of the nineteenth century as wage supplements paid by employers to employees with children as a means of avoiding more general wage increases. During the 1930s, the idea that these benefits could be used for pro-natalist purposes appeared, and all employers were required to contribute to a fund which then distributed benefits to all employees with children. The present system of family allowance payments, which emerged just after the Second World War, is regarded as one of the most extensive and generous systems in the world (Kahn and Kamerman 1994).

The pro-natalist spirit of the French system is still in evidence, with benefits that are relatively much more generous for larger families. Family allowances in France consist of a large number of different cash transfers. However, a basic universal benefit for all families with two or more children less than sixteen years of age is by far the most important, accounting for about half of total expenditures. All political parties now agree on the merits of extending this basic benefit to families with just one child, although this has not yet been done in an era of fiscal restraint.

Over the past twenty years a concern with aiming benefits toward the most needy families has emerged. A number of means-tested or categorical (or both) child allowances have been established. For example, there are special benefits for children in single-parent families, for handicapped children and for very young children (Kahn and Kamerman 1994). All child allowances are funded through a 7 per cent payroll tax levied on employers or on the self-employed (USDHHS 1992); family allowance transfers are not taxable income (OECD 1993). There is also tax relief for families with children.

Germany

The goal of preserving the traditional family has been the dominant influence on family policy in Germany. German family allowances were established in 1955 as a form of wage supplement and were originally payable only to fathers with three or more children. For obvious reasons, pro-natalism could not be an explicit policy goal so soon after the Second World War, but the benefits had an implicit pro-natalist design. Over time, cover-

age was extended and the value of the transfers increased (Kahn and Kamerman 1994). Currently, all families with children under sixteen (or under twenty-one if unemployed, or twenty-seven if full-time students or invalids) receive family allowance payments financed from general revenue. Payments per child increase for additional children. For example, families receive twice as much for the second as for the first child, 4.4 times as much for the third as for the first and 4.8 times as much for the fourth and each subsequent child (USDHHS 1992). High-income families receive the same benefit as lower-income families for the first child, but only 1.4 times as much for the second child and 2.8 times for the third and each subsequent child (Gauthier 1993). As in France, family allowances are not subject to income taxation (OECD 1993).

Fathers, when present, are still the recipients of family allowance payments in Germany, in keeping with a policy perspective favouring the traditional family. However, it is also clear that family allowances are intended to help with the costs of childrearing. German family allowances (and tax concessions for children) were recently (1991) increased following a federal court ruling that all parents have the right to benefits that ensure a basic standard of living for their children (Kahn and Kamerman 1994).

Finland

Family allowances in Finland emerged in 1943 from a pro-natalist agenda. More recently, however, Finnish policy has been characterized as devoted to universalistic principles (Kahn and Kamerman 1994). Family allowances are viewed as a means of providing social support for all families with children. Benefits, financed through general revenue, are universally available to all families with children less than sixteen years old. The real value of family allowances in Finland in 1990 was about three times what it was in 1951 and about 30 per cent above the 1982–7 value (Mikkola 1991).[3] Per-child payments increase as the number of children in the family increases

(USDHHS 1992). In 1993, a young child supplement to the family allowance as well as tax concessions for children were eliminated as a result of budgetary pressures. To help compensate for these measures, the level of basic family allowances was increased (Kahn and Kamerman 1994). Family allowances are not subject to income tax (OECD 1993).

Sweden

As in the other European countries, early family allowances in Sweden were intended to increase birthrates. However, as in Finland, concern has shifted over time to broader goals of economic security and equality (OECD 1994). Swedish family allowances, financed through general revenue, are now universally available to families with children under sixteen (or less than twenty if full-time students). Higher per-child benefits are received for third and subsequent children: for the third child, the benefit is worth 150 per cent of that for the first; for the fourth child, 200 per cent; for the fifth and subsequent children, 250 per cent. The increments for additional children were increased to current levels in 1989 (Sundstrom 1991). Child allowances are paid monthly and are not subject to income taxation (OECD 1993).

Canada

In Canada, we have recently abandoned universal transfers for all families with children—which were similar in design to many of the European benefits but much lower in value—in favour of child benefits available only for children in lower-income families. We have thus moved away from the European approach of acknowledging social responsibility for all children and toward the US approach of regarding children as the private responsibility of their parents, except when parents are unable to supply basic needs. Canadians have been persuaded that it is somehow wasteful to pay family allowances to higher-income families, although there has not been the same general concern, for example, over the larger benefit well-to-do families receive from the childcare expense deduction.

Currently, the Canadian child benefit system consists of a basic child tax benefit and an earned income supplement. While the basic benefit is $1,020 per child per year, it is 'taxed back' so that only low-income families actually receive the full amount; middle-income families receive smaller and smaller benefits as their incomes increase; higher-income families receive nothing. The earned income supplement is a wage subsidy with a maximum value of $500 paid to parents with low but positive earnings. The earned income supplement also becomes smaller and smaller as incomes increase, and disappears entirely for families with net incomes over $25,921. There is no general tax relief for dependent children.

The current Canadian child benefit system thus differs significantly from those of the European countries. Most importantly, the Canadian system is not universal; only about 62 per cent of families with children receive cash transfer (assuming that the post-1993 system of child tax benefits and earned income supplements delivers benefits to about the same proportion of families as the pre-1993 refundable child tax credit). Also, because benefits are delivered through the tax system, a family's benefit entitlements is always established with a lag—a fall in income will eventually mean an increase in benefits, but not until several months after the next income tax form is filed.

Finally, the level of benefits provided in Canada is much lower than that offered in any other countries studied (see Table 5). Before 1993, Canadian family allowances and refundable child tax credits provided transfers to families with children which, on average, constituted 3 per cent of median gross family income.[4] Since 1993, the average value of child tax benefits and earned income supplements is estimated to constitute 3.5 per cent of median family income. In Germany, the average value of family allowances constitute 4.2 per cent of median gross income; in Sweden, 7.7 per cent; in Finland, 8.1 per cent; and in France, 13.3 per cent. Moreover, the coun-

Table 5: Cash Transfers for Children: Canada vs. Selected European Countries

	Canada 1991	Canada 1993	Finland 1991	France 1984	Germany 1984	Sweden 1987
Level of benefits						
Average child benefits received by families with children/median country gross income (%)	3.0[a]	3.5[a]	8.1[b]	13.3[b]	4.2[b]	7.7[b]

Sources: [a]Canada 1992 and Luxembourg Income Study; [b]Luxembourg Income Study.

tries chosen for analysis in this chapter are not the ones with the most generous child benefit systems. Norway, Australia, Belgium, and Luxembourg provide even more generous child allowances than France (Gauthier 1993).

ADVANTAGES OF THE EUROPEAN APPROACH TO CHILD BENEFITS

The European child benefit systems offer at least three advantages relative to that of Canada.

First, universal family allowance systems require no calculations to establish eligibility. Cheques can simply be mailed each month to all families with children. Administratively, it is an extremely simply program design.

Second, each of the European family allowance programs is a more effective poverty alleviation tool than the Canadian system. Canadians are not used to thinking of universal family allowance payments as a potential poverty alleviation tool—perhaps because our benefit levels have always been so low. Yet it has been shown that the higher the average level of child benefits, the more successful a country is likely to be at preventing poverty among families with children (Phipps 1995). Of course, simple arithmetic says that a fixed pot of money spent entirely on the poor could go further toward alleviating child poverty than the same funds distributed equally to all families. However, the key question is, would the same total funds always be available if child benefits were

received only by the poor, particularly if the poor seemed to be receiving quite generous transfers? It is quite possible, particularly during difficult economic times, that benefits would be cut as a result of concerns about deficits or about transfers interfering with work incentives. In other countries, generous child allowance payments have proven extremely popular and their real value has increased over time, while the real value of Canadian benefits has been allowed to fall. When the Thatcher government attempted to replace universal family allowances with a child benefit aimed toward low-income families, public pressure led to the abandonment of this plan, leaving universal benefits in place (Gauthier 1993). Such popularity ensures that low-income households continue to receive generous benefits.

Third, the universal nature of the European benefits provides better security for families with children in an era when parental income is increasingly insecure. Generous child benefit cheques received monthly by all families with children in the European countries provide an excellent means of helping families cope with sudden reductions in income through, for example, the loss of a job. On the other hand, *lack* of responsiveness to year-to-year changes in family incomes is a characteristic of the new Canadian system (Kesselman 1993). In Canada, eligibility for any child benefit is assessed based on the previous year's income tax returns. Adjustments necessary as a result of changes in income are made 1 July. If an individual loses his or her job on January 1 of 1995 and is without employment throughout the year, evidence of the drop in income will not be available until April of 1996. Child benefits will not be adjusted until July of 1996. Thus, the family will wait from January 1, 1995, until July 1, 1996, for the receipt of any benefits. And, as noted above, economic insecurity is a fact of life for many Canadian families with children, particularly when parents are young.[5]

As well, longitudinal data for the United States indicates that many more families fall into poverty within a year than are measured to be poor based on annual income (Ruggles and Roberton 1989). Relatively few of these families have sufficient income to carry them through even a relatively short spell of reduced income. Yet most bills (rent, groceries) must be paid at least monthly, causing considerable hardship to families with even temporarily low income. A child allowance received monthly—particularly if it is relatively generous—can thus be an extremely effective and administratively simply way of increasing the economic security of Canadian families with children.

Maternity or Parental Benefits in Canada and Europe

In Canada, maternity and parental benefits are conceived as labour market programs—benefits to provide parents who have significant past labour force attachment with time at home with their new children before they return to paid employment. Administration of maternity or parental benefits through the unemployment insurance program is unique and clearly illustrates the labour market orientation of the Canadian system. In contrast, while all of the European countries offer benefits that are linked with past earnings, they also offer at least some benefits to new parents without recent histories of paid employment. Thus, European maternity or parental benefits offer some assistance to all new parents; Canadian

maternity or parental benefits assist only some paid employees who are new parents, and then only if they will be returning to their jobs. In general, the European programs offer benefits to more people, at a higher level of compensation and for a longer period than we do in Canada.

PROGRAM COMPARISONS

France

In France, pro-natalism is again very evident in the design of maternity and parental benefits that are considerably more generous for third and subsequent children. Maternity benefits have been available in France since 1946. To qualify for cash benefits, a woman must have had at least 1,200 hours of paid employment in the year before the child's birth and she must prove that her insurance coverage by the social security system has been in place for ten months by the date of delivery (David and Starzec 1991).[6] The duration of benefits varies with the number of children the mother already has. For the first two children, she is entitled to sixteen weeks of paid leave (six prenatal and ten postnatal) at a basic rate of 84 per cent of daily earnings, with both a ceiling and floor (USDHHS 1992). For third and subsequent children, the mother is allowed twenty-six weeks of paid leave (eight weeks prenatal and eighteen postnatal) at the same rate (David and Starzec 1991). (Employers often top up benefits to 100 per cent of previous earnings.) Additionally, all women are entitled to an income-tested child allowance from the fourth month of pregnancy, and nursing mothers are provided with a monthly allowance or milk coupons for four months (USDHHS 1992).

A childrearing leave entitles parents with a minimum of one year of paid employment before the birth or adoption of the child to an additional two-year leave following the maternity leave. The childrearing leave may be taken by either the mother or the father. During this period, the parent's job is protected, and he or she is entitled to social benefits from the job.

Since 1985, parents of a third or subsequent child have been eligible to receive a childrearing allowance while on childrearing leave. Eligibility is contingent only on previous work history (the parent claiming it must have had paid employment for at least two of the ten years preceding the birth or adoption of the child); there is no income test. Benefits are paid until the child's third birthday (David and Starzec 1991). For one year preceding the child's third birthday, the parent receiving the allowance can return to work part-time, retaining half the cash benefit. Only one parent may claim the benefit. The allowance was about $547 per month (in 1990 terms) in 1989, over half the guaranteed minimum wage (David and Starzec 1991).

Germany

In Germany, two major programs exist for new parents. The first is a program for labour force participants; the second offers payments to any new parents who remain at home to care for their young children. Since the payments for stay-at-home parents would not be enough to support a single parent with no other sources of income, and since the recipients are not supposed to engage in paid labour, the payments are clearly intended to reinforce the traditional family.

In Germany, all women with twelve weeks of insurance, or continuous employment from the tenth to the fourth month preceding confinement (this includes unemployment beneficiaries and the insured self-employed), are eligible for fourteen weeks of paid maternity leave (six weeks before and eight weeks after the birth). Paid employees receive 100 per cent of their net covered earnings (based on an average for the past three months). The standard benefit is a flat rate, but employers must top up the flat-rate benefit for higher-income employees. Maternity benefits are not taxable.

In keeping with the desire to support traditional husband-and-wife families with stay-at-home mothers, a new government-financed childrearing benefit was introduced in 1986. This benefit is available at a flat rate of about $405 per

month (1990) for six months and on a means-tested basis for an additional eighteen months. (This was increased from twelve months in 1993.) Over 97 per cent of eligible families take the childrearing benefit for the full period. Sometimes called 'an honorarium for motherhood', the benefit is intended to enable families to care for infants and toddlers at home. Legally, the benefit can be taken by either the father or the mother, but in practice it is almost always taken by the mother unless the father is unemployed. Families are eligible for benefits regardless of past employment status, so about half of all claimants are stay-at-home mothers without recent labour force attachment (Kahn and Kamerman 1994). A beneficiary may not have more than twenty-nine hours paid employment per week while receiving childrearing benefits.

German parents (either mothers or fathers) are also entitled to an annual allotment of five days per child (compensated with 100 per cent of salary) for the care of sick children. Also, breast-feeding mothers are entitled to work two hours less per day with full salary (CACSW 1986).

Finland

The Finnish maternity and parental benefit system provides the most choices for new parents. Every new mother, regardless of previous employment status, is eligible to receive maternity allowance, provided she has resided in Finland for the six months preceding confinement (Mikkola 1991). The duration of cash maternity allowances is 105 days, which may be taken anytime from five weeks before the baby's birth to 9.5 months after the birth; a further 170 days of parent's allowance, compensated at the same rate, may be taken by either mother or father, although the mother must decline to take the benefit for the father to be eligible.[7] The total duration of maternity and parental benefits is thus about forty-six weeks.

For women with paid employment in the period preceding the birth, the benefit paid is 80 per cent of previous wages, not subject to a ceiling, while women who have no previous work history can collect the minimum allowance of about $277 per month (1990) (Mikkola 1991). While there is no ceiling, the earnings replacement rate is gradually reduced to 30 per cent for individuals with annual taxable income over approximately $22,849 (1990) in 1991 (USDHHS 1992). Cash benefits are taxable.

Finland also offers childrearing allowances together with job-protected parental leaves from the end of the maternity or parental benefits until the child is three years old. These may be taken by either parent. Basic compensation during this period is equal to the minimum benefits for parental leave, about $277 (1990) per month. The allowance increases if there are at least two other children under the age of seven at home. Parents may also choose to use childrearing funds to pay for childcare in or out of their own homes. About 80 per cent of eligible families take the childrearing leave for, on average, an additional fourteen months beyond the first forty-six weeks of maternity or parental benefits (Kahn and Kamerman 1994).

Finally, Finnish parents are entitled to 60 days of paid leave per year to care for a sick child at home (USDHHS 1992).

Sweden

In Sweden, parental benefits are designed to encourage the continued labour force participation of new parents. Mothers or fathers are entitled to twelve months of benefits compensated at 90 per cent of previous earnings, to a ceiling of about $78 (1990) per day in 1991, plus an additional three months with a small, flat-rate benefit. These benefits are universally available, regardless of previous labour market participation, as long as the parent is covered by the national health insurance. Multiple births qualify the parent for an incremental six months of benefits for each additional child (Sundstrom 1991). Finally, and quite separately, parents are entitled to unpaid childcare leave until the child is eighteen months. Since the paid leave may be taken at any time before the child reaches eight years, it is possible to arrange many different combinations of paid and unpaid leave, offering new parents a great deal of flexibility in their approaches to work and family life.

Parents are also entitled to paid temporary leave for the care of sick children (up to ten years of age) of up to sixty days per child per year, compensated at 90 per cent of foregone earnings. Until the child is eight years, employers must grant parents the right to a six-hour workday with prorated pay (Gauthier 1993; Kahn and Kamerman 1994).

Canada

In Canada, maternity and parental benefits are available to some workers through the employment insurance system, although it is more difficult to qualify for maternity or parental benefits than for regular employment insurance (EI), and the maximum benefit period is shorter. To qualify for maternity or parental benefits, individuals must have twenty weeks of insurable earnings (with at least fifteen hours per week or at least $121 of earnings per week in 1989). Successful claimants are then eligible for fifteen weeks of maternity benefits compensated at 55 per cent to 60 per cent of previous earnings to a ceiling of $429 per week (1994). Parental benefits, which may be taken by either mothers or fathers, are available for a further ten weeks on the same terms. Maternity and parental benefits are taxable income. Canada does not offer childrearing benefits, a general program of paid leave for the care of sick children, or any special provisions for nursing mothers.

ADVANTAGES OF THE EUROPEAN APPROACH TO MATERNITY AND PARENTAL BENEFITS

Reduced Strain for Two-Earner and Single-Parent Families

A first major advantage of all the European maternity and parental benefit systems is that they are better designed to reduce the strain that a growing number of Canadian families (both two-earner and single-parent) face—the strain of combining work outside the home with parenting responsibilities.

France and Germany offer basic paid maternity leaves that are comparable with the Canadian system, but also offer extended childrearing leaves that allow new parents (either mother or father) the option of a longer period of time at home with new children without giving up jobs previously held. In Germany, this leave is paid. In France, the leave is paid only for third and subsequent children. French childrearing leaves are contingent on past labour force attachment. In Germany, on the other hand, childrearing benefits are available to all families, regardless of past labour force status. However, parents in receipt of childrearing benefits can work no more than nineteen hours per week and can only work at the job previously held. Thus, during the period of potential leave, a German parent is effectively forced to choose between paid employment and parenting; traditional gender roles are hence reinforced.

The Finnish system provides parents with more flexibility. The basic Finnish maternity or parental benefits are available, regardless of past labour force status, for about double the potential duration of benefits in Canada; in addition, paid childrearing leave is available until the child is three. Parents who choose to return to paid employment before the child is three have the option of working only six-hour days, retaining 25 per cent of the childrearing allowance as partial compensation for the associated income loss; alternatively, the childrearing allowance can be used to help pay for childcare for parents returning full-time to paid employment. Parents can thus choose the combination that best meets their needs.

In Sweden, new parents are encouraged to participate in the paid labour force; childrearing leaves are not available. However, basic parental benefits are extremely flexible. A new parent can take an initial full-time leave, followed by part-time paid leave and part-time paid employment, in almost any combination. The intent is to support new parents in combining parenting and paid employment.

Finland, Sweden and Germany also provide paid leave for the care of sick children, a reality that causes many Canadian parents logistical nightmares. Germany also recognizes the right of a new mother to paid time off for nursing.

The key point of all such policies is the recognition both that a growing majority of families now combine parenting and paid employment, and that without help from facilitative policies, enormous strains are created. Typically, these strains are disproportionately borne by mothers, since in all countries studied, traditional gender roles prevail despite the growth in female labour force participation. In Germany, only 1.3 per cent of childrearing leaves are taken by men, most of whom would otherwise be unemployed (Schiersmann 1991). In Finland, fathers took only 2 per cent of all parental leave days (Mikkola 1991).

Longer paid leaves provide new parents with the option of spending more time with infants during their first years of life. Not only does this make life easier for sleep-deprived new parents, but it may have important consequences for parent-child interactions. As one example, mothers breastfeed longer in the European countries than in Canada—an average of 8.5 months in Sweden (Waldenstrom and Nilsson 1994) compared to 4.3 months in Canada (Greene-Finestone et al. 1989).

Higher rates of compensation, especially for basic maternity or parental leaves, help European families cope with the financial strain of adding a new member to the family. Also, more families are covered. In Canada, relatively stringent eligibility conditions must be satisfied, resulting in the exclusion of, for example, the self-employed, workers with low weekly hours or earnings and workers with fewer than twenty weeks of work in the previous year. Given poor conditions in the labour market, particularly for young adults in their family formation years, significant numbers of new parents are excluded from benefits.

Increased Equality between Men and Women in the Paid Labour Market and Increased Economic Security for Women

The idea of parental rather than maternity leave is that by offering fathers the opportunity to stay home to care for their children, traditional gender roles will begin to erode, allowing both mothers and fathers to combine childcare and paid employment. However, as noted above, the reality everywhere still seems to be that mothers take the leaves. Thus, the real gender-equity advantage of the extensive child-related leaves, particularly in the Scandinavian states, seems to be that these policies make it easier for women to combine home and workplace responsibilities. More continuous labour force participation contributes to increased job-related skills and experience with the likely outcome of higher wages. This may be one important reason why gender-earnings ratios are more favourable for women in the European countries than in Canada (see Table 2).

Better labour market outcomes for women also have the distinct advantage that women are better able to support themselves financially in the increasingly likely event of divorce or separation. This helps to reduce the economic vulnerability of women both following a separation and within a marriage. A growing body of evidence indicates that women's power within marriage increases as their earned-income contributions increase (Phipps and Burton 1992). It is also true that women may be less likely to remain in a bad relationship if there is no economic need.

Furthermore, these facilitative policies offer an enormous advantage to single mothers, who must cope alone with both home and workplace responsibilities. The results in Europe seem very positive—rates of labour force participation for European single mothers are high, especially in the Scandinavian countries where policies are most facilitative (see Table 2).

Advance Maintenance Payments

In each of the European countries studied, the state guarantees maintenance for the child by providing a cash transfer in cases where an absent parent does not pay child support, pays only infrequently or does not pay enough. Like the European countries, Canada has a growing population of single-parent families. Unlike the European countries, single-parent families in Canada are extremely insecure. A study of the significant differences in outcomes for single parents in Europe versus Canada suggests one extremely important new policy option—advance maintenance payments.

While shockingly little information about the receipt of child support is available for Canada, a Department of Justice study indicated that 68 per cent of divorces involving children received court orders for child support. Of these, only two-thirds of non-custodial parents made payments regularly during the first year, and compliance is known to fall as time passes (Finnie et al. 1994). In Canada, some attention has recently been given to the design of enforcement mechanisms to ensure that non-custodial parents (typically fathers) pay. All provinces and territories now have automated, government-run enforcement programs, and the federal government contributes by garnisheeing funds such as income tax refunds and unemployment insurance when support payments are not being made. Guidelines for child support wards have also recently been recommended (Dept. of Justice 1995).

Despite these efforts, it is still true that if a non-custodial parent chooses not to contribute to the maintenance of his (or her) children or is unable to pay, the child suffers the consequences. Current child support policy thus treats children as the private responsibility of the parents. On the other hand, we offer disabled contributor's child benefits and orphan's benefits to the unmarried children of Canada Pension Plan contributors who become disabled or die. The availability of month benefits of $154 (1992) per child provides some insurance for children against the risk of income loss resulting from the death or incapacitation of a parent (Hess 1992). In effect, society shares in costs which would otherwise be borne exclusively by the child. The idea of advance maintenance payments is similar, providing children with some insurance against loss of income following the divorce, separation or non-marriage of their parents. Such programs have been available in European countries for many years.

Program Comparisons

France
Family support allowances have been available in France since 1970 for children with a parent who is not meeting child-support obligations. The amount paid is about $87 (1990) per child.

Germany
In Germany, a limited system of tax-free advance maintenance payments has been available since 1980. These benefits are available only to single parents who do not receive support payments required by court order. Moreover, they are provided for a maximum of only three years or until the child reaches age six. The maximum payment is $158 (1989) per month. Thus payments are at a much lower level than those available, for example, in Sweden, and receipt of the child-support benefit results in a 50 per cent reduction in family allowance payments (Schiersmann 1991).

Sweden
The Swedish advance maintenance system is the oldest and most developed. Established in 1964, the basis for this system is the belief that children should not be penalized for an absent parent's inability or unwillingness to pay support (Kamerman and Kahn 1983). In 1990, advance maintenance payments were cash benefits equal to about $284 (1990) per month per child less than 18, tax free (Sundstrom 1991). The intent is

that the cost of the advance should be recovered from the absent parent. In 1983, it was estimated that about 38 per cent of expenditures were recovered in this way (Kamerman and Kahn 1983). The effect of this comprehensive system of advance maintenance payments on the incomes of single mothers is striking—100 per cent of Swedish single mothers received child support (either directly from the non-custodial parent or from the state) (Phipps 1993). Maintenance payments are as important a source of income for Swedish single parents not in the labour force as social assistance (Kamerman 1984).

Finland
A similar program is available in Finland, where the monthly allowance in 1990 was $103 per month. Single parents who receive less than this amount in child support from absent parents (perhaps because of the non-custodial parent's inability to pay) receive a partial benefit from the state to bring them up to the state-guaranteed monthly level (Mikkola 1991). These child support payments are not income-tested and are not taxable.

Canada
The fact that we do not provide *any* publicly supported advance maintenance payments is another example of how Canadian policy tends to regard children as private rather than public responsibility. If the non-custodial parent is unable or unwilling to pay, the child suffers the consequences. With an advance maintenance system in place, the rest of society would share this burden.

How would advance maintenance payments work? One scenario is as follows:

- Child-support payments would be set according to recommended guidelines and collected from the non-resident parent's income, just as income taxes are withheld or EI premiums are collected.
- The government would guarantee minimum child-support payments for *all* children,

regardless of the income of the custodial parent, financed through general revenue.[8]

The government would pay nothing in cases where support payments above the legislated minimum are received. But, just as any child is eligible for orphan benefits, any child not receiving sufficient child support would be eligible for the advance maintenance benefits, whether his or her mother is rich or poor (i.e., advance maintenance payments are not intended to be another form of social assistance). In practice, children with higher-income custodial mothers are more likely to be receiving child support because higher-income women are more likely to have been married to higher-income men who can subsequently afford to pay (Garfinkel 1994).

Summary Discussion

The discussion of socioeconomic indicators for Canada at the start of this chapter indicated several sources of economic insecurity or strain for Canadian families: (1) an increasing number of two-earner and single-parent families who do not have a stay-at-home mother to cope with the inevitable day-to-day responsibilities of child and home care (e.g., a sick child); (2) high rates of unemployment and growing 'non-standard' employment, particularly for younger Canadians, so that fewer families can rely on a continuous inflow of earnings; and (3) extremely high levels of economic vulnerability for a growing population of single-mother families.

Many of the same social trends are evident in Europe, but the associated negative outcomes are not always present (e.g., single-parent families are not particularly poor in the European countries). One very important reason for differences in outcomes between Canada and Europe is that the European countries offer more extensive and generous policies for families. Thus, when we look for solutions to our problems, Canadians can learn much from the Europeans.

Of course, there are differences that might make simply importing policies from one country to another difficult. For example, Canada is more heterogeneous in terms of geography, language, and ethnicity than the European countries studied. As well, the constitutional division of responsibilities between the federal and provincial governments seems to have made it more difficult to implement new social policies in Canada than in the other countries here.[9]

Obviously, the space constraints of a single chapter limit discussion to only a few policy areas. This chapter focuses on three European policies that are significantly different from those currently available in Canada, that would help to reduce economic insecurity for Canadian families and that seem most likely to have some hope of acceptance or adoption in Canada because they are reasonably consistent with some currently popular ideas about social policy in Canada. These popular ideas include (1) the belief that something should be done about high levels of child poverty; (2) the view that both fathers and mothers should try to enter the labour force to support themselves and their children; and (3) the concern that debts and deficits are out of control, and, hence, that we should not spend much more on almost anything. This chapter does not argue for or against these ideas, but merely suggests that they are not commonly held in Canada today. In the final analysis, we must be careful not to take currently popular ideas too seriously. One of the most important lessons to learn from international comparisons of policy is that our ideas are not the only ones possible—there really are different ways of thinking about social policy.

For each of the sources of vulnerability noted above, this review of European policies suggests at least one idea that could help and that we should seriously consider for adoption in Canada.

First, we should recognize the difficulties faced by a majority of Canadian families in balancing home and workplace responsibilities by offering more flexible maternity and parental leaves and benefits. This could remove an enormous burden of stress from Canadian families. For example, allowing parental leaves to be taken half-time (for twice as long) while parents returned to work half-time would not cost more but would increase the flexibility for families. Similarly, allowing parents even a small number of paid days off for the care of children each year would make life much easier for both two-earner and single-parent families without being extremely costly. Such changes are in the Swedish tradition of expecting labour force participation of everyone. This seems more suited to current Canadian thinking than, say, a move to initiate a German-style childrearing benefit to help support stay-at-home mothers. Childrearing benefits would not be in keeping with the current Canadian emphasis on labour force participation for all. Not only would more flexible maternity and parental leaves and sick days for children help families, but they could also be expected to yield productivity gains that would help offset the costs as stress is removed from current employees and new workers are able to enter the labour market.[10]

In Sweden, Finland, and Germany, almost all new parents are eligible for some maternity, parental, or childrearing benefits. Coverage in Canada is much narrower and shrinks as unemployment increases or non-standard employment grows. Since it is currently more difficult to qualify for maternity and parental benefits than to qualify for regular EI benefits, we should, as a first step, consider reducing entrance requirements to match those for regular EI benefits. This would extend coverage to many more new parents. As a second step, we should think about extending coverage to workers with low wages or low hours, perhaps with a flat-rate floor on benefits. This would provide maternity or parental benefits to the growing numbers of Canadians, particularly young people and women, who are in the labour force but who are unable to find 'good jobs'. While these changes in coverage would improve

the economic security of many Canadian families, they would not involve major changes in the basic structure of existing programs. And, because EI is administered at the federal level, changes would be relatively easy to implement.

The maternity, parental, and childrearing benefits available in the four European countries studied offer higher rates of compensation for a longer period of time than those available in Canada. Thus it would be desirable to increase expenditures on programs that are so potentially beneficial to both Canadian families and Canadian employers. Unfortunately, this might be a harder policy change to sell in the current Canadian policy environment. But if we do not expand benefits, we should at least be careful that we do not move even further away from international standards, if EI is downsized and maternity benefits, as part of the EI system, are reduced at the same time.

Second, the generous family allowances available in each of the European countries studied are central to their lower rates of child poverty. Thus, we should reinstate family allowances paid monthly to all families with children. Furthermore, the value of these allowances should be at least equal to the benefits currently received by low-income families. This would provide a reliable source of funds to help families with basic needs during periods of income shortfall and would be an important way of helping Canadian families face an increasingly insecure labour market. This is particularly true for young Canadian parents, many of whom are increasingly unlikely to be covered by EI.

Universal cash transfers for children are administratively simple, since no calculations of entitlement must be made. Universal cash transfers are also unlikely to discourage labour force participation because no benefits are lost as earnings increase. Evidence from the European countries indicates that generous universal cash transfers for children are very effective in reducing child poverty. Thus, a return to universal family allowances would suit the Canadian social policy environment in many ways and, obviously, would be relatively easy to implement. The increased expenditures required to improve the generosity of family allowances might be opposed as too expensive, although obviously we can spend more on families and still be fiscally responsible if we are prepared to increase taxes or to make yet more cuts elsewhere.

Third, we should design a system of advance maintenance payments for single-parent families not receiving child-support payments (or receiving only infrequent or inadequate payments). This system would help reduce the economic insecurity of single-mother families. With advance maintenance payments in place, we all share in the cost of non-payment by a defaulting non-custodial parent rather than forcing the child alone to pay.

It is important to note that many other family benefits are available in each of the European countries studied. For example, Finland, France, Sweden and to a lesser extent Germany offer much more comprehensive public childcare than we do in Canada. Housing allowances are also available in all four countries. While income-tested, these benefits are nonetheless received by 80 per cent of single-parent families and 30 per cent of two-parent families in Sweden (see Sundstrom 1991). There are also ideas from Europe that could help reduce the insecurity associated with high rates of unemployment in Canada. For example, all four European countries offer a second tier of unemployment insurance benefits to unemployed individuals without past labour force attachment. These benefits are offered for an unlimited duration although at a lower level of compensation than the very generous basic UI benefits. (Second-tier UI benefits differ from social assistance in that individuals must be searching for work in order to qualify.) Such a program could be of particular benefit for Canadian youth.

Before concluding that any of these European policies should be considered for adoption in Canada, it is important to address the argument raised by critics of the European welfare states who claim that more generous programs necessarily mean a less efficient economy. Canada has the least generous welfare state of the countries studied here, so, by this argument, we should have the best economic performance. However, there is little evidence that this is true (see Table 3).[11] The average Canadian rate of unemployment for the period 1983 to 1991 was 9.5 per cent, while the equivalent for Finland was 5 per cent and for Sweden, 2.1 per cent. Canada has had the lowest growth in real earnings, although growth in GNP per capita is comparable with the other countries. Our inflation record is better than the group average, but our deficit position is worse. Similarly, Sweden and Finland offer the most generous social programs, and thus by the reasoning above should have the worst economic records. Again, this is not the case (Table 3). Historically, unemployment rates have been lower and inflation rates higher than in Canada. Growth of GNP per capita has been better in Finland and worse in Sweden compared to Canada. Earnings growth in both Finland and Sweden has been better than in Canada. Thus, it is not obvious from the historical data that less generous social programs—such as are available in Canada—mean better economic performance or that more generous social programs—such as are available in Sweden and Finland—lead to inferior economic records.

Critics of European welfare states have been delighted to hear of economic hardship in these countries in the last few years and have gleefully announced the 'death of the social democratic dream' (Klebnikov 1993). It is certainly true that economic conditions are currently extremely unfavourable in Finland and Sweden (see Table 3), but there is little evidence that welfare states are to blame. In Sweden, for example, an OECD report documents major expansion of the welfare state during the 1960s and 1970s followed by excellent economic performance with much lower rates of expenditure increases in the

1980s, which in turn was followed by poorer economic performance.[12] Other factors appear to have been more important than social programs in causing economic decline. For example, economic conditions in Finland took a dramatic turn for the worse following the breakup of the Soviet Union, which resulted in the sudden loss of 20 per cent of Finland's export market. Economic conditions deteriorated dramatically in Sweden after a major policy shift to deregulate financial markets. Unemployment rates for Germany increased significantly after re-unification. (German data include East Germany from 1991 onward.)

Of particular interest is the fact that European family policies have remained basically untouched, despite very difficult times. In Finland, generous family allowances are a given, for all political parties (Kahn and Kamerman 1994). Similarly, in France, 'the likelihood that family policy will be spared cuts related to budgetary austerity is all the greater because of a broad political consensus on the principle of family protection' (David and Starzec 1991: 90).

The evidence so far is that no substantive cuts are being made to social welfare programs in the European countries studied here.[13] Apparently, people in these countries believe they can still afford generous social programs even though they are not as rich as we are in terms of per-capita income; indeed, most of these programs were introduced at a time when per-capita incomes were even lower than they are today. Can we afford more generous programs? The evidence says we can if we really want to. Perhaps, then, the most important thing to take from the Europeans is a vision of 'a society in which everyone is precious' (Kahn and Kamerman 1994) and social programs are a priority.

Conclusion

What can we learn from the Europeans about improving the economic security of Canadian families with children? Plenty. Although there are important differences across France, Germany, Finland, and Sweden, family policies in each of these countries reflect a tradition of acknowledging social responsibility for children; Canadian policies, like those in the United States, often reflect the attitude that children are the private responsibility of their parents. Policies offered in Europe are more extensive and generous, and outcomes for families in all cases look much better than outcomes in Canada. Finally, more generous welfare states have *not* led to economic disaster—our economic record is no better in Canada despite our rather cautious programs for families.

Notes

1. The term 'married' refers to both legal and common-law relationships.

2. Poverty estimates were obtained using microdata from the Luxembourg Income Study. For each country the most recent data available were used, but survey years differ across the countries. Data for Canada and Finland are from 1991; data for Sweden are from 1987; data for France and Germany are from 1984. To ensure consistency in poverty measurement across the countries, this chapter adopts the approach of defining a family as poor when gross income is less than 50 per cent of median gross income for the country. (All incomes are adjusted for differences in family needs using the equivalent scale recommended by the OECD, 1982.)

3. Finland also offers tax deductions for children worth about as much as the family allowances.

4. Since family allowances were subject to a clawback for high-income families and were counted as taxable income for the purposes of income tax,

this overstates the level of benefits available in Canada at the time.

5. Of course, the current Canadian system could be made more responsive by income testing more often and reconciling benefits at tax time, but this would substantially increase administration costs.

6. Wives and daughters of insured persons can also be insured.

7. Multiple births qualify the parents for an additional 60 days of benefits (USDHHS 1992). Thus, total duration of benefits is 246 days for adoptions, 275 days for single births and 335 days for multiple births.

8. Garfinkel recommends that advance maintenance be available only for children with court orders for child support (Garfinkel 1994). Eichler argues that all children be eligible (Eichler 1993).

9. While there are federal-state government disputes in Germany, they do not appear to be of the same magnitude as those in Canada, perhaps because

Germany is geographically smaller and less economically and culturally diverse (Michelmann 1986).

10. A comprehensive childcare system would be an extremely important tool to facilitate labour force participation by parents. I do not discuss this option here.

11. To avoid comparing performances in any given year when countries may be at different stages of the business cycle, averages over a number of years for each indicator are reported in Table 3.

12. See OECD Economic Surveys (1994). Of course, it is true that deficits will increase when unemployment goes up in a country with generous transfer programs.

13. The only major change to transfer programs noted in the 1994 OECD report on Sweden was a reduction in the earnings replacement rate for social insurance programs to 80 per cent with the introduction of a one-day penalty without pay.

References

Canada, Canadian Advisory Council on the Status of Women (CACSW). 1986. *Report of the Task Force on Childcare* (Ottawa: Author).

Canada, Department of Justice. 1995. *Federal/Provincial/Territorial Family Law Committee's Report on Child Support* (Ottawa: Public Works and Government Services).

David, M.-G., and C. Starzec. 1991. 'France: A Diversity of Policy Options' in *Child Care, Parental Leave, and the Under 3s: Policy Innovation in Europe*, eds S.B. Kamerman and A.J. Kahn (Westport, CT: Auburn House).

Economic Council of Canada. 1990. *Good Jobs, Bad Jobs: Employment in the Service Economy* (Ottawa: Author).

Eichler, M. 1993. 'Lone Parent Families: An Instable Category in Search of Stable Policies' in *Single Parent Families: Perspectives on Research and Policy*, eds J. Hudson and B. Galaway (Toronto: Thomson Educational Publishing).

Esping-Andersen, G. 1990. *The Three Worlds of Welfare Capitalism* (Princeton, NJ: Princeton University Press).

Finnie, R. et al. 1994. *Child Support: The Guideline Options* (Montreal: Institute for Research on Public Policy).

Garfinkel, I. 1994. 'The Child-Support Revolution', *American Economic Association Papers and Proceedings* 84 (2) (May): 81–5.

Gauthier, A.H. 1993. *Family Policies in the OECD Countries* (Oxford: University of Oxford, Department of Applied Social Studies and Social Research).

Greene-Finestone, L. et al. 1989. 'Infant Feeding Practices and Socio-demographic Factors in Ottawa-Carleton', *Canadian Journal of Public Health* 80 (3) (May/June): 173–6.

Hess, M. 1992. *The Canadian Fact Book on Income Security Programs* (Ottawa: Canadian Council on Social Development).

Jäntti, M., and S. Danziger. 1992. 'Does the Welfare State Work? Evidence on Antipoverty Effects from the Luxembourg Income Study', The Luxembourg Income Study, Working Paper 74.

Kahn, A.J., and S.B. Kamerman. 1994. *Social Policy and the Under-3s: Six Country Case Studies. A Resource for Policy Makers, Advocates and Scholars*, Cross-National Studies Research Program (New York: Columbia University School of Social Work).

Kamerman, S.B. 1980. 'Childcare and Family Benefits: Policies of Six Industrialized Countries', *Monthly Labour Review* 103 (11): 23–8.

———. 1984. 'Women, Children, and Poverty: Public Policies and Female-Headed Families in Industrialized Countries', *Signs* 10 (2): 249–71.

———, and A.J. Kahn. 1983. 'Child Support: Some International Developments' in *The Parental Child-Support Obligation*, ed. J. Cassety (Toronto: Lexington Books, D.C. Heath).

———. 1988. 'Social Policy and Children in the United States and Europe' in *The Vulnerable*, eds J.L. Palmer, T. Smeeding, and B.B. Zorrey (Washington: Urban Institute Press).

Kesselman, J.R. 1993. 'The Child Tax Benefit: Simple, Fair, Responsive?', *Canadian Public Policy* 19 (2): 109–32.

Klebnikov, P. 1993. 'The Swedish Disease' *Forbes* 151, 11: 78, 80.

Lefaucheur, N., and C. Martin. 1993 'Lone Parent Families in France: Situation and Research' in *Single Parent Families: Perspectives on Research and Policy*, eds J. Hudson and B. Galaway (Toronto: Thomson Educational Publishing).

Michelmann, H. 1986. 'Comparing Policy-Making in Two Federations' in *Challenges to Federalism: Policy-Making in Canada and the Federal Republic of Germany*, eds W. Chandler and C. Zollner (Kingston, ON: Institute of Intergovernmental Relations, Queen's University).

Mikkola, M. 1991. 'Finland: Supporting Parental Choice' in *Child Care, Parental Leave, and the Under 3s: Policy Innovation in Europe*, eds S.B. Kamerman and A.J. Kahn (Westport, CT: Auburn House).

Nordic Council. 1994. *Women and Men in the Nordic Countries: Facts and Figures 1994* (Copenhagen: Nordic Council of Ministers).

Organisation for Economic Co-operation and Development (OECD). 1991, 1994. *Employment Outlook* (Paris: Author).

———. 1993. *Taxation in OECD Countries* (Paris: Author).

———. 1994. *OECD Economic Surveys: Sweden* (Paris: Author).

Phipps, S.A. 1993. 'International Perspectives on Income Support for Families with Children', paper (Halifax: Department of Economics, Dalhousie University).

———. 1995. 'Taking Care of Our Children: Tax and Transfer Options for Canada' in *Family Matters: New Policies for Divorce, Lone Mothers, and Child Poverty*, eds J. Richards and W.G. Watson (Toronto: C.D. Howe Institute).

———, and P. Burton. 1992. 'What's Mine is Yours? The Influence of Male and Female Incomes on Patterns of Household Expenditure', Discussion Paper 92–12 (Halifax: Department of Economics, Dalhousie University).

———. 1995. 'Sharing Within Families: Implications for the Measurement of Poverty among Individuals in Canada', *Canadian Journal of Economics* 28 (1) (Feb.): 177–204.

Pulkingham, J. 1995. 'Investigating the Financial Circumstances of Separated and Divorced Parents: Implications for Family Law Reform', *Canadian Public Policy* 21 (1): 1–19.

Ringen, S. 1987. *The Possibility of Politics: A Study in the Political Economy of the Welfare State* (Oxford: Clarendon Press).

Ruggles, P., and W. Roberton. 1989. 'Longitudinal Measures of Poverty: Accounting for Income and Assets over Time', *Review of Income and Wealth* 35 (3): 225–82.

Schiersmann, C. 1991. 'Germany: Recognizing the Value of Child Rearing' in *Child Care, Parental Leave, and the Under 3s: Policy Innovation in Europe*, eds S.B. Kamerman and A.J. Kahn (Westport, CT: Auburn House).

Sharif, N., and S. Phipps. 1994. 'The Challenge of Child Poverty: Which Policies Might Help?', *Canadian Business Economics* 2 (3): 17–30.

Smeeding, T.M. 1991. 'US Poverty and Income Security Policy in a Cross National Perspective', The Luxembourg Income Study, Working Paper 70.

Sundstrom, M. 1991. 'Sweden: Supporting Work, Family and Gender Equality' in *Child Care, Parental Leave, and the Under 3s: Policy Innovation in Europe*, eds S.B. Kamerman and A.J. Kahn (Westport, CT: Auburn House).

United States, Department of Health and Human Services (USDHHS). 1992. *Social Security Programs Throughout the World—1991*, Social Security Administration Publication No. 61–006 (Washington: Author).

Waldenstrom, U., and C. Nilsson. 1994. 'No Effect of Birth Centre Care on Either Duration or Experience of Breastfeeding, But More Complications: Findings from a Randomised Controlled Trial', *Midwifery* 10 (1) (March): 8–17.

Wallace, C., and J. Myles. 1994. *Relations of Ruling: Class and Gender in Postindustrial Societies* (Montreal: McGill-Queen's University Press).

Wong, Y.-L.I. et al. 1992. 'Single-Mother Families in Eight Countries: Economic Status and Social Policy', The Luxembourg Income Study, Working Paper 76.

Chapter 33

This article provides us with much more than a comparison of Sweden's excellent family policies with Canada's poor support of families. Rianne Mahon *traces the history behind the legislation that has made Sweden one of the countries where families are well supported.*

Welfare State Restructuring and Changing Gender Relations: The Politics of Family Policy in Sweden and Canada

Rianne Mahon

In the formative years of welfare states, the failure of the male breadwinner's wages to cover the family's basic needs constituted an important problem.[1] Pension systems, disability allowances, and unemployment and sickness insurance can be seen as supports for families when the breadwinner was temporarily or permanently unable to perform his role. Mother's allowances were designed to sustain 'deserving' families that lacked a male breadwinner. Social policies did not assume dominance of the male breadwinner family form, however, in all countries (Jenson 1986). More importantly, this type of family is on the decline in all OECD (Organisation for Economic Co-operation and Development) countries, yielding place to the dual-earner family.

The emergence of the dual-earner family does not eliminate the need for supportive social policies, however: it simply changes it. Time-pressed dual-earner families find it hard to perform the reproductive work, daily and intergenerational, formerly done by housewife-mothers. Nor is it easy to substitute housework with services—from food preparation to childcare—purchased on the market, because these activities, on the whole, remain labour intensive and thus relatively expensive. To some extent, families respond by deciding to delay—or even to avoid—having children, but this only exacerbates the problem posed by ageing. The latter means a rising dependency ratio (too few working age adults to support an ageing population). Contemporary states are thus coming under pressure to develop policies that support the dual-earner family and to encourage that family to have children (Esping-Andersen 1999: ch. 4).

It is important, of course, not to equate the emergence of the dual-earner family with equality of the sexes. While having a job can give women economic independence from men within the family, its impact on overall gender equality depends on a variety of other conditions. The choices states make, in turn, profoundly affect these conditions. To a great extent, their responses thus far have followed patterns established during the heyday of the male breadwinner family form.[2] Thus 'conservative' welfare states have largely continued to favour the male breadwinner and support the dependent position of housewife-mothers. 'Liberal' welfare states prefer to leave as much as possible to the market and/or family, overtly intervening only to help the worst off. This model perpetuates both gender (the 'double burden') and class inequalities (O'Connor et al. 1999). It is the 'social-democratic' states that have generally been the most active in supporting the dual-earner family through provision of new services—family leave policy and the like. The latter go farther toward establishing the conditions for gender equality, and do so in a way that mitigates class inequalities as well.

In this chapter, the family policies of 'liberal' Canada will be compared to those of 'social-democratic' Sweden. As we shall see, their policies pretty well conform to expectations. Canada's policies assume that families' market-derived income will allow them to purchase the goods and services they need. The poor are provided some assistance, but it is increasingly geared to getting them to work, even if the pay is too low to cover the added expenses. This is in marked contrast to the policies of the Swedish state, which continues to provide a wide range of high-quality services supportive of the dual-earner family. Universal and generous child allowances, combined with strong parental leave insurance programs, complete the package. The Swedish welfare state has also had an impact on the labour market. It has generated 'postindustrial' jobs, matching the performance of the North American economies, while largely avoiding the tendencies to income polarization that have come to characterize the latter (Esping-Andersen 1999). These policies are described in greater detail in the first section.

It would be a mistake, however, to stop here, with the liberal Canadian and social-democratic Swedish models frozen in time and in space. Such models do not dictate history but rather are the products of past struggles, and unfinished ones at that. Thus, the rest of the chapter takes a closer look at the politics that shaped contemporary childcare arrangements in both countries. As we shall see, the establishment of social-democratic style childcare policies in Sweden was not a foregone conclusion in the 1960s, when the dual-earner family became the principal policy object, nor are its core features uncontested. With regard to Canada, there have been moments when it looked as if the liberal mold would be broken in childcare as in health care. In both countries, feminists had an important role to play in the struggle to establish strong public supports for the dual-earner family. In each country, however, the way

they sought to influence policy was affected by their respective national political contexts.

Family Policy in Canada and Sweden: An Overview

Family policies—policies targeted at households with dependent children[3]—have long formed an important component of welfare states. In both Canada and Sweden during the formative years, the male breadwinner family form constituted the underlying assumption of most policies. In both countries, the state stepped in to deal with cases of family failure or when the breadwinner's wage was deemed inadequate to cover his family's basic needs. Since the 1960s, both have moved to accept the dual-earner household as the emergent norm but they have done so in different ways. These differences are largely consistent with patterns established in the earlier period, patterns that reflect the imprint of social-democratic (Sweden) and liberal (Canada) state characteristics.

The Swedish welfare state is usually taken to exemplify the social-democratic model that was constructed in two phases. In the first phase, steps were taken to develop a basic social security system, founded on the principle of universality. Pensions and other basic benefits were thus made available to all citizens. Although at this point the Swedish system still offered only flat rate benefits, these were set at a fairly generous level. Swedish family policy fit the pattern. Thus children's allowances established in 1947 were set at a decent level and made available to all.[4] Nevertheless at this stage, although the Swedish welfare state worked to mitigate the effect of class inequality, it helped to entrench gender inequality and difference.

To be sure, in the 1930s the universe of political discourse had included visions of a gender as well as class equality (Hirdman 1994). And aspects of these visions were translated into policy. Thus, as individual citizens, Swedish women were included in universal social programs like the basic pension. In the 1930s, working mothers won the right to work after marriage and the right to one month's maternity leave with some financial compensation (Hobson 1990). Yet the dominant pattern of policy compromises to emerge from the turmoil of the 1930s focused on the housewife-mother. Universal child allowances, good quality housing (especially for larger families), and various forms of maternity assistance positively supported the modern housewife-mother who was also to heed the advice of experts as she went about her tasks of childrearing and housework. Such active support given the housewife-mother *as caregiver* went beyond the principle of maintenance that is the hallmark of the male breadwinner welfare state (Sainsbury 1994).

Contemporary Swedish family policies conform to the social-democratic pattern, as it came to be construed in the 1960s. The model is still founded on the principle of universality but aims to build a broader basis of support, by speaking to the concerns of middle-, as well as working-class, citizens. High-quality public services and social insurance systems with generous income replacement rates are the means for building such cross-class solidarity. It was also in the 1960s that Swedish family policy came to actively support the dual-earner family in a manner that has done much to mitigate gender inequality in the labour market. This 'gender equality' model of family policy 'supports gender equality at home and in the workplace, with a child centered focus, through lengthy paid parental leave for both parents, income support, flexible work hours, part-time work options, family leave (e.g., "sick child" leave), and child care services' (Stroick and Jenson 1999: 60).

Since the 1960s, the Swedish state has thus accepted the need to provide working mothers with services supportive of economic equality. Notable among these is the publicly financed system of childcare. Between 1960 and 1980, the number of preschool children in publicly

financed daycare rose from 13,000 to 219,000 and by 1993 the number of places had nearly doubled again (LO 1995: 11). In 1988, 73 per cent of Swedish children under six had a place in daycare (Baker 1995: 212). In the first decade there was considerable reliance on municipally supervised family daycare, but now the majority of Swedish children are in municipal daycare centres. In the 1980s, the bourgeois parties began to push for public support for commercial daycare and in the early 1990s, introduced legislation to this effect. The latter was, however, rescinded when the Social Democrats returned to office in 1994. Today a small percentage of Swedish children are in private non-profit (cooperative, church-run, etc.).

Swedish family policy also came to include a generous system of parental leave, until recently, insured at 90 per cent of one's income.[5] Established in 1974, this system was successively expanded so that Swedish parents are now eligible for a full year's leave at the higher (income-related) rate and an additional six months at a flat rate. To be eligible, they need to have worked 240 days before the mother's confinement but if an additional child is born within two years of the previous one, parental leave is compensated at the full (90 per cent) rate. There are also generous provisions for leave (up to sixty days per annum) to care for sick children. Since the late 1970s, Swedish parents can reduce their workday from eight to six hours until the child is in school, with employment security.

Although this system has done much to ease the care burden of dual-earner families, and does so in ways that advance gender equality, it falls short of the mark. Thus mothers are the ones who take the majority of 'parental' leave.[6] Despite data showing a persistent tendency for mothers to take 95 per cent of parental leave, Swedish governments resisted pressure to introduce a 'father quota' until the early 1990s. Moreover the provision allowing the reduction of the normal working day to six hours for parents of young children contributes to the relatively high rate of part-time employment among women. While more than 75 per cent of Swedish mothers are employed, nearly half of them work part-time. Nor has Swedish family policy been immune to the effects of the economic crisis, which hit at the start of the 1990s, pushing unemployment to heights not seen since the 1930s. Neo-liberal ideas have, moreover, gained in strength within Swedish discourse. In response, elements within the Social Democratic Party have moved to embrace some of these ideas. Nevertheless, the social-democratic imprint—and the 'gender equality' model embedded in it—remains clear. It is in marked contrast to family policy in Canada.

Canada fits the 'liberal' pattern, albeit with important social-democratic inflections. In other words, the key reforms of the 1940s and especially of the 1960s embodied the principles of universality and solidarity without thereby eradicating the liberal bias toward means-tested programs targeted at the needy.[7] Moreover, levels of compensation have remained low in comparison with Swedish rates, leaving room for the creation of an American-style private social-security network. Canadian family policy conforms to the liberal pattern perhaps better than many others.

Canada's first universal family policy measure, the Family Allowance which came into effect in 1947, put money in the hands of all mothers but the amount provided has never approached the Swedish level.[8] For the first two postwar decades, the family allowance system moreover constituted the sole element of family policy that was universal in coverage. With the exception of those on social assistance, Canadian policy assumed the norm was an independent wage earner 'whose family situation entered the public purview only at tax time, when the exemption for dependents (non-earning spouses and children) was claimed. . . . Families were left to their own decisions, and their own resources, about who would care for children and whether one or two parents would be employed' (Stroick

and Jenson 1999: 63). Thus, unlike the Swedish system, Canada largely turned a blind eye to those providing care—although the family allowance cheque did go to the main caregiver (usually the housewife-mother), rather than the male breadwinner as it did (and does) in a number of European systems.

In the early 1970s, there were plans to replace the Family Allowance with an income-targeted scheme, but popular pressure was still strong enough to prevent this. In fact, a minority Liberal government, dependent on the support of the social-democratic New Democratic Party (NDP), substantially increased benefits and expanded coverage to include immigrant families with landed status (Baker 1995: 128–9). From 1979, however, the value of the Family Allowance was steadily reduced and in 1992 the Conservative government abolished it entirely in favour of the Canada Child Tax Benefit. The latter targeted middle- and lower-income families, with the amount falling as incomes rose to the point that families with net incomes of over $70,000 received nothing (Baker 1995: 129). The Canada Child Tax Benefit (CCTB) subsequently became part of the National Child Benefit—a federal-provincial program geared to children whose parent(s) are on social assistance or form part of the working poor.[9]

In the 1940s, working mothers were even more grudgingly acknowledged than their housewife-mother sisters were, and then only when they were considered important to the war effort. Thus, through a special wartime Dominion-Provincial cost-sharing arrangement, the federal government covered 50 per cent of the costs of daycare for women working in essential industries. The program, however, ended with the war.[10] The federal government would not become involved in childcare again until the 1960s and then it did so as part of its overhaul of the social-assistance system. From 1966 to 1996, the federal government made funds available to the provinces, on a cost-sharing basis under the

Canada Assistance Plan, to subsidize daycare spaces for those 'in need or in danger of becoming in need'.

In the 1970s, the sections of the act applicable to daycare were amended allowing the provinces to include a wider swathe of income earners and making operating grants available to centres that offered subsidized spaces. Although this did expand the scope somewhat, the program retained its classically liberal features, targeting the needy. Upper- and middle-income families are assumed to be able to look to the market to meet care needs not being met by the family. Some relief—the Child Care Expense Deduction, introduced as part of the 1971 overhaul of the tax system—was, however, made available in the form of tax deductions for receipted expenses up to a specified amount. This, too, is typical of liberal welfare states.

This system left the initiative to the provinces and thus sanctioned a very uneven development of daycare across the country, in coverage as well as form of provision. Today Quebec has the most 'social-democratic' system, with the highest share of publicly run and financed centres and a new commitment to make daycare available to preschool children at $5 a day. Alberta also has one of the higher coverage rates but much of this is provided by commercial operators. For the most part, this system has not been able to provide anything near the coverage of its Swedish counterpart, forcing upper- and middle-income families to look to the informal sector to meet their needs. By the mid-1990s, although 35 per cent of families on social assistance had children in centre-based and regulated care, only 19 per cent of families with mothers employed or studying had places for their children (Stroick and Jenson 1999: 65). In fact, the majority of families are forced to look to care outside of the formal sector entirely. Increasingly, federal and provincial policies positively encourage this.[11] When the CAP was replaced with the Canada Health and Social Transfer in 1996, moreover, not only were funds reduced substantially but any pretense at national standards was abandoned.

Canada's leave policy for parents shows its 'liberal' colours, too. The federal government introduced special regulations for maternity leave in 1941. Such leave was unpaid but, for a while after the war, the federal Unemployment Insurance Commission granted unemployment insurance benefits to pregnant women who applied (Burt 1990: 201). This practice was soon stopped, however, and from 1950 to 1957, married women were ineligible to receive unemployment insurance unless they met special employment criteria (Ursel 1992: 235).

In 1971, amendments to the Unemployment Insurance Act provided maternity leave insurance at the same rate as unemployment insurance. This is also the case in Sweden but there parental leave is covered under its own act—and, of course, the replacement rate (90 per cent, now 80 per cent) is much higher than Canada's has been (65 per cent, now only 55 per cent). Moreover, fathers were only included in the Canadian system in 1990 whereas in Sweden they became eligible in 1974. Funded leave provisions are also shorter in Canada. Until 1990, it was only fifteen weeks. The 1990 reforms added ten weeks and, in the Speech from the Throne, in the fall of 1999, the Canadian government also promised to extend parental leave to one year. While this officially matches the length of time Swedish parents can take leave at the enhanced rate, the Canadian replacement rate is substantially lower. Moreover, with the reforms to the UI system—now (un)'Employment Insurance' (EI)—fewer and fewer women qualify (Porter 1998; CLC 1999).

Thus Swedish and Canadian family policies each bear the characteristics of the wider welfare states in which they are embedded. Sweden stresses the provision of high-quality public services (in this case daycare), a universal child allowance that makes a meaningful contribution to the income of all families with children, and a generous income-replacement scheme for funding parental leave. A 'father month' has recently been introduced into the latter, in order to induce fathers to take some of that leave. Canada's offers an inadequate patchwork of daycare services, in which federal subsidies have only been available for lower-income families, leaving the tax system to mitigate the financial burden of the rest. The tax deduction, moreover, only applies to those with receipted expenses, thus leaving out the majority of parents who have to rely on the informal sector. The one universal program—the family allowance system—never approximated the generosity of Sweden's and has now been abolished, making way for the finely targeted National Child Benefit. Canada does have a parental leave system, with a promised extension that will make it almost as long as the Swedish. Yet the replacement rate is a miserly 55 per cent and the changes to 'employment' insurance mean that many women do not qualify for benefits.

This suggests that the main typology available for comparing welfare states does have insights to offer those interested in assessing these two sets of family policies. Yet it would be a mistake to give what is only a system for classification a life of its own. It is therefore worth taking a closer look at the making of family policy in each country. A comprehensive treatment however is clearly beyond the scope of this chapter. We shall, therefore, focus on two policies—daycare and parental leave.

Sweden: Renovating the People's Home for Wage Earners of Two Genders

As the foregoing brief overview suggests, the roots of Sweden's 'social-democratic' and 'gender equality' family policy can be traced to the 1960s. The Swedish labour movement played an important part in the making of this welfare state but it was Swedish feminists who ensured that a 'gender equality' dimension was added to it.[12] To be sure, those who argued for equality of the sexes were

aided by favourable economic circumstances. The Swedish economy enjoyed boom conditions well into the 1970s, with tight labour markets, and this coincided with the shift from goods to services (a sector which tends to be strongly 'feminized' in most OECD countries). The decision to look to Swedish women, rather than immigrants, to meet labour-market needs certainly made it easier to hear feminist voices that began to argue for gender equality in the 1960s. The concern over falling fertility rates also helps to explain why, rather than turning a blind eye to women's mothering role, the Swedish state sought to meet these demands by developing appropriate childcare arrangements. Yet politics, including feminist politics, were necessary to turn these 'facts' into signs that new arrangements were needed.

Feminist politics in Sweden were, of course, affected by the institutional terrain. Thus feminists organized inside the existing party system, especially within the Social Democratic and Liberal parties. The party system was itself in flux, creating new openings for feminists. The demise of the alliance between the Social Democrats and the Agrarian (now Center) party contributed to a new fluidity in party politics at a time when the SAP (Social Democratic Party), the Liberals and the Center party were discovering the growing strata of white-collar workers. Although the existing party system generally proved capable of absorbing these new social forces, to do so the parties had to open up to new ways of thinking about social relations.

The growing political salience of white-collar workers, along with a simmering revolt by blue-collar workers, in turn sustained the wave of important policy innovations which came to characterize the Swedish model of social democracy—and also left their stamp on the new childcare arrangements. Thus the Rehn-Meidner version of 'Keynes plus' policy was finally implemented and its promise to maintain full employment was extended to women. The government also erected a new tier of social insurance benefits based on the income-replacement principle and made good on its commitment to provide high-quality public services (Martin 1978; Esping-Andersen 1985). With this, the material basis was laid for cross-class 'wage earner' solidarity which stood in marked contrast to the divisive 'public-private' arrangements that came to characterize the liberal American welfare state.

It took feminists, however, to make the point that wage earners now came in two sexes. Ginger elements in the Liberal and the Social Democratic parties articulated a feminist-humanist vision: men and women alike should become fully human by making it possible for women to work and for men to care. The 1961 publication of an important essay by a young Liberal, Eva Moberg, is usually credited with having re-ignited demand for a world in which men and women were simultaneously to play two roles, with the assistance of the (social-democratic) state. Similar ideas were being raised by young Social Democrats in the party journal, *Tiden*.

Although the main proponents of the feminist-humanist vision were divided by party allegiance, an important network of activists cutting across party lines was formed in the mid-1960s. Known as 'group 222', the group included women and men who were influential in the trade unions, party circles, and national media. Their agenda included tax reform, educational and labour market policy reforms, supportive social services including daycare, and a new form of child support that would combine the already generous child allowance with reimbursement for parental homecare during the child's first year. Such reforms only became feasible, however, as the activists engaged in a struggle to win over opponents in both the Social Democratic and Liberal parties. They did so initially by emphasizing women's 'right to choose' between paid work and staying at home.

The notion of 'choice', concretely expressed in the feminist-humanists' proposal to establish a care allowance, held a convenient ambivalence that was conducive to the formation of compromises within parties and in Swedish society as a whole. The care allowance was essentially a child bonus system, to be financed by a payroll tax, that would make it feasible for women/parents to choose to stay at home with young children or to work full-time. The proposal appealed to traditionalists within the Social Democratic and Liberal parties. It also made it easier for the Liberals to work out a common family policy with their new allies in the Center Party where more traditional views prevailed. Ironically, given later developments, in the 1960s only the Conservative party opposed the care allowance.

In the mid-sixties, however, the balance tipped in favour of the working mother. One of the forces helping to shift the balance from 'choice' and the care allowance to working mothers and daycare was LO, the blue-collar trade union central formally associated with the Social Democrats. Since the early 1960s, LO had been concerned about projected labour shortages and had begun to look to married women to meet these. In the early sixties, LO and the employers association, SAF, agreed to abolish separate women's wages and by the mid-sixties LO had become a leading advocate for the expansion of public daycare. LO staffers connected with Groups 222 played an important role in engineering this shift but to do so they had to learn to cast their arguments in ways that fit with the latter's class-centred identity.

The Liberals too moved away from the care allowance to favour public spending on daycare. They differed with the Social Democrats, however, on the relative weight to be accorded family home daycare and municipally run daycare centres. For the former and their Center party allies, family home daycare was not only cheaper; it also preserved parental 'choice' (now between different forms of daycare). Most importantly, it did so in ways that allowed parents to choose the milieu that most closely approximated the home (Kyle 1979: 185). For LO, TCO, and many Social

Democrats, however, public institutions were the best way to provide high-quality childcare to all. Here the pedagogical advantages of public institutions were stressed in a discourse emphasizing equal opportunity between classes as well as between the sexes. Thus like the schools which were then being expanded to provide *all* children with at least secondary education, public daycare could be justified as a way to erase disadvantages arising out of working-class origins. In fact, both forms of daycare rapidly expanded. Between 1965 and 1980, the number of spaces in municipal daycare centres leapt from 11,900 to 136,400 while the number of places in family care grew from 6,000 to 88,500 (Hinnfors 1995, Table 11: 50).

The decision to fund the rapid expansion of daycare had not banished the notion of a care allowance. The Center party continued to seek a 'care wage' to be paid to those who chose to stay at home and look after their young children. Despite their growing ambivalence toward this notion, the Liberals continued to support the idea of an allowance that could be used to pay for daycare or to defray the costs of raising children at home. A third option—parental leave—which clearly favoured a two-earner family norm, began to take shape as the decade came to a close. This idea first appeared in LO's 1969 family policy document and the report of the joint LO-SAP Equality Commission. The TCO too embraced the notion of *parental* leave in its 1971 family policy document, giving the Social Democrats the support they needed.

In 1974, the new parental leave insurance scheme, which originally offered six months of leave to either parent, became law. Like the other pieces of the 'wage earner' model, the new scheme was based on the income-replacement principle. It thus not only appealed to both white- and blue-collar women workers but also provided an inducement for the often higher-paid fathers to take their share of the leave. In this respect, it marked an important symbolic victory for feminist humanists. Subsequent extensions of

the leave period (currently, twelve months with the more generous income replacement) have made it easier for fathers to take their share. That it is still women who take the majority of 'parental' leave (over 90 per cent), however, suggests that more was needed. Swedish feminists recognized this but they did not succeed in their efforts to provide the institutional supports for full gender equality.

Feminist-Humanist Reform Stalled; Choice, with a Neo-Liberal Inflection

The feminist-humanist vision articulated in the sixties was flawed to the extent that it ignored the power relations that sustained gender inequality. This is less true of the 1970s when feminists within the Social Democratic Party adopted a more radical discourse. The radicalism fit the times as the unions and the SAP responded to workplace unrest by raising the banner of industrial and economic democracy. The notion of 'women's oppression' did not seem out of place when 'class oppression' was again openly debated. Recognition of women's oppression, in turn, made clear that it was not enough to enable fathers to choose to participate in childcare. Steps would have to be taken to force them to do so. Among the means for doing that were the introduction of quotas to ensure that leave was shared by both parents and the adoption of the six-hour day as a new norm which would give men and women alike the 'time to be human'.

Both proposals were placed on the agenda by a radicalized Social Democratic Women's League (SSKF). The demand for a six-hour day was advanced in the document produced by six young Social Democratic women, *The Family in the Future: A Socialist Family Policy* (1972). The SSKF supported this vision and worked to put the work time issue on the political agenda by publishing a report on the question. The six-hour day was included in the proposals for the SAP's new party program but at SSKF's 1974 conference, the unions' ambivalence became apparent. For LO, there were more important demands, like a fifth week of vacation, reduced hours for shift workers, or securing the inclusion of part-time workers in collective agreements (Karlsson 1990: 161–3).

A possible compromise between the SSKF and the unions was floated in the 1975 report of the Commission on Family Support: parental leave could be modified to allow parents of very young children to reduce their work time for up to twenty months while receiving partial compensation for wages foregone. Although this represented a step back from the idea of a six-hour day for all, the suggestion that a father's quota be simultaneously introduced sought to assuage SSKF (Baude 1979). The government's proposed reforms to the leave legislation failed to mention the father month (Bergvist et al. 1999). It took bold action by a small group of social-democratic women MPs to make the proposed father month part of the SAP's 1976 election platform.

By this time, however, the radical wave had crested and the economic crisis, which earlier had hit many other OECD economies, had reached Sweden. The Social Democrats lost the 1976 election and would not return to office until 1982. The coalition governments that were in office from 1976 to 1982 brought together the Liberal Party, whose conception of the modern family was not far from that of the Social Democrats, and the Center and Conservative parties, who clung to the old idea of a 'care wage'. The compromises they arrived at served to institutionalize a 'one and three quarters' solution rather than the fully egalitarian vision which inspired the feminist-humanists.

Thus in 1978 parental leave was extended to nine months, with the last three at a flat rate that was unlikely to be attractive to the usually higher paid fathers. The additional three months could be used to reduce the working day for one of the parents, but with no requirement that both parents utilize this option, it has primarily been exercised by mothers. That same year, legislation was introduced which made it illegal to deny parental leave while the child was under eighteen months or to refuse a parent's request for a six-hour day until the child started school. The language remained the gender neutral language which the feminist-humanists had introduced into Swedish political discourse but the institutional supports for turning that into full equality were not forthcoming. In 1982 the Social Democrats returned to office committed to restoring full employment while simultaneously eliminating the deficit. While the SAP maintained its commitment to daycare, the father month and the six-hour day were brushed aside. No further steps toward improving the model were to be taken in that decade.

Thus, instead of the egalitarian family with two earners (and two active parents), the one and three-quarters wage-earner family has become the norm, leaving many women economically dependent on their men and on the state. To be sure, public funds continued to be channelled into the expansion of the daycare system throughout the 1980s and parental leave was (temporarily)[13] extended. Yet, in the absence of a quota, parental leave remained to a large extent maternity leave. The legislation of a right for 'parents' to reduce their work time to three-quarters until the youngest child reached school age similarly helped to institutionalize the one and three-quarters solution. Moreover, the argument for 'choice' and the related care allowance were returning to the political agenda, this time with a marked neo-liberal inflection. Thus not only had the reforms stopped short of realizing the dream: the very achievements were clearly not invulnerable.

The reinsertion of choice can be traced to the actions of a newly politicized employers' association (SAF) dedicated to dismantling social-democratic Sweden. An important part of SAF's campaign was a propaganda drive celebrating individualism and the associated demand for variety, as the harbinger of a new societal model. The latter rejects the belief, held by the Liberals, feminist-humanists, and Social Democrats alike, that a strong public sector constitutes a vital support for individual development. Rather, markets were presented as the best way to meet the multiplicity of needs and interests found in civil society. SAF was also prepared to challenge the social-democratic welfare state more concretely, by funding private alternatives. Thus along with private health clinics and private health insurance, SAF and the Swedish Federation of Industry financed the establishment of a private, for-profit daycare company, Pysslingen, named after a character in a popular Swedish children's story.

The Social Democrats answered the challenge by introducing legislation banning private for-profit daycare and regulating the growth of other non-public forms (Olsson 1990: ch. 5). In the parliamentary debate that ensued, choice was defended by all three bourgeois parties (and, *sotto voce*, elements within the SAP itself), in the name of respect for 'difference'. And the Social Democrats did gradually increase the range of options in the system by making subsidies available to parental cooperatives and daycare centres run by voluntary associations, including churches, while holding fast against the principle of for-profit daycare.[14]

The bourgeois parties' celebration of choice also embraced the old proposal for a care allowance and, with it, the opportunity for a 'parent' to choose to stay at home with young children beyond the time allotted under the parental leave legislation. Ironically, the threatened reappearance of the housewife-mother occurred just when the Swedish women's movement was preparing a new push for equality in Swedish society, focused on parity representation in public life and pay equity in the labour market. The 1991 election is important in this respect, for it brought a coalition of bourgeois parties to office and thus made it possible for the latter to legislate choice. At the same time, the *drop* in women's representation in parliament led not only to talk of the formation of a new women's party but also

to the establishment of an autonomous women's network, the 'support stockings'.

The recharged feminist movement was, however, able to utilize existing tensions between the Liberals, who continued to defend their version of the feminist-humanist ideal, and the Center and Christian Democratic parties, who championed the housewife-mother. Thus, when national subsidies for daycare were rolled into a new system of block-funding to municipalities in 1992—a move which could have made it easier for the latter to renege on their commitments to provide daycare—the egalitarian line was strong enough to insist on putting into legislation a national commitment to provide daycare spaces for all children who wanted or needed them. In addition, the Liberals also managed to introduce the first quota into the parental leave system—a father month which could not be traded to the mother. They were, however, unable to resist the introduction of a care allowance.

Both the care allowance and the law rendering commercial daycare centres eligible for public subsidies were rescinded by the Social Democrats when they returned to office in 1994, while the father month was left intact. Yet this did not mean that the Swedish childcare system was again secure. Having accepted financial deregulation in the 1980s, and later, joined the European Union, the Swedish Social Democrats felt constrained to work within the circumscribed space permitted by international financial markets and EU convergence requirements. In response to a run against the Swedish currency, the Social Democrats cut the compensation rate for parental leave (and other social insurance programs) to 75 per cent. They also imposed stringent fiscal requirements on the municipalities, making it more difficult for the latter to meet their obligations to expand (let alone to maintain) a quality daycare system. Although once the deficit was under control, the Persson government raised transfers to municipalities and counties explicitly to improve the quality of education, health, and childcare, layoffs continued. In childcare, the child:adult employee ratio went up from 4.7 in 1991 to 6.7 in 1996 (*Dagens Nyheter*, 30 April 1998). In the spring of 1999, urban centres like Stockholm witnessed demonstrations by parents and staff against the fall in daycare standards.

The picture may not be all that bleak, however, and here again feminist activists have played an important part. The latter were given an opportunity to influence the development of government policy in all areas after the 1994 election. Their efforts bore limited fruit in the mid-1990s. Yet as the state's financial position improved—and when the trade unions had shown the government the strength of their opposition to its labour market policy reforms—a feminist impact became visible in two key initiatives. First, special increments on top of block fund transfers to the counties and municipalities were made available with the express purpose of restoring social services.[15] The commitment involves more than a matter of money as the government's appointment of a Care Commission indicates. It is also intended to improve both the quality of service and the quality of jobs (including pay structures) in this largely female-dominated sector of the labour market (Mahon 1999).

The Persson money is not enough to guarantee the desired result. While not a federal system, the Swedish state system allows the municipalities considerable scope in determining the rules governing service delivery. This poses a real problem at a time when neo-liberal coalitions committed to privatization and contracting out govern the three main urban centres. Even social-democratic municipalities have raised daycare fees and introduced other restrictions in order to meet the requirement of balanced budgets. Nevertheless the SAP is committed to a maximum daycare fee and the 1999 budget statement set aside the funds necessary to make this a reality by 2003. Finally, while this SAP government is no more eager to reduce the normal working day, the SSKF has found an important new ally within the

movement in the Metal Workers Union. Moreover, the minority SAP government is reliant on the feminist Left Party and a Green party also keen on work time reductions. There is a real chance that this government may take an important step toward providing the institutional conditions for gender equality.

Canada: Social Liberalism's Patchwork of Childcare Arrangements[16]

The beginning of the break with the male breadwinner model in Canada—the first federal peacetime subsidies for childcare (included in the Canada Assistance Plan of 1966)—cannot be attributed to the feminist mobilization, but is rather the result of inter-governmental bargaining.[17] Women were more active in the second phase when the politics of 'equitable access' added an important layer of popular participation to the policy process. This time the women's movement formed part of the struggle to establish a set of childcare arrangements very similar to those already in place in Sweden. Women did not fight alone, however. The struggle for the social-democratic-feminist alternative was waged by the women's movement in alliance with the unions. This struggle formed part of a broader move to 'coalition politics'.[18]

As in Sweden, the move away from the breadwinner model began when labour markets were tight, job growth was increasingly concentrated in the service sector, and women's labour force participation was on the rise. And, in Canada as in Sweden this was also a time when new political openings appeared. With the merger of the Trades and Labour Congress and the Canadian Congress of Labour to form the CLC, and the newly formed alliance of the latter with the NDP (formed in 1961), the labour movement seemed poised to challenge the old line parties. The wave of wildcat strikes in the mid-1960s and the struggle of the public sector workers for collective bargaining rights gave class-based issues a new salience. The New Left in anglophone Canada helped to spawn a movement for an independent, socialist Canada (the Waffle) and, in Quebec, the unions and the women's movement helped to shape the new nationalist visions that blossomed during the Quiet Revolution. Aboriginal groups began to mobilize against the government's attempts to redefine Indian status and to forge their claims as Canada's First Nations.

The federal Liberal government's first response was a spate of new social policy legislation. From the mid-1960s on, however, the social policy reforms took place in the shadow cast by the rediscovery of poverty, which helped to derail the drive for universality. This put its stamp on childcare policy: federal support for daycare came as part of the first shot in Canada's war on poverty. Thus federal support for daycare formed part of the larger package of social assistance reforms, bundled together in the Canada Assistance Plan (CAP) of 1966. Through CAP, the federal government agreed to share daycare costs with the provinces on a fifty-fifty basis. The inclusion of the program in CAP did not mean that the federal government was prepared to play the kind of leadership role that the Swedish government was preparing to take on at that time. Rather, CAP provided assistance for those 'in need, or likely to become in need'. It thus established a pattern that has prevailed until CAP was abolished in 1996— means-tested daycare subsidies for low-income parents who meet locally established criteria.

The CAP initiative, moreover, was less the result of partisan debate than discussions within the bureaucracy, though here consultation and negotiations involving federal and provincial officials had a critical part to play (Haddow 1993: chs 2 and 3). Haddow documents the labour movement's relative invisibility in the debates surrounding the formation of CAP but his account implicitly provides evidence of the even more glaring absence of women's organizations. Rather, daycare seems to have been included under CAP as a by-product of intergovernmental negotiations over other matters. What appears to have happened is this. The decision to include provincial mothers' allowance programs in the new cost-sharing arrangements brought poor mothers into the system of shared federal-provincial concern. Daycare, in turn, seems to have been added as a result of federal concerns to thwart the inclusion of provincial workfare schemes by adding a 'rehabilitative service' element—training, vocational counselling, job placement, and the like—to existing cost-shared social assistance programs. In this sense, Canada seems to have been following the pattern then being established in the United States where the war on poverty included an attempt to get single mothers off social assistance and into the labour force (Michel 1999). Yet there was a 'made in Canada' side to this too in that there was growing pressure for daycare, articulated primarily by social workers concerned about the lack of support for the growing numbers of mothers. Within the federal bureaucracy, the latter were supported by the lone representative of official feminism at the time, the chief of the Women's Bureau (Finkel 1995; Mahon 1998).

In contrast to daycare, the move to publicly financed maternity leave focused on the right of all women as workers and mothers. In 1971, amendments to the Canada Labour Code granted women the right to seventeen weeks of maternity leave while modifications to the federal Unemployment Insurance Act provided income replacement for fifteen weeks for those who had worked twenty weeks over the last year.[19] Like the Swedish legislation, these reforms were based on the income-replacement principle, but they offered a much lower rate. As the Cook Task Force (Task Force on Child Care 1986: 28) was later to note, 'the actual replacement income of all maternity leave claimants is . . . below 60 per cent when averaged over the entire leave period. Each claimant must first survive a two-week period without benefits.' Given the relatively low level at which the maximum insurable earning level is set, many middle-income women got less than 50 per cent. The low replacement rate is typical of Canada's social-liberal welfare state and reflects the relative weakness of the Canadian Left but the failure to consider including fathers reflects the still limited influence of second-wave feminism on public policy.

Toward the end of the 1960s, a feminist-humanist discourse similar to, but more modest than, its Swedish counterpart, began to enter the universe of political discourse. The report of the Royal Commission on the Status of Women (1971) constituted the first attempt to codify this new understanding of gender relations. In it, as Burt (1986: 117) notes, glimmered a vision of a future in which men and women would be able equally to participate in the worlds of paid work and parenting. Yet the Royal Commission was still rather hesitant to advocate policies designed to produce this new world. Nonetheless, it argued the need to 'lift daycare out of the context of poverty' and replace it with a universal system designed to appeal to 'all families who need and wish to use it' (1971: 268 and 270). As an alternative means for subsidizing daycare, the Commission suggested not only capital grants to be made available under the National Housing Act but also a care allowance rather similar to that proposed earlier in Sweden.[20] Thus in the section on taxation, the Commission argued for a child-care allowance to 'be paid to all mothers whether the parents themselves care for the children or pay for the substitute' (1971: 304).

The role envisaged for the state was informed by the principles of social liberalism and a humanist feminism that had much in common with Swedish feminism of the early 1960s. Unlike its Swedish counterpart, however, it could not benefit from connections with a labour movement strong enough to secure a social-democratic welfare state. Although the Canadian labour movement formed part of the ferment attending the 1960s wave of reforms, it was not in a position to shape these developments. Rather it was

the governing Liberal party that established the Royal Commission and it was to a Liberal government that the latter would report.

The Commission's report did help to bring about the 1971 introduction of an income-tax deduction for childcare. More importantly, the terms of CAP, applicable to daycare, were changed to allow subsidies for centers and for a broader income group. Here the Interdepartmental Committee on the Status of Women, set up to advise the government on how to implement the report's recommendations, played an important role (Mahon, 1997). In the 1970s, too, several federal programs—notably the short-lived Local Initiatives Program (LIP) and DREE grants, the main instrument of federal regional policy, added modest improvements to Canada's daycare infrastructure (Friendly 1994). Yet the femocrats and their supporters in the daycare advocacy community did not feel they were strong enough to put daycare out of CAP and make it a universal policy.

Thus neither the Royal Commission nor the femocrats who sought to realize its agenda were able to mount an effective challenge to the basic liberal parameters of the established model. Canadian daycare policy retained its liberal, class-divided character: income-tested subsidies for the needy and tax deductions for the better paid. It was only in the 1980s that an opportunity appeared to remodel this liberal edifice according to a social-democratic-feminist blueprint. Unfortunately, these plans came forward just as the state was abandoning 'social' for 'neo' liberalism. In the 1980s, the emergent 'popular sector' would mount a challenge to this 'corporate agenda' strong enough to block the Tory alternative, but not strong enough to advance its own.

A Social-Democratic-Feminist Model of Childcare for Canada?

From the 1970s through to the early 1980s, the federal government was guided by a philosophy of 'social liberalism plus' and this gave activists a sense that more was possible. Thus in economic policy, the Trudeau Liberals experimented with 'Keynes plus' measures, including tripartism, whereby the unions were offered a chance to participate in the formation of economic policy in exchange for accepting wage controls.[21] In Canada, moreover, such measures came wrapped in the language of a (liberal) nationalism directed at American control of the economy.[22] Although a liberal emphasis on poverty continued to mark Canadian social policy, the emphasis shifted to less intrusive forms of needs-testing and to rehabilitative services like training and counselling. In the area of labour market policy, too, the state began to recognize that women formed an important part of the labour force but that they, like other 'equity' groups, needed pay and employment equity measures to achieve equality (Cameron 1996). The government's embrace of 'social liberalism plus' thus created an environment in which it was possible to imagine social-democratic-feminist alternatives.

Second, feminists chose to organize for new childcare arrangements through 'coalition politics', forged in the trenches of civil society rather than the stale corridors of party politics. This choice has to be seen in relation to the failure of Canada's conventional parties, schooled in the principles of brokerage politics, to respond adequately to the challenges posed by social movements in the 1970s (Brodie and Jenson 1988). Thus modern Quebec nationalism quickly escaped Lesage's Liberal Party, finding new, more radical homes in the trade unions, in artist and community groups—all of whom constitute the popular base of the then-new (and social-democratic) Parti Québécois. Left nationalism in anglophone Canada initially found a home in the New Democratic Party, but the Waffle was soon ousted. This widened the gap between the NDP and a whole generation of left intellectuals and activists (Bradford and Jenson 1992). The CLC-affiliated unions continued officially to support the NDP but the unions, too, increasingly turned to mobiliza-

tion in civil society to advance their aims. Although feminists were certainly sought to influence the mainstream parties, the latter were not as ready as their Swedish counterparts to welcome these new forces (Vickers, Rankin, and Appelle 1993: 55).

The new social movements were not, however 'at a distance' from the state itself, in the sense that many came to rely on state financial support. Under the banner of Trudeau's 'just society', the Liberal government adopted the principle of equitable access and established a variety of programs designed to mitigate the 'political poverty' of social assistance recipients, aboriginal peoples, environmentalists, and others. As a result,

> By the mid-1970s Canada's postwar citizenship regime had evolved to include *both* countrywide institutions which addressed citizens as individuals *and* programmatic acknowledgment of intermediate groups which recognized and represented particular *categories* of citizenship. This regime recognized both individual and collective rights of citizenship. It accepted the legitimacy of the intermediary associations of civil society in the representation of interests (Jenson and Phillips 1996: 112).

The state's recognition of the right to equitable access may, nonetheless, have been guided by a liberal-pluralist conception of policy making. According to the latter, each group should become involved in its appropriate policy network and leave the 'interest aggregation' function to parties (and to the bureaucracy). Yet in Canada, the groups began to develop mechanisms of cooperation, giving birth to the pattern of coalition politics that, in the 1980s, would pose a challenge to traditional structures of representation.

Through the National Action Committee on the Status of Women (NAC), the Canadian women's movement has developed an institutionalized forum for a wide range of women's groups which facilitates coordination and mutual support across policy areas. Formed in 1972 out of 31 member groups, a decade later NAC could boast over 200 member groups. NAC also became involved in alliances with other groups, including unions. NAC's picket-line support for some of the key struggles of union women in the late 1970s and early 1980s helped to give birth to a 'working-class feminism', which complemented the stance of the more theoretically inclined socialist feminists who were coming to form an important element within NAC.[23] On the union side, feminists organizing within unions in turn helped to open the latter up to alliances with the women's movement. These experiences laid the foundation for the coalitions that, *inter alia*, would lead the struggle for social-democratic-feminist childcare in the 1980s.

The pattern was already visible in the struggle for maternity/parental leave. In 1979, the common front forged by public-sector unions in Quebec took up the issue and secured twenty weeks of maternity leave at full pay. Given the concentration of women in the social/public service sector, the agreement affected nearly one-quarter of the female workforce in Quebec (Task Force on Child Care 1986: 31). The Canadian Union of Postal Workers (CUPW) made maternity leave the central issue in its 1981 strike, a strategy deliberately designed to build alliances. Other unions have followed suit so that by 1992 'paid maternity leave had become relatively common, negotiated for almost one-half of the workers covered by major contracts' (White 1993: 90). The struggle was not confined to the collective bargaining front, however; the women's movement and the unions also supported the demand to extend the right to parental leave to all wage earner citizens and they made some important inroads. Thus the 1985 revisions to the Canada Labour Code added the right to an additional twenty-four weeks leave to 'any employee who has the care or custody of a newborn child' (Task Force on Child Care 1986: 22). This was the first

federal move to recognize the rights and responsibilities of both parents to combine paid work and parental care.[24] In 1990, changes to the Unemployment Insurance Act offered *parents* an additional ten weeks of benefit on top of the original fifteen. Maternity and parental leave provisions in Canada, of course, remain less generous than the Swedish system, even after the latter has been reduced by deficit-reduction initiatives. Nevertheless, the alliance of women's groups and unions did manage to establish a beachhead in the longer struggle for a social-democratic-feminist alternative. They have thusfar been less successful on the daycare front.

Despite the inclusion of daycare in the Royal Commission's report, it was not until the 1980s that daycare became a priority issue and NAC began to work with the labour movement and early childcare advocacy groups toward this end. The first step in forging such an alliance was taken by the Ontario Coalition for Better Day Care, a coalition of groups organized under the aegis of the Ontario Federation of Labour. Throughout the 1980s, the Coalition remained an important force for universal, public daycare, at both the provincial and federal levels (Friendly 1994: 146). An equally important role would be played by a group—the Canadian Day Care Advocacy Association—formed out of the second Canadian conference on daycare. The conference endorsed the demand for universally accessible, comprehensive, high quality daycare, to be provided under the auspices of public or non-profit organizations.[25] It also called for the establishment of a federal committee to look into childcare policy (Friendly 1994: 151).

In the dying days of social liberalism, the advocates of a new daycare system seemed to have had an impact. The Abella Commission on Equality in Employment was clear that public commitment to women's equality meant state support for a universal daycare system of high quality. On the eve of the 1984 election, the Minister Responsible for the Status of Women established the Cook Task Force to develop proposals for a comprehensive system of childcare and parental leave. During the 1984 election, daycare was highlighted in the televised leaders' debate organized by the women's movement.

The Cook Task Force delivered what the majority of groups had called for. In addition to recommending parental leave, the Task Force recommended the establishment of a high quality, universally accessible daycare system, to be funded by a new inter-governmental cost-sharing arrangement. Unfortunately, its advice would be received by a government determined to complete the break with social liberalism begun in the last years of the Liberal government, and to establish a neo-liberal agenda. Moreover, while there were feminists within the Tory party, the New Right was also well represented as was evident in the support for REAL women in the Tory caucus.

Like the Swedish conservative parties, the Tory's response included a return to the softer 'choice' option. It thus gave several billion dollars in the form of 'tax assistance to families *with the express intent of permitting them to chose among different child care options, including the choice of one parent remaining at home*' (Phillips 1989: 166, emphasis added). To be sure, the Tory strategy also proposed a Canada Child Care Act to replace CAP as a source of federal funding for daycare, with $4 billion to be allocated to this over the next seven years.[26] Although the proposed Child Care Act hinted at a break with CAP's welfare bias, in practice it would have allowed the federal government to put a ceiling on expenditures—something it could not then do under CAP. And, like their Swedish counterparts, the Tories wanted to make for-profit daycare centres eligible for government subsidies.

Although the government was able to pass the Canadian version of the care allowance, the women's movement, acting in concert with other members of the emergent popular sector, mobilized effective opposition to the Tory childcare act

which died on the government's order paper when the 1988 election was called. Here NAC worked in close concert with daycare advocates, unions, and other popular groups (Friendly 1994). During the 1988 election, in which the Pro-Canada Network played an important role in Free Trade Agreement (FTA) a key issue, an alternative vision of childcare was part of the popular sector's agenda. With opponents of the FTA split between the NDP and Liberal parties, the Tories were able to form the next government with less than a majority. The childcare act was not, however, revived.

During the lead-up to the 1993 election, the CDCAA and its allies mobilised to put the social-democratic-feminist alternative back on the agenda. The Liberal victory seemed to offer a chance to make real gains. Thus the Liberals' 'Red Book' promised to promote the expansion of daycare through the establishment of a new cost-sharing arrangement with the provinces[27] and offered to devote $720 million to this end over the next three years. There were, however, two provisos: an annual growth rate of 3 per cent had to be achieved and a sufficient number of provinces had to agree to participate.

The Liberals won that election and Minister Axworthy's 1994 social security review declared that childcare was central to 'work, learning and security'. The follow-up document on 'Child Care and Development' provided more detail on the Liberals' plans to establish 'a national framework of principles to guide and consolidate investment in childcare and development' (Friendly 1994: 2). Concerns about the government's fiscal situation—and the impending referendum on sovereignty in Quebec—helped to derail this initiative, however. The 1995 federal budget certainly dashed any hopes that a breakthrough was imminent. Instead, CAP and the Established Programs Financing Act were replaced by the Canada Health and Social Transfer (CHST), a block-funding arrangement that placed no obligation on the provinces to allocate funds to daycare. The CHST also meant a significant reduction in transfers to the provinces—a drop of

33 per cent between 1995–6 and 1997–8 (Bach and Phillips 1997: 241).

The issue was kept alive, however, and in December, the federal government announced that it was prepared to offer the provinces $630 million over five years to expand and improve daycare provision—as long as a sufficient number of provinces agreed to participate. While a number of provinces did express interest, the federal government unilaterally withdrew its offer in February 1996. At the same time, the speech from the Throne announced that the federal government would no longer utilize its spending power to launch new social-policy initiatives without the agreement of the majority of provinces. The subsequent intergovernmental agreement on the National Child Benefit seemed to confirm that social services, such as daycare, were the exclusive jurisdiction of the provinces.[28] Like the CHST, the agreement does not include any measures that enable the federal government to ensure that the provinces spend the money on daycare: the agreement leaves it to the provinces to choose how to reinvest the funds saved.

The failure of the Liberals to act on their Red Book promises has to be seen in its economic and political context. For most of the 1990s Canada has struggled with slow growth, high unemployment, and a substantial deficit-debt. In this respect, its situation has not been unlike Sweden's—though both countries are now projecting substantial surpluses. In addition, the crisis of Canadian federalism, especially the inability to find an acceptable solution to Quebec's status, has enhanced the trend to decentralization—while cutting intergovernmental transfers—found in many OECD countries, including Sweden. In the 1980s the turn to neo-liberalism had been countered, with some success, by a coalition of popular forces that included the daycare groups. Yet the latter's very success was increasingly met by efforts to undermine them. As Jenson and Phillips (1996) argue, Tory and Liberal governments have worked to dismantle their means of advocacy within the bureaucracy and to diminish their credibility in civil society.

If the story were to end here, the conclusion would have to be that Canada's childcare arrangements have stayed within their liberal mold, despite decades of struggles for change. Worse still, the form of liberalism has changed, going from the more encompassing 'social liberalism' of the 1960s and 1970s, to the neo-liberalism of the dying decades of this century. Thus while CAP-subsidised daycare places targeted the 'needy', revisions to the Act in the 1970s opened the way for provincial/municipal decisions to include middle-income groups. Moreover, CAP funds could only be used to provide daycare in non-profit auspices. Although this system never came near to providing an adequate number of places, the replacement of CAP by the CHST removed any pressure on the provinces to spend on daycare. The Liberals' decision *not* to live up to the promises made in 1993 has to be seen in relation to the National Child Benefit System, which focuses on the children of the working poor as well as those on social assistance. This supports the growing polarization on the labour market, in effect subsidizing low wage jobs (Myles 1988). As both federal and provincial governments show an increasing willingness to provide subsidies for informal care, the daycare branch of the labour market becomes even more of a low-pay female ghetto. This is in marked contrast to the Swedish government's commitment to renewing the public sector in a manner that recognizes the value of care work. It also goes against the arguments of the childcare community in Canada.[29]

This is not, however, the end of the story. The struggle for an adequate childcare policy continues. In February 2000, the federal and provincial governments[30] concluded a new 'Social Union Framework Agreement' (SUFA), which seemed to provide the childcare advocacy community a new opening. Among other things, the agreement committed the parties to ensuring access 'for all Canadians, wherever they live or move in

Canada, to essential programs and services of reasonably comparable quality' (Phillips 1999). The campaign is supported by experts in early childcare, the broader policy community, and the coalition that has focused public attention on child poverty (CLC 2000). The trade unions have taken an active part,[31] just as they earlier did for maternity/parental leave. There are also influential supporters within the Liberal caucus like Toronto MP John Godfrey.

Thusfar, the main result has been the promised extension of parental leave to one year, promised in the fall 1999 Speech from the Throne. If it is left at that, the campaign will have failed. As we noted above, changes to the (Un)Employment Insurance program, through which parental leave is funded, have cut the replacement rate (to 55 per cent). More importantly, as the CLC has shown, the new eligibility requirements mean that the number of women EI claimants has dropped 26 per cent over two years (vs. 18 per cent for men).[32] The government's own advisors, however, concur with the CLC that the EI rules have made it harder for women to qualify for unemployment insurance *or* for parental leave. More broadly, *if* the balance within the federal cabinet remains in favour of using half the expected surplus to finance new expenditures rather than cutting taxes and *if* enough of the provinces can be brought on board, then perhaps steps will be taken to ensure that all Canadian families have 'access to (childcare) services of reasonably comparable quality.' These are, of course, rather large 'ifs'.

Conclusions

The textbook picture of the 'social-democratic' Swedish welfare state and its 'liberal' Canadian counterpart has been confirmed by this study of the two countries' childcare arrangements, but only in part. Thus, it is true that Swedish childcare arrangements conform to the model of the high quality, universal welfare state designed to strengthen wage-earner solidarity, but our story has also shown that the model was not built overnight. There was little room for the working mother in the original design and there is no reason to expect that the renovations of the 1960s would have recognized that wage earners come in two sexes had Swedish feminists not organized to press their claims. In addition, the construction came to a halt before all the features (i.e. the introduction of quotas to the parental leave system; the six-hour day for all) could be added. Childcare arrangements in Canada, also established in the 1960s, conformed to the (social) liberal pattern but there have been serious campaigns to remodel these according to a social-democratic-feminist design. Feminist action has been important to both stories but feminists have had to work with other forces to achieve their ends.

Both countries have felt the turn to neo-liberalism and, in both, neo-liberalism has brought the policy associated with the earlier 'choice' option—some form of a care allowance—back onto the policy agenda. New Right rhetoric aside, however, the reappearance of the care allowance is not really about increasing 'parents' ability to choose between paid work and the care of young children. In both countries, families have become increasingly dependent on the paid work of both parents and neither the Swedish care allowance nor the Canadian child tax credit were set at levels sufficient to compensate for the lost income. The introduction of care allowances thus does not aim to return mothers to kitchen and child. If such measures win the day, they will simply support existing trends to labour-market polarization. Under these conditions, cross-class and cross-gender 'wage earner' solidarity could become historical artefacts as men and women with 'good' jobs pay other women to look after their children—often for longer hours—while many women (and an increasing number of men) join the new industrial reserve army.

The forces of neo-liberal 'globalization' lend support to these tendencies in both countries.

Yet, as we have seen, there are important capacities for resistance. In Sweden, the women's movement and the unions appear to have helped to tip the balance in favour of the renewal of the social-democratic welfare state, and there is even the promise of new steps toward full gender equality. In Canada, childcare advocates and their allies have shown a remarkable tenacity. At present, Canada's family policy clearly retains a strong liberal stamp, but neo-liberalism is but one element in the universe of political discourse, albeit one strongly backed by big business and its campaign for tax cuts. The 'social' liberalism that helped legitimate such 'social-democratic' reforms as medicare remains alive in civil society, as numerous polls over the last decade have shown. Its persistence both reflects the effects of past struggles and constitutes one of the strengths on which advocates of a social democratic/gender equity family policy for Canada can draw today.

Notes

Earlier versions of this chapter appeared in *Social Politics* 4 (3) (1997) under the title 'Child Care in Canada and Sweden: Policy and Politics' and in *Women's Organizing and Public Policy in Canada and Sweden*, eds L. Briskin and M. Eliasson (Montreal: McGill-Queens 1999). I would like to acknowledge financial support provided by the Social Science and Humanities Research Council of Canada, to thank Ann Britt Hellmark for her help in collecting information on Sweden and various Canadian colleagues, especially Susan Phillips, Jane Jenson, Penni Richmond, and Martha Friendly, for their insights.

1. In North America, the term *welfare* is often reduced to social assistance—government transfers to members of society who are unable to work due to age, illness, disability, or other responsibilities. In this paper the term has a broader referent, in that it includes all social policies. The latter can come in the form of public provision or financing of social services like education and health; income transfers (in the form of social assistance, social insurance or basic grants to citizens such as family allowances); and regulations.

2. This classification scheme is based on the work of Esping-Andersen, the mainstream theorist whose work has attracted the friendly but critical attention of many feminists. See Esping-Andersen (1985, 1990, 1999).

3. I take this definition from O'Hara (1998: 2). O'Hara suggests that such policies can include (1) direct and indirect cash transfers; (2) services for families like childcare, home visiting, family centres; (3) labour market legislation targeted at workers with families such as maternity benefits and parental leave; (4) legislation (marriage and divorce laws); and (5) public services like health care, education, and housing. The overview provided in this section focuses primarily on the first three.

4. In the 1960s, special increments were made available to families with more than two children. The allowance applies until the child reaches the age of twenty if he or she is still studying and twenty-three if disabled.

5. This figure has changed several times in the 1990s as both bourgeois and social-democratic governments cut benefits and services to deal with rising deficits. The unions and the Social Democratic Women's League, however, put pressure on the party to restore the replacement rate first to 80 per cent (it had fallen to 75) and, as soon as possible, to 90 per cent. Both understand that this is crucial for maintaining broad support for the public system.

6. In 1987, although 25 per cent of fathers took some leave, the average length was only 47 days versus 265 for mothers (Baker 1995: 176). While leave for care of sick children had come to be more evenly shared between the parents, since Sweden's unemployment rate rose to join that of the majority of OECD countries in the 1990s, fathers have been less inclined to take such leave. Their use of sick leave for childcare fell by one-third between 1987 and 1997 (O'Hara 1998: 17).

7. Family Allowances and the Old Age Security reforms of the immediate postwar years were universal programs based on a flat rate payment. Some of the main reforms of the 1960s and 1970s moved in the direction of universality and solidarity—the expansion of public education including the postsecondary level; Medicare, the Canada and Quebec Pension Plans; and reforms to Unemployment Insurance. On Canada's welfare state from a comparative perspective, see Myles (1988, 1995), O'Connor (1989), and Haddow (1993).

8. Baker notes that in 1975, Sweden's child allowance was equivalent to 146 per cent of Canada's. By 1991 that had risen to 465 per cent. (Baker 1995: 127, Table 4.2). For a critical feminist analysis of the decision to adopt a universal family policy, see Ursel (1992).

9. When families are eligible for the full amount (incomes of $25,921 or less), the CCTB only provides $1,020 annually per child as compared to the estimated annual costs, exclusive of childcare, of raising a child of $5,700 ($8,600 if childcare costs are included) (Stroick and Jenson 1999: 79–80).

10. For a wonderfully detailed analysis of the wartime policy and what happened in Ontario after the wartime supports were terminated see Prentice (1993).

11. BC has long made subsidies available for informal care but the neo-liberal restructuring of welfare states has given rise to a new interest in this form of provision. Thus the federal government provides subsidies for informal care through its 'Working Income Supplement' for those in training programs. The Harris government is encouraging the expansion of unregulated care and the government of New Brunswick has reserved 400 spaces in unregulated care for parents whose jobs or schedules make it difficult to access centre services (see Stroick and Jenson 1999: 61–71 for more details).

12. The Swedish Social Democratic Party (SAP) has been formally allied with the blue-collar trade union central, LO, for over a century. The white-collar unions, organized around the TCO and SACO, retain a non-partisan stance though TCO members have tended to vote for the social democrats.

13. With the onset of a new economic crisis in 1990, the SAP government rescinded the additional six months at the higher compensation rate.

14. When the bourgeois parties took office in 1991 they made it possible for commercial daycare to receive government subsidies, but the social democrats rescinded this legislation on their return to office in 1994.

15. Named after the Swedish prime minister, these funds will have amounted to some 25 billion Swedish Crowns (about $5 billion Canadian—a substantial amount for a country with a population equivalent to Ontario's)—by 2002. See Mahon (1999) for more details.

16. The term *social liberalism* is actually a Swedish term designed to distinguish between laissez-faire and the more social-democratic versions of liberalism. I have decided to apply it to Canada's welfare state—at least as it developed in the 1960s and 1970s—because it helps to capture the blend of liberalism and social democracy adopted by the federal Liberals (and, to a lesser extent, the Tories) at that time. To this was added in the 1970s a more activist stance vis-à-vis the economy which I label *social liberalism plus*.

17. The Federation des Femmes du Quebec (FFQ), formed eight years before NAC, included a demand for daycare in their agenda. The Quebec women's movement was very involved in redesigning Quebec society, a process unleashed by the Quiet Revolution (Begin 1992).

18. During the 1970s, there was an increasing number of examples of such coalition politics, forged in the trenches of civil society. Nevertheless, the emergence of a 'popular sector' is perhaps best dated from the Macdonald Royal Commission on the Economic Union and Development Prospects for Canada (1982–95).

19. The Canada Labour Code only applies to workers in federally regulated industries—a small percentage of the whole labour force. The majority of the workforce is governed by provincial legislation. Federal legislation has, however, often acted as something of a pacesetter. Unemployment insurance, moreover, is a federal scheme, which applies

to all workers. Burt argues that the government chose to implement maternity leave insurance through UI because it has exclusive jurisdiction in this field and thus could circumvent the still-reluctant provinces (1990: 203).

20. They also recommended that daycare centres be included in housing developments 'including university buildings' (where young feminists were organizing for daycare); that Health and Welfare establish an advisory service to aid the provinces and territories and that the latter establish childcare boards to plan, regulate and support the development of a network of daycare centres. Ontario had already established a regulatory and advisory branch but most other provinces still lack such a mechanism for enforcing standards.

21. By Keynes plus I mean the whole plethora of post-Keynesian policy instruments that add a supply-side activism to the original focus on macro-economic demand management. These measures were not without their limitations nor were they by any means unambiguously progressive. Nevertheless this form of liberalism did accept an active role for the state in the economy and hence gave more radical demands a certain legitimacy.

22. Again I do not wish to suggest that liberal nationalism posed a serious challenge to foreign control. Yet the presence of a nationalist element within the federal government helped to make the Left nationalist project seem less utopian.

23. On working-class feminism, see Maroney (1987). On NAC support for the strikes at Fleck and elsewhere, as well as on the rise of socialist-feminists within NAC see Vickers et al (1993).

24. Parents were given the right to share the additional leave (if both were employed under the jurisdiction of the Canada Labour Code—a pretty big 'if') and they also had the right to reinstatement in their former jobs or ones equivalent thereto, upon return to work.

25. The term 'comprehensive' means recognition of a diversity of needs. In other words, the policy should support a range of options, to be worked out at the local level (Friendly 1994: 163). Both the Abella and Cook reports recognized the different needs with particular reference to First Nations, 'visible minorities', and the disabled as well as those living in rural areas.

26. In the version tabled in the House, provinces were given the option of staying with CAP or moving to the new program that did not restrict funding to subsidized spaces for low-income families. It was intended, however, that funding through the new program would diminish as daycare capacity expanded. In other words, it was not an open-ended program where the federal government had to match every dollar spent by the lower levels of government.

27. Forty-forty with parental fees covering the remaining 20 per cent. This would have left parents responsible for a larger share than in Sweden (10 per cent) but nonetheless represented a major breakthrough.

28. Through this the federal government enriched the Canada Child Tax Benefit available to all low income families (including the working poor), reducing the funds the provinces would have to pay out of the CHST or their own revenues to support low income families with children.

29. The main report of the Steering Committee for the Human Resource Study of Child Care in Canada argued, inter alia, for equitable wages, benefit levels, and working conditions, as well as a public commitment to a trained and competent workforce (Beach, Bertrand, and Cleveland 1998).

30. Minus Quebec—but, alas, that is the way federal-provincial arrangements have been functioning for some time now.

31. The CAW's August 1999 agreements with the Big 3 automakers included a childcare package, with the provision that if a new national policy were adopted, the companies' share of costs would drop accordingly. The CLC is involved in the campaign, inter alia, through sponsorship of a postcard campaign. *The Globe and Mail*'s decision to run a year long series on families with young children (launched fall 1999) also seemed promising.

32. See CLC website (Social Justice—Women and Unemployment Insurance) 12/14/99 and the concluding chapter to Porter's (1998) dissertation.

References

Abella, Judge R.S. 1984. *Report of the Commission on Equality in Employment* (Ottawa: Government of Canada).

Bach, S., and S. Phillips. 1997. 'Constructing a New Social Union: Child Care Beyond Infancy?' *How Ottawa Spends 1997–98 Seeing Red: A Liberal Report Card*, ed. G. Swimmer (Carleton University Press).

Baker, M. 1995. *Canadian Family Policies: Cross-National Comparisons* (Toronto: University of Toronto Press).

Baude, A. 1979. 'Public Policy and Changing Family Patterns in Sweden, 1930–1977' in *Sex Roles and Social Policy: A Complex Social Science Equation*, eds J. Lipman-Blumen and J. Bernard (London: Sage).

Beach, J., J. Bertrand, and G. Cleveland. 1998. *Our Child Care Workforce: From Recognition to Remuneration* (Child Care Human Resources Steering Committee).

Begin, M. 1992. 'The Royal Commission on the Status of Women in Canada: Twenty Years Later' in *Challenging Times: The Women's Movement in Canada and the United States*, eds C. Backhouse and D. Flaherty (Montreal: McGill-Queen's University Press).

Bergqvist, C., J. Kuusipalo, and A. Styrkarsdottir. 1999. 'The Debate on Childcare Policies' in *Equal Democracies: Gender and Politics in Nordic Countries*, eds C. Bergqvist et al. (Oslo University Press).

Bradford, N., and J. Jenson. 1992. 'The Roots of Social Democratic Populism in Canada' in *Labor Parties in Post-Industrial Societies*, ed. F.F. Piven (London: Polity).

Brodie, J., and J. Jenson. 1988. *Crisis, Challenge and Change: Party and Class in Canada Revisited* (Ottawa: Carleton University Press).

Burt, S. 1986. 'Women's Issues and the Women's Movement in Canada Since 1970' in *Politics of Gender, Ethnicity and Language in Canada*, eds A. Cairns and C. Wiliams (Toronto: University of Toronto Press).

———. 1990. 'Organised Women's Groups and the State' in *Policy Communities and Public Policy in Canada: A Structural Approach*, eds W. and G. Skogstad Coleman (Toronto: Copp Clark Pitman).

Cameron, B. 1996. 'From Equal Opportunity to Symbolic Equality: Three Decades of Federal Training Policy' in *Changing Spaces: Gender and State Responses to Economic Restructuring in Canada*, ed. I. Bakker (Toronto: University of Toronto Press).

CLC. 2000. *Analysis of UI Coverage for Women*. www.clc-ctc.ca/policy/ui/wom-ui-00e.html

Esping-Andersen, G. 1985. *Politics Against Markets: The Social Democratic Road to Power* (Princeton, NJ: Princeton University Press).

———. 1990. *The Three Worlds of Welfare Capitalism* (London: Polity Press).

———. 1999. *Social Foundations of Postindustrial Economies* (London: Oxford University Press).

Finkel, A. 1995. 'Even the Little Children Cooperated: Family Strategies, Child Care Discourse and Social Welfare Debates, 1945–1975' *Labour/le travail*.

Friendly, M. 1994. *Child Care Policy in Canada: Putting the Pieces Together* (Toronto: Addison-Wesley).

Haddow, R. 1993. *Poverty Reform in Canada, 1958–1978* (Montreal: McGill-Queen's University Press).

Hinnfors, J. 1995. *Familjepolitck, samhällsförändringar och partistrategier 1960–1990* (Almquist and Wiksell).

Hirdman, Y. 1994. 'Social Engineering and the Woman Question: Sweden in the 1930s', *Swedish Social Democracy: A Model in Transition*, eds W. Clement and R. Mahon (Toronto: Canadian Scholars' Press).

Hobson, B. 1990. 'No Exit, No Voice: Woman's Economic Dependency and the Welfare State', *Acta Sociolgica* 33.

Jenson, J. 1986. 'Gender and Reproduction or Babies and the State', *Studies in Political Economy* 20: 9–45.

———, and R. Mahon. 1993. 'Representing Solidarity: Class, Gender and the Crisis of Social Democratic Sweden', *New Left Review* 201: 76–100.

———, and S. Phillips. 1996. 'Regime Shift: New Citizenship Practices in Canada', *International Journal of Canadian Studies* 14 (Fall): 111.

Karlsson, G. 1990. *Manssamhället till behag?* (Stockholm).

Kyle, G. 1979. *Gästarbeterska i manssamhället* (Lund).

LO. 1995. Barnomsorg—för barnen och jämställdheten LO.

Mahon, R. 1997. 'The Never-Ending Story Part I: Feminist Struggles to Reshape Canadian Day Care Policy in the 1970s', paper presented at the Workshop of the Research Network on Gender, State and Society held in conjunction with the Social Science History Association meetings, Washington, DC, 16 Oct.

———. 1999. 'Swedish Social Democracy and the Quest for Social Justice at the Close of the Twentieth Century', presented at the conference New Left/New Labour and the Quest for Social Justice, Victoria, BC, 11–12 Sept.

———. Forthcoming. 'The Never-Ending Story: The Struggle for Universal Child Care Policy in the 1970s' *Canadian Historical Review*.

Maroney, H.J. 1987. 'Feminism at Work' in *Feminism and Political Economy*, eds H. Jon Maroney and M. Luxton (Toronto: Methuen).

Martin, A. 1978. 'Dynamics of Change in Keynesian Political Economy' in *State and Economy in Contemporary Capitalism*, ed. C. Crouch (London: Croom-Helm).

Michel, S. 1999. *Children's Interests? Mothers' Rights: The Shaping of America's Child Care Policy* (New Haven: Yale University Press).

Myles, J. 1988. 'Decline or Impasse? The Current State of the Welfare State', *Studies in Political Economy* 26.

———. 1995. *When Markets Fail: Social Welfare in Canada and the United States* (Geneva: United National Research Institute for Social Development).

O'Connor, J. 1989. 'Welfare Expenditure and Policy Orientation in Canada in Comparative Perspective', *Canadian Review of Sociology and Anthropology* 26 (1): 127–50.

O'Connor, J.S., A.S. Orloff, and S. Shaver. 1999. *States, Markets, Families: Gender, Liberalism and Social Policy in Australia, Canada, Great Britain and the United States* (Cambridge: Cambridge University Press).

O'Hara, K. 1998. *Comparative Family Policy: Eight Countries' Stories,* CPRN Study No. F-04 (Renouf).

Olsson, S. 1990. *Social Policy and the Welfare State in Sweden* (Lund).

Phillips, S. 1989. 'Rock a Bye Brian: The National Strategy on Child Care' in *How Ottawa Spends 1990–91*, ed. K. Graham (Ottawa: Carleton University Press).

———. 1999. 'Canada's Social Union Framework Agreement: Implications and Opportunities for the Voluntary Sector', unpublished paper prepared for National Voluntary Organizations.

Prentice, S. 1993. *Militant Mothers in Domestic Times: Toronto's Postwar Childcare Struggle.* Ph.D. diss., York University.

Porter, A. 1998. *Gender, Class and the Welfare State: The Case of Canadian Unemployment Insurance.* Ph.D. diss., Sociology, York University.

Royal Commission on the Status of Women in Canada. 1971. *Report of the Royal Commission on the Status of Women in Canada* (Ottawa: Government of Canada).

Sainsbury, D. 1994. *Gendering Welfare States* (Newbury Park, CA: Sage).

Stroick, S., and J. Jenson. 1999. *What Is the Best Policy Mix for Canada's Young Children?* CPRN Study No. F-09.

Task Force on Child Care. 1986. *Report of the Task Force on Child Care* (Cook) (Ottawa: Status of Women Canada, Government of Canada).

Ursel, J. 1992. *Private Lives, Public Policy: One Hundred Years of State Intervention in the Family* (Toronto: The Women's Press).

Vickers, J., P. Rankin, and C. Appelle. 1993. *Politics As If Women Mattered: A Political Analysis of the National Action Committee on the Status of Women* (Toronto: University of Toronto).

White, J. 1993. *Sisters and Solidarity: Women and Unions in Canada* (Toronto: Thomson Educational Publishers).

Index